ADULT DEVELOPMENT
AND
AGING
FIFTH EDITION

ADULT DEVELOPMENT
AND
AGING

FIFTH EDITION

Bert Hayslip Jr.
Julie Hicks Patrick
and
Paul E. Panek

KRIEGER PUBLISHING COMPANY
Malabar, FL
2011

Original Edition 1989
Second Edition 1993
Third edition 2002
Fourth Edition 2007
Fifth Edition 2011

Printed and Published by
KRIEGER PUBLISHING COMPANY
KRIEGER DRIVE
MALABAR, FLORIDA 32950

FROM A DECLARATION OF PRINCIPLES JOINTLY ADOPTED BY A COMMITTEE OF THE AMERICAN BAR ASSOCIATION AND A COMMITTEE OF PUBLISHERS:
This publication is designed to provide accurate and authoritative information in regard to the subject matter covered. It is sold with the understanding that the publisher is not engaged in rendering legal, accounting, or other professional service. If legal advice or other expert assistance is required, the services of a competent professional person should be sought.

Library of Congress Cataloging-in-Publication Data

Hayslip, Bert.
  Adult development and aging / Bert Hayslip and Julie Hicks Patrick. — 5th ed.
    p. cm.
  Includes bibliographical references and index.
  ISBN-13: 978-1-57524-308-5 (alk. paper)
  ISBN-10: 1-57524-308-3 (alk. paper)
  1. Adulthood. 2. Aging—Psychological aspects. I. Hicks-Patrick, Julie. II. Title.
  BF724.5.H39 2011
  155.6—dc22

                                                                          2011012119

10 9 8 7 6 5 4 3 2

To Paul E. Panek, Ph.D.

(1947-2007)

—a loving father and husband,

and a good friend and colleague.

Contents

Preface to the Fifth Edition

You are about to be introduced to adulthood and aging. What should you make of all of the information you will gather? Perhaps we can provide you with a few guideposts to help you organize what you will read. Because each chapter deals with a somewhat different aspect of adult development, it might be easy for you to lose sight of the fact that changes in each area of our lives are interwoven with changes in other areas. As we discuss in Chapter 1, it would be unusual to observe that what happens to us as young adults is completely independent of events we experience as middle-aged or older persons. Likewise, development in certain areas of our lives does have an impact on other aspects of our existence. Our physical development (Chapter 2), for example, influences our relationships with others (Chapters 4 and 5) as well as our intellectual and cognitive skills (Chapter 3) and our personality and self-image (Chapter 6). Moreover, having a supportive network of family and friends (Chapters 4 and 5) is crucial to our well-being (Chapter 10), and our well-being is often influenced by our experiences in the context of work and retirement (Chapters 7, 8, and 9). How we sense and process what happens to us (Chapter 2) is the foundation for most of our experiences and relationships. Of course, we all live with the knowledge that our skills, relationships, careers, and indeed, all that is important to us will be changed forever when our lives come to an end (Chapter 12). The point we want to make is that our adult lives are quite dynamic and, while we have discussed these various aspects of adult development as if they were separate from one another, in reality we should try to understand our own development as adults as something that is amazingly complex. Rarely do decisions and choices that we make, or fail to make, fail to impact us in many different ways.

We also want to stress that how your life will play itself out in all its complexity will likely be different from that of your friends, siblings, parents, and grandparents. Each person travels a unique path. As adults, we are constantly being bombarded with what is "normal," and we often forget that what is normal for one person may not necessarily be so for the next. Moreover, what was normal for our parents or grandparents may not apply to us, or to our children, for that matter! There are individual differences in how our lives progress; let us learn from these differences so that we can lead happy, fulfilling, and productive lives.

Last, we want to remind you that although younger and older adults are different in many ways, they nevertheless have much in common. This is especially important because we live in a culture that often pits the young and the old against one another. Kuhn and Bader (1991) have expressed this sense of commonality nicely in the following ways:

1. Both younger and older persons are not often taken seriously.
2. Many younger and older persons are either physically or emotionally dependent and need to be taken care of.
3. Both younger and older adults have trouble in the job market.
4. Both younger and older persons experience significant body changes.

5. Because of our biases about age changes in competence, both younger and older persons are likely to be denied input into decisions that may affect them.
6. Both younger and older persons have a wealth of learning and experience before them . . . and behind them.
7. Both younger and older persons can make a difference in their world. Both are free to initiate social change.

To this we add that both younger and older persons are, will be, or have been parents, children, workers, caregivers, citizens, lovers, learners, and grievers. Most important, younger and older persons are people with good and bad qualities, strengths and weaknesses, and goals and accomplishments that are important to them. Each lives life as he or she sees it.

Recognizing that our lives are complex, that we do differ from others, yet realizing that we share much in common with those who are younger or older than ourselves can help us to age well. We can set realistic goals for ourselves, learn to cope with stress and change, enjoy our relationships with others, and perhaps most importantly, be happy.

In this fifth edition, we have again focused on creating a text that is truly student-oriented and student-accessible. Consequently, we have placed additional emphasis on the applied aspects of adult development and aging so that students can appreciate both the usefulness of basic research in these areas and the relevance of this material to their own lives and the lives of those they know.

Our text is organized topically rather than chronologically, since many of the topics are equally relevant to both older adults and younger adults. Aging is best thought of as an ongoing process, not easily segmented into discrete stages that are mutually exclusive. Yet some aspects of young adulthood, middle age, or late adulthood are unique and need to be understood in the context of biological change and/or psychosocial factors distinct to each life period. For these reasons, our discussion of issues relevant to adults and aged persons varies both within and between chapters.

We believe that organizing the material topically also helps you understand adulthood in a more integrated manner, making it more likely that topics in different chapters will be seen as interrelated rather than as independent of one another. The chapters are also arranged so as first to lay the groundwork for your thinking about adult development, and then to deal with basic psychobiological processes (i.e., biology of aging, sensation/perception), followed by topics that are distinctly psychological (i.e., learning/ memory, intelligence, and personality). The latter chapters are predominantly psychosocial and/or clinical in their orientation (i.e., work/ retirement, mental health/psychopathology, intervention/treatment, and death/dying). This chapter organization reinforces the text's dual emphasis on basic and applied research.

We continue to provide a breadth of coverage and presentation in this edition. For example, references have been updated to include the newest studies on a variety of topics; most of the references cited are 2000 or later, save a small number of unique and/or classic studies. Moreover, there is a balance between theory and application that is reflected in how material is presented in each chapter.

Because the field of adult development and aging is a dynamic, changing one, high-interest topics that are current and relevant to the lives of both younger and older adults are discussed, such as grandparent caregivers to their grandchildren (Chapter 5), elder abuse (Chapter 4), the impact of stereotypes on older persons (Chapter 1), improving health care for older persons (Chapter 1), motherhood in midlife (Chapter 4), centenarians (Chapter 1), caloric restriction and aging (Chapter 2), new patterns of retirement (Chapter 8), emerging adulthood (Chapter 1), personality disorders (Chapter 10), women's career development (Chapter 7), stress and coping (Chapter 6), intellectual and memory training with older adults (Chapter 3), the impact of job loss on young adults (Chapter 7), bridge employment and unretiring (Chapter 8), memory impairment (Chapter 3), the impact of engaged lifestyles on older persons (Chapter 3), drug use and abuse in older adults (Chapter 10), family caregiving (Chapters 4, 10, and 11), mild cognitive impairment (Chapter 10), preventing Alzheimer's disease and cognitive decline (Chapter 10), successful aging (Chapter 10), the psychological effects of physical aging (Chapter 2), homosexuality (Chapter 4), end of life decision making (Chapter 12), psychological hardiness (Chapter 6), Medicare coverage of mental health care (Chapter 11), strength-based approaches to aging (Chapter 10), and psychotherapy with dying persons (Chapter 12). In addition, we have expanded our coverage of dementia and the functional disorders in Chapter 10, psychotherapy in Chapter 11, everyday memory and learning in Chapter 3, as well as discussing more fully the developmental aspects of grief and bereavement as well as psychotherapy with dying persons in Chapter 12, the concluding chapter in the text.

We have retained the "Check Your Learning" feature which we hope will enhance your understanding of the material as you read through a chapter, rather than waiting until its end to determine what you do and do not understand. Throughout each chapter, key terms appear in boldface type at their first usage, to call your attention to their sig-

nificance. In addition, in each chapter, a summary and a list of key terms and concepts cue you to the most important issues just discussed. Review questions test your comprehension of the material throughout each chapter.

We have also retained another feature that we are excited about: the inserts with the heading "Adults Speak" in nearly every chapter. In these quotes and excerpts, people of various ages describe in their own words how they are facing a number of aging-related issues. We think these inserts will make the text material come to life for you—and maybe some of them will even strike a chord of familiarity! Other boxed inserts throughout the text highlight high-interest topics and applications, such as hospice care, grandparenting, euthanasia, marriage and parenting, physical aging, sexuality in later life, training older workers, therapy with people suffering from dementia, the Baby Boom generation, and centenarians.

A complete glossary at the end of the text assists you in defining terms used throughout the text. We believe that these features will not only make your learning easier and more effective, but also make this learning more personally meaningful to you.

We hope you like what we have done with the fifth edition of our text!

Bert Hayslip Jr.
Julie Hicks Patrick
Paul E. Panek

Chapter 1
Adulthood and Aging:
A Personal Journey

As adults, many of us are reminded nearly every day that we are growing older. We each have our personal opinions and views about how we or others should age, or what "normal aging" looks or feels like. Some of us dread getting older, while others indeed look forward to being older. However, before we begin our discussion of adult development and aging, it is important to understand that we have been "aging" since the moment of our birth, and that aging is the result of the **normal** process of development.

Learning about adult development and aging is important and valuable for many reasons. It can lead us to new insights about understanding our own lives, as well as strengthen our relationships with our children, parents, or grandparents. It can help us set realistic and attainable goals for ourselves in the future. It can help us separate myth from fact, and normal from abnormal aging processes. It can guide the choices we make now to ensure a healthier and happier future. It can enable us to be more effective and empathic in how we do our jobs.

Think about the years that lie ahead of you as a journey that we all must travel. For some of us, the journey may be a difficult one, while for others it may be a pleasant trip. Nevertheless, as with any journey, there are many routes to take, and some are more difficult than others. While we cannot predict with certainty which of the many routes your personal journey will take, we will provide some road signs as guides that might be helpful.

In this text we will explore the effects of a variety of biological, psychological, social, and cultural factors on development during the adult years. In order to accomplish this complex task, we have organized the text topically rather than chronologically. Every topic is relevant to each phase of the life cycle, that is young adulthood, middle age, or late adulthood. As the importance of each of these factors on behavior and development sometimes differs for adults at different points in their lives, our discussion of issues relevant to young adults,

Figure 1-1. Adulthood can be thought of as a journey we all must travel.

1

persons of middle age, and older persons often varies within and between chapters. Additionally, we will stress the implications of these issues for everyday life. Further, where appropriate, we will elaborate on gender and racial/ethnic differences in adult development since these factors can influence the process of development. For example, such factors often affect our longevity and health. In addition, to aid in your understanding, **Check Your Learning** exercises appear at various points in each chapter.

Aging: Complex and Multidimensional

In order to adequately study and understand the complex process of aging, we must keep five important ideas in mind about development and aging. It is: (1) multidimensional, (2) continuous and dynamic, (3) pluralistic and involves multidirectional change, (4) a universal characteristic of all living organisms, and (5) to be viewed within the context of historical time and culture.

The normal aging process is **multidimensional** since it affects us simultaneously on a number of dimensions of behavior and functioning (Panek, 1997). These are: (1) **Sensory-Perceptual**, such as vision, hearing, and selective attention; (2) **Biophysiological**, for instance, the cardiovascular system and central nervous system; (3) **Cognitive/ Intellectual**, for example, intelligence, learning, and memory; (4) **Personal-Interpersonal**, such as self-concept and interpersonal relationships; and (5) **Cultural-Environmental**, for example, ethnicity and occupation.

Because we do not age "in parts," each of these above dimensions or sectors of development overlaps with and affects the others. For example, declines with age in the Sensory-Perceptual Dimension (e.g., decreased hearing ability) can lead to changes in the Cognitive/Intellectual Dimension (e.g., incorrect interpretation of verbal instructions regarding a task), that in turn can effect the Cultural-Environmental Dimension (e.g., inappropriate behavior or poor job performance), which subsequently effects the Personal-Interpersonal Dimension (e.g., criticism from family members as a result of the person's poor performance or behavior which negatively affects the person's self-concept).

Continuous and Dynamic

Adult development is a continuous, holistic and dynamic process, which makes adulthood difficult to segregate into discrete or independent stages. Consequently, factors or issues that affect people during adulthood should be viewed rather as interrelated, and as a whole rather than as independent factors or events. As noted previously, since we do not age "in parts," each of the five dimensions presented above overlaps with and affects the others. Thus, development and aging are best understood and viewed in a holistic manner.

Generally speaking, we will focus our discussion on what can be considered **normal aging** as opposed to **pathological aging**. There are two types of "normal" aging (Abeles, 1997), **optimal** or **healthy** aging, and **typical** aging. Normal aging involves changes in functioning and behavior in the various dimensions that are inevitable. They occur as the natural result of maturation or the passage of time, and these changes in varying degrees affect all of us as we age. Optimal or healthy aging refers to the aging of individuals who have no identified physical illness, while typical aging describes the aging of individuals who have one or more medical conditions that become prevalent in later life. Pathological aging refers to changes with age that are the result of abnormal conditions or disease processes, rather than to age per se.

Pluralistic and Multidirectional

Adult development is **pluralistic** and **multidirectional**. Development which is **pluralistic** means that development can take many forms, of which gains and losses in specific behaviors are but of one type. Consequently, many different types of abilities and behaviors have different courses in terms of onset, direction, duration, and termination (Baltes, 1987). **Multidirectionality** suggests that change during the life cycle can take on many forms or directions. That is, some abilities will decrease with age and others will increase with age, while others will not change with age.

A Universal Characteristic

Development and aging are universal characteristics of all living organisms and thus entail and imply change. Baltes, Reese, and Nesselroade (1988) stated that in order to adequately understand changes in the context of adulthood and aging, one must consider three types of influences: (1) **age-normative**, (2) **history-normative**, and (3) **non-normative** influences.

Age-normative influences are factors that are general to the process of development and are highly related to chronological age. Although the timing in terms of onset may vary for different persons, or for different subgroups of people, these influences generally affect persons of a specific age in a particular manner. Age-normative influences can be the result of either biophysiological processes, such as the onset of puberty or menopause, or social-environmental factors such as mandating a specific age for marriage, getting a driver's license, or retirement. It is easy to underestimate the influence of age-normative views, but many college students would feel uncomfortable if the student sitting next to them were a 14 year old or an 84 year old. We often have a sense of what behaviors and activities are "on-time" for individuals of varying ages.

History-normative influences are events that occur at a specific point in time (day, month, or year) and theoretically affect everyone in that society or culture. These events can have either a short-term or long-term effect upon individuals in that particular society or culture. However within a given culture, these influences can have different effects on individuals as a function of age. For instance, if a war were to be declared, the most profound effect of this would be on younger adults, who, because of their age would be called upon to fight the war. Nevertheless, this does not mean that the spouse, children, and family members of the individual called to fight in the war will remain unaffected. The short-term effects of history-normative events are actions such as delaying marriage or starting a

family, going to college (or postponing going to college), or entering or not entering a particular occupation.

Non-normative influences are factors that cannot be attributed to the normal process of development or to the impact of historical change events. These tend to be idiosyncratic, in that these events exert influences on a particular individual. Thus, non-normative events tend to increase the differences among individuals. For example, having an accident, becoming seriously ill, winning the lottery, or being fired from your job are all examples of non-normative events.

Each of these influences is considered ongoing and interactive in terms of its effect across the life span. Moreover, each of these factors exhibits different levels of influence on the individual at different points in the life cycle. Age-normative influences are often considered to be the result of maturation and are under genetic control. Thus, they have the most pronounced effect during childhood and old age. History-normative influences are most pronounced among adolescents and young adults, and non-normative events increase in significance with increasing age (Baltes et al., 1988; Danish, 1981).

The Context of Time

To the extent that there is something systematic and age-related about our behavior, the **age continuum** serves as our individual time line (Neugarten, 1973), which begins at birth and ends with death. This age continuum serves as a focus or basis for the interactions of each of these dimensions, e.g., sensory-perceptual, personal-interpersonal, etc.

Also, each of these dimensions is itself changing along a **historical time continuum** (Neugarten & Datan, 1973). Each point in history serves as a reference point, and thereby defines the larger context for our development. Thus, in addition to changes in individuals, we must consider changes in our culture that vary with the ebb and flow of historical changes that help to define the context of development. These cultural changes affect us at each phase of the life cycle (see Chapter 9).

We call this historical continuum **contextual time.** We might draw several samples of a person's behavior at various chronological age points in time; each must be considered a small slice of the individual's life in the context of sensory-perceptual, biophysiological, cognitive/intellectual, personal-interpersonal, and cultural-environmental factors.

Time, age-normative influences, history-normative events, and non-normative influences all interact to shape the people we become. McIlroy (1984) refers to the long-term effects of history-normative influences as **cultural ethics**, which are the prevailing attitudes, values, and beliefs shared by members of society at a particular time, or of a specific generation within a society. History-normative influences can thus have significant and long-lasting effects on the behavior, attitudes, and values of members of a specific generation or cohort. A **generation** or **cohort** refers to persons born at a particular historical time period or era whose experiences are unique, and particular to when they were raised and/or grew up, matured, aged, and died. Events such as 9/11, the AIDS epidemic, wars, or economic ups and downs may help to define a distinct cohort of individuals who share similar attitudes and experiences (see also Hudson, 2002). Thus, these and other events make each generation unique compared to individuals born earlier or later. For example, the cohort of individuals who were born between 1925 and 1945 is called Traditionalists (Smola & Sutton, 2002). The work ethics and values among members of this generation are "practical, "patient, loyal and hard-working," "respectful of authority," and "rule followers" (Dittman, 2005; Patterson, 2005).

Another example of a cohort is the **Baby Boom generation**, which refers to the group of individuals born between 1946 and 1964 (Abeles, 1997). The Baby Boom generation was the first to be free of many potentially fatal childhood diseases, such as smallpox and whooping cough. This generation grew up with television and experienced Woodstock, Vietnam, free love, and the drug culture. The work ethics and values among baby boomers are "opti-mistic," "teamwork and cooperation," and "effecting change" (Dittman, 2005; Patterson, 2005; Smola & Sutton, 2002). This generation grew up embracing the psychology of entitlement and expected the best from life (Smola & Sutton, 2002).

Persons born between 1965 and 1980 are members of what has been referred to as **Generation X**. Gen X-ers grew up with financial, family, and societal insecurity; rapid change; great diversity; and a lack of solid traditions (Smola & Sutton, 2002). They are technically competent, comfortable with diversity, change, multitasking, and competition; they believe in similarities rather than differences (Smola & Sutton, 2002).

A majority of you reading this text are members of the **Millenials** generation, persons born from 1981 to present (Patterson, 2005). This is the first generation to be born into a wired world (Smola & Sutton, 2002). The work ethics and work values of this generation are described as "hopeful," "meaningful work," "diversity and change valued," and "technology savvy" (Dittman, 2005; Patterson, 2005). Millennials are expected to be the first generation since the 1960s to be socially active (Smola & Sutton, 2002).

Person-Environment Interaction

Our viewpoint is that the concept of person-environment interaction provides an excellent perspective from which to view the process of development and change during adulthood. Person-environment interaction suggests that all aspects of human behavior and performance are the result of the interaction or transactions between individuals and their environment (Panek, 1997). Thus, successful adaptation and adjustment during adulthood require persons to be selective in their choice of stimuli, responses, and behavior, and to compensate for changes in ability or health that result from the aging process in order to optimize their behavior and performance (Baltes, 1997). In order to successfully age, adapt, and cope, individuals must continually match their skills to the demands of the environment, which is also changing. This can be

Box A

Baby Boomers

Although there is some debate over the exact years marking its beginning and its ending, the Baby Boom generation refers to the very large group of individuals born between 1946 and 1964—almost 80 million people. The Baby Boom was created by delays in marriage and childbearing due to World War II and the prosperity that followed. We sometimes separate this generation into the Early Boomers, born before the early 1950s, and the Late Boomers, born thereafter.

Consider that in 20 to 25 years, the ratio of older to middle-aged persons will be 253 to 100, according to Census figures. If this doesn't make you aware of the tremendous shift in our population base due to the Baby Boom generation, consider that in the year 2021, Bill Clinton, Donald Trump, and Sylvester Stallone will be 75. Drew Carey and Madonna will be 63. Barack Obama will be 60. Demi Moore and Tom Cruise will be 59. All of these well-known people are either early or late Baby Boomers.

In response to the sheer numbers of people growing up in the late 1940s and early 1950s, our society has changed in many ways. For example, thousands of new elementary schools were built in the 1950s to accommodate the young Baby Boomers. Colleges and universities also expanded rapidly to meet the demands of this new generation.

The Baby Boom generation was bound together by a number of significant cultural changes. For example, they were the first generation to be free of many potentially fatal childhood diseases, such as diphtheria, polio, smallpox, and whooping cough. Boomers grew up with television—Mickey Mouse, Superman, Roy Rogers, Howdy Doody, and American Bandstand, plus Barbie and Ken, I Like Ike, Elvis, and the Twist. Later on, Woodstock, Kent State, Gloria Steinem, Vietnam, the Beach Boys, the Beatles, Bob Dylan, the Pill, a concern for women's rights and for the environment, the Civil Rights movement, and the drug culture of the 1960s and 1970s separated the Baby Boomers from their "materialistic, traditional, middle-of-the road" parents. Boomers spawned the development of the record industry, amusement parks, the convertible, and fast foods, notably McDonald's.

This "bulge" in our population is now middle-aged. They are confronting the realities of raising children and caring for aging parents, as well as dealing with the physical realities of aging themselves—crow's feet, double chins, and potbellies. In general, Baby Boomers are more highly educated, are married, have children later in life, start work later, and are more likely to have two incomes than their predecessors.

Given the anticipated advances in preventing and treating major fatal diseases and their risk factors and interventions that may slow the rate of biological aging, it is likely that those age 65+ will increase from 38.7 million in 2008 (U.S. Census Bureau, 2008) to between 99 million and 108 million by 2050 (Olshansky, Goldman, Zheng, & Rowe, 2009). These estimates are considered to be more accurate and significantly higher than those developed based on Census data. The implications are far-reaching. We have not adequately planned for this number of older adults accessing medical care, seeking jobs in the work force, and providing valuable human capital to the community.

Table 1-1

Components of Transactional Model

Component	Description and Example
Degree of individual competence	Degree of individual competence The diverse collection of abilities and skills the person possesses, e.g., sensory processes. Each of these abilities or skills levels is unique to the person and varies over time between minimum and maximum limits that are specific to each person.
Environmental press	The demands from the environment impinging upon and affecting the individual, e.g., demands or requirements of the task, job, or situation.
Adaptive behavior	The outer manifestation of individual competence, e.g., in the work environment, adaptive behavior can be considered the observable performance on the job.
Affective responses	The inner unobservable aspects of the individual-environmental transaction, including the person's evaluation and emotional reaction to the environment, e.g., if a person is critical of self-performance, that person may become angry or depressed.
Adaptation level	The point or level where the person is functioning at a comfortable level relative to the external demands. Beyond this comfort zone, positive affect decreases and becomes negative as the demands push the person past an adaptation level, e.g., if the person's adaptation level is driving 55 miles per hour, 60 might be challenging, attempting to drive 65 miles per hour would cause the person discomfort and may result in an accident.

Source: Adapted from Lawton and Nahemow (1973) and Panek (1997).

illustrated by the transactional model of Lawton and Nahemow (1973) (see Table 1-1). The components of the transactional model are: (1) **degree of individual competence**, the diverse collection of abilities and skills the person possesses. These are unique to the person and vary in terms of performance levels over time; (2) **environmental press**, the demands from the environment impinging on and affecting the individual; for example, stimuli from the environment while driving a car; (3) **adaptive behavior**, the observable manifestation of the person's performance in a specific situation, e.g., the actual driving behaviors while in a car; (4) **affective (emotional) responses**, the unobservable aspects of the person-environment transaction, including the person's evaluation of and emotional reaction to the environment; for example, labeling ourselves as incompetent having failed an exam leading to anger and depression, and (5) **adaptation level**, the point at which the person is performing at a comfortable level relative to the external demands of the environment or situation. Beyond this comfort zone, positive affect decreases and becomes negative as the demands of the environment push persons past their adaptation level.

To illustrate this transactional model, if a person's adaptation level is typing 90 words per minute, 100 might be challenging, and attempting to type 120 words per minute would likely lead to more mistakes. The transactional model views aging in terms of continued adaptation to the demands and pressures from the external environment as well as to the internal changes in physical and cognitive functioning that take place during the entire life cycle. Consequently, regardless of our age, in order to deal effectively and competently with our environment, we must engage in tasks and activities that match our ability levels (see Chapter 9).

Developmental Niche

The concepts of person-environment fit and adaptation level are very similar to what has been termed a **developmental niche** (Super & Harkness, 1986; Wachs, 1996). Generally speaking, a person's developmental niche is defined in terms of the culture or environment in which the individual best functions. In theory at least, persons select those environments in which they can function most comfortably—those that are most congruent with their skills and abilities productively, that enable them to express their convictions and values, and that allow them to mature in the context of the roles they occupy such as parent, spouse, or worker. One's school or work environment, neighborhood, or even the region of the country in which one lives may help or hinder one's health, well-being, or work performance. We will revisit the concepts of person-environment fit and developmental niche in Chapter 9, when we discuss the social-environmental context in which we age.

Ways of Describing Change

The primary focus of research and theory during adulthood is to identify and explain change within the person over time, called **intra-individual change**—changes within an individual over time on any behavior, ability, trait, or skill, e.g., how your learning or memory skills change over time. To the extent that these changes are associated with chronological age, they are termed **age-related changes,** since they are assumed to be the direct result of the aging process. **Individual differences** are differences between individuals in any ability, trait, or characteristic. To illustrate, if your hair color is black and your significant other's hair is brown, that is an individual difference in hair color.

As noted previously the process of aging proceeds at different rates for different people. Some individuals begin to lose their hair during their late 20s or have white hair by their mid-40s. Others do not lose any hair, or their hair does not turn white until their late 60s. Therefore, when we discuss various topics throughout this text, such as psychomotor ability, intelligence, memory, or vision, you should realize that at any point during adulthood, people are very different from one another even at identical ages. Hence, not all individuals of a given chronological age will share the same attitudes or have similar abilities or performance levels. In fact, it is not uncommon for individual differences to become greater with increasing age (Nelson & Dannefer, 1992). Simply put, older persons are more different from one another than are younger persons. Also, as intra-individual changes become more dramatic, differences between persons also widen. Consequently, there are differences both within and between individuals at all points in adulthood.

Intra-individual differences refer to differences among traits, behaviors, abilities, or performance levels within a specific individual at any point in time. An example would be the differences among your grades for the various courses you are taking this term. For instance, you may be receiving an A in this course, a B in Mathematics, and a C in English.

The course of development may also vary in terms of the extent to which these factors are working together, or in **synchrony**, or at cross-purposes with one another, or **out of synchrony**. We all go through smooth and bumpy periods in our lives, where we are more or less in or out of sync with others as well as with physical or social changes in our everyday lives. To illustrate, one may wish to marry but not find a suitable mate, illness may interfere with one's career plans, or one may be forced to retire prematurely due to poor health or company policy. Likewise, life stages, e.g., midlife, are best understood in terms of social changes that make them crises for some and not for others (Moen & Wethington, 1999).

Check Your Learning 1-1

Identify the following terms and concepts:

> Normal aging
> Pathological aging
> Life cycle
> Person-environment interaction
> Transactional model
> Developmental niche
> Typical aging
> History-normative influences
> Non-normative influences
> Age-related changes
> Traditionalists
> Millennials
> Age continuum
> Individual time line
> Historical time continuum
> Contextual time
> Adaptation level
> Optimal aging
> Age-normative influences
> In/out of synchrony
> Cultural ethics
> Generation X
> Baby Boomers

• Why is learning about the normal aging process important?

• What is person-environment interaction, and why is it important to the study of adult development and aging?

• Why is the process of adult development and aging considered a continuous, holistic, and dynamic process?

• What is the relationship between person-environment interaction and a developmental niche?

• What are the differences among intra-individual change, individual differences, and intra-individual differences?

• Describe how age-normative, history-normative and non-normative influences affect behavior and life span development.

• Why is adult development and aging considered multidimensional, multidirectional, and pluralistic?

Learning Activity: Ask six persons: "At what age does adulthood begin? At what age does middle-age begin? At what age does old age begin?" Summarize your findings. Where are there differences by gender? Where are there differences based on the person's age?

Developmental Research Designs

Throughout this text we will be referring to various age differences and age changes on a variety of traits, abilities, and skills, such as cognitive functioning, personality traits, attitudes, and psychomotor skills. In order for you to have a greater understanding and appreciation of these presented age differences and age changes, we need to briefly discuss developmental research. The goal of developmental research is to determine if any relationship exists between chronological age, or the processes that account for aging, and some other factor of interest such as intelligence, interpersonal relationships, memory, and so forth. That is, our goal is to derive an **age function**, which is a picture of how age and our variable of interest are related. For example, what role does age or aging play in shaping our memory processes? This role of age (versus other factors) in accounting for our variable of interest is a question of internal validity.

Traditionally, the measurement of age effects on behavior has been undertaken by the use of one of three basic developmental research designs: **cross-sectional, longitudinal,** and **time lag.** Each design has its own unique purposes, advantages, and disadvantages. Prior to our presentation of these three research designs it is important to understand four terms: age, cohort, time of measurement effects, and confounded.

Basically, **age** refers to the chronological age (**level of maturation**) of the participants in the study. **Cohort** (or generation) refers to a common set of experiences that identify members born at a particular point in historical time; these separate them from others born earlier or later. For example, persons who have experienced such events as the Great American Depression or the Vietnam War may differ on their attitudes and behavior. Thus, each cohort grows up with different attitudes, experiences, skills, and values (see our discussion above of cultural ethics). **Time of measurement effects** are influences that affect all persons, regardless of age or cohort, at a given point in time such as the aftermath of September 11, 2001. Finally, **confounded** means that the effects of at least two factors such as age or cohort cannot be disentangled, thus making the results of a study difficult to interpret.

It is important to point out that these three research designs are descriptive. That is, the data they yield may or may not indicate that chronological age *causally* relates to whatever we are studying such as intelligence or attitudes. Therefore, while each design can help to derive an age function, which is a picture of how our variable of interest is related to age, based on the findings from each design, they can only describe the fact that the particular variable does or does not likely vary with chronological age. However, they cannot explain why. This question involves a statement about causality, or explanation.

Cross-sectional designs compare individuals who vary in age at a specific time of measurement.

For example, we could select a group of 20-year-olds, 40-year-olds, and 60-year-olds in 2005, administer measures assessing the same variables of interest (e.g., an intelligence test) to all participants, and then we would compare the performance on the variables of interest between the age groups.

The cross-sectional research design measures age differences or what can be considered average interindividual differences, that is, the normative and average performance for members of that age group on the variables of interest. Although this research design can be quite useful in establishing normative trends, it does suffer from a number of weaknesses. Perhaps the most serious weakness is that the results are confounded by both age and cohort effects. Specifically, it is difficult to determine if the results are due specifically to age of the participants or due to different cumulative generational experiences of the different age groups. As a result of these factors, cross-sectional designs often tend to magnify age differences between the age groups on the variables of interest.

Longitudinal designs involve comparing individuals of the same age at different times of measurement. For instance, we would administer measures assessing the variables of interest to a group of 20-year-olds in 1990, administer the same measures to the same individuals in 2000 when they are 30, and then administer the same measures to the same individuals in the year 2010 when they are age 40. We are interested in determining how performance on the variables of interest changes from one time of measurement to the next time of measurement and so on.

Thus, the longitudinal research design measures age changes or average intra-individual change, i.e., change within a person over time (with age). Even though this research design permits us to estimate average intra-individual variability with age on the variables of interest, it also has weaknesses. In this case, the most serious weakness is that the results are confounded by both age effects and time of measurement effects—a short-term influence that is or is not present before or after a given time of measurement, e.g. the Kennedy assassination, the

Challenger or *Columbia* disasters, or the events of September 11, 2001. Consequently, longitudinal designs generally minimize or underestimate age changes in the variables of interest.

Time lag designs assess some aspect of cultural change rather than age effects, and may therefore help us explain more clearly the results of either a cross-sectional or longitudinal study. Time lag designs involve at least two separate times of measurement on the variables of interest, involving individuals of identical ages from different cohorts. For example, we could measure performance on the variable of interest in two groups of individuals: those age 20 who are from the 1960 cohort, measured in 1980; and in 2000, we would measure performance on the same variable of interest in persons who are age 20, who are members of the 1980 cohort. If for example, our groups were to score similarly, then we would be in a better position to argue that both cohort and time of measurement effects (each reflecting some aspect of cultural change) are largely irrelevant to the age differences or age changes we assessed with the cross-sectional and longitudinal designs, respectively.

Time lag studies are a valuable source of information to the extent that cultural changes, and not age-related factors, are responsible for such things as political attitudes or persons' attitudes toward the roles they play or with regard to social/environmental issues. However, the most serious weakness of the time lag design is that time of measurement is confounded with cohort (generation) effects. Thus, if our groups were not to score similarly, we could most likely eliminate age-related factors as important, but would still have difficulty explaining exactly why our groups differed: were they different because they were members of different cohorts, or because they were tested at different historical times?

In an attempt to address the inherent weaknesses in the three traditional developmental research designs, Schaie (1965, 1970) proposed a more complicated set of approaches, each derived from the three traditional designs. These are the **time sequential, cohort sequential,** and the **cross sequential**

designs. Specifically, each involves sequences of cross-sectional, longitudinal, or time lag studies. Schaie's approach is considered a trifactorial one, where three factors, age, cohort, and time of measurement, are the dimensions of interest.

Time sequential studies replicate a cross-sectional study at a new time of measurement, allowing for independent (unconfounded) estimates of age and time of measurement effects. Time sequential studies assume that cohort effects are minimal.

Cohort sequential studies replicate a longitudinal study utilizing different cohorts. In this study time of measurement is considered irrelevant. Therefore, cohort sequential studies allow us to independently estimate age and cohort effects.

Cross sequential studies are a more general case of the time lag design. Cross sequential studies allow age to be confounded, and make possible independent estimates of cohort and time of measurement effects.

In general, each design rests upon a distinct set of assumptions about which component is irrelevant or confounded (based upon the researcher's knowledge or research data). In the case of each design, threats to the external validity of the above basic designs is enhanced via their replication (remember we only have a single cross sectional, longitudinal, or time lag comparison), and threats to the internal validity of each design are addressed via the assumption (based upon sound research and theory or actual data) that a specific factor's influence is minimal (1 of 3 factors will necessarily remain confounded in each sequential design), allowing us to independently estimate the effects of the remaining two.

Thus, each sequential design, being a more general case of one of the three more basic designs, tries to deal with validity issues by assuming one of the three components (age, cohort, time) to be irrelevant, therefore allowing for unbiased estimates of the remaining two. They allow us to **generalize** from one set of findings to another set of findings in examining their stability over time, cohort, or age. Each design asks a somewhat different question, and, everything else being equal, is more appropriate for some topics than others.

In addition to each of the above strategies we use to collect data from adults, there are other considerations to keep in mind when conducting and interpreting adult developmental research (see Baltes, 1968). As our samples are generally composed of volunteers, persons who do so may not represent everyone in whom we are interested. Those who volunteer may be brighter, healthier, more highly educated, or differ in terms of their gender or marital status from those who do not volunteer. This problem is referred to as **selective sampling.** Persons who are alive to be studied may not represent all persons who are members of a given birth cohort. Those who survive may be more likely to be married, be female, be more highly educated, or be more adaptive in coping than those who have not survived. This problem is referred to as **selective survival.** Persons often change in ways that have more to do with nearness to death than to the effects of age (see Chapters 2 and 12). Thus, we may be measuring what is termed **terminal change or terminal drop,** rather than the effects of development or aging. Persons may also improve over time because they have been repeatedly assessed. Their scores are therefore subject to the effects of **practice,** rather than to the effects of age. Persons may drop out over time in longitudinal or cohort sequential designs. Who is available to be reassessed may be different (perhaps they had performed better on our measures of interest) from those who chose to drop out of our study. This is referred to as **selective dropout** or **selective attrition**. Last, persons may be more or less likely to change over time based upon their initial scores. Statistically, the scores of those who initially score higher are more likely to decline because the initial score was already high. That is, there is more room to decline than to increase if you have already scored near the top of the scale. Those who score lower earlier are therefore more likely to change positively (improve) relative to how they had scored earlier. For this reason, on subsequent tests, the scores of people who initially score very highly or very lowly approach

the mean or average for the group. This phenomenon is referred to as **regression to the mean**. These influences (selective sampling, selective survival, terminal change, practice, selective dropout, regression to the mean) all need to be taken into consideration, in addition to those factors discussed above (age, cohort, time of measurement), when interpreting the results of the above designs, as they influence how much faith we can have in our findings' accurately representing real developmental (age-related) change.

A summary of each of the designs we have discussed here appears in Table 1-2. In addition, the above influences on each basic design's findings, of which one needs to be aware, are also presented in Table 1-2.

Who Are Adults? Who Are Older Persons?

Generally, the primary criteria used in assigning the above labels to particular individuals, including ourselves, is chronological age, which simply refers to the number of years that have passed since birth. However, age has many meanings and may be conceptualized in a variety of ways such as functional, ideal, personal, and cognitive in nature, in addition to chronological (Staats, 1996). Consequently, age is not a simple concept.

Additionally, experts in the field of adulthood and aging (e.g., Abeles, 1997) have expressed great dissatisfaction with the use of chronological age as a meaningful indicator of change, since age-related changes or differences observed in terms of personality or behavior are not always due to age per se, but to other factors such as underlying biological changes or cohort influences. Thus, while chronological age may help us organize our knowledge about people and their behavior, it does not allow us to explain the how and the why of behavior. Hence, at best one should view chronological age as an index of change, just as inches are an index of a person's height, rather than a cause of change.

We have found it difficult to move away from the use of chronological age to explain or predict

Table 1-2

Developmental Research Designs

Design	Purpose	Confounded Factors/Limitations
Cross-sectional	Measures age differences at a single time of measurement	Age differences are confounded with cohort differences, selective sampling, selective survival, terminal change. Findings are time of measurement specific.
Longitudinal	Measures age changes over several times of measurement	Age changes are confounded with time of measurement, selective sampling, selective survival, terminal change, practice, selective dropout, regression effects. Findings are cohort specific.
Time lag	Measures cultural change; age held constant	Cannot separate time of measurement and cohort effects.
Time sequential	Replicates a cross-sectional study over time; separates time of measurement and age	Cohort is confounded in all comparisons.
Cohort sequential	Replicates a longitudinal study over cohorts; separates age and cohort	Time of measurement is confounded in all comparisons.
Cross sequential	Time lag study can be generalized over multiple times and cohorts; separates time and cohort	Age is confounded in all comparisons.

behavioral change, because it is often linked by law to the accessibility of specific goods, services, and benefits. To illustrate, at age 16 you can get a driver's license, at 18 you can vote, at 21 you can purchase alcohol, and at 65 you can retire. The use of chronological age in this manner is called **legal age.** Although this use of age lacks scientific precision, it does mandate a specific standard for making decisions about people that relate to persons of a given age with equal applicability.

Birren's Three Types of Age

Birren (1964) suggested that in order to discuss the age of a person in a meaningful way, we must consider three types of age: **biological age,**

psychological age, and **social age.** Each of these types of age is thought to be independent of one another. For instance, a person's biological age does not necessarily affect his or her psychological and social ages, and vice versa. In reality, however, for most individuals they are somewhat related.

There are two aspects to **biological age.** First, it can be considered to be the relative age or condition of the individual's organ and body systems. For example, does the 80-year-old individual's cardiovascular system or nervous system in fact function like those of the typical 80-year-old? It is quite possible for an 80-year-old who has remained physically active through exercise to have a cardiovascular system characteristic of someone much younger.

Adults Speak

On Reaching 40

A few middle-aged people may experience a midlife crisis, and react by becoming anxious or depressed. They may make sudden, unwise, or irrevocable changes in their lives. However, many people see middle age simply as a time to reevaluate the direction of their lives. They often set new goals for themselves, realizing that they no longer have unlimited time to get things done.

As one 43-year-old woman says, 'I think being 40 caused me to kind of stop and take stock . . . . I wondered if I wanted to be a professional organist all my life." She has since returned to school to pursue a degree in counseling.

Her most sobering realization at turning 40 was that I'm not going to have time to do everything. . . . Like I always had the idea of going to medical school. That's not going to be a possibility now. . . . It's kind of a splash of cold water when you realize that some of the things you thought you would be doing just aren't going to happen."

Her advice to young people? "Shake loose and look at all the possibilities."

The perception of the richness in life that people can experience in their middle years is supported by a recent survey of over 8,000 middle-aged individuals by the MacArthur Foundation to understand the multitude of factors contributing to successful development and happiness in adulthood. The results indicated that less than a quarter of persons surveyed felt that they had experienced a midlife crisis. Indeed, their well-being and control over their lives had improved over the last decade, and while they had some complaints (high blood pressure, back problems, arthritis, anxiety/depression, stomach trouble), their perception of the stability of their marriages, commitment to raising their children, sex lives, and striking a balance between work and family, were positive, though this varied by gender.

Source: MacArthur Foundation Research Network on Successful Midlife Development, www.mac found.org

On the other hand, a 30-year-old who has lived a very sedentary life-style (a couch potato!) and engaged in poor dietary and health practices (e. g., a diet high in cholesterol, lack of exercise, cigarette smoking) may have the cardiovascular system characteristic of someone much older.

The other aspect of biological age is an individual's present position relative to potential life span, which is how many years the organism or person could theoretically live. This varies from species to species. For example, flies have a potential life span of days, dogs 15 to 20 years, and humans 115 years. Consequently, a given chronological age has vastly different meanings for different species. An age of 15 years is of course meaningless when applied to a fly, while to a dog it implies the later stages of the life cycle, and it represents adolescence for a human being. Thus the same chronological age carries a very different meaning from species to species. While biological age should not be viewed as synonymous with chronological age, for most humans they are generally quite similar.

Psychological age refers to the adaptive capacities of an individual such as one's coping ability, problem-solving skill, or intelligence. Most often we infer psychological age from observations of a person's behavior in everyday situations or on the basis of interviews or test performance. While our psychological age may be related to both chronological and biological age, it cannot be fully described by their combination. For example, although an individual may be chronologically 90 years of age and bedridden with severe arthritis, that person may keep abreast of current local and world events, be alert and conversational, and have sound reasoning skills. This individual's capacities in these areas might therefore be more similar to those of persons in their 20s.

Social age refers to the habits, behaviors, beliefs, attitudes, and activities of an individual relative to the expectations of society. Others' beliefs about these behaviors are often called developmental tasks, which are age-specific expectancies, in terms of the acquisition of specific skills, behaviors, and activities. They often also vary as a function of culture, race, ethnicity, or gender. Developmental tasks are useful in that they provide individuals with a system of age norms or age-appropriate behaviors and activities. As an illustration, have you ever told one of your friends, whom you view as acting like a child, to "act your age"? Society tends to positively reinforce individuals for acting in an age-appropriate manner and to implicitly punish individuals for violating these norms or expectations. Accordingly, social age is somewhat related to chronological, biological, and psychological ages but is not completely defined by them. For instance, someone who is chronologically 80 years of age may share similar attitudes, habits, clothing preferences, and leisure activities typical of people in their 20s or 30s.

Functional Age

There are a variety of definitions for **functional age**. However, they all share the assumption that one's functional age is an index of one's capacities or abilities, which can range from performance on a particular job to the condition and functioning of various organ systems in the body. To illustrate, although a person has a chronological age of 40, the condition of his or her cardiovascular system may be similar to that of a 30-year-old (similar to Birren's biological age). Another way of viewing functional age is with regard to performance. For example, a person who is 40 years of age chronologically, but

who performs on the job, and is just as productive as someone who is 25 years of age, would have a functional age of 25. The primary goal of this view of functional age is to find a replacement for chronological age as a criterion for hiring, job change, and retirement. At present, both views of functional age are limited in that they still are in part defined by chronological age. We will examine the implications of functional age regarding the assessment of work performance in greater detail in our discussion of aging and work (Chapter 7).

Another way to look at age is to examine it from the inside. How do people define age from their own perspective? There are a number of "self-perceived" or attitudinal ages, such as **ideal age** and **personal age**. Each of these types of age can be considered **subjective**, since age in these contexts can have different meanings to individuals at different points in the life cycle. For instance, a 6-year-old may view a 15-year-old sibling as an adult. Fifteen-year-olds may consider themselves adults, while most parents view them as children. Most 30-year-olds consider themselves adults, yet a 20-year-old may view a 30-year-old as middle-aged, or even old. Likewise, many 60-year-olds may see themselves as middle-aged and reserve the term *old* for someone who is 75 or 80, and consider a 30-year-old as a "youngster." Thus, personal age is how old persons feel they are, while ideal age is the age they would like to be.

In general, people report feeling younger than they really are more often than they report feeling older than their actual age (Barnes-Farrell & Piotrowski, 1989). However, in this study, the proportion of people reporting feeling younger increased with age, while the opposite was true for younger people. Moreover, the magnitude of this discrepancy also increased with increased age. Similar results were reported by Montepare and Lachman (1989), who however found that this was more true for women than for men. Polls (*Your Health*, 1996) show that more than 75% of Baby Boomers believe that they look younger than their actual age. The same polls indicate that for persons age 30 to 34, middle age starts at age 40, while for people aged 44, they believe that middle age starts somewhere between ages 45 to 50. Most Americans think that old age begins in a person's early 60s (Speas & Obenshain, 1995). Accordingly, terms such as young or old are relative in nature and often depend on one's personal perspective.

Also, women tend to fear age-associated losses more than men do and perceive themselves as "old" at a younger age than do men (McConatha, Schnell, Volkwein, Riley, & Leach, 2003). Because of the high cultural value placed on women's reproductive potential and activities, it has been widely assumed that middle age, and the associated decrease in reproduction-related demands and potential, would pose a particular challenge to women's self-image and sense of purpose (Stewart, Ostrove, & Helson, 2001). However, women felt more identity certainty, generativity, confidence, and concern about aging in their 40s than they recalled feeling in their 30s (Stewart et al., 2001).

Further, research (e.g., Stewart et al., 2001) has confirmed both that adults of all ages share a view of middle-aged people as particularly competent, productive, and responsible, and that middle-aged adults generally feel that they are more in command of themselves and their worlds than adults of other ages; this is consistent for both men and women.

At this point, you might ask yourself: how old do I feel? When do you feel adulthood begins? Middle age? Old age? What does it mean to be mature? Interestingly, both middle-aged and older persons equate maturity with a selfless attitude and being able to accept change (Ryff, 1989). Just as there are different definitions of age, there are a variety of perspectives on how to characterize stages or periods in the life cycle.

Periods of the Life Cycle

As noted previously, the two most widely used methods of classifying individuals to periods of the life cycle are by either age or by developmental tasks. Each of these methods has advantages and disadvantages. Using either of these criteria for classification has led to numerous schemes proposed to define the stages or periods of adulthood. Since

these designations are often arbitrary, they should not be considered absolute or distinct. Their primary value is to simply help us organize and describe adult life. One of the most widely accepted age criteria classification system is that of Levinson (1986). Levinson classifies the periods of the adult life cycle into: **early adulthood** (17-45 years), **middle adulthood** (40-65 years), and **late adulthood** (60+ years). Neugarten (1976) suggested that late adulthood can be separated into **young-old age** (65-75) and **old-old age** (75+). While such classifications may be convenient, they too frequently mask the distinctive individual patterns of adaptation to changes that occur with increasing age (Feifel & Stack, 1987). Older people are different not only from the young, but also from each other, even within the same age category.

As individuals proceed along the life course, entrance to and exit from these purported stages are gradual. For example, according to Levinson, early adulthood theoretically ends at about age 45, and middle adulthood begins at age 40. The 5-year span (ages 40 to 45) thus serves as a **midlife transition** during which the stage of early adulthood draws to a close and the stage of middle adulthood begins. Similarly, between the stages of middle adulthood and late adulthood is a 5-year span (ages 60 to 65) for the **transition to later life.**

The **developmental task** approach uses behaviors and activities such as marriage, entering or leaving the workforce, as the criteria for classification. As we noted above, this is important as society tends to positively reinforce individuals for acting in an age-appropriate manner and to implicitly punish individuals for violating or departing from those norms. While developmental tasks are often seen in normative terms, they often vary as a function of factors such as culture, gender, and occupation. Thus issues defining developmental tasks and norms for behavior are always relative, and never absolute (Arnett, 1994).

Emerging Adulthood

Arnett (2000) has argued that the period of young adulthood needs revision, and terms this new stage **emerging adulthood,** beginning with the late

Box B

Changing Views about Adulthood:
Emerging Adulthood, Midlife, and Later Life

Our ideas about adulthood are undergoing a shift, in part a function of the comparatively recent interest in those persons whom we have for the most part ignored in our study of adults: younger and middle-aged persons. This is in contrast to the comparatively more established interest in the study of childhood, adolescence, and later life. This shift suggests that we are thinking in a more flexible manner about how the adult life span is to be organized. Rather than define adulthood in rigid, chronological terms, we are moving toward an experiential perspective, where the **quality** of the choices and behaviors persons make are key in defining the phases of adulthood.

For example, **emerging adulthood** has replaced both adolescence and young adulthood, encompassing the period for most adults, between ages 18 and 25. It is succinctly defined by Erikson's notion of **moratorium**: being able to try on new ways of defining oneself and relating to others in many contexts—work, family, with regard to one's peers—much as one shops for a new coat or dress, trying many on until the one that fits best is chosen. Tanner (2006) defines this process in terms of **recentering**: experiencing a shift in the power of decision-making from one's parents to oneself—"parental regulation is replaced by self-regulation" (p. 27), where the individual is now in the process of making commitments that are lifelong in nature—to one's career, to one's spouse, and to one's children. In so doing, the boundaries between oneself and one's family of origin are becoming more well-defined. Yet, more adults negotiate this transition toward more freedom with less support, and fewer definitive guidelines regarding what to do and how to do it than ever before. Putting off marriage until later in one's 20s or 30s, spending more time in college, and being more likely to

make more residential moves are all indicators of this shift (Arnett, 2000). This results in great heterogeneity among persons at this point in their lives. Arnett (2006) discusses **five key features of emerging adulthood**. It is (1) **the age of identity explorations**, especially in the areas of love and work; (2) **the age of instability**, where freedom, novelty, and excitement are accompanied by great instability; (3) **the self-focused age**, where emerging adults have few commitments and obligations to others, leaving them more time and energy for self-exploration and autonomy; (4) **the age of feeling in-between**, because in some ways, emerging adults do not see themselves as adolescents, but neither do they see themselves as adults (e.g., accepting responsibility, making independent decisions, being financially independent); and (5) **the age of possibilities**, where individuals are hopeful and optimistic about the future, and they recognize that they now have the opportunity to overcome family, personal, or economic hardships and difficulties, and to "steer their lives in a different and more favorable direction before they enter the commitments in work and love that structure adult life" (Arnett, 2006, p. 13).

A second example relates to our changing views about **midlife**, in contrast to a complete ignorance of this phase of adulthood, or upon midlife as a period of crisis and personal upheaval, whose beginnings are impossible to define chronologically and whose end is signaled by retirement. Are people "over the hill" or "does life begin" at 40? In some respects, middle age has been negatively defined in terms of age 50-60 "triggers" that signal when one is no longer young (Karp, 1988), e.g., when one's body changes, when one is now a senior person at work, or when one's parents or age peers die. Indeed, our views about midlife itself are undergoing a transition or rebirth (Wahl & Kruse, 2005). Even if one chooses to view midlife in chronological terms, recent evidence suggests that it may, for some people, begin as early as age 30 and last until at least age 70 (National Council on Aging, 2000). Indeed, the entry and exit years for midlife vary with age, with such limits increasing for those who are older (Lachman et al., 1994). Rather than simplistically defining midlife in terms of crisis, brought about by the empty nest, by fears of aging, or in terms of Eriksonian generativity, it is better to see midlife in terms of the variety of activities and roles in which individuals are embedded. Middle-aged persons may be not only raising children or grandchildren, but also caring for parents and grandparents. They may be in the process of either launching their children or reabsorbing them after the death of a spouse, the loss of a job, or after divorce or a serious illness. They may have reached the zenith of their careers, be pursuing entirely new careers, or be saddled with debts associated with college tuition or nursing home costs. They may be planning for retirement or faced with redefining their careers, having been downsized from their jobs. They may be in good health, or be coping with the effects of menopause or the climacteric, breast or prostate cancer, high blood pressure, a heart attack or stroke, or the effects of lifestyle issues, e.g., obesity, high cholesterol, or smoking (see Lachman, 2001). On the other hand, increases in life expectancy, improvements in health care, and greater attention to lifestyle issues have redefined the upper limits of midlife. Midlife can be a stressful period, but instead of seeing such events and pressures as negative, they instead are viewed as challenges—mountains to be scaled, problems to be solved.

Likewise, reflecting this revised manner of thinking about adult development, later life has now been differentiated in terms of the **young-old** (age 65-74), the **old-old** (age 75-84) (see Neugarten & Neugarten, 1987), and the **oldest-old** (over age 85), or what Baltes (1997) has termed the "fourth age." Moreover, **cente-narians** (persons living to at least 100 years of age) have now emerged as the more recently discovered older adult. Each subcategory of older persons is faced with the task of coping with varying degrees of impairment and/or alternatively, can be seen as survivors, persons who are resilient in the face of change and adversity.

A last example of this shift in views about adulthood is reflected in Hudson's (1999) **cyclical view of adulthood**. Rather than think strictly in terms of stages or phases of development that make adulthood predictable and stable, Hudson argues that adulthood has been reinvented. Life is less predictable, to a greater extent full of change, challenge, and indeed, contradiction and instability, relative to the adulthood that our parents and grandparents experienced. The cyclical view of adulthood suggests that persons are engaged in a perpetual cycle of **self-renewal**, where issues of one's identity, the meaning of work and leisure, one's needs for intimacy, play, and creativity are expressed/defined and reexpressed/redefined continually, as is the search for personal meaning and recognizing the importance of compassion for others and contributions to the world beyond oneself. Adult development is therefore expressed as a series of cycles of change and continuity in the context of a world that is complex, unstable, and sometimes unpredictable. Self-renewing adults are adaptive, connected to others, future-oriented, and resilient in the face of change and adversity. According to the cyclical view of adulthood, conflict and loss are just as much a part of life as are joy and fulfillment. Adults of all ages are constantly in the process of renewing and reinventing themselves in the context of constancies and universals in life that are meaningful and important to them, such as the need for intimacy or the development of a viable personal identity. The very notion of cycles suggests that certain themes are repeated over time, but also reflect the fact that these themes are played out differently at different times in persons' lives.

These changing views about adulthood will

hopefully reflect persons' awareness of the decreasing power of chronological age to predict behavior and to serve as a yardstick by which adults can be understood or categorized. Perhaps ultimately, our society will indeed become an ageless one!

teens and lasting through the 20s, with the focus being on ages 18-25. According to Arnett, sweeping demographic shifts have taken place over the past century which has made the late teens and early 20s a distinct period of the life cycle, characterized by change and exploration of possible life directions. Thus, emerging adulthood is neither adolescence nor young adulthood, and is characterized by independence, but not with the responsibilities of marriage, parenthood, and work. The emerging adult is consumed with exploring the many directions life might take, in terms of love, personal values and opinions, and work. For this reason, Arnett (2000) suggests that emerging adulthood is the most volitional of all life stages. While it may be ambiguous (one is neither an adolescent nor an adult), it presents one with many opportunities for the exploration of one's personal identity. In emerging adulthood, there are no norms, since it is a period of exploration. Overall, the years of emerging adulthood are characterized by a high degree of demographic diversity and instability, reflecting the emphasis on change and exploration. It is only in the transition from emerging adulthood to young adulthood in the late 20s that the diversity narrows and the instability eases, as young people are more likely to make more enduring choices in love and work.

It is important to realize that emerging adulthood is not a universal period but a period that exists only in cultures that postpone the entry into adult roles and responsibilities until well past the late teens (Arnett, 2000). Consequently, emerging adulthood would be most likely to be found in countries that are highly industrialized or postindustrial. In these cultures, marriage and parenthood are typically postponed until well after schooling has ended, which allows for periods of exploration. So too is middle age or late adulthood culture-specific.

Transitions in Adulthood

Transitions are important developmental events which can occur in adulthood. According to Schlossberg (1989) there are seven types: (1) **Elected**, which are based on individual choices such as leaving home and changing jobs; (2) **Surprises**, when the unexpected happens, e.g., winning the lottery, being fired from your job; (3) **Nonevents**, is when the expected does not happen such as never finding a suitable mate, never receiving the expected promotion at work; (4) **Life on hold**, which are transitions waiting to happen such as waiting for the last child to graduate from high school; (5) **Sleepers,** transitions which occur slowly over time, such as becoming overweight and out of shape, or becoming bored with your job; (6) **Double whammies**, when the person experiences multiple significant events almost simultaneously, such as retiring and losing your spouse, or having a baby and developing a serious illness; and (7) **Legal/chronological transitions**, that when reached will confer certain legal rights or responsibilities for the person, for example, voting at age 18, retiring at age 65.

Check Your Learning 1-2

Identify the following terms and concepts:

Age function
Time of measurement
Age differences
Time sequential studies
Cross sequential studies
Age-appropriate behaviors
Chronological age
Transitions
Emerging adulthood
Intra-individual differences

Longitudinal design
Selective sampling
Selective dropout
Regression to the mean
Cohort
Confounded
Age changes
Cohort sequential studies
Legal age
Attitudinal age
Ideal age
Functional age
Personal age
Individual differences
Intra-individual changes
Cross-sectional design
Time lag design
Selective survival
Practice effects
Terminal change/terminal drop

- What are some of the common definitions of age?

- What are the two most widely used methods of classifying persons to periods of the life cycle? What are some of the advantages and disadvantages of each method?

- Why are developmental tasks important to adult development and aging?

- What are the seven types of transitions which persons could experience during adult development and aging?

- Compare and contrast the cross-sectional, longitudinal, and time lag research designs.

- What is Schaie's tri-factorial approach?

- Define and give an example of Birren's three types of age.

Learning Activity: Ask a young adult, a middle-aged person, and an older adult what they consider to be the major developmental tasks associated with young adulthood, middle age, and old age.

An Aging Society: Attitudes and Implications

Demography is affected by birth rates, mortality rates, and immigration (Vincent & Velkoff, 2010). Based on past trends and current conditions, demographers attempt to estimate the proportion of various groups within a population in the future. These projections can vary from one source to another depending on the statistical and mathematical algorithms used and how the demographers weigh the importance and likelihood of future advancements in medicine. Regardless of which set of demographic projections one reads, however, it is clear: during the last three decades, America has been growing older. Longer life expectancies coupled with a general decline in the birth and death rate has led to a dramatic shift in the proportion of older adults within the general population (Vincent & Verkoff, 2010). Life expectancy has increased from 70 years in 1970 to 75+ years in 2000. The percentage of persons aged 65 and older was approximately 4% of the population in 1900 and approximately 13% in the year 2000 (see Table 1-3). Further, the median age in the United States has increased from 30 years in 1980, 32.1 in 1990, 34.6 in 1996, and approximately 36 at the turn of the century; it is expected to be 42 by 2030 (Howell, 1997; U.S. Bureau of the Census, 1997). The fastest growing subgroup is persons over 85 (Abeles, 1997), the majority of whom are women (Howell, 1997). Similar trends are observed in other industrialized nations of the world.

In view of these facts, it is easy to see why the United States and other industrialized nations are becoming an **aging society**, since the number of "older" persons is proportionately larger over time than that for "younger" individuals (see Table 1-3). Moreover, among older adults, we anticipate an increase in those over the age of 85 (see Table 1-4) and those over age 100 (see Box C). This shift in demographics will have major implications for society (Howell, 1997; Vincent & Verkoff, 2010).

1. It will lead to a change in the demand for products and services associated with older

consumers. Advertisers were quick to grasp the significance of the aging trend and have reacted accordingly to attract older consumers, e.g., dental adhesives, specialty vacations, and long-term care insurance.

Table 1-3

Percentage of United States Population Age 45+ Years and Age 65+ Years 1900 to 2000.

Year	45+ Years	65+ Years
1900	17.8%	4%
1920s	20.7%	4.7%
1940s	26.7%	6.8%
1960s	29.3%	9.2%
1980s	30.3%	11.3%
2000	22.1%	13%

Sources: U.S. Bureau of the Census (2004). *U.S. interim projections by age, sex, race, and Hispanic origin.* Washington, DC; U.S. Bureau of the Census Bicentennial Edition, *Historical Abstract of the United States, Colonial Times to 1970,* Washington, DC; Schick (1976), *Statistical Handbook on Aging Americans,* Phoenix: Oryx Press.

2. Passage of legislation prohibiting age discrimination, disability discrimination, and mandatory retirement has enabled older workers to remain on the job longer; this will substantially impact the workplace. Employers need to adapt, such as in the design of tasks, and personnel practices such as hiring, training, evaluating, and compensation will need to be modified (see Chapter 7).
3. There will also be major economic impact on society; for example, the health care system, educational institutions, welfare, etc., will need to be modified.
4. Government at local, state, and national levels will be significantly affected since "older" persons will be a substantial voting block.

Attitudes toward Aging

For many of us, aging continues to be mysterious, often surrounded by ignorance, stereotypes, and biases. The study of attitudes toward older adults can be described as voluminous and often contradictory (Ferraro, 1992). Despite the demographic changes in the U.S. population and the acquisition of new knowledge and research findings, views about the aging process and later adulthood continue to be clouded by misinformation. It is for this reason that subscribing to common **myths of aging** can affect attitudes toward our own aging pro-

Table 1-4

Projected Number of Millions in United States Population: Age 65+ and Age 85+ Years.

Year	Census Estimates		Social Security Administration		MacArthur Foundation	
	65+	85+	65+	85+	65+	85+
2030	72.1	8.7	70.4	7.4	75.9 – 78.3	10.3 – 12.1
2050	88.5	19.0	80.8	15.1	99.3 – 107.7	27.0 – 34.7

Source: Olshansky et al. (2009).

Box C

Centenarians

About 1 in every 10,000 Americans is currently age 100 years or older (Perls, Bochen, Freeman, Alpert, & Silver, 1999), and the odds of living to 100 are likely to double in the near future (Perls, 2006). It is estimated that in 2050, approximately 610,000 Americans will be age 100 or older (Olshansky et al., 2009). Several studies examining centenarians are currently in the field around the world. From these studies, we have learned much about the correlates of longevity, as well as the physical and cognitive changes exhibited among the oldest old.

Current research suggests that just as with other age groups, centenarians show marked individual differences in some areas and strong similarities in other areas. Most individuals who live to be 100 years demonstrate a high degree of functional independence well into their 90s and more than half (53%) experience delays in the onset of or absence of chronic health conditions such as heart disease, nonskin cancer, and stroke (Perls, 2006). In terms of cognitive impairments associated with Alzheimer's disease and other forms of dementia, although there is an increase in dementia with age, the risks seem to plateau in the late 90s (Perls, 2006).

Centenarians show marked inter-individual differences and may be very different than stereotypes would suggest. For example, a recent telephone survey with 100 individuals ages 99+

years revealed that many centenarians are socially engaged, attentive to their health, and keep current with pop culture and technology (Evercare, 2010). For example:

82% talk to or otherwise communicate with family and friends every day.
72% laugh or giggle every day.
62% engage in daily spiritual activities.

To stay healthy, at least once a week:

41% walk or hike.
32% do gardening.
6% practice Tai Chi, yoga, or meditate.
5% play a sport such as basketball, tennis, baseball, or soccer.
4% ride a bike.

They keep current with technology and pop culture, too. In fact,

12% have listened to music on an iPod or similar device.
11% have watched a video on YouTube.
8% have sent a text or instant message.
2% have used Facebook.
1% have tried Nintendo's Wii Fit.

None, however, reported using Twitter or voting for a contestant on a reality show (but 56% said they knew who Simon Cowell is).

cess and aging persons themselves. Some of these myths include: older adults show little interest in sex, they tend to be inflexible, they lack creativity and are unproductive, and they have great difficulty in learning new skills (Abeles, 1997).

Some of these myths or beliefs can be traced as far back in history as Biblical times, and appear in the writings of Shakespeare (Covey, 1989). These myths lead to **stereotypes** (overgeneralizations) of

older adults, and are the result of a lack of experience and knowledge, as well as selective exposure to older adults. According to Cuddy, Norton, and Fiske (2005) extensive research indicates that the stereotype of older persons is mixed, that is, both positive and negative in tone. Specifically this stereotype views elderly people as warm (positive), but also incompetent (negative). Likewise, we may unfairly characterize young adults as being preoccupied with sex and drugs, lazy, or lacking in ambition, or see middle-aged persons as experiencing a crisis. Indeed, the overgeneralized notion of "crisis" has recently been extended in the popular press to not only the aging of Baby Boomers (Mellor & Rehr, 2005), but also to young adults facing the transition from young adulthood to mature adulthood (Robbins, 2005), paralleling the assumption that midlife is a crisis and that young adults, lacking mentors to guide them through emerging adulthood (Arnett, 1994), are facing a crisis of responsibility and success. While it is undoubtedly true that some young adults and middle-aged persons experience a crisis of sorts, whether persons, by virtue of their age, are predisposed to experiencing a crisis, is questionable.

All of these assumptions reflect generalizations about others with whom we may have little regular contact or experience; they reflect the tendency for persons to describe members of their own age group more specifically and those of other age groups more generally (Curtiss & Hayslip, 2000). This may be an artifact of the ageist society in which we live, where age is used as a criterion for expectations about our behavior (see above), and persons are unlikely to have regular contact with persons who are not members of their birth cohort. Regarding work, they may reflect the influence of age norms for certain occupations (see Chapters 7 and 8).

Research by the American Association of Retired Persons (Speas & Obenshain, 1995) demonstrates that Americans' knowledge, perceptions, and attitudes about the aging process and the elderly have changed and are generally now more positive. These researchers report that less knowledge of aging leads to negative views as well as being associated with a high level of anxiety about aging.

It is important to note that attitudes toward aging differ as a function of culture. For example, Oberg and Tornstam (2003) found rather positive attitudes toward old age in Sweden, while McConatha et al. (2003) found that although negative stereotypes about older people are widespread in both the United States and Germany, they appear to be even more prevalent in Germany. Respect for the elderly is built into the social fabric of most Asian countries (Ingersoll-Dayton & Saentienchai, 1999). The concept of **filial piety** demonstrates that respect and care for parents and the aged are deeply entrenched in Asian cultures. Ingersoll-Dayton and Saentienchai (1999) found that although while the expressions of respect for the elderly are changing in Asia, respect remains a central value in these cultures. However, there is some evidence suggesting that this is changing and that ageism is now pan-cultural (see Cuddy et al., 2005).

Overall, although attitudes toward aging have improved substantially during the last decade, the study of such attitudes toward older adults continues to be quite enigmatic because of the complexity and multidimensionality of attitudes. However, the literature is quite clear in suggesting that the more exposure individuals have to older adults, just as with any group of individuals, the more attitudes tend to be positive (Abeles, 1997; Howell, 1997).

Implications for Adults

As you read about the various dimensions of adult development in this text, think of them in relationship to one another and their influence on your own development. Also, consider how changes in these dimensions over the last decade have affected development in adulthood. For example, how have advances in medical care and social services impacted changes in life expectancy (Chapter 2)? How do changes in observable physical appearance (Chapter 2) affect interpersonal relationships (Chapters 4 and 5) and one's personality and self-concept (Chapter 6)? How have changes in men's and women's roles affected marriage and parenting (Chapters 4 and 5)? How have changes in the workplace affected career choice among younger and middle-aged persons (Chapter 7)? How have changes in life expectancy affected the ability of adult children to care for their parents and grandparents (Chapters 5 and 10)? How has divorce affected the role of grandparent (Chapter 5)?

Understanding adult development in this way will help you realize that your own development

Box D

Age Stereotypes and Stereotype Threat

Persons tend to stereotype others whom they perceive to be different than they are, which leads to many unfortunate consequences. **Attitudinal generalizations** about older or younger persons, or **stereotypes**, are related to social discrimination, foster negative attitudes toward oneself and others, create physical, emotional, and social distance between the person who holds such beliefs and the object of such attitudes, and affect interactions between younger and older persons. For example, persons may address older adults in a patronizing, demeaning, or childlike manner, termed **elderspeak** "Aren't we looking good today!" (Ryan et al., 1986). This may be based upon physical cues and/or the person's age which serve as cues for such behavior. Older persons become victims of such attitudinal generalizations about them. Their self-esteem suffers, they lose self-confidence, and they may withdraw from others and reduce their participation in meaningful activities (Hess, 2006).

Recent work (see Hess, 2006) suggests that aging attitudes are complex, have emotional, cognitive, and behavioral aspects to them, and can be positive (golden ager, perfect grandparent) as well as negative (severely impaired, recluse) (Hummert, 1989). Often, persons who are the objects of such stereotypes internalize them, which contribute to their being the very victims (or beneficiaries) of the stereotypes that they ironically believe to be true as they apply to others. Examples of such stereotypes are that younger persons are hardworking and ambitious or that they are lazy, that such persons are obsessed with sex, drugs, or material things; that middle-aged persons are either mature and responsible, or are experiencing a crisis or breakdown, or that older persons are wise and experienced, or are physically and mentally impaired.

Recently, adult developmental researchers have explored the impact of being exposed to negative or positive stereotypes on persons' performance and well-being—the impact of **stereotype threat**. Such threats can be **situational** in their influence, or they may be **internalized** early in life as a function of repeated exposure to them via, for example, the media or in the context of family influences. Exposure to both positive and negative stereotypes of aging has predicable effects on older persons, assuming exposure to such influences activates previously held beliefs about aging. When exposed to negative stereotypes, older persons' cognitive (memory) performance is negative (Levy, 1996), and persons holding negative stereotypes demonstrate more hearing loss over time (Levy, Slade, & Gill, 2006). Exposure to such stereotypes also negatively impacts responses to stress (Levy et al., 2000), compared to persons exposed to positive stereotypes. On the other hand, holding positive stereotypes of aging predicts better recovery and more positive expectation of recovery from acute myocardial infarction (heart attack) (Levy et al., 2006), and is correlated with better functional health and less mortality (Levy et al., 2002). Indeed, how you think about your own or others' aging can have both positive and harmful effects on you. How important is age to you in understanding your own or others' behavior? How old is too old to be a surgeon? A police officer? A dentist? A teacher? A pilot? A bus driver?

and aging is best understood in **relative** terms, that is, relative to how each of these dimensions in your own life is interacting across the life cycle and relative to changes in each dimension across contextual time.

Check Your Learning 1-3

Identify the following terms and concepts:

  Aging society
  Filial piety
  Stereotypes
  Stereotype threat
  Centenarians

• To what extent is the aging process still surrounded by misinformation, stereotypes, and biases?

• What is an aging society?

• What are the current attitudes toward aging in the United States? How do these attitudes compare to other cultures?

Learning Activity: Ask five persons "What are the three phrases/words that come to mind when you hear the term *older adult*?" Summarize your findings. Classify the responses as positive, negative, or neutral.

Summary

Aging is **complex, continuous, holistic, dynamic, multidirectional, pluralistic,** and **multidimensional**. It affects us simultaneously on a number of dimensions: **sensory-perceptual, bio-physiological, cognitive/intellectual, personal-interpersonal,** and **cultural-environmental,** with each dimension affecting and being affected by each other dimension during the life span.

To the extent that there is something systematic and age-related about our behavior, the **age con**tinuum serves as our individual time line, which begins at birth and ends with death. This age continuum serves as a focus or basis for the interactions of each of these dimensions.

The concept of **person-environment interaction** suggests that all aspects of human behavior and performance are the result of the interaction or transactions between individuals and their environment. Thus, the successful adaptation and adjustment during adulthood require persons to be selective in their choice of stimuli, response, and behavior, and to compensate for changes in ability or health that result from the aging process in order to optimize their behavior and performance. A person's **developmental niche** is defined in terms of the culture or environment in which the individual best functions.

Adult development is continuous, holistic, and dynamic, which makes adulthood difficult to separate into discrete or independent stages. **Normal aging** involves changes in functioning and behavior in the various dimensions that are inevitable and normal. **Pathological aging** refers to changes with age that are the result of abnormal conditions or disease processes, rather than to age per se. In order to adequately understand change in the context of adulthood, one must consider three types of influences: **age normative, history normative** and **non-normative** influences. There are several ways of viewing change, **intra-individual changes, individual differences,** and **intra-individual differences.**

The goal of developmental research is to determine if any relationship exists between chronological age, or the processes that account for aging and some other factor of interest, that is, to derive an age function which is a picture of how age and our variable of interest are related. There are three basic developmental research designs: **cross-sectional, longitudinal,** and **time-lag.**

Categorization into phases of life is usually done on the basis of either chronological age or developmental tasks, both of which have advantages and disadvantages. There are a variety of ways of viewing age, such as **chronological, biological, psychological, social,** and **functional ages,** as well as a number of self-perceived or attitudinal ages such as personal age and ideal age.

Our country has been growing older; this is called an **aging society**. Longer life expectancies coupled with a general decline in the birth and death rates have led to a dramatic shift in the proportion of older adults in the general population. These demographic changes have many implications for society. Despite such changes, views about aging continue to be clouded by much misinformation. The resulting **stereotypes** about older adults are the result of lack of experience and knowledge, or selective exposure to older adults. Recent surveys indicate that Americans' knowledge, perceptions, and attitudes about the aging process have changed and are generally more positive.

Chapter 2
Aging: Biophysiological, Sensory, and Perceptual Processes

As you learned in Chapter 1, **biological aging** is a gradual and progressive decline in functioning, which generally results in death (Austad, 2009). We can further differentiate between life span, the biological limit for a species to live, and life expectancy, an estimate of remaining time to live for a member of subgroup within a species. As you might suspect, few members' life expectancies match the species life span.

Although historically, there have been several explanations for why we age and for differences in life span across species, current research suggests that three general theories are viable: (1) rate-of-living, (2) programmed senescence, and (3) evolutionary senescence (Austad, 2009). The **rate-of-living** theories state that maintaining and repairing our bodies requires energy. As damage increases, it requires more energy to repair our bodies. Eventually, there is more damage than we have biological energy to repair. This approach is similar to the idea of general wear-and-tear. Many of you have probably heard of another sub-type of the rate-of-living approach that focuses on the damage caused by oxygen-free radicals that result as a function of normal metabolic processes. Although such damage may occur, it is unlikely that free radicals are the "cause" of aging (Austad, 2009).

In contrast, **programmed senescence** is an explanation of aging that posits a role for specific "clocks" or genes which control the aging process (Austad, 2009). Extensive research suggests that the life span of any organism, or how long a member of a species will live on the average, is ultimately determined by an inherited genetic program (Hayflick, 1988, 1994). Thus, this genetic theory of the aging process proposes that there is a genetic program that sets the average upper limit of the life span for all species. All cells reproduce a specific number of times and then die. Hayflick (1994) has demonstrated that normal human cells reproduce themselves 50 times (± 10 times), then they die, which has been termed the **aging clock**. For example, the may fly has an average life span of only one day, the dog's life span is 12 years, a horse's life span is 25 years, while the human's life span is 70+ years (Shock, 1977). Also, individuals who have long-lived parents and grandparents live, on the average, longer than those who do not, and identical twins' life spans are more similar than those of fraternal twins (Hayflick, 1994).

Evolutionary senescence also posits a role for genes, but argues for a later timing of the genetic effects and a different mechanism responsible for them. Evolutionary senescence states that genes may be responsible for aging, but because these traits are not expressed prior to reproducing offspring, the genes remain in the gene pool and are not eliminated through natural selection (Austad, 2009).

Longevity and Life Expectancy

Longevity reflects that proportion of the upper limit of our potential life span (approximately 120 years) we actually achieve. In contrast, **life expectancy** is the average length of life for a member of a given species. Human life expectancy has exhibited a significant increase from the time of the ancient Greeks to the present. Life expectancy at birth in ancient Greece in 500 B.C. was 18 years, 25 years in ancient Rome (A.D. 100). However, if an ancient Roman lived to her fifth birthday, she could expect to live another 43 years. Thus, life expectancy changes for an individual as a function of time survived. In addition to genetics and time survived, other important contributors are environment and life style.

The increase in life expectancy since 1900 can be attributed to factors such as: improved housing, sanitation and hygiene, the development and use of antiseptics, the passage of public health laws, immunization for childhood diseases, improved medical care and medical practice, and better nutrition. Since 1950, the increases in life ex-pectancy have been relatively small because for middle-aged and older adults, the primary causes of death for both men and women are chronic diseases such as cardiovascular diseases and cancer, which, generally speaking, currently do not have a cure. These two diseases account for three-fourths of all the deaths of older adults (Kastenbaum, 2009). The likelihood of having a chronic illness increases with age, and it is not uncommon for people in their 80s and 90s to have more than one chronic illness. On the whole, the conditions that are most common among older age groups require more care, are more disabling, and are more difficult and costly to treat than the conditions that are more common for younger age groups. In contrast, most young adults die of accidents or violence. Thus, until medical science discovers cures for cancer and the various forms of cardiovascular disease, life expectancy will continue to show only minor increases. However, as you learned in Chapter 1, increasing life expectancy and decreasing birth rates result in a larger percentage of older adults living than at any other point in history. This demographic shift challenges several social and political systems, including education, health care, Social Security and Medicare, housing, transportation, industry and the work force, and families.

Factors Related to Life Expectancy: Intrinsic and Extrinsic

Research has demonstrated that there are a number of factors related to life expectancy. These factors are classified as either intrinsic/primary factors or extrinsic/secondary factors.

Intrinsic Factors

Intrinsic/primary factors are generally considered fixed or permanent, since they are inherited or otherwise related to universal biological and physiological processes (Timiras, 1988), and set the limits for our maximum potential life span. These are: **genetic inheritance, gender, ethnicity, and health condition.** Their impact varies with other primary or secondary factors, since humans do not develop in a vacuum, nor does each factor function in isolation.

Genetic Inheritance

As noted previously, our inherited generic program sets certain limits for the potential life span (Austad, 2009). Simply put, long-lived parents tend to have long-lived children. However, this relationship is quite complex, since the expression of this basic genetic program can be altered by many internal and external factors. For example, how long you live in relation to your parent's life span will depend on the interaction with other intrinsic and extrinsic factors such as nutrition, stress, and exercise. Thus, one might say that heredity "deals the cards," but we "play the hand."

Gender

In most nations, females are expected to live longer than males born in the same year by a margin of 7 to 8 years. Though we cannot definitively explain this, there are two commonly held hypotheses: (1) females have a genetic program for a longer life than males; and/ or (2) females are the stronger and healthier members of the species; thus, they live longer. Another explanation may be that the greater life expectancy of females results from other primary or secondary factors (Vincent & Velkoff, 2010).

In 2010, women make up about 57% of those over age 65 years. Female life expectancy has long exceeded male life expectancy. Although this trend is likely to continue for at least the next 40 years, the gender gap in life expectancy is narrowing. This narrowing is related to an increase in the life expectancy of men, rather than a further increase for women. The convergence of life expectancy extends to the oldest old, as well, with women decreasing from 67% of those over age 85 currently to only 61% in 2050. Just as the changing age structure in the nation will affect social and economic indicators, the changing gender ration within the oldest members of our population will also affect society (Vincent & Velkoff, 2010).

Ethnicity/Race

In the United States, Caucasians generally live longer than members of non-white minority groups. Among adults age 65 and over, there is less racial diversity than in the population as a whole. In fact, about 87% of older Americans are white alone, 9% African American alone, and 3% Asian alone. Hispanics comprise about 7.1% of all older Americans (Vincent & Velkoff, 2010). However, significant growth is expected in the next few decades, with projections suggesting growth for all non-white groups and for mixed racial groups (Vincent & Velkoff, 2010). This is especially important because members of minority groups experience more chronic health conditions, more serious symptoms, and at younger ages than their non-white peers (Kawachi, Daniels & Robinson, 2005). Three current explanations are offered for these observed racial disparities: (1) racial disparities reflect biological differences in susceptibility to diseases, (2) racial disparities reflect socioeconomic (SES) differences related to nutrition and medical access, and (3) both biological and SES effects exist and interact to create a "multiple -jeopardy" effect (Kawachi et al., 2005). Research is currently exploring these issues, which have important implications for communities, services, and policies.

Health Condition

Disease and chronic health conditions certainly can lead to death, but they can also cause physical pain, emotional distress, functional disability, and economic hardship. The top causes of death among older adults are heart disease, cancer, and cerebrovascular disease (CDC, 2007). Moreover, the probability of having multiple chronic conditions (e.g., arthritis, hypertension, cataracts, heart disease, diabetes, and osteoporosis) increases with age (Karlamangla, Tinetti, Guralnik, Studenski, Wetle, & Reuben, 2007).

Yet, in spite of the increase in the number and severity of chronic conditions with age, the majority of older adults report themselves as being in good or excellent health, with about 64% of community dwelling people aged 65 to 74 reporting their health to be good, very good, or excellent (Cagney, Browning, & Wen, 2005). As you might expect based on the discussion of race, more whites than African Americans report excellent/good health (69.4% versus 56.4%; Spencer et al., 2009). The match between objective and subjective assessments of health is not perfect, however. Spencer and colleagues report evidence that even at the same level of objective health status as whites, African Americans are less likely to report excellent health, displaying "health pessimism."

Extrinsic Factors

Extrinsic or secondary factors modify the limits projected for life expectancy by the intrinsic factors. Although, individuals do not have any control over the primary factors, they can exercise control over the secondary factors to a large extent. Among the most common extrinsic factors associated with a decrease in life expectancy are: smoking, adiposity (being over fat), high blood pressure, physical inactivity, and high blood glucose (Danaei, Rimm, Oza, Kulkarni, Murray, & Ezzati, 2010). These factors interact with intrinsic or other extrin-

Box A

Health Care and Aging

A report by the American Association of Retired Persons (AARP, 2005), entitled "Reimaging America," argues that the problems many older Americans have in getting and affording good health care have less to do with Medicare and Medicaid, and more to do with our health care system itself. A large, complex, and poorly co-ordinated health care system contributes to the problem, over and above the growing numbers of older persons and the expenditures for health care, especially during the last two months of life.

Indeed, AARP argues that the health of older Americans is improving: the prevalence of disability is declining, fewer persons are entering nursing homes. Ultimately, this will result in health care savings for older persons, especially since more people are working while in retirement, postponing retirement, and therefore more capable of contributing to defraying the costs of health care, though the likelihood of being poor in later life is still high (4 in 10 will be poor sometime after age 60).

AARP makes the following recommendations:

- Put a greater emphasis on preventative health care (e.g., in preventing obesity and diabetes, developing healthy lifestyles).

- Conduct more biomedical research to treat and cure chronic illness.
- Minimize the number of persons who are uninsured (1 of 6 older persons has no health insurance).
- Enhance the availability of prescription drugs to persons who need them (hence the implementation of the Medicare Prescription Drug Improvement and Modernization Act of 2003).
- Improve the quality of health care in long term care.
- Stress the more careful screening of persons to detect health problems earlier.
- Create better home-based and community-based care.
- Invest in "liveable" communities (affordable/appropriate housing that encourages mobility and access to services).
- Keep Social Security solvent.
- Help persons build their retirement assets.
- Help persons work longer who desire to do so.

Though not discussed by AARP, another important solution to solving the health care crisis is to **reduce inequality in health and access to health care** among older persons as a function of gender, race and ethnicity, level of education/socioeconomic status, and age (see Zarit & Pearlin, 2005).

sic factors. Results of a new study examining the effects on longevity due to four extrinsic factors in isolation and in combination suggest that Americans could easily increase life expectancies by four to five years (Danaei et al., 2010). Alone, smoking and high blood pressure exerted the greatest negative effects on life expectancy. The researchers estimate that modifying these risk factors would reduce the risk of dying from cardiovascular diseases

and diabetes by 69%–80%; the risk of dying from cancer could be reduced by 29%–50%.

Aldwin, Spiro, and Park (2006) suggest that personality and coping skills are also factors in life expectancy. Hostility, anxiety, neuroticism, and depression can contribute to worse health and a shorter life span, whereas adopting an optimistic stance toward life, having some control over what happens to you, being emotionally stable, having religious or spiritual resources, and having good coping skills (see Chapter 6) can all contribute to better health, more life satisfaction (optimal aging, see Chapter 1), and a greater life span. Snowden (2001) found that among successfully aged nuns, being happy, maintaining one's curiosity, being thankful for what one has, having a deep sense of spirituality (see Valliant, 2002), and having a sense of community all helped persons to age well, despite physical frailty and illness.

Nutrition and Diet

Avoiding obesity and eating a diet low in animal fats is beneficial to our health. Although dietary restrictions that lead to low blood-cholesterol levels may not be directly related to longevity, they are related to decreases in high blood pressure and cardiovascular disease, conditions which may shorten life. Nutritional factors are related to more than just life expectancy. Chronic nutritional deficiencies in older adults (and in young adults as well) can lead to vitamin deficiencies, which in turn may have negative effects upon various organs and organ systems in the body. These deficiencies can eventually lead to disorders which resemble dementia (see Chapter 10). Nutrition and diet are significantly affected by economics at all age levels, since it may be difficult to eat nutritious meals if one does not have the economic resources to purchase nutritious food (Zohoori, 2001). Thus, many communities and agencies sponsor programs for elderly people to provide meals that are free or at greatly reduced cost based on the person's ability to pay. These programs serve two important purposes: they provide people with nutritious meals, and they provide opportunities for social interaction (see Chapter 9).

Climate and Physical Environment

Every species has specific requirements in terms of temperature and climate in order to sustain life. For instance, tropical birds cannot live for a prolonged time in a cold climate. Additionally, exposure to hazardous chemicals, high noise levels, and pollution can affect life expectancy, directly

or indirectly. To illustrate, if you work on a job in which you are repeatedly exposed to dangerous chemicals or live in a city with a high pollution level, these factors have the potential of either contributing to disease or possibly reducing your life expectancy.

Exercise and Activity

Regular physical exercise throughout life has many positive physical and psychological effects for both men and women. These include improved cardiovascular and respiratory-system functioning, better muscle tone, as well as improvements in functional status, anxiety, depression, mobility, and mortality among older adults (Lee & Paffenbarger, 2000). Exercising for a half hour twice a week significantly increases the health and mobility of men and women with serious chronic ailments, reduces or prevents the onset of heart disease, improves family relationships, enhances sex life, lessens loneliness, improves mood and self-confidence, and, reduces the risk of hip fracture (Aldwin, Spiro, & Park, 2006).

Exercise and physical activity have been shown to positively influence mood changes by reducing anxiety and stress. By increasing fitness and physical functioning ability, physical activity has also been shown to enhance a sense of accomplishment and create feelings of efficacy, particularly among older adults (Netz, Wu, Becker, & Tennenbaum, 2005). For these reasons, exercise such as running is often prescribed as a treatment for depression (see Chapter 10). A program of physical exercise, in combination with a healthy diet, will contribute to less weight gain, lower blood pressure, lower risk of heart attacks and strokes, and lower cholesterol levels (Netz et al., 2005).

Education and Economic Status

In general, the higher one's educational level and economic status, the longer one is likely to live (Kinsella & Wan He, 2009). The increases in life expectancy that have been observed during the past 30 years have occurred almost entirely among those who have at least finished high school. In 2000,

Box B

Caloric Restrictions: Of Mice and Men

In the 1930s, Clive McCay and colleagues at Cornell University used mice to examine the health effects of a low calorie, nutrient rich diet. Specifically, these diets included 30% fewer calories than mice normally consumed, but with retained or improved nutritional value of the food. They began their studies when the mice were adolescents. Results indicated that the calorie-restricted animals experienced reductions in the severity of age-related diseases and increased their longevity by 30%. Since then, results of caloric restrictions have been replicated in a variety of species, including yeasts, flies, worms, and fish. The age at which calorie restriction is started, the degree of restriction, and the specific type of animal all seem to influence the degree of benefit that results. Starting caloric restriction earlier in the life span seems to result in stronger effects than when it is started in adulthood. However, even when begun in adulthood, caloric restriction has resulted in a 10–20% increase in longevity (Fontana & Klein, 2007). In addition to increasing the quantity of life, caloric restriction may increase the quality of life. In the lab, calorie-restricted mice experience reductions or delays in a variety of chronic conditions, including diabetes, atherosclerosis, autoimmune diseases (like arthritis), respiratory diseases, and cancer (Fontana & Klein, 2007; NIH, 2006).

Encouraged by the evidence with mice and other species, researchers are actively studying whether the benefits of calorie restriction can reduce or eliminate chronic disease and extend the life span of primates (NIH, 2006). Primates such as rhesus monkeys are an ideal group within which to study the effects of caloric restriction: rhesus monkeys have a shorter life span than humans (27 to 40 years) and experience similar age-related changes, including diabetes, cancer, and cardiovascular disease (Colman et al., 2009). Promising results

are emerging from a longitudinal study with rhesus monkeys, which began in 1987 (Colman et al., 2009). Seventy-six adult rhesus monkeys were randomly assigned to either a free feeding control group or to a 30% calorie restricted diet. Over the course of the study, significantly fewer monkeys in the calorie restricted group died of age-related causes than in the control group (13% versus 37%) (Colman et al., 2009). Relative to the monkeys which were free-feeding, calorie restricted monkeys had less total body fat, had smaller declines in lean muscle mass, showed no evidence of pre-diabetes status, had a 50% reduction in cancer, showed a 50% reduction in cardiovascular disease, experienced one-third the rate of arthritis, and had healthier brains (Colman et al., 2009).

Some of the earliest evidence supporting the benefits of caloric restriction in humans derives from the Biosphere 2 project. In the early 1990s, eight men and women lived in an experimental closed, self-sustaining ecological system. Due to crop failures within the dome, these adults ate a 22%-reduced calorie diet for 18 months. Although they lost weight, they also experienced a reduction in blood pressure and blood lipids, both of which are known risk factors for coronary heart disease (Fontana & Klein, 2007). One of the residents of Biosphere 2 was Dr. Roy Walford, whose seminal work in caloric restriction informs much of the current research in this area.

Few scientific studies of caloric restriction in humans have been reported. However, some promising results are emerging. Heilbronn and colleagues examined the effects of 6 months of calorie restriction, with or without exercise in 48 adults. Results showed that after 6 months, core body temperature, resting metabolism, and fasting insulin levels were reduced in adults eating a calorie restricted diet (Heilbronn et al., 2006).

Despite the benefits observed across non-primates, monkeys, and humans, there is some doubt as to whether caloric restriction is a practical means of extending longevity for most people. Most Americans find it challenging to adhere to a nutrient-rich diet with a 30% reduction in calories consumed (NIH, 2006).

life expectancy for a 25 year old with a high school diploma or less was 50 years. For a person with some college, life expectancy was nearly 57 years. Although similar trends were seen across race and gender, the education effect was especially strong among older adults (Meara, Richards, & Cutler, 2008). Education is positively associated with access to medical care, more effective use of medical care, more health promoting behaviors, and fewer risky health behaviors (Kinsella & Wan He, 2009). Globally, there is an increase in the number of individuals completing secondary school (Kinsella & Wan He, 2009). Currently, older Americans have a relatively high level of formal education, with nearly 75% having finished high school (Census, 2008)

Work and Work Satisfaction

There is a clear relationship between working conditions, work satisfaction, and life expectancy (Panek, 1997). As noted previously, working in hazardous conditions, such as being exposed to pollution or dangerous chemicals, potentially shortens one's life expectancy. Also, individuals who have high work satisfaction tend to have higher self-esteem and a more positive outlook on life than those who are dissatisfied with their work. Indeed, being passionate about one's work can contribute to greater quality of life, better health, and a longer life span (Amick et al., 2002). The type of work one performs is also highly related to socioeconomic level and other secondary factors related to life expectancy. We will have more to say about the relationship between aging and work-related issues in Chapter 7.

Interpersonal Relationships

Positive interpersonal relationships, such as those with friends, spouse, or significant other, ex-

ert a positive influence on life expectancy (Gruenewald et al.2009). The presence of valued others makes us feel worthwhile and reduces feelings of isolation, loneliness, and depression, and provides necessary and beneficial psychological and social support. Further, research on the relationship of marital status to health and longevity has shown that widows and widowers are at greater risk of mortality and poor health than are their counterparts (Quandt, McDonald, Arcury, Bell, & Vitolins, 2000).

Also, having animals as pets has been shown to facilitate psychological well-being in people of all ages (Cusack & Smith, 1984). Such relations are more critical to us as we get older due to the deaths of friends, relatives, our spouse, and pets. We will discuss interpersonal relationships further in Chapters 4 and 5.

Cognitive/Intellectual Factors

Individuals with better or higher cognitive and intellectual abilities tend to live longer; this is often referred to as the **wisdom factor** (Birren & Renner, 1980). Life expectancy and survival are related to sudden and dramatic declines in cognitive/intellectual performance from a few days to a number of years prior to death. As an illustration, Kleemeier (1962) administered an intelligence test on four occasions, at 2 to 3 1/2-year intervals during a 12-year period, to 13 older adult males, and observed that the performance of all participants decreased over the 12-year period, and there were substantial individual differences in the magnitude of this decline. Then it was observed that the decline in test scores was faster and greater in magnitude for those who died following the last retest than those who survived. This decline was labeled terminal drop (see Chapter 1). However, we should be cautious about terminal drop. For instance, the poor physical health of the individuals who died in these studies may have been responsible for the observed decrease in test performance, rather than cognitive factors. Also important to life expectancy is our **ability to avoid and cope with stress** (Siegler, 1989); this is important in light of the transactional model we discussed earlier (see Chapter 1). We will discuss personality, stress, and coping more fully in Chapter 6. In reviewing the influences on life expectancy, it might be helpful to think about those factors that you can and cannot alter. Perhaps it's time for a change?

Check Your Learning 2-1

Identify the following terms and concepts:

> Intrinsic/primary factors
> Wisdom factor
> Life expectancy
> Terminal drop
> Extrinsic/secondary factors
> Aging clock
> Longevity
> Health disparities

- What is the major assumption of a theory of aging emphasizing genetics?

- Distinguish between longevity and life expectancy.

- List and discuss the four intrinsic factors related to life expectancy.

- How has life expectancy changed from ancient to modern times? What factors are responsible?

- Discuss several implications of increased life expectancy for society.

- List and discuss the top five causes of death among older adults.

- List and discuss any four of the extrinsic factors related to life expectancy.

Biophysiological, Sensory, and Perceptual Processes

Many people define aging in terms of the changes experienced in their everyday physical, sensory, or physiological functioning. These may be mild, such as aches and pains, or they may be severe and life threatening, for example, heart disease or cancer. It is important to distinguish between changes that are the result of the biophysiological processes, called **primary age changes**, from those that are due to inactivity, poor eating habits, or disease, termed **secondary age changes**. Primary age changes are experienced by everyone, while secondary age changes may affect some people and not others. Indeed, many of the physical changes that people experience as they get older are secondary to primary aging. For instance, having wrinkles is a consequence of factors such as sun exposure which are secondary to the basic processes of aging. These changes can affect our self-esteem, mobility, relationships, behavior, and influence decisions made about us by others. Consequently, knowing what physiological, sensory, and perceptual changes actually occur as one gets older can help us adjust to and cope with these changes.

The Biophysiology of Aging

During young adulthood, most physiological and physical functions are at their most efficient levels. By the middle to late 20s, most of the physical growth and development of muscles, internal organs, and body systems have reached a plateau. Thus, most individuals in their 20s and 30s view themselves as being at their peak regarding health and physical condition. Because such biophysiological changes are not directly experienced by most young adults, and thus have little impact on their behavior, this creates the illusion of young adulthood as a stable period. It is

Figure 2-1. Regular exercise is critical to muscular-skeletal health in adulthood.

during our 40s and 50s, when these physical and biophysiological changes begin to affect behavior and performance that we take note of them. This has been explained in terms of the **Multiple Threshold Model of Identity and Physical Aging** (Whitbourne, 1999), wherein we are more or less sensitive to some aspects of biological and physical aging versus others, dependent upon their potential to affect our adaptation and adjustment. For example, we may be more sensitive to changes in our appearance (e.g., the elasticity of our skin), or changes in our sensory abilities (e.g., vision and hearing) than to whether our kidneys or autonomic nervous systems are functioning as they should. While we will highlight the major age changes that occur in various organ/body systems, it is important to realize that there are individual differences among persons of all ages regarding these changes; some persons age more rapidly than do others, and persons vary in those aspects of biological aging to which they are sensitive (their thresholds vary).

For some persons, even those in their 20s, a sensitivity to aging-related changes in their skin or body shape, causes them to resort to the use of antiaging products (moisturizers, eye wrinkle cream, hair dyes, skin firming lotions), begin an exercise program, lose weight, or even have plastic surgery. A 24-year old woman said "instead of starting when you're 40 or 45, you might as well start now . . . vanity is probably the main reason I started using anti-aging products, as superficial as it is" ("Not too young for anti-aging," *Dallas Morning News,* December 26, 2005). Interestingly, both men and women seem to be susceptible to such pressures to continue to look young.

Muscular-Skeletal System

The muscular system begins to change noticeably during the mid-30s, including changes in overall muscle strength, muscle mass, and muscle tone, and a redistribution of fat and subcutaneous tissue (Panek, 1997). The degree of loss differs widely

---

Over the Hill?

Over 3500 *USA Today* readers aged 35 to 43 were asked to say what bothered them most about aging as well as what they missed about youth. In many cases, their responses suggested that they do not distinguish between aging and disease or life-style. Moreover, they often failed to realize that many of the physical and psychological changes they experienced could be totally avoided, or at least minimized, by exercise, diet, or decrease in stress level. Here is a summary of the *USA Today* findings:

"What bothers you most about aging?" For men, tiring quickly (31%), bad back (19%), poor memory (12%), sags and wrinkles (6%), and diminished sex drive (5%) were the most troubling. For women, sags and wrinkles (28%), tiring quickly (26%), poor memory (15%), bad back (11%), and diminished sex drive (4%) were the most distressing.

"Which body part has aged the most?" For all respondents, the waist (35%), face (20%), back (19%), knees (14%), and feet (13%).

"What do you miss most about youth?" Can't stay up late (64%), can't play sports without getting stiff (18%), can't drink as much (10%), and can't touch toes (8%). Before 40, people complained most often of weight gain. After 40, they were most distressed by failing eyesight.

This increased awareness of bodily changes and acceptance of them is illustrated by several comments:

A 35-year-old man said, "Everyone else reaches for a beer after the ball game. I reach for Ben-Gay."

A 43-year-old woman said, "I'm beginning to feel as if aspirin is one of the four basic food groups."

A 41-year-old man stated, "My favorite exercise is a nice, brisk sit."

To what extent do these opinions mirror reality? How are they influenced by myths and stereotypes of growing older?

It need not be all bad, For example, an over-40 woman proclaimed, "Sure there are some things I'd like to change, but I ain't bad for 42. I'd love to show how good this age can be!"

Many take such changes in stride and can even make light of the physical realities of middle age. As one 42-year-old woman quipped. "Recently, I found myself shopping for support shoes and a sexy teddy on the same day. Reality versus illusion."

Source: The ache age. (1989, December 29-31). *USA Weekend*, pp. 4-5.

---

among various muscle groups, and the rate and degree of loss is influenced by one's level of physical activity. Thus, if one exercises regularly, age-related muscle atrophy can be minimized.

Further, aging affects collagen and elastin, which are two common proteins found in all con-

nective tissues, muscles, joints, and bones. With advancing age these fibrous proteins become thicker, less elastic, less soluble, and tend to mass and replace existing tissues (Whitbourne, 1999). Age-related changes in collagen and elastin fibers are associated with various external signs of growing older, such as wrinkling of the skin, sagging muscles, and slower healing of cuts and injuries.

On average, all of the skeleton in the body has been transformed to bone by age 18, at which time we achieve our maximum height (Roseman, 1990). Thereafter, due to increased loss of calcium, increased porosity, and erosion, the bones start to become more brittle, and the articulating surfaces begin to deteriorate. Also, flexibility in connective tissues and joints decreases, and as the bones weaken, they become less capable of supporting the body and are easily broken (Vercruyssen, 1997). These changes can limit one's mobility and contribute to arthritis (Ferrini & Ferrini, 1993). Moreover, due to the settling of bones within the spinal column, changes in body curvature, and shrinkage of the intervertebral disks and vertebrae, individuals may shrink 1 to 2 inches in height over the life span.

Although both men and women tend to lose bone mass as they age, the process usually begins earlier and proceeds more rapidly in women due to a reduction in estrogen levels (Merz, 1992). **Osteoporosis** is a disease characterized by progressive decline in bone density (Rowe & Kahn, 1987), and is most common among women. With osteoporosis, bone mass actually deteriorates, posture declines, and it is much easier to fracture the spine, hips, and other stressed parts of the skeleton. The disease progresses slowly, often with no pain or visible symptoms, making it difficult to detect. However, with proper nutrition, specifically a diet with calcium supplements, and regular exercise, the chances of developing osteoporosis can be reduced.

Cardiovascular System

At approximately age 25, heart rate is at its peak efficiency and by age 45 decreases to 94%, to 87% by age 65, and to 81% by age 85 (Panek, 1997). Further, the heart loses about 1% of its reserve pumping capacity each year after age 30, reducing the amount of oxygen delivered to the tissues by red blood cells, which are deployed less efficiently because the vessel walls, thickened with rigid collagen deposits, lose their ability to dilate and con-

tract in response to the heart's pumping action (Merz, 1992).

However, many of the debilitating effects of cardiovascular changes are the result of disease, not a consequence of normal aging. In fact, coronary disease accelerates the effect of aging on the functioning of the heart (Lakatta, 1990). During middle adulthood, the frequency of coronary artery disease, cardiovascular failure, and hypertension begins to increase, where such illnesses are generally the number one cause of death in men over 40.

Heart disease is a type of cardiovascular disease. In addition to heart disease, the term encompasses a variety of heart conditions such as high blood pressure and stroke. **Coronary heart disease** is caused by a narrowing of the coronary arteries, which results in a decreased supply of blood and oxygen to the heart. A **heart attack** is caused by the sudden blockage of a coronary artery, usually by a blood clot. With advancing age more women than men have hypertension.

Other parts of the body are also targets of blood vessel disease, including the brain, which is subject to cerebrovascular disease. **Stroke** occurs when blood is cut off to a region of the brain due to weakened or blocked cerebral arteries or a rupture with bleeding (hemorrhage) into surrounding tissues. Loss of blood may result in permanent damage to the brain cells and related cognitive or physical disability or death. Stroke affects one-and-a-half times as many men as women, and survivors can be left with permanent disabilities. Although the structures within this system show signs of change and degeneration with age, these disorders are highly dependent on both genetic and environmental factors such as smoking, stress, diet, and exercise (Panek, 1997). People can reduce their risk of stroke and cardiovascular disease by making changes in their diets and life-styles (Lakatta, 1990).

Immune System

The human immune system protects us not only against microorganisms that invade the body but also against atypical or mutant cells that may form in the body. The immune system carries out this protective function by generating antibodies that form special cells to engulf and digest foreign cells and substances. The aging process has a marked impact on the functioning of the immune system. Production of antibodies reaches a peak during adolescence and then declines thereafter.

The immune system starts to decline at around age 30, which makes it harder for the body to fight off illnesses (Miller, 1990). Also, after age 65, hemoglobin and red blood cell count decrease and white blood cells, which fight off viruses and bacteria, lose their effectiveness. The functioning of this system is further hampered by the gradual degeneration of the thymus, which is responsible for educating T-lymphocytes to coordinate the body's defense system (Merz, 1992).

Respiratory System

The maximum breathing or **vital capacity** of the lungs decreases progressively between 20 and 60 years of age (Ferrini & Ferrini, 1993), and is due to a loss of elasticity in the joints of the rib cage and the lung tissue itself, as well as weakened muscles that support the lungs. Also, as the lungs age, they become less elastic and are no longer able to inflate or deflate completely. Thus, they cannot take in as much oxygen, thereby affecting how much oxygen reaches needy tissues (Merz, 1992). However, the primary harmful effects to the lungs are caused by environmental factors such as smoking and the inhalation of noxious agents (e.g., asbestos), which have been linked to disorders of the respiratory system such as lung cancer, asthma, and emphysema.

Digestive System

The digestive system works less efficiently with aging due to slower action of the muscles that move through the system, reduced acid production, and impaired ability to absorb nutrients. Metabolism begins to slow at around age 25, and there is some decline in the secretion of gastric juices and in the metabolism of proteins and fats (Whitbourne, 1999). For these reasons, it is not uncommon to begin to noticeably gain weight, even when being careful about diet and exercise. For each decade thereafter, the number of calories required to maintain one's weight drops by at least 2%. Also, there is an increase in body fat (Ferrini & Ferrini, 1993), and people generally accumulate fat around the middle of their torsos.

The most serious disorders associated with age in this system are **colon cancer** and **diabetes**. Next to lung cancer, colon cancer claims more lives than any other form of the disease (National Cancer Institute, 2004). While the incidence of colon cancer is highest among white men, when detected early this type of cancer can be arrested with surgery. Diabetes is a metabolic disorder that can cause a number of debilitating symptoms, including blindness, damage to various organs of the body, and in some cases death, and its frequency increases with age (Ferrini & Ferrini, 1993). Overall however, the primary consequence of age changes in this system is that more time is needed for digestion and metabolizing substances (Merz, 1992), which is important when prescribing medications to older persons (see Chapter 11).

Excretory System and Endocrine System

The primary age-related changes in the excretory system are a gradual reduction of blood flow to the kidneys, coupled with a reduction in nephrons (filtering units), which impairs the kidneys' ability to extract wastes from the blood and concentrate them into urine (Merz, 1992). This affects the ability of the kidneys to excrete medications from one's system. Regarding the endocrine system, although hormone-secreting glands shrink as we grow older, their performance does not appear to be significantly affected by normal aging (Merz, 1992).

Skin and Hair

Often, it is the external and observable changes in our body, such as wrinkles in the skin and graying hair that remind us that we are aging. While these age-related changes are cosmetic, they are nevertheless the result of internal biophysiological processes. These changes include the following: the flexibility of collagen fibers decreases, which inhibits the skin's ability to conform to moving limbs; "age spots" **(lipofuscin)** become more numerous; and the skin begins to lose elasticity and wrinkles appear, although exposure to the sun plays a significant role in this process (Ferrini & Ferrini, 1993). The loss of small blood vessels and subcutaneous fat with age also contributes to dry, wrinkled skin. In addition to a decrease in pigment in the hair, loss of hair is common after age 30 in men and after menopause in women.

Many of these changes contribute to changes in our body image. Indeed, such changes have an impact on both men and women as they age, and are assigned different meaning based on gender: younger women are more sensitive to such changes as they impact their physical attractiveness, while older women are less sensitive to such changes (Kaminiski & Hayslip, 2006). In contrast, men as they age become more sensitive to the functional consequences of changes in their bodies; they simply cannot do what they were able to do when they were younger (Kaminiski & Hayslip).

Central Nervous System

Our ability to think, reason, and act in response to incoming stimulation from the environment depends on the integrity of our central nervous system (CNS). The CNS, which is composed of the brain and the spinal cord, is critical to learning, memory, and other cognitive processes (see Chapter 3).

Gross Cerebral Changes

The CNS reaches its peak in terms of functioning neurons by age 30 (Howath & Davis, 1990). The principal age-related changes in the CNS occur in the brain and are highly subject to, and moderated by, disease or "pathological" aging. Also, the aging of the CNS occurs at different rates for different people and varies by health status. With age the number of cells in the CNS , and the overall size of the brain, decrease (Scheibel, 1992). Between the ages of 20 and 90, the brain loses from 5 to 10% of its weight. By age 80, there is a 7% re-

duction in overall cerebral hemisphere mass (Merz, 1992). Some areas of the brain shrink more than others; for example, the cerebral cortex (the gray matter that handles higher mental skills, behavior, and perception) loses as much as 45% of its cells (Merz, 1992). Brain volume also declines, especially after age 50, by approximately 15 to 20%. As the volume of brain tissue shrinks, the brain's appearance changes. The **gyri** (swellings of the brain) become smaller, and the fissures or **sulci** (valleys between the gyri) widen (Scheibel, 1992). Finally, the volume of the ventricular fluid increases, compressing adjacent tissue, which leads to increased ventricular size.

Neuronal Changes

The primary structural change in the aging brain is the loss of neurons, or nerve cells, which receive and transmit information. By age 30, the brain begins to lose thousands of neurons a day (Merz, 1992). When a neuron dies, all its connections, including the small spaces between neurons called **synapses** (and there are thousands per cell) also die. Synapses help integrate information from various parts of the nervous system, occur on the cell body and the dendrite of the neuron, and are the sites of the neuronal electrical and chemical activity in the nervous system. With age, cell bodies change in appearance and accumulate lipofuscin, which interferes with neuronal function.

Extending from each cell body are **dendrites**, whose function is to receive incoming information from other neurons. While they are normally intricately intertwined, with age this organization becomes simplified, and eventually the cellular dendrites disappear altogether, meaning that less information is received by each neuron (Whitbourne, 1999). Consequently, less information can be transmitted via the axon to other neurons, muscles, and glands. Also with age, **neurofibrillary tangles** are more likely to develop, which means nerve fibers in the cell body and dendrites increase in number and become interwoven, which interferes with cell functioning. These neural tangles are found in normal brains but are especially prevalent in the brains of people with certain forms of dementia (see Chapter 10).

With age, and especially in certain forms of dementia, **senile plaques** are more likely to form (see Chapter 10). Senile plaques are abnormally hard clusters of damaged or dying neurons, present in specific areas of the brain such as the hippocampus, which interfere with neuronal function. As neurons die, certain types of glial cells (supportive brain cells) increase in size and perform their function of providing nutrients to brain cells less adequately (Selkoe, 1991).

The brain's structures may also degenerate due to a reduction in cerebral circulation, which can result from either normal age-related changes in cardiac output or from heart disease. Heart disease creates a progressive narrowing (**atherosclerosis**) and hardening (**arteriosclerosis**) of arterial walls. Blood flow may be shut off altogether by **infarcts** (blood clots) of varying sizes or by stroke.

The cortex of the brain is organized into **hemispheres** that function somewhat independently of one another and mediates many complex behaviors and functions. The left hemisphere controls speech, language and verbal activity, and mathematical and symbolic skills, while the right hemisphere controls spatial and complex perceptual abilities. Right hemisphere functioning appears to decline at a greater rate with age than does left-hemisphere function (Whitbourne, 1999).

Various functional areas of the cortex controlling sensory experience lose neurons, particularly the occipital (visual), parietal (skin and muscle senses), and parts of the temporal (hearing) and frontal (motor control) lobes. In the various areas of the associative cortex that control higher cognitive functions, such as long-term memory, abstract reasoning, and symbolization, as well as coordinate the sensorimotor areas, the loss is less severe (Whitbourne, 1999). Also, degeneration is found in certain areas of the brain stem, which connects the cortex with the spinal cord.

The production of **neurotransmitters** (chemical messengers that carry impulses to and from cells and the brain) slows down with age. With fewer agents available to carry information, translating the brain's message into action takes longer, and synaptic transmission and coordination are impaired (Merz, 1992). Neurotransmitter deficits in certain areas of the brain stem seem to be linked to disturbances in sleep patterns, short-term memory deficits, and overarousal (Whitbourne, 1999).

With appropriate stimulation or experience, however, neuronal connections may be regenerated, or neuronal loss may be lessened. This seems to be particular to an area of the brain called the hippocampus, which is responsible for the control of filing new experiences into long-term memory (Scientific American, 1998). We call this potential for new growth **plasticity**. It is the redundancy of neurons in the cortex, resulting in more frequent activity by fewer cells or more constant activity by healthy cells, that makes such plasticity possible (Scientific American, 1998). Transmitter substances in these areas remain relatively constant, and thus wisdom, abstract reasoning, judgment, foresight, and long-term memory may be relatively unaffected by aging (Bondareff, 1985). Overall, we can compensate for deficits in memory, fine motor coordination, or learning new information by relying on experience, planning, and organizational skills to maintain effective functioning on an everyday basis (see Chapter 3).

Check Your Learning 2-2

Identify the following terms and concepts:

  Coronary heart disease
  Osteoporosis
  Colon cancer
  Neurofibrillary tangles
  Atherosclerosis
  Senile plaques
  Neurons
  Synapses
  Multiple threshold model
  Heart attack
  Stroke
  Diabetes
  Vital capacity

Plasticity
Arteriosclerosis
Dendrites
Lipofuscin
Primary/secondary aging

- What are the major age-related changes in the muscular-skeletal system? What are some of the implications of these age-related changes?

- What are some of the normal age-related and disease processes associated with the cardiovascular system?

- Distinguish between primary and secondary aging.

- What are the primary age-related changes in the immune system?

- What factors are primarily responsible for disorders of the respiratory system?

- What are the most serious disorders associated with the digestive system and age?

- What are the primary effects of the agerelated changes in the skin and hair?

- What are some of the major age-related changes to the central nervous system? What are the major implications of these changes?

- What are some of the pathological changes to the central nervous system often associated with age? What are the implications of these changes?

- What is the multiple threshold model of identity and physical aging? Why is it important?

Reproductive System

There are a number of age-related changes in the reproductive system which has implications for sexual interest and activity. Some of these major changes for males (Leitner & Leitner, 2004; Merz, 1992) are: increased time is required for erection; the penis does not get as hard or extend to its maximum length; the force of ejaculation and volume of seminal fluids decrease; orgasm is briefer and the refractory period increases. For women, with increasing age (Merz, 1992): production of vaginal lubricant becomes slower, the vaginal canal constricts in size and vaginal walls become thinner, orgasm is briefer; these changes may result in pain during intercourse.

The primary hormonal change associated with aging for females is **menopause**, which refers to the cessation of menstruation, accompanied by decreased estrogen production, often accompanied by symptoms such as hot flashes or night sweats (Merz, 1992). Following menopause, only a minority of women reported a loss of sexual desire (APA Monitor, 1991). It is important to realize that there is no evidence that any of these changes, in themselves, affect an older person's ability to engage in normal sexual activity. Further, while these normal age-related changes do not prevent arousal or orgasm (Abeles, 1997), they may have important implications for one's well-being, as evidenced by enthusiasm for such drugs as Viagra and Cialis. Research is beginning to question to meaning assigned to menopause, seeing it instead as a positive change, wherein women should be encouraged to develop coping skills to deal with changes in their bodies and in their emotions that menopause often brings (DeAngelis, 2010).

Sexual Interest and Activity:
Life Span Trends

Sexual interest is primarily a psychological experience and pertains to a person's desire to engage in sexual behavior, and sexual activity refers to engaging sexual behavior. Although there is great variability in attitudes, sexual needs, and behavior among all individuals during all phases of adulthood (Hodson & Skeen, 1994), there are a number of generalizations we can reach regarding sexuality in a life span perspective.

Figure 2-2. Intimacy and togetherness are an essential aspect of sexuality at any age.

First, there is a discrepancy between interest and actual **sexual activity**. Interest and desire are always higher than activity. Investigations report that sexual interest remains fairly constant throughout most of life and does not begin to decline until after age 75 (Hodson & Skeen, 1994). Many lines of research demonstrate that men show more interest in sex than women (Peplau, 2003). Further, across the life span, men rate the strength of their own sex drive as higher than that of their female age-mates (Peplau, 2003). Moreover, although activity level decreases with age, people are still generally satisfied with their activity level (Matthias, Luben, Atchison, & Schweitzer, 1997).

In a large-scale study of adults aged 57 to 85, Lindau, Schumm amd Laumann (2007) found that more than 75% of those questioned remained sexually active, though the frequency of sexual behavior did wane a bit with increased age, and 25% of sexually active adults reported avoiding sex to deal with sexual difficulties. Healthier people and those with partners were more likely to have active sex lives; on the contrary, sexual activity may contribute to better physical health among such persons.

Also, the quality of the marital or interpersonal relationship affects sexual activity. The closer and warmer the relationship, the greater the potential for sexual activity. Research indicates that although sexual intercourse may occur in a casual relationship, it is more likely to occur in a monogamous dating relationship (Oliver & Hyde, 1993). Generally, women tend to emphasize sexuality within the context of committed relationships, compared to men who have more permissive attitudes toward casual premarital and extramarital sex. In terms of gay men and lesbian women, like heterosexual women, lesbians tend to have less permissive attitudes toward casual sex and sex outside a primary relationship than do gay or heterosexual men (Peplau, 2003). Prior to marriage, individuals of both genders tend to be faithful to their partner in the relationship, but we may have many sex partners as we move from one relationship to another, a pattern which is called serial monogamy.

Consequently, being married (or in a committed relationship) is highly related to sexual activity because of the availability of a partner. But, after marriage, the frequency of intercourse generally declines because of the demands of work, parenthood, and because sex is balanced with the other rewards of a marital relationship. For instance, Cross (1993) found the percentage of married men and women who have sexual relations at least once a week to decline from 80% in their 20s to 37% in their 60s. Matthias et al. (1997) found that the main predictors of sexual activity were being married, having more education, being younger and being male, and having good social networks, while the main predictors of sexual satisfaction were being sexually active, being female, having good mental health, and having better functional status.

In this light, it is important to understand that sex has different meanings during the various phases of adulthood (Pedersen, 1998). Sexuality in young adulthood is characterized by the desire to become sexually experienced and knowledgeable, perhaps as a prelude to marriage (Masters, Johnson, & Kolodny 1992). To illustrate, Masters et al. (1992) identified two patterns of sexual behavior in young adults: experimenters, who value proficiency and variety in sexual behavior; and seekers, who reserve intercourse for serious relationships. On the other hand, for many older couples, simply touching one another and embracing are highly sexual in nature; this may help them cope with a loss of sexual capacity due to normal aging or disease. Indeed, older men and women seem to be more willing to talk openly about sexuality, more likely to identify sexuality as a key component to their mental health, and to turn to a health practitioner for help with difficulties in their sexual health (Sexuality in Midlife and Beyond, American Association of Retired Persons, 2004).

There are gender differences in preferred frequency of sexual activity. Research (e.g., Peplau, 2003) suggests that it is usually the man who wants to have sex more often than the women does. Thus, actual frequency of sexual activity may reflect a compromise between the desires of the male and female partners. In gay and lesbian relationships, sexual frequency is decided by partners of the same genders, and lesbians report having sex less than gay or heterosexual men (Peplau, 2003). Also, women appear to be more willing than men to forgo sex or adhere to religious vows of celibacy. Overall, for women, an important goal of sex is intimacy within the context of a committed relationship, which is less true for men. However, it is important to note that there is a problem in obtaining accurate data on this topic since males may tend to exaggerate their sexual experiences while females may underreport their sexual experiences (Oliver & Hyde, 1993).

Finally, there is a consistency in sexual behavior. Over a 6-year period George and Weiler (1981) found that the most common pattern of married men and women ages 46 to 71 years was stability of sexual interest and activity (58%). Only 20% reported decreased sexual activity with their partner.

The oldest participants (65+ years) were most likely to report a sexual decline. Thus, the frequency of sexual activity in later life corresponds directly to the importance one places on sexuality earlier in life (George & Weiler, 1981).

However, research (e.g., Peplau, 2003) suggests that in comparison with men's sexuality, women's sexuality tends to have greater plasticity. Specifically, women's sexual beliefs and behaviors can be more easily shaped and altered by cultural, social, and situational factors. Additionally, factors such as educational level, religion, and acculturation are more strongly associated with women's sexuality than with men's.

Factors Involved in the Decline of Sexual Interest and Activity

There are a number of factors involved in the decline of sexual activity and interest for males and females such as: preoccupation with career or other activities, mental or physical fatigue, poor physical health, lack of a partner, psychological reasons (e.g., anxiety), and individual attitudes and beliefs (Abeles, 1997), i.e., that sexual activity in late life is abnormal (Pedersen, 1998). It is, however, difficult to determine which is the most important reason for the decrease in sexual activity and interest during the course of the life span, since each of these factors or reasons may interact. To illustrate, difficulty in maintaining an erection for males can result in a lower self-concept . Hence, the great interest in Viagra and Cialis among middle aged and older men from the late 1990s to the present!

A number of medical conditions have been found to be related to decreased sexual activity such as heart attack, prostate surgery, hysterectomy, arthritis, and cancer (Matthias et al., 1997). The side effects of medications can also interfere with sexual activity (Abeles, 1997). However, one's physical condition or health may not reduce activity per se, but rather beliefs about physical condition, such as anxieties about a heart ailment or enlarged prostate may explain declines in sexual activity. Thus, fear and misinformation can be just as harmful as can hormonal changes. Although sexual activity may

---

Adults Speak

Sex after Sixty

Contrary to the popular notion that sexual interest and prowess disappear in aging adults, research shows that many members of the over 60 set continue to lead active sex lives. Here are some excerpts from personal observations offered in group discussions that were conducted in a retirement community after the participants saw a film on sexuality and aging.

A 68-year-old married man: I have to admit that I used to think that older people didn't have sexual relations. I never really thought about it in personal terms, though, so when I got to my sixties and found my needs were still there, I wasn't all that surprised.

A 72-year-old woman: I think that the thing that surprises people is that we even think about sex, but why shouldn't we? If sex is still fun, and doesn't cost anything, and you've got a person you love to be with, it's no sin.

A 76-year-old widow: I say that you're as young as you think you are. If you think you're over the hill, you will be in a hurry. If you leave all the fun to younger people, you'll just sit in a rocking chair feeling old.

An 81-year-old man: To me, it's like knowing how to ride a bicycle. Once you learn, you never really forget. Even though my friends don't talk much about sex except to make jokes, I think about sex and even have dreams about it. And a couple of years ago, when I was having trouble with my prostate, my doctor was certainly surprised when I told him I still have sex twice a week.

A 71-year-old widow: I think it's perfectly all right to stop having sex whenever you want to. When my husband was still alive, we continued to love one another long after we stopped having sex.

A 70-year-old married woman: You have to admit that sex isn't exactly the same when you get older. I enjoy myself, and I know my husband does, but the passionate responses simmered down years ago, and sometimes I think we respond more out of memory than excitement.

A 69-year-old widower: One thing that nobody ever talks about is the pressure you get from women if you're an eligible man who is reasonably healthy and secure. They flirt, they hint, they make outright propositions — and I don't always like it, although I must admit that sometimes I do. But it's embarrassing to find that you've got a willing partner and you're not capable.

Source: Masters, Masters, & Kolodny (1992).

---

decline in females due to factors such as preoccupation with career or other activities and worries about health, as in the case of males, the primary cause of decreased sexual activity in older women is the lack of an available partner.

Sexual dysfunction refers to difficulties or impairments in normal sexual functioning. It is estimated that at least half of all married couples at some time may be affected by some form of sexual dysfunction (McCary & McCary, 1982). The incidence of sexual dysfunction increases with age for both men and women, mostly because of an increase in chronic health problems and increased medication use (Abeles, 1997). For instance, men with diabetes often report erectile difficulties, and diabetic women often experience sexual dysfunction. However, sexual dysfunction can also be attributed to psychosocial factors, such as fear of failure, guilt, and low self-esteem. Some examples of sexual dysfunction for males are: (1) erectile dysfunction, when intercourse is unsuccessful 25% of the time or more, due to an inability to have or maintain an erection; (2) premature ejaculation, which is the absence of voluntary control of ejaculation; and, (3) retarded ejaculation, an inability to ejaculate into the vagina, although the person may be able to ejaculate through other means of simulation, e.g., masturbation. For females, examples are: (1) orgasmic dysfunction, the inability to reach orgasm; and (2) vaginismus, which are severe involuntary contractions of the muscles surrounding the vaginal entrance that makes intercourse too painful.

In conclusion, many factors affect sexual behavior during the course of the life span. These range from physiological factors such as a longer time needed for the penis to become erect in men, and for women lower levels of estrogen, to health factors such as cardiovascular disease and hypertension, drugs and alcohol, and to psychosocial factors, e.g., attitudes and apprehension (Leitner & Leitner, 2004).

Check Your Learning 2-3

Identify the following terms and concepts:

> Menopause
> Sexual interest
> Serial monogamy
> Sexual dysfunction

- Describe the discrepancy between interest and sexual activity during adulthood.

- Describe how the quality of a marital or interpersonal relationship affects sexual activity during adulthood.

- How does the meaning of sex vary during the various phases of adulthood?

- How do males and females differ in their preferred frequency of sexual activity during adulthood?

- Discuss the factors that are involved in the decline in sexual interest and activity during adulthood.

Sensation

Sensation is the reception of physical stimulation and the translation of this stimulation into neural impulses, and perception is the interpretation of sensory stimulation. For instance, imagine yourself walking across campus, and off at a distance you see someone approaching you. When you are able to more closely examine this person's features, you realize it is one of your friends. Here we see the distinction between sensation—the reception of a shape or form by the visual system—and perception— the interpretation of this form as a friend. In real life, sensation and perception are closely intertwined. Our ability to cope and interact with our environment is in large part due to our ability to detect, interpret, and respond appropriately to sensory information (Kline & Scheiber, 1985), and there are clear relationships between perceptual processes and many other behaviors and traits, such as driving accidents, personality, and learning style. Thus, as we discuss these changes, try to determine what implications they have for the person in terms of everyday functioning. Further, we shall see that aging has a pervasive but differential effect on the senses (Stevens, Cruz, Marks, & Lakatos, 1998). Thus, aging has more significant effects on some sense modalities than on others. Therefore, aging does not cause a uniform decline in all senses.

Sensory Processes: Vision

Peak visual functioning is achieved during late adolescence or early adulthood, and it is fairly constant through adulthood. Functioning then begins to decline during one's late 50s and early 60s. Beginning in early adulthood, many of the eye structures begin to change, causing some loss of efficiency and effectiveness in functioning. Some of these normal age-related changes in the structures in the visual system (Kline & Scialfa, 1997;

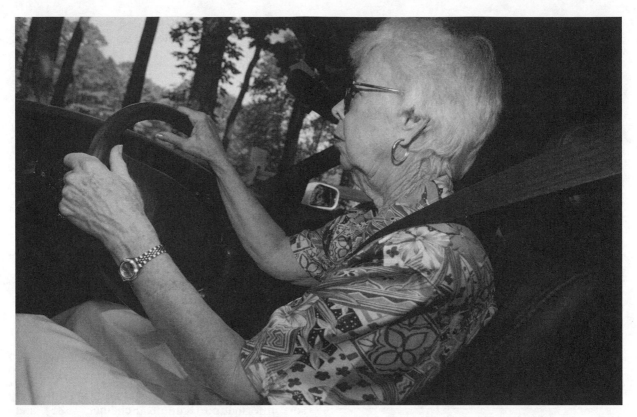

Figure 2-3. Adequate sensory and perceptual skills are crucial to activities such as driving.

Scheiber, 2006) are: (1) the lens gets thicker, yellows, and becomes more opaque, resulting in less light being projected onto the retina; (2) the ciliary muscles get weaker, affecting the focusing capability of the lens; (3) the aqueous humor changes, which provides metabolic support for the lens and cornea, and the aqueous outflow may decline and could contribute to the increase in intraocular pressure associated with glaucoma; and (4) the pupil's resting diameter declines, called senile miosis. These structural changes result in changes in various visual abilities or functions, which have consequences for the person's behavior and functioning. For instance, problems with eyesight represent the leading reason given by both older men and women to limit or avoid driving (Raglan, Satariano, & Macleod, 2004).

Visual impairment affects up to 10% of persons over age 65 (Rudberg, Furner, Dunn, & Cassel, 1993) and, next to cancer, the loss of vision is the most feared consequence of aging (Verrillo & Verrillo, 1985). Diabetes is a major cause of blindness for individuals at all age levels. The leading causes of severe age-related losses in vision are cataracts, glaucoma, and macular degeneration (Kline & Scialfa, 1997; Schieber, 2006).

Changes in Visual Abilities

Absolute threshold, the minimum level of stimulus energy required to see an object, increases with age (Kline & Scialfa, 1997). Thus, older persons may need more light to, for example, read the newspaper. Also, since they may not see well in the dark, they may be hesitant to go out at night. The **difference threshold** (how different two stimuli must be to be seen as such) also increases with age. Thus, older persons may have more difficulty in adjusting light levels to read comfortably.

Accommodation is the process whereby the eye adjusts its focus both near and far in order to gain clarity. With aging, there is a decrease in the ability of the eye to focus and/or refocus on objects at varying distances (Panek, 1997). A problem of accommodation associated with aging is **presbyopia,** which is a decline in the eye's ability to focus on near objects, and is due to a loss of elasticity of the lens. This is why many individuals in middle age start to need glasses for reading or for working with objects that are close to them. Also, given the problems of refocusing with advancing age, older drivers may accidentally miss important signs (Panek & Reardon, 1987), or they may compensate for this increased accommodation time by driving more slowly.

Visual acuity is the ability to resolve detail. It is equated with the accuracy of distance vision compared with that of a "hypothetical normal person," which is measured by means of a Snellen chart, consisting of a standardized series of letters, numbers, or symbols that must be read from a distance of 20 feet. The ability to read this chart is termed **static visual acuity**. If an individual with normal vision can read a designated letter on the Snellen chart at a distance of 20 feet, this is called 20/20 vision. A person who can distinguish at only 20 feet a letter that a person of normal vision can distinguish at 100 feet is said to have a visual acuity of 20/100.

Visual acuity tends to be relatively poor in young children, but improves in young adulthood, and shows a slight decline from the mid-20s to the 50s. Beyond this point, the rate of decline is accelerated. The average static visual acuity for persons 65 and older is 20/70. Decreased visual acuity creates difficulties in reading, watching television, and reading labels on medicine bottles. Providing more ambient light or making objects larger and more distinct (termed **contrast sensitivity**) seems to lessen the older person's difficulty in this area (Long & Crambert, 1990; Schieber, 2006).

There are also age decrements in **dynamic visual acuity** (Long & Crambert, 1990), which is the ability to accurately identify a moving target, such as a television message, a weather warning, or a street sign seen from a moving car. The more quickly the target is moving, the more older people are disadvantaged. The decrement with age in dynamic visual acuity appears to be related to changes in the thickness of the lens and the size of the pupil.

Regarding **color vision**, with increased age there is increased difficulty in discriminating among the blues, blue-greens, and violets—the low to middle range of the visible light spectrum—and much better successes in discriminating among the reds, oranges, and yellows, the upper middle to high range of the visible light spectrum (Kausler, 1991). Color vision deficits are more apparent when levels of illumination are low and when fine discriminations in shades of a particular color are being made (Fozard, 1990). The consequences of distortions in color vision can range from minor such as choosing two different colored socks, to severe, such as an inability to differentiate medication tablets by color.

Adaptation is the change in the sensitivity of the eye as a function of change in illumination. Dark adaptation is increased sensitivity to light in a dark environment, and light adaptation is increased sensitivity to light in a light environment. For example, when you enter a dark movie theater, your pupils will automatically expand in order to increase the amount of light entering your eyes (**dark adaptation**). This process takes about 30 seconds. The reverse happens when you leave the theater, that is, your pupils will automatically contract to cut down the amount of light entering your eyes (**light adaptation**). This process requires a shorter time than does dark adaptation.

The time required for both of these processes increases with age (Kline & Schieber, 1985; Schieber, 2006). The primary consequence of this change is that it will make you more susceptible to environmental hazards during the first few minutes of being in a differently illuminated environment. For instance, coming out of a theater into bright sunlight may temporarily blind you, to the point where you stumble off the curb.

Relatively bright light that results in unpleasantness or discomfort and/or interferes with optimum vision is termed **glare,** and is produced when light rays are diffused via a change in the composition of the vitreous humor. An example of this process occurs during night driving when you view the headlights of oncoming autos. The negative effects of glare on performance increases with age from age 40 on. For middle-aged and older drivers, this temporary blindness resulting from glare can easily cause an accident.

Visual field is the total extent of physical space visible to an eye in a given position—the whole area you see when your head is in a fixed position, and for a young adult is typically 180 degrees, and by age 70 decreases to approximately 140 degrees; the **peripheral field** is the outer area of your overall visual field and shrinks several degrees per decade after age 45 (Kline & Schieber, 1985; Schieber, 2006). The more your visual field is restricted, the more you must turn your head to see what you used to see "out of the corner of your eye," with your peripheral vision. This decline is significant since a great deal of important information from the environment comes to us from the peripheral visual field.

Sensory Processes: Hearing

The ability to hear decreases quite dramatically across the life span, to a level sufficient to compromise performance on a wide variety of daily tasks such as engaging in normal conversation, hearing the telephone, or hearing verbal instructions regarding the use of medications. These decreases are a function of both normal aging and external forces (Kline & Scialfa, 1997) such as occupational noise, pharmaco-therapeutic agents, industrial chemicals, and rapid changes in ambient pressure. A number of medical conditions, such as diabetes, ear infections, and cardiovascular disease affect hearing (Strawbridge, Wallhagen, Shema, & Kaplan, 2000). With aging, there are a number of changes in the structure of the outer, middle, and inner ear that may have implications for receiving auditory information. These include: an accumulation of fluid in the middle ear; atrophy and degeneration of hair cells in the cochlea; loss of auditory neurons; and

wax buildup (Fozard & Gordon-Salant, 2001; Merz, 1992; Panek, 1997).

As we age, the absolute threshold for the lowest level of sound that can be heard increases with age, meaning that sounds must be louder to evoke a response as we grow older. There is also a loss in the ability to hear higher frequencies of sound that occurs as part of the normal aging process. The most common auditory disorder associated with aging is **presbycusis**, which is a progressive bilateral (meaning both ears) loss of hearing for tones of high frequency due to changes in the auditory system. Although hearing ability decreases with age, the most dramatic decrements in hearing result from environmental exposure, rather than age per se (Davis, 1991). Therefore, many industries require workers, when working in environments with high noise levels, such as airline baggage handlers, to wear protective ear plugs (Panek, 1997). The ability to detect changes in the pitch of sounds is called pitch discrimination, and it declines with age (Davis, 1991). The ability to differentiate pitch is not only important for listeners of music, but it is also an important factor in the perception of speech.

The Effects of Age-Related Changes in Hearing

Hearing impairments are progressive, irreversible and affect 23% of persons over age 65 (Rudberg et al., 1993). At any age impairments in hearing may produce detrimental changes in one's behavior and one's interaction with the environment and others (Panek, 1997). For example, hearing impairment alters a person's ability to communicate with others and thus can seriously affect interpersonal relationships (Strawbridge et al., 2000). The magnitude of adjustment problems experienced by individuals with hearing disorders is directly related to the severity of the hearing disorder and at what age it began. The later in life it begins, and the greater its severity, the greater the adjustment problems individuals experience. This is assumed to be the result of either of the following: (1) not being able to hear adequately leads to lower self-concept, or (2) not being able to hear adequately leads to feelings of paranoia—"Are those people talking about me?" For instance, if people have to speak quite loudly for you to hear, they may not want to interact with you in a social situation if they feel embarrassed by talking loudly. In turn, you may avoid conversations with others, causing you to feel less confident and more isolated. Thus, hearing impairment is associated with multiple negative outcomes, including depression, loneliness, altered self-esteem, and diminished functional status (Strawbridge et al., 2000). Although most people with a hearing loss can benefit from using a hearing aid, a majority do not wear a hearing aid for a variety of reasons such as cost, stigma, or vanity (Strawbridge et al., 2000).

Finally, research (e.g., Strawbridge et al., 2000) suggests that there are gender and ethnic/racial differences in hearing impairment. Specifically, men's hearing impairment is worse than women's, and white Americans have higher rates of hearing loss than do African Americans.

Sensory Processes: Taste and Smell

Although we are exposed to numerous tastes and smells every day, we know comparatively little about what exactly happens to them as we age, compared to the other senses. Our taste (**gustatory system**) and smell (**olfactory system**) senses work interactively. To illustrate, when you have a cold and your nose is stuffed up, you are often unable to taste your food. However, for presentation purposes, we will discuss these two systems separately. As we will see, losses of taste and smell are common in elderly persons and can result from normal aging processes, certain disease states (such as Alzheimer's disease), medications, surgical interventions, and environmental exposure (Schiffman, 1997).

We are able to detect four basic taste qualities: **sweet**, **salty**, **bitter**, **sour**, and the controversial taste quality termed **umami** (Moject, Christ- Hazelhof, & Heidema, 2001). An example of umami is mono-

sodium glutamate (MSG), which is described as salty with a greasy aftertaste. The receptors for taste are the taste buds which are on the tongue, and the taste buds for each of the four basic taste qualities tend to be clustered on specific locations on the tongue. The taste buds become fully developed in early adolescence and remain relatively unchanged until the mid-40s, when signs of atrophy begin to appear. The specific age-related changes in the taste system include: a gradual decrease in the number of taste buds; a loss of elasticity in the mouth and lips; decrease in saliva; and fissuring of the tongue.

However, although the majority of studies show decreases in taste sensitivity as we age (Moject et al., 2001) the cause of taste changes in normal aging in the absence of disease and medications is not fully understood (Schiffman (1997). In fact, as we age, we are still able to detect all four taste qualities, although there are considerable differences between young and old persons in the sensory perception and pleasantness of food flavors (de Graaf, Polet, & van Staveren, 1994). In most cases the sense of taste is not totally absent but rather it is reduced or distorted (Schiffman, 1997). Nonetheless, deficits in taste sensitivity may not only reduce the pleasure and comfort from food, but represent risk factors for nutritional deficiencies as well as adherence to specific dietary regimens. Also, it generally appears that the decline in taste sensitivity with age is more pronounced for men compared to women.

Many older adults express numerous taste complaints in a restaurant or at home, such as "the food is tasteless" or is "too salty." This may be is due to the influence of psychosocial factors, such as illnesses, medications, smoking, problems in personal adjustment, attitudes toward self, or feelings of abandonment. For example, complaints about the ability to taste foods may indicate mild degrees of depression or side effects of medication prescribed for a health problem (Bischmann & Witte, 1990).

Olfactory losses with age, like taste losses, result from normal aging, certain disease states (such as Alzheimer's and Parkinson's disease), medications, surgical interventions, and environmental exposure (Schiffman, 1997). Most studies suggested that the sense of smell is even more impaired than the sense of taste.

During the aging process, anatomical and physiological changes also occur in the structure of the upper airway, the olfactory epithelium, olfactory bulb and nerves, hippocampus and amygdaloid complex, and hypothalamus, including reductions in cell number, damage to cells, and diminished levels of neurotransmitters (Schiffman, 1997). Thus, even in healthy older adults, olfactory losses can result from one or more causes. Also, studies have not usually observed gender differences in odor detection with age (Larsson, Finkel, & Pedersen, 2000).

When familiar objects no longer smell the same, the result might be as mild as diminished sensory enjoyment, or as severe as disorientation (Russell, Cummings, Profitt, Wysocki, Gilbert, & Cotman, 1993). Clearly, deficits in olfactory sense can have some potentially disastrous consequences both at home and in the workplace. For example, the decrease in the ability for older workers to detect odors with increasing age would have a pronounced effect in occupations where failure to detect low levels of toxic substances can lead to health risks (Panek, 1997). At home, the impaired ability of older persons to recognize the scent of natural gas may contribute to the increased number of gas-related accidents in their homes (Russell et al., 1993).

Somesthesis

Sensitivity to touch, vibration, temperature, kinesthesis, is pain are collectively known as **somesthesis**, and results from normal and intensive stimulation of the skin and viscera (Panek, 1997). Age-related declines in sensitivity in each of these senses can be attributed to a decreased number of sensory receptors for each sense. Age changes or differences in these senses vary by the part of the body involved. For example, sensitivity of the feet starts to decrease at an earlier age than does that of the forearm.

Regarding **touch**, sensitivity appears to remain relatively unchanged through about age 50 to 55, with a rise in the absolute threshold (decreased sensitivity) thereafter (Whitbourne, 1985), attributed to a loss of touch receptors. As with the other somestestic senses, **vibratory sensitivity** differs by the part of the body stimulated. For example, vibratory sensitivity is better for the wrists, elbows, and shoulders than for the ankles, shins, and knees (Kenshalo, 1977), and it appears the lower extremities are more affected by age than the upper extremities. With age there is a slight rise in the absolute threshold for both **cold** and **warmth** (Whitbourne, 1999), which is termed **thermal perception** (Harju, 2002), resulting in an impairment of the ability of the temperature-regulating system to cope with extreme environmental temperatures. Consequently, older adults may be more susceptible to hypothermia, heatstroke, and frostbite, more readily than younger adults.

In terms of **kinesthesis**, there are two forms of movement, passive (the individual is stationary but is in a vehicle or apparatus that is moving, e.g., in an airplane or on a moving sidewalk), and active (actual movement of the body or body parts, e.g., walking). Active movement is relatively unaffected by age, while there is a decline in the ability to detect passive movement (Ochs, Newberry, Lendhardt, & Harkins, 1985).

Falls are the third leading cause of accidental death for all ages in the United States, behind automobile accidents and unintentional poisoning. Among those age 65+, falls are the leading cause of death from unintended injury (CDC, 2009). More than one-third of older Americans fall each year, with 20-30% experiencing moderate to severe injuries. Falls increase the risk of death. Although women are more likely to fall than are men, older men are more likely to die as a result of a fall. There do not seem to be differences in the rate of falls between Caucasian and African American older adults, but both groups have higher rates than Hispanic adults (CDC, 2009). The effects of falling can be quite debilitating. Being unable to walk or fearful of walking can contribute to isolation from others, the sense that one is no longer able to walk without help, and thus depression. Factors that contribute to falls include: impaired balance, muscular weakness, inflexibility, slow and inadequate adjustments to environmental objects, cardiovascular disease, reduced leg strength, mental confusion, hearing and vision impairments, medications, decreased or failed input from the kinesthetic receptors, and arthritis (CDC, 2009).

Pain thresholds vary substantially between individuals and between parts of the body in the same individual. This occurs in part because the experience of pain is more than just sensory—it is cognitive, motivational, personality-related, and cultural in nature. Thus, pain is a universal, enigmatic, and highly subjective phenomenon (Zarit, Griffiths, & Ber, 2004). Overall, research suggests a curvilinear relationship between age and pain increasing up to the age of 50, decreasing through age 85, and then increasing again (Zarit et al., 2004).

Perception

There are a variety of perceptual processes, and each has major implications for everyday functioning during adulthood (Kline & Scialfa, 1997). Three of the most important are **vigilance**, **perceptual/cognitive style**, and **selective attention**. Each plays a significant role in our everyday behavior and successful adaptation to the demands of the environment.

Vigilance is the ability to maintain attention on a task for a sustained period, and is very important for driving, assembly-line work, air-traffic controllers, and for other persons whose attention must be maintained for fairly long periods of time (Panek, 1997). Although performance on vigilance tasks decreases with age, the young-old differences on vigilance tasks can be attenuated with practice (Paraman & Giambra, 1991). Performance varies as a function of a number of factors, such as the nature of the task, the sensory modality studied, the length of time one is expected to be vigilant, time one has to respond, memory, the number of items to be monitored, and fatigue (Kausler, 1991).

Perceptual/cognitive style more or less sets the stage for those aspects of the environment that one attends to (Rogers, 1997). One aspect of cognitive style is **field dependence/ independence**. People

who are considered field-dependent make judgments that are heavily influenced by the immediate environment, while field-independent persons' judgments are not. There is a shift from field dependence to independence during adolescence, continuity during adulthood, and a return to field dependence during old age (Panek, Barrett, Sterns, & Alexander, 1978; Rogers, 1997). This shift toward field dependence with increased age has been found to be related to driving performance and accident involvement (Rogers, 1997). Thus, field dependence is related to higher accident involvement.

Attention plays an important role in almost all areas of our daily lives, including reading this book and taking notes in class, and in order to effectively function we must be able to selectively attend to particular aspects of this information and ignore others. Thus, **selective** or **divided attention** is an essential aspect of perception, information processing, and everyday behavior (Panek & Rush, 1981). A good example is attempting to read this text while your roommates are carrying on a conversation and listening to music. The ability to maintain and reorient attention decreases with age. For most adults, reorientation of attention (switching from one task to another) is more difficult than its maintenance (focusing on one task) or vigilance. Moreover, the difference in performance between the two components of selective attention, maintenance and reorientation, is magnified with increasing age. Even when not distracted by irrelevant information, older people are deficient in selective attention relative to young and middle-aged persons (Barr & Giambra, 1990). While the performance of both young and old individuals declines as the tasks increase in difficulty, the decline is generally greater and more rapid for older adults. When the attentional demands of the task decrease, the performance of older adults improves (Lorsbach & Simpson, 1988). Further, the more distractors, demands on memory, anxiety, and the greater the task complexity, the worse the performance (Kline & Scialfa, 1997). To illustrate, when confronted with difficult or complex tasks, older adults often respond anxiously (Hayslip, 1989), which can interfere with attentional resources in situations where mental effort is expected, as can depression and fatigue (Hayslip, Kennelly, & Maloy, 1990).

Slowdown in Behavior and Performance

One of the most documented age-related changes is a slowdown in behavior and performance (Vercruyessen, 1997). As suggested by Smith and Brewer (1995) it is widely recognized that growing old is accompanied by changes in speed of performance, with older people typically performing more slowly than younger people on activities that emphasize rapid responding. From age 40 onward, accuracy appears to be emphasized at the expense of speed in performing a psychomotor task (Panek, 1997), which is called the **speed versus accuracy trade-off.** This slowdown in behavior has generally been studied with **perceptual-motor reaction time** (PMRT) tasks. These tasks involve the speed of response to some external or internal stimulus. The study of PMRT performance during adulthood is very important because many situations in our everyday life involve reacting to stimuli quickly and accurately.

Successful performance on these tasks involves a great deal more than just a single motor response because the person must: (1) perceive that an event has occurred, (2) decide what to do about it, and (3) carry out the decided-upon action. Thus, poor performance can often be attributed to one or more of these other factors rather than to just the speed of motor performance. There are few age declines in simple tasks (one stimulus associated with one response such as pressing a key when a light comes on), or choice tasks (one stimulus associated with one response, but there is more than one stimulus-response pair, e.g., typing). Age declines in complex tasks (numerous stimuli and responses, which are not paired, e.g., driving an automobile) are substantial (Kausler, 1991). The most pronounced age differences are in the **decision** or **premotor time** component of reaction time (time from the onset of the stimulus to initiating the response), compared to the **motor time** component (time from response initiation to response completion) (Vercruyssen, 1997). That is, it takes older adults a longer time to initiate the response than those who are younger. Also, research suggests that older adults are more variable than young adults in reaction time performance and demonstrate greater intra-individual variability compared to young adults (Hultsch, MacDonald, & Dixon, 2002). Training, however, can improve both the pre-motor and motor aspects of reaction time (Baylor & Spiduso, 1988). In this respect, older drivers have more difficulty in anticipating collisions while decelerating, especially at higher speeds (Anderson, Cisneros, Saidpour, & Atchley, 2000).

Although age-related slowing is well documented, it is still largely unexplained (Salthouse, 1993), though this slowdown is mediated predominantly by **central** rather than **peripheral** factors (Panek, 1997; Vercruyssen, 1997).

There have been many "central" explanations proposed for the slowing of behavior with age which can be classified into one of two general categories: the neurobiological ("hardware") and psychological ("software") perspectives (Vercruyssen, 1997). The neurobiological ("hardware") perspective attributes the slowdown to changes in the CNS such as: changes throughout the CNS and/or neuropsychological processes (Birren & Fisher, 1995); interference from distracting neural noise (background sounds from neuronal irregularities) (Welford, 1977); structural and cell loss due to genetics, disease, or disuse (Salthouse, 1985).

In addition to a generalized slowing of central nervous system functions, aging disrupts decision-making processes and higher cortical functions (Fozard et al., 1994). These decision-making processes and higher cortical functions are the basis of the "software" perspective. Explanations from the psychological ("software") perspective attribute slowing to some higher order central process, rather than to specific changes in the CNS. Examples include: information overload and task complexity (Cerella, Poon, & Williams, 1990); memory changes (Salthouse, 1985); reduced arousal/activation and inability to maintain preparedness (Birren et al., 1990); increased cautiousness, rigidity, and/or lack of flexibility.

Table 2-1

Examples of the Effects of Sensory Decline with Age upon Interacting with the Environment

Sensory System	Structural/Anatomical Changes	Functional/Ability Changes	Possible Behavioral Implication
Gustatory	Decreased taste buds (papillae)	Inability to correctly determine taste qualities	Loss of appetite Distorted taste Decreased socialization
Olfactory	Degeneration of neurons on olfactory bulb	Inability to correctly detect and determine various odors	Loss of appetite Distorted odors Inability to detect the presence of potentially harmful odors
Somesthesis (touch, vibration, temperature, kinesthesis, pain)	Decreased number of sensory receptors for each somesthetic sense	Inability to correctly detect stimulation from the environment	Exposure to potentially dangerous temperature levels Susceptibility to falls Inability to discriminate among clothing materials
Visual	Deposits forming on lens Atrophy of ciliary muscles	Decreased ability in accommodation Decreased visual activity Decreased visual field Absolute/difference thresholds increase	Difficulty in reading Difficulty in mobility Difficulty in driving Difficulty in writing letters Difficulty in watching television Decreased activity
Auditory	Wax buildup Accumulation of fluid in middle ear Degeneration of hair cells in the basal coil of cochlea Loss of auditory neurons	Increased absolute threshold Difficulty in pitch discrimination Hearing loss Difference threshold increases	Inability to hear on the telephone Inability to hear during normal conversation Difficulty in hearing questions on intelligence test Difficulty in interpersonal communication

Implications:
The Effects of Biophysiological, Sensory, and Perceptual Changes on Everyday Life

The physical, biophysiological, sensory, and perceptual changes associated with aging we discussed have many significant implications for everyday functioning. Some of these are highlighted in Table 2-1. These changes can affect our self-concept, our interactions with others and with the environment, and our health.

In light of these many changes, middle age can be a particularly difficult time of transition, change, confrontation, and crisis for some. It may be seen as a time of confrontation between the realities of one's present life and the myths and dreams of one's youth. The greater this discrepancy, the greater the potential for stress and crisis. While this self-examination is usually associated with middle age, it can occur at any point in the life cycle. Seeing ourselves, our peers, and our parents aging physically and eventually dying, as well as watching our children growing up and entering adulthood, often results in the first realization that we are in the middle of the life cycle. Individuals at this point in the life cycle are often called members of the **sandwich generation** (see Chapter 5). That is, they are caught in the middle between meeting the demands and needs of their children and the demands and needs of their aging parents. For some people, such demands, on top of the growing discomfort with their own aging, can be overwhelming. This stress may contribute to alcohol or drug abuse, family violence, impaired social and work performance, or depression. Others, however, are able to cope with caregiving demands (see Chapters 4, 9, and 10) and with the physical realities of growing older.

Check Your Learning 2-4

Identify the following terms and concepts:

Sensation
Absolute threshold
Difference threshold
Presbyopia
Static vs. dynamic visual acuity
Dark adaptation
Peripheral field
Sandwich generation
Vigilance
Field dependence/independence
Perception
Accommodation
Somesthesis
Visual acuity
Light adaptation
Presbycusis
Decision/pre-motor time
Motor time
Selective attention

- Describe the age-related changes in taste and smell sensitivity. What are some of the effects of these changes for a person?

- Describe how age-related changes in the visual system affect a person's everyday interaction with the environment.

- Describe the age-related changes in somesthesis. What are some of the effects of these changes for a person?

- Describe the age-related changes in pain sensitivity.

- Describe the age-related changes in vigilance. What are some of the implications of the age-related decrease in vigilance for a person?

- Describe the age-related changes in selective attention. What are some of the implications of the age-related decrease in selective attention ability for a person?

- What are some of the effects of the biophysiological, sensory, and perceptual age-related changes on a person?

- What is the speed versus accuracy tradeoff? What factors contribute to the slowdown in behavior and performance with age? What are some of the implications of this slowdown?

- Compare and contrast the neurobiological ("hardware") perspective with the psychological ("software") perspective in explaining the slowdown in behavior and performance with age.

Learning Activity: Ask two people over age 50: "What types of physical, sensory and perceptual changes have you experienced? How have these changes affected your behavior?"

Summary

There is no single theory that adequately explains all aspects of why we age. However, current research suggests a fundamental assumption that the life span of any organism, or how long a member of a species will live on the average, is ultimately determined by an inherited genetic program.

Life expectancy has exhibited a significant change from the time of the ancient Greeks to the present. The most significant increases in life expectancy in the United States occurred between 1900 and 1940; increases have been relatively minor since then. The increase in life expectancy since 1900 can be attributed to a variety of factors such as improved housing, sanitation and hygiene, and better nutrition.

Intrinsic/primary factors and extrinsic/secondary factors are related to life expectancy, where **intrinsic factors** set the parameters for our maximum potential life span. The major intrinsic factors related to life expectancy are genetic inheritance, gender, ethnicity, and health condition. **Extrinsic factors** modify the limits projected for life expectancy by the intrinsic factors. The major extrinsic factors influencing life expectancy are nutrition and diet, climate or physical environment, exercise and activity, interpersonal relationships, work and work satisfaction, education and economic status, cognitive/intellectual factors, and personality and stress avoidance.

For many of us, aging is defined in terms of the changes we experience in our everyday physical, visual, or physiological functioning. We distinguished between changes that are the result of the biopsychosocial processes of aging (**primary** age changes), from those that are due to inactivity, poor eating habits, or disease (**secondary** age changes). In this context, experiencing wrinkles or gray hair may lead to loss of self-esteem for some individuals, as explained by the **multiple threshold model of physical aging**.

Beginning in early adulthood, there are in fact a number of internal biophysiological changes taking place, which will eventually show up as external physical changes, or changes in behavior and performance later in life. Especially during middle age, we become acutely aware that there are numerous age-related changes in many body systems such as the **muscular-skeletal**, **cardiovascular**, **central nervous**, and **reproductive systems**, which have numerous implications for our everyday functioning.

There is a discrepancy between **sexual interest** and **sexual activity** during all phases of adulthood; interest is always higher than activity, with gender, age, health, and marital status contributing to this discrepancy. Moreover, there is a consistency in sexual behavior over time.

The age-related changes in the ability to **detect**, **interpret**, and **respond** to visual and auditory information often compromise performance on a wide variety of daily tasks, such as reading medicine labels and comprehending speech. The most serious decreases in hearing are the result of environmental factors such as exposure to high levels of **noise**, rather than age per se. Food complaints and **taste** aberrations among older people are based, not on sensory decrements, but on factors such as problems in personal adjustment, attitudes toward self, or feelings of abandonment. Declines in the **somesthetic** senses such as touch and pain can be attributed to a decreased number of sensory receptors for each sense. Three of the most important perceptual processes for everyday functioning are **vigilance**, **perceptual/cognitive style**, and **attention**. Extensive research has documented decreases in these perceptual processes with age. Moreover, one of the most documented age-related changes is a slowdown in behavior and performance. From age 40 onward, accuracy appears to be emphasized at the expense of speed in the performing a psychomotor task, which is referred to as the **speed versus accuracy trade-off**.

While there are marked declines in **peripheral** (sensory and motor) mechanisms and processes, such deficits account for relatively little of the overall slowing of performance. In contrast, age differences in response speed are mediated predominantly by **central** rather than peripheral factors. Among the many explanations for the slowing of decisions and movements in older adults are two major types of theories, **neurobiological** ("hardware") and **psychological** ("software") perspectives.

Learning  Intelligence

Cognitive Processes in Adulthood

Universities now face the prospect of declines in the numbers of students who are 18-22 years of age with the proportion of older students predicted to increase relative to younger students (National Center for Educational Statistics, 2005). As the demands of older employees and older students increase, educators will face the challenge of designing appropriate learning environments for such persons who want to either upgrade their existing skills or learn new skills (see Figure 3-1). This may be especially important to many adults. Not being able to learn new procedures at work or being unable to remember others' names can be embarrassing and detrimental to one's personal and professional well-being. Moreover, forgetting an important doctor's

Figure 3-1. It is not uncommon to see older persons attending universities to pursue their goals.

appointment or when to take one's medication can have serious consequences for one's health.

All of us suffer from memory lapses or have difficulty in learning new information from time to time. Yet, it is when people reach their 40s and 50s that even temporary slips of memory or difficulty in learning new ideas sensitize them to the fact that "they must be getting old" or worse still, that they might be suffering from Alzheimer's disease (see Chapter 10). For those older persons who value their brain, such difficulties may cause them to lose their self-respect, or other people may indeed expect less of them because they are forgetful. Rather than read a new book, try a crossword puzzle, or attend a lecture, the adult learner gives up. Thus, learning difficulties or memory loss with increased age become a self-fulfilling prophecy for some middle-aged and older persons (see Figure 3-2). Memory failures in an older family member might even cause a son or a daughter to consider institutionalizing a parent. In contrast, few college students would worry about forgetfulness on an exam or in an everyday social situation (e.g., in forgetting a phone number, someone's name, or an address). In thinking about memory and aging, it is important to distinguish between normal, maturational changes in our memory skills that are independent of disease, which have been termed **age-associated memory impairments (AAMI)** (Crook et al., 1986), and pathological changes in memory, which are due to the effects of disease or injury, for example (see Chapter 10) Alzheimer's disease or multi-infarct dementia (Cherry & Smith, 1998). While age differences in memory depend on the nature of the

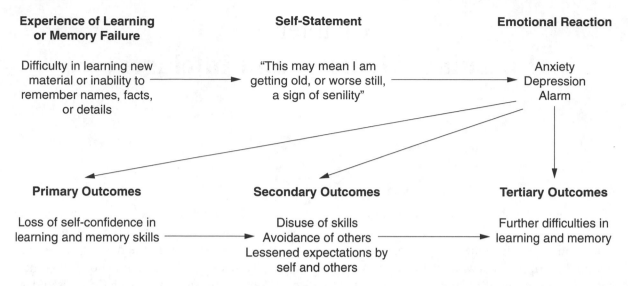

Figure 3-2. Learning and the Cycle of Memory Loss.

memory system and associated processes, what it is that one is trying to remember, and how one assesses memory (Cherry & Smith, 1998), there are great differences among adults in the nature of their memory skills (Powell, 1994).

Age-associated memory impairments (see Figure 3-3) occur for six basic reasons:

1. The ability and efficiency of our brain cells to carry electrical and chemical messages decline because of changes in the chemical-sand structures of our brains.
2. Sensory changes (declining vision, hearing) and attentional interference reduce the integrity of information entering the cognitive system and our ability to retrieve it.
3. Current life-style factors may interfere with our cognitive system. Cigarette smoking, alcohol, poor nutrition, and lack of exercise interfere with the brain's functioning.
4. Overall health factors and the presence of certain diseases are associated with impaired memory functioning. Hypertension, Type 2 diabetes, and sleep apnea can interfere with blood flow and oxygen uptake in the brain.
5. Chronic stress, including posttraumatic stress disorder (PTSD), can interfere with a range of memory abilities.

6. Other emotional factors, including depression and anxiety, can directly interfere with memory via altered brain chemicals, and indirectly interfere with memory via self-perceptions and motivation (Crook & Adderly, 1998).

Typical AAMI

Although there are wide individual differences in the rate and extent of AAMI, we can observe some general trends. Youngjohn, Larrabee, and Crook (1991) tested more than 1,500 adults on their ability to learn and remember written information. Their results are presented in Figure 3-3. As shown, there were substantial age differences from young adulthood to old age. In a similar study conducted in Italy (Crook, Zappala, et al., 1993), adult age differences are substantial for both immediate recall and delayed recall (1 hour after initial learning) of names. In fact, the ability of the oldest adults to recall names was particularly poor, with an average decline of 74% from the initial learning. Imagine how difficult it would be to be a successful college student if your ability to remember names and other written information was so poor!

Fortunately, as people age, they attempt to cope with changes they associate with the process of growing older by either developing new skills or finding ways of compensating for losses in their

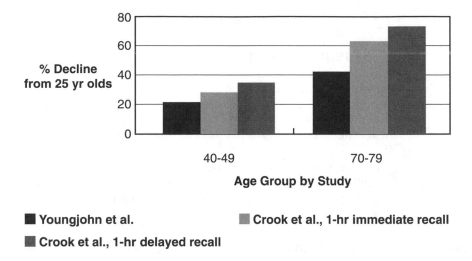

Figure 3-3. Extent of age-associated memory impairments (AAMI) in two studies.

skills (Baltes & Baltes, 1990). Many of the techniques older adults use to optimize their memory and learning performance are helpful for younger adults, too. For example, maintaining good health and avoiding the negative effects of chronic stress, alcohol abuse, and fatigue are important for learners of all ages. Making a concerted effort to learn and remember information, and using a variety of sources of information (listen to the lecture, take written notes, read those notes later, think about the information) increase learning and retention.

What Are Learning and Memory in Adulthood?

Learning is often understood in terms of the **acquisition of stimulus-response (S-R) associations** (Kausler, 1991), while forgetting (a loss of memory) is caused by a weakening or breakdown of these associations. The stimuli (S) may lie in your environment (a sound causes you to turn your head) or be produced by you yourself (a sensation of pain in your leg causes you to walk more slowly). These stimuli often evoke a particular thought or image, (e.g., the sound I heard means class is over), which then mediates an external response (R), such as putting one's notes away and leaving the classroom. In contrast, the **information processing approach** stresses that learning and memory are best under-

stood in terms of the **registration, encoding, storage,** and **retrieval** (all types of cognitive processes), and the adult learner is viewed as an active processor of information (Schwartz & Reisberg, 1991). For example, we might organize or categorize information as we often do when trying to remember grocery items to be purchased or in learning and recalling persons' names at a party.

Memory: Structure and Process

Memory in adulthood can be understood by studying **memory structures** and **memory processes** (Hoyer & Verhaeghen, 2006) (see Figure 3-4). This approach suggests that there are distinct

---

Check Your Learning 3-1

Define the following terms and concepts:

Learning
Memory
Age-associated memory impairments
S-R associations
Information processing

- Why are learning, memory, and intelligence important to us in adulthood?

Table 3-1

Memory Structures and Aging

Memory Stores	Defining Characteristics
Sensory Memory	Rapid decay (for example, 1/2 second), preattentive in nature. Aging decline is slight and depends on sensory integrity.
Short-Term Memory (Primary, Secondary Memory)	Limited to what can be consciously retained at present, decays if not further processed. Reliable but modest age declines occur in both active and passive aspects. Age deficits reflect the nature of how material is actively processed, stored, and retrieved.
Long-Term Memory (Tertiary Memory)	Permanent and unlimited capacity. Age effects depend upon the datedness of material and extent of rehearsal.

- What is the distinction between learning and memory?

- What is an information processing approach to learning?

structures or "hypothetical entities" defining memory. These memory stores differ in function and duration, and in some degree, in content. Thus, each memory store serves a different function within our multistore system (see Table 3-1) and memory "failures" differ across each system (Schacter, 2000).

Sensory memory (SM) is not really "memory" at all. Rather, SM is said to be preattentive or precategorical. It may serve as a kind of attentional filter, working directly with the raw physical aspects of incoming stimuli. Information in SM decays very rapidly (within 1/3 to 1 second) unless it is filtered into other memory systems for additional processing. The classic example for sensory memory involves the common experience of still "hearing" the last few notes of a song after we have turned off the radio. There are few clear age differences/age changes favoring young adults regarding sensory memory (Kausler, 1994). Indeed, it may

be difficult to demonstrate that sensory memory even exists for elderly adults who may be experiencing serious sensory or attentional deficits. Some researchers have suggested that information decays more slowly for older adults, leading to added processing interference.

Short-term memory (STM) is the hypothetical place in which we can both store and manipulate incoming information for brief periods (up to 30 seconds)). STM is the kind of memory we use when we look up a telephone number and keep it in mind just long enough to call it. If the number is busy, we must look the number up again. The classic example of STM casts it as a desk top. There is limited space on a desk top. If we try to pile too much on the desk, information gets lost. However, we can organize and group similar bits of information to make it easier to work on our cluttered desk. There is a trade-off however: we can store so much information on our desks that we no longer have adequate room to actually work and organize. STM is similar. We have a limited processing capacity, but good organization can help us to deal with more information in a more efficient manner. Due to the trade-off between storage capacity and work space, some people refer to this memory process as working memory (WM). In general, there are age differences in STM (Hultsch & Dixon, 1990; Kausler, 1994; Smith, 1996). Using a **digit span task**, where digits of varying span lengths (2-7 digits) are read to the individual who repeats this span in the same order, young adults can repeat about 6 digits. In contrast, older adults can repeat about 5.5 forward digits. In many ways, the forward digit span task assesses storage capacity. Larger age differences are seen when participants are asked to repeat the digits in reverse order. For example, the experimenter might say, " 1, 5, 3" and the participant is expected to say " 3, 5, 1." In this backward digit span task, young adults can recall about 5 digits and older adults about 3 (Gregoire & Van der Linden, 1997; Hultsch & Dixon, 1990). The backward span task represents both the storage and manipulation processes involved in STM; thus, it is not surprising that even the young adults remember fewer items in a backward span task than in a forward span task.

In addition to having a smaller storage capacity in STM, older adults may be slower or less efficient in searching the content of the STM, and they may organize information to be stored less efficiently (Kausler, 1991). Moreover, older adults rehearse to-be-remembered items less actively and search for such items less efficiently. This contributes to short-term memory deficits (Kausler, 1994). In order to ascertain whether age differences in STM/WM were due to storage differences or processing differences, Swanson (1999) tested several age groups on a variety of STM tasks. He concluded that capacity in STM may peak around age 45. As the underlying biological and cognitive system begins to age, older adults have less capacity in the STM (Swanson, 1999).

Often when people talk about "memory," they are referring to either **short-term memory** or to **long-term memory (LTM)**. LTM is a permanent and unlimited capacity to store both remote events and recent events. Remembering what you read five minutes ago, recalling what you ate last week, or knowing the name of your first grade teacher are all bits of information that are stored in LTM. Re-

searchers studying LTM typically use questionnaires or experimental procedures to gather data on LTM.

In terms of age differences in LTM, results are often mixed. If researchers are studying history and geography facts, older adults tend to remember better than younger adults; recall for names, however, favors younger adults (Hoyer & Verhaeghen, 2006; Smith, 1996). Interpreting these differences in LTM is difficult, however, given the confounding of the age of the individual and the age (datedness) of that which is to be recalled (Botwinick, 1984). That is, when we ask someone to recall an event, name, etc., from long ago, we may be assessing many things. For example, people who know more, because they are older or are more experienced and educated, may actually appear to show poorer long-term memory because what they have stored is more complex and extensive. Thus, it may appear that persons who have less material to search through are more likely to appear to have better memories! However, older persons with a greater storehouse of personally meaningful information may be able to recall accurately a greater percentage of what they know, perhaps because they have rehearsed it more often. Older persons have accumulated more knowledge, and have rehearsed more often that which is personally important to them (Kausler, 1994).

As opposed to memory structures, a newer approach to memory emphasizes **memory processes** that explain how material is transferred from one memory store to another (see Figure 3-4).

Registration refers to whether the material is literally heard or seen, i.e., its size or loudness exceeds one's sensory threshold. This is a prerequisite for further processing such information. If, for example, an older adult suffers from sensory loss, e.g., poor eyesight, it is unlikely that what has been presented visually will be adequately registered. **Encoding** refers to the process of giving meaning to information in working memory that has entered the sensory store. Creating a visual or verbal mediator (a rhyme or an image) to help you learn and recall a list of words reflects encoding. **Storage** suggests that information, having been encoded in

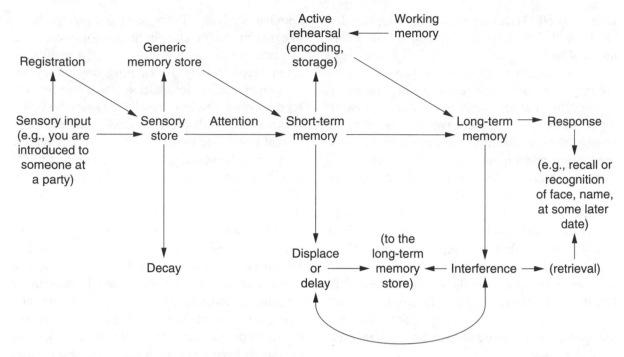

Figure 3-4. Links between memory stores via memory processes.

working memory, is then organized in a general-to-specific pattern, where general categories are first created, within which more specific categories are developed. It appears that older adults are less likely to spontaneously organize or to use **mediators,** and they store information less efficiently (Kausler, 1994). They are **role learners**. A good way of expressing the distinction between encoding and storage is that encoding involves establishing a memory trace, whereas in storage, this trace is maintained (rehearsed) until it can be retrieved (Kausler, 1994).

Retrieval is, quite simply, the "getting out" of the information that presumably has been registered, encoded, and stored. If you are anxious, that anxiety may make it difficult for you to retrieve what you have in storage. This explains the "tip-of-the-tongue" phenomenon we have all experienced. If you cannot recall a name or a date on an exam, we would say that something **interferes** with either your learning (acquisition [encoding] and storage) or your recall (retrieval) of that information. In working with both younger and older adults, we want to minimize those factors that make interference more

likely and capitalize on situations that allow for positive gains from previous learning experiences and situations.

Understanding Learning and Memory in Adulthood

Current research suggests that the ability to learn and remember with age is highly dependent upon a number of factors. Finding out exactly where a person's memory problems are can be accomplished via the use of a recognition format (e.g., as in a multiple choice test) versus a recall format (simply asking individuals to recall what they can, as in an essay exam). Deficits in recall performance only allow us to infer retrieval as the locus of the problem, as recognition tests provide learners with clear retrieval cues to guide their search for an answer. If one were to have a memory deficit in both recall and recognition situations, this would suggest not only retrieval but also encoding and storage problems. Typically, recognition formats show fewer age differences than do recall tasks, highlighting retrieval as a critical skill that is essential to both short-term and long-term memory (Hoyer & Verhaghen, 2006; Poon, 1985).

In explaining everyday cognitive functioning, it is important to understand the adult learner in the context of many interacting systems, i.e., the family system and the cultural system (Sinnott, 1989). In addition to the learner's memory system, other systems influence how learning and memory function in everyday life, such as motivational, perceptual, or sensory systems.

As a general rule, whether one is a superior learner or has a good memory is relative to (1) the nature of the information to be learned, (2) the needs, abilities, and motives of the individual, and (3) the requirements of the situation in which one uses the learning and memory skills (Cockburn & Smith, 1991; Hultsch & Dixon, 1990). For this reason, those interventions that we might use to help people improve their learning and memory skills must be flexible. Different approaches will work best for some (e.g., organizing material to be learned), while for others, these same methods will fail miserably. Indeed, it is important to acknowledge that different memory improvement methods are likely to be equally effective with adults (Verhaeghen, 2000). Thus, many methods, assuming they have scientific credibility, are likely to be helpful in improving one's memory skills.

Enhancing Learning and Memory in Adulthood

Most of us get jittery when we must respond quickly in a situation, and older persons are no exception. Older persons recall the fewest correct words when they are not given sufficient time to respond referred to as **task pacing**. Increasing the time available to search and retrieve a correct response seems to be more important in lessening age differences in learning and memory (Monge & Hultsch, 1971). In addition, encouraging and training adults in the use of **verbal mediators** (a verbal association involving the words to be learned) or **visual mediators** (a mental picture involving the words to be

linked) seem to help matters greatly (Canestrari, 1968).

One approach to improving memory performance capitalizes on different memory systems. This approach recognizes that memory processes can be classified as either **explicit** (conscious and under our control) or **implicit** (unconscious and outside of our general awareness). Similarly, memory aids can be external (sticky-notes, calendars) or internal (mental images, silly songs). Cameron Camp and his colleagues have formalized these constructs in such a way that they can be used to help us both encode and retrieve information. See Box A for a detailed description of this **E-I-E-I-O method**.

Helping the adult learn to manage anxiety about failure is also very important (Hayslip, 1989). For example, you have at some time probably been so "psyched-up" for an exam that this extra energy or emotion actually interfered with your performance. In these situations, perhaps you did not listen carefully to the instructions or failed to read each question carefully. Should you manage to be more relaxed yet still alert, you can focus on the requirements of the task at hand, and your performance would likely improve. This is based on a **fixed resources** view of the adult learner's attentional capacity (Smith, 1996), where persons must divide their attention when they are anxious, or when they are confronted with a complex task or a simple task requiring a complex response. This leaves them few resources with which to deal with the task itself and respond appropriately (Smith, 1996). A common example of such a situation might involve driving at night on a strange highway. Dealing with your fears about whether you might be lost causes you to miss road signs or perhaps actually causes you to drive faster when you should be driving slower so that you can read these signs. Encouraging adults to drive more slowly or to stop, try to relax, get out the map, or get out of the car to get their bearings would be helpful. Learning to program a computer and running a new computer program are also complex tasks that demand a great deal of concentration and attention. They often are also physically

Box A

The E-I-E-I-O Method

Memory processes can be categorized as either **explicit** (deliberate, conscious) or **implicit** (unconscious). These two systems work somewhat independently of each other, giving us great flexibility in how information enters and is retrieved from our cognitive system. For example, people with amnesia, by definition, cannot consciously access certain information. They may wander into a police station or hospital and not be able to tell any one what their name is. This is explicit memory impairment. However, if such people are handed a telephone, they can often dial a friend or relative's phone number! This is implicit memory success. In addition to operating separately, the systems age differently, with implicit memory often being preserved even in the face of Alzheimer's disease (Camp et al., 1993).

Our strategies for remembering information are also quite flexible, and can be classified as either **external** (outside our heads) or **internal** (mental imagery). Using multiple kinds of memory and multiple strategies can significantly improve our ability to encode and retrieve information.

Students are often fascinated with the various mnemonic strategies, especially those that can be classified as internal-explicit. These include such techniques as **first-letter** and the **method of loci**. Most of us know at least a few first-letter mnemonics. For example, to what do ROY G BIV or HOMES refer? The answers are: Red, Orange, Yellow, Green, Blue, Indigo, Violet—the colors of the optical spectrum, arranged by wavelength; and Huron, Ontario, Michigan, Erie, Superior—the Great Lakes. Sometimes we make more elaborate aids, such as: My very educated mother just served us nine pizzas. (The nine planets in order from the sun). The method of loci is an ancient memory technique that relies on creating mental images of items-to-be-remembered and a familiar location. For example, if you wanted to remember a list of items you needed from the grocery store (e.g., bananas, coffee, and bread), you could associate each item with a specific place in your living room. You then would mentally walk through your living room and say, 'the couch is long and has curved ends, just like bananas. The coffee table reminds me that I need to buy coffee. The throw rug is tan, like the crust of the bread I want." Although first-letter and method of loci techniques differ somewhat, they both rely on your conscious effort (explicit) and take place inside your head (internal). These can be highly effective, but most of us would probably rely on the external-explicit strategy of making a list!

	Memory Strategy	
Memory system	**Internal** (inside our heads)	**External** (outside our heads)
Implicit (Occurs without our conscious awareness or effort)	Spaced retrieval, some biological responses, phobias	Classical and operant conditioning; some cue in the environment triggers recall
Explicit (Requires conscious attention and effort)	Mental imagery, song, first-letter, method of loci (each is a **mnemonic device**)	Memo books and PDAs; external reminders that we deliberately create

and mentally fatiguing. Many of you have probably had some difficulty with computers because of computer phobia. Taking breaks to relax and being able to manage your fears make working with computers easier. Moreover, if one is depressed, becoming fatigued makes the learning and or retention of new material particularly difficult (Kennelly, Hayslip & Richardson, 1985). Factors such as anxiety or depression are termed **noncognitive**, that is, they influence one's performance on a learning or memory task (cognitive) skills per se.

Check Your Learning 3-2

Define the following terms and concepts:

E-I-E-I-O method
Sensory memory
Noncognitive influences
Registration
Encoding
Storage
Retrieval
Pacing
Self-efficacy
Method of loci
Keyword method
Fixed resources
Short-term memory
Long-term memory
Working memory
Recall
Recognition

- How are memory stores different from one another?

- To what extent does memory store performance decline with age?

- To what extent are there age declines in memory processes?

- How might an adult's memory problems be identified?

- What types of mediated learning techniques have been used with adults?

- How can noncognitive factors influence learning and memory in adulthood?

Learning and Memory in Everyday Life

What we know about learning and memory in everyday adult life has grown from our interest in studying the basic processes of learning and memory in the lab. Ultimately, however, what psychologists and educators know about these basic processes is important to the layperson if it can be used to predict and improve our everyday cognitive functioning. Practical memory refers to use of our learning and memory skills to cope with the everyday demands that are made on us in real life. The use of our memory skills depends upon our beliefs about, and estimates of our memory skills, termed metamemory (Dixon, 1989). Related to **metamemory** is (1) memory self-efficacy—the confidence one has in one's memory skills, (2) memory management—the strategies and techniques one uses to make best use of one's memory, (3) memory remediation—the efforts we make to improve our memories, and (4) memory fears—concerns about memory loss that affect us personally (Reese, Cherry & Norris, 1998). Reese et al. (1998) found older persons to report that they could remember important dates (birthdays, anniversaries), but not names, used external memory aids most often, wanted to improve their memory for names and for verbal information, and linked the loss of their independence to memory failures.

These findings suggest much potential for enhancing everyday memory performance among middle-aged and older persons. This might be achieved by providing in concert (a) skills for memory improvement, (b) skills to best use one's existing memory skills, and (c) techniques to cope with fears over memory failures. We all have had difficulty in remembering where we put our keys, what we have read, what someone has said to us, or when an important appointment is. This emphasis on the context in which we use our learning and memory skills is emphasized in recent discussions of everyday memory, problem solving, and decision making (Marsiske & Margrett, 2006). It is perhaps because older adults are subject to the effects of context that age differences between younger and older persons are subject to numerous moderating influences; i.e. when the context of problems is interpersonal in nature, age differences are less apparent (Thornton & Dumke, 2005).

Education and the Adult Learner

Lifelong education is a powerful means by which to "normalize" the roles older persons play in our society, as well as to preserve the adult's sense of personal dignity, enabling persons to grow personally (Beder, 1989). This predisposition toward learning for **self expressive** (internal) reasons versus seeing learning as **instrumental**—related to achievement (external)—has been termed **learning style** (Pearce, 1991). Alternatively, **learning styles** have been defined in terms of whether one is a physiological/ perceptual learner (e.g., one who learns best visually, orally, or tactually), a cognitive learner (e.g., one who learns best via clearly stated directions or by example), or an affective/personality learner (e.g., one who learns best via collaboration and receiving positive feedback) (James & Maher, 2004). The important point to make here is that adults learn in very different ways—what works for one person may not work for another, depending upon that person's learning style.

Regardless of one's goals, we should encourage adult learners, who could be as young as age 25, in the pursuit of educational goals that are meaningful to them personally. By doing so, we strengthen the perception that one's mind can still work quite well!

Predictions about adult learners suggest that they will be more diverse and more highly educated. Not only will education help individuals maintain their survival skills, but it will also help persons leaving the work force who wish to be retrained for new careers (Sterns & Gray, 1998). Wanting to learn new skills may be influenced by changes in one's career plans or may simply reflect a desire to acquire new knowledge for its own sake. For many adults, one's skills, interests, and abilities must lead to the attainment of a well-defined goal (a college diploma, a new or better job, preparation for a future life role). In contrast, painting, creative writing, or gardening may lead to a desire to learn new skills. For many middle aged and older adults, a change in their values about what is personally important motivates them to seek out new opportunities for learning. Thus, their values influence, and are influenced by, their learning style.

Findsen (2005) argues that it is necessary to consider the social cultural context in which adults and older persons learn in order to fully understand the education of adults and lifelong learning. In this respect, he draws on what we know about learning in general as well as about older persons' personal and social lives, separating informal learning (in everyday life), nonformal learning (educational activities carried out outside the formal educational system), and formal learning (learning that is institutionalized: traditional age-graded and hierarchical in nature). Learning, adult education, and **lifelong learning** ultimately, if they are meaningful, should contribute toward enhancing the quality of adults' lives, and be focused on possibilities—what could or ought to be, rather than what is (Findsen, 2005, p. 21). Education and learning, in their many forms, should be personally meaningful and empower older learners so that they can participate equally in society, with equal access to societal resources, programs, and services. In defining adult education and lifelong learning, Findsen (2005) stresses that learning evolves from the issues that confront adults and older persons in their everyday lives: effecting change in the culture's response to them, making possible continuing independence and decision making, enabling adults and older persons to better cope with technological change, being treated by others as individuals rather than as a member of a group, and enabling persons to better deal with death, grief, and loss.

Intelligence—The Psychometric Approach

Our ideas about intelligence in adulthood have been heavily influenced by research derived from the **psychometric tradition**, focusing on the assessment of an individual's testable intelligence via the use of distinct scales. This approach assumes that scores obtained from these scales reflect real qualities (abilities) that exist within the person. The answer to what intelligence is influences one's ideas about the development of intelligence or its assessment. Current ideas about intelligence have evolved from being very philosophical in nature to being more empirical and objective, and currently reflect intelligence as an **intelligence quotient (IQ)** based on **deviations** from the mean, where each person's IQ is expressed in terms of the extent to which it differed or deviated from an average of 100 for persons of a given age range. It is important to realize that an IQ of 100 which indicates "average" intelligence is arbitrary; the figure could just as easily be 150 or 60! Moreover, the particular items that appear on any intelligence test are a function of the test constructor's own beliefs about what exactly intelligence is. Thus, an individual's test score is somewhat arbitrary. You might more easily understand this point if you think about your grade point average. For any number of reasons, that number will also be somewhat arbitrary—relative to the particular courses you have taken, your energy level, state of health, whether you were motivated to do well during a particular semester, your family or work responsibilities, and whether or not your course load was a heavy one. Someone with an undergraduate GPA of 3.8 who has few responsibilities, whose academic load is light and composed of beginning-level courses, might not be seen as doing as well as someone whose GPA was 3.0 but who worked fulltime, was raising a family, and whose course load was a comparably heavy one, composed of more difficult upper-level courses. In this case, who is the better student?

The most commonly used test of "intelligence" among psychologists and educators today is the Wechsler Adult Intelligence Scale (WAIS). The WAIS tests yield an IQ score that is age-normed. An IQ obtained by a highly intelligent 6 year-old differs dramatically in scope from a highly intelligent person of age 30. In addition, the WAIS tests, which must be individually administered, include verbal tasks that assess how much information a person knows (see crystallized intelligence, below) and performance tasks which assess how one applies existing intellectual skills (see fluid intelligence, below). The performance IQ tasks have time limits. These two aspects of intelligence, the content versus the application of our intellect, are influenced by different factors and may relate differently to later success in school settings, work settings, and life in general. For example, scoring high in verbal scales of the WAIS such as vocabulary, comprehension (of facts), or information (breadth of information) may reflect one's formal educational background or simply be a function of an avid interest in reading and acquiring diverse facts. Being intelligent in this sense may predict success in fields such as library science or English but do little in explaining why an individual would have difficulty in following directions or reassembling a lawn mower engine!

In terms of age differences, early cross-sectional studies (Doppelt & Wallace, 1955) found that overall WAIS performance peaked between ages 20 to 34, and then declined slowly with age until about age 60, with more severe declines afterward. However, longitudinal studies typically display an increase in overall WAIS performance with age (Schaie & Labouvie-Vief, 1974). A number of studies using the WAIS have found a **classic aging pattern** in intelligence (Botwinick, 1984), where a decline in performance scores, relative to stability in verbal scores, is seen.

Check Your Learning 3-3

Define the following terms and concepts:

Practical memory
Metamemory

Memory management
Classic aging pattern
Lifelong education
Learning style
Deviation IQ

• Why is learning style important to understanding the adult learner?

• Why is practical memory important in adulthood?

• Why is an IQ of 100 arbitrary?

___

Crystallized (Gc) and Fluid (Gf) Abilities

The distinction between **crystallized (Gc)** and **fluid (Gf) abilities** is especially suited to adult development in that both intelligences are defined in such a way that predictions about developmental change are possible (Horn & Hofer, 1992). What is perhaps most distinctive about fluid ability is that it can be measured by tasks in which relatively little advantage comes from intensive or extended education and acculturation (Horn, 1978), while crystallized ability reflects more organized, systematic, acculturated learning. Gc is determined by purposeful, "acculturational" learning provided by societal institutions, such as the home environment or the school (and by implication, the work environment). It is conceptually similar to the WAIS Verbal IQ. In contrast, Gf is fluid, or fluctuates with the demands made on us in novel situations, and is determined by idiosyncratic, largely self-determined causal learning influences. Gf is akin to the Performance IQ of the WAIS tests. Gc crystallizes or takes on a definite form or character with experience—our early learned skills are the basis for those acquired later on in life. In some cases, where the problem or situation demands that we manufacture a novel response to it, Gf will come into play, whereas when previously learned skills are required, Gc will be called upon. Gf is thought to increase and then decline over the life span, whereas Gc should generally increase or remain stable over the adult years (Horn & Hofer, 1992). The distinction between fluid (Gf) and crystallized (Gc) intelligence suggests that

in adulthood, a complex picture of intelligence is necessary. As each ability exhibits a different path of development, a global measure of intelligence (IQ) fails to separate crystallized and fluid intelligences.

Ackerman (2000) has investigated domain-specific knowledge, an attribute of Gc in young and middle-aged persons. With increased age, scores on 10 of 18 knowledge domains, e.g., chemistry, music, art, law, physics, electronics, increased. Generally speaking then, middle-aged persons' scores were higher than those of younger persons, and such scores were positively related to Gc. Considerable variation can be observed both within and across individuals in Gf and Gc functioning, due to effort, fatigue, anxiety (Hayslip, 1989), personality-related interests (Ackerman, 1996), or attentional lapses (Horn, 1978).

Another important finding from this area of research involves the nature of the relationship between Gc and Gf. In children and younger adults, there is often some distinction between these two types of intelligence. In fact, many types of learning disabilities in children are diagnosed, in part, based on a child having a significantly higher Gf than Gc (Wechsler, 1982). However, as we age, these two types of intelligence may become more integrated, and thus, less distinct (Hayslip & Sterns, 1979; Sinnott, 1998). Thus, the nature of intelligence may change as we age.

A practical implication of the fact that multiple intelligences exist is that one need not see oneself as more or less intelligent, relative to others, in an overall sense. Rather, it is more accurate to say that some individuals are brighter than others with regard to certain classes of abilities but not others. For example, the highly educated older individual may have excellent verbal skills or command a wealth of information, but do poorly in visualizing relationships between objects in space, a critical skill in assembling or disassembling an engine. Moreover, this person, despite being highly educated, may still have difficulty in understanding and recalling directions.

The very complexity of intelligence indicates that we all can develop our skills in some areas to perhaps compensate for deficiencies in other areas (Baltes, 1997). One can observe this frequently among many older adults who maintain and even make an effort to improve their vocabulary skills, while shying away from tasks or situations in which they cannot use their past experience to their advantage. These situations are often seen as too difficult, personally irrelevant, or simply requiring too much effort (Hayslip, 1989). Thus, these adults develop those skills that are already intact, while neglecting those skills that they do not see as critical or where everyday life experience does not demand their use (Hayslip, 1988).

Thurstone's Primary Mental Abilities Theory

In contrast to IQ as a "general ability" underlying intelligence, Thurstone's theory of primary mental abilities (PMA) specifies several factors: **spatial reasoning** (visualizing figures in space), **perceptual speed, numerical ability, verbal relations, word fluency, memory, and induction.** In contrast to the WAIS tests, tests of PMAs can be obtained in group settings. The spatial reasoning tests include measures of figural relations, in which people have to recognize rotated letters and shapes. Perceptual speed is measured by asking people to perform proofreading tasks. Numerical ability is assessed using mathematical computation problems. Verbal relations include measures of analogies and vocabulary. Word fluency tests ask people to generate members of different categories (e.g., list names of animals that begin with the letter "M"). Memory tasks include paired associates in which people study pairs of words (table—river) and are later given one of the words as a cue to recall its partner. Induction tasks tap into logic and the ability to discern patterns (e.g., what comes next in this series of letters: A B A B __? Now try this one: 1, 2, 4, 7, 11, 16, ___? Keep reading for the answers!)

Primary mental abilities have served as the framework within which Schaie has conducted perhaps the most extensive studies of adult intellectual development to date (see Schaie, 1979, 2005), beginning with a series of cross-sectional and longitudinal studies that began in 1956 that have become known as the Seattle Longitudinal Studies of Ag-

ing. Initially, a cross-sectional comparison of over 500 adults ranging in age from 20 to 70 years of age (spanning seven different cohorts) was carried out. In 1963, a new cross-sectional sample was drawn, and, in addition, a 7-year longitudinal follow-up of those tested in 1956 was begun using a battery of PMA scales. In 1970, a new random sample was taken and follow-ups of those interviewed in 1956 and 1963 were conducted. Additionally, new random samples from those originally tested in 1956 and 1963 were also drawn. In 1977, 1984, 1991, and 1998, this process was essentially repeated (Schaie, 1996, 2005).

Data from the first cross-sectional study conducted in 1956 suggested that different types of abilities demonstrated diverse age-related peaks of functioning. Schaie found PMA inductive reasoning to peak early, whereas spatial, verbal meaning, word fluency, and number all peaked later. Thus, young adults would be more likely to know that the next entry in the A B A B series would be B and in the 1, 2, 4, 7, 11, 16, __ series would be 22 because each number increases by a factor of 1 + previous increase.

In addition, the 1963 data found evidence for a time of measurement effect, where those tested in 1963 were superior to those tested in 1956 who were at comparable ages. Schaie's data also suggested that cohort differences were more important in explaining the cross-sectional or longitudinal age effects found for many abilities than was chronological age (Schaie & Willis, 1996). His findings also indicated that in early adulthood and in very late adulthood, age effects on abilities within cohorts might also be substantial. Further, analyses suggested positive cohort effects, i.e., more favorable performance for successively younger cohorts, for verbal meaning, space, and reasoning. For number, cohort effects were minimal, while for word fluency, cohort effects were slightly negative, where younger cohorts scored more poorly. Thus, the extent to which age decrements in intelligence vary depends upon (1) **the type of ability examined** and (2) **cohort membership** (see Schaie, 1996, 2005). Cross-sectional and longitudinal replications of 7-year (1956 vs. 1963; 1963 vs. 1970) follow-up analyses yielded similar findings. The third cross-sectional (1970) study yielded substantial time of measurement effects, with advantages to those tested in 1970 for all PMA factors except word fluency. Similarly strong time of measurement effects are observed at other occasions of testing as well (Schaie, 2005).

The notion that more recent cohorts are "smarter" than their parents or grandparents at comparable ages is known as the **Flynn Effect** (Flynn, 1999). In the past 50 years or so, the average IQ score has increased world-wide by 5 to 25 points. Most of this increase has been in Gf. Several explanations for this increase in the raw IQ score have been offered, including: a fast-paced life-style that encourages people to work well under time constraints (remember, the Performance IQ tasks have time limits), better nutrition, better early childhood medicine, and better education among parents who then provide stimulating home environments (Czaja, 2001; Neisser et al., 1996).

Perhaps most important thing to learn from Schaie's study of adult intelligence is that cognitive decline with age is not entirely biologically based, nor is it irreversible. In most cases, the age decrement in intelligence may be reduced or intensified depending upon the interaction of the sociocultural environment (whether it is stimulating or not) and cohort (with different cohorts aging intellectually in unique ways.) Thus, there is no universal true decline. Schaie's data also indicate that declines in ability are largely restricted to those age 70 and over, especially the very old (Baltes, 1997).

Many older people, depending on their health, educational background, and social engagement sustain and even improve their skills, while others decline much earlier in life. Recent analyses from the Seattle Longitudinal data suggest an important role for these noncognitive factors (Schaie, 2005). One of the tasks in the test battery asks people to read a written passage and change all the lower-case letters to capitals and vice versa. People who make a lot of mistakes are viewed as more rigid in their cognitive style. Interestingly, people who were more rigid showed greater cognitive declines. It appears that the ability to roll with the punches is good for our intellectual functioning!

The Information Processing Approach to Intelligence

The **information processing** perspective (Sternberg, 1985) stresses the person as an active processor of information contained in a problem or in the real world. Individuals develop logical operations and strategies by which to understand and analyze information presented to them. Those who support this approach focus upon component processes that are a function of the interaction between task influences and person influences (Salthouse, 1992). Examples of component processes would be encoding, storage, retrieval, rule formation, and pattern analysis. In addition to specific component processes, information processing researchers focus on an executive processor, which selects and supervise the use of these processes, and processing resources, referring to the energy or space available within the person to carry out cognitive operations or processes (Salthouse, 1992). Impairments with age in terms of speed or accuracy of performance may exist in each of the above elements required to process information. Generally speaking, age declines in intelligence are seen in terms of the speed, capacity, or efficiency of central processing resources (e.g., working memory, attention, processing speed) (Salthouse, 1998). Ideally by using an information processing approach to intelligence, we may discover and foster the component skills that individuals of all ages may use on an everyday basis.

Check Your Learning 3-4

Define the following terms and concepts:

Psychometric intelligence
Primary mental abilities
Crystallized ability
Fluid ability
Multiple intelligences

Adults Speak

Views about Intellectual Growth and Change

Some of us have fairly negative expectations about our intelligence and learning ability as we grow older, and hold similar views about older persons themselves. Yet, not all adults share this rather pessimistic view. Still others are somewhat ambivalent. There is much truth in the notions that "what you see is what you get" and "use it or lose it" when it comes to the aging of our cognitive skills.

A 29-year-old man said, "I believe older people can be taught new ideas. I do not believe they are as capable of learning as someone who is younger. I feel this is so because they do not like to learn new things. They would rather stick with what has worked in the past. However, I do respect older people for their wisdom about life. Older people obtain lots of information from experience . . . I also believe intelligence increases with age if it is worked at."

A 44-year-old woman had this to say: "An old person is without hope. An old person has a "wearingout" attitude written on his face because society looks and judges old people this way. Most people think of grey hair, wrinkles, stooped posture, lack of metabolic functioning, and hopelessness when old age is mentioned. Wrong! If the older person is willing to learn, behavior modification is possible. I am certain that a person's willingness to survive motivates activity. Intelligence is a capability. If you don't use, you lose. It is that simple. Barring disease, age has no impact on intelligence. Now wisdom, that's a whole different ballgame!"

A 70-year-old woman said that "One should keep changing and not get in a rut. I believe the learning process continues across the lifespan, providing one wants to learn. At the moment, I am in a rut! . . . Intelligence does not increase. Its manifestations change, but it does not decrease either . . . A person becomes old around the age of 60. Other characteristics would be slowing down and grey hair." (There was a tone of resentment in her response).

Cohort effects
Time of measurement effects
Information processing
Emotional intelligence
Flynn effect

- What does Schaie's PMA research tell us about intelligence and aging?

- Why do crystallized and fluid abilities change in adulthood?

- What is the practical implication of multiple intelligences in adulthood?

- What are the outstanding characteristics of an information processing approach to intelligence?

Piagetian Abilities and Aging

Under the assumption that older people regress back to an earlier level of development, many researchers have investigated performance on Piagetian tasks of intelligence among aged people (Blackburn & Papalia, 1992), where older persons are thought to regress from formal operations back to concrete operational or, in some cases, to a preoperational level of thinking (Piaget & Inhelder, 1969). These studies collectively reveal age differences in Piagetian task performance—older individuals are less able to successfully solve tasks which require the transformation of number of objects, or deal with changes in the weight or volume of different objects (Blackburn & Papalia, 1992). However, deficits in Piagetian task performance are rarely found in healthy, educated elderly persons, and errors on these tasks are even common among younger persons (Kausler, 1991). While older people might solve such tasks more slowly or simply make more errors, they are, however, capable of solving them.

Postformal Operations

Rybash, Hoyer, and Roodin (1986) have suggested that Piaget's formal operational stage of cognitive development is of limited use to the adult developmental theorist and research. **Formal operational thinking** is characterized by a rational, logical, abstract, deductive approach to problem solving and understanding the world; formal operational thinkers ignore the context in which the problem to be solved is embedded. In the real world, everyday problems may be ambiguous and ill-defined. Rybash et al. (1986) note that "real-life problems, in contrast to formal operations problems, are 'open' to the extent that there are no clear boundaries of a problem and the context within which it occurs" (p. 32). For example, what is the problem confronting a woman who is deciding whether or not to have a child? **Postformal operational** thinkers would see this decision as influenced by a number of factors, for example, her self-concept, demands on her time via her career, her socioeconomic status, whether she has the support of her husband and her relationship with him, whether she has other children, as well as her health. How she defines this problem, as well as its solution, depends on the particular factors that influence and are influenced by her decision to have or not to have a child. Postformal reasoning is therefore relative; that is, knowledge is temporary rather than absolute (as in formal operations). We often solve a problem only to realize that there are new things to learn and new questions to ask. We enter into the adult work world with a specified set of skills that we think will enable us to be successful only to find that our success brings new challenges and problems. Most importantly, postformal thinking is adaptive; it helps us identify and solve real-life problems in adulthood (Sinnott, 1996).

Many adult developmental researchers have explored age differences in the extent to which older versus younger adults engage in formal or postformal thinking (Sinnott, 1996). Labouvie-Vief (1985), for example, presented to children and adults of varying ages a story of a woman whose husband had come home drunk. Each was asked what the woman might do if he indeed did come home drunk again. With increased age, respondents were more likely to give answers that recognize different situations (contexts). Thus, they were able to entertain other interpretations of the problem. Postformal thought therefore represents a different style of thinking, rather than reflecting a new stage of cognitive growth. Adults may also think in different ways about how to solve problems because these problems are emotionally salient (Blanchard-Fields, 1986; Sinnott, 1996).

Factors Affecting Intelligence in Adulthood

We have suggested that cohort effects may modify the aging of intelligence. Yet, there are a number of other influences on whether we see declines in intelligence with age. For example, sensory deficits in hearing and vision may put many adults at a disadvantage (Sands & Meredith, 1989). Indeed, Baltes and Lindenberger (1997) assert that one's sensory abilities are the bedrock upon which intelligence rests. Persons who are in poor physical and mental health tend to perform more poorly on a measure of fluid ability (Perlmutter & Nyquish, 1990). Zelinski et al. (1998) found high blood pressure, strokes, and diabetes to all adversely influence intelligence later in life. Another factor found to influence intelligence in adulthood is education, where those who are more highly educated tend to age less, intellectually speaking, though for those who are initially more able, declines may be more rapid because they have more to lose (Alder et al., 1990). Moreover, an emphasis on speed unfairly penalizes those adults who respond slowly in timed tests (Kausler, 1991), and slower performance could result from lessened ability to process information

Figure 3-5. Exercising mental skills is critical to their maintenance over the lifespan.

quickly (Kausler, 1991; Schaie & Willis, 1996) (see Figure 3-5).

There may also be a relationship between personality factors and intellectual performance. Perhaps persons who have adaptive personalities age better intellectually, or intelligence may permit more flexibility in adulthood. In one study, older persons who were more anxious about their intellectual skills had higher Gc scores, utilizing defense mechanisms that protect them from feelings of self-worthlessness and failure and/or a loss of control over their real life environments (Hayslip, 1988). One personality characteristic that may be especially relevant to intelligence in adulthood is **self-efficacy**. Self-efficacy refers to a belief in one's ability to perform a task successfully (Bandura, 1989). Individuals

with positive self-efficacy expectations perceive difficult tasks as challenges. They see failure as related to their effort and therefore under their control. Thus, they have an emotional resilience to difficulties (Bandura, 1989). Lachman and Leff (1989) reported that over a 5-year period, control beliefs about one's skills did not predict changes in intellectual functioning. However, changes in intellectual control beliefs were predicted by fluid intelligence, and the authors suggest that the impact of negative stereotypes about older adults' cognitive abilities may cause such changes. However, decrements in perceived changes in one's ability over time may also contribute to declines in intelligence (Schaie, Willis, & O'Hanlon, 1994).

Schaie and Willis (1996) have emphasized the impact that the complexity of our everyday environment may have on cognitive performance. Individuals in optimally complex environments who are reinforced for "using their heads" may develop higher cognitive skills that generalize to other situations and may be better in problem solving. Schooler (1987) suggests that one complex environment during adulthood that may be beneficial is a cognitively challenging work situation.

It thus appears that in addition to age and cohort, a number of factors influence intelligence in adulthood. As some people are affected by some factors and not others, intellectually, aging is better seen as an individual phenomenon. That is, individuals should be understood in terms of their own personalities, life histories, health, and education, as well as the nature of the everyday environments in which they live.

Intelligence and Everyday Life

In 1957, Demming and Pressey developed tests "with content and tasks more natural or 'indigenous' to adult life" (p. 144) because of the inadequacy of then current tests to measure adult abilities. They chose items from several sources: newspapers and popular reading material, records of daily activities, and questions directed to individuals. They found that people scored progressively lower on traditional psychometric tests of intelligence across the lifespan but the reverse pattern was evidenced on their "indigenous" tests.

These kinds of studies prompted some researchers to call for more research on **everyday intelligence**, or "cognition in the wild" (Landauer, 1989, p. 116). However, measuring everyday intelligence has proven to be anything but easy, and there are very diverse opinions about this new area of research (Hayslip, 1989; Willis, 1996). More recently, the everyday adaptive aspects of everyday intelligence have been emphasized, such as the skills one uses in shopping, map reading, cooking, reading schedules and ads, and understanding directions (Allaire & Marsiske, 1999; Diehl, 1998; Marsiske & Willis, 1995). Although some studies have failed to find strong associations among measures of cognitive ability and performance on everyday tasks (e.g., Cornelius & Caspi, 1987), most report at least moderate associations, with correlations ranging near .50 (Allaire & Marsiske, 1999; Diehl et al., 1995). Diehl et al. (1995) found that Gc and Gf directly influence how well a person solves problems related to daily living tasks. However, everyday intelligence includes far more activities than completing activities of daily living, and the skills necessary for shopping, cooking, and reading schedules may differ in important ways from other everyday activities (Ackerman, 2000).

Other research on everyday cognition has examined the kinds of strategies that people use to solve real-life problems. These strategies may represent a combination of Gc and Gf. For example, Patrick and Strough (2004) examined older adults' advice offered in response to hypothetical vignettes that featured an older adult who was considering moving to a new home. They found that people who were thinking about moving to a new home themselves and those who knew of other adults who were contemplating this kind of transition offered more strategies to solving the problem. Adults who were thinking about making a relocation in their own lives were more likely to advise the hypothetical person to seek assistance from others and to engage in more

cognitive kinds of problem-solving strategies. So, from whom do older adults seek advice in their own lives? These same researchers find that family members, especially spouses, are the preferred source of information (Strough, Patrick, Swenson, Cheng, & Barnes, 2003). As we will discuss in the next chapter, family members are especially important for older adults' cognitive performance.

An additional area in which everyday cognition researchers are examining older adults' skills is that of decision making. Two areas have been investigated: medical decisions and consumer decisions. In both areas, older adults tend to seek out less information than younger adults (Hershey, Walsh, Read, & Chulef, 1990; Johnson, 1990; Meyer, Russo, & Talbot, 1995). However, questions remain regarding whether older adults are making good decisions. In recent work, Patrick and Murphy (2004) compared the quality of decisions made by younger, middle-aged, and older adults who completed everyday consumer tasks. They found that although no age differences emerged in the overall quality of the decision people made, significant age differences did emerge in the strategies that decision makers used. Interestingly, when these researchers examined the combined effects of age, strategy, and decision quality, they found that low-quality decision makers, especially older adults, tended to focus too quickly on a few of the consumer choices, ignoring other potentially good products. Combined with other research in this area, older adults, who may have more health factors, less education, and more anxiety about their intellect (Meyer et al., 1995), and who prefer to consult with family members (Strough et al., 2002), may choose to make "fast" decisions rather than careful, high-quality decisions. This has implications for the ways that older adults select, optimize, and compensate regarding their skills.

Optimizing Intelligence in Adulthood

On the assumption that declines with age in intelligence are not irreversible, many investigators have developed training programs to help older adults enhance their intellectual skills. Baltes and Willis (1982) concluded that for older persons skills training can in fact enhance fluid intellectual skills. For those who had simply been allowed to practice items measuring Gf, no specific pattern of improvement was found. Indeed, Schaie and Willis (1986) have demonstrated that training can apparently reverse 14-year declines in PMA performance (see also Schaie, 2005). Over a 7-year interval, intellectual performance still exceeded their original levels 7 years earlier. Hayslip (1989) found that providing older persons with anxiety-reduction techniques, such as substituting success self-statements for failure self-statements (Meichenbaum, 1989) and relaxation were almost as effective as direct specific rule-based training, yielding superior performance relative to no training. Moreover, practice seemed to help all persons, regardless of whether they were trained or not. These findings vividly demonstrate that aging need not be characterized by loss and decline, and that if given the opportunity, older adults can indeed continue to grow intellectually. To optimize intellectual performance, older adults can use a number of strategies to help them compensate for declines in their intellectual skills brought on by disease or obsolescence of skills that once were more functional. Thus, the **plasticity** and everyday adaptive value of one's skills in adulthood should be emphasized (Hoyer & Rybash, 1994).

Newer Theories about Intelligence and Aging

Baltes (1987, 1997) has proposed a theory of life-span intellectual development that suggests a **dual process** concept of intellectual development, emphasizing a distinction between the **mechanics** of intelligence, which are the basic cognitive skills such as speeded performance, or Gf, and the **pragmatics** of intelligence, which reflect more organized systems of knowledge, e.g., social intelligence, wisdom, Gc. The mechanics of intelligence are more structural and involve basic skills such as logic, information processing, and problem solving. The

pragmatic aspect of intelligence is more applied or adaptive and thus reflects intelligent behavior in a specific context or situation. Even under the best conditions regarding mechanics, younger persons will outperform older persons, while the opposite is true for the pragmatics of intelligence. Baltes (1997) sees intelligence in adulthood as enabling individuals to **selectively optimize** (enhance) their continued growth, or to **compensate** for biological/social losses by narrowing their frame of reference. That is, they apply their pragmatic abilities only to problems that affect them personally. All of this is accomplished within the context of each individual's own life history and current life situation.

Sternberg (1988) argues that three aspects of intellectual functioning underlie our adaptive behavior, termed a **triarchic theory** of intelligence. The **metacomponents** of intelligence, which are executive processes, enable us to plan what we are going to do, monitor while we are doing it, and evaluate it after it is done. More specific to the task are **performance components**, which are the actual mental operations (e.g., encoding, making inferences, making comparisons) people use to solve specific problems. A last dimension of intelligence is the **knowledge acquisition component**, which helps us gain new knowledge. Separating new versus old, and relevant from irrelevant information in solving a problem, and being able to form new knowledge by combining specific bits of information into a new whole are aspects of knowledge acquisition. For example, surgeons or lawyers must learn to recognize what is important, and be able to put things together to form a theory about a legal case or make a diagnosis. Berg and Sternberg (1985) found younger adults to be superior in most metacomponents of intelligence as well as in the performance components. Older adults have more difficulty in defining problems to be solved, in managing their attention to solve problems, and in monitoring solutions effectively. These skills may, however, improve with practice. Likewise, making inferences and combining and comparing information are impaired in older persons. It may be that

Box B

Does an Engaged Lifestyle Help Us Age Better Mentally?

Some persons certainly do age better than do others, intellectually speaking. We all know people who despite being in their 80s and 90s, are still "sharp as a tack." Why might this be? Does it have anything to do with what we do with our daily lives? Are we stimulated mentally? Do we watch TV or solve crossword puzzles? Do we read books or read the comics? Do we challenge ourselves mentally by doing challenging, difficult, and stimulating things?

Recently, there has been much interest in the effects, if any, of leading an **engaged lifestyle** on intellectual and cognitive aging, and even the effects of such lifestyles on dementia (see Chapter 10). Do such lifestyles help? Many people believe so, while many do not. Answers to this question depend upon who one asks.

For example, in the **Nun Study**, longitudinal work by Snowden (2001) suggests that nuns whose linguistic skills (indicating that they were well read and curious) were better early in life seemed to be less likely to develop Alzheimer's disease, and if they did so, they seemed to be less severely affected. McCormick and his associates (2006) found that regular (and varied) physical exercise protected persons against Alzheimer's disease. Kleigel, Zimprich, and Rott (2004) stress the importance of early education and lifelong intellectual engagement on cognitive functioning among centenarians. Newson and Kemps (2005) based upon cross-sectional and longitudinal studies also found lifestyle activities to promote cognitive growth in later life. A review of cognitive and physical exercise by Hogan (2005) suggests that each can lead to **multisystem resilience** (cardiovascular, physical, and musculoskelatal) in older

persons that can promote better everyday functioning, while the review by Hayslip and Maiden (2005) found that the effects of an engaged lifestyle are both positive in some studies and minimal in others. Still others (Salthouse, 2006) conclude that there is no conclusive evidence for the positive impact of an engaged lifestyle on one's intellectual and thinking skills later in life; neither the rate of cognitive decline nor its prevention seems to be affected by engaging in stimulating everyday activities.

The key factor to consider in answering this question is that engaged lifestyles and rates of decline or levels of performance in later life may be **correlated**, but not necessarily **causally related**. Their relationship is explained by a **third factor**, being it physical and mental health, how often one practices the skills that are crucial to everyday functioning and decision making, or how highly educated one is. An importance piece of this puzzle may be the **personality** of the older person. If one is intellectually curious, values stimulating conversations with others, enjoys mental challenges (e.g., Sudoku, crossword puzzles, anagrams) and learning new things, he or she will create a lifestyle that is stimulating. It could also be that persons who live engaged lifestyles have more **cognitive reserve**, and so while they do lose some of their abilities as they age, they appear to function better because they have this "cushion" to fall back on. The problem of whether an engaged lifestyle is helpful should challenge us to make the most of our intellectual lives, be it in elementary school, college, in the world or work, or later in life. Indeed, there may be some truth in the "use it or lose it" philosophy of cognitive aging!

Box C

Wisdom and Aging

One important aspect of the pragmatics of intelligence is the role that wisdom plays in helping older adults to continue to flourish and grow throughout life. Paul Baltes and Jacqui Smith have explained what wisdom is and how to measure it in adults. Wisdom emphasizes expert knowledge in life pragmatics and can be defined very precisely.

Family of Five Criteria for Wisdom

1. Rich factual knowledge about life matters
2. Rich procedural knowledge about life problems
3. Life-span contextualism: Knowledge about the contexts of life and their temporal (developmental) relationships
4. Relativism: Knowledge about differences in values and priorities
5. Uncertainty: Knowledge about the relative indeterminacy and unpredictability of life and ways to manage

Using verbal protocols where persons reflect on how they would go about dealing with real-life problems pertinent to both young (life planning) and old (life review) adults, these researchers discovered that middle-aged and older adults indicated a greater awareness of uncertainty and seemed to be able to deal better with problems specific to their age. This exciting work suggests that wisdom, though it is often seen as characteristic of old age, evolves and is continually transformed throughout adulthood. Young people are therefore also capable of wisdom under certain circumstances.

Comment on the following:

Life Planning

Joyce, a widow aged 60 years, recently completed a degree in business management and opened her own business. Although she has been looking forward to this new challenge, she has just heard that her son has been left with two small children to care for. Joyce is considering several options. She could plan to give up her business and move to live with her son, or she could plan to arrange for financial assistance for her son to cover child-care costs. What should Joyce do and consider in planning for her future? What extra information would you like to have available?

Life Review

Martha, an elderly woman, decided to have a family and not to have a career. Her children left home some years ago. One day Martha meets Ann, a friend whom she has not seen for a long time. Ann had decided to have a career and no family. She has retired some years ago. This meeting causes Martha to think back over life. What might her life review look like? Which aspects of her life might she remember? How might she explain her life? How might she evaluate her life retrospectively?

the knowledge acquisition components that are based on experience do not decline with age, especially if they are critical in helping people to cope with new situations (Cunningham & Tomer, 1991).

Each of the above aspects of intelligence helps us to cope with and to use our experiences to adapt to our everyday environment. Consider the person who must learn a new job or adapt the job to fit

---

Box D

Creativity and Aging

Consider the following views about creativity:

"If you haven't cut your name on the door of fame by the time you've reached 40, you might just as well put up your jack-knife." (Oliver Wendell Holmes, poet)

"A person who has not made his contribution in science before the age of 30 will never do so." (Albert Einstein, physicist)

"Age is, of course, a fever chill that every physicist must fear. He's better off dead than living still when once he's past his thirtieth year." (Paul Dirac, physicist)

"When age is in, wit is out." (William Shakespeare, poet and playwright)

Do you think that these statements are true?

Indeed, we can cite many examples to the contrary. Benjamin Franklin, Galileo, Tennyson, Grandma Moses, Michelangelo, Leonardo da Vinci, Alexander Graham Bell, and Eubie Blake all produced significant and important creative work well into later life.

Precisely defining and measuring creativity can be very elusive, however. Creativity has been alternatively defined as (1) a process such as problem solving or reason, (2) something that one produces, e.g., a painting or a poem, (3) a characteristic of the person, such as the ability to use objects in unique ways, or (4) an act of persuasion, as when one impresses others with one's creativity. In this respect, creativity is akin to a distinct type of leadership (Simonton, 1990, 1998).

Simonton reaches several conclusions about creativity at any age, based on an exhaustive review of the literature as well as his own research:

1. **Decrements with age in creative potential will not, by the end of one's career, transform a creative person into a noncreative one.** Most creative persons die before their creative potential is exhausted.

2. **The amount of decrement varies by discipline in a consistent and predictable manner.** In some of the arts and in mathematics, the drop is severe, while in literature or history it may be minimal.

3. **When we define creativity in terms of the ratio of quality works to total works produced, the age decrement vanished.** While those younger persons who are generally more productive are also more likely to produce something creative, older persons simply produce less "rubbish."

4. **Productivity later in life depends on the individual's initial level of creative potential.** Those with less potential will begin making creative contributions later in life, while those with more potential will be more consistently creative.

5. **If extrinsic factors do interfere with the exercise of creativity, their effects can be lessened.** Physical illness, the multiple demands of work and family, or work stress can be lessened or coped with. Assistants can be hired to do more tedious tasks, or those that are more mundane and technical.

6. **We need not assume that the age decrement in creativity proves that corresponding declines occur in basic cognitive skills.** Intelligence and real-life

creativity are not identical, and even persons who are older can resume creative activity after a period of intellectual loss.

How do you define creativity? What do you predict for yourself in later life?

new skills or needs. If either of these approaches fails, a new job must be found that is different from the old job. Each aspect of intelligence is also involved when we deal with words, numbers, or figures, e.g., in knowing that a stop sign looks different than a caution sign.

Check Your Learning 3-5

Define the following terms and concepts:

Postformal operations
Self-efficacy
Everyday intelligence
Pragmatics vs. mechanics
Triarchic theory of intelligence
Creativity
Wisdom

• What are postformal operations? Why are they different from formal operations?

• What factors influence intelligence in adulthood?

• By what means can intelligence be improved in adulthood?

• What role do the pragmatics of intelligence play relative to the mechanics of intelligence?

• What are the three elements of Sternberg's triarchic theory? Are there age differences in each?

• How does a complex environment promote intelligence in adulthood?

Summary

In this chapter we discussed learning, memory, and intelligence, all of which must be inferred from our behavior and performance. **Learning** in its most basic sense involves the making of stimulus-response (S-R) associations. **Memory** loss (or forgetting) refers to the breakdown of these associations. Research in learning and memory in adulthood separates a **structural approach** (sensory, short-term, long-term) and a **process approach** (registration, encoding, storage, and retrieval) to memory. Deficits with aging occur at the encoding and retrieval stage of memory processing and in the secondary memory stores. Memory and learning deficits, where they exist, can be lessened in learners of all ages via a number of different types of interventions such as the method of loci. Learning and memory performance can also be improved by a number of noncognitive interventions such as reducing anxiety about failure and treating depression. Recently, attention has been directed to the study of learning and memory in ecologically valid contexts. The context in which learning occurs has been recognized as an important factor in the design and implementation of adult education and lifelong learning programs. These programs serve a number of diverse needs of the adult learner.

The **psychometric approach** to intelligence treats intelligence as a structural concept; it is composed of various well-defined abilities that relate to one another in various ways. A number of theories about how intelligence is structured have been proposed. The two-factor theory of **crystallized** and **fluid intelligences** and the Thurstone **primary mental abilities** (PMA) approach have most influenced research on intelligence in adulthood. The information processing approach to intelligence specifies the underlying processes individuals use when they behave intelligently. Extensions of Piagetian formal operations to postformal operations have also opened up.

Intelligence does and does not decline with increased age, depending upon how one chooses to define and measure it. Research by Schaie and by Horn has confirmed the complex nature of intelligence in adulthood. Its growth and development depend upon both the influence of the immediate environment (time of measurement) and the cultural differences between cohorts of individuals born at different points in historical time.

Recent attempts to explain intellectual development emphasize the **pragmatics** versus the **mechanics** of intelligence and Sternberg's **triarchic theory**, which sees intelligence as both an information processing ability and an adaptive characteristic. A great deal of work has demonstrated that adults can improve their intellectual performance by a number of means, such as practice, cognitive skill training, or anxiety reduction training. Recently, the application of intelligence to everyday life has received some attention. **Everyday intelligence** may reflect the adaptive role that our intellectual abilities play in helping us cope and maintain our independence as we grow older.

Chapter 4
Socialization and Interpersonal Relationships: The Nuclear Family

Relationships with others play a vital role in affecting the quality of our lives in adulthood and are critical to our satisfaction with life, self-concept, and physical health. Some of these relationships are positive, while others are negative, as in the case of **Intimate Partner Violence** (IPV, see Box A). Weiss (1974) suggested that interpersonal relationships can serve any one of six functions: (1) **Attachment**, feelings of intimacy, peace, and security as found in relationships with spouses and very close friends; (2) **Social integration**, a sense of belonging to a group with whom one shares common interests and social activities; (3) **Reliable alliance**, knowing that one can count on receiving assistance in times of need, a function often provided by kin; (4) **Guidance**, having relationships with persons who can provide knowledge, advice, and expertise; (5) **Reassurance of worth**, a sense of competence and esteem obtained typically from work colleagues; and (6) **Opportunity for nurturance**, being responsible for the care of others, such as one's children. People with whom we share a relationship play an important role in socialization. Thus, interpersonal relationships and socialization are intertwined.

Families are the primary context in which the individual members' developmental tasks and interpersonal processes are experienced and negotiated. Within families, all generations celebrate rites of passage, maintain a sense of lineage, and educate other generations about the life events that are to come (Knight & Qualls, 1995). In order to adequately understand socialization from a life-span perspective, we will discuss a number of diverse but related topics, such as roles, friends, families, parenting, and grandparenting, in this chapter and in Chapter 5. Each of these plays an important part in the socialization process, and therefore affects our relationships with others.

The family is a dynamic, reciprocal, changing system, composed of individuals who are themselves changing and of family members who both influence and are influenced by the others. Since the family changes over time, in order to retain its identity, supportive, and socializing functions, it must be flexible enough to absorb the entry, exit, and reentry of its members into the family system without interfering with individual development (Goldenberg & Goldenberg, 1991).

The view of the family as a **dynamic system** fits well with the idea that the intact nuclear family has given way to a diversity of family forms. We must also recognize that there are individual differences in the timing of life events such as marriage, parenthood, or retirement, and periods of transition between stages within and between families (Wethington et al., 2004). Consequently, all families are unique. Your definition of "family" depends on a variety of factors including your personal views, religious orientation, sexual preference, and moral value system. Thus, it is very difficult to present an all-encompassing definition of family. What is clear is that the once "traditional" family consisting of a lifelong "bread winner," a lifelong "homemaker," and two children, has undergone significant transition (Kreider & Elliott, 2009). In 1970, 40% of American households included two married parents and

Box A

Intimate Partner Violence and Child Maltreatment

Intimate partner violence (IPV), intentional lethal and non-lethal acts of violence committed by current or former spouses, romantic partners, and dating partners, declined from 1993 to 2005 (Catalano, 2007), but continues to account for a high percentage of the violent crimes committed in the United States. IPV accounts for 11% of all homicides; of IPV homicides, 78% of the victims are women, with 22% of the victims being men (Catalano). Among all homicides in which a woman is killed, one-third result from IPV. IPV accounts for about 3% of all homicides in which a man is killed (Rennison & Welchans, 2002). In terms of non-lethal IPV, rates have declined (Catalano), but continue to represent a significant problem for many couples. As shown below, the rates of non-lethal IPV vary as a function of race, gender, and age (Catalano), as well as the measures used (Hamby, 2009).

However, there is some debate in the field of IPV regarding how best to quantify IPV, particularly when making gender comparisons of the rates of perpetration. When community-based family surveys are used, females perpetrate between 20 and 35% of IPV (Hambry). When examining self-reported injury data, 32% of men and 50% of women who report IPV also report an injury (Rennison & Welchans). Of these men and women, 4% and 5% respectively, report medically serious injuries requiring hospital or emergency care (Rennison & Welchans).

Other forms of interpersonal violence occur within the family, as well. In 2008, about 1% of children were the victims of **child maltreatment**. Although boys and girls are equally likely to experience maltreatment, rates vary by age. Of children experiencing maltreatment, 33% were younger than age 4 years, 24% were ages 4 to 7 years, and 19% were ages 8 to 11 years. The majority of maltreatment cases involve neglect (71%), with 16% involving physical abuse and 9% involving sexual abuse. Mothers alone are more likely to be the perpetrator (40%) than either fathers alone (18%) or both parents together (18%) (U.S. Dept. of HHS, 2010).

Rates per 1000 when non-lethal IPV is defined as criminal acts*

	12-15 yr	16-19 yr	20-24 yr	25-34 yr	35-49 yr	50-64 yr	Age 65+
Men	0.6	1.7	2.4	2.6	1.5	0.4	—
Women	2.5	17.4	21.3	15.5	8.1	1.5	0.2

***Source:** Catalano (2007).

their children, compared to 23% in 2007 (Krieder & Elliott, 2009).

Socialization

Through the process of socialization we acquire the skills, values, and behaviors to function in the roles we currently occupy or will occupy in the future. Socialization is a **dynamic**, **lifelong**, and **bidirectional** process between children, parents, and others such as grandparents. Each member of this circle represents a host of personal and historical-cultural influences that have a dynamic effect on other individuals and the family as a whole. For example, parents and grandparents attempt to instill specific beliefs, attitudes, and behaviors in the younger members of the family, while simultaneously the younger members of the family modify these in light of current social-cultural factors, which in turn may modify the attitudes and beliefs of the parents and the grandparents.

Critical to our discussion of socialization is the concept of **roles**. Roles are culturally determined guidelines and expectancies in terms of behaviors, traits, and characteristics expected of individuals who occupy a specific social position in society (Hagestad & Neugarten, 1985). According to **social learning theory**, roles are the direct result of learning and experience. To illustrate, as others reinforce or reward us for behaving in certain ways, or modeling behaviors they feel are appropriate for us based on factors such as our age, gender, ethnicity, and occupation (Steinmetz, Clavan, & Stein, 1990), these expectations are eventually **internalized**. Subsequently, individuals are assumed by others to know what is expected of them in their roles, and in turn, these roles are influenced by society's norms, values, and attitudes.

During the course of adulthood each of us will develop and modify a variety of complex roles that we will occupy for varying lengths of time. Some of these critical roles we will play during adulthood include parent, spouse, friend, community citizen, and grandparent. Each of these roles gives meaning, organization, and structure to our lives, and the loss or change in our roles can lead to anxiety, tension, and emotional distress. In some cases, role expectations may conflict, as when one must take time away from the parenting role to fulfill the requirements of the occupational role. This can lead to **role strain**, which is a feeling of anxiety and tension as a result of having less than enough time to fulfill each of one's roles, or **role overload**, in which the demands of one or more of one's roles exceeds the person's capacity to meet the demands of these roles, e.g., having little time to care for a chronically ill child and working in a time-consuming occupation. Stressful events in one part of a person's daily life associated with one role can often "spill over" into other parts of life, e.g., having a bad day at work and then acting negatively toward children at home (Fincham & Beach, 2010).

Roles in Adulthood

As adults, we are expected to acquire and perform behaviors associated with many roles simultaneously. Often, age serves as a normative criterion with regard to both role entry and exit, and influences the types of socialization agents (parents, coworkers) with whom we have contact.

Rosow (1985) classifies roles in terms of their characteristics. These are: (1) **Institutional role** types, which assume a given status, with accompanying well-defined roles, such as occupation, gender, or age; (2) **Tenuous role** types apply to people in definite social positions (status) who do not have well-defined functions or roles, such as aged people or the unemployed; and, (3) **Informal role** types, which have no institutional status but have definite roles attached to them, for example, the family scapegoat or blackmailers.

Each type of role assumes a varying degree of importance across the life span, and each can assume positive or negative status. For instance, as we get older, institutional role types decrease in relative importance, while tenuous role types increase in relative importance. With increased age, important, well-defined roles are lost and replaced with less well-defined ones, which has important implications for the socialization of, and attitudes toward, older people (see Chapter 1). Specifically, this contributes to the perception of late adulthood as a roleless period of life (Rosow, 1985), since very few roles, with the exception of senior citizen, retiree, and grandparent, are available to older adults in our society. Since roles we occupy contribute substantially to our identity and self-esteem, the unavailability of viable roles can have negative effects on us personally as well as on our relationships.

Role Transition and Role Change

As we progress through the life span, we are constantly shifting roles (George, 1990). **Role shifts** occur in two ways: through **role transition**, such as from mother to grandmother, or through **role change**, such as from student to professor. While role transition is simply the process of evolving from one form of a specific role to another form of that same role, role change involves the complete shift from one type of role to a different one. For this reason, the shift from father to grandfather is substantially less difficult than from husband to widower. In order to maintain a positive self-concept throughout the life span, new social roles must be adopted to replace those that are lost (George, 1990). This is accomplished by becoming involved in new activities that can provide new roles. For instance, one might shift from the role of bank president to president of the senior adult volunteers' organization.

The most current research on roles focuses on a life span orientation in which role transitions are viewed along a **life trajectory** (Ferraro, 2001), with a growing recognition that adults face multiple turning points and role transitions across the life span (Marks, Bumpass, & Jun, 2004). Thus, there is increasing attention on emerging adults' departure from (and sometimes return to) the parental home (Arnett, 2000), the transition to marriage (Blair, 2010), and the transition to parenting both for younger adults (Leerkes & Burney, 2007) and middle-aged adults (Friese, Becker, & Nachtigall, 2008). Research continues to examine family caregiving, widowhood, and retirement as mid- and late-life transitions (Wethington, Kessler, & Pixley, 2004). Each of these topics is discussed in depth in the current or subsequent chapters.

Interpersonal Relationships in Adulthood

Kahn and Antonucci (1980) have used the term **convoy** to describe the interpersonal support system we all utilize to help us cope with change. This concept helps describe the importance of interpersonal support networks at all phases of the life span, especially in old age (Rowe & Kahn, 1998). The interpersonal convoy serves as a **psychological buffer** to help support us in times of stress and change such as divorce, illness, retirement, job loss, and death; it includes friends, professional or work

relationships, and close family members. We also provide a support function for the members of our convoy, that is, that we can support others as a member of their convoy allows them to support us.

Adults with well-defined convoys of support can generally cope with changes more effectively than those without. A typical convoy includes supportive relationships with others that are both intimate and stable, as well as those that are more role-bound, instrumental, and changing (Kahn & Antonucci, 1980). However, convoys do change over time due to divorce, marriage, death, relocation, job change, or illness, wherein the convoys of older person are less dense, smaller, and more homogenous than those of younger persons (Cornwell et al., 2008; Winningham & Pike, 2007). Moreover, as we will discuss, social partners within our convoy are sometimes a source of negative interactions.

Socioemotional Selectivity Theory

Carstensen and her colleagues have systematically examined the structure and function of the social convoy. They find that the composition of the convoy differs from person to person and changes as our life circumstances change over the course of the life span, providing us with different types and levels of support at different times and in different situations (Carstensen, 1992, 1995). Beginning in adolescence or early adulthood, people begin a **selection** process by which they strategically and adaptively cultivate their social networks to optimize social and emotional gains and minimize social and emotional risks (Carstensen, 1992, 1995).

Carstensen uses **socioemotional selectivity theory (SST)** to explain why such changes occur. SST is a life span model of social motivation, viewing changes in the social convoy as both functional and adaptive. Within this model, social support networks serve three central functions: (1) development and maintenance of identity, (2) a source of information, and (3) emotional regulation. The importance of these goals varies as a function of life stage (Carstensen, Isaacowitz, & Charles, 1999; Lang & Carstensen, 1994). Moreover, it may be more accurate to say that it is our perception of remaining time, rather than life stage, per se, that influences these goals.

SST states that as we age and the perception of how much time we have remaining becomes more limited, the social goals that we pursue and the people with whom we interact narrow considerably (Carstensen et al., 1999). The social interactions of young people are motivated by a concern for information and identity formation. Therefore, children, adolescents, and younger adults typically have numerous relationships. However, not all of these relationships are particularly meaningful or emotionally rewarding. As young adults, we might tolerate a network member who often irritates us because he or she is an important source of wisdom or other information. In contrast, older adults are motivated by emotional "connectedness." Thus, as we age, it is the third function of emotional regulation that relates directly to the structure and quality of the social convoy (Carstensen et al., 1999). Older adults are less willing to invest their remaining time on relationships that may not have the opportunity to develop, nor are they interested in the potentially negative interactions associated with less familiar partners. Thus, older adults tend to retain only those network members who help to satisfy emotional needs (Carstensen et al., 1999). In keeping with these ideas, research has shown that with age, one's spouse becomes increasingly more important as a source of emotional support (Carstensen et al., 1999; Lang & Carstensen, 1994).

SST has been supported across different age groups, cohorts, and cultures. There is strong evidence that our perception of time-remaining influences our social interaction preferences (Lang & Carstensen, 1994). Younger people will demonstrate preferences for familiar partners, similar to the behaviors of older adults, when faced with time constraints such as a terminal illness or an impending residential relocation far from home (Carstensen et al., 1999). Fung and Carstensen (2002) reported evidence of SST in residents of Hong Kong. As Hong Kong was preparing to become part of the nation of China after a 100-year separation, residents of all ages preferred to spend more time with their closest family members. As the scheduled time

of the political transition approached, the stronger the desire was to interact with those who were especially central in their lives. Within months after the transition, younger adults again preferred to spend free time with a wide variety of network members. Similarly, 2 weeks after the terrorist attacks on the United States on September 11, 2001, Fung conducted telephone interviews with hundreds of residents of mainland China. Given the perception of more limited time, most Chinese residents preferred to spend time with their closest family members. Several weeks later, younger adults relaxed a bit and preferred to spend time with their friends. Thus, even young adults sometimes prefer to maximize emotional support over informational goals, especially when they perceive an uncertain or limited future.

Other Approaches to Understanding Relationships in Adulthood

Attachment (Bowlby, 1969) is the foundation of an individual's basic sense of trust in others, and usually develops during the first year of life. **Trust** develops from individuals' experiences with their primary caretakers—mother, father, grandparent, or other relatives. These early experiences serve as the foundation on which other relationships are built and serve as the basis for **attachment theory** (Ainsworth, 1989). According to this perspective, if these first relationships are negative, we may have difficulty in forming and maintaining interpersonal relationships later in life such as friendships and developing a warm and meaningful relationship with a significant other. Therefore, one's **attachment style**, which is established very early in life, serves as the guiding principle in developing intimate relationships during adulthood. For example, issues of abandonment, closeness, disclosure, secure or insecure attachment—all play a role and contribute to the type of partner one seeks, as well as determine the ability to form and maintain an intimate relationship (Cicirelli, 2010; Holmes & Johnson, 2009).

Holmes and Johnson (2009) recently reviewed the empirical literature that addresses the role of attachment histories in adult romantic love. These researchers found that persons with "secure" attachments described their relationships as happy, friendly, and trusting. They accepted and supported their partner despite the partner's faults and tended to have longer lasting relationships than persons with other attachment styles. Individuals with "anxious" attachments had relationships marked by emotional highs and lows, extreme sexual attraction, jealousy, and obsessive preoccupation with their partners. Finally, persons with "avoidant" attachments tend to have relationships characterized by fear of intimacy, emotional highs and lows, and jealousy. Thus, one's attachment style serves as the guiding principle in developing intimate relationships during adulthood.

Two types of attachment relationships, **vertical** and **horizontal**, are necessary for normal development (Hartup, 1989). Vertical attachments are the first to form and involve people who have greater knowledge and social power than the child and provide protection, security, and satisfaction of basic needs. It is within this context that our basic social skills develop. Horizontal attachments begin to emerge about the third year of life. They are relationships with other individuals who have the same amount of social power as oneself, that is, child-child relationships. These relationships are characterized by reciprocity and egalitarian expectations. They provide the framework in which children elaborate and enhance their basic social skills. Within these relationships, the complexities of cooperation and competition are mastered, and intimacy in social relations is first achieved. Both vertical and horizontal attachments are maintained during adulthood. To illustrate, learning to relate to one's supervisor or teacher is an extension of vertical attachments, while relationships with coworkers, adult siblings, or one's spouse are extensions of earlier horizontal attachments.

Sibling Relationships

For many of us, an important part of our inner social network involves our brothers and sisters. Indeed, 80% of adults and older persons have at least one living sibling (Connidis, 2010). Our rela-

Figure 4-1. Sister-sister pairs often remain close as adults.

tionships with our siblings depend on a variety of factors such as gender and differences in age (among the siblings). It appears that earlier interaction patterns developed among siblings tend to be maintained into adulthood and old age. That is, siblings who had a close relationship during childhood also tend to be close during adulthood. In general, feelings of closeness increase with age, while conflict between siblings dissipates (Cicirelli, 1985). Regardless of age, sister-sister pairs are closer than either brother-brother or mixed-sex pairs, and although siblings tend to maintain some form of regular contact throughout their adult years, this contact is generally not extensive (Cicirelli, 1985). Siblings can provide considerable interpersonal support to individuals in times of crisis (Matthews, Werkner, & Delaney, 1990) and can act as trusted confidants (Cicirelli, 1989). Finally, although sibling rivalry dissipates with age, it may continue to occur in some situations, such as when there is an inheritance, but not in others, such as illness (Connidis, 2010).

Finding a Partner

In order to discuss **finding a partner** who serves as an important part of our personal convoy, it is first meaningful to understand why individuals are first attracted to one another. A variety of factors tend to facilitate attraction and interpersonal relationships (Fincham & Beach, 2010), some of which may result in marriage. These are: **familiarity** and **propinquity**, **satisfaction of personal needs**, **similarity**, **predictability**, and **reinforcement**.

Familiarity and Propinquity

In order for people to meet and become **familiar** with each other, they must have some form of regular contact, association, or physical proximity. Through regular contacts such as being in a class together or working in the same department, individuals have more opportunities to develop and nurture interpersonal relationships. We are attracted to individuals who satisfy our **personal needs** and desires, such as those for love, emotional support, affiliation, and intimacy. Individuals with needs for strong emotional support tend to be attracted to individuals who will meet these needs; and individuals who seek wealth are attracted to those with great financial resources. Also, individuals are attracted to those who complement their needs or compensate for their real or perceived deficiencies. This is referred to as **complementarity**, and simply means that opposites attract. Thus, people often gravitate toward those with complementary needs. We tend to be attracted to individuals who are **similar** to us in terms of socioeconomic level, race, religious beliefs, and education level. For example, women and, to a lesser extent, men preferred roommates who possessed similar values. Similarity of attitudes, personality, demographic characteristics, and beliefs are one of the strongest predictors of interpersonal attraction. Furthermore, being similar to other individuals allows us to **predict** how they will react to specific events and situations. Research indicates that predictable people are liked, while unpredictable people are usually disliked. People tend to be attracted to those who **reinforce** and support their own opinions, values, and ideas, or share similar interests. Such individuals provide mutual support for one another. Similarity tends to be the most important factor in maintaining relationships over time (Huffman, 2007).

Although these factors help explain how individuals are initially attracted to each other, they do not explain the individual's choice of a particular marriage partner from a group of potential mates who may qualify on a number of these factors. Table 4-1, on the following page, presents brief descriptions of a number of theories related to interpersonal attraction. Ultimately, however, the selection of a partner is highly subjective and based on many personal and individual preferences.

Check Your Learning 4-1

Identify the following terms and concepts:

> Socioemotional selectivity
> Role strain/role shifts
> Socialization
> Role overload
> Attachment/attachment styles
> Convoy

- How do we acquire our various roles during the life span?

- How is the process of socialization different for adults and children?

- List and describe three role types.

- Compare and contrast role transition and role change.

- What is an interpersonal convoy? Who composes an interpersonal convoy? What function does the interpersonal convoy play during adulthood?

- Compare and contrast vertical and horizontal attachments.

Table 4-1

Theories of Interpersonal Attraction

Theory	Description
Parental models	We are attracted to individuals who possess traits similar to our opposite-sex parent.
Filter theory (Udry, 1974)	Selection is based on a hierarchical set of "filters," which include propinquity, attractiveness, similarity of social backgrounds, consensus on specific topics, complementarity, and readiness.
Stage theory	Couples progress through stages, including: 1) the **stimulus stage**, where observable characteristics (e.g., attractiveness or occupation) dominate, 2) the **values comparison** stage, where evaluations of mutual interests, attitudes, personal beliefs, and needs are made, and 3) the **role stage**, where the couple makes clear their feelings about each other.
Attachment theory (Ainsworth, 1989)	During adolescence, the young person seeks a partnership with an age peer, usually of the opposite sex in which the reproductive, care-giving, and attachment systems are involved.
PXO theory	**PXO theory** (Murstein, 1982) contends that the nature and quality of interactions between two people have are influenced by four causal conditions: P variables (attributes specific to the person), X variables (physical and social environment), O variables (attributes specific to the other or target), and PXO variables (variables that are unique to the relationship between P and O, such as the fit between the two people).

- List and describe four factors which tend to facilitate attraction and interpersonal relationships.

- What are the major theories of interpersonal attraction?

Romantic Love

During the period of young adulthood, roughly ages 20 to 34 years, many adults seek out a romantic partner, growing out of what Erikson (1963) terms a person's **intimacy needs**. Intimacy is the ability to experience an open, supportive, warm relationship with another person, without fear of losing one's identity in the process of growing close. Intimacy implies the ability for mutual empathy and mutual regulation of needs. It is this ability to share oneself with another that is perhaps the central component in the establishment of intimacy. If you are unable to develop intimacy, you may experience conflict in your relationships, delay marriage, or not marry at all. Current research suggests that within committed relationships, intimacy is a function of self-disclosure and responsiveness of one's partner. Although both of these factors influence intimacy, self-disclosure seems to be particularly important for men, whereas partner responsiveness seems to be especially important for women (Laurenceau, Barrett, & Rovine, 2005). In addition to intimacy, two other components define love: physical and sexual **passion** and a **commitment** or decision to love another and to maintain that love (Sternberg, 2007).

There are many definitions and subtypes of love (see Sternberg, 2007). Moreover, there is a general developmental sequence of love styles (Butler, Walker, Skowronski & Shannon, 1995). For example, Hendrick and Hendrick (1986) found that "eros" love (characterized by passion and intimacy) is the preferred style of young adults. "Storge" love (described as high intimacy and commitment, but more moderate passion, i.e., friendship-based love), and "pragma" love (relationship is a means to an end, practical love) become increasingly important with age. Butler et al. (1995) found that "young" love is characterized by a degree of possessiveness, dependency, and selflessness that decreases with age, and the general structural conceptions of love remain relatively constant into middle age. Thus, there is a relation between age and some specific love styles. In a recent study with 2000 adults from ages 18 to 65+ (AARP, 2009), 80% said they thought that love could last a lifetime. Age differences were observed, however, with 94% of those ages 65+ and 65% of those ages 18 to 24 feeling that love could last.

Figure 4-2. Being happily married requires the use of many problem-solving and communications skills.

Marriage

Reflecting the different types of love, adults choose to marry for a variety of reasons. For some, it is a response to the **social clock**, in that one "should" get married within a particular age range (time), such as age 20, 30, or 40. Going much beyond this range may evoke criticism, or at the very least, a stream of questions from peers or relatives, as well as lead to one's own anxiety about "marriage-ability." Others marry for security or to compensate for perceived social and/or personal inadequacies. Of course, others marry as an outgrowth of their commitment to maintain their love (Sternberg, 2007). However, many persons have unrealistic expectations regarding what married life will be like, and

in adjusting to being married, these expectations may have to be modified (Huffman, 2007). For a variety of views on marriage, see **Adults Speak: Marriage.**

Alternatives to Marriage

Although most adults marry at least once, a growing number are either delaying first marriage or foregoing marriage altogether. Currently, the average age at first marriage is around 27 years for men and 25 years for women. For both men and women, these ages represent a 5-year delay compared to the 1950s (U.S. Bureau of Census, 2006). These trends give rise to three groups of adults: cohabiting partners, gay and lesbian couples, and the single-by-choice. Each is discussed further.

Marriage

People marry for many reasons, some of them wise and others not so wise. Among those who marry, there may be a relationship between why one marries and the later success of that relationship. Consider the diversity of the following views:

Heather (age 21): "I want to get married in the future. I want to be sure that I really love the person and that the person really loves me. I don't want to make a mistake, but if I do, I won't stay married. I'll get a divorce as soon as I realize that I've made a mistake. I've had a couple of casual intimate experiences, but I'm not so quick to do that now because of AIDS."

Joan (age 30): "I guess I got married for all the wrong reasons. At the time it was the thing to do. Here are all my friends getting married, what am I gonna do? I'm a senior in college, that's pretty old. I better start thinking about marriage. I don't know what else I can do. I can teach but that's not enough.

"The person I married was a very popular man and I was a very insecure person, very insecure; and I thought, well, golly, I'm going with this person and everybody likes him, so maybe if I marry him, everybody will like me! The man I married, I didn't feel he really listened, but I did feel security. That, and not knowing what I'd do when I graduated—that's why I got married."

Ann (70 years old): "Arthur and I met at a USO dance. While we were dancing, we discovered that we had grown up near each other in New Jersey and that we had even attended the same high school. I really believe it was love at first sight. We met on the fifteenth of December and married on the twenty-fifth.

"I was 22 and Arthur was 25 when we married. We shared 30 years together. He died of a heart attack in 1973.

"I have positive feelings about marriage. We had such a good one, he was a good friend and confidant, we worked and played together and it was good. When we fought, it was over little petty things."

A 45-year-old woman says: "I think that marriage is a wonderful thing. I say that even though my first marriage did not work out. I think that my first marriage did not work because the people who were involved felt quite a bit of pressure. I mean my ex-husband and I loved each other very much. However, there were other circumstances that created some pressure for us both.

"For example, I do not think that my mother liked my first husband very much. Sometimes I wonder if our parents got along much at all. I mean, his parents and my parents were from such different backgrounds and had different interests.

"However, with my second husband, things were quite different. There was not that much pressure from our parents. We came from much more similar backgrounds and our parents got along well together."

A 53-year-old woman had very definite views on why she married: "I married my childhood sweetheart. I felt that I would always get married. I wanted that to be my lifestyle. It was also what everyone did. At 18, with limited exposure to the world, I don't think I was very farsighted about what I expected from a marriage. I was just in love. I think you always use your parents as role models. There are always certain things you see in your parents' relationships that you like or dislike. You promise yourself that you will do it differently or the same. Whichever the case may be. Today it is a mix. At times I feel like it is active and passive, but in retrospect and with a more mature perspective, it is give and take. There are certain areas where I give more and he gives more in some areas. It all evens out."

Cohabitation is a living arrangement in which two adults who are not legally married are involved in a sexual relationship. It is difficult to obtain accurate estimates of the number of cohabiting couples, in part, because the Census definitions categorize all nonrelated adults sharing a residence as "nonfamily" households (Kreider & Elliott, 2009). Thus, nonfamily households include unmarried heterosexual couples, gay and lesbian couples, friends sharing a home, and households with boarders. Between 1970 and 2007, the United States saw a 4% increase in the number of households in which at least two unrelated adults coresided (Kreider & Elliott, 2009), with 40% of women ages 15 to 44 years reporting ever having cohabitated (Bramlett & Mosher, 2002). Cohabitation is often a precursor to or substitute for marriage, or a testing ground for marital incompatibility (Bramlett & Mosher, 2002). Most cohabiting relationships last between 1 1/2 to 5 years, and when they end, 60% result in marriage and 40% in a breakup.

The percentage of previously married people (divorced, separated, or widowed) who cohabit is higher than the percentage of never-married people who cohabit (Bramlett & Mosher, 2002). Premarital cohabitation is associated with higher probability of divorce; but this is less accurate for couples who are a little older when they start to cohabitate and for whom religion and stability are important (Bramlett & Mosher, 2002).

Gay and Lesbian Couples

Gay and lesbian relationships involve a personal commitment by gay or lesbian individuals to each other to live together as married partners (domestic partners), despite the failure of many states to legally sanction their relationship. Although enumerating gay and lesbian as couples is challenging, it is estimated that more than 600,000 gay and lesbian couples were co-residing and living as married in 2000 (Peplau & Fingerhut, 2007). Partners share or take individual responsibility for specific roles and duties within the relationship. Many same-sex partnerships are quite enduring and satisfying.

Lesbian relationships are likely to develop out of close same-sex friendships, and lesbian women are more likely to establish long-term relationships than gay men. Further, lesbian women generally describe their relationships as stable, sexually exclusive, and extremely close (Peplau & Fingerhut, 2007). Although gay men are interested in developing long-term relationships, they are less likely than lesbian women to be sexually exclusive; relationships among gay men are most often described as multiple short-term relationships. Gay and lesbian couples report many of the same factors expressed by heterosexual couples regarding quality relationships, such as closeness, trust, good problem-solving and conflict resolution skills, openness, and perceived social support. Gay and lesbian couples generally perceive less social support from family members (Peplau & Fingerhut, 2007).

Single Adults

Single adults are those individuals who have never been married, are widowed, or are divorced. Of this group (now a majority), 60% have never been married, 15% are widowed, and 25% are divorced (U.S. Bureau of Census, 2005). Individuals who never marry do so for a variety of reasons such as personal choice, professional/occupational demand, and caring for parents or family members. Older never married persons, however, may be better adjusted than widows of the same age, never having to cope with the death of a spouse. This may also be because they have experienced living alone, being independent, and doing things for themselves for a long time. Further, they do not experience the dramatic changes in lifestyle that can occur as the result of losing a spouse, and they have developed friendship networks independently of a spouse (Connidis, 2001). However, research does show that in late life, never-married adults have fewer members in their social networks than do married adults, due to fewer family members (Dykstra, 2006).

Within the diversity of the Baby Boomer generation is the increase in the number of openly gay men and lesbian women, many of whom enter late life as single adults. The stereotyped portrayal of older lesbian-gay-bisexual (LGB) adults has described these individuals as isolated, lonely, and depressed. In contrast, researchers speculate that same-sex orientation can facilitate successful aging. At some point in life, a self-identified LGB person goes through a coming-out process, an often lengthy and ongoing series of realizations that can occur at any stage of life (Biblarz & Savci, 2010). This process may provide a sense of **crisis competence** that buffers a person against later crises (Kimmel, 2004). In addition, the role changes of aging may be less severe for LGB adults, primarily because gender roles are more flexible for this group than they are for same-aged heterosexuals (Biblarz & Savci, 2010).

According to Friend's (1991) theory of successful aging, achievement of a positive sexual identity as an LGB adult places that individual at a distinct advantage for continued adaptations to the challenges of aging. The cornerstone of this theory then is achievement of a positive identity based on rejection of the bias and stereotypes of the larger group (i.e., heterosexuals). After rejecting society's negative evaluation, LGB adults reconstruct a set of attitudes, feelings, and values that allow for an affirmative self-identity, the emergent psychological attributes of crisis competence, and flexible gender roles (Friend, 1991). From this perspective, self-identity of older LGB adults may be greatly determined by their social context, which in turn will influence their adaptation to aging (Reid, 1995).

There is evidence that older lesbian women fare particularly well compared to older gay men (Claes & Moore, 2000; Friend, 1991). Evidence suggests that gay men may exhibit lower levels of well being because they are members of a community which extols youth, physical attractiveness, and sexual prowess (Claes & Moore, 2000). Bennett and Thompson (1990) found that gay men may experience **accelerated aging**, that is, they are considered old at an earlier age than their heterosexual counterparts, with gay men being "old" at age 30.

Many areas of concern for aging gay and lesbian women are the same ones as for most aging heterosexual adults—loneliness, health, and income. Recent work by Kimmel, Rose, and David (2006) has contributed to adapting late-life issues such as retirement planning, sexuality, legal concerns, grandparenting, physical and mental health, substance abuse, cultural and ethnic diversity, needs for social services, and end-of-life decision making to address the unique concerns of older gay men and lesbian women. These approaches emphasize the resilience, coping, and successful adaptation to aging in the face of discrimination and oppression against gay, lesbian, and transgendered persons. In addition, the authors describe a model agency (SAGE—Services and Advocacy for GLBT Elders) dedicated to delivering quality social and medical services to this population.

Transitions and Turning Points in the Family

Childfree or Childless?

Most emerging adults report that they would like to become a parent (Yaremko & Lawson, 2007). In a large study with more than 12,000 adults, the most popular reason cited for wanting children by both men and women was that idea that children are "fun" (Langdridge, Connolly, & Sheeran, 2000). However, whether and when one becomes a parent is influenced by a variety of factors, not all of which are under a person's direct control. Read **Adults Speak: On Parenthood** for a variety of views on becoming and being a parent. Increasingly, many adults are delaying or forgoing entry into the parent role.

Adults Speak

On Parenthood: It All Depends on Your Point of View

Heather (age 21): "I'm not ready for motherhood. You don't have a life after you have kids. I have a friend with a baby; she always has trouble finding sitters. I babysat for her once: the kid didn't like me and it cried the whole night. I was so glad when she came to get it. It's harder to have a career when you have kids. I mean you need to work less hours and then you have to mess with doctors' appointments and stuff like that. I think it will be a long time, if ever, before I have a baby."

Jean (age 30): "I tried to be a good mother but I always had to be at work and I couldn't afford daycare so they spent a lot of time alone. My two sons really gave me a hard time; they wouldn't do their schoolwork and they had lots of behavior problems at school.

"My daughter did good school work and behaved well there, but she and I fought terribly. The kids didn't get to spend time with their real dad; he remarried and had a new family. I didn't pick very good role models for them either. We don't visit much; they call or come by to see if I'll babysit. Most of the time I do, it's like a second chance. I love them and I'm proud of them."

Ann (age 70 years old): "I feel like I was a good mother. I loved them and I showed it to them by hugging and kissing them and by listening to anything they wanted to tell me. I was strict. We had rules and if they broke them I punished them. I didn't push it off on their daddy. They were good boys; even during the sixties when our friends' children were taking drugs, our kids didn't. They wore long hair and trashy clothes, and peace symbols the priest said were actually satanic symbols. We were concerned but tolerant. I'm very proud of them"

A 21-year-old woman says: "Do I want to be a parent? It all depends on my life situation and whether I feel it would be fair to bring a child into the world at that time.

"Are there certain things I would like to wait for? Yes, economic stability, parental stability, marriage stability. I feel the world right now has so many problems; I would be really unfair to bring a child into the world unless you feel you can give a very stable, realistic environment. Not protective, but where you can teach that child how to live in the world he is going to be brought into.

"What values are important to instill in my children? Honesty, not being judgmental or hypocritical, being able to have a basic understanding about the realism of life and not the quantitative things that society tries to bring upon you, be your own person and have your own opinion about things."

An 80-year-old woman states: "Is there anything I wish I had done differently with my children? I regret that I wasn't more affectionate and expressive. I don't think they were slighted. My sisters and I are still that way. My parents were not affectionate. I didn't know how to be. The last few years in my life there have been more hugs and kisses than ever. I ask my kids sometimes if I was a mean old witch. They assure me that I wasn't. . . .What values did I want to instill in them? Along the same lines as my parents did. Honesty, strive to be your best. If I was in trouble in school, I was in trouble at home. The same goes for my children. These were definitely achieved."

A 25-year-old man wrote: "Becoming a parent is not a gradual thing. Instead, it is instantaneous and a little otherworldly, like waking up one morning to a new gravity and having to learn to drink coffee without spilling on the ceiling.

"A good deal of anxiety generally precedes it. But one adjusts to parenthood quickly—so quickly, in fact, it is difficult to realize one has adjusted to anything at all. Parents learn to walk, talk, breathe, and think in a world of whole new universals. But because they learn to do it so swiftly, new parents often don't realize anything has changed until long after it has already happened. By that time, spilling coffee on the ceiling is as natural as spilling it on the floor."

Much of what we know about the effects of not being a parent comes primarily from the experience of women. As noted in relation to the lack of research on men in other family roles (e.g., Patrick & Tomczewski, 2008), this lack of information on men may be the result of the very small number of men who do not parent, the reluctance of men to participate in research, or a failure of researchers to ask questions that are relevant to men's experiences in the family. In the small literature on the effects of not becoming a parent, however, there is evidence that similar patterns hold across men and women (Dykstra, 2006). In addition, the majority of the evidence suggests that single and coupled gay and lesbian parents provide love and support to their children in ways that are similar to one- and two-parent heterosexual families (Biblarz & Stacey, 2010).

Due to choices in contraception and increases in educational attainment, about 20% of American women ages 40 to 44 years have never given birth; approximately equal numbers are childless by choice as are childless due to infertility (Livingston & Cohn, 2010; Plotnick, 2009).Some of these women will later become mothers, either by giving birth (see Box B); adopting children, or becoming a step-parent (Livingston & Cohn, 2010). Others will remain without a child; approximately one-third of these women are likely to continue to long for motherhood, feeling that they are incomplete (Kotter-Gruhn, Scheibe, Blanchard-Fields, & Baltes, 2009).

For a variety of reasons, individuals and couples may make a conscious decision not to have children. For example, being child-free may allow each partner to focus on the other and their respective careers, not wanting the responsibility or commit-ment associated with raising a child. However, couples who choose not to have children often experience pressure from family members and friends. Although negative public perceptions of the child-free are less harsh than in previous generations (Livingston & Cohn, 2010), negative stereotypes may still linger. For example, adults who choose to remain child-free may be viewed as selfish and less well-adjusted

Regarding the long-term effects of remaining childless (or child-free), most research shows no negative effects. Although the social networks of people without children is smaller than those of parents (Dykstra, 2006), childless adults do not report feeling more lonely or depressed than adults with children (Kotter-Gruhn et al., 2009; Koropeckyj-Cox, 1998). Moreover, there are economic benefits related to not being a parent that are experienced by both child-free couples and unmarried child-free women (Plotnick, 2009).

Transition to Parenthood

Although parenthood and the roles associated with it are crucial for child development, individuals often become parents without any formal training in how to parent. You learn how to parent on the job! There is some evidence, however, that girls are better socialized to the role of parent than are boys. For example, several pre-parenting experiences may be more available to girls, including babysitting, volunteer work, and other opportunities that place them in contact with children and their parents (Coleman & Karraker, 2003). At emerging adulthood, women report a stronger desire to become a parent as do men (Yaremko & Lawson, 2007). Women also report having twice as much contact with children (Leerkes & Burney, 2007) and more

Box B

On Becoming a Mother After Age 40

Approximately 6% of American women ages 40 to 44 are childless due to **infertility**; another 2% in this age group are still planning to give birth (Livingston & Cohn, 2010). With the advances in **assistive reproductive technologies**, an increasing number of middle-aged women are giving birth for the first time. In fact, in 2008, more than 7,600 babies were born to women over the age of 45 in the United States (Livingston & Cohn). In an interview study with 79 middle-aged couples who were becoming parents for the first time, Friese, Becker, and Nachtigall (2008) examined issues of identity and stigma related to late parenting.

Women reported **negative age stereotypes** related to giving birth past age 40.

"Being 40 can be a very intimidating experience because you're doing it with a lot of women who are a lot younger than you and who seem so much more adept!" (p. 69, Friese et al.)

"I know I've embarrassed people. Like if they say, 'Does your granddaughter want' something or other and I say 'my daughter.' But I say it tough. I was probably more sensitive to that when my kids were younger and more willing to educate people rather than embarrass them. But I don't feel as though I owe explanations in all circumstances." (p. 70, Friese et al.)

"I started bleaching my hair when I was pregnant with the twins. I saw a picture of myself and thought: 'Oh my God. When I'm holding these babies, and they see pictures of me in their infancy, I don't want to look like their grandmother." (p. 70, Friese et al.)

Women also reported **positive age stereotypes** and the "extraordinary woman" stereotype.

"And that just feels—it makes me feel so good . . ."(when others compliment her) . . . and I go, 'This is hard.' You know, this is hard because you're 48 in a lot of ways."(p. 70, Friese et al.)

"I go to the playground, and I see these 20- and 30-something moms, and they're sitting there talking about getting their nails done and they'll do their shopping at Nordstrom's or whatever. And I'm usually sitting on the slide or the sandpit with the kids. It's a total difference of priorities. I've lived enough life that I can make my kids my priority and not think twice about it, where they still need more time for them. It's more a tug of war. So I think if many people in society would actually stop and think about it, it's not as bad as they think." (p. 70, Friese et al.).

Source: Friese C., Becker G., Nachtigall R.D. (2008). Older motherhood and the changing life course in the era of assisted reproductive technologies. *Journal of Aging Studies*, *22*, 65-73.

knowledge about children and child development than do men (Ribas & Bornstein, 2005).

In a study of expectant parents, similar levels of enthusiasm and anxiety about becoming parents were expressed by men and women, although the specific areas differed by gender (Delmore-Ko, Pancer, Hunsberger, & Pratt, 2000). Among these expectant parents, women were concerned about the physical and instrumental demands of caring for an infant, whereas men tended to focus on a broader perspective, mentioning areas of concern from infancy through emerging adulthood (Delmore-Ko et al., 2000). Both men and women tended to underestimate the effects that a child would have on their overall lifestyles, including time, finances, and activities. Many experienced an increase in depression during the first 18 months after the birth of their child (Delmore-Ko et al., 2000).

Figure 4-3. Raising happy children is a full-time job!

Work to Family Spill-overs

Indeed, living with and raising children is a major stressor for most couples. These stressors are increased when both parents work outside the home. Today, in 83% of households comprised of two parents and at least one child, both parents work (Campos et al., 2009). Among married childless couples, nearly all are employed outside the home (Kreider & Elliott, 2009). Thus, the **dual-career** family is the modal family style in the United States. When both spouses work outside the home, it is necessary to negotiate how to divide household tasks, including cleaning, cooking, bill-paying, and if necessary, child care. Often, each partner assumes responsibility and authority for specific duties and tasks within the family, and these are generally stable. Clearly, when both partners are employed, it requires a redefinition of roles and duties within the family. During late life, many couples must re-negotiate these household duties, as one partner retires and the other remains in the work force (Winston & Klepfer, 2000).

Crouter and Manke (1997) suggest that there are three distinct types of dual-earner family lifestyles: high status, low status, and main-secondary. Each type has its own pattern of role relationships, costs, and rewards. In the high status category, both persons had high prestige careers, earned high salaries, and were very involved in their positions/jobs. Although the division of housework was more equal than in the other two groups, these couples experienced the greatest amount of role overload, had lower levels of love and marital satisfaction, and more marital conflict than the other two groups. Although low status couples worked as many hours on their jobs as couples in the high status category, their jobs were of lower prestige, such as secretary, salesperson, carpenter, and substitute teacher. This group had the lowest amount of role overload and marital conflict, and the highest scores in marital satisfaction and love for their spouse. In the main-secondary lifestyle, generally, husbands were in the primary position, with higher occupational prestige; they worked more hours and had higher work involvement than their wives, who typically worked part time. Women in this category tended to have less education and tended to have more household responsibilities.

Changes in women's education levels and the economy have combined such that many women now earn more than their husbands do. For men with traditional sex role attitudes, this may result in negative perceptions of marital quality (Brennan, Barnett, & Gareis, 2001). Additional evidence of **work-to-family spillover** and **family-to-work spillover** is provided by Wierda-Boer, Gerris, and Vermulst (2009). They collected responses from 276 dual-earner couples with between 1 and 4 children. Women reported more child care duties and felt more restricted by the parental role than did men. Although men and women did not differ in their reports of work stress, women report more negative effects on their work due to family stress and men reported more interference on their family time due to work stress (Wierda-Boer et al.). Another trend, which developed between 2007 and 2010, is likely to negatively affect couples and families. As record numbers of men lost their jobs in construction and manufacturing due to the economic recession, more women became the sole wage earner. More than 2 million American women were the sole economic support for their husband and children in 2009 (Hartmann, English, & Hayes, 2010). The full effects of this trend will not be manifested for several more years (see Chapter 7).

Marital Satisfaction

Being happily married is dependent on a number of factors, and it is difficult to say in an absolute sense what characterizes all satisfying marriages. However, research has identified a number of factors related to marital satisfaction. These are: approach to conflict resolution, communication, pleasurable interaction, attributions one makes for a partner's behavior, perceived support from one's partner (Bradbury, Fincham, & Beach, 2000) and a high degree of disclosure (Laurenceau et al., 2005). Specifically, happily married couples solved problems by mutually talking them out, enjoyed each other's company (they enjoyed being with and interacting with each other), openly communicated with each other, and were able to disclose personal issues and openly express their emotions.

Further, marital satisfaction varies with both time and age; there appears to be a curvilinear relationship between marital satisfaction and stage of the life cycle, with marital satisfaction peaking before children are born and after they leave home. The transition to parenthood is associated with decreased marital satisfaction and less marital happiness (Bradbury et al., 2000; Kurdeck, 1999). These decreases are attributed to the new demands and stressors related to the birth of the first child. For example, parents may lack the training and skills required for parenting, sleep patterns are altered, economic resources are strained, and potential conflict over child care activities may emerge, all of which lead to stress in the marital relationship. Additionally, the new baby interferes with the dynamics between the husband and the wife. Therefore, having children clearly affects the marital relationship.

Marital satisfaction at mid- and late-life differs from that at earlier stages of marriage. That is, the factors which influence the formation and establishing of a good relationship are different from those involved in maintaining a rewarding relationship (Schmitt, Kliegel, & Shapiro, 2007). Evidence suggests that marital satisfaction increases steadily throughout middle age, after adult sons and daughters leave the parental home (Gorchoff, John, & Helson, 2008), termed the **empty nest**. However, this increase in marital satisfaction is directly related to the day-to-day interaction patterns within the couple. For example, after adult children depart, couples report an increase in enjoyment of their time together (Gorchoff et al., 2008). Those marriages characterized by shared activities, felt emotional support from their spouse, and reciprocity tend to report higher marital satisfaction (Schmitt et al., 2007). Thus, what seems to be important is the content and quality of the interaction between members of the couple. Using a behavior observation task, Henry, Berg, Smith, and Florsheim (2007) investigated two dimensions of marital satisfaction, actual behavior exhibited by one's partner and perceptions of the partner's behavior. Participants included 106 couples in their 40s and 98 couples in their 60s. Each couple participated in a discussion task in which they talked about an area of disagreement, a collaborative route-planning task in which they devised a plan to complete a series of errands, individual reports of their partner's behavior, and measures of marital satisfaction. In general, the older couples reported higher marital satisfaction than the middle-aged couples, especially the husbands. Older couples also perceived more positive behaviors from their spouse in both the discussion and route-planning tasks. Perhaps more importantly, older couples perceived fewer negative behaviors from their spouse during the discussion about an area of disagreement. Comparing these perceptions to the actual behavior exhibited by the partners confirmed these findings: older adults exhibited more positive behaviors and fewer negative behaviors than did the middle-aged adults.

Check Your Learning 4-2

Identify the following terms or concepts:

> Empty nest
> Dual-career/dual-earner couples
> Intimacy needs
> Family life cycle
> Social clock

- What are some of the reasons why people marry?

- Describe the developmental changes in love.

- Describe the factors related to martial satisfaction. How do they change with age?

- What do we mean in stating that the family is a dynamic system?

Divorce

Divorce is now a more common end to a marriage than is death (Fincham & Beach, 2010). In the United States, four **contextual factors** are associated with divorce: age at the time of marriage; socioeconomic level; personality traits; and, a family history of divorce (Amato, 2010; Bramlett & Mosher, 2002). In terms of age, divorce is particularly high among couples who marry under the age of 20 and among those who marry in the late 20s or older. It is assumed that those who marry young (under 20) are emotionally immature (Blair, 2010) and those who marry late in life may be too independent to make the compromises necessary for a successful marriage. The influence of socioeconomic level is a combination of the factors of educational level, employment status, occupational level, and income level. The relationship among each of these specific factors and divorce is quite complex. For instance, divorce rates are higher among couples with low levels of education and low income levels. Finally, children of divorced parents are more likely to get divorced than children from intact marriages. It is suspected that because children from divorced families view divorce as an acceptable strategy for resolving marital problems and conflicts (Bramlett & Mosher, 2002).

Specific interpersonal factors, individual characteristics, and life events are associated with divorce, as well (Amato, 2010). Personality traits such as degree of autonomy, identity, negative emotionality, closeness, disclosure, and hostility are related to divorce. For example, marital stability often depends on each of the partners achieving a sense of personal identity, a balance in power, emotional intimacy, and mutual respect. Interpersonal communication within the couple also predicts divorce. The **demand-withdrawal** pattern, in which one partner pushes a topic or area of conflict and the other actively avoids it, is associated with divorce (Bradbury et al., 2000). Stressors and life events may also tax a couple's ability to remain married.

In addition to IPV, discussed in Box A, one particularly challenging event is **infidelity**. Infidelity, or extramarital romantic and/or sexual relationships, has increased for both men and women across the past 40 years (Fincham & Beach, 2010). Among adults age 40 and younger, the rates of infidelity are approximately equal. The group which has experienced the largest increase in extramarital relationships includes men ages 65 to 90 years, a change that is associated with the availability of drugs like Viagra and other treatments for erectile dysfunction (Fincham & Beach, 2010). A newly emerging area of conflict for couples relates to **cybersex** and other forms of on-line infidelity. About one-third of married men and women report using the internet for sexual purposes. The majority (66%) of adults who develop on-line romantic relationships eventually have a physical sexual relationship with their on-line partner. Even in the absence of a physical relationship, however, the partner often feels emotionally betrayed and views the relationship as infidelity. In addition to the perception of betrayal, cybersex taxes one's income and may jeopardize one's employment if the internet is used at work (Fincham & Beach, 2010). All of these threats to the marital union may lead to dissolution of the marriage.

During the past 20 years, the **divorce** rate has risen substantially, and it is estimated that nearly 50% of all current first marriages will end in divorce. It is estimated that 1 in 5 first-time marriages will end in divorce within the first 5 years, with another 1 in 3 ending in divorce before the 10th anniversary (Bramlett & Mosher, 2002). Statistics indicate that the probability of divorce is highest during the first years of marriage and peaks somewhere between 2 and 4 years. The median duration of a marriage currently in the United States is 7 years.

However, as is the case with other aspects of our lives, the Baby Boomers are changing what we thought we knew about divorce. As predicted by socioemotional selectivity theory, mid-life may be a time of pruning the unsatisfying relationships from our social network (Carstensen et al., 1999); thus, it is not surprising that more midlife adults are ending their **long-term marriages**. A recent AARP study of more than 1,100 divorced adults ages 40 and 60 years shows that: women initiate the split more often than men, many men (26%) report being unaware that their marriage was in trouble, and the majority of women (75%) and men (81%) were involved in a serious relationship within 2 years after the divorce (AARP, 2004). Thus, middle-aged adults adapt to the transition presented by a midlife divorce.

Just as people make the decision to marry for a number of reasons, they choose to divorce for a variety of factors, such as a breakdown of mutuality, changing interests, or singular focus on job responsibilities. The issues of conflict and tension are most evident during the early years of marriage when each partner must learn to adapt, adjust, and compromise on issues such as financial matters, work schedules and positions, sex, household tasks, and social activities. The reasons for a midlife divorce differ between men and women. For women, abuse, infidelity, and substance abuse top the list. Men say that they sought a divorce at midlife because they fell out of love or that the couple had different values or lifestyles (AARP, 2004).

Coping with Divorce

Divorce is a painful, disruptive experience for the entire family and often leads to more life changes. Divorce generally leaves one of the partners with a deep sense of failure and rejection and is associated with a number of significant losses. These losses are in the area of finances, social networks and support, social roles, self-concept, and material possessions (Bramlett & Mosher, 2002).

For example, the loss of financial resources can lead to a decreased standard of living resulting in moving from a big house in a nice neighborhood and driving an expensive car to living in an efficiency apartment and driving a used car.

Divorce also leads to a loss of social networks and support. That is, divorced persons lose contact with family and friends who were established as a result of the marriage relationship (Kunz & Kunz, 1995). Additionally, there is a loss of social roles such as husband, wife, mother, or father. Divorce is especially negative and stressful for the person being left, who feels a deep sense of failure and rejection, which can lead to a negative self-concept and a lowered self-esteem. The stressors related to divorce can also lead to health or psychological problems such as depression (Bramlett & Mosher, 2002). Further, the person must deal with feelings of guilt, sorrow, and anger. Berman and Turk (1981) have identified six specific stressors associated with divorce: contacts with the former spouse, parent-child interactions, interpersonal relations, loneliness, everyday practical problems (such as cleaning, transporting children to school and to activities), and financial problems.

Divorce creates a new set of difficulties for people. One may need to find a new place to live, learn to manage on a day-to-day basis, arrange for child care, make new friends, find a new job, or establish credit. This may be especially difficult for women who have never worked outside the home, as well as for middle-aged and older women. There are increasing numbers of middle-aged and older adults divorcing (Connidis, 2010). For midlife and older women, the transition from married to single life can be particularly difficult. They often find that they are unprepared for lives as divorced single people. Women of all ages emerge from divorce with a decrease in their standard of living due to less income. There is also severe stress associated with loss of support caused by the loss of friendship networks, which are usually couple-oriented.

Often, people who have custody of the children must serve as "both parents." Arrangements for custody, alimony, and visiting rights create ad-ditional difficulties to overcome. There literally may not be time to see others socially or become intimately involved with another person. Many, overwhelmed by these pressures and lacking help and support from others, become depressed, suffer physical or work difficulties, or have difficulty in forming new relationships with others, further isolating them from support they need. Women report more anxiety and conflict prior to separation, while men experience more practical problems during the year following divorce.

The effects of divorce on the person who initiates the divorce are substantially different than for the person who is being left. The person who initiates the divorce does not experience many of the negative psychological factors associated with divorce such as depression, negative self-concept, or lowered self-esteem (Amato, 2010).

Although the immediate aftereffects of divorce are very stressful for all involved, many divorced individuals report feelings of enhanced self-esteem and ultimately do establish other meaningful romantic relationships (AARP, 2004; Bramlett & Mosher, 2002). This having been said, if one can think of divorce as a healthy life transition, ex-spouses will have accomplished three tasks: letting go of the old relationship, reestablishing new ties with others, and where children are involved, redefining the parental role (Amato, 2010).

Remarriage and Blended Stepfamilies

Since 75% of divorced mothers and 80% of divorced fathers remarry, usually within 3 years, many children are exposed to a series of marital transitions and household reorganizations. Though married with children is still a prominent pattern in the United States, a number of these families are **blended stepfamilies** (Kreider & Elliott, 2009). Individuals often describe their second marriage as being somewhat better than their first on a number of dimensions; however, divorce rates for remarried individuals is somewhat higher than for first marriages. Adults in a second marriage report fewer disagreements about money, less positive communication, and less negative communication, relative to their first marriages (Sweeney, 2010).

One particular group is at a higher risk. The group of remarried adults who have the most difficult adjustment problems are those in which both husband and wife have children from previous marriages living in the household. Although the stepparent role has become common in the United States (Amato, 2010; Sweeney, 2010) there are no rules for stepchildren and stepparents to follow; that is, they don't know how they're supposed to act toward each other. Just as losing a parent can be stressful, so can gaining a parent be stressful (Cherlin, 1996). Therefore, one of the biggest challenges **stepparents** face is developing favorable relationships with their stepchildren. Doing so is much more difficult for stepmothers than for stepfathers. Also, among stepfamilies, the addition of new biological children from the current marriage detracts from relationships between stepmothers and their stepchildren, but may add to those between stepfathers and their stepchildren (Sweeney, 2010). When biological children are added to the remarriage, either from the current or a previous marriage, the conditions surrounding the stepmother role may become even more demanding. Because the role of the father is usually not as closely tied to the children as is the role of the mother, stepfathers may be less likely to experience such role conflict. Thus, stepmothers, more often than stepfathers, experience greater difficulty in rearing their stepchildren and have a harder time finding satisfactions with their stepchildren than with their biological children (Sweeney, 2010). This is especially true when stepparents become biological parents for the first time.

Generally, studies of stepfamilies have compared children living in stepfamilies to those in nuclear families and/or single-parent families on global measures of psychosocial adjustment or cognitive functioning. They have found negligible differences in psychological outcomes for children living in stepfamilies and nuclear families (Amato, 2010). Yet, all children do not respond equally. The three factors that have been consistently found to affect a child's response to remarriage are age, temperament/personality, and gender. The period of adjustment to remarriage appears to be longer for older children, who usually adapt better over the long term to remarriage. Like younger children, however, older children and adolescents experience pain and anger when their parents divorce. However, they may be better able to assign responsibility for the divorce, resolve loyalty conflicts, and adapt to a new family.

Children who are temperamental and less adaptable to change are more likely to be the target of criticism, anger, or anxiety on the part of a parent and stepparent, and they are less able to cope with the situation. The negative effects of divorce, life in a single-parent family, and remarriage are more pervasive for girls than for boys (Amato, 2010). Clearly, children vary in their response to the remarriage of their parents. Stepfamilies do not necessarily experience stress and difficulty (Amato, 2010).

Single-Parent Families

Due to the high divorce rate and the number of children being born to unmarried parents, the percentage of **single-parent families** has been increasing during the past few decades (Amato, 2010; Biblarz & Stacey, 2010). Approximately 25% of families are headed by one parent (Kreider & Elliott, 2009). Of these families, the vast majority are headed by women, since the courts traditionally favor mothers where physical custody of children is concerned. Generally, the younger the children, the more likely they are to be living with the mother, while older boys are more likely to be living with the father.

There are four types of single-parent families: (1) a household maintained by a parent with at least one child under 18 years; (2) a household with one parent but no children under 18 years of age (however, sons and daughters over 18 live in the household); (3) a related subfamily, in which the single parent and children live in a house maintained by a relative, such as a young mother and her children living in the home of the mother's parent; and (4) an unrelated subfamily (Kreider & Elliott, 2009).

An unrelated subfamily lives in a house maintained or shared with someone to whom the subfamily is not related. An example is a divorced man and his children living with a friend and his children.

Single-parent households represent about 25% of U.S. households with children. In 2007, approximately. 2.5 million single-father households and 8.3 million single-mother households existed (Kreider & Elliott, 2009). Fathers who head single-parent families tend to be older, more highly educated, raising children who are older, raising fewer children, and more financially stable than single mother families (Kreider & Elliott).

The area of single-parent families is emotionally and politically charged, with a stereotype that children raised in single-parent families have poorer outcomes,. When other important factors are controlled (such as income and neighborhood), the research does show that two loving and involved parents are better than one for most child outcomes. However, rarely are all other factors equal between single- and two-parent households. In two-parent families that show a high degree of conflict, child outcomes might well be improved by transitioning to a single-parent household (Biblarz & Stacey, 2010).

Check Your Learning 4-3

Identify the following terms or concepts:

> Blended families
> Related subfamily
> Single parent families
> Cohabitation

- What are some of the negative effects of divorce for the person?

- What four factors are associated with divorce?

- What are some "losses" associated with divorce?

- What are some of the effective methods of coping with divorce?

- What are some of the potential difficulties experienced by blended families?

- What are some of the reasons for cohabitation?

- What are some of the reasons people choose to become parents?

Summary

Relationships with others play a vital role in affecting the quality of our lives in adulthood and are critical to our satisfaction with life, our self-concept, and our physical health. Through the process of socialization we acquire the skills, values, and behaviors to function in the roles we currently occupy or will occupy in the future. It is a **dynamic** process, and throughout the life span we are constantly undergoing or anticipating socialization. Also, **socialization** is a **bidirectional** process between children, parents and others. Each member of this dyad has a dynamic effect on other individuals and the family as a whole.

Roles are culturally determined guidelines that tell people what is expected of them in terms of behaviors, traits, and characteristics anticipated by others and are the direct result of learning and experience. Role expectations may conflict, leading to **role strain** or **role overload**, in which the demands of one or more roles exceed the person's capacity to meet the demands of these roles. Stressful events in one role can often spill over into other roles. As adults, we are expected to acquire and perform behaviors associated with many roles simultaneously, and throughout the life span we are constantly shifting roles either through role transition or role change.

The interpersonal support system or **convoy**, composed of family and friends, serves as a psychological **buffer** to help support us in times of stress and change. The composition of the convoy differs from person to person and changes as our life circumstances change, providing us with different types and levels of support at different times and in different situations. Theories emphasizing **socioemotional selectivity** or **attachment** can explain the process by which our convoys of support are formed and maintained in adulthood.

A variety of factors tend to facilitate attraction and interpersonal relationships, some of which may result in marriage, such as **familiarity** and **propinquity**, **satisfaction of personal needs**, and **reinforcement**. There are a number of theories which attempt to explain how these factors interact in the selection of a mate, such as parental models and filter theory.

For a variety of reasons, the "traditional" family has undergone significant change, and now the **dual-earner** family is now the modal family style in the United States. Although there are many advantages to being a dual-career couple, there are also many difficulties.

Often, the marital relationship is the central part of our interpersonal convoy. People get married for a variety of reasons. Assuming that love is central to most marriages, the general structural conceptions of love remain relatively constant into middle age, although there is a relation between age and some specific love styles.

Marital satisfaction varies with both time and age. There appears to be a curvilinear relationship between marital satisfaction and stage in the life cycle, with marital satisfaction peaking before children are born and after they leave home. Good marital relationships are characterized by mutual respect for one another, commitment and responsibility for meeting each other's needs, and concern for one another's happiness and welfare. Persons who are happily married report strong emotional support and understanding from one another; they feel that their good and bad qualities are accepted by the other spouse.

During the past few decades, the **divorce** rate has risen substantially. Divorce creates a new set of difficulties for people and often leads to many lifestyle changes. This may be especially difficult for women who have never worked outside the home, as well as for middle-aged and older women. Most divorced individuals remarry. As a result, many children are exposed to a series of marital transitions and household reorganizations. Although married with children is still a prominent pattern in the United States, a number of these families are **blended stepfamilies**. Stepfamilies do not necessarily experience stress and difficulty.

The American family is in transition. Although many adults remain **childless**, most become **parents**. Due to the high divorce rate, the percentage of **single-parent families** has been increasing during the past few decades. Of these families, the vast majority are headed by females. **Gay relationships** involve a personal commitment by gay or lesbian individuals to each other to live together as married partners (domestic partners). Gay and lesbian couples experience many of the same joys and challenges as their heterosexual counterparts. **Cohabitation** is a living arrangement in which two adults who are not legally married have a sexual relationship. Cohabitation is often either a precursor to or substitute for marriage, or a testing ground for marital incompatibility. Individuals who never marry remain unmarried for a variety of reasons such as personal choice, professional/occupational demands, and caring for aging parents or other family members.

Chapter 5
Interpersonal Relationships:
Our Personal Network

Our Personal Network of Support

In addition to our immediate family, our convoy is also shaped by other interpersonal relationships during adulthood. In this chapter we focus on other members of our **personal convoy** including friends and members of our extended family such as grandparents. In addition, we focus more closely on the predictions made by the socioemotional selectivity theory (SST) in relation to friendships.

As you learned in Chapter 4, Carstensen's SST is a life span model that explains change and stability within the social support network. Moreover, SST views these changes as both functional and adaptive. SST suggests that one's perception of time is linked to the social goals that one pursues and the people one selects to fulfill those goals (Carstensen et al., 1999). As a person ages, the three central functions of social interaction are modified so that available social partners satisfy emotional needs (Carstensen et al., 1999). Two of the functions, development/ maintenance of identity and information gathering, decline with age as there is a decreased need for ego identity and information. The third function, which relates directly to the quality of social networks (emotional regulation), is maintained and assumes greater centrality with increasing age.

Social support can take several forms, including **emotional** or affective support, **instrumental** support, and **information** and advice (Sorkin & Rook, 2006). Emotional support includes sympathy and affection. Instrumental support involves the provision of goods and services. Advice or infor-

mational support is especially important in terms of seeking health and financial information. In late life, this support most often is provided by inner circle family and friends. A comprehensive view of the function of social interaction is particularly important in research on older adults, where social support may be a key determinant of successful aging (Krause, 2001; Lincoln et al., 2010).

However, not all social interactions with our network members are positive or beneficial. Although SST suggests that we prune unsatisfying relationships from our network, family members are rarely removed completely. Thus, some social relationships have a "cost" associated with them in terms of **negative interpersonal interactions**. Rook (2009) suggests that because interpersonal conflict arises even in the closest relationships, both negative and positive aspects of interpersonal ties should be examined in models of social interaction.

Negative Interpersonal Interactions

As you learned in Chapter 4 in the context of marital conflict, negative interactions may arise in our personal relationships. Evidence suggests that these negative interactions, although infrequent, may exert powerful negative effects on both physical and emotional well-being (Lincoln et al., 2010). In a study with more than 900 adults ages 65 to 90 years, Sorkin and Rook (2006) report that more than half had experienced a negative interaction during the previous month. The negative interaction occurred with an adult son or daughter (33%), spouse (15%), other family member (21%), or friends (23%). The most common type of negative interaction was receiving unwanted advice (47%). Other common negative interactions involved unsympathetic behavior, a failure to receive needed help, and rejection or neglect (Sorkin & Rook, 2006).

Gender Differences in Social Support

In addition to age-related changes, there are gender differences in social support and social interaction. Although causal mechanisms have not been identified, it is hypothesized that gender differences in social support are due to differences in socialization that begin in infancy and persist throughout adulthood and into late life (Mehta & Strough, 2009). Older women in particular have been socialized to develop, maintain, and utilize social support resources more so than men (Rook, 2009). There is also evidence that gender differences extend to the source and nature of emotional support received. Across the life span, women tend to be more intimate with their social contacts than do men. They also report more confidants than men, although men report having more social acquaintances (Rook).

That older women may rely more heavily on friends than men may be a function of the nature of friendship. Friendship ties tend to be more egalitarian and have lower expectations for tangible support (Rook, 1987; Sherman et al., 2000) than do family ties. Although women may have closer ties than do men, these ties are also more burdensome for women than they are for men (Moen, 2001).

Friendships

Friends compose an important part of our social network and can be important sources of support and affection for many adults. They can give our lives meaning and help give us guidance, support, and perspective on the problems and situations that we encounter. Among older adults, social support is a significant predictor of physical health, psychological well-being, and mortality (Charles et al., 1996; Krause, 2001). Differences in the nature of social interactions within one's network can contribute to differences in well-being. Specifically, friendships can contribute to a person's psychologi-

cal well-being (Carlson-Jones & Vaughn, 1990; Rowe & Kahn, 1998) and provide supportive exchanges such as sharing intimacies as well as giving and receiving assistance and emotional support. To illustrate, Williams and Solano (1983) have found that, among college students, feelings of loneliness are primarily determined by whether people with whom they had both intimate and meaningful friendships shared the same view about them. Larson, Mannell, and Zuzanek (1986) found that, among retired adults, friendships were an even greater source of satisfaction than were family members. Patrick, Cottrell and Barnes (2001) report that the positive effects of friendship may be especially pronounced for older women. Many factors contribute to the selection of our friends, including characteristics such as honesty, self-disclosure, understanding, kindness, sympathy, perceived similarity, proximity, gender, race, marital status, ethnicity, religion, occupation, and educational level. The relative importance of each of these factors will vary as a function of the type of friendship and the age of the individuals involved. Stevens-Long (1984) suggests that friendships among adults are defined in terms of **mutuality**, that is, mutual self-disclosure, mutual commitment, and equally mutual expectations of the relationship, termed **equity**. Thus, friendships can have an important socializing influence on us, and help to strengthen our personal convoy.

Friendship can also connote a wide range of dyadic relationships, including those with acquaintances with whom one has an occasional pleasant interaction, relationships with congenial companions with whom one spends quite a great deal of time in activities of mutual concern or interest, and close, intimate relationships with one or a few particularly valued persons whose company one seeks intermittently (Ainsworth, 1989). Thus, we must distinguish between categories of types of friends.

Interest-Related and Deep Friendships

Researchers suggest there are two major categories or types of friendships. These are **interest-**

related, and deep (or intimate) friendships. Interest-related friendships are based on some similar lifestyle, activities, or interests between the individuals, such as sports, pets, or hobbies. These are usually short-lived and entirely context specific (Ainsworth, 1989). Further, they are often quite superficial and do not provide emotional closeness (Carstensen, 1992). During the course of the life span, interactions with more casual social contacts, which provide fewer affective rewards, become less satisfying and frequent (Carstensen, 1992). Deep friendships are those in which there is an intimacy between the individuals going beyond an interest, that is, based on a feeling of personal closeness to another individual. Friendships of this type involve affectional bonds and endure despite circumstances that may make proximity or contact difficult (Ainsworth, 1989). As reported by Carstensen (1995), although interactions with close friends wax and wane over adulthood, feelings of emotional closeness remain stable. Further, while rates of interaction with acquaintances decline steadily from early adulthood on, interactions in significant relationships increase. That is, interactions with a core group of social partners, from whom people derive emotional gains, become more frequent, satisfying, and emotionally close over the adult life course (Carstensen, 1992). The presence of a "significant other" or confidant provides emotional support (Brody, Litvin, Hoffman, & Kleban, 1995), and these close relationships can help stabilize our convoy of support throughout our lives. Once deep friendships are formed, they tend to be permanent and are usually broken only by death.

Our Personal Network

Our interested-related friends and deep friends compose an important part of our personal network, and most people of all ages report, on average, a personal network of 8 to 11 members (Rowe & Kahn, 1998). The size of this personal network is relatively stable across the life span, although the composition of the network often changes over the course of life. These changes in the composition of our personal network are the result of factors such

as death, changes in jobs, retirement, change in residence, or moving to another city or state.

In this context, there are age and gender differences in friendship patterns (Johnson & Troll, 1994). People between the ages of 35 to 55 years tend to report having larger social networks than people who are older or younger (Rowe & Kahn, 1998). There is a great difference in the meaning of friendship to men and women. Women place more importance on friendships and engage in trusted relationships, while men usually have more superficial, less emotionally close relationships (Barer, 1994). Thus, women tend to cultivate more deep friendships (Johnson & Troll, 1994). Therefore, women have more extensive social networks and throughout the life span are better able than men to rally social supports to meet their needs. A recent study of older men and women found that for older women, receiving emotional support from one's friends was associated with increases in positive psychological well-being (Patrick, Cottrell, & Barnes, 2001). Although men tend to have a greater number of friendships overall, and are more likely to report having opposite-sex friendships, they are described as less close than those of women. Women usually have only other women as close friends (Antonucci, 1985; Mehta & Strough, 2009). In a comprehensive review, Mehta and Strough (2009) discuss the possible reasons that sex-segregation in friendship occurs throughout life, maintained by several factors including **behavioral compatibility** and **third-party determinants**. Behavioral compatibility relates to similar types of activities and energy levels. Third-party determinants relate to others' ideas about appropriate behavior. As a life span phenomenon, sex-segregation in friendship begins in infancy and childhood. These early experiences influence with whom a person plays and interacts, shaping one's communication and interaction style. These childhood experiences then influence our patterns of behavior in romantic relationships and in the workplace.

The importance of distinguishing between deep and interest-related friendships was highlighted by Roberto and Scott (1986), who studied the importance of **equity** in older people's satisfaction with friendship. Equity in a relationship refers to the perception that the costs of giving something to the friendship are at least equal to the rewards. These researchers found that older people who felt they were part of an inequitable relationship were less satisfied with that friendship. Where these relationships involved best friends, however, satisfaction was high regardless of their equity. Men were involved in more equitable friendships than were women and were more intimate and self-disclosing. Women had fewer but more diverse friendships, reported being more intensely involved, and were more concerned about equity. This study suggests that intimacy needs may be defined and fulfilled in different ways for older men and women. While this component of the personal convoy may differ greatly by gender, there are many positive effects of a confiding relationship on the quality of life for both older men and women (Connidis & Davies, 1990).

Intergenerational Relationships

Intergenerational relationships are interactions between individuals of different cohorts or generations. They most often occur within the context of the larger family or kinship network composed of aunts, uncles, cousins, grandparents, parents, and children. Intergenerational contacts can serve many functions for the person, as that person progresses through time and interacts with other family and generation members differently. Each member of the kinship network constantly renegotiates the interdependencies that bond and bind each of them together. There are many individual and cultural differences in intergenerational relationships, since family values and patterns clearly vary as a function of ethnicity and race.

Given increased longevity and better health, the likelihood of an aging yet healthy parent living with an adult child and grandchildren as a **multigenerational household** is increasing (Harrington, 1992, U.S. Bureau of the Census, 2000). However, relationships between family members of different gen-

Figure 5-1. Grandparenthood is a crucial dimension of intergenerational relationships.

erations tend to be better when the individuals do not live in the same household and everyone feels autonomous (Sussman, 1985). Children and adults enjoy visiting with their older relatives and vice versa, but they prefer to do it on a voluntary and mutual basis.

Studies indicate that one of six older adults lives with an adult child, and that this proportion is higher among disabled elderly persons (Spitze, Logan, & Robinson, 1992). As most caregivers are women, the burden of responsibility for an impaired family member usually falls on them. In this light, while women are quite willing to adjust family schedules and help with the costs of health care to help an elderly parent, they are generally not willing to adjust work schedules or share households. For both children and parents, receiving emotional support or help in money management is more acceptable than is receiving supplemental income.

Kinship Networks

Within the family kinship network, individuals usually give assistance to and interact and visit with the other members of the family (Silverstein, 2006). This assistance is provided by adult children and other members of the extended family such as cousins and grandparents. Older people are both recipients and donors of help, and, in general, emotional ties are strong between parents and children (Rossi & Rossi, 1990). When there are differences, parents usually report being closer to their children than their children are willing to acknowledge (Bond & Harvey, 1988); this is termed the **generational stake** (Bengtson et al., 1990).

The primary functions of families of all types, in all cultures and societies, are to provide care and socialization for the young and serve as a network of support, i.e., the convoy, and identity for individuals within the family or clan unit. For each individual within the family, there are specific roles and expected behaviors. When individuals have a mutual understanding regarding what these roles are, the family can perform its socializing and caregiving functions more effectively (Goldenberg & Goldenberg, 1991). All families, however they are specifically constituted, establish rules and communicate and negotiate differences between members to help them define themselves and cope with change (Goldenberg & Goldenberg, 1991). Family **solidarity** is a source of support and identity for many adults (Bengtson, Rosenthal, & Burton, 1990). The **solidarity model** is discussed in Box A.

Filial responsibility is the perceived obligation regarding the various types of services and social support that children should provide for their older parents. A study by Horne, Lowe, and Murry (1990) found that college students believed it likely they would care for one or both of their parents, and that they viewed such care with anxiety. These researchers also found that women exhibited more anxiety than men regarding the provision of such care (see Box B). Most older adults prefer to turn to relatives, rather than to friends, neighbors, or formal sources, when they need assistance (Thomas, 1993). Again, this can lead to role conflict, financial strain, and fatigue in the caregiver. Finley, Roberts, and Banahan (1988) found that filial responsibility in caring for an aging parent varied by gender of the child, maternal/paternal kinship status of the parent, how far away the parent lived from the child, and how much role conflict children felt about caregiving, particularly for an in-law or parent. However, contemporary patterns of social change suggest that such reliance on family support could become problematic in the future. Trends toward smaller families and women's increased labor force participation suggest that there will be fewer "child hours" available for parent care in the future (Thomas, 1993). Given these changes in the demographics of the family, health care, and longevity, providing care for an elder member of the family is now a typical experience (Pearlin, Mullan, Semple, & Skaff, 1990; Pearlin, Pohli, & McLaughlin, 2001).

Filial responsibility continues to serve as an ideal in many Asian cultures, where it is based on the values of respect, responsibility, family harmony, and sacrifice (Sung, 1990). In filial responsibility, ideally there are "no strings attached." Help is given freely, rather than out of a sense of obligation. Overall, it appears that the quality of help is more important than the quantity of help (McCullock, 1990). However, stress related to filial responsibility and other factors can lead to atypical interpersonal relations. One of these can be elder abuse.

Elder Abuse

Many states have passed mandatory reporting laws for **elder abuse**, and instituted protective service programs that work with aged persons (Wolf & Pillmer, 1994). Shiferaw, Millelmark, Wofford, Anderson, Walls, and Rohrer (1994) consider three categories of behaviors as defining elder abuse, including physical and emotional abuse, exploitation, and neglect. A recent study shows that more than 11% of older Americans report experiencing at least one form of maltreatment during the past year. Although correlates of each form of mistreatment varied somewhat, the lack of social support emerged

Box A

The Solidarity Model and Aging Parents

Negative stereotypes about older families persist. It is not uncommon to characterize older adults as "greedy geezers," who place huge burdens on both the family and society (Pillemar & Suitor, 1998). Decades of empirical study, however, reveal a picture of families in which aging parents play a key role. Most of this research has been guided by the **solidarity model** proposed by Bengtson & Schrader (1982). This model examines intergenerational relations in terms of normative solidarity, affectional solidarity, consensual solidarity, associational solidarity, functional solidarity, and structural solidarity.

Normative solidarity refers to perceptions that one is experiencing usual or typical life events. Indeed, the phenomenon of aging parents is normative. Most older Americans are parents, with 75-80% having at least one living child (Hagestad, 1995). This, coupled with increased longevity, increases the likelihood of living in a four- or five-generation family. Thus, one can simultaneously have aging parents and be an aging parent.

Affectional solidarity refers to shared feelings of esteem and affection. The parent-child bond is the strongest familial bond (outside of marriage) and continues to be important to both children and aging parents (Aday, 1997). However, there is some evidence that these relations may be more important to aging parents, giving rise to the generational stake hypothesis (Pillemar & Suitor, 1998).

Consensual solidarity refers to the degree to which generations agree about social, cultural, and political views (Aday, 1997). We know that attitudes and expectations are in flux currently, making it difficult to adequately gauge the effects of consensual solidarity (Cutler & Hendricks, 2001). Some research suggests that this aspect of intergenerational solidarity is especially important for immigrants and first-generation families (Aday, 1997; Luescher & Pillemar, 1998).

Associational solidarity is indexed by the frequency of contact between the generations. Associational solidarity is high, with 80% of older parents having some contact with an adult child at least once a week (Hagestad, 1995).

Functional solidarity, the exchange of goods and services, flows bidirectionally across contiguous generations. Aging parents may provide child care, financial assistance, and advice; adult children may provide help with household chores, home repairs, and personal care (Bengtson, Rosenthal, & Burton, 1996). In late life, parents tend to receive more than they give (Cutler & Hendricks, 2001). When aging parents require assistance, it is family members who provide the bulk of that care. Reciprocity, however, continues to characterize relations with aging parents. Even when aging parents are receiving assistance from their adult children, older parents may continue to provide a range of support, including emotional, and tangible support in such areas as child care and household tasks (Cutler & Hendricks, 2001; Ingersoll-Dayton, 2001).

Structural solidarity focuses on living arrangements. Throughout American history, and continuing through today, separate but proximate households is the norm (Hareven, 2001). Only about 20% of the noninstitutionalized elderly reside in households in which two or more generations are present (Coward & Netzer, 1995). As one might expect, the percentage of older adults co-residing with a younger generation increases dramatically with advanced age, with nearly half of adults over age 90 who live in the community sharing a residence with at least one younger generation. African-Americans are more likely than European-Americans to live in multigenerational homes (Coward & Netzer, 1995).

Box B

Caregiver Stress

For older adults, the caregivers in order of choice are spouses, then daughters, daughters-in-law, and other relatives. Services provided by family members include everything from housing, transportation, and financial assistance to the more basic personal care services such as personal care services, e.g., bathing, dressing (Knight & Qualls, 1995). Research (e.g., Rosenthal, Martin-Matthews, & Matthews, 1996) indicates that women have traditionally cared for elderly parents in need. In addition to facing the demands of their parents, parents-in-law, husbands, children, and grandchildren, these women also must deal with the demands of their jobs. These multiple demands can lead to stress related to role conflict and financial matters, which can have psychological, social, and physical effects for the caregiver.

However, there are individual differences in the perception and significance of stressors such as caregiving (Krause, 1994). For example, Spitze, Logan, Joseph, & Lee (1993) found that giving help to parents increases men's distress, while giving help to adult children enhances women's well-being. Thus, Spitze et al. (1993) suggest that women are unaffected by the multiplicity of roles while, for men, there is strain from conflicting roles.

Family caregivers of cognitively impaired older people feel strained and burdened by the demands of caregiving (Novak & Guest, 1992). Caregivers of elderly relatives with serious disabilities, such as dementia, report elevated rates of depressive symptoms, sleep disorders, social isolation, lowered morale, and physical disorders (Knight & Qualls, 1995).

as one of the strongest correlates for each type of mistreatment (Acierno et al., 2010).

Abuse is willful infliction of physical pain, injury, or mental anguish; unreasonable confinement; or the willful deprivation of services which are necessary to maintain a care recipient's mental and physical health. **Physical abuse** involves acts of violence that may result in pain, injury, impairment, or disease, e.g., pushing, striking, slapping, force-feeding, improper use of physical restraints or medications. **Psychological abuse** is conduct that causes mental anguish in an older person, e.g., verbal berating, harassment, or intimidation; isolating the person from family, friends, or activities; threats of punishment or deprivation. Generally speaking, persons are less likely to recognize psychological abuse than physical abuse (Childs, Hayslip, Radika, & Reinberg, 2000).

Exploitation is the illegal or improper use of disabled adults or their resources for another's profit or advantage, for example, stealing money or pos-

sessions or coercing the older person into signing contracts (Childs et al., 2000). Violation of one's rights occurs when caretakers ignore the older person's rights and capacity to make decisions for themselves, such as forced placement in a nursing home or denying the older person the right to privacy. A recent study suggests that financial exploitation is the most common form of elder abuse, with approximately 5% of older adults being financially exploited each year (Acierno et al., 2010).

Neglect is the lack of services necessary to maintain mental and physical health of a disabled person living alone or not able to render self-care. **Physical neglect** is characterized by a failure of the caregiver to provide the goods or services that are necessary for optimal functioning or to avoid harm, e.g., withholding of health care, adequate meals, failure to provide physical aids such as eyeglasses, hearing aids, or false teeth. **Psychological neglect** is the failure to provide a dependent elderly person with social stimulation, e.g., leaving the older per-

---

Box C

The Sandwich Generation

Middle-aged individuals are sometimes referred to as the sandwich generation. This term has two levels of meanings. Structurally, it refers to middle-generation cohorts sandwiched between older and younger cohorts in the population. Individually, it refers to simultaneously having relations with adult children, as they enter and adjust to adulthood, and aging parents, as they deal with issues of later life. Members of this sandwich generation are presumed to face potential stresses from the combined and competing demands of their intergenerational roles as parents and children (Ingersoll-Dayton, 2001).

Despite the attention that this construct has drawn in the popular press, Pearlin, Pioli, and McLaughlin (2001) submit that the notion of a sandwich generation may be misleading. First, many of the conflicts middle-aged adults report are due to competing roles in general, not competing generations. Second, conflicting obligations or "sandwiching" can be experienced by anyone who assumes the caregiving role. Research in this area must be viewed in the larger context of generational reciprocity across the life span. It is only in later life, after age 85, that older adults begin to receive more support than they provide (Uhlenberg, 1996). However, even though relatively few middle-aged adults are actively involved in assisting their children and parents, either individually or in combination, at any particular time (Bengtson et al., 1996), there may be substantial burdens for those who are.

---

son alone for long periods of time, failing to provide companionship, changes in routine, news, or information. Financial or material neglect is failure to use available funds and resources necessary to sustain or restore the health and well-being of the older adult.

Typically, abusers are relatives of the victim or the caregiver of the victim (Hwalek, Neale, Goodrich, & Quinn, 1991), such as the spouse or grandchildren (Shiferaw et al., 1994). Physical or psychological abuse may also result from stress and frustration stemming from the daily demands on an adult child's physical, psychological, and financial resources in caring for an aging parent. Other contributing factors include financial dependency on the victim and substance abuse (Hwalek et al., 1991). Feeling guilty about not caring for a parent and having a history of violence are also critical factors in the abuse of the elderly (Costa, 1984).

The American Medical Association (1992) proposed four theories on the causes of elder abuse. **Transgenerational** or **family violence** theory asserts that violence is a learned behavior. Individu-

als who have witnessed or have been victims of family violence may deal with their problems in a like manner. **Psychopathology** theory suggests that some form of psychopathology of the caretaker, such as alcoholism, drug addiction, or severe emotional problems predispose the caretaker to violence. **Disability** theory suggests that some form of medical, functional, or cognitive disability of the elderly person increases dependency and vulnerability, and therefore the risk for abuse or neglect. **Dependency** theory suggests that the caretaker may be dependent, especially economically, on the older adult, which leads to resentment and, when combined with other factors, may predispose to mistreatment.

Cultural Variations in the Kinship Network

Race and ethnicity have a very powerful influence on intergenerational relations. Specifically, there are ethnic or racial norms regarding familial obligations or expectations. Many elders from other countries still have a strong sense of ethnic identity and therefore have different worldviews, norms, and beliefs that may have impact on their adjustment to

Box D

Aging Parents as Caregivers

Although most parents look forward to launching their sons and daughters into an independent adulthood, some adult children are not able to live independently. Parents of adults with chronic disabilities may experience an extended parenting in which the roles they enacted during early childhood continue into that child's adulthood. When sons and daughters experience such lifelong disabilities, it is often aging parents who provide assistance. Two types of chronic disabilities are associated with this extended parenting: developmental disabilities, including mental retardation, and chronic mental illness, such as schizophrenia.

Providing continued parental assistance to an adult son or daughter with a chronic disability is associated with a host of satisfactions and burdens for aging parents, especially aging mothers (Patrick & Hayden, 1999). Mothers of adults with chronic mental illness report particularly high levels of caregiving burden, even when they do not co-reside with their son or daughter. Even in these situations, however, the parent-child relation is characterized by high levels of affectional and functional solidarity (Patrick & Hayden, 1999). As in other aging families, the flow of assistance between aging parents and adult children with disabilities is often bidirectional. Greenberg (1995) report that most mothers of adults with serious mental illness receive help from their adult offspring at least "some of the time."

old age as well as on their ability to cope with frailty and chronic life stresses (Mui, 1993).

Extended families represent a significant proportion of families in the African-American community (Wilson, 1989). The African-American extended family serves as a mechanism for meeting the physical, emotional, and economic needs of individuals at all age levels (Sussman, 1985). There is a strong sense of familial obligation that underlies this family support network (Wilson, 1989). Research suggests that Hispanic elders consistently have higher levels of interaction and support from their children than do either African-American or white elders (Mui, 1993). Similar findings were reported by Markides (1983), who reported that Mexican-American and African-American families tend to provide more contact and support in the care of aged family members than do white families. Family may be a particular strong source of support among Latino and African-Americans, compared to whites (Jackson, Antonucci, & Gibson, 1990). Such support may help aged people maintain an independent lifestyle to avoid nursing home

care, but increased contact with one's family may not always be positive for all family members. However, within the extended African- American family network, elderly persons are usually the donors of services rather than receivers (Wilson, 1989).

In view of the diversity among older minority individuals, one must be especially cautious about generalizing about kinship networks among ethnic and racial groups. Each racial or ethnic group responds differently to available social services, holds different values regarding relationships with whites, and interacts differently with service providers who might aid the family in caring for an elderly member.

Check Your Learning 5-1

Identify the following terms and concepts:

Equity
Mutuality
Deep (intimate) friends
Sex-segregation in friendship

Figure 5-2. A sense of the family constitutes an important component of many adults' identity.

Intergenerational relationships
Negative interpersonal interactions
Extended family
Interested related friends
Personal network
Kinship network
Elder abuse
Filial responsibility
Filial maturity
Generational stake

• What factors contribute to our selection of friends?

• Who composes the kinship network? What is the function of the kinship network?

• Describe and discuss racial and ethnic influences on intergenerational relationships within the extended family.

Widowhood

Numerous researchers have demonstrated that the death of a spouse is the most difficult and disrup-

tive role transition that an individual may confront throughout the life course (Bradsher, Longino, Jackson, & Zimmerman, 1992). The death of a loved one is a severe psychological blow and disruptive to daily life, causing grief, depression, tension, anxiety, confusion, and a profound sense of loss (Faberow, Gallagher-Thompson, Gilewski, & Thompson, 1991). While most of us associate widowhood with later life, the death of a spouse can occur at any time during the life cycle. There is a fairly high predominance of widows compared to widowers in old age, for two primary reasons: (1) there is a difference in life expectancy between males and females in favor of females; (2) as is the social custom in most cultures, men tend to marry women younger than themselves.

The widowhood event is not an uncommon life experience among persons who have lived to a very old age, especially among women. By age 75, about 25% of all males and 67% of all females are widowed (Bradsher et al., 1992). Generally, men do not usually become widowers until after age 85. Thus, widowhood is considerably less common for men.

Emotional reactions to widowhood are complex and can include denial, anger, relief, and guilt. Widowhood can, under some conditions, predispose people to serious illness or death, due to isolation from others, loneliness, or preexisting health difficulties (see Chapter 12). Bereavement is often overlooked as a possible cause of disease in elderly persons and as a factor that aggravates preexisting disorders. Thus, it can produce physical effects that in older persons may be passed off as normal age changes (see Chapter 12). To illustrate, Rosenbloom and Whittington (1993) found that widowhood produces negative effects on eating behaviors generally, and significantly reduces both the overall and specific nutrient quality of the older widowed person's diet.

Persons who are widowed are **vulnerable** in many ways and need active support, not only immediately after the death but also for many months afterward. In most cases, the grief that accompanies the death of one's spouse is very personal and intense. Resolution of these feelings may require a great deal of time and support; and for some, it is never resolved (see Chapter 12).

Becoming a widow or widower seems to cause many different types of problems. For example, Thompson, Breckenridge, Gallagher, and Peterson (1984) investigated multiple indices of self-perceived physical health for older widows and widowers, ranging in age from 55 to 83 years, 2 months following the loss of their spouse and compared them to a nonbereaved control group. Results indicated that widows and widowers reported significantly more recently developed or worsened illnesses, greater use of medications, and poorer general health ratings. These differences were independent of gender and socioeconomic level. Further, Thompson, Gallagher-Thompson, Futterman, Gilewski and Peterson (1991) observed that the experience of grief persists for at least 30 months in both older men and women who have lost their spouse. Also, women reported more distress than men regardless of bereavement status.

Widows are better able than widowers to develop and sustain intimate relationships; they tend

Figure 5-3. Reactions to widowhood can be quite varied.

to form confidante relationships with other widowed women, whereas widowed men, who had relied on their wives for their emotional needs, are often left with no one (Barer, 1994). Most men do not expect to outlive their wives, and thus they are not generally prepared for the bereavement process (Barer, 1994). Therefore, since widowhood differentially affects friendship patterns, women are less isolated than men (Johnson & Troll, 1994). Also, widows spend more time and provide more help to family and friends than do older married women (Gallagher & Gerstel, 1993). Widows who experience declines in their standard of living may have to return to work for economic reasons (Staats, Partlo, Armstrong-Stassen, & Plimpton, 1994). While widowhood later in life is quite stressful, conjugal bereavement in young adults also leaves men and women emotionally scarred (Allen & Hayslip, 2000). A unique aspect of widowhood in young adulthood is that the death of one's spouse is typically unanticipated, whether accidental or due to illness.

Being widowed is so common, especially during late middle age and old age, that society has ascribed a variety of roles to widows (Lopata, 1975). For some women, the role of a widow is to work to keep the family together and keep the husband's memory alive; they are not supposed to be interested in other men. For women whose lives have evolved more independently of their husbands all along, role changes are less drastic, although these women are of course still lonely and grieve for their husbands. It is important to recognize that women adjust to the loss of their husbands in idiosyncratic ways, depending on age at widowhood, health, socioeconomic level, race, and ethnicity (Bengtson et al., 1990). Comparatively speaking, we still know very little regarding widowers, though there is a growing awareness among researchers that the resilience of older widows may have been underestimated (see Chapter 12).

Remarriage among Widows and Widowers

With increasing age, the tendency to remarry following the death of a spouse decreases, although remarrying can be an effective coping mechanism for dealing with the problems and concerns of widowhood (Gentry & Shulman, 1988). Also, the tendency to remarry following the death of a spouse is highly related to the age and gender of the widowed individual. Widowers are more likely than widows to remarry, especially with advancing age. For a variety of reasons, less than 20% of males over age 65 remarry, and less than 5% of females over age 55 remarry. First, given gender differences in life expectancy, there are simply fewer available males with advancing age. Also, females tend to be in better health than males with advancing age; thus widows may not want to risk losing another spouse to a health-related problem. In contrast, older males are usually unprepared or inexperienced in the skills required to live alone, such as cooking, cleaning, and grocery shopping. When individuals do marry following the death of a

spouse, especially after age 50, they tend to marry someone they have known for a long time and to do so for companionship and affection (Bengtson et al., 1990, Connidis, 2010).

Grandparenting

Being a grandparent is generally viewed as a developmental task of middle or late adulthood. For many, having a grandchild may be considered a symbol or marker of middle age or getting old. Individuals who are overly concerned with being considered young may react with anxiety when others know they are old enough to be grandparents. Because life expectancy has increased, the chances of becoming a grandparent have also increased. However, current demographics suggest that there is great diversity in the age and social status of grandparents (Kornhaber, 1996). The once-popular image of the grandparent as a kindly, elderly person in a rocking chair is often inaccurate. Grandparents are more likely to be men and women who are much younger, employed, and even have adult children still at home! This same individual may also be caring for a mother or father who is quite old. Some people become grandparents in their 30s and 40s while others do not become grandparents until their 60s or 70s. Because of this variability, it is not surprising to find that grandparenting is a **tenuous role**, having no clear criteria for what constitutes appropriate behavior (Rosow, 1985). It is for this reason that grandparenting is largely an individual experience.

The grandparent-grandchild relationship may now extend over 20 years (Whitbeck, Simons, & Conger, 1991). However, this interaction is likely to be different when grandchildren are little and grandparents are in good health than when grandchildren are adolescents and grandparents are frail.

Factors that Affect Grandparenting

Whether one finds grandparenting satisfying depends on numerous factors, such as race and ethnicity; gender; age of the grandchild; number of grandchildren; geographic distance; the age, health,

Adults Speak

Remarriage after Widowhood: Harold and Nancy

Harold is 67 years old, and has been a university professor for over 30 years. He retired 2 years ago and now teaches part-time. He is outgoing and friendly, is in good health, and takes care of himself. He was married to Chris, whom he met in college, for 43 years. Together, they raised two sons and a daughter, all of whom are happy, well-adjusted adults. Harold is the proud grandfather of two boys.

For the last 7 years of their marriage, Chris suffered from Parkinson's disease, which eventually left her nearly helpless and bedridden. Harold cared for his wife until the day she died. Chris's death hit Harold very hard. Despite the loving support of his family, he took long drives by himself and often ate out alone.

Nancy is 68 years old and has three children and four grandchildren. She divorced her husband 18 years ago and did not look forward to getting married again. In fact, she enjoyed being single. She is a fun loving, kind person who has a wonderful sense of humor and quite obviously enjoys other people.

Harold and Nancy have known one another since high school, and in fact were sweethearts during their high school days together. Harold played on the football team and had lots of girlfriends, while Nancy did well in school, and was very attractive and popular. Because they grew up together, they had many friends in common, and saw each other at the yearly high school reunion. They were good friends despite the fact they went their separate ways after high school. Nancy and Chris also knew one another well.

One year after Chris died, Nancy and Harold met at the annual high school reunion. They were dancing to the Platters, having a good time, and fell in love. Harold insists that Nancy locked the seat belt in her car so that she could kiss him, but Nancy denies this. Several months later, they got married. They had a small wedding with their immediate families there to offer love, support, and good wishes.

Nancy describes Harold as fun loving, with a wonderful sense of humor. She feels quite lucky to have him, and says, "We could do nothing and have a good time." She thought about marriage carefully, not wanting to be disappointed and hoping that their relationship would not be changed by getting married. "I was afraid things would change, as they might for other people who don't know one another so well."

Harold, too, was somewhat concerned: "I was afraid my children would not approve."

Having known one another for over 50 years has proven to be a big advantage, as has having finished raising their children. Nancy says, "We just have fun, and he's the same all the time. He'll start a conversation at 2 A.M. and keep you in stitches. We don't have the problems some young people have, such as paying for a house and a car, raising children, and worrying about money."

Harold and Nancy both feel very strongly about how happy they are and expect to be. "We can both be ourselves, and we don't feel censored or judged at all. You know, it's so good it's scary. We just don't have to work at it, yet we both have our individual interests." Harold enjoys woodworking and playing golf, and Nancy enjoys playing bridge.

It is clear that marrying Harold has been wonderful for Nancy, who spent many years single. "It's been lots better than I ever dreamed it could be. He could make any woman happy."

For Harold, marrying Nancy meant an end to days of feeling very lonely and somewhat lost without Chris. "I just never thought my life would turn out this way."

and quality of the relationship between the grand-parent and their adult child; and marital status of the grandparent (Kornhaber, 1996; Thomas, 1986). Positive yet voluntary relationships with grandchildren and a close relationship with the adult child often contribute to how grandparents perceive their role (Johnson, 1988; Hayslip & Page, 2011; Shore & Hayslip, 1994).

Race and **ethnicity** affect grandparenting styles, values, and roles (Kornhaber, 1996). In such cases, grandparents may serve in the roles of the family historian or living ancestor who teaches the grandchildren ethnic traditions, experience, culture, and history. To illustrate, Cherlin and Furstenberg (1986) and Pearson, Hunter, Ensminger, and Kellam (1990) investigated differences in grandparenting styles between African-Americans and whites and noted a variety of differences. For example, African-American grandparents had almost twice the degree of involvement with their grandchildren than whites. Compared to whites, African-American grandmothers' parenting involvement was substantial, especially in the areas of control, support, and punishment. Schmidt and Padilla (1983) studied Mexican-Americans, African Americans, and whites, and found that the Mexican-Americans belonged to larger, more multigenerational families, reported higher satisfactions relating to their grandchildren, and had a greater degree of intergenerational contact.

Gender also affects grandparenting roles and styles (Kornhaber, 1996). Traditionally, the grandfather is viewed as the head of the family, while the grandmother is viewed as its heart (Rosenthal & Marshall, 1983). Research indicates that grandmothers anticipate the role earlier than grandfathers and get involved sooner. Further, children tend to favor grandmothers over grandfathers. Roberto and Stroes (1992) found that grandchildren reported that while grandparents were influential in teaching and modeling values such as sexual, religious, and political, they also reported stronger relationships with grandmothers than grandfathers. Also, grandmothers are more likely to have frequent contact with grandchildren (Uhlenberg & Hammill, 1998;

Reitzes & Mutran, 2004). Finally, in a study of high school students, Shea (1988) found that students had more contact with maternal grandparents, and that contact with the maternal grandmother received the most favorable evaluations.

Age of the grandchild is a significant factor in the activities and roles played by grandparents (Kornhaber, 1996). That is, grandparents play specific and different roles at different times in their grandchildren's lives. Specifically, when the grandchildren are young, the grandparent roles focus primarily on direct care and involvement, such as play and child care. During adolescence, the grandparent roles revolve around listening, supporting, and serving as the family historian.

Number of grandchildren in addition to age also plays a significant role in the amount of contact with grandparents (Uhlenberg & Hammill, 1998). As would be expected, as the number of grandchildren increases, the frequency of contact with each grandchild decreases, because one's time and resources are limited.

Geographic distance is the strongest predictor of whether grandparents will have frequent or infrequent contact with grandchildren (Uhlenberg & Hammill, 1998). The closer the geographic distance, the more opportunity for interaction. Thus, geographic distance significantly influences opportunity for contact between grandparents and grandchildren. Overall, most grandparents would like to maintain contact with their grandchildren. Physical proximity facilitates this interaction and distance decreases it. As discussed later in this chapter, newer technologies are helping long-distance grandparents to maintain relationships with their grandchildren and other family members.

Age of the grandparent also plays a significant role in contact with grandchildren and the types of activities grandparents engage in with their grandchildren (Kornhaber, 1996). The age when one becomes a grandparent can greatly influence satisfaction in the role. As the age of the grandparents increases, the less able they are to get involved with "active physical" interactions with the grandchildren, e.g., active playing and sports. Instead, with increasing age, grandparents provide more emotional support or advice to the grandchildren.

Health of the grandparent is an obvious factor in determining the contact and types of interactions with grandchildren. It can affect one's vitality, types of activities engaged in, and emotional readiness to be a grandparent (Kornhaber, 1996).

The **quality of the relationship between the grandparent and the adult child** also affects the grandparent role. Research (e.g., Uhlenberg & Hammill, 1998) consistently demonstrates that the quality of the relationship between a grandparent and child affects the quantity of contact between the grandparent and that set of grandchildren. That is, the adult child serves as a gatekeeper for the grandparent-grandchild relationship. Furthermore, it makes a difference if grandparents are linked to a set of grandchildren through a daughter or a son. Maternal grandparents are more likely than paternal grandparents to have frequent contact with grandchildren (Uhlenberg & Hammill, 1998).

The **grandparent's marital status** has a significant effect on the frequency of contact with grandchildren, especially for grandfathers (Uhlenberg & Hammill, 1998). For example, divorced older men have far less contact with their adult children and grandchildren than married ones. Further, widowed grandfathers may have less contact with their grandchildren than married ones because they lack a wife to facilitate the maintenance of family ties. Marital status of grandmothers also may be significant because a lack of a spouse may weaken ties to children and grandchildren, or reduce resources needed for traveling to visit the grandchildren. Overall, for both grandmothers and grandfathers, the ordering from most to least likely to have frequent contact with grandchildren is married, widowed, remarried, and divorced. Finally, divorce presents particular problems for grandparents, especially following remarriage. When adult parents remarry, stepgrandparenting often creates more problems than satisfaction. Because grandparents have no biological ties to their "new" grandchildren, their role in a reconstituted family is often ambiguous and stressful, which complicates the

difficulties blended families already face (Novatney, 1990).

Meanings of Grandparenthood

Whether grandparenting is satisfying seems to be principally dependent upon the relationship with one's adult children (Cherlin & Furstenberg, 1986). If that relationship is positive and lacks conflict, the grandparent role is likely to be more fulfilling to all involved. Conflicts often pertain to three issues— responsibility for raising the grandchildren, relations with adult children, and feelings about being a grandparent (Hayslip, Shore, Henderson, & Lambert, 1998; Thomas, 1990).

Grandparenthood means different things to different people. How one perceives this role most likely influences one's style of grandparenting. Meaning is also affected by the quality of one's re-

Figure 5-4. Grandparents can serve as role models and emotional companions for their grandchildren.

lationship with the grandchildren. Thomas and King (1990) found that both white and minority young adult grandchildren believed their grandparents were good role models and good sources of advice and support. Indeed, it is common to find that grandparents and grandchildren both give and receive tangible material and emotional support to one another (Bengtson et al., 1990). This type of mutually satisfying, reciprocal relationship strengthens one's convoy of support.

Other satisfactions derived from the grandparent role include making one feel younger, carrying on the family line, and providing things for the grandchildren that they were unable to provide their children. Overall, grandparenting is an individual experience, with a diversity of opinions held by individuals regarding their roles as grandparents. Thus, on one end of the spectrum we have individuals who are totally immersed in the grandparent role and the lives of their grandchildren, in the middle are individuals who look at grandparenting as only one of many roles that they occupy, and on the other extreme end of the spectrum are individuals who for a variety of reasons have little interest in grandparenting or contact with their grandchildren.

Styles of Grandparenting

The literature on grandparenting suggests that there are many **styles** or **types** of grandparenting, and that these are affected by a number of individual, environmental, and socioeconomic factors (see Table 5-1). One of the primary factors that distinguishes among the styles of grandparenting is the authority and control over the grandchildren. On one end of this continuum is the **surrogate parent**, who will exercise authority and control over the grandchildren both in the presence and absence of the parent(s). For example, at the dinner table, if the grandchild were to engage in a behavior that was considered inappropriate, the grandparent will reprimand the grandchild. At the other extreme is the **fun-seeker** grandparent who does not exercise any authority and control over the grandchildren. In the middle of the continuum are the **formal, res-**ervoir of family wisdom**, and **distant figure** styles who will exercise authority and control over the grandchildren only in the absence of the parent, or on the authority of the parent.

The **distant figure** style is very common due to society's mobility. It is important to note that although this type of grandparent may be distant in terms of physical proximity to the grandchildren, they may be close emotionally. Further, when visiting with the grandchildren, the distant figure grandparent may take on characteristics of the other types of grandparenting styles such as the fun-seeker or surrogate. Overall, the styles of grandparenting vary over time and situations for the grandparent. Further, there are vast individual differences and diversity regarding grandparenting styles.

Given the above discussion, it is not surprising to find the role of grandfather is viewed as less salient than that of grandmother, and because of this, there is very little research regarding the significance and function of grandfathers (Kivett, 1991). However, grandfathers make unique contributions to the family network such as reservoirs of wisdom and role models for those not regularly exposed to male family members (Kivett, 1991; Thomas, 1989).

Generally, maternal grandmothers and paternal grandfathers tended to display closeness and warmth toward their grandchildren. In contrast, maternal grandfathers and paternal grandmothers appeared to manifest the most negative attitudes toward their grandchildren. Thomas (1986) found grandmothers to be more satisfied with their role than grandfathers. This was perhaps due to their relative familiarity with intimate family relationships, having been principally responsible for raising their own children. Men who expressed satisfaction were older, had active relationships with their young grandchildren, and were happy with their involvement in the tasks of child rearing.

Grandparent-Grandchild Contact

Information on grandparent-grandchildren contact is important, since most of our contact with and attitudes toward older adults are partly influ-

Table 5-1

Styles of Grandparenting

Type of Grandparent	Characteristics
Formal	Highly interested in their grandchildren. Although they often care for their grandchildren, they are not viewed as primary or surrogate caretakers. Have authority and control over the children in the absence of the parents.
Fun-seeker	Involved in playful, frequent relationships with their grandchildren. Do not exert any control or authority over grandchildren. View being with their grandchildren as a leisure activity.
Surrogate parent	Primary caretakers of the children. Active involvement in raising the children. Enforce family discipline and rules. Very common.
Reservoir of family wisdom	Provide special skills, resources, and knowledge to younger members of the family. Comparatively rare and usually associated with the grandfather.
Distant figure	Contacts are infrequent, usually on holidays. Perceived as benevolent and emotionally involved, yet remote in terms of geographical distance.

Adapted from: Cherlin & Furstenberg, 1986; Neugarten & Weinstein, 1964; Tomlin & Passman, 1991.

enced by our interactions with grandparents or other elderly relatives. For example, Kennedy (1990) reported that college students' perceptions of grandparent and grandchild roles were generally positive, indicating affection and respect for grandparents. African-American students saw the grandparent role as a more active one in the family than did white students, reflecting racial and cultural differences in perceptions of the extended family network (Bengtson et al., 1990).

Kivett (1991) in a study of African-American and white grandfathers found that: (1) the grandfather role is more affectionate than functional among both older African-American and white men; (2) there is a higher centrality of the grandfather role among older African-American than older white men, which indicates that such African-Americans tend to be more involved in the lives of their grandchildren than whites; (3) social and dependency factors, other than proximity, are of little relative importance in the grandfather-grandchild relationship; (4) as a group, African-American men show greater variation in both the structural (number of grandchildren) and functional dimensions (association and helping) of the role. This variability appears to be related to: (a) the African-American family's flexibility in expanding and contracting sources to meet the specialized needs of various extended family members, and, (b) the flexibility of African-American male family roles.

Overall, grandparenthood can indeed be satisfying to those who value the role, who have the opportunity to interact with grandchildren, and whose relationships with their adult children are positive. As Troll (1980) has noted, the real value of grandparenthood for many middle-aged and elderly adults is that it reinforces the sense of family. Wilcoxon (1987) terms such people **significant grandparents**. That is, these grandparents derive a great deal of satisfaction in knowing that the "family theme" is being carried on by their grandchildren, even if their contacts with their adult children and their children's children are minimal. However, there is a preference for fulfilling voluntary, nonparental relationships with grandchildren among grandparents (Shore & Hayslip, 1994). Simply being older does not guarantee that one will derive a great deal of personal satisfaction from having grandchildren. As with many things in life, the grandparent role must be actively shaped if it is to have meaning for both grandchild and grandparent.

Custodial Grandparents

Due to the increasing number of single-parent families and families where both parents work outside the home, the surrogate parent style (Cherlin & Furstenberg, 1986) is becoming more common. Surrogate parent grandparents are often the primary caretakers of the children. For many grandparents, caring for a grandchild after an adult child has divorced is a full-time job. Such grandparents are termed **custodial grandparents** (Hayslip & Goldberg-Glen, 2000; Hayslip & Page, 2011; Shore & Hayslip, 1994).

A growing number of children depend on their grandparents for their primary care (Hayslip & Patrick, 2003; Kornhaber, 1996). For example, in 1970, approximately 2.2 million children under the age of 18 lived in grandparent-headed households, and by 1993 this number has grown to 3.4 million, and in 1996 to approximately 5 million. This number grew by 16% from 2000-2008, and indeed by 6% alone from 2007-2008, based upon 2008 Census Bureau data (Grandparents raising kids: Rising

number, rising stress, *Dallas Morning News*, September 1, 2010).

Given the diversity in which traditional grandparents define their roles, it is not surprising that caregiving grandparents are quite diverse with regard to cultural background, race and ethnicity, gender, the reasons for assuming care of their grandchildren, health status, and age (Hayslip & Patrick, 2003). Moreover, such grandparents may need to reactivate long-unused parenting skills, and may need more support from others in raising their grandchildren and coping with the demands of this newly acquired role (Hayslip & Kaminski, 2005). They consequently may especially benefit from support groups, where information, mutual support, and a sense of commonality can be fostered (Smith, 2003).

Technology and Social Support

Adults over age 50 years are the fastest growing group of technology consumers (AARP, 2009). The most common uses among this group include social support, leisure and entertainment, and information-seeking, including health information (Wagner, Hassanein, & Head, 2010). Rather than replacing face-to-face or telephone contact, **computer-mediated communication** resulted in a net increase in contact with members of one's social support network. In one survey of internet users, 66% of the older adults said that technology increased their contact with friends and family; 83% reported no change in in-person contact and 65% reported no change in telephone contact (Sum, Mathews, Pourhasem, & Hughes, 2009). Due to geographic differences, computer-mediated communication may facilitate contact across generations. Among older adults who relocated to a retirement community four years previously, contact with friends and family via email occurred 15 to 21 times per month for older men and women, respectively (Waldron et al., 2005). In addition to helping older adults maintain their social support networks, support programs are being implemented with family caregivers, as well (Kinney & Cart, 2006).

Box E

Custodial Grandparents

For a variety of reasons such as physical abuse and divorce, many grandparents have had to assume full-time custodial responsibility for their grandchildren, even though they do not have legal custody (Hayslip & Page, 2011). In a study of 200 custodial and traditional grandparents, Shore and Hayslip (1994) found that the disadvantages of reassuming the parental role outweighed the advantages. Custodial grandparents tended to be: younger, more likely to be the mother's parents, in poorer health and with fewer social and economic resources, less highly educated, and more likely to be raising boys. The common difficulties reported by custodial grandparents were:

- Less satisfaction with grandparenting

- Less meaningful grandparenting

- Impaired or strained relationships with their grandchildren

- Isolation from friends because of their parental responsibilities

- Overloaded and confused about their roles as parents and grandparents

- Likely to be caring for children who had behavioral or school difficulties, for which these grandparents were less likely to seek help

On the other hand, grandparents who raise their grandchildren do so out of a commitment to the family and out of genuine concern and love for their grandchildren. Indeed, in spite of the challenges they often face, they are quite **resilient** and adapt well to their newly acquired roles as parents. With adequate financial and medical resources, and with the support of others, custodial grandparenting can be meaningful and fulfilling to both grandparents and grandchildren.

Check Your Learning 5-2

Identify the following terms or concepts:

Custodial grandparents
Significant grandparents
Formal grandparenting style
Reservoir of family wisdom
Surrogate parent grandparents
Distant figure grandparenting style
Fun-seeker grandparenting style
Widowhood
Computer-mediated communication

- What are some of the negative effects associated with the death of a spouse?

- What are some of the major gender differences in widowhood?

- What is the likelihood of remarriage among widows and widowers?

- Why is grandparenting considered a tenuous role?

- List and describe some of the factors that determine if grandparenting is considered satisfying.

- What does it mean to be a grandparent?

- What issues usually lead to conflict between grandparents and their adult children?

- What are some of the gender differences in grandparenting?

- What are some of the challenges facing grandparents caring for their grandchildren?

Summary

Friends compose an important part of our convoy and can be important sources of support and affection during all phases of the life span. Many factors contribute to the selection of our friends, and importance of each of these factors varies as a function of the type of friendship and the age of the individuals involved. There are two major types of friendships, **interest-related**, based on some similar lifestyle, activities or interests between the individuals, and **deep (intimate)**, those in which there is an intimacy between individuals based on a feeling of personal closeness to another individual. Our interest-related and deep friends compose our **personal network**.

Intergenerational relationships are interactions between individuals of different cohorts or generations, and most often occur within the context of the larger family or kinship network composed of aunts, uncles, cousins, grandparents, parents, and children. The primary functions of families of all types, in all cultures and societies, are to provide care and socialization for the young and serve as a network of support and identity for individuals within the family or clan unit. For each individual within the family, there are specific roles and expected behaviors.

Filial responsibility is the perceived obligation regarding the various types of services and social support that children should provide for their older parents. Caregiving is often associated with stress for the caregiver.

Race and ethnicity have a very powerful influence on intergenerational relations; there are ethnic or racial norms regarding familial obligations or expectations. **Extended families** represent a significant proportion of families in the African-American community.

The death of a spouse has been described as the most difficult and disruptive role transition that an individual may confront throughout the life course. While most of us associate **widowhood** with old age, the death of a spouse can occur at any time during the life cycle. Widowhood is considerably less common for men. Emotional reactions to widowhood are complex and can include denial, anger, relief, and guilt. Widowhood can, under some conditions, predispose people to serious illness or death, due to isolation from others, loneliness, or preexisting health difficulties. The tendency to remarry following the death of a spouse is highly related to the age and gender of the widowed individual.

Being a **grandparent** is generally considered to be a developmental task of middle or late adulthood. For many, having a grandchild may be considered a symbol or marker of middle age or getting old. Grandparenting is a **tenuous role**, having no clear criteria for what constitutes appropriate behavior. It is for this reason that grandparenting is largely an individual experience. The grandparent-grandchild relationship may now extend over 20 years, though this interaction is likely to be different when grandchildren are little and grandparents are in good health than when grandchildren are adolescents and grandparents are frail.

Whether one finds grandparenting satisfying depends on numerous factors. Positive yet voluntary relationships with grandchildren and a close relationship with the adult child often contribute to how grandparents perceive their role. Grandparenthood can indeed be satisfying to those who value the role, who have the opportunity to interact with grandchildren, and whose relationships with their adult children are positive. Increasing numbers of grandparents are caring for their grandchildren. Such persons are termed **custodial grandparents**.

Chapter 6
Personality and Adaptation

Defining Personality in Adulthood

This chapter deals with personality and adaptation in adulthood. Not only do we change in some ways as we get older, but our ways of coping with change also have a major impact on our health, relationships, intellectual functioning, and even on our very survival (Field, 1991; Gold & Arbuckle, 1990; Mroczek, Spiro, & Griffin, 2006; Pearlin & Skaff, 1995; Ruth & Coleman, 1996). For these reasons alone, it is an important dimension of adult development to understand.

Personality can be defined in many ways, and this has implications for its measurement, relationship to coping, and therapy. For example, an approach to personality emphasizing **variations** in our **behavior** across situations is in contrast to one emphasizing **consistency** in our behavior that is determined by our **underlying qualities**. According to the behavioral perspective, our behavior can vary from day to day, or from situation to situation. If our behavior (personality) is stable across time, it is because the situations have not changed. The other approach assumes that there exists an underlying set of qualities or **traits** that give meaning to the individual's behavior in most situations, which accounts for stability in personality across time (Costa & McCrae, 1989). Rather than think solely in terms of these extremes, we can better understand personality along a **continuum**, where those who emphasize internal processes and constructs (e.g., ego, id, superego) or qualities (traits) are on one extreme, and those who emphasize observable behaviors in response to the immediate environment

are at the other end of this continuum. In between the extremes of our continuum lies the **cognitive view**, emphasizing the **perception** of oneself in studying personality (Ryff, 1984). Whether personality changes occur depends upon whether the individual perceives or recognizes this change. The **social learning** perspective stresses that individu-

Figure 6-1. Successful adaptation to the process of aging is a hallmark of personality in adulthood.

als **construct** a set of internal standards to govern their own behavior in the absence of external guides (Bandura, 1989). Through the observation of valued, competent **models**, whose behaviors are internalized, personality development takes place. Individuals who maintain a stable personality are able to better cope with experiences that do not agree with these established constructs (Pearlin & Skaff, 1995).

In thinking about approaches to personality in adulthood, you should resist the temptation to say that approach A is "better" than approach B. Rather, differing approaches are more or less **useful** (Hall & Lindzey, 1985) in studying personality change in adulthood.

Stability and Change in Adult Personality

Thinking about personality in terms of stability versus change with age has a number of important everyday implications. We do seem to change in some readily observable ways as we age—in our tastes and interests, for example—while in more fundamental ways we are in many respects the same people we were when we were young. Many of us have compared ourselves with others at special times in our lives—when we marry, when we first become parents, or when we retire. In so doing, we realize that everyone's life does not turn out the same. This is because different persons adjust to these events in distinct ways. For example, high school graduation opens up new possibilities for some of us. We feel enthusiastic and optimistic about the future. We may go away to college or begin our careers. For others, graduating brings an end to a happy, if not secure period in their lives. Now, they must make decisions about an uncertain future. They react by feeling overwhelmed, and thus the future is closed off to them. They may remain at home simply to be close to their parents, or have difficulty in making new friends. Rather than feeling excited about the future, they seem threatened by it.

The answer to whether people change as they age depends upon (1) one's **definition of stability** or **change** (whether we are studying the stability of averages or the stability of individual differences), (2) one's **theoretical biases**, (3) the particular **design** (e.g., cross-sectional versus longitudinal) used to gather our facts about personality, (4) the **level** of personality that one studies, and (5) how one **assesses** personality (see Mroczek, Spiro, & Griffin, 2006). Depending upon these factors, personality can be at once stable, and yet changing in adulthood. This should perhaps confirm your own self-assessment. In some ways, you are much like you were years ago. In other ways, however, you may have changed (Edelstein & Segal, 2011).

Recent reviews of the literature on personality change and stability in adulthood (e.g., Caspi, Roberts, & Shiner, 2005; Mroczek, Spiro, & Griffin, 2006) have tended to emphasize the importance of **individual differences in personality change** in adulthood. That is, some persons change, while others do not, consistent with the influence of many factors. For example, life events (disorderly careers, marriage, divorce, role stress and overload, the death of a spouse, remarriage) can all influence personality change. Exposure to such influences may also interact with our genetic makeup, so that depending upon one's predisposing characteristics, a given environmental event may or may not influence our personality over time. Not only can personality be affected by life experiences, but it can also influence them. For example, our personality makeup may influence our susceptibility or reaction to illness, how long we live, the quality of our relationships with others in adulthood, and our experiences as parents (Caspi et al., 2005; Mroczek et al., 2006).

Check Your Learning 6-1

Define the following terms and concepts:

Personality
Stability
Trait
Social learning
Cognitive theory of personality
Personality as a continuum of views

- What general approaches exist to define personality?

- What do we mean by the continuum of views about personality?

- What factors influence whether personality is stable in adulthood?

- How can stability be defined?

Stage Theories of Adult Personality Change

Erikson

Erikson (1963) sees personality development (specifically **ego** development) in terms of eight psychosocial crises, which can be resolved positively or negatively. Erikson's **psychosocial crisis** theory is an **age-graded** approach to ego development. Difficulties in resolving earlier crises can seriously interfere with adults' resolving later crises. Furthermore, each crisis, regardless of its resolution, comes to help redefine later crises. For example, trust (characterizing infancy) and industry (characterizing early childhood) are played out several times over one's life in dealing with, respectively, the issues of intimacy (young adulthood) and generativity (middle adulthood) (Logan, 1986). Likewise, one's identity (characteristic of adoles-

cence) undergoes several transformations if one marries, has children, divorces, gains and loses a job, retires, or suffers the loss of one's spouse. These crises are **epigenetic**; that is, they arise out of a **maturational ground plan** and eventually come together to form the **whole individual**. For our purposes, we will discuss those especially applicable to adulthood (see Figure 6-2).

For example, the trust-mistrust crisis, which is especially relevant to being cared for in a timely way, may reemerge in young adulthood, when we often crystallize our feelings about educational or career goals, our ideals, and relationships with a partner. Each of these requires the ability to project oneself into the future, and requires **trust in one's own skills** and abilities, and more importantly a **sense of trust in time itself**; one must have faith that goals will be realized. The crisis central to young adulthood, **intimacy versus isolation**, requires the individual to be able to merge with another person (e.g., a parent, spouse, child) to form a relationship that is built upon mutual trust and love (Logan, 1986); such a relationship is **mutual**. One's ability to form such a relationship is a function of the individual's previous efforts in establishing a stable sense of **ego identity** (versus **identity diffusion**) in adolescence. If one's identity is poorly formed or not formed at all, the crisis of **intimacy** will be perceived as threatening. This inability to

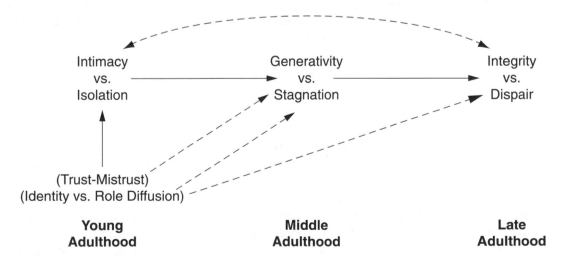

Figure 6-2. Erikson's Psychosocial Crises of Adulthood.

commit oneself to another person, or in a sense merge one's identity with that of someone else, is termed **isolation**. Anyone can feel isolated from others, regardless of age.

Characteristic of middle age is the crisis of **generativity versus stagnation**. To be generative literally means **to generate**—to **produce** things or people that symbolize one's continued existence after death—a reexpression of the **industry versus inferiority** crisis of early childhood. Generativity may be expressed by being productive in one's work (in writing or teaching), personal creativity (in finding a novel solution to a problem, in painting an original picture), or most directly in having children, caring for them, raising them to become adults. In contrast, **stagnation** implies a withdrawal from others—being self-indulgent, bitter, and isolated. A change in identity will likely accompany this process as well. Intimacy will be redefined to include relationships with one's children or perhaps a few trusted friends.

Integrity versus despair characterizes old age, and implies a sense of **completeness**, of having come full circle. Persons who have integrity have, through the process of **introspection** (looking inward and examining what one finds), been able to integrate a lifetime full of successes and failures to reach a point where they have a "sense of the life cycle." Despairing individuals fear death as a premature end to a life (good or bad) that they have not been able to take personal responsibility for, while those who have a sense of integrity accept death as the inevitable end of having lived. A recent therapeutic approach (validation) discussed in Chapter 11 extends Erikson's approach to help older adults experiencing severe confusion and dementia.

Levinson's Life Structure

Another stage approach to adult personality development is that of Levinson, who conducted an intensive study of 40 men aged 35-45 to investigate the process by which these men created a **life structure,** defined as a coherent relationship between one's own goals and the roles one plays in various life arenas, e.g., career, family, marriage, social roles (Levinson, 1978, 1986). The life structure evolves through a sequence of distinct periods, and is shaped by decisions that each individual makes at varying times in adulthood (see Table 6-1).

Although criticized for focusing solely on men, subsequent work suggests that Levinson's approach applies to women as well (Harris et al., 1986; Levinson & Levinson, 1996; Reinke et al., 1985; Roberts & Newton, 1987). Women went through the same transitions as do men, and these changes were experienced at similar ages. However, **gender splitting** permeated every aspect of these women's lives, including how they defined themselves, the availability and choice of careers, and their roles within marriage. Gender splitting was also seen in the perception that it was "unnatural" for a woman to be the head of the household, an executive, or a leader. In addition, men and women may experience periods of crisis at different ages, with men reevaluating around age 40 and women reevaluating nearer to age 30. While the 1990s brought about many changes in men's and women's roles, gender inequity in the workplace remains and conflicts between men and women regarding gender discrimination and harassment remain as issues to be resolved (Levinson & Levinson, 1996) (see Chapter 7).

Any approach to personality development emphasizing developmental stages (Erikson, Levinson) is more properly viewed as a **descriptive** framework within which to view individual development, rather than as **prescriptive** in nature—reflecting a desire to "predict" the crises of adult life. From this perspective, challenges to our identity, and sense of mastery or **self-efficacy** (Bandura, 1989) are brought about by "marker events" (birthdays, occupational changes, marriages, births of children, divorces, retirement, having one's picture taken), which cause us to compare ourselves at present with ourselves in the past. We then can project into the future some ideal that we have set for ourselves. Depending upon the nature of the event and the adaptiveness of our efforts to cope with that event,

Table 6-1

Levinson's Changes In the Life Structure

Age	Life Structure State	Major Characteristics
17-22	Early adult transition	Reevaluation of pre-adult relationships
22-28	Entering the adult world	Creation of provisional life structure in the context of the dream
28-33	Age 30 transition	Revision of the life structure in the context of work, fatherhood, and marriage
	Potential crisis	Age 30 for women Age 40 for men
40-45	Midlife transition	Substantial reevaluation of the making new choices regarding a new life structure, taking on role of mentor at work
50-55	Age 50 transition	Possible further revision of the life structure established earlier
55-60	Late adult transition	Terminates middle adulthood; preparation for late adulthood

Source: Levinson (1978).

a "crisis" may be experienced. For example, while some people shrug off routine physical exams, for others this alerts them to the possibility that in the future something may go wrong with their bodies, even if they pass with flying colors. Instead of alleviating their fears, the physical magnifies them. Thus, how persons **cope** with such changes seems to be most important. Developmental stages are really attempts to explain the behavior of individuals at a given point in their lives that are exhibited most of the time (Lerner, 2002). They may or may not apply to you personally.

Check Your Learning 6-2

Define the following terms and concepts:

Epigenetic
Trust
Generativity
Intimacy
Ego identity
Integrity
Stage
Introspection
Life structure
Prescriptive vs. descriptive
Self-efficacy
Gender splitting

- How do Erikson's psychosocial crises reemerge later in life?

- What is the life structure? How does it change in adulthood?

- Does Levinson's work apply to women?

Non-Stage Approaches to Personality In Adulthood

Riegel's Dialectics of Adjustment to Developmental States

Klaus Riegel (1975, 1976) suggests that the **process** of resolving crisis is really most crucial—that the periods of stability that come between a "crisis" are the exception, rather than the rule. For Riegel, the cultural-historical context in which we live influences whether or not a crisis is experienced at all (Riegel, 1976). If society is "in synch" with individual life events, no crisis will occur (see Chapter 1). For example, while childbirth at age 20 normally would not be seen as a crisis, it could be considered as such, depending upon the culture's prohibitions about birth control, day care, abortion, equal job opportunities, or single parenthood. In such a case, having a child could present a major problem for a young woman. Similarly, depending upon a man's options in retirement such as access to part-time work or viable volunteer roles, leaving the work force may or may not precipitate an "identity crisis."

As developmental stages are culture-specific, as the culture changes, the nature of the "crisis" requiring one's adaptation will also change (Riegel, 1976). For example, raising children in the new century is very different from what it was in the 50s! While parents may have worried about the influence of Elvis or whether their children drank beer, smoked cigarettes, or impregnated an underage girl, they now must deal with drug abuse, violence in the schools, suicide, and AIDS. According to Riegel, "crises" create the necessity for problem solving and decision making, which may further change our environment. For example, in disciplining our children, our relationships with them will change. This may work against us in that we feel less close to our children and they rebel against us. In other cases, it works to our benefit and we feel loved and appreciated by our children. In the former case, if things get more "out of synch" a crisis might be precipitated. Thus, for example in midlife, a crisis could

exist borne of the synchrony between persons and their cultures (Rosenberg, Rosenberg, & Farrell, 1999).

Cognitive Personality Theory

A cognitive approach to personality emphasizes the **perception** of one's experiences. From a cognitive point of view, personality is one of many factors that **mediate** one's response to life events (Thomae, 1980). This view about personality suggests that how we **appraise** what happens to us can assist us in **evaluating** events (assessing the degree of threat or change) and **modifying** our **response** to the situation change or task to be coped with (Lieberman, 1975; Thomae, 1980). **Accurately** appraising a situation can also enable us to better utilize our resources (e.g., financial, physical, psychological, interpersonal) to deal with change. It brings us into "synch" with changes in our lives (Ruth & Coleman, 1996).

For example, those who consistently look on the bright side of things tend to be happier, more well-adjusted persons who can overcome adversity. Seligman (1991) calls such persons **optimists**. Reker (1997) defines optimism as ". . . .the human capacity to transcend temporal boundaries, to anticipate a positive future, to hope. Optimism is defined as looking forward to many desirable events and being very confident that these will take place" (p. 710). Optimism has been shown to be directly related to better subjective physical health, better medical outcomes after serious illness, and psychological well-being (Reker, 1997; Scheier & Carver, 1985). One mechanism through which optimists enjoy these positive outcomes may be related to their tendency to view themselves as able to modify the environment. Because they believe they can effect a change in their environment, optimists respond in appropriate ways.

Whitbourne's Identity Styles

Another approach to personality emphasizes the concept of **identity style** (Whitbourne, 1986, 1987). An individual's identity style is that person's manner of representing and responding to life experiences. As individuals interact with others in the environment, they begin to separate the **self-as-agent** from the **self-as-object**. It is through the particular identity style of the individual that experiences are processed to contribute to ourselves. These identity styles can be **assimilative, accommodative**, or **balanced**. In identity assimilation, new experiences are fit into the existing identity of the individual, while in identity accommodation, one's identity is changed to fit a new experience.

As persons have new experiences or interactions with others, they attempt to fit these into how they see themselves along those dimensions that are important to them. For example, if it is important to be a loving parent, the experiences with one's children will be processed in a way that reinforces the perception of oneself as a loving father or mother (Whitbourne, 1987). In other words, these new experiences are **assimilated** into one's existing identity. Likewise, if being productive is an important aspect of the self, then retiring will be processed in a way that complements one's view about oneself as productive. Experiences for which one's identity must be changed (or **accommodated**) so the individual can cope with them are those that are most discrepant from the individual's views about self. In some cases, assimilation is simply not possible. For example, if divorce separates a parent from the children, or an employee is forcibly retired, such experiences cause persons to redefine themselves. The self is accommodated or changed to fit these new events in one's life. Successful development or adaptation occurs when there is a balance between identity assimilation and identity accommodation. For example, when one must discipline a child, this experience can be assimilated in one's identity as a loving parent via "I am disciplining my child because I love him." Yet, this same experience may require that one's identity as a loving parent be accommodated to fit the negative experience of being violent, of a child's crying, or of feelings of hurt and guilt at having to discipline one's child. Thus, one's identity may shift to incorporate

the necessity for limits on the type of discipline one uses—"I love my child, but maybe I am not the perfect parent. Perhaps I should seek advice from my spouse."

Whitbourne (1987) found several forms of both identity assimilation and identity accommodation among adults; some were more adaptive than others. Assimilative persons by contrast have a controlling style, and will need to win most arguments, while accommodative individuals will give in without considering any alternatives because they lack confidence in their ideas or because they need to please others. In support of the value of identity styles' ability to predict behavior, Sneed and Whitbourne (2003) found that in a sample of adults from their 40s to 80s, that identity assimilation was positively related to age and negatively related to self-reflection, while identity accommodation was negatively related to age and to more self-reflection and self-awareness. Older adults are therefore more assimilative (taking a new experience in light of one's existing identity) than are younger adults.

Adapting to Change

As aging involves adaptation to physical change and to new roles, it is not surprising that people with each identity or coping style will cope with stress and change differently. For example, becoming defensive, withdrawing, bring in denial, or acting out, which are all **emotion-focused coping** styles, may be helpful in an emergency. In contrast, seeking advice and information and solving problems each a form of **problem-focused coping**, are more advantageous when making an important new purchase such as a car or a house (Pearlin & Skaff, 1995; Roth & Cohen, 1986).

Recent research is moving beyond describing different coping efforts to focus on the **match** between coping with various aspects of the crisis and the coping strategy employed. Life events vary in seriousness and in the degree to which they can be controlled, for example, your bedroom window is broken versus your spouse has Alzheimer's disease. In these cases, a combination of emotion-focused and problem-focused coping might be appropriate. You might use emotion-focused coping to deal with your anger about the window, but ultimately, you must find a way to repair or replace the window. For controllable aspects of a situation, problem-focused coping is often more useful. For emotional or uncontrollable aspects of the problem, emotion-focused coping is appropriate, For example, Kinney and her colleagues (Kinney, Ishler, Cavanaugh & Pargament, 2003) found that over time, religious coping, a kind of emotion-focused strategy, was helpful in reducing the stresses of providing care to a spouse with Alzheimer's disease (see Chapter 10).

Trait Approaches to Personality and Aging

Traits are inferred "mental structures" which motivate and guide one's behavior across a variety of situations or across time (Hall & Lindzey, 1985). Traits structure or give meaning to our behavior. By using traits, one can understand whether through development, people "sort themselves out" (are differentiated) along a number of bipolar trait dimensions: for example, as they age, some people become more aggressive than do others (Lerner, 1996).

This approach is often heralded as more objective for studying personality in adulthood than those relying upon, for example, clinical interviews (McCrae & Costa, 1990). The trait approach has, however, been criticized as essentially ignoring the whole person, focusing instead on the characteristics (traits) themselves (Caspi & Bem, 1990). It is also descriptive, and not explanatory in nature (Lerner, 2002).

Costa and McCrae's Five Factor Approach

Costa et al. (1983) found stability in what they term the NEO trait model of personality: **N (Neuroticism)—E (Extroversion)—O (Openness to Experience)**. Later, two other factors (**Agreeableness** and **Conscientiousness**) were added to form a **five factor model** of personality (Costa & McCrae, 1989).

Persons higher in neuroticism tend to be higher in anxiety, depression, self-consciousness, vulnerability, impulsiveness, and hostility. Evidence suggests, however, that the life experiences of people who are higher in neuroticism differ substantially from those who are lower in neuroticism. It appears that people who are higher in neuroticism experience more negative life events, evaluate those events as more negative, and react less positively to those events than peers who are lower in neuroticism (Costa & McCrae, 1992). Extroverts tend to be high in attachment, assertiveness, gregariousness, activity, excitement-seeking, and positive emotions. Persons high in openness to experience have high scores on ideas, feelings, fantasy, esthetics, actions, and values. Agreeable individuals are trusting, cooperative, and sympathetic, while conscientious persons are competent, feel a sense of duty, and are both planful and self-disciplined; they are especially good problem solvers (Costa, 1991).

Reliable group-level differences exist for the Big Five. Relative to men, women tend to be higher in neuroticism, lower in extroversion, lower in openness to new experiences, higher in agreeableness, and higher in conscientiousness. Age differences are minimal, as these traits are stable across time for individuals. Barring some major non-normative or life-altering event (winning the lottery, religious conversion, psychotherapy), stability at the domain level is the norm (Small, Hertzog, Hultsch, & Dixon, 2003). Small to moderate changes may occur for some **facets** or aspects within each broad trait domain (Bleidorn, Kandler, Riemann, Angleitner, & Spinath, 2009).

In contrast to a trait approach to personality in adulthood, Hooker and McAdams (2003) have argued for a **process approach** to understanding personality, where traits are only one of many elements. Others are as follows:

*   One's goals
*   One's motivations
*   Self-regulatory processes; one's self-efficacy and expectations of being able to produce certain outcomes in life
*   Life stories; how persons understand them-

selves, which is something they create to make their lives meaningful and purposeful.

All these elements are necessary to fully understand personality in all of its richness and uniqueness in each adult. Though this approach is new, it stands in sharp contrast to a trait approach to personality, and clearly parallels changes over time that we all experience privately that are so much a part of us—our feelings, how we organize our lives, and what motivates us to reach the goals we have set for ourselves.

Personality Assessment

We must also realize that whether certain dimensions of personality show stability or change is partly influenced by how personality is assessed. **Projective tests** (e.g., ambiguous pictures, inkblots) for example, often show **change**, such as increased interiority, (turning inward emotionally with increased age), whereas **structured interviews** or **standardized personality inventories** often portray a picture of **stability**. Personality inventories of a self-report nature may be subject to the effects of **response set**, for example, guessing, choosing extreme responses or neutral responses, answering in socially desirable unduly positive terms (Carstensen & Cone, 1983; Kozma & Stones, 1986); response set may be especially important when dealing with personal issues. Whether personality appears to change with age or not also depends on whether one's data were gathered **cross-sectionally** (more change) or **longitudinally** (less change) (see Chapter 1).

Why do individuals tend to be stable over time? Part of the reason may be genetic. For example, Pederson et al. (1988) and Pomin et al. (1988) studied 99 pairs of identical twins reared together versus those reared apart and found that there was a genetic influence on neuroticism and extraversion. Bergman et al. (1988), however, found that both environment and heredity interact in complex ways to influence personality in adulthood. While individuals with different personalities may react to the environment by changing it, when faced with novel life changes, one's preexisting characteristics (e.g., emotionality) are often accentuated (Caspi & Bem, 1990). A broader aspect of the contextual influences on personality emphasizes the **historical context** (Kogan, 1990) of events to which persons are exposed and with which they must cope (see Chapter 9). Although we know less about how historical change influences personality (Bem & Caspi, 1990), an exception is research by Elder and Caspi (1986), discussed in Box A.

However, certain life events or health conditions may influence a person in such a way that an individual displays **instability** in personality traits. A limited number of research studies are emerging that address the issue of instability. Although we all experience some normal day-to-day fluctuations in our mood, those individuals who display more pronounced variations may be at risk for certain neurological and psychological disorders (Strauss, McDonald, Hunter, Moll, & Hultsch, 2002).

Check Your Learning 6-3

Define the following terms and concepts:

> Dialectics
> Identity styles
> Balanced
> Emotion focused vs. problem focused
>   coping
> Appraisal
> Assimilation
> Accommodation
> NEO model
> Process approach

- What are the benefits and costs of an accommodative identity style? Assimilative? Balanced?

- What picture of personality change does the NEO model paint?

- What evidence is there for the influence of historical (cohort-specific) factors on personality in adulthood?

Box A

Adaptation to Change and Cohort Membership

Elder (1979) compared two older cohorts—children of the Oakland Growth sample (1920-1921 cohorts) and those of the Berkeley Guidance sample (1928- 1929 cohorts) in their respective adolescent years (The Great Depression of the 1930s) and again 30 years later. Elder found that (1) the impact of the Depression was specific to and more pervasive in the Berkeley cohorts, (2) males were more severely affected than were females, due to their being deprived of a father figure at this time in their lives, and (3) in Berkeley families who were experiencing marital difficulties prior to the Depression, its impact on personality (e.g., submissiveness, self-inadequacy) was far more negative. Elder concluded that the earlier the Depression occurred in the lives of boys, the more negative was its impact, while the effects of the Depression on girls were opposite. Thirty years later, especially for the father-deprived boys in the Berkeley sample, psychological health was greater. This appeared to be due in part to their experience in the military (WWII, Korea), which caused them to marry later (hence more emotional support), and go on to become college educated (G. I. Bill). They were in some cases also able to escape jobs that were not satisfying and family situations that were emotionally aversive. While the deprived Berkeley males had been rated somewhat less healthy these differences were small 30 years later. What enabled these individuals to cope with the negative effects of the Depression, father absence, and marital discord? They seemed to have developed the cognitive skills of **positive comparison** (things are not so bad compared to the Depression) and **selective ignoring** (looking for the good aspects of the Depression) (Elder, 1979, 1986).

Caspi and Elder (1986) studied the 1900 cohort at age 30 of the Berkeley Guidance sample 40 years later and found that having had more adaptive skills (being good problem-solvers, being more emotionally healthy) predicted life satisfaction depending on social class. While having had higher intellectual and social skills was crucial for middle-class women, having been emotionally healthy was most important for middle-class women. For working-class women, having lived through the Depression lowered life satisfaction, while the Depression enhanced life satisfaction for middle-class women. Caspi and Elder suggest that women from lower socioeconomic classes were socialized in such a way as to interfere with the learning of coping skills to deal with stress. On the other hand, many middle-class women, not having had to deal with previous stressful experiences (the Depression), were ill-prepared to deal with the potentially negative impact of growing old.

Similarly, Stewart and Healy (1989) found that the impact of changing women's roles on women themselves was influenced by when such changes were experienced in the life cycle and by cohort membership. For example, older cohorts of women, whose traditional identities were already formed, were less affected by the women's movement. In contrast, younger cohorts of women whose identities were still being formed felt more pressure to combine work and family. For the earlier born cohorts, parental models were most influential.

Not only have cohort effects have been found to influence personality for less recently born persons, but such influences are important for more recently born persons as well. For example, Twenge (2000) found more anxiety among college students in the 1980s than in the 1950s, which she attributes to feeling less connected with others and to a more stressful and threatening environment. Twenge (2001) also found reliable cohort differences among college students in self-reported extraversion, with this characteristic increasing over time (1965-1995).

- Of what significance is being "in synch" or "out of synch" in adulthood?

- What do we mean by a process approach to personality in adulthood?

Personality and Adjustment to Aging

Activity and Disengagement

The issue of coping with change can in part be understood in light of the difference between **activity theory** and **disengagement theory** (see Chapter 9). Activity theory suggests a **positive** relationship between activity (i.e., involvement in social roles, interpersonal relationships, solitary activities, formal commitments) and life satisfaction or morale (Lawton, 1975; Havighurst, Neugarten & Tobin, 1961; Lemon, Bengtson & Peterson, 1972; Maddox, 1965). Disengagement theory (Cumming, 1963, 1975), on the other hand, suggests the opposite. Not only is decreased involvement beneficial, but the process of disengagement is a **mutual** one. That is, society and the individual withdraw from one another, with benefits to both. The individual gains because unwanted commitments can be given up, and the individual can disengage from others and become more self-absorbed. Society gains because younger, more productive individuals can replace those who are older. It is, however, important to distinguish between **psychological** disengagement, i.e., being emotionally uninvolved in the outside world, and **social** disengagement, i.e., not being formally committed to social roles and activities. Disengagement may also be involuntary, via relocation or poor health, or voluntary, as in avoiding a stressful situation.

Kansas City Studies

The Kansas City studies, which speak to how persons with different personalities cope with life changes, were a series of cross-sectional and longitudinal studies of nearly 1,000 people conducted by Neugarten and her colleagues. The Kansas City data yielded four clusters of personality types, broken down into eight specific patterns of adaptation,

Figure 6-3. Activity theory suggests that older adults who remain both physically and mentally active cope more adequately with aging.

each varying along a high, medium, or low continuum of role activity and yielding varying levels of life satisfaction; see Table 6-2 (Neugarten & Hagestad, 1976; Neugarten, 1968).

The study of personality style measures personality at the level of **socioadaptational processes**. Neugarten and her colleagues also found that on an **intrapsychic** level, aged individuals utilized less energy in dealing with the outer world, compared to more energy that was invested in one's own "impulse life," termed **interiority** (Neugarten, 1977). Hayslip, Panek, and Stoner (1991) found no cohort or time of measurement differences in personality functioning, reinforcing Neugarten's age-related interpretation of interiority.

Based on the Kansas City studies, as well as work by Mass and Kuypers (1975) and by Haan

Table 6-2

Personality Clusters and Adaptation

I. **Integrated**—well-functioning, complex people who are psychologically intact and competent; high in life satisfaction.
   A. **Reorganizers**—maintaining high levels of activity; their lives have been successfully reorganized after retirement.
   B. **Focused**—showing moderate levels of activity, but their involvement is selective.
   C. **Disengaged**—well-integrated, life-satisfied individuals who are not active; their disengagement is voluntary and preferred.
II. **Armored or Defensive**—very achievement-oriented, hard-driving individuals who experience anxiety about aging that must be controlled by defenses; they maintain control over, rather than are open to, their own desires and inner needs; less highly (moderately) life satisfied.
   A. **Holding On**—aging is seen as a threat; these individuals hold on to their past; their high levels of activity defend them against their fears of growing old.
   B. **Constricted**—these people defend against aging by withdrawing from others and become preoccupied with losses and deficits; this constriction permits them to maintain a sameness in their lives to ward off the inevitable losses of aging.
III. **Passive-Dependent**—less highly life-satisfied, for whom a source of happiness in life is letting others care for and make decisions about them.
   A. **Succorance-Seeking**—very dependent upon others who may be both moderately active and life-satisfied, but whose physical/emotional needs are met by leaning on someone else.
   B. **Apathetic**—markedly passive, not very active, medium life satisfaction; most likely always passive and apathetic, and

aging simply reinforces this pattern of meeting one's needs.
IV. **Unintegrated**—physically and emotionally incapacitated; low levels of life satisfaction.
   A. **Disorganized**—grossly psychologically dysfunctional, not active, but maintaining themselves in the community.

---

and Block (Block, 1971; Haan, 1972; Haan, Millsap, & Hartka, 1986), perhaps the most important influence on styles of adaptation to aging is **personality type** (Filsinger & Sauer, 1978; Mass & Kuypers, 1975; Neugarten, 1977). This view suggests that individuals form distinct characteristic "styles" of coping that are **maintained** across time. However, some styles of adapting produce higher levels of life satisfaction or morale than others. These personality types cover the continuum from activity to disengagement, though they are somewhat different for men versus women (see Table 6-2).

Life Events in Adulthood

The study of individuals experiencing specific life events provides an opportunity to observe changes within individuals including changes in routines, roles, relationships, and views of self. Life events can be catalysts for physical and emotional illness, or can cause personal growth. Still others serve as antecedents for behavioral change (Gassinger & Schlossberg, 1992). Neugarten (1976) suggests that life events are much more likely to be stressful if they occur **off-time** than when they are **on-time**. Life events also vary in terms of **probability of occurrence**. High probability events are normative (see Chapter 1) and are defined as those life events which are usually expected and predictable (e.g., marriage, birth of children, launching of children, and retirement). Low probability (non-normative) events are those events which are unpredictable and affect either a great number of

---

Box B

Coping with Life Events

In recent years, psychologists have begun to study a personality disposition termed **hardiness**. We sometime use the term **resilient** to refer to psychologically hardy persons. Hardiness involves a sense of personal control, commitment, and appreciation of challenges that can influence a person's adjustment to a specific life event and his or her overall psychological and physical well-being (Crowley, Hayslip, & Hobdy, 2003). Actual research results regarding the role of hardiness have been equivocal. In order to determine whether psychological hardiness was associated with adjustment to life events, Crowley and her associates examined two events that differed in controllability and predictability.

Crowley et al. (2003) studied a group of 88 individuals who had become unemployed due to layoffs, resignations, or terminations. A second group of 227 adults had recently experienced their youngest child leaving home, a transition that is sometimes referred to as the empty

nest. These two events represent common, and often stressful, adjustments in adulthood. They differed, however, in the degree to which people perceive the events as predictable. Most parents expect that their children will leave home and fully enter the adult world, but few adults anticipate losing their job.

The results indicated several interactions among hardiness, life event, and coping. For example, hardy individuals who were facing job loss used more problem-focused coping (planful coping) and more cognitive reappraisal. These individuals also experienced better emotional well-being. In contrast, hardy individuals who were experiencing the empty nest were less planful but engaged in more positive reappraisal than less hardy parents. The relation between hardiness and adjustment to the empty nest was smaller than the relation between hardiness and adjustment to job loss, offering additional support for the **matching hypothesis** (see text).

---

people at a single point in time, or small numbers of people over time (e.g., floods, involuntary job loss, sudden onset of a life-threatening illness). In an examination of expected and unexpected life events, Crowley et al. (2003) compared the coping responses of adults who experienced two distinct life events (see Box B).

Stress and Coping in Adulthood

Day-to-day stress and coping with major life changes are a normal part of life. Stress can be found on the job, at school, at home, and in our personal lives. For example, changing your job to a higher paying job, though positive, can lead to stress, just as a negative event such as the death of a close friend

can be stressful (Holmes & Rahe, 1967). Our response to stress involves both psychological and physiological reactions.

When individuals are confronted with a life change, they engage in a series of cognitive appraisals which lead to behaviors which may or may not be successful in helping them adapt to change. **Primary appraisals** allow persons to evaluate the event in terms of its being positive, neutral, or stressful and negative (Lazarus & Folkman, 1984). **Secondary appraisal** allows the individual to decide upon what options are available to cope with the event, if a chosen course of action is possible, and if the behaviors chosen will produce positive or negative outcomes. **Tertiary appraisal** or **reappraisal** allows one to incorporate new information into the

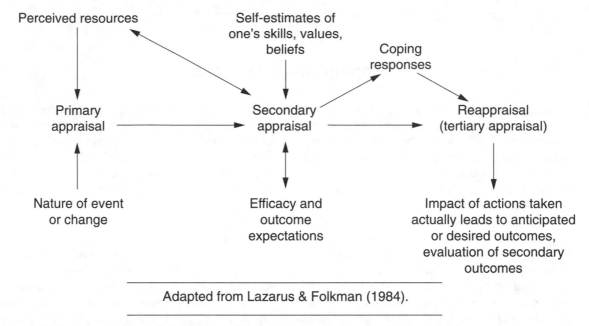

Adapted from Lazarus & Folkman (1984).

Figure 6-4. Process Approach to Personality: Adaptation to change.

situation. At this point, one might evaluate whether the course of action taken was effective; in other words, "Did things actually work out as I planned? Are there outcomes that I did not anticipate?" (see Figure 6-4).

Consider the individual who is offered a promotion, which is evaluated as positive (primary appraisal). The next decisions are, "Do I have the skills to actually do the job? Can I get along with new coworkers?" (secondary appraisal). Also, assuming positive efficacy expectations ("Can I cope with this?") (Bandura, 1986), the person must then evaluate whether the promotion will lead to desirable outcomes, such as higher pay, or better hours or working conditions (secondary appraisal).

Let's suppose that our worker actually accepts this promotion. Tertiary appraisal may be necessary because as it turns out, time with family needs to be sacrificed, or little contact is possible with former coworkers or friends in order to do the new job well. Such reappraisal might also be necessary because the individual could not cope with the unanticipated side effects of earning more money (excess money is spent foolishly), or of having more responsibility (failing to ask for advice from others, feeling over-

whelmed or isolated from others). At this point, the individual might choose to be reassigned back to the old job because the **costs** of accepting the promotion outweigh its **benefits**.

Our emphasis on stress and coping processes also highlights the individuals' beliefs about **personal control** over events or personal commitments to a set of values and ideals as influences on how people assess and respond to change over the life span (Lazarus and Delongis, 1983; Pearlin & Skaff, 1995). With increased age, individuals may pull away from commitments they have made earlier in their lives because of poor health or nonreward (they fail to get a promotion). Such changes are adaptive—they allow the individual to cope with stress. Similarly, individuals as they age may decide that they lack **primary control** over events in their lives, and consequently exert **secondary control** over such events by **reinterpreting** what these events mean to them personally (Schulz & Heckhausen, 1996). Primary control is directed to the external world, while secondary control is directed at the self. Individuals may also **redefine** what **goals** they see as important to reach (Brandstadter, Krampen & Greve, 1987). Through such processes, persons can maintain their self-esteem, establish satisfying relationships with others, and develop new interests and skills.

A few cross-sectional studies do suggest age differences in **coping styles**, utilizing a cognitive framework to examine the relationship between stress and coping (see Pearlin & Skaff, 1995). For example, McCrae (1982) found younger adults to more frequently use hostility or fantasy to cope with life events, relative to middle-aged adults. Boerner (2004) found older persons with lower levels of disability to use accommodative coping (changing oneself to fit an event or the environment), while middle-aged persons with greater levels of disability also used accommodative coping. This suggests that persons can cope with events over which they have no control by changing themselves rather than by changing the event—a good example of secondary control. However, the similarities across age in coping styles (e.g., taking rational action, seeking advice, denial, isolation) outweighed the differences. McCrae (1989) found that older persons used less interpersonal aggression to deal with stress, were more forgiving, and less likely to take out their frustrations on others. Most studies suggest a consistent pattern in coping styles, which is maintained into late adulthood.

Check Your Learning 6-4

Define the following terms and concepts:

Life events
Primary appraisal
Secondary appraisal
Tertiary appraisal
Primary control
Activity theory
Personality type
Positive comparison
Selective ignoring
Secondary control
Disengagement theory
Coping style

- By what process do adults evaluate life events that they experience?

- What is the general adaptation syndrome?

- By what processes do adults adjust to change?

- Why is one's personality type important to understanding stress and coping in adulthood?

- What impact does age have on coping style?

- How do life events and life experience influence the stability of personality?

Summary

This chapter dealt with personality stability and change, as well as with how personality affects the aging process to influence how persons cope with changes in their lives. Personality can be understood along a **continuum** of emphasis, from a focus upon unobservable processes to one choosing to use observable behavior as the unit of personality.

Several factors affect the stability of personality in adulthood: for example, **different views about adult personality** (Erikson, Levinson, Whitbourne, Riegel, Costa, and McCrae), and a bias whether one predicts either stability or change in personality with age. In addition, the researchers' biases about **activity** and **disengagement**, the **level** at which personality is studied, **how stability is defined**, how personality is **measured**, and the particular **developmental design** (cross-sectional, longitudinal) are all considerations in trying to determining whether and how individuals change or not as they age.

Riegel's **dialectical** theory, Thomae's **cognitive theory of personality**, and Whitbourne's **identity style theory** are each consistent with the mediating role that personality plays in affecting and being influenced by experienced life events. Cognitive approaches stress the **interpretation** or **appraisal** of life events and experiences as critical to adaptation and coping.

While most individuals may face age-graded sets of tasks or events, they cope at a **socio-adaptational** level with these tasks in ways that are more or less adaptive, consistent with their established life histories. At an **intrapsychic level**, there is much evidence for increased **interiority** with age.

While cross-sectional data often present a picture of apparent age change, studies of adult personality reveal that **cohort** differences do exist for many psychological **traits**. Longitudinal studies paint a clear picture of stability with age in personality, relying upon psychometric scales to measure personality traits. The issue of personality change and stability in adult years is complex, subject to the effects of many influences.

Chapter 7
Occupational Selection and Work

Given current life expectancy predictions, we will most likely spend at least 40 years of our lives in the workforce. Indeed, next to sleeping, many of us will spend more time working during our lives than in any other activity. Assume that you enter the work force at age 25 and work 40 hours a week for the next 40 years, retiring at 65—that is 76,800 hours of work over the course of your life! Add to that the 4 years (or more) that you have spent in college preparing for this career. Depressing or exciting? Indeed, even before we enter college, most of us have probably spent a good deal of time in high school preparing for our life's work. With this in mind, it is perhaps an understatement to say that work has a major influence on many aspects of our lives throughout our adult lives!

Our work role is critical to our identities as adults since our occupation will affect and helps to determine what society expects of us in terms of behaviors and activities. Such expectations might include manner of dress, social and recreational activities, personal conduct, and values. How well we conform to these work role expectations determines how we are viewed by others and by our occupational peers. Obviously, as work is often connected to income, working for many adults reflects the necessity to support themselves and their families, i.e., "to put food on the table."

Occupational Roles and Their Selection

The selection of an occupation is one of the most important decisions made during our lives since it has a major influence on many intrapersonal and interpersonal aspects of adult development. Indeed, Brown (2002) argues that career decisions are really **value decisions**, where some values are retained, and others are given up or distorted during career decisions. Thus, what kind of person you are to become, what kinds of friends you want, where you want to live, and what is important to you to strive for are all examples of such value decisions. For example, you may feel that earning more money is important to you and that influences what kind of career you choose as well as whether to change jobs within that career. Now, what will you do if that "dream job" comes along—the one you never thought you would get? What if you will earn less money if you take it? What if it requires that you move away from the city in which your parents live? These are examples of the value decisions that we are often forced into making when we choose careers, change jobs, or even change careers—tough choices and important ones! Receiving career counseling is therefore really about clarifying your values—what is and is not important to you now and perhaps, in the future.

For this reason, it is understandable that the occupational role one plays is a major influence on many facets of development in the adult years, regardless of whether work is viewed as a blessing or a curse (Niles & Harris-Bowlsbey, 2005). Work generally occupies a central position in our adult lives, serving as a basis for our self-concept, contributing to our self-esteem, and influencing our identity. It also influences where our children go to school, how much autonomy and free time we have, how much training or continuing education we engage in, and whether and/or how much vacation we take.

The *extent* of work's influence on our identity and lifestyle depends on how central work is to our identity, whether we are self-employed or work for others, whether we are doing manual labor or not, and whether we are viewed as either expendable commodities or as valued resources as employees. In this context, it is not surprising that in young adulthood, both men and women who are either working or going to school have higher self-esteem than do those who are unemployed or hold part-time jobs, and for young women, as well as women in midlife, being employed contributes to feelings of well-being (Stein, Newcomb, & Bentler, 1990). Thus, work can produce intrinsic satisfaction for the individual beyond that derived from economic gains.

Although the occupation one selects is very important, career choices are often made with little thought or assistance. Also, many extraneous and unpredictable influences are involved in this process, such as economic factors, the accessibility of educational and training opportunities, and supply-and-demand market conditions. In addition, individuals may get "locked in" to jobs by accident, or take jobs they thought were only temporary, only to end up spending their entire lives in these jobs. In this respect, in one study of nearly 800 high school and university students, over 70% of young adults reported that their career choices were influenced by "chance" events (Bright, 2005). Furthermore, many people who thoughtfully choose their careers find out that they "**plateau**" in young and middle adulthood. That is, their career has leveled off, and further advancement is not likely, which can lead to frustration and perhaps a career/job change.

It is for these reasons that (a) decision-making about careers is no longer limited to adolescence and young adulthood but continues throughout the life cycle, and that (b) there is now an increasing emphasis on career guidance and placement (Niles & Harris-Bowlsbey, 2005). In order to deal with work and career issues, school systems, colleges, and state and local agencies are implementing career-planning programs for people of varying ages (see Box A). These programs can be quite successful in facilitating appropriate career decision-making for individuals at all age levels.

Niles and Bowlsbey (2005, p.5) suggest that career choices in the future will be more complex than today. Workers will be asked to develop "a variety of skills, behaviors, and attitudes to manage their careers effectively." **Managing one's career** effectively will require the ability to (1) continuously learn new skills, (2) tolerate ambiguity and cope with change, (3) acquire and use occupational information effectively, (4) interact competently with fellow workers, (5) adjust quickly to changing work demands, and (6) use technology effectively (Niles & Bowlsbey, 2005, p. 5). How do you stack up when it comes to these skills?

Hall (1996) can be credited for the earliest, most straightforward position regarding the changing work environment, highlighting the need for **self-management** due to turbulence in the world of work. Hall articulated seven guidelines concerning career development based on his review of the state of career development in organizations (see Davis, 2009):

1. In today's chaotic job environment, organizations cannot outline progressively ordered career paths for their employees and should not waste effort trying to do so.
2. Of necessity, responsibility for about 80% of career development belongs to the employee.
3. Employees must identify and develop new *career competencies* instead of focusing on skills specific to a job; a component of these new competencies must be "meta-skills," the skill of acquiring new skills.
4. Organizations should encourage employees' efforts to assume responsibility for their careers, focusing organizational attention on broader organizational objectives.
5. Organizations should provide information and support for employees who pursue career development.

Box A

Changing Assumptions Underlying Effective Career Counseling

Not everyone can make work choices. Some individuals do have the ability and resources to exercise some control over the work that they do. Others must work simply to survive economically. They cannot choose what they do, where they work, or with whom they work.

Work is not separate from other aspects of life. We now recognize that work is intimately related to family life, friendship patterns, mental health, and physical health. In effect, persons making career choices are making life choices that are life designing.

The world of work is unpredictable and even chaotic. Technology, economic pressures, globalization, and the changing demographics of the workforce contribute to the unpredictability of work. This makes the definition of particular career patterns exceedingly difficult. Employees who trained for a particular career and have stayed in that career for the bulk of their work lives are

becoming increasingly rare. How can we best help people to deal with this state of affairs? What of people who lack technological skills?

Career choices are now seen as dynamic. They become a series of decisions people make over the course of their work lives. Multiple careers, trial-and-error careers, dealing with the need to develop new skills, and coping with the loss of their jobs and job stress are ongoing realities for today's workers as well as those of the future. Adults (even older adults) and not just adolescents make career choices that shape their lives in powerful ways.

Effective career counseling is now more broadly defined. It may extend over many years as persons' careers change. It is not limited to providing information about work, but it must incorporate work in the context of family, friendships, stress, and the values persons hold about life and the personal choices they make in many aspects of their lives.

Sources: Fouad (2007), Savickas et al. (2009).

6. Wide degrees of freedom of movement for employees should be allowed for in the organizational structure.

7. Career development support should be included within a strategic human resource management process that grows out of the larger strategies and priorities of the organization (Hall, 1996, pp. 348 -349).

In this light, the well-planned, predictable career plan driven by a "career ethic" (McCortney & Engels, 2003) is a thing of the past and likely applies to only a minority of individuals. This is

due to a variety of factors ranging from downsizing and the resulting unemployment and job change that comes with it, the growing importance of technology (being "replaced" by a computer), and the tendency for persons to define their careers in increasingly personal terms, rather than solely in terms of being occupationally "successful"—having prestige and power, being well-known in one's field, earning a great deal of money. Indeed, persons are now more likely to engage in a series of "mini-careers," characterized by "mini-stages" of exploration-trial-mastery-exit, moving in and out of a given career, and moving along when necessary for personal or professional reasons (Niles & Bowlsbey, 2005).

The terms **career development** and **occupational development** are used to describe a semi-organized, coherent pattern of jobs that lead us to some implicit (subjective) or explicit standard level of performance or goal. Career development implies that a variety of deliberate decisions are made about a job/occupation, versus holding a more or less random, unrelated series of jobs just to get by financially. In light of the changing world of work we discussed above, we could argue that career development per se is less relevant today than in the past!

In today's world, key to making good career choices, especially in young adulthood and midlife, are attributes of flexibility, job mobility, and the need to constantly upgrade one's skills to "keep up" (Taylor, 2005). Persons project a "possible occupational self" into the future when they contemplate a career (Meara, 2005), and thus, occupational choices become a *series* of decision one makes, based upon numerous personal, social, and economic factors (Sauermann, 2004), others' expectations (Mani, 2004) and the influence of the family (see below).

Theories of Occupational Choice and Career Development

Theoretical perspectives on career choice can be classified into three types of approaches (Ackerman & Beier, 2003). These are: (1) trait-oriented approaches that include vocational interests as well as personality and ability, e.g., Holland's; (2) developmental approaches such as Super's; and, (3) social learning theory-oriented.

Holland's Trait Congruence Approach

Holland's (1994) theory is a trait-factor approach, which predicts that vocational selection and satisfaction will be determined by **congruence** or fit between an individual's attributes and vocational interests. Thus, individuals will choose an occupation that is a fit with their personalities, the types of interpersonal settings in which they function, and the lifestyles associated with specific occupations.

By doing this, we can express ourselves, best apply our skills as we believe them to be, and take on work roles that are compatible with our personalities. Holland views these personal-social factors as more important to occupational selection than the performance requirements of the occupation. Hence, trait-oriented approaches such as Holland's focus mainly on the congruence of individual differences in personality, vocational interests, abilities, and different occupations (Akerman & Beier, 2003).

Super's Lifespace Lifespan Approach

Super's theory of occupational development is a self-concept approach that is presented within a lifespan or developmental framework, and it is for this reason that we discuss it extensively here. Super's is a developmental approach that delineates different stages of career development over the lifespan. Also, according to this theory persons select an occupation that allows for the expression of their self-concepts. Super proposes that occupational development is a progression of career stages that result from modification of the individual's self-concept and adaptation to an occupational role. These five distinct stages are the (1) **implementation stage**, (2) **establishment stage**, (3) **maintenance stage**, (4) **deceleration stage**, and (5) **retirement stage**. Individuals can thus be located along a continuum of **vocational maturity** throughout their occupational lives. According to Super (1990) the more consistent that individuals' vocational behaviors are with what is expected of them at different ages, the more vocationally mature they are considered.

In Super's **implementation stage**, characteristic of later adolescence, individuals take on a number of temporary positions (trial occupations) in which they begin to learn behaviors related to the work role. This "trial work period" is generally very unstable; persons may suffer from **career indecision** at this point (Lee, 2005). As an individual's self-concept becomes more definite, he or she begins to move toward a specific occupational choice and enters the **establishment stage**. This usually occurs during young adulthood and is characterized by stability in occupation, productivity, and advancement. Although individuals may change jobs or positions, they rarely change vocations. Also during this stage, greater congruence is achieved between the individual's self-concept and occupational role. Following the establishment stage is a period of transition that usually occurs during late middle adulthood (ages 45 to 55 years), called the **maintenance stage**. This is the time when individuals prepare to decrease their occupational activity, since they either feel they have already attained their occupational goals or realize they will never attain these goals. This is referred to as a career "plateau," and it means maintaining but no longer striving and achieving. People in this situation are occupationally stable, yet they may be frustrated by the realization that some of their goals are unattainable. By the mid-50s, individuals begin to enter the **deceleration stage**, during which they begin to prepare for retirement, more actively consider what leisure activities are important to them, and begin to separate themselves from the job. This period is quite difficult for those to whom work has been the most important part of their lives. Finally, there is the **retirement stage**, in which individuals formally divorce themselves from the work role. Depending on a variety of factors individuals may "psychologically" retire from their jobs many years prior to actual retirement.

Super's lifespace lifespan vocational theory (Super, Savickas, & Super, 1996) stands out in its focus on career development beyond the adolescent years. In this respect, Osipow and Fitzgerald (1996) argue that most vocational theories concentrate on the initial career selection/implementation process that usually takes place in one's early to mid-20s, likely reflecting the emphasis western social institutions place on this initial career selection. Although these theories typically discuss early environmental and internal influences on this initial selection, Osipow and Fitzgerald argue that they fail to conceptualize how these and other influences affect career development beyond the early adult years, despite the fact that the majority of career related occurrences take place in mid to late adulthood.

Within each of Super's above developmental stages are distinct *developmental tasks*. Relevant to adulthood are Super's ideas of exploration, which involves deciding on an occupation (see above). This stage involves three tasks: **crystallizing, specifying,** and **implementing**. When *crystallizing*, the person is faced with determining what field and level of work he or she is interested in, whereas, during the *specifying* task, the individual selects and commits to a chosen occupation. Finally, when *implementing,* the individual makes plans related to attaining a position in the chosen career and carries them out.

Exploration is followed by establishment (see above), which challenges the worker to obtain a secure job within the occupation he or she has selected. There are three developmental tasks to master within this stage: **stabilization, consolidating,** and **advancing**. *Stabilization* requires the individual to settle down, support oneself, make maximum use of one's abilities and interests, and make one's position in an organization or field secure by assimilating to its culture and performing the job well. Establishing status within one's occupation is the goal of the *consolidating* task, and moving up within one's career reflects the challenge of the *advancing* task.

During the maintenance stage (see above), one is concerned with preserving status and security in the chosen occupation, provided the choice has been made to remain in the occupation for the next several years. The three developmental tasks of this stage (**holding, updating,** and **innovating**) reflect the notion that in order to maintain one's position, one is required to increase one's skill set and outpace those who may be competing for the same job. The employee is concerned with *holding* and improving one's position when faced with those competing for the same job by *updating* one's skills and knowledge to stay current. Finally, *innovating* centers around the need or expectation that one will make unique contributions to the field.

Last, workers in the deceleration stage (see

above) demonstrate the desire or need to transition from active worker to retiree. Such persons often experience decreased emotional and physical energy for work related activity, a characteristic of the **decelerating** task. **Retirement planning** involves planning for and anticipating one's retirement and **retirement living** involves the actual act of retirement, making up the two final tasks of this stage.

Super argues that one's career development does not cease once one reaches adulthood, though it is generally irreversible, orderly, patterned, and predictable. Accordingly, while Super initially assigned age ranges to each of these stages, he later added the construct of **recycling** to his theory. Whereas the **minicycle** refers to the repetition of the stages as one progresses through each stage to the next, the **maxicyle** is the term Super gave to the whole lifestage process. Here Super acknowledged that although people within the age ranges may certainly find themselves with the assigned stage concerns, this does not necessarily have to be the case (Super, Osborne, Walsh, Brown, & Niles, 1992). People are generally more susceptible to recycling though the exploration, establishment, and maintenance stages, as may be the case when one switches career fields. Accordingly, Super hypothesized that the disengagement stage and associated substages may be more highly related to age than others (Super, Thompson, & Lindeman, 1988). Super also acknowledged that persons can have concerns related to many stages and developmental tasks simultaneously. For example, a person can have establishment and maintenance concerns at the same time if one is concerned with increasing one's skills within a profession to increase marketability as one considers applying at other, more established or prestigious companies within a field.

Social Learning Theory

Social learning theory (Krumboltz & Henderson, 2002) approaches of career choice examine person-environment interactions and their influences on career decision making (Ackerman & Beier, 2003). It emphasizes the individual's sense of self-efficacy in making good decisions, career barriers, and expectations about how one's career will "turn out" (Lindley, 2005). From this perspective parents and family members can serve as models for career choices, and their work attitudes and behaviors can exert a powerful influence on career choices (Berrios-Allison, 2005). Also, new or interesting career paths are opened to students in high school through participation in activities and programs such as job shadowing and career day. Further, career decisions may extend well into one's 20s (Arnett, 2000) as the emerging adult experiments with a variety of career roles.

Family influence and individual factors such as self-esteem and perceived ability must also be understood in light of cultural influences. Cultural attitudes and expectations varying by gender, socio-economic status, or ethnicity may well modify the family's influence on an adolescent's choice of career. For instance, U.S. culture views career choice as a way of self-actualization and fundamentally as individual choice, while Asian Americans view career choice as mutually beneficial for themselves and their families (Tang, Fouad, & Smith, 1999). Consequently, Asian Americans may not choose a career based on their own interests or intentions but on the whole family's mission (see Box B).

A social learning approach to career choice incorporates the influence of historical changes in what careers are "hot." For example, engineering, social service, and teaching have been desirable at different times in the past 20 years, while currently, healthcare, business, and high-tech careers are highly popular. Such an approach might also emphasize the influence of culture.

Gottfredson's Compromise and Circumscription Approach

Gottfredson (2002) understands career choice in terms of the **compromises** people make in choosing a career, often being victimized by sex-typed expectations about what men and women should do with their work lives. Persons therefore are heavily influenced by what they or others believe is appropriate for their gender, less influenced by pres-

Box B

Culture and Diversity in Career Development

Our views about career choice, work, and career development are increasingly influenced by culture, and, more generally, workplace diversity. Indeed, **cultural pluralism**, broadly defined, now embraces our approach to helping persons with career choice, reflected in what is termed **multicultural counseling** (Niles & Bowlsbey, 2005), or **cultural competence**.

From this perspective, what are the **key issues** to be considered regarding our views about work, career choice, and career development?

1. Do we view career choice and development as universal or culture-specific? Should career counseling be the same for everyone or should it consider cultural differences in the meaning of and opportunities for career choice?
2. How does the counselor's **ethnocentrism** (belief in the superiority of one's own culture) influence the counseling process? While individualistic cultures emphasize an individual's abilities,

interests, and choices, collectivistic cultures emphasize the influence of the family or group. Thus one set of values may not support the other in helping persons who are not members of the dominant culture make career choices.
3. How **acculturated** (adopting the behaviors, values, and language of the dominant culture) the client is influences how effective we can be with persons who have, for example, immigrated from another country into the United States. Moreover, a client may or may not be as acculturated as his or her family, and thus may not share the values of the culture of origin.
4. To what extent has the individual defined himself or herself in terms of **race, gender, sexual orientation,** or **disability status**? For some persons, these attributes may be central to them, while for others they may not. Understanding the basis for a given client's **identity** is key to **values-oriented** career counseling (Brown, 2002).

---

tige of the career, and even less so by whether their career choice is personally fulfilling to them. For this reason, persons search for careers that are "good enough," but not ideal for them in light of their interests and skills. **Circumscription** involves elimination of unacceptable career alternatives primarily based upon gender and prestige. In adulthood, circumscription and compromise come about, according to Gottfredson, because children internalize notions of social inequality long before they pursue their dreams in terms of a career or vocation, i.e., that boys and girls are inherently different in terms of what careers might suit them best. Gottfredson's compromise and circumscription ap-

proach suggests that early intervention and education are therefore critical in allowing adults to make career decisions unfettered by biases about gender by exposing them to the full range of occupational possibilities open to them.

Other Approaches to Career Choice and Career Development

Other, more recent ideas about career choice involve the role of **cognition** as a factor in how we process experiences in making career decisions (Lent, Brown, & Hackett, 2002). Thus, our behaviors, values, personalities, specific skills, and contextual/environmental factors all come together to influence **self-efficacy**—our self-confidence in, expectations about, and goals for ourselves in making career decisions and choices. Peterson et al. (2002) emphasize how we **process information** about careers in making career choices. Key to this approach is the fact that we make career choices and decisions via (1) acquiring knowledge about careers and about ourselves, (2) our ability to communicate about, analyze, synthesize, apply value to, and execute career decisions, and (3) metacognitive skills such as self-talk, self-awareness, and the monitoring of and control over our thoughts, emphasizing such skills as the storage, coordination, and retrieval of career information. A last newer approach is Brown's (2002) **values-based approach,** which centralizes values clarification in the process of making career decisions: What is important to us in doing so? What kind of person do we want to be? What goals are we setting for ourselves?

Niles and Bowlsbey (2005) argue that many theoretical perspectives on career development are limited because they were based upon linear/predictable models, which assumed individuals moved through predictable career stages (e.g., Super) and the view that a person has a single career. Additionally, these perspectives ignore individual differences. Accordingly, career theorists and counselors must come to grips with the facts that many people will not be able to follow a simple linear career trajectory and that family and economic constraints may impact career patterns. A change in perspective about careers is emphasized by the fact that in the future, extended and multiple careers will become the norm as more and more workers chose to remain on the job because of either economic necessity or for personal fulfillment.

Changing Careers in Midlife

It seems clear that people, through career choices and job changes, eventually select themselves (or "drift") into occupations where they are better able to cope with the demands of a particular job/occupation. Also, for a variety of reasons such

as financial situation and family obligations, job change and career options may be limited for many individuals. Yet, middle-aged individuals seem to be most vulnerable to "job loss" and middle adulthood can be especially pivotal occupationally. For example, rather than being upwardly mobile, some individuals seem to focus on the stable, fulfilling aspects of their careers. For others, the mid-career phase is a largely negative one, characterized by dissatisfaction and restlessness.

However, some people do change careers in middle adulthood. Such changes may be **horizontal**, from one career to another, or **vertical**, to a higher level of responsibility (Osipow, 1983). Many people experience several vertical career changes in their lives. Both types of changes come about for a variety of reasons. Family changes such as divorce, widowhood, adult children leaving home, a desire for more income, status, or security; philosophical differences with one's employer; and dissatisfaction with how one's skills are used are all common reasons for career changes. Finally, since some people are never able to enter the career of their first choice, these individuals attempt mid-career life changes or pursue entirely new careers after retirement.

Overall, factors such as lack of interest, incongruity with one's occupation, a lack of consistent and diversified interests, fear of failure, or a history of emotional problems, but not age, predict career change. This suggests that regardless of age some people are more likely to change careers than others. At present, it clearly would be inaccurate to state that midlife is necessarily a period of occupational upheaval for men or women.

Work in Context—A Midlife Crisis?

That some persons change careers in midlife or lose their jobs at this time (see below) might suggest that these events constitute a crisis. Indeed, portraits of midlife often emphasize such events as the empty nest, menopause, or the **midlife crisis**, but our knowledge about these events and other key experiences in midlife is limited (Lachman, Lewkowicz, Marcus, & Peng, 1994). Realistically,

Figure 7-1. Career upheaval can be potentially stressful for many middle-aged individuals.

midlife is characterized by both gains and losses (Baltes, 1997). It is a time to engage in a process of appraisal and evaluation, and a time to look back to see what has been done and to look ahead to see what is left still to do. Thus, it is a time for reassessment with the possibility for making changes (Lachman et al., 1994)

The 50s is a kind of **fulcrum decade**, a turning point in the aging process, during which people, more sharply than before, are made to feel their age (Karp, 1988). As the 50s progress it becomes harder to avoid the recognition of really growing older. Particular events occur, such as the deaths of parents and friends, being in the middle of three generations, being the oldest at work, and becoming grandparents, which inevitably make aging a prominent part of self-consciousness in the 50s. For these reasons the 50s is a **decade of reminders.**

In midlife, there may be increased stress in several domains, while at the same time midlife is seen as the peak period for competence, ability to handle stress, sense of control, purpose in life, productiv-

ity, and social responsibility. Thus, the midlife adult is potentially well equipped with psychosocial resources to handle role overload. The gains are primarily the psychological and social realms with increased control, competence, and respect. Losses are primarily in the physical realm, involving appearance, energy, and health. Stress is common in several areas, including family, fulfilling responsibilities, relationship with children, and finances. However, it should be emphasized that negative life events are distressing or depressing *only* insofar as an individual values, identifies with, or is committed to the domains in which these events occur (Thoits, 1992). Moreover, women and men may attach different meanings and definition to stress, and the sources or causes of stress may be different (Iwasaki, MacKay, & Risstock, 2004).

Most women tend to feel pressured or are expected to take on the responsibilities of household work and care for children, aging parents, and other family members (Iwasaki et al., 2004). In contrast, most men appear to have the privilege or option of not taking on this responsibility; thus, they tend to primarily focus on themselves and their careers (Iwasaki et al., 2004). Research on women of several generations has suggested that women's regrets about their lives often focus on missed opportunities for education and career development (Stewart & Vandewater, 1999). Levinson's (1996) research suggests that middle-aged women of the "baby boom" generation may have more serious regrets at midlife if they pursued marriage and motherhood roles, but not careers, during early adulthood. One might predict that in the future, as women centralize the role of work to a greater extent, that the impact of work stress on them will indeed resemble that of men.

It remains to be seen just how prevalent the midlife crisis really is, as well as the influence of midlife on career development. Some people do not experience a crisis or even a period of occupational transition, and there are individual differences in how people respond to dissatisfaction if it is experienced at all.

Check Your Learning 7-1

Identify the following terms or concepts:

> Work role
> Midcareer life changes
> Vocational maturity
> Career crisis
> Vertical career changes
> Value-based approach
> Career plateau
> Career development/occupational
>   development
> Midlife crisis
> Horizontal career changes
> Career self-management
> Decade of reminders

- What is the significance of "work" during adulthood?

- What skills might one develop to cope with the world of work?

- What are the major assumptions of Holland's theory of occupational choice?

- What are the major assumptions of Super's theory of occupational choice?

- What are the major assumptions of the social learning theory of occupational choice?

- What is the compromise and circumscription approach to career choice?

- What factors influence whether midlife is a time of crisis?

Learning Activity: Ask three individuals how they decided on their current job/career. Did they enter the job/career on the basis of rational decision-making or for some other reason (s)?

Career Patterns: Men

While it seems clear that particular career patterns are less likely to exist in the future, and there is some indication that labor force participation rates for men and women are becoming more similar in inducstrialized nations (Huang & Sverke, 2007), it is interesting that Havighurst (1982) identified several career patterns for men that did vary in terms of orderliness or stability. These were: **conventional**, a typical career path from trial (trying out several jobs) to stable employment, characteristic of managerial, skilled, and clerical workers; **stable**, common among professionals (e.g., managers, physicians, dentists, lawyers, and college professors); **unstable**, characterized by trial-stable-trial career patterns, common among domestic, semiskilled, and clerical workers; and **multiple-trial**, characterized by frequent job changes, with no one job type predominant, also characteristic of clerical, semiskilled, and domestic workers. Indeed, in light of the uncertainty of today's job market, we would predict that conventional and stable patterns would be less common, while unstable and multiple-trial patterns would be more common, today and in the future.

Recently, the role of holding **gender stereotypic** views as an influence on men's and women's career choice has begun to be studied, finding that interest in a given career per se dominates men's career choices, while for women, interest in others ("I like to help people") or altruism seems to drive career choice (Fouad, 2007). For men, more traditional, masculine career choices seem to be related to holding anti-feminine attitudes, seeing oneself as tough, holding in one's emotions, and homophobia (Fouad, 2007).

Career Patterns: Women

Although most women in the United States are employed in the paid workforce, they have lower wages than men, are concentrated in different occupations, and are thinly represented at the highest levels of organizational hierarchies (Eagley & Wood, 1999). Women are challenged by balancing the roles of worker and mother, and are more likely work part-time and have their careers interrupted by having to move because of a husband's work relocation or because of childbirth/child-rearing. While the number of women in the work force climbed 37% from 1960 to 2002 (Gilbert, 2005), according to Cox (1994) the relative absence of women in upper management positions is often attributed to a **"glass ceiling"** that poses an impenetrable organizational boundary where they can see, but not reach, the apex of corporate power end status. It prevents the progress of women above middle management levels in organizations on the basis of gender rather than for lack of ability to handle jobs at higher levels. Van Vianen and Fischer (2002) found among non-management, but not management, that women expressed less masculine cultural preferences (being less ambitious), and even those who were ambitious experienced work-home conflicts.

Most managerial women are found in entry level or supervisory positions such as restaurant manger, office manager, and buyer; this concentration of managerial women in the lower ranks may be due to their relatively recent entrance into management positions in business and industry, structural barriers constructed by society and organizations that result in the glass ceiling effect, and personal biographic characteristics that affect how well women are able to adjust to corporate culture (Sachs, Chrisler, & Devlin, 1992). Kirchmeyer (2002) found that career interruptions, having an unemployed spouse, and family responsibilities principally accounted for the disadvantage women had in managerial career progression (see Hoffnung, 2004). Valcour and Ladge (2008) found that having one's first child later in life and having more time since having had one's last child predicted greater career success among women, while favoring a husband's career, working part-time, or changing jobs more often predicted less such success.

Overall, interest in women's career development is comparatively recent and it seems that women's career paths are more variable than those of men (Farmer, 2002). Recently however, Huang and Sverke (2007), relying on data collected over a nearly 30-year period, confirmed that women's career trajectories are more diverse, relative to those of men, with women's career patterns described as **upwardly mobile** (entrepreneurs in small business, professionals, associate professionals [finance, sales, administration] upward) , **stable** (associate professionals, stable at lower level occupations, stable service and sales workers), **downwardly mobile** (unskilled workers), **fluctuating** (drifters), and **being outside the labor market** (not being employed for the most part). Those women whose careers were upwardly mobile and stable were more common, while those whose careers were fluctuating or downwardly mobile were much less common, and restricted to women in lower-level occupations. Interestingly, professional women experienced the most work-to-family conflict (work interfering with family life). Huang et al. (2007) characterized these career patterns as either **work-centered, family-centered,** or **work and family combined.**

As women and men approach career decision making differently, these gender differences are likely magnified when considering the choice of gender-non-traditional occupations (Tokar & Jome, 1998). Interestingly, this variability among women

Figure 7-2. Men and women often display diverse patterns of career change.

relative to men is reflected in the former's expectations and timing of retirement while they are still working (Wong & Hardy, 2009).

Despite continued discrimination, the demands of dual-career marriages, and lagging behind men in earnings, women are highly committed to their chosen career paths. It is important to acknowledge the contributions of the Women's Movement during the 1960s to the diversity we currently observe in women's career paths. For example, Harmon (1989) studied two groups of women, those who were 18 in 1968 who were reassessed at age 30 in 1981, and a separate group of 18-year-olds in 1983. College freshmen and adult women of the 1980s were similar in terms of their career aspirations, and were more specific than those in 1968 regarding desirable occupations. Historical changes in women's roles seem to have produced women who are more aware of the need for women to be employed and who are more likely to consider nontraditional careers than their age peers in the 1960s. Indeed, having women as mentors (McBride, 2003), having better access to training opportunities to

improve work skills (Stern, Song, & O'Brien, 2004), and a growing trend against defining careers (e.g., teaching, nursing) as "feminine" (Smulyanm, 2004) that contribute to a changing organizational culture (Jandeska & Kraimer, 2005), all contribute to a more supportive work climate for women. While some women "opt-out" for motherhood over career, they are in minority (Gilbert, 2005).

The term **reentry** has generally been used to describe women reentering the labor force after an absence (e.g., in raising their children) ranging from a few years to as many as 35 years (Padula, 2001). Typical reentry women are between 25 and 54 years of age (Padula, 2001) and are either women who left the labor force to raise families and then returned to work after varying periods of time, or are returning to work as a result of divorce or death of a spouse. These women, having lost their primary source of support, need to secure employment. However, the largest group of individuals now entering the workforce are women over 40 years of age and married women with young children. As the rate of growth of women in the labor force is likely to increase at a faster rate than that of men, the proportion of women in the labor force will also grow; it was predicted to grow to 48% in 2008 (Schwerrha & McMullin, 2002). Unfortunately, a lack of work experience for some women results in limited opportunities and lower earnings. A majority of such women work in retail sales and administrative support services, occupations for which the average wages are often below those of the total workforce.

Widows qualify as **displaced homemakers** (Morgan, 1989). Younger widows and widows who experience declines in their standard of living are more likely than other widows to seek employment (see Chapter 12). In contrast, older widows are soon disinclined to look for work, in part because access to Social Security and perhaps private pension income lessens the pressure to seek employment. Staats et al. (1995) found the quality of life of older working widows to be lower than that of other older workers. Also, these researchers reported that the income of the working widow is lower than other older workers. Displaced job-seeking women, because of age and a lack of work experience and out-dated skills, generally face multiple barriers upon labor force reentry. Such women need training, advice on how to find jobs, other supportive services, and income.

Occupational Stress

The increasing demand of constant change for many employees has heightened workers' stress reactions, resulting in severe psychological turmoil for some. McCortney and Engels (2003) in discussing the impact of unemployment, note increased suicide rates, substance abuse and addiction, homelessness, violence, and other mental health problems associated with the inability to cope with job loss. Another outcome of having to adapt to the constant changes that occur in today's work environment is **job burnout** (Angerer, 2003). As workers are over-loaded in job cultures that penalize "pushing-back" or complaints about one's work environment, they increasingly experience feelings of exhaustion, cynicism, and alienation. Although work continues to contribute to people's identity development in adulthood, the Western world has seen a steady decline in the traditional work-ethic and organizational loyalty. This is caused by demands for increased productivity as resources are diminishing, resulting in critical sacrifices in workers' personal time with family, ignorance of their health, and having to make connections with friends by workers that they perceive as a necessary burden in order to keep their jobs.

Organizations seem to have diminished in loyalty to their employees as well (e.g., the CEO of General Electric Jack Welch's approach of firing the bottom 20% of employees; Delta Airlines defaulting on their employees' pensions), all of which points to a declining trend in reciprocal loyalty between workers and their employers (Hall & Mirvis, 1996). This trend is increasingly common in today's world of work as workers and employers see one another in adversarial terms.

In a classic study of work stress, Osipow, Doty, and Spokane (1985) studied over 300 employed men and women in five age ranges: below 25, 25 to 34, 35 to 44, 45 to 54, and 55+, finding that people under age 25 experienced the most psychological and interpersonal strain. For people over 25, strain in general declined consistently with age. Perhaps older people are better at coping with strain or have left jobs that are stressful? Further, younger people reported distinct types of stresses at work, such as having unchallenging work, experiencing conflict between the values or objectives of different people at work, or being in an aversive physical environment. On the other hand, older people reported that work overload and being responsible for others at work were more stressful to them (MacLennan, 1992).

With increased age, most people tend to change coping styles to those that are more effective, such as adopting more recreational activities, better self-care, and more effective use of time. With increased age, people make better use of social support to cope with job stress. Consistent with the differential impact of work stress on persons in adulthood, beginning workers are anxious about entry into a field and holding their first job; middle-aged workers worry about peaking in their careers; and older workers are concerned about obsolescence, redundancy, and extrusion. Additionally, work hours, leave policies, and needs for child and eldercare are all potential sources of conflict for parents, particularly working mothers on whom most of the responsibility for the family generally falls (MacLennan, 1992).

There are also gender differences in terms of occupational stress. In general, studies have suggested that managerial and professional women encounter unique sources of stress associated with their minority status and gender, and that these stressors contribute to higher levels of overall stress compared with their male counterparts (Iwasaki et al., 2004). Multiple-role strain is a major source of stress or overload for employed women and men, but the reality remains that working women typically spend more combined time on work and family responsibilities than do men (Iwasaki et al., 2004).

The cumulative demands of multiple roles can result in **role strain** of three types, **overload, interference from work to family,** and **interference**

from family to work (Duxbury, Higgins, & Lee, 1994). Overload exists when the total demands on time and energy associated with the prescribed activities of multiple roles are too great to perform the roles adequately or comfortably; interference from family occurs when family-role responsibilities hinder work performance, e.g., a child's illness causes one to miss work, and interference from work to family arises when work-role activities interfere with one's family responsibilities, e.g., long hours at work prevent the performance of duties at home.

What seems to be key, especially regarding the relationship between family and work, is one's **emotional state**, where some persons seem to be more likely to experience conflict between their roles as employees and their role in the family than are others, where being **psychologically resilient** or **hardy** and possessing the ability think about the demands of life without getting angry are especially advantageous in handling work-family conflicts (Eby, Maher, & Butts, 2009).

Duxbury et al. (1994) found that mothers experience more role overload, interference from work to family, and interference from family to work than do men. This suggests that combining paid employment with responsibilities at home is more problematic for women than it is for men because their family and combined work and family demands are higher, and thus, female workers experience greater amount of stress because of higher pressure and the difficulty in juggling work and home responsibilities compared with male workers. Alternatively, males typically report experiencing stress primarily centered on their work lives (Iwasaki et al., 2004). These findings are consistent with the idea of the "double day" or "second shift" which are terms used to explain multi-role stress where employed women are primarily responsible for work inside the home in addition to their work outside the home (Iwasaki et al., 2004).

In addition to work and family stressors commonly experienced among working men (e.g., workload, working environment, people relationships, work-home conflicts), researchers have identified key sources of stress that are pertinent to working women. For example, work-related stressors include problems related to discrimination and prejudice such as career blocks, sexual harassment, being "token" women who work in nontraditional jobs (e.g., male-dominated organizational structures and climates), performance pressure, gender stereotyping, isolation, and lack of models (Iwasaki et al., 2004). Stress experienced by women working in male-dominated industries or male-dominated professions is frequently exacerbated by gender-based barriers (Iwasaki et al., 2004). Another source of work stressors represents specific stressors associated with ethnic/minority women such as racism, sexism, and bicultural stressors. Finally, both men and women can experience stress as a result of **sexual harassment in the workplace** (See Box C).

Fortunately, some employers are assisting their employees in coping with work stress by implementing wellness programs, providing resources for middle-aged persons caring for their parents, providing eldercare benefits, and even assisting in the formation of caregiver support groups (*Hello mom— goodbye retirement*, CNN.com/living, October 22, 2008)

The Loss of One's Job: The Impact on Individuals and Families

Currently, global competition is the single most powerful economic fact of life, leading some companies to downsize to increase their competitive advantage. Indeed, the effects of involuntary job loss can last as long as 2 years, impair one's physical health, and cause depression (Price, 2002). Indeed, a Gallup poll indicated that 61% of Americans feared losing their jobs (www. http://inhome.rediff.com/money/2004/mar/17bpo1.htm).

In the context of employment, laid-off workers who return to the job market must often take huge pay cuts because downward mobility is the rule rather than the exception. Jobs are not only being lost temporarily because of a recession. Rather, they are also being wiped out permanently as a result of

---

Box C

Sexual Harassment in the Workplace

Sexual harassment is a form of sex discrimination that violates Title VII of the Civil Rights Act of 1964. According to the U.S. Equal Employment Opportunity Commission in the Fiscal Year 2004, the EEOC received 13,136 charges of sexual harassment. Of those charges, 15.1% were filed by males.

Unwelcome sexual advances, requests for sexual favors, and other verbal or physical conduct of a sexual nature constitute sexual harassment when this conduct explicitly or implicitly affects an individual's employment, unreasonably interferes with an individual's work performance, or creates an intimidating, hostile, or offensive work environment.

Sexual harassment can occur in a variety of circumstances, including but not limited to the following:

- The victim as well as the harasser may be a women or a man. The victim does not have to be of the opposite sex.
- The harasser can be the victim's supervisor, an agent of the employer, a supervisor in another area, a coworker, or a non-employee.
- The victim does not have to be the person harassed but could be anyone affected by the offensive conduct.
- Unlawful sexual harassment may occur without economic injury to or discharge of the victim.
- The harasser's conduct must be unwelcome.

It is helpful for the victim to inform the harasser directly that the conduct is unwelcome and must stop. The victim should use any employer complain mechanism or grievance system available.

Source: U. S. Equal Employment Opportunity Commission.

---

new technology, improved machinery, and new ways of organizing work.

Organizations of this century will differ dramatically in structure, design, and demographics from those of the 20th century. Demographically, they will be far more diverse. They comprise more women at all levels, more multiethnic, multicultural workers, more older workers, workers with disabilities, robots, and contingent workers. Also, the racial composition of the United States is changing as minorities continue to increase in proportion and their labor rates continue to increase. The Hispanic labor force is the most rapidly rising and will eventually be larger than the African American workforce (Schwerha & McMullin, 2002). The constant sequence of mergers, acquisitions, and reengineering has made organizational tenure very unpredictable. Thus, workers of today and of the future have to be able to adapt to changing circumstances and prepared for multiple careers. In any event, loss of self-esteem, feelings of alienation and depression, family discord and abuse (see Chapter 4), alcoholism, and, in some situations, even suicide (see Chapter 10) are the result of such unforeseen negative events in people's careers. Many individuals even feel they are responsible for losing their jobs, contributing to depression and feelings of failure.

In a classic study of the impact of job loss on adults, DeFrank and Ivancevich (1986) found that the personal impact of job loss and/or unemployment on individuals can be quite debilitating, causing declines in physical health and self-esteem, depression, anxiety, or suicide. Moreover, job loss has potential psychological, economic, and social effects on all members of the family. Indeed, while unemployment can have devastating effects on self-esteem and relationships with the family, psychologically hardy, resilient individuals fare better in coping with the loss of their jobs (Crowley, Hayslip, & Hobdy, 2003).

Many factors influence individuals' responses to the loss of their jobs (DeFrank & Ivancevich, 1986). While loss of a job means loss of both income and status, age is a more important predictor of responses to job loss, with middle-aged men being more vulnerable than older or younger men. However, Lahner and Hayslip (2005) found younger employees to be more negatively impacted by the downsizing of fellow employees than older employees, perhaps because of the former group's more restricted job-seeking experience should they themselves lose their jobs, the unexpected loss of employee peers with whom one expected to be working for a long time, or because of the latter group's anticipation of retirement. Consistent with this finding is that younger employees experience more job insecurity and are more likely to see job turnover as a possibility than are older workers (Cheng & Chan, 2008). It is important to realize however, that how people perceive this loss, their degree of social support, their existing coping skills, and how long they are unemployed all contribute to how they respond to job loss (Hayslip, 2011).

While at one time, it was believed that job loss was not particularly devastating for young individuals (Allen & Staffensmeir, 1989), given today's economy, unemployment rates for young adults greatly exceed the national average of about 10%, reaching nearly 14% for young adults between the age of 20 and 25 (National Bureau of Labor Statistics, 2009a, 2009b), with 25% of unemployed young adults saying that they have given up looking for work.

In understanding job loss, it is important to differentiate forced unemployment (layoffs, downsizing), health-related unemployment (a serious illness, an injury, a chronic health condition such as diabetes-related obesity or COPD via smoking)

and voluntary withdrawal (quitting a job) from the workforce. A clear understanding of the effects of unemployment is moreover hampered by the attributions employees make regarding the reason for unemployment, depending upon the degree of control they feel they have in the loss of their jobs.

While the primary victim of job loss is the employee, unemployment also has pervasive effects on the family as a whole (Hayslip, 2011). Indeed, the effects of involuntary job loss can create many challenges that are both direct and indirect in understanding the impact of job loss on families. For example, in addition to the loss of income, families must cope with the realignment of role responsibilities that accompany job loss as well as the secondary effects of unemployment on family members' physical and mental health. For many families, there is a stigma attached to not only being victims of unemployment, but also in some cases, having to deal with the foreclosure of their homes and the loss of status in the community linked to the loss of income.

Individuals vary in terms of the impact that forced unemployment has on them and their families. For some, its effects are indeed negative in terms of impaired physical and mental health (even when controlling for pre-job loss levels of functioning and health); the research literature is clear in this respect (Blau, 2008). Persons do grieve over the loss their jobs: their identity is undeniably changed, friendships are lost, and the very stability of the family is threatened. For some, such feelings lead to suicide, complicating further the family's adjustment to job loss.

Individuals who are older and who have been in labor force for a long time are perhaps more negatively affected in that the loss of their jobs interrupts what has been a long career or precipitates an earlier than anticipated retirement. For these reasons, it makes sense that there would be a negative relationship between age and job turnover (Panek, 1997). That is, as age increases, individuals are less likely to leave their current positions.

Yet, while such persons may have the economic resources to withstand the loss of income accom-

Box D

Unemployment among Young Adults: An Intergenerational Experience

More and more young adults are returning home to live with their parents after graduating from college. Why? For many, it is because they could not find work. Also the period of young adulthood is more elongated than before (Arnett, 2000), young adults are taking longer to finish their educations, and the law passed under the Obama administration lets parents keep their children on their health insurance until they are 26 ("The long road to adulthood is growing even longer," *The New York Times*, Cohen, 2010). Young adults are increasingly more likely to rely on their parents for financial support. This new life transition is principally explained by the bleak job prospects for young adults in view of the recession of late, where the unemployment rate for young adults greatly exceeds the national average.

Not only does a child's moving back home end the empty nest period for parents (1 in 7 parents say their adult child has moved in with them, according to research conducted by the Pew Research Center), but it requires sacrifices on their part because of the extra money they must spend that they had hoped to set aside for retirement. At the same time, it gives them the opportunity to reconnect with and know their children as adults. This elongated period of dependence on parents has been termed **adultescence** by David Morrison, founder of *Twentysomething,* a consulting/research firm focusing on young adults.

According to 2008 Census data, 30% of adults aged 18-34 lived with their parents. In the face of not being able to get that first job, divorce, or unemployment, young adults adjust to moving back home by taking part-time work or returning to school to get a graduate degree. Some, however, give up on looking for work altogether, believing that that dream job is out of reach for them. Some, as a newly graduated 23-year old with a degree in emergency management termed it, adjust by "moochin' off my parents" until they can find employment. He said his "self-esteem is at an all-time low" not being able to find a job after looking intensely for 6 months. As a 25-year-old remarked at having to move back home, "It's not something you plan on trying to start life as an adult." A 29-year old who lost her job said "I resisted it for awhile, a loss of independence, pride thing going on."

For both generations, this life transition requires adjustments. Parents can adjust by setting limits and insisting that their children "pull their weight" at home (e.g., helping out around the house, contributing to paying for car insurance or a cellphone). At the same time, extending the "safety net" to a child gives many parents great satisfaction. Rather than make their children feel guilty or inferior, they support them out of love until the job situation improves. Importantly, parents, as do adult children, should realize that this situation will eventually change for the better. As one parent put it, whose son is moving out and whose other son will soon follow, "We were empty nesters once for about four months. It will be fine when it happens again." According to the Bureau of Labor Statistics, 40% of young adult job seekers are "discouraged"- they have given up looking for a job. Avoiding such discouragement can be achieved by adult children setting new, and more immediate goals for themselves, and in supporting the family to the extent that they can. Remaining optimistic and taking a proactive stance to getting even part-time work are very important in being able to feel good about oneself in the face of an adverse job market.

Box E

Primary Obstacles or Risks to Job Change for Older Workers

- **Rule and strategy changes**. The most difficult kinds of changes for older workers may be those that "alter the rules and strategies" they used successfully to develop their occupational career (or current job), such as company loyalty, cooperation with others, independent thinking, and individual initiative.
- **Technological dominance.** When the knowledge and skills acquired over years of experience become less important than being able to use the latest technologies, older workers are likely to view the job change as a threat, rather than a challenge for growth. The threat occurs because new technologies can often undermine competitive advantage enjoyed by the older workers, such as knowledge and skills learned with prior experience, and force them to compete with younger workers in areas where the younger workers are more skilled.
- **Threat to their self-concept.** Older workers may resist job changes that threaten their self-concept. As persons mature and develop on their jobs, they achieve a level of psychological success, such as sense of task success and feeling of competence. By midcareer, workers may become more concerned about protecting themselves from failure (which they would perceive as a blow to their self-concept), and establish career/job routines that minimize risk taking.
- **Age stereotypes.** When supervisors believe that older workers are less capable of learning new skills, more resistant to change, unable to keep up with the workload, and a general burden to the organization, they are less likely to commit training dollars to what is perceived to be a poor return on their investment. Furthermore, if older workers themselves internalize such stereotypes, they can become self-fulfilling prophecies and reinforce any age stereotypes that may be held by their employer.

Source: Bailey and Hansson (1995).

panying unemployment, finding another job may be more difficult because they are perceived as too expensive to hire, untrainable, or simply too close to retirement, and therefore a poor risk in terms of remaining with the company. In this respect, there appear to be four primary obstacles or risks to getting a new job for older workers, and overcoming such obstacles is key to an older person's gaining work after losing a job (see Box E).

Other the other hand, younger, newer employees may be more highly trained in terms of the currency of their skills and have not yet developed the expectation that their careers will be stable. Younger

persons, however, are unlikely to have accumulated the financial resources to tide them over in the face of extended joblessness, and they may be faced with expenses (e.g., house or childcare payments, the costs of raising children) for which they have little financial resources to meet, given their lack of savings. Such differences parallel those for persons with white collar jobs versus those with blue collar jobs, with job loss affecting the latter more seriously. Laid-off workers who return to the job market must often take huge pay cuts because downward mobility is the rule rather than the exception. Rather than be scientists, teachers, or computer programmers, they take low paying jobs, e.g., stocking shelves at a hardware store (*Working Longer a Growing Trend for Americans*, Associated Press, September 1, 2008).

Individuals who are self-employed also face different challenges that those who work for others; the former may have more flexibility in seeking a new line of work, but also are likely to be more negatively impacted if they do not have health insurance or cannot file for unemployment benefits. Indeed, adding to the tenuousness of their situation, many have made no preparations for retirement (Denay & Kim, 2008). The impact of job loss on individuals and families also varies with whether the family is a single earner one, whether the parent is single, the extent of social support that is available, the ages of the children, and the potential for reemployment and/or mobility (Hayslip, 2011).

Coping with Job Loss

How individuals cope with the loss of their jobs, i.e., to the extent persons cope adaptively or not, has implications not only for them, but also for their families (Hayslip, 2011). In addition to increased depression, anxiety, worry, hostility, and anger, individuals may turn to alcohol or drug use as a means of coping with feelings of loneliness, alienation, and pessimism about the future. This, under certain circumstances, may lead to spousal abuse, marital friction and stress, depression in one's spouse, or divorce as a direct consequence of unemployment. The effects of unemployment are also indirect via becoming isolated from friends, particularly if the latter are still employed. For children, job loss may precipitate family conflict or unduly harsh or abusive behavior on the part of the parent(s), leading to poor school performance, drug use, smoking, or delinquent behavior. The unemployed parent may be seen as having less status in the family, and in the case of fathers, be seen as less worthy of respect or as someone whose authority in the family has been lessened. On the other hand, unemployment can create the opportunity to learn new skills or pursue a new career, which can create an atmosphere of hope and optimism within the family.

Adapting a strategy of positive reappraisal (see Chapter 6) for both the individual and the family can be helpful, wherein seeking employment or receiving new job training may help family members to feel more cohesive and empowered. Such effects may be greater if the unemployed family member's former job was not challenging, hazardous, or not satisfying. In this respect, expressive writing has proven helpful in coping with job loss; this likely benefits the entire family as well.

While unemployment means loss of income and status, as we noted earlier in this chapter, age is an important predictor of how persons cope; middle-aged men are most vulnerable. This threatens their family's financial future in having to spend money set aside for retirement, or having less money to spend on a child's college education. Money spent on travel to visit children and grandchildren may be limited. Middle-aged persons seeking employment are confronted with the dual constraints of finding appropriate jobs in a tight economy and finding employers receptive to hiring older workers. Middle-aged and older workers may face difficulties in adapting to new methods and techniques and, in certain jobs, in maintaining the pace and rhythm of work. They may be unable to gain access to training programs and run a greater risk of not only long-term unemployment, but also greater difficulty in getting rehired. Complicating matters, middle-aged and older persons may be concerned about their ability to do new work, feel they are too old, or find retraining opportunities, when they become available, to be more difficult than they expect. In addition to middle-aged males, for older, poorly educated persons who have low self-esteem, job loss is also quite devastating as they have the lowest expectation of finding a new job.

When people lose their jobs, they must find ways of reorganizing their non-work lives, assessing themselves realistically yet positively. Ultimately, they must distance themselves from the loss of their jobs and remind themselves that there is more to life than work. Simply put, they still have their families upon which to depend for emotional support. Indeed, interventions to help persons cope

Box F

Suggested Coping Strategies for Those Who Have Lost a Job

1. Accept the feelings of denial, a profound sense of loss, anger, and feeling unproductive; they are normal and predictable reactions to the loss of a job. So too is feeling fearful, and feeling that the future is bleak or uncertain.

2. Move toward a constructive and proactive stance toward getting a new start: work on your resume, refresh your interviewing skills, talk to others who have lost their jobs. Ask for advice, but maintain your independence of thought.

3. Strive to regain and maintain control over your life. You have a choice in how you respond to being laid off. You can feel overwhelmed and defeated, and you can seize this as an opportunity. Do not let your feelings about the situation or the persons who caused it to interfere with your efforts to move on with your life.

4. Examine your health insurance and financial situations. Cut unnecessary expenses as soon as possible. Develop an economic plan. Take advantage of any counseling, job search, or job training opportunities. Do not give yourself "time off" after the loss of your job. This will make it more difficult to return to a state of emotional normalcy.

5. Develop a satisfying, consistent, and constructive routine. Set daily goals: creating your resume, making phone calls, writing letters, conducting job searchers, going to interviews, contacting future employers, maintaining friendships. Keep this schedule every day and do not deviate from it. A lack of effort or action leads to worry and depression. Having a routine allows you to focus on what you can control.

6. Take care of your health and value your family and friends. They are your lifeline throughout all that you have gone through.

7. Keep positive, keep learning, examine all your options, and don't give up!

Source: Adapted from "Job loss: How to cope" (2006), http://careerplanning.about.com/od/jobloss/a/job_loss.htm

---

with job loss must be holistic in nature—they must include the family, and especially the spouse. Responses to unemployment are influenced by the quality of the (marital) relationship, the mutually supportive skills of each person, and perhaps most importantly, the *meaning* for the family that the loss of the job has, i.e., can the family survive in the face of unemployment? Clearly, the transitions families face in the event of job loss are potentially negative. However, individuals and families can survive unemployment and grow closer in the face of the adverse circumstances that losing a job can create.

As the unemployment rate among older persons continues to rise (Johnson, 2009; National Bureau of Labor Statistics, 2009) and indeed approaches that for persons who are younger, it is indeed unfortunate that older persons also have the lowest expectation of finding a new job (Johnson, 2009). In this respect, AARP has called for efforts to support older unemployed persons: subsidize more health insurance premiums for those who have lost jobs, give older unemployed persons the same earned income tax benefits that younger persons get, enforce age discrimination laws in hiring and firing decisions, and extend unemployment insurance (*bulletin.aarp.org*, January-February, 2010).

Complicating matters is the fact that middle-aged and older persons are often concerned about their ability to learn new skills (see Chapter 3), may feel they are too old, and may find retraining more difficult than they expected. While older persons may find new learning more meaningful to them personally, getting opportunities may be especially difficult for older workers, as organizations often encourage them to retire early rather than helping them navigate the job change process.

Industrial Gerontology

Due to a variety of reasons, such as economic and personal factors, increased longevity, and federal legislation, more individuals are remaining longer in the workforce. Thus, the United States and other industrialized nations are currently experiencing a "greying" of the workforce (Panek, 1997). Between 1985 and 2000, the number of workers between the ages of 45 and 65 years grew by 41%, while the number of workers in the 16 to 35 years age group declined slightly, and this trend is expected to continue (Hedge, Borman, & Lammlein, 2006). At the end of the last century the median age of the labor force was age 40, and the number of workers over the age of 55 was predicted to jump and did jump another 46% during the first decade of the 21st century. Thus, America and its labor force are changing. Most significantly the working population is becoming older and the characteristics of workers and of the workplace itself are changing due to technological changes and business turbulence (Hardy, 2006).

While mandatory retirement, health, and the physical demands of work force some persons to retire, the new reality is that more people are putting off retiring and therefore working longer because they cannot afford to do otherwise. The threat of Social Security benefits diminishing; the impact of the recession of 2008-2009 on the stock market— affecting what people can save for retirement via an individual 401k plan (versus earning a pension through one's employer or through the state or federal government); more restricted and more ex-pensive health care coverage; and diminished and/or less reliable employer-provided pension earnings are all factors that suggest people, at least in the near future, will stay on the job longer than before (see "The jilted age," Greenhouse, 2009, *New York Times*).

These technological, business, and demographic changes necessitate a rethinking of the traditional models of career stages. As such, extended and multiple careers will become the norm. Further, with the virtual abolishment of mandatory retirement for many Americans, a large number of older workers choose to remain in the labor force. In addition, the workforce is increasingly female and diverse (Staats, Colbert, & Partlo, 1995). For these reasons, business and industry must consider the needs and abilities of the older worker as important (Hedge, Borman, & Lammlein, 2006).

The study of the older worker is referred to as **industrial gerontology**. Who is the older worker? According to the Work in America Institute (1980), anyone, regardless of occupation, aged 55 years or above is an **older worker**. However, this designation is a general one and varies substantially from one occupation to another. For instance, 35 may be considered old for a professional athlete but relatively young for a surgeon.

Attitudes toward Older Workers

Business and industry, as well as younger workers, hold a number of common, and generally negative, stereotypes of older workers (Panek, 1997). These imply that older workers do not do well in training and retraining (You can't teach an old dog new tricks); are not comfortable with new technologies; are rigid, not flexible and have difficulty in adapting to change; and lack the desire/motivation to get ahead. The most widely accepted negative stereotype of the older worker is that job productivity and performance decline with age (Hedge, Borman, & Lammlein, 2006). On the other hand, older workers have much experience to bring to the job, and the impact of age on work performance varies by the nature of one's work (e.g., jobs that involve speed and strength versus those involving experience, wisdom, and judgment (Hedge, Borman & Lammlein, 2006). Indeed, Bambrick and Bonder (2005) found older employees to see work in terms of enhancing their self-concept, as a means of giving back to the community, and as a way of staying involved. Being more selective in the kinds of work one does, especially when one's work is difficult, and compensating for losses in speed and physical strength are also characteristic of the adaptations to work that older employees make to remain productive and enjoy their work (Yeung & Fung, 2009).

In an extensive study of 11 corporations (Sticker, 1997), employers were asked their opinions of older workers. The universal response, consistent with the results of earlier studies, was a recitation of the positive stereotype, extolling the qualities older workers bring to the workplace (the older worker is perceived as stable, reliable, responsible, trustworthy, possessing a strong work ethic and seriousness concerning the work). However, when asked if they were hiring or making an effort to retain older workers, the response was no. Even though older workers were highly valued for their characteristics such as reliable and responsible, these were not considered as important to the firms that were studied. Flexibility, innovativeness, and being technologically current were more favorable traits.

Sticker (1997) argued that these positive and negative stereotypes make older workers desirable, in limited numbers, for certain low-pay, low-skill jobs, particularly where their maturity serves to stabilize an otherwise very young labor pool. Yet such stereotypes inhibit employers from recruiting older workers for, or retaining them in, well-paid jobs that require a significant level of professional and technical skills. Overall, the many unfounded attitudes and beliefs about older workers generally stem from a lack of knowledge and understanding about the aging process (Hedge, Borman, & Lammlein, 2006) and/or, in many instances, are not supported by research. Underscoring the negative attitudes held toward older workers are the findings of Erber and Long (2006) who found that forgetfulness and slowness were attributed to older employees to a

greater extent and were attributed to older workers' declining skills. Also, as an indication of older workers' negative expectations about their work lives, Zacher and Frese (2009) found that with increasing age, workers were more likely to anticipate the end of their careers and to see fewer opportunities open to them at work.

Age Norms of Occupations

The same chronological age can take on different meaning, relative to the age distribution of the job or occupation in which it is embedded. That is, jobs and occupations have "age norms." These age norms may shape both the expectations of the individual, as well as the group (Rosen & Jerdee, 1988), and involve the classification or categorization of individuals into groups based on age. This results in shared beliefs regarding the "appropriate" age at which an individual either should or should not occupy a particular occupation (Panek Staats, & Hiles, 2006). Unfortunately, age norms for occupations often contribute to false beliefs and stereotypes about the capabilities of older workers (Hedge, Borman, & Lammlein, 2006).

Age norms suggest that occupations may be viewed as more or less appropriate for different individuals based on their chronological age (Cleveland & Hollman, 1990). By way of illustration, Gordon and Arvey (1986) found that many occupations (e.g., security guard, jeweler, mayor), were classified as "old age jobs," while other occupations (e.g., file clerk, hospital attendant, dental hygienist), were classified as "young age jobs." Further, they observed a positive correlation between the actual age distribution in an occupation and the classification of the occupation based on chronological age.

The proportion of older men employed in executive and managerial occupations tends to be reasonably high, reflecting, undoubtedly, age-related gains in experience that make these men attractive as managers and executives (Hedge, Borman, & Lammlein, 2006). The proportion of workers employed in what might be considered more physically demanding occupations, such as laborers,

---

Adults Speak

Vic

Vic is 59 years old. He is married and has two children and three grandchildren. He is unassuming and pleasant to be around, and he works extremely well with people. After working in the computer industry for 30 years, he decided to go into business for himself. He acquired a printing business and handled all aspects of computerized billing, graphics, and delivery for over 5 years. When the economy worsened in the 1980s, he was forced to sell his business, but his troubles had just begun. Over the next 4 years, he repeatedly applied for positions for which he was highly qualified and was passed over for someone younger.

He is now, finally, employed in a home-security business monitoring alarms via a computer terminal. Over the past 4 years, he figures he has been turned down for jobs he was highly qualified for at least 30 times. He was often told, "You're really overqualified for this job. You would be bored and the pay would be an insult to you." Even though Vic really wanted these jobs, he felt that these were simply excuses to reject him because of his age. Vic concluded by saying, "These years have probably been the worst period of my life. I had lost my mother, then my father. I told a friend one day, `You really get to the point where you say, is there ever going to be an end to this?' It was a devastating experience."

---

shows a drop with age, although almost as many middle-aged men can be found in this occupational category as among executives and managers. The oldest male workers are usually in farm occupations. Age differences in occupational distribution are somewhat less pronounced among women, who, regardless of age, show a clear tendency toward concentration in a very few occupations, most notably those classified as service or administrative, which includes clerical work (Rix, 1990). Also, occupations that require a high degree of training and experience, such as dentist, college professor, and physician, are generally associated with being older.

The study done by Panek et al. (2006) of 60 occupations reinforces these conclusions. These researchers found perceived optimal performance and recommended retirement age were correlated (related) but differed as a function of the perceived demands (e.g., cognitive, physical, psycho-motor) associated with the occupation. Specifically, raters suggested the earliest recommended retirement ages for the two clusters of occupations with the highest perceived physical demands (high risk, e.g., firefighter; trades, e.g., plumber), compared to the two clusters of occupations with the lowest perceived physical demands (professionals, e.g., physician; white collar, e.g., sales representative) (See Box G).

Also, determining an individual's career success/progress is partly based on the age norm characterizing various career tracks. For example, specific age norms for occupations designate whether an individual is considered a "fast-tracker," "on time," or "reached a plateau" with respect to career progression and/or advancement.

It has been suggested that instead of judging workers by their chronological age, it is of more value to judge them in terms of **functional age**, that is, in terms of what they can do (see Chapter 1). This has led to attempts to derive measures of functional ability required for each job and to place individuals, regardless of age, in jobs that best match their abilities. However, research has not been overly supportive of the functional-age approach in industry. Thus, the courts have generally upheld chrono-

---

Box G

Does Age Make a Difference to You?

When asked, most of us might state that a person's age makes no difference to us in our personal relationships, but we often "think twice" about older people in specific occupational contexts. Consider the following list of individuals in specific occupations. Ask yourself, "Would I feel differently about this person if I learned that he or she were older than I thought, say, 60, 65, or 70?" If your health or well-being or that of your family were "on the line," would you feel safer with someone younger? Evaluating your reactions may make you more aware of your own ageist biases!

Your family doctor
Your dentist
Your barber or beautician

The person driving the school bus your children take every day
The salesperson at a shop
Your therapist
The lab technician doing your blood work
The receptionist in an office
Your surgeon
The airline pilot flying the plane in which you and your family are passengers
Your children's teacher
Your pharmacist
Your mechanic
Your lawyer
The electrician rewiring your house
The nurse in your doctor's office
The telephone operator taking your message

---

logical age as a valid criterion for retirement decisions (Avolio & Panek, 1981).

Ageism in Employment

Ageism refers to the process of systematic stereotyping of and discrimination against people because they are old, just as racism and sexism do on the basis of skin color and gender. Although it is against the law, implicit and explicit **ageism in employment** occurs for both genders in all types of jobs. Nearly 2 decades ago, Davies et al. (1991) reported that between 60% and 90% of employers agreed that age discrimination occurred. To illustrate, the unemployment rate for adult males 55 to 64 years of age is higher than for those aged 25 to 54 years, a trend that has been common for the past 30 years, and once out of work, older workers are likely to remain unemployed much longer than younger workers (Hardy, 2006). When reemployed, they often find jobs at lower pay, requiring less skill, and at lower occupational levels. For older minorities, employment problems are especially severe (Freeman & Williams, 1987).

Since older adults experience more prolonged unemployment, they are also more likely to become discouraged and drop out of the work force altogether (*AARP Bulletin*, January-February, 2010). Understandably, discouraged unemployed older workers are likely to have significantly lower job-search self-efficacy expectations, more disorderly work histories, longer periods of current unemployment, and higher reported levels of depression, social isolation, and psychological discouragement (Hedge, Borman, & Lammlein, 2006).

Older workers tend to be unemployed longer than younger workers for a variety of reasons. First, because they have seniority, they tend to remain in declining industries and occupations until the jobs finally disappear as a result of economic or technological change. Second, older workers tend to have lower levels of formal education and, therefore, are excluded from positions with higher requirements. Third, they have less mobility, due to greater responsibilities and obligations, compared to younger workers. Finally, they have less well-developed job-seeking attitudes and skills compared to younger workers, since they may not have interviewed for a job in many years. Contributing to the problem is that many traditional personnel selection tests and interview procedures may be unfairly discriminating against older job applicants (Sterns & Alexander, 1987). That is, selection tests may not have norms for older workers, or may measure abilities that decline with age but have nothing to do with actual job performance (Stagner, 1985).

Age Discrimination in Employment Acts (ADEA)

Discrimination against workers as a function of age may even begin at age 30 in some occupations. The problem of age discrimination has been so severe that federal laws were enacted to prohibit it. The legislation was titled the **Age Discrimination in Employment Acts (ADEA)**, and it was originally passed in 1967 but amended in 1974, 1978, and 1986. This legislation protects workers between the ages of 40 and 70 years (Panek, 1997). Specifically, the ADEA of 1967 specified protection of workers from age discrimination between the ages of 40 and 65 and promotion of employment opportunities for older workers capable of meeting job requirements. In 1974 the act was amended to include coverage of government employees at the local, state, and federal level. In 1978 it was amended to change coverage to age 70 and to abolish mandatory retirement altogether for federal employees. In 1986 the act was further amended to remove the maximum age limitation, with certain exceptions. Since January 1987, older persons have, with a few exceptions, been legally entitled to remain at work for as long as they wish, assuming their performance is adequate. Thus, the ADEA has effectively eliminated mandatory retirement for the vast majority of American workers (Clark & Quinn, 2002). Australia and the United States are the only countries that prohibit companies from making their employees retire at a certain age (Edwards, 2004).

Further, it is a violation for employers to fail or refuse to hire, to discharge, or in other ways to discriminate against any individual with respect to compensation or other terms or conditions of employment because of age. Finally, workers cannot be limited, segregated, or classified in a way that might adversely affect their status as an employee because of age. However, this legislation is not universal; it does not cover all employees in all occupational settings. Exempt from this legislation are employers of less than 20 people, and jobs where age is a **bona fide occupational qualification (BFOQ)**. Although age discrimination is against the law, it still exists today, either subtly or overtly. Overall, the enactment of the ADEA and the virtual elimination of mandatory retirement by Congress in 1986 have resulted in employers becoming more sensitive to using the worker's chronological age as a basis for employment decision making (Avery & Foley, 1988). The ADEA defines "older workers" as individuals aged 40 and older (Waldman & Avolio, 1993).

Even in light of federal legislation, the issue of age discrimination has been and continues to be a problem. For example, Sterns and Alexander (1987) reported that a national workforce survey indicated that more than 80% of American workers believed that employers discriminate against older employees. Reflecting a continuing concern over age discrimination at work, in 2009 over 27,000 workers filed age discrimination complaints, a 29% increase over 2007 ("The jilted age?", Greenhouse, 2009, *The New York Times)*. For better or worse, from its inception the ADEA has allowed employers to consider an individual's age in employment decisions when the employer can show that age is a BFOQ, and reasonably necessary to the normal operations of the business.

Because age discrimination can be subtle, there are no reliable statistics on how many middle-aged and older workers actually experience age discrimination and under what circumstances. However, recent (2005) information from the Equal Employment Opportunity Commission indicates that perceived "unlawful discharge" was mentioned in over 50% of cases filed, the next two most frequent claims were "hiring and/or terms and conditions of employment," and "layoffs." In conclusion, discrimination against older workers did not evaporate with the passage of the ADEA; often it just

---

Box H

Generational Stereotypes of Worker Characteristics

Traditionalists (1925-1945): Practical, patient, loyal and hard-working, respectful of authority, follows the rules.

Generation X (1961-1980): Skeptical, self-reliant, risk-takers, maintains a balance between work and home life.

Baby Boomers (1946-1960): Optimistic, team player, ambitious, workaholic.

Millennials (1981- present): Hopeful, desirous of meaningful work, values diversity and change, technologically skilled.

Source: Patterson, C. (2005), *Generational diversity: Implications for consultation and teamwork.* Paper presented at the Meeting of the Council of Directors of School Psychology Programs on generational differences, Deerfield Beach, FL. Cited in Dittmann, C. (2005). Generational differences at work. *Monitor in Psychology*, June, p. 55.

---

becomes harder to prove (Hedge, Borman, & Lammlein, 2006). On the other hand, a recent Supreme Court ruling made it easier for employees over the age of 40 to file age discrimination suits. On a positive note, in late 2007, Congress passed the Fair Treatment for Experienced Pilots Act, which raised the age of mandatory retirement for currently employed pilots to age 65; they had formerly been forced to retire at age 60.

Changing Age Discrimination in the Workplace

How do we change age discrimination in the workplace? Hardy (2006) has several solutions: (1) improve the "fit" between older employees' skills (speed, physical strength, speed of information processing versus experience, handling unfamiliar situations, loyalty), (2) educate employers (and the public) about the strengths and weaknesses of older workers, (3) utilize the skills of persons who have retired (encouraging them to become mentors for younger employees) (it is becoming less common for persons to retire completely—see below), (4) develop a better understand of what older employees can and cannot do, and develop training pro-

grams with this in mind, and (5) more carefully consider job redesign with older workers as a focus, especially with regard to the impact of technology in the workplace.

An additional factor to consider is the workplace environment itself, wherein younger and older employees may not interact or understand one another well. In this respect, encouraging productive and open-minded mentor-mentee relationships (Some Boomers Struggle with the Role of Mentor, *Dallas Morning News*, June 10, 2003), and breaking down generational stereotypes of workers and employees (see Box H) are important. Such stereotypes lead to misinformation and hostility, undermining communication; they may be related to different values systems about work held by persons as they age (e.g. lessening the importance of work, less importance placed on pride in one's work) as well as differing values about work held by different generations (valuing promotion, being selfish, feeling less loyalty to the company (see Dittmann, "Generational differences at work," *Monitor in Psychology*, June, 2005, pp. 54-55). In the face of age discrimination, many older job seekers strive to maintain their skills, change their own work-related expectations, alter their physical appearance, use different language, and unfortunately, sometimes alter their resumes (Berger, 2009).

Check Your Learning 7-2

Identify the following terms or concepts:

"Greying" of the workforce
Ageism in employment
Bona fide occupational qualification (BFOQ)
ADEA
Reentry workers
Industrial gerontology
Functional age
Occupational stress
Glass ceiling effect

- Describe Havighurst's career patterns for men.

- Why is career development more complex for women compared to men?

- List and describe career patterns for women. Which are most common? Least common?

- What is the nature of age differences in perceiving and coping with pressures (stress) in the workplace?

- What are some of the gender differences in occupational stress?

- Discuss the three types of role strain which can result from the demands of multiple roles.

- What are some of the reactions to job loss? Do these reactions differ as a function of age?

- How is the family impacted by job loss?

- What are some of the ways organizations of the 21st century will differ from those of the 20th century?

- Who is the "older" worker?

- What are some of the stereotypes and generalizations that business and industry hold regarding older workers?

- What are "age norms" for occupations? Are such norms helpful or hurtful?

- What are the Age Discrimination in Employment Acts (ADEA)? Why were these acts needed? What are some of the protections under these acts?

- How can age discrimination be changed?

Research on the Older Worker

Exactly what do we know about older workers? Is there a basis for the claim that older workers are unproductive? As workers vary in their skills, defining expectations about older employees based upon their work experience, quality of their work, and attitude, rather than upon their age is best (Hardy, 2006). Hedge, Borman, and Lammlein (2006) argue that older workers can perform jobs just as effectively as younger workers if they (a) can avoid physical and mental declines, (b) maintain their health, (c) have and can utilize their accumulated experience and expertise, (d) are flexible in how they approach their work, (e) have jobs which do not change drastically/are stable in nature, (f) receive support from fellow workers and supervisors, and (g) get the job training that is appropriate and necessary for their job as older workers. In a meta-analysis (an analysis of many findings based upon multiple studies) of the literature, Ng and Feldman (2008) found that age was (a) unrelated to work performance and performance in work training programs, (b) positively related to prosocial behaviors at work and safety behavior, and (c) negatively related to counterproductive (drug use, tardiness, absenteeism and sickness-related absenteeism) workplace behavior. These are all positive work attributes that most employers value and can take advantage of in selecting prospective employees.

Caveats: Age and Work

Research on the relationship between age and job satisfaction as well as age and job performance sometimes yields mixed results (Panek, 1997). Moreover, the exact relationship between age and job satisfaction is complex. Thus, although these are important questions, they are difficult to answer and findings often vary as a function of a number of factors, such as type of occupation studied, the performance criterion used, characteristics of co-workers, quality of supervision, and how performance is evaluated. Also, the sources or determinants of work performance change with the actual length of time a person has occupied a given job. To illustrate, in occupations where physical strength is required for job performance, such as manual labor, older workers may show performance decrements due to changes or declines in physical functioning, while in other occupations, where these abilities are not highly related to successful performance, such as college professor, little age decrement in per-formance is observed. In terms of experience, it is important to note that the definition and conceptualization of experience are difficult such as the time in the current job, seniority, or time in the organization. Though the effects of experience at a job may counteract the effects of age, existing research is too equivocal to draw conclusions on whether age differences in performance can be reduced or eliminated with task experience.

There is some evidence for an age decrement in performance on tasks where speed is a major component (see Chapter 2). The age-speed-performance relationship has been quite difficult to study in industrial settings for a number of reasons. For example, with advancing age and job tenure, individuals tend to be promoted to supervisory positions. Therefore, it is difficult to compare speed of performance of young and old workers on the same job. Also, when older workers are employed in positions where speed is important, they are often able to compensate effectively for any decrease in speed through experience with the job. Thus, they may know shortcuts and use more efficient methods of doing their jobs. For these reasons, we still know very little that is conclusive regarding the actual relationship between age and speeded job performance.

In many industries and occupations, there may be very little or no age-related decline in productivity. Although we have discussed that there are clear age-related changes in physical capacity as well as in certain aspects of cognitive functioning, hearing, vision, and psychomotor speed (see Chapters 2 and 3), it is not yet clear if these changes actually affect job performance (Panek, 1997). Overall, the effects of the slowdown in performance and the older worker vary as a function of the occupation and particular duties within a job (Vercruyssen, 1997). However, there is a tendency for older individuals to leave jobs placing a premium on speeded sensorimotor performance.

Obviously, health is an important variable affecting the ability of persons to work, and health problems increase gradually as age increases (see Chapter 2). Yet, there is considerable variation among individuals, and while for some, physical capacity may start to decline in middle age, this may not be true for others. When it occurs, however, decreasing health and physical condition can have negative effects on job performance and safety in jobs with high physical demands, e.g., construction laborer. Many older employees leave such jobs because they indeed are too demanding in a physical sense.

Physical limitations do increase sharply with age, as does the severity of the limitations (Panek, 1997). For example, workers aged 65 to 69 are three times as likely as workers 45 to 54 and six times as likely as those 35 to 44 to report severe functional limitations, and these limitations include impairments in seeing, hearing, speaking, lifting or carrying, walking, using stairs, and getting around outside, as well as inside, and can obviously affect work performance. In this respect, a **work disability** is defined as a health problem or disability which prevents someone in the household from working or which limits the type or amount of work in which they can engage. Although decreasing health and physical condition can have negative effects on jobs with high physical demands, innovations in technology are increasingly making one's physical abilities less critical to one's performance at work. Also, with age, people may improve in knowledge and wisdom which might well offset some of the physiological changes that could potentially affect job performance (Berkowitz, 1988).

Older workers appear to be less likely to be injured on the job and accident rates for most occupations tend to decrease for older employees (Panek, 1997). Nonetheless, when illness or injury do occur, they are more likely to be associated with longer-term absence; for such persons, more work time will be lost and injuries are more likely to be fatal or lead to permanent disability (Sterns et al., 1985). Thus, the impact of illness or injury varies across persons.

One also needs to consider the impact of family life events on job performance. Thus, divorce, providing care for a member of the family, and death of a spouse can be potentially disruptive to job performance or result in a return to or entry into the workforce. To illustrate this point, caregiver problems and requirements are often translated into workplace problems such as lateness, absenteeism, changed work schedules, impaired work performance, and job turnover (Panek, 1997). For employers and employees alike, many hours at work are lost to the demands of caregiving (see Chapters 10, 11, and 12), and some persons quit their jobs to care for an ill or dying family member.

Gender may play a role in explaining the impact of such events on work performance. Iwasaki et al. (2004) suggest that female managers emphasize that personal or work relationships involving other people contribute to their experiences of emotional stress. They cared about other people who were important to them. In contrast, male managers do not discuss the issue of emotional stress involving relationships, and tend to consider relationships less personally and less emotionally then their female counterparts (Iwasaki et al., 2004).

Job Skill Training

Because we live in a highly technological, rapidly changing world, both on and off the job, training and retraining are important issues for workers of all ages. **Skill obsolescence** is often a major factor in the voluntary withdrawal of middle-aged men from the workforce. Skill obsolescence is serious problem for older workers, and describes a worker who has fallen behind in the ability to use new techniques or master new skills in present jobs. That is, obsolescence occurs when the demands of a job become incongruent with a worker's knowledge, skills, and abilities. The negative consequences associated with obsolescence include clogged channels of promotion, lower morale among other workers, and lower overall productivity of the department or unit. Consequently, two of the major challenges for organizations now and in the future will be to retain employees with potential for important work contributions and to retrain employees whose skills have become obsolete (see Box I).

Fortunately, the growing awareness that older adults can be trained and retrained in both the laboratory and industrial settings has led to the development of training principles and methods that recognize the unique attributes of the older adult worker. Consequently, one major issue today is assuring equitable access to training opportunities for older adult workers since current policies and practices regarding training may exclude older employees. Indeed, Armstrong-Stassen and Templer (2005) found fewer than 10% of employers to provide training opportunities for their older employees. Importantly, jobs that are stimulating and cognitively complex (see Chapter 3) may actually positively influence an older person's job performance by challenging the employee to thinking more actively about what one is doing at work and how to best maintain one's job skills (Hedge, Borman, & Lammlein, 2006).

Box I

Meeting the Needs of the Older Worker

The American Association of Retired Persons (AARP) advocates retraining midcareer and older employees, based on the philosophy of the aging worker as a resource to the employer. To be used effectively, this resource must be properly conserved and managed, but can yield an employee who is productive and happy on the job throughout his or her career. This is in contrast to the philosophy of the employee as an asset that decreases in value with time. As a result of this philosophy, training older employees is not cost effective because their value lessens the longer they stay on the job. Employees who are midcareer and beyond face several problems: (1) career burnout, (2) career plateau, and (3) career obsolescence. AARP suggests several solutions to each career difficulty.

Problem: Career Burnout
Look for signs such as absenteeism, poor job attitudes, lower quality of work, complaints about being overworked.
Solutions:
1. Job redesign or rotation.
2. Special temporary assignments.
3. Reassignment as mentors or trainers.
4. Stress-management training.

Problem: Career Plateau
Solutions:
1. Assign projects that use the employee's special skills.
2. Give more frequent feedback about performance.
3. Provide alternative career paths.
4. Provide training and development opportunities.

Problem: Career Obsolescence
Solutions:
1. Retrain to sharpen current skills or learn new ones.
2. Encourage involvement in professional organizations.
3. Encourage continuing professional education to keep up with new developments.
4. Establish a career-planning system.
5. Encourage older employees to consider career options and career contingency plans.
6. Hold career-planning workshops
7. Start a career-information center.

In designing a training program, AARP recommends the following.

1. Build a long-range plan. In this way, each employee's skills can be best used and developed so that both employee and company benefit.
2. Use performance appraisals as a source of training and development planning. Knowing what strengths and weaknesses employees have enables an employer to design training to best help each develop new skills or maintain skills that have deteriorated.
3. Survey training needs and develop a list of priorities based on input from employees.
4. Develop flexible ideas about training. Training can be skill-specific, interpersonally oriented, formal, or informal in nature, and can even involve retirement planning. It might include alternatives to total retirement such as temporary work assignments, part-time work, or consulting.

Table 7-1

Factors to be considered in the design of training programs for older workers.

Factor	Description and Example
Motivation	Older workers need to be encouraged and motivated to participate in training programs. Older workers have often been out of school for many years and may have a fear of failure or an inability to compete against better or more recently educated younger workers.
Structure	A careful task analysis should be carried out to develop the training material and content, as well as determine the sequence of training. The training sequence should be in terms of increasing complexity. After mastery of the basic skill, more difficult or complex aspects are introduced. This increases self-confidence and reduces fear of failure.
Familiarity	The use of former and familiar elements and skills on a new task facilitates the acquisition of new learning. Therefore, whenever possible, training programs should be constructed on the basis of past knowledge and abilities.
Organization	Research indicates that many older workers have been found to have difficulty organizing information adequately. Therefore, training programs should be organized so that the knowledge can be built on at each step or phase in the program.
Time	Older workers often take longer to learn a new task, but when given sufficient time, older workers usually perform as well as younger workers. Therefore, training programs for older workers should have a slower presentation rate and longer periods of study.

Source: Adapted from Panek (1997).

Training older adult workers may require changes in traditional training methods to accommodate special needs and limitations of some individuals. Complicating matters, some older workers often fail to recognize threats of obsolescence and are reluctant to pursue training or retraining (see Hedge, Borman, & Lammlein, 2006). A number of training approaches such as the discovery method, active learning, and programmed instruction have been effective with older workers. Also, certain techniques, such as self-paced learning, experiential training, on-the-job coaching, or prag-matic training are more effective in teaching older workers. For example, Rosen and Jerdee (1985) reported that in-service training and retraining provided older adult workers with the opportunity to strengthen knowledge and skills. Factors that should be considered in the development of training programs for older adults are presented in Table 7-1.

What Lies Ahead?

Visser and Beatty (2005b) point out that by the year 2020, more than half the workforce will be age 40 or older. Indeed, projections suggest that fully 60% of the workforce will be classified as older (Fullerton, 2005). In addition, relative to today's workforce, that of tomorrow will likely be more ethnically diverse. In light of the slowing of the birthrate and mortality at older ages, this shift in the proportion of older to younger workers is likely to make more demands on companies to train, retrain, and retain older workers, even beyond traditional retirement age (see Chapter 8). This is important in the sense that the work place will be more competitive and even more dominated by technology in the future than it is today. It will also shift from a goods-producing to an information/services-producing economy, and the demand for higher skilled jobs will be greater than for lower skilled jobs (Patel, 2005). Indeed, such skills are those that only 20% of the current workforce currently possess: technology and communication skills; critical thinking, creativity, and information management; personal (e.g., being open to change, having self-insight) and interpersonal skills, as well as community-building skills (Patel, 2005).

In the future, more women will comprise the workforce, and workers will assume more responsibility for paying healthcare costs (this indeed already happened in 2006 as the proportion of health care costs older persons will pay to supplement Medicare was increased, especially so for higher income older persons), as well as for supplementing their retirement incomes. The average age at which one will no longer work will increase, in part because persons will not be able to afford to retire as early as they did earlier, because they are healthier, and because they will value productive, meaningful involvement to a greater extent (Visser & Beatty, 2005b).

For these reasons, new strategies for recruiting and retaining older workers will need to be developed, wherein their needs and interests in working will have to be thoroughly understood, so that they remain committed to the organization, are satisfied with the work they are doing, are unlikely to seek other employment, and are more likely to put off retirement (Fyock, 2005; Taylor, Shultz, &

Doverspike, 2005). In order to be fully committed to training and retaining older workers, stereotypical, ageistic attitudes must be replaced by more realistic ones among employers and employees alike (Dunn, 2005), emphasizing the development of work environments that foster self-confidence among older workers, building skills slowly and specifically, using training approaches that emphasize the older worker's life and work experience, and via the incorporation of the principles of learning as they apply to older persons (see Chapter 3), creating a learner-friendly atmosphere for the acquisition of new skills.

Key to making such changes is revising our approach to career development, stressing the active and ongoing nature of one's career, wherein flexibility, meaningful involvement, a reward system that encourages continued learning and retraining, and challenge are all important (Russell & Visser, 2005; Sterns & Sterns, 2005). In addition, team-building, a greater emphasis on intergenerational relationships and on mentoring, recognizing the balance between work and family caregiving, and emphasizing diversity will likely define the workplace of the future (Finkelstein, 2005; Keene, 2005; Markos, 2005). This is in contrast to a lockstep, stage-like approach to career development, which predicts disengagement from the workforce later in life.

Ethnicity, Culture, and the Older Worker

Japan is the only industrialized country with a history of policy efforts to improve labor market opportunities and increase labor force participation among older people ((Raymo, Liang, Sugisawa, Kobayashi, & Sugihara, 2004). Thus, Japan serves as a model for how industry can make effective use of older workers. Older workers in Japan represent the norm rather than the exception. Japan is the most rapidly aging developed country in the world.

Pathways into post-retirement jobs depend, to a large extent, on characteristics of the career job. All firms have a mandatory retirement age of 60 or under, and three out of four Japanese firms rehire retired workers or continue their employment beyond the official retirement age. For those retiring from larger companies with lifetime employment policies and reemployment programs, it is not uncommon to continue working for the same company or to be transferred to an affiliated company (Raymo et al., 2004). As a rule, however, these rehired or retained workers step down from managerial or supervisory positions to posts of lesser responsibility. Older workers selected for reemployment typically are relegated to lower status jobs, have less responsibility, and are paid substantially lower wages. Japanese employers, with government encouragement, also actively help recent retirees search for new jobs if necessary. Others may find employment in different types of work such as self-employment or facilitated through work agencies. Self-employment is very common among older Japanese (Raymo et al., 2004).

Often, in Japan, changes from physically demanding jobs, such as assembly line work to less physically stressful positions, often occur as early as the late 40s for Japanese workers. Toyota Motor, Nissan Motor, and Matsushita Electric (Panasonic) are among the many corporations engaged in job redesigning for an aging labor force. In doing so, employers are responding to current and anticipated labor shortages, government pressure to increase older workers labor force participation, and the perceived need to heighten morale among workers. Japanese employers are generally willing to make work adjustments to maintain the older worker's productivity and interest in the job. Approximately 55 percent of firms have a formal policy to help older workers remain healthy and productive through job transfers, reduced working hours, or changes in work operation and physical environment.

However, the rate of aging and the projected age structure of the population in the 21st century have caused considerable adjustments in the human resource policies of Japanese employers (Clark & Ogawa, 1996). Population aging has produced a rapid escalation in the cost of social security and other retirement programs. These cost pressures

have stimulated government efforts to prolong worklife. Specifically, with aging of the labor force, firms are reconsidering their commitment to lifetime employment and have been altering their retirement policies. Changes in human resource policies include reduced reliance on seniority pay systems (change to merit), new human resource policies for older workers, increases in the age of mandatory retirement, greater use of policies that allow reemployment after mandatory retirement, and assistance in the placement of retired workers.

Business and industry worldwide is beginning to address the demands of the changing and aging workforce. For example, the Volvo plant in Uaddevalla, Sweden, is being ergonomically designed, such as designing tools that are less physically demanding, to accommodate a workforce where 25% will be over age 45 and 40% are women.

Check Your Learning 7-3

Identify the following terms or concepts:

Career plateau
Work disability
Career burnout
Skill obsolescence

- What is the relationship between age and various aspects of work?

- What roles can experience, health, and job demands play in influencing older persons' job performance?

- What are some of the changes in training methods required to accommodate older workers?

- What are some accommodations made in other countries to enhance the employment of older workers?

Summary

Our work role is critical to our identities, self-concept, and self-esteem. Our occupation determines how our time is spent, who our friends will be, our attitudes and values, and our lifestyle. There are three major approaches to occupational choice: **trait oriented**, **developmental**, and **social learning theory**.

Men and women differ in their career patterns, but each is highly complex and subject to the influence of opportunity, economic constraints, family influences, and decision-making skills. While many advocate **occupational developmental tasks** particular to distinct life stages, **occupational/career development**—defined as a coherent pattern of jobs—is a lifelong process, influencing and being influenced by events in other areas of one's life. Young adulthood is often an upwardly mobile occupational period, but yet many young adults experience a great deal of stress and disappointment at not finding a job. Likewise, **middle adulthood** may or may not be occupationally stable, and in midlife, some people change careers for economic and personal reasons.

Since the 1980s, companies have continued to downsize, making workers vulnerable to **job loss**, which can lead to many problems, e.g., psychological, financial, and stress. Stress in the workplace varies as a function of many factors, e.g., personal, environmental, and age.

Organizations and other workers often hold **stereotypical** views toward older workers such as "they cannot learn new skills." However, research has generally dispelled many of these negative beliefs. But in spite of the evidence, organizations continue to give credence to many of these negative views, resulting in policies and procedures which may indirectly or directly discriminate against older workers.

Chapter 8
Retirement and Leisure

Retirement and Leisure in Adulthood

It is quite likely that most of you reading this text will eventually retire, withdrawing from the workforce either voluntarily or involuntarily. Retirement has an effect on the retiree, the family, and society. Therefore, it is important that we be aware of the issues and factors that will affect us at that time, in order to plan appropriately for both the event and the roles associated with being retired. Retirement is at once a specific *event*, a *role*, and a *process* (Atchley & Barusch, 2003). Consequently, retirement should be viewed as a process, not as a single, abrupt event. Moreover, persons often engage in **gradual retirement** by reducing their time at work prior to formal retirement, enabling them to plan for retirement. As we learned in Chapter 7, some persons, i.e., those who are self-employed, often do not plan for retirement. Do you think this is wise?

Just as many do not put a great deal of preparation into choosing a career and rely on incomplete or inaccurate information (see Chapter 7), so too is retirement planning a last thought for many workers. They begin to think about life after retirement when they are approaching their likely retirement age, which traditionally has been viewed as 65, though this is changing as of late. People are putting off retirement due to fears about not being able to maintain their lifestyles (Retiring at 65 out of Reach for Most, *Dallas Morning News*, November 11, 2009). They may also put off retiring because they are caring for an aged parent or a grandchild (see Chapters 4 and 5), and so they cannot afford to support themselves in retirement and afford all the expenses that accompany raising a child or caring for an ill parent. Unfortunately, based upon a 2009 report by the Sloan Center on Aging and Work, employers may underestimate the impact of this trend on their workforce due to the number of older employees or to employers' fear about not being able to afford health care for older or retired employees (*Gerontology News*, May, 2010).

When persons do eventually retire, they often discover that retirement involves a change in lifestyle as well as changes in the roles they play and in their personal identities. Alternatively, rather than seeing retirement as a new identity, persons may simply add the "retiree" identity to that of worker (Atchley & Barusch, 2003). Such an identity shift may cause the person to relate differently to others, and he/she in turn may be treated differently by them.

It is commonly assumed that one of the major consequences resulting from retirement is a dramatic increase in the amount of time for leisure pursuits and activities. Indeed, a discussion of leisure is part of many companies' retirement-preparation programs.

As with retirement, an all encompassing definition of **leisure** is difficult, since one person's leisure activity may be an occupation to another. To illustrate, let us suppose someone's primary occupation is bank management and his or her hobby or leisure activity is coin-collecting and coin-dealing. Should this be considered a leisure activity, since it is related to one's occupation and involves making money? Or, consider a history teacher who during nonwork time travels around the country visiting historical sites—is this leisure? Thus, leisure satisfaction may be **intrinsic**—one engages in leisure for its own sake, because it is enjoyable or relaxing, or it may be **instrumental,** and lead to the attainment of some other goal.

Retirement

Rationales for Retirement

There are two rationales for retirement. First, it allows individuals to enjoy their remaining years in pursuit of hobbies or leisure activities, after having spent the major portion of their lives producing goods and services for society and/or a particular organization. Thus, retirement is viewed as a "thank you" for a job well done. Most people retire between 62 and 65 years of age, though this is changing, in part because of economic pressures, and differing patterns of retirement (Atchley & Barusch, 2003; Hardy, 2006). In this respect, older (over age 75) persons may adopt such a view, reflecting their experiences over time at work emphasizing hard work, loyalty to an employer, and occupational stability (Hooyman & Kiyak, 2011). In contrast, middle-aged and younger older persons' views about work and retirement may differ substantially, with many not retiring at all, delaying retirement, returning to work after retirement, or working part-time in retirement. Winston and Barnes (2007) found that Baby Boomers rejected the traditional notion of retirement, saw retirement in terms of their personal needs and values, and chose to integrated work and leisure. Such persons were still concerned about their health, getting adequate healthcare, and their financial status after retirement. The second rationale for retirement is that it allows for a constant, predictable, and orderly flow of workers through the workforce. Retirement makes possible the replacement of older workers with younger ones who are considered by the organization as being more productive and efficient.

Regardless of which of these two rationales is correct, the number of retired individuals increased dramatically in the industrialized nations during the 20th century. For example, in 1900, approximately 70% of men over age 65 were employed. By 1960, the figure dropped to 35%, and by 1975, to 22%. In 1984, only about 11% of older adults were still in the work force. By 1988, this figure had dropped to less than 10% (AARP, 1990). These figures of late have increased somewhat, however.

Why did the percentage of older adults who are retired continue to increase? A number of factors explained this trend. First, during the 20th century, the United States progressively shifted from an agricultural to an industrial base (Atchley & Barusch, 2003). Moreover, the United States shifted from a nation where the majority of individuals were self-employed (e.g., as farmers and craftsmen) to one where most people work for others. When individuals were self-employed or involved in a family business, they worked until they died or became disabled. Therefore, the decrease in the number of older adults who are still in the work force was a reflection of the shift in the percentages who work for themselves versus those who work for others.

Second, life expectancy increased substantially during the 20th century (Seman & Adler, 1998); more individuals are alive to retire today than in previous years. Before 1900, very few individuals lived to be 65 years or older. Those who lived longer tended to be those who were in the best health. Therefore, they were able to remain on the job longer. While, with improved health care and medical technology, life expectancy has increased, some (but not all) individuals' abilities and capacities may nevertheless decline in old age. Therefore, although individuals live longer, some are not physically able to continue to work, so they leave the work force. So the decrease in the percentage of older adults in the work force was a reflection of the fact that more individuals are living longer.

The third reason was the continued development of formal retirement systems and pensions, as well as legal factors. Since individuals tend to work to support themselves and their families financially, if no provision is made to do so when they retire, they will continue to work. The United States was one of the last Western industrialized nations to provide retirement benefits for older adults. It wasn't until 1935 that the Social Security

Act was passed, mandating that people over 65 who had worked a certain length of time were eligible for benefits. By contrast, some form of retirement system was in place in Germany in 1889 and in the United Kingdom in 1908. Each year, additional financial plans (e. g., pensions, tax shelters, IRAs) become available, allowing individuals to plan for their economic security during retirement. For this reason, more and more individuals were covered under some form of pension or retirement plan, and a greater percentage of individuals were able to leave the workforce (Quinn & Burkhauser, 1990). In addition, since the law specified at what age one is eligible for retirement benefits, organizations and institutions could then "legally" set mandatory retirement ages and force individuals from the workforce when they reach that age.

A fourth reason for the decrease in the number of older workers was increasing productivity due to technological advancements. That is, advanced technology, such as computers and industrial robots, was taking over many occupations. Since older workers are often viewed as unproductive, they are considered expendable and are encouraged to retire early. Again, the net result was a decrease in the overall number of older adults in the workforce.

Finally, during the last part of the 20th century, there was a change in attitudes toward work, the meaning of work, and the support of nonworking members of society (Hardy, 2006). Many individuals had moved further away from the belief that the major purpose in life was to work and be active. This was replaced by the belief that the purpose of work was to attain self-actualization and/or obtain money necessary to pursue other interests (Hooyman & Kiyak, 2011). Furthermore, many people often had more to lose (i.e., experiencing work stress or age discrimination) than to gain by continuing to work. Therefore, with successive cohorts, during the 20th century, greater percentages of American felt that, rather than continue to work to support themselves in old age, they should retire and let others support them through Social Security and pension plans (Atchley & Barusch, 2003).

Recently, this trend toward more retirees has changed somewhat: while older labor force partici-

pation was at 43% in 1950, in 2004, it was less than a third; yet, in 2004, 23 million persons over age 55 were in the workforce, and this represented an *increase* of 1 million over the previous year (AARP, 2004). Indeed, forecasts are that older workers will continue to increase their participation in the workforce through the next decade (AARP, 2004). Interestingly, while labor-force participation decreased steadily since 1900 for men, the participation rate for women increased during this same period.

This increase in the older workforce may be explained by the following: (a) increasingly more persons have not saved adequately for retirement, (b) there are fewer private industry supported pension plans (a major airline abandoned its employee pension plan in late 2005), (c) persons have lost money in the stock market and consequently put off retirement, (d) persons have lost health benefits, making retirement less attractive financially, and (e) the age of eligibility for full Social Security benefits has been raised (AARP, 2004), and is currently being discussed as one means of avoiding the bankruptcy of Social Security.

These facts support analyses which suggested (accurately) that the trend toward early retirement may have ended and that the 21st century will be characterized by later, not earlier, retirement (Clark & Quinn, 2002). If persons retire earlier, their post-retirement lives would have to be increasingly financed privately (savings, deferred compensation through pension); this is now less likely as such programs are being restructured to encourage later retirement, lessening the burdens on employers (Hardy, 2006).

Early retirement increases persons' dependence upon Social Security and/or private savings, but makes it more likely that persons will enjoy a longer period of relative good health which decreases their costs for healthcare and prescription drugs and enables them to be active for a longer period of time. Many persons having retired early take advantage of the opportunity to pursue new careers, travel, or spend time with friends and family. Putting off retirement heightens fears about not being able to enjoy retirement due to failing health or the death of a spouse. Likewise, dependent upon the economy and the real estate market, persons may end up spending more on housing than they would otherwise would have had they retired earlier (Bidwell, Griffin, & Hesketh, 2005; Hooyman & Kiyak, 2011). Societally, putting off retirement is beneficial because adults will contributing longer as taxpayers and will not be supported by Social Security for as long, relative to having retired earlier. The problem is that one cannot predict the future with certainty —one's plans for retirement may or may not play out as imagined.

Unretiring

Some persons "unretire" for economic or personal reasons (Hardy, 2006), which is more likely during the first 2 years after retirement. This more common among persons in their early to mid-50s, lasting an average of 4 years, and often involves a lower paying job with fewer hours, and may involve self-employment. **Unretiring** is distinct from bridge employment (see below), or partial retirement. In this respect, a new aspect of career counseling involves helping retirees make decisions about whether to enter and if they do return to the workforce, what jobs or careers might be best for them (Harper & Shoffner, 2004). As noted by Hardy (2006), individuals are increasingly more likely to abandon retirement altogether and return to the work force.

Some individuals unretire by founding an entirely new business (More older Americans start own businesses, *USA Today*, May 25, 2010). As a 65-year old recently retired man put it, "I was a Navy photographer when I was young (when I was in my 20s), then I got diverted into a finance career for about 30 years. When I was 64, I got out of the finance business and tried to figure out what I wanted to do when I grew up." His new vocation is entitled Photo Safari Yosemite, which takes tourists to the best photo-taking locations in the national park (*USA Today*, 2010).

Bridge Employment

In the past, the stereotypical retirement meant that an individual terminated employment in a full-time career job and fully retired; that is, they stopped working altogether. However, while evidence suggests that while still prevalent, this pattern is not the only or perhaps even the typical way that most Americans are retiring (Clark & Quinn, 2002). Instead, while some older people are using phased retirement programs in career jobs, others are moving into **bridge employment** jobs (Atchley & Barusch, 2003) that ease the transition from full-time career employment into retirement (Clark & Quinn, 2002). Bridge employment refers to the labor force participation patterns observed in older workers between their career jobs (jobs held 10 years or more) and complete labor force withdrawal (Schultz, 2003, p.215). Today, many persons in their 50s, 60s, and early 70s engage in some form of paid employment which could be classified as bridge employment.

Bridge employment is not new. For instance, Quinn and Burkhauser (1990) found that among those who left career jobs, more than one-fourth did something other than retire altogether, such as accepting part-time employment. Myer (1991) found that there were actually four different post-career paths: (1) part-time employment in one's previous position, (2) either part-time or (3) full-time employment on a new job, and (4) full-time retirement. In this study, which path people chose was influenced by economic factors such as existing wealth, pension, and Social Security benefits, as well as the availability of training or job opportunities. Many retirees seek "bridge jobs" that span the time between leaving a career job and full-time retirement (Schultz, 2003).

Bridge employment tends to be an important element in the transition from full-time employment to full-time retirement, and it fulfills certain psychological needs for older adults who have retired (Schultz, 2003). Research, although limited, suggests as Baby Boomers approach retirement age, many intend on opting for bridge employment rather than withdrawing completely from the workforce (Dendinger, Adams, and Jacobson, 2005). In this respect, Jones and McIntosh (2010) found that in occupations for which labor shortages are anticipated, e.g., nursing and pharmacy, employers were

Figure 8-1. Impairments to health can affect adjustment to retirement.

quite invested in retaining or attracting retirees who could meet such shortages. In addition, they found that the odds of unretiring were greatest when bridge employment was sought within the same organization for which one had worked prior to retirement. In this respect, Hedge, Borman, and Lammlein (2005) note that executive, administrative, managerial, educational, and technological fields will be most severely affected by the increasing number of Baby Boom retirements. Thus, unretiring and bridge employment, though distinct from one another, may benefit the employer and employee alike.

Adjustment to Retirement

Because retirement entails discontinuity from previous behavioral patterns and economic positions, retiring individuals must adapt and make a major life transition (Adams & Beehr, 2003). In reality, it involves a *series* of adjustments and decisions that impact oneself, one's family, and one's friendship networks (Szinovacz, 2003). These adjustments highlight the need for "self-management" of one's career, where the individual makes deci-

sions, rather than being viewed as solely reactive (Sterns & Kaplan, 2003).

Viewed as a social institution, retirement can have positive societal consequences (see above) and outcomes that are social in nature. It can provide a late-life opportunity for further self-development and the achievement of life satisfaction. However, under some circumstances the effects of retirement can be negative, where anxiety and fear associated with retirement is strongest for people who are described as neurotic—the shy, the lonely, and those who expect to have little control over their lives after retirement (Robinson, Demetre, & Corney, 2010; Van Solinge & Henkens, 2008). Such persons may be attached to their jobs, cling to the role of worker as a source of their identity, be fearful of what will happen to them after retiring, be unable to do their work as well as they once did, be unhappy with the jobs or careers, or have experienced the loss of friends at work because of their job changes, deaths, or retirements (Barnes-Farrell, 2003).

At one time, it was believed that the process of post-retirement adjustment was gradual, and as

Table 8-1

Stages of Retirement

Stage	Characteristics
Honeymoon	The euphoric honeymoon stage occurs immediately after retirement and lasts roughly 6 months. Retirees are very enthusiastic and look forward to doing things they have not had time to do. They might begin new projects and look forward to what the future will bring. Often, individuals become very involved in a variety of physical activities such as golf, bowling, tennis, or jogging.
Disenchantment	This phase begins 13 to 18 months after retirement. There is less involvement in physical activities, and people experience an emotional letdown. They find that their expectations of retirement have been unrealistic or that they have underestimated the change that retirement brings. In this phase, they also come to terms with the loss of structure that working gave their daily lives. They see less of their working friends, often feel lost or bored, and tend to focus on the past. This is the phase that is considered the most difficult.
Stability/reorientation	The last phase, 19 months and up, is characterized by stability, or a reorientation to the day-to-day realities of being retired. In this phase, the retiree finds a predictable and satisfying daily routine and lifestyle. A new circle of friends is established, and choices and decisions about the future can be made with confidence.

Source: Ekerdt & Bosse, 1985.

Ekerdt and Bosse (1985) suggested, individuals may progress through several phases of adjustment to retirement. These are: the **honeymoon** phase, the **disenchantment** phase, and the **stability** or **reorientation** phase (see Table 8-1). Pre-retirement training that is effective should lessen unrealistic expectations of the retirement experience. These unrealistic expectations are likely responsible for the honeymoon and disenchantment phases of adjustment. That retirement is gradual is consistent with the fact that not everyone who retires fully disengages from the workforce. Indeed, as the institution of retirement changes (see above), the notion of stages of retirement adjustment is likely to need revising. Perhaps these stages will be elongated as individuals retire later and for different reasons than in the past.

Reflecting this *process* view of retirement adjustment, Pinquart and Schindler (2007) found three types of persons who adjusted to retirement differently: those for who retirement satisfaction declined soon after retiring but increased afterward, those who experienced retirement positively but yet reported less positive overall life satisfaction, and those who experienced a small and temporary increase in retirement satisfaction. These patterns were quite variable across many characteristics, such as health, SES, marital status, employment history, and gender. Indeed, couples may not agree on the wisdom of retiring or when to retire, complicating the retirement decision for many persons.

Although the vast majority of men and women look forward to retirement, are happy with this time, and suffer no ill effects as a result of labor force withdrawal (Hooyman & Kiyak, 2011), some people do experience negative effects following retirement. Indeed, involuntary retirement, e.g., forced retirements due to company policy, and/or declining health, can have negative influences on emotional satisfaction, self-image, emotional stability, and interpersonal relationships (Reis & Gold, 1993). Szinovacz and Davey (2005) found that nearly 1/3 of the workers they surveyed perceived their retirement as involuntary, due to health problems, feeling displaced by someone younger at work, or caregiving responsibilities. Szinovacz and Davey (2004) also found that when retirement is involuntary, and when the person one is (or soon may be) caring for is more functionally impaired (see Chapter 10), symptoms of depression are more likely. Overall, results of studies regarding the effects of retirement are mixed (Kim & Moen, 2002). Specifically, for some individuals the retirement experience may promote a sense of well-being, as workers move out of demanding and/or stressful jobs. However, the retirement passage itself may lead to diminished well-being as individuals lose their occupational attachments, their social network of coworkers, and a major source of their identities (Kim & Moen, 2002).

Retirement is not simply a state but a complex process embedded in prior psychological resources as well as gendered experiences. Men tend to experience increases in their morale as they undergo actual transitions into retirement, feeling released from the pressures of their jobs, which is beneficial for their psychological well-being (Kim & Moen, 2002). On the other hand, women come to retirement with higher levels of depressive symptoms and lower levels of morale, personal control, and perceived income adequacy (Kim & Moen, 2002).

Factors Related to the Decision to Retire

The decision to retire is influenced by a variety of factors, including the kind of retirement options available, the benefits associated with them, estimates of inflation trends, the person's financial commitments, the level of job satisfaction, perceived health status, labor market conditions, and societal retirement norms (Adams & Beehr, 2003; Atchley

& Burusch, 2003). Consequently, the decision is affected not only by personal circumstances, but also by the wider economic and social context. However, for both men and women, the two primary factors affecting the decision to retire are health status and finances. However, it is not easy to state conclusively why people retire because the decision is often a personal one and the result of a number of factors. Further, these reasons are highly related to each other and thus, should not be considered independent. For example, it is difficult to prove that retirement per se *causes* poor health or depression, and whether retirement is voluntary or involuntary seems to be more predictive in this respect (Hooyman & Kiyak, 2011).

This being said, for both men and women the primary factors influencing the *decision to retire* are **financial situation**, **health**, **occupational level**, **age**, **gender**, **work satisfaction**, and **personal attitudes**. Each of these factors can be categorized as either **personal** (health, economic situation, attitudes toward work/retirement, and degree of social support), or **institutional** (workplace conditions, employer policy, public policy, economic conditions, and societal values) (Robinson, Coberly, & Paul, 1985). Since the "institutional" factors are out of the control of the individual, e.g., the company's mandatory retirement policy, they will not be our primary focus.

Financial Situation

Reviews of research on the predictors of retirement decisions consistently conclude that finances, in some form or other, are the strongest single predictor of the decision to retire (Beehr, Glazer, Nielson, & Farmer, 2000). Specifically, individuals are generally more likely to leave the workforce if they can financially afford to retire than if they cannot. Since individuals need a certain level of income to maintain their lifestyle after retirement, those who were enrolled in pension/retirement plans or know they will have a secure income when they retire tend to have a more positive attitude toward retirement (Solinge & Henkens, 2008). Those who do not feel secure often experience stress and anxiety.

It is the individuals at the lower occupational levels who tend to have the lowest retirement benefits, since the level of these benefits is related to earnings. These are the very individuals who are subject to mandatory-retirement rules. Given their relatively low earnings while working, these individuals, in most cases, have not had extra money to put aside for retirement. It is persons in these groups that are usually adversely affected by retirement, especially in terms of financial resources.

While dual-career couples tend to make the decision to retire collaboratively, taking into account each person's personal circumstances, the husband's earnings and pension entitlements exert a stronger effect on the wife's retirement decision than do the wife's on the husband's (Smith & Moen, 2004).

Physical and Mental Health

One of the most important factors influencing both males' and females' decisions to retire following finances is their health status (Beehr et al., 2000; Lowis et al., 2009; Wilson & Palha, 2007). Health status plays a very important role both for individuals who are subject to mandatory retirement rules and those who are not. Poor health makes working burdensome and difficult. While some individuals who retire early due to poor health do so voluntarily, others do so involuntarily. These people are forced to retire abruptly because they do not have the option of working part-time, or can't "phase out" of work gradually by reducing the hours they work overtime; they cannot support themselves on a part-time income because their expenses remain fixed. Thus, they retire because they have no other alternative.

Also, being in good health is a reason given for retiring. In a classic study exploring retirement and health, Clark and Spengler (1980) reported that there appear to be two types of individuals who choose to retire early (62 years of age or earlier). These were (1) individuals in good health, with financial resources, who desire additional leisure time, and (2) individuals in poor health. Once individuals with poor health retire, they often find that their health affects the plans they had made for themselves for retirement. In some cases, however, their health may improve as they are relieved of the burden and responsibility of working, especially if there was a high degree of stress in the workplace. Despite the advantages of good health in retirement, Wilson and Palha (2007) argue for greater efforts at health promotion among retired persons.

Occupational Level

An individual's occupational level plays a very important role in the decision to retire, be it voluntarily or due to mandatory retirement policies (Hooyman & Kiyak, 2011). Individuals at the highest occupational levels, such as doctors, lawyers, senior executives, and other professionals, are less likely to retire early and more likely to continue working in some capacity beyond the normal retirement age (Hedge, Borman, & Lammlein, 2005). These individuals usually continue to work at a reduced level, as consultants or summer replacements, or they may work on special assignments and cases. As they usually have high levels of expertise and commitment, they may choose or be encouraged to continue working in some capacity in their profession. When individuals in this occupational category do retire, it is primarily due to poor health.

At the middle occupational level are individuals who are lower-level executives and middle managers within organizations. People at this occupational level often choose early retirement for two reasons. First, they may realize their careers have reached a plateau, and they choose to leave early because they have nothing to gain by staying on. Moreover, they are still young enough and may be in good enough health to enjoy retirement activities. Second, companies often offer an attractive early retirement package to those in target positions who retire early. For example, maximum retirement benefits for retirement at age 65 result in a pension of 45% of base salary. Individuals may be encouraged to retire at age 60, at which point they will receive a pension of 42% of the baseline plus free insurance until age 68. Therefore, the individual has little to gain financially by staying on the job. In tough economic times, it may actually be to both the company's and the employee's advantage to retire early. Younger, less senior employees, can be paid less. For some people, however, adequate retirement income cannot replace the feeling of doing a good job and of being needed and depended on. Early retirement is, unfortunately, quite common in positions where younger workers are viewed as more productive than older ones, or when younger workers can perform the same duties for significantly lower pay than older ones. The company's rationale in this case is higher productivity for lower cost.

The majority of workers in the United States fall into the categories of skilled (e.g., tool-and-die maker), semiskilled (e.g., electrician's assistant), and unskilled (e.g., food service) employees. Individuals in these three categories usually retire when they can receive retirement benefits. Also, because these are often low-status jobs, offering few opportunities for the exercise of autonomy or responsibility, and often having considerable physical demands, these individuals retire early (Wilson & Palha, 2007).

Gender

Research indicates that gender plays a role in the decision to retire (Beehr et al., 2000). Recent demographic trends such as increases in women's workforce participation, increased longevity, and decreased retirement age suggest that retirement should be considered a "couple phenomenon" (Kim & Moen, 2002). That is, many spouses do not retire simultaneously, resulting in various combinations of employment and retirement within couples (Kim & Moen, 2002). In general, women seem to hold more positive expectations of retirement than men, where research indicates that women were more likely to retire if they are needed to care for someone, while men were more likely to keep working (Beehr et al., 2000).Thus, working women may find that family obligations create pressure to retire. Therefore, the decision to retire may be related to factors such as her husband's health condition or an interest in pursuing leisure activities. For instance, a woman may retire early in order to care for a sick and infirm husband or grandchildren.

Work Satisfaction

It is not surprising that many individuals enjoy working and wish to work as long as they can, particularly if they are in good health. Therefore, when one retires, one gives up not only the economic advantages but these additional benefits as well. For this reason, individuals who are satisfied with their jobs continue to work longer than individuals who are dissatisfied. Because those in higher occupational levels have higher work satisfaction, it is difficult to discuss job satisfaction without keeping in mind its relationship to occupational level. Thus, as you would expect, the more satisfied workers are with their jobs the less likely they are to retire (Topa et al., 2009).

Generally, just prior to retirement, work satisfaction begins to decrease in relation to overall life satisfaction (Atchley & Burusch, 2003). This may be because individuals are beginning to disassociate themselves from their jobs. Also, people who report their health to be relatively poor, are more likely to retire, especially if they are also dissatisfied with their job, or feel that they are unable to cope with its demands. According to Robertson (2000) a reason many workers cite for taking early retirement is changes in corporate culture and changes in the nature of their particular jobs. Specifically, it was the changes in managerial styles, the productivity demands made on people, the ways in which people were treated and regarded by the company, along with other considerations such as timing and financial incentives that made early retirement more attractive than continuing to work for the company (Robertson, 2000).

Attitude toward Retirement

Most findings about retirement adjustment treat retirement as a normative experience, and reflect the fact that up until recently, persons would retire early if they could. It will be interesting to discover whether the same factors that influence retirement adjustment for previous cohorts apply to future cohorts (e.g. the Baby Boomers) or to more recent cohorts who are more likely to work longer and retire later.

In this respect, Valliant (2006) studied over 700 men who had recently retired and who had been born around 1929; these men entered young adulthood in a period of prosperity, just after the end of WWII. Valliant found that the happiest men were those who were wealthier, in better health, had successful marriages, and were active volunteers (see Chapter 9). Importantly, they enjoyed their leisure time—they had "developed a capacity to play." Interestingly, these men had retired at a *later* age. In contrast, Valliant found that men with physical disabilities, mental illness, or unhappy work relationships were less happy as retirees and had retired earlier. Success at work did not predict happiness in retirement. Collectively, this suggests that happiness in retirement is a complex phenomenon, and reinforces the personal attitudinal aspect of retirement, its relationship to marital happiness, and the independence of work success and happiness in retirement. It also underscores the role of satisfying leisure activities in later life; we will discuss leisure more completely later in this chapter.

Check Your Learning 8-1

Identify the following terms or concepts:

Retirement
Gradual retirement
Unretiring
Personal vs. institutional influences
Bridge employment

- What are the personal factors related to retirement?

- What are the two rationales for retirement?

- Why did the number of retired individuals increase during the 20th century?

- What changes in retirement are expected during the 21st century?

- What is the perspective of Baby Boomers toward early retirement?

- What are the three phases of adjustment to retirement?

- Can retirement lead to negative effects for the person?

- What factors are related to the person's decision to retire?

Learning Activity: Ask several retired persons why they chose to retire. How has their life and lifestyle changed since retirement?

Retirement Preparation

Research indicates that in addition to factors such as one's financial situation, attitudes toward work, and support from one's spouse, preparation for retirement is also considered important when one is considering retirement. In a classic study of retirement preparation programs, Ekerdt, Vinick, and Bosse (1989) found that workers were more likely to retire if they foresaw a good pension awaiting them, if they held positive retirement attitudes, if they engaged in informal and formal retirement preparation, and if their retirement occurred at older ages.

To avoid financial crises and other retirement-related problems among retirees, many companies implement pre-retirement-planning programs for workers of all levels and ages, though the above discussed efforts by AARP to open up job possibilities for older workers may impact this trend, as might the cost of funding pensions for retirees. In an extensive review of the available literature at the time, Ekerdt (1989) indicated that there are two major types of information common to all pre-retirement programs. The first type of information is regarding the company's financial benefits, Social Security, and any other financial matters. The second type is advice, counseling, and suggestions concerning such topics as health care and services, leisure activities, legal matters, and changes in lifestyles.

Who Prepares for Retirement?

The more highly educated and better off financially one is, the more likely the person is to prepare for retirement (Taylor & Doverspike, 2003). Alternatively, for those who are less highly skilled and more poorly educated, retirement preparation activities are less frequent. This suggests that for those who cannot afford to retire—that is, those who have held the lowest-paying jobs and consequently contributed less to company pension plans and Social Security—special efforts may be needed to induce anticipation and planning for retirement. In this respect, affluent Baby Boomers are more likely to engage in retirement preparation than their predecessors (Taylor & Doverspike, 2003). Issues of individual variability in retirement adjustment and its relationship to planning, ethnic/racial diversity and retirement as it applies to women are likely to become more important in the retirement planning process (Taylor & Doverspike, 2003). Based upon a meta-analysis of available research, Topa et al. (2009) found that previous work involvement and greater previous job satisfaction most strongly predicted retirement planning. Health, negative working conditions, and retirement attitudes were less important in this respect.

It seems that a majority of Americans do not report engaging in any systematic, self-initiated retirement preparation at present, due to their putting off retirement (see above). Moreover, at one time, there was some misunderstanding about retirement provisions among even those who had company-sponsored pensions (Ekerdt, 1989). Indeed, the prevalence of retirement-preparation programs is difficult to assess (Ekerdt, 1989), where estimates depend upon on how such programs are defined and the extensiveness of what is offered, where programs should encompass both planning and counseling.

Part of the problem is that the preparatory behaviors persons engage in are poorly understood. Muratore and Earl (2010) found that such behaviors could be understood in terms of those related to the protection of the public, self-insurance, and

self-protection, and that persons varied in each of these respects as a function of age, gender, income, and their own self-assessed readiness to retire. Family support in preparing for retirement is critical (Greller & Richtermeyer, 2006), as is the ability to accurately assess one's financial needs in retirement in the context of having confidence in the government, i.e., Social Security and Medicare (Kim, Kwon, & Anderson, 2005). Likewise, the ability of the couple to agree upon and collaboratively carve out a likely retirement scenario for themselves influences retirement planning (van Solinge & Henkens, 2005), wherein women spend less time thinking about retirement life (Jacobs-Lawson, Hershey, & Neukam, 2004). In light of these findings, if we view retirement as a process, programs with multiple goals are likely to be most effective.

One of the difficulties in evaluating both the prevalence and efficacy of retirement planning lies in the fact that not everyone who could enroll in a formal program does so (Campione, 1988). In an extensive study of retirement planning, Turner, Scott, and Bailey (1990) found that, among nearly 2800 university employees, only a few had engaged in any more than financial planning, a problem especially common among those less well-off financially. Higher education, greater family income, being male, and increased age related to more financial planning (Turner et al., 1990). People who are experiencing job burnout and for whom leisure activities are important may also choose to retire earlier (Rowe, 1990) and therefore engage in both formal and informal planning to a greater extent. Likewise, the changing nature of retirement, the impact of lifelong learning, career management, and the trend toward later retirement pose challenges for those assessing the efficacy of retirement preparation (Taylor & Doverspike, 2003).

That the work and retirement scenario for many persons is changing influences behavior at work, prior to retirement, and during retirement. One may or may not put off retirement because of the stock market's performance, the demands of caregiving, the cost of healthcare, or concerns about the viability of Social Security and Medicare. For many, retirement preparation behaviors reflect messages that one receives via financial planners that stress investing wisely, saving, and (depending upon whom one listens to), stress either caution or boldness in terms of playing the odds in the stock market. Clearly, the events of 2008-2009 (the recession, government bailouts of banks and companies such as AIG, the car industry, or Fannie Mae) have caused people to carefully consider their options in terms of retirement preparation. Scary times, indeed!

Is Retirement Preparation Effective?

Assuming that one can prepare for retirement, retirement preparation seems to have many advantages. In that workers can and do retire unexpectedly, the anticipatory socialization that accompanies early planning could be viewed positively; that is, one is not caught unprepared. The later planning begins, the greater the risk of making costly and potentially irreversible decisions. Preparing for retirement should encourage attention to the future, for example, health maintenance and income security, rather than a focus solely on the present, that is, career advancement. Retirement planning should also be beneficial because one's identity and circle of friends will not likely revolve around work after retirement.

In reality, retirement preparation is both advantageous and disadvantageous (Ekerdt, 1989; Taylor & Doverspike, 2003). In addition to benefiting individuals, it lessens turnover by increasing morale. While early retirement may be beneficial for those with viable work alternatives, good health, and sufficient interpersonal and emotional resources, many people choose to work longer, especially if they anticipate a drop in income and enjoy their work. For such individuals, adopting a retirement-oriented mind-set as a function of a retirement-preparation program may actually be counterproductive!

Overall, whether retirement planning is effective often depends on the criteria one uses to measure program efficacy. Clearly, while programs can facilitate short-term attitude change, long-term change in attitudes and their translation into actual retirement-planning behaviors may be minimal, es-

pecially if one's health or life situation changes after retirement. Those who enroll in such programs and who benefit to the greatest extent may be more likely to engage in retirement planning anyway (Taylor & Doverspike, 2003). That is, their participation is itself a form of planning (Glamser, 1981). For all of these reasons, definite conclusions about whether programs are effective in a long-term sense cannot be reached, especially if we see retirement adjustment as a *process*. Indeed, the realities of retirement may force people to redefine what is desirable or even attainable, undermining styles of adaptation and/or goals they may have established in the program years earlier. Unfortunately, there is very little data regarding pre-retirement planning among women, and what information is available is often ambiguous. Thus, we need to learn more about women's involvement in pre-retirement planning programs.

Effects of Retirement

Many, if not most, men and women make the transition from work to retirement fairly easily. Szinovacz (2003) suggests a **continuity theory** explanation for those who do not experience any negative effects as a result of retirement. According to this perspective, after retirement the person continues her or his personal identity through the expansion and development of other roles, rather than the work role. These roles provide self-esteem for the retired person. Calasanti (1996) has also proposed a **crisis** explanation to account for those individuals who experience negative effects as a result of retirement. This explanation suggests that since the occupational role serves as the major source of cultural and personal validation, and serves as the nexus around which all other roles revolve, retirement negatively affects self-identity, and subsequently has other negative effects on one's physical and mental health, and on his/her relationships. Further, research indicates that Americans, particularly men, place a greater emphasis on work compared to Europeans (Leitner & Leitner 2004). Also, European men have the advantage over American men in adjusting to the extensive free time of retirement years because during their working years they experienced larger blocks of free time (5 or 6 weeks of vacation time), whereas many American men have not (Leitner & Leitner, 2004).

Simply put, some individuals experience difficulties in retiring, while a majority of others do not. The negative adjustment to retirement for a minority of individuals is most likely due to financial or health problems, or both, rather than retirement per se.

Lochenhoff et al. (2009) found persons who were high in neuroticism (see Chapter 6) and low in extroversion to be less satisfied with retirement, and those high in extroversion to be more active in retirement. These authors also found that over time, retirees increased in agreeableness and decreased in activity (see Chapter 6). Interestingly, Type A individuals seem to adjust to both voluntary and involuntary retirement equally well (Swan, Dame, & Carmelli, 1991). Overall, persons who expect to exert control over their post-retirement lives, who are well- adjusted, who have a well-developed network of support and close family ties tend to report greater satisfaction in retirement (Hooyman & Kiyak, 2011; Lowis, Edwards, & Burton, 2009). What interferes with retirement satisfaction among women appears to be the "impingement" of their husbands into their "worlds-as-lived" (Bushfield, Fitzpatrick, & Vinick, 2008).

One of the major positive aspects of retirement is that it may allow increased time for social and leisure activities, especially if the individual has adequate money and is in good enough health to engage in these activities. In fact, self-worth may increase after retirement if an individual is able to transfer the self-esteem derived from the previous job to current activities. It appears that the most important condition for an individual to adjust well to retirement is activity—doing something. Thus, after retirement, many individuals begin or resume their education or do volunteer work.

Societal Effects of Retirement

Retirement can also affect society, which, in this case, refers to other workers in one's company, other individuals in general, and society's institu-

tions. One of the major effects retirement has on society pertains to the allocation of economic resources. Retired individuals need goods and services such as senior centers, recreational facilities, and housing that often require reallocation of resources from other age groups or programs, accompanied by resentment or hostility on both sides. In contrast, Europeans are likely to be generous to older people, and more willing to support them (Edwards, 2004); the European attitude is, "we're in this together and sooner or later we're going to become older, and we'll need some help."

Another societal aspect of retirement is that it affects one's industry or company both positively and negatively. On the positive side, it gives the company a somewhat objective yet arbitrary method— chronological age—of replacing higher paid, older employees with lower paid, younger employees (Hooyman & Kiyak, 2011). Furthermore, chronological age as the sole criterion for retirement affects all workers equally, since they will all eventually reach that age. This provides the company with a practical administrative procedure that is objective and avoids potential charges of discrimination, favoritism, and bias (Panek, 1997).

On the negative side, organizations must provide economic support—contributions to a pension plan, medical insurance, and life insurance—for individuals who are no longer producing for the company. From the company's perspective, retirees are taking from the system but are not contributing to it. Employers may offer early retirement programs, but they can be costly. Companies may also be faced with the need to retrain workers whose skills have become obsolete, yet feel pressure from other workers to eliminate such programs.

For other employees in the retiree's company, retirement allows for upward mobility in positions and pay increases, and for orderly and planned progression of workers throughout all levels of the organization. At the same time, the younger workers who occupy the positions vacated by retirees now have the greater responsibility and demands of these higher positions. They must contribute to the pension and benefits system in order to support retirees. The same can be said of most workers; that is, since they are working, they are contributing to the support of individuals who are not working. Because our population is "graying," there are more and more retirees to be supported by fewer and fewer workers. On the other hand, if recent trends continue, more older persons will remain in the work force for longer periods of time, creating more competition with younger workers who are desirous of getting jobs.

Check Your Learning 8-2

Identify the following terms or concepts:

> Preretirement planning
> Crisis explanation for retirement
> Continuity explanation for retirement

- Is preretirement preparation effective?

- What are some of the major implications of retirement for the person?

- What are some of the major implications of retirement for society?

The "New" Retirement

Key elements of the new retirement landscape include the demise of mandatory retirement, significant changes in Social Security incentives and the nature of pension plans, and improving health and greater life expectancy, all resulting in a desire by many persons to continue working longer than they otherwise would have (AARP, 2004; Clark & Quinn, 2002; Hardy, 2006).

Many persons who put off retirement relate this to changes in the physical demands of many jobs and labor shortages that force employers to attract older workers (AARP, 2004). Indeed, in 2003, AARP conducted a "Staying Ahead of the Curve" survey of 2001 employed men and women between the ages of 50 and 70, and found many to want to continue working for a variety of reasons, the most important being the need for money and for health benefits (AARP, 2004). To help matters, AARP es-

tablished a program entitled "Best Employers for Workers over 50," which honors those companies whose policies and programs do the best job of attracting and retaining older employees. In early 2004, AARP created the Foundation Senior Community Service Employment Program, and formed a hiring partnership with Home Depot, the second largest retailer in the nation. This program encourages the hiring of older workers. It provides community service employment opportunities for persons over the age of 55 to obtain new job knowledge and skills and break the "silver ceiling" (AARP, 2004).

Members of the Baby Boom generation (see Chapter 1) were predicted to be nearing retirement at a time when the institution of retirement was itself undergoing a transformation (Lewis, 1998). In fact this contributed to reversing the 50-year trend toward "earlier" retirement. The Baby Boom generation presents retirement researchers with many new questions, since they are distinct from previous cohorts in many ways (Ekerdt, 2010). These differences encompass demographic factors as well as psychological factors (Taylor & Doverspike, 2003). For example, compared to previous cohorts, the Baby Boomers are in better health, have a better financial situation, and have the highest level of education (Taylor & Doverspike, 2003). Consequently, Baby Boomers will make major changes in how Americans retire. Rather than retiring abruptly and at earlier ages, as was true for previous cohorts, they will stretch out their working lives, moving in and out of new and varied careers, and are likely to view retirement as a process, not as a single event.

Research on work and retirement is evolving in response to these generational shifts. Not only do different cohorts of men and women attach different meaning to retiring, but retirement can also be considered a behavior—as an *outcome* of decisions about work and life that have been made previously, and as a *cause* of changes in well-being, health, or relationships with others (Ekerdt, 2010). Clearly, we need to learn more about (a) future generations' perceptions of the nature and timing of retirement, (b) the impact of the labor market on retiring, (c) the quality of retirement pensions, and (d) the experience of being a retiree (Ekerdt, 2010).

The Changing Face of Retirement

It is likely that the retirement of the future will differ from the retirement of the past. Retirees are likely to be faced with increasing health care costs because fewer employers will offer retiree benefits. Benefits packages and eligibility criteria will change, forcing retirees to spend more of their retirement income on health care, especially with increased copayments, spending limits, and lessened benefits for workers hired at older ages (Fronstin & Salisbury, 2005). Thus, there exists a lag in or a discrepancy between what persons want to do with their retirements and what they will be able to accomplish. Ultimately, it may take organizations several years to respond to the availability of older workers. Such changes as career development programs may be difficult and expensive to implement quickly enough. They will likely require changes in higher education (see Chapter 3) or aging organizations themselves (see Chapter 9) to meet the requirements of an increasingly learning-hungry cohort of older persons returning to school to enhance their skills, thereby meeting shortages of skilled persons in many fields such as nursing or education (Bass, 2005). Persons who are partially retired or unretired may eventually outnumber those who are fully retired, defined by the Department of Labor as persons who collect Social Security benefits and who work less than 20 hours per week (Beatty & Visser, 2005). Thus, our ideas about work and retirement, to include the wisdom of preparing for retirement, adjustment to the role of retiree, and the personal and societal effects of retirement, are likely to undergo a change in the next decades. Stay tuned for new developments!

Leisure

Leitner and Leitner (2004) discuss the meaning that leisure may have for adults and older persons, wherein meaningful leisure activities are those that contribute to the quality of life for such persons, enhance life satisfaction, and for these reasons, lessen mortality. McGuire, Boyd, and Tedrick (2004) have discussed leisure as the embodiment of the "Ulyssean adult"—the person who is on life's journey seeking adventure and opportunity, named after Ulysses, whose adventures, as discussed in the *Odyssey*, began when he was 50 and ended in his 70s. Viewed from this perspective, leisure can take many forms, be it competitive sports or solitary reading, and is considered to have two defining characteristics: perceived freedom of choice and intrinsic motivation (Kelly, 1996). Indeed, leisure has a simplistic quality to it; persons can derive joy and satisfaction from the simplest of activities (McGuire et al., 2004).

Regardless of whether we associate leisure with retirement, leisure activities can maintain or enhance cognitive functioning (e.g., playing bridge), lessen loneliness and depression, reduce bone loss and improve bone density (lessening the risk of fractures), and improve one's balance and strength. Indeed, while participating in sports, dance, music, art, or drama can all be beneficial to adults and older persons, such activities must be an expression of **leisure competence**—valuing leisure for its own sake, rather than defining it solely in terms of activities. Not surprisingly, persons who hold more positive attitudes toward leisure, who view growing older with more enthusiasm, who are in better health, and who have been involved in leisure earlier in life are more likely to engage in meaningful leisure activities (Leitner & Leitner, 2004). Programs providing opportunities for leisure involvement may exist at senior centers, assisted living facilities, nursing homes, or as discussed below, in retirement communities, where individuals locate themselves along a continuum that defines leisure lifestyles. We discuss such lifestyles later in this chapter.

For our purposes, we will define leisure activity as any activity in which individuals engage during free time (Stebbins, 2004). Such activities are typically non-paid in nature (Hooyman & Kiyak, 2011). This definition does not distinguish between activities that are related to a job and those that are

Figure 8-2. Developing meaningful leisure activities is important to leisure competence.

not, nor whether the activity involves purely self-enjoyment (**intrinsic**) or earning money (**instrumental**). Moreover, this definition does not distinguish between *choosing* to have leisure time, as when taking time off from work, taking a vacation, or spending weekends or evenings engaged in an activity, and having leisure time *imposed upon* the individual, as when one is forced to use vacation or sick times lest it disappear, or is laid off or forcibly retired. As work becomes more intrinsically meaningful, the distinction between leisure and work is more difficult to make. Indeed, because work structures our lives, its impact on and relationship to leisure is substantial (Stebbins, 2004).

Types of Leisure Activities

Although almost any activity can be considered a leisure activity, researchers generally group leisure activities into five major categories (Scott & Willits, 1998; see Table 8-2). It is important to note that these categories are not independent. For example, reading books and then discussing them with a group of other persons would be both a solitary as well as social/cultural leisure activity. Leisure activity is very important since research has consistently demonstrated that leisure activity is related to mental and physical well-being in old age (Cohen, 2005). Persons make gradual shifts in leisure involvement that are purposefully selective, in light of one's health, likes, dislikes, and values (Baltes, 1997); this allows them to feel valued as persons, even into very late life (Menec, 2003; Johnson & Schaner, 2005). Thus, participation in activities provides opportunities for both personal development and social interaction and support, wherein building networks of

Table 8-2

Types of Leisure Activities

Type	Example
Sports	Play tennis, softball, golfing.
Intellectual	Read books; learn about a topic of interest.
Socializing	Visit with family and friends; go to parties.
Creative/artistic	Paint; play a musical instrument.
Formal Organizations	Participate in school, community, religious groups.

support and providing the opportunity for meaningful interactions with others seems to be the major contribution of leisure (Hooyman & Kiyak, 2011).

In light of the changing nature of retirement, especially for Baby Boomers, definitions of leisure, and the role that leisure plays in adulthood may each need to change. Gibson (2006) notes the importance of changing definitions of work and leisure as well as the increasing role of leisure in relating to well-being in later life. Indeed leisure may free persons of the "busy ethic" of later life, which stresses the need to be continually active in order to age well (see Gibson, 2006).

Learning to Live with Leisure

Americans have generally subscribed to what is often described as the **Protestant work ethic,** which views work as sacred and something to be enjoyed. Basically, one is expected to be a working and contributing member of society. For this reason, leisure activities have generally been equated with idleness, something to be engaged in by only

the young and retirees. To illustrate, Hooker and Ventis (1984) found a commitment to the work ethic to relate negatively to life satisfaction in retirees. Indeed, we have been made to feel guilty about actively engaging in leisure activities—that is, not working and enjoying ourselves. In fact, many Americans do not know how to relax when they are not working at their jobs. On their days off, they mow the lawn or paint the house.

It is important to recognize that leisure is contextual in nature. How it is defined, how we experience it, and whether it is satisfying are relative to many factors—family lifestyle, work values, gender roles, and relationships with others.

Leisure competence is understanding the meaning of leisure for you personally, as well as acting on that understanding through your involvement in meaningful leisure activities. As with retirement, it is perhaps best to state that the development of leisure competence is a learning process (Peacock & Talley, 1985). That is, people do not suddenly become aware of leisure in retirement. A *process* approach has the advantage of reframing retirement more positively, rather than seeing it as leading to the "problem" of developing leisure activities.

In this respect, Stebbins (2004) argues for the construct of **serious leisure**, reflecting the enthusiasm and dedication to leisure pursuits among hobbyists, amateurs, and volunteers, analogous to those who are workaholics. Serious leisure pursuits are seen as a substitute for overinvolvement at work, providing one with a new lifestyle and identity and enhancing one's relationships with others; serious leisure is "not constrained by the need to make a living" (Stebbins, 2004, p. 121). Thus, leisure involvement can promote successful aging by allowing individuals to more fully engage in everyday life and prevent age-related physical and cognitive decline (Jopp & Hertzog, 2010).

Lifespan Trends in Leisure Activities

Leisure patterns, like other aspects of human behavior, are believed to exhibit both change and continuity across the lifespan (Scott & Willits,

1998). Specifically, leisure activities vary as a function of the phase of the adult lifespan, and they are influenced by a variety of factors. That is, while there appear to be common types of leisure activities adults engage in which vary with age, other forms of leisure activities are nevertheless common to all adults (Kelly, 1983). Moreover, leisure activities change according to the current needs, abilities, and health of the individual (Janke & Kleiber, 2008).

While there are individual differences in the choice of leisure activities in adulthood, the three most important factors in determining leisure activities appear to be health, economic resources, and time constraints (Burrus-Brammel et al., 1985). For example, you may wish to spend your spring break at the beach, but if you cannot afford the plane fare or do not have a car (and cannot get a ride), you're likely to be stuck at home!

Young Adulthood

During young adulthood, the majority of leisure activities tend to be **active** and focus outside the home. These include outdoor reaction activities such as exercising, jogging, playing sports, and going to movies, shows, and restaurants. The primary focus of these leisure activities is active "doing" and/or participation. Many young adults also spend time in **passive** leisure activities such as reading, watching television, surfing on the internet, playing video games, or just relaxing.

Young adults report that they engage in leisure activities for various reasons. These include personal interest, a means of coping with pressure and stress, and meeting individuals with similar interests. Thus, during young adulthood, leisure activities are important because they provide a means of relaxation from daily pressures experienced on the job, the commute to work, at home, and in the family. Consider an individual who works as a stockbroker in a high-pressure situation for 8 or more hours a day, followed by a 1-hour commute home every evening through heavy traffic. This individual may enjoy getting away from those pressures by engaging in fishing at a quiet pond.

Another reason leisure is important is because it may permit one to feel self-actualized or fulfilled. Since individuals often enter fields or jobs they are not interested in, leisure activities may serve as compensation for the lack of self-fulfillment attainable on the job. For example, an individual might want to be an artist but constantly be told it is not possible to earn a living in that endeavor. This individual, in order to achieve some economic security, may obtain a degree in accounting or engineering, yet spend lots of leisure time painting.

Leisure activities also provide a social outlet for meeting others with similar interests, such as stamp collecting, softball, bowling, and dancing. Therefore, although during young adulthood, individuals engage in all five categories of leisure activities (see Table 8-2), for the most part leisure activities can be characterized as "active" in nature.

Middle Adulthood

Middle age serves as a transition between the active leisure orientation of young adulthood and the passive leisure style of later adulthood. Individuals begin reducing the frequency of action-oriented activities such as participation in sports, and increasing the frequency of passive-oriented activities such as reading (Kelly et al., 1986). For instance during middle age, outdoor action activities such as playing team sports declines (Iso-Ahola, Jackson, & Dunn, 1994).

There are two primary reasons for this change. First, declining health may limit participation in action-oriented activities for some people. Second, individuals begin to select activities that they can continue into later adulthood. Often, these new activities are somewhat related to the activities of young adulthood. For example, instead of playing softball, the individual now spends leisure time being an umpire. Instead of long-distance jogging, the individual now takes up walking or biking.

Middle-aged people also often participate in leisure activities by becoming involved in civil organizations, joining clubs, or enrolling in adult education courses that deal with topics they have always had an interest in but have never had the time or opportunity to explore (see Chapter 3). These topics range from academic areas to genealogy and pets. Leisure activities may also provide an outlet where social relationships can be developed and maintained. Since fulfilling leisure activities can lead to greater life satisfaction and better adjustment to retirement in older adults, it is important to at least begin to develop leisure activities in adulthood that can be continued into retirement.

Later Adulthood

Disengagement theory (see Chapter 6) holds that, as a person ages, there is a tendency to psychologically and socially withdraw or disengage from the environment (Griffin & McKenna, 1998). This can cause a reduction in leisure activities, especially those engaged in outside the home. Alternatively, **activity theory** suggests that, because of a positive relationship between activity levels and life satisfaction, older adults tend to replace lost roles and activities with new to maintain activity levels (Griffin & McKenna, 1998).

Although some older adults engage in active leisure activities, the majority are involved in passive leisure activities. These include watching television, reading, or socializing with friends. For example, Strain, Grabusic, Searle, and Dunn (2002) found that solitary activities, such as watching television and listening to the radio, are cited as the most popular pursuits among this age group, whereas sports and exercise programs are activities in which participation is least likely. As persons age, other activities such as cooking, running errands, attending community meetings, checking the mail, housekeeping, gardening, handyman-type work around the house, or simply sitting quietly occupy an increasing proportion of persons' time, especially if they are of the "oldest-old" (age 75 and older) (*Bureau of Labor Statistics*, American Use Time Survey, 2006).

While leisure involvement may decline for widows (Janke & Kleiber, 2008), in many instances, older adults must develop new leisure activities because of economic and physical health factors, reducing their involvement in former leisure activi-

ties. For many older people, being involved in some form of activity is critical to feeling positive about themselves. This implies that leisure competence is itself an important construct in understanding adulthood.

Although older adults participate in similar types of leisure activities as young and middle-aged adults, the overall frequency of participation decreases with age. As mentioned above, there is a shift from action-oriented activities to passive-oriented ones with age.

In a longitudinal study of leisure activities, Glamser and Hayslip (1985) conducted a 6-year longitudinal investigation of the impact of retirement on participation in leisure activities. They surveyed 132 male workers aged 60 and older who were employed in semiskilled positions regarding the types and frequency of their leisure activities. Activities were arranged into one of four major categories: (1) **cultural**, e.g., attending plays and movies; (2) **physical**, e.g., playing golf; (3) **social**, e.g., visiting with family or friends; and, (4) **solitary**, e.g., reading books, watching television. They found that, during the 6-year period, the overall level of leisure activity declined. However, there was a substantial amount of individual change in leisure activity and substantial social disengagement following retirement. The greatest decline was in social activities, followed by cultural, then physical activities. Interestingly, stability across time was found for physical activities—the most common pattern was continued nonparticipation.

In a classic study of leisure in adulthood, Kelly et al. (1986) investigated leisure activities in four age groups—40 to 54 years, 55 to 64 years, 65 to 74 years, and 75 years and older—in a small midwestern city. These researchers assessed overall activity level and identified 28 kinds of leisure, which were reduced to 8 major types. These types were cultural, travel, exercise and sport, family leisure, outdoor recreation, social activities, community organizations, and home-based activities. Kelly et al. (1986) found both consistency and differences in leisure activities with age. In terms of differences with age, there was a decline in overall activity level, sport and exercise, and outdoor recreation. There was **continuity** in a number of core activities such as family, social, and home-based activities. Results also indicated that for the 40-to-54 and 55-to-65 age groups, travel and cultural activities were important. For the 65-to-74 age group, social and travel activities predominated, and for the oldest age group (75 years plus), the most common leisure activities were family- and home-based activities.

McGuire, Dattavio, and O'Leary (1986) identified **limiting factors** and **prohibitory factors** in a study of outdoor recreational activities across the lifespan. Limiting factors reduce participation, while prohibiting factors prevent it altogether. Most people, regardless of age, stressed that lack of time, people, and poor health were major constraints both limiting and prohibiting activities, with health taking on more importance with age. Interestingly, constraints of income, safety, access to transportation, and lack of information did not change across age levels. While lack of money seemed to affect most people, lack of time was an important issue, especially to middle-aged people, and not having a companion increased as a barrier among older adults.   Life events or transitions can also have an impact of participation in leisure activities (Janke & Kleiber, 2008; Strain et al., 2002). For example, losing a spouse or partner can affect participation in activities such as dancing, traveling, or playing bridge.

Finally, although often overlooked, transportation has a profound impact on an individual's quality of life, lifestyle, and participation in a variety of leisure activities, especially for older adults. Adequate transportation allows the individual access to shopping facilities, medical services, social contacts with others, and participation in activities of all types. Lack of available transportation affects a large percentage of older adults.

Patterns of Leisure during Retirement

Researchers have been interested in studying the lifestyles of individuals during retirement, since later life adaptation is strongly related to activity and social context outside the home (Zimmer et al., 1995). These lifestyles are often referred to as **leisure lifestyles**. It is common for organized leisure activity programs to be provided in assisted living environments as well as older adult communities (see Chapter 9). In this respect, an active leisure lifestyle appears to have positive effects on human health (Iso-Ahola et al., 1994).

It is important to note that the benefits of leisure involvement extend to young adults, especially if they come from disadvantaged backgrounds (Feinstein, Bynner, & Duckworth, 2006). Moreover, early (childhood) involvement in leisure-related physical activity seems to predict levels of physical activity in young adulthood (Kjonniksen., Anderssen, & Wold, 2009).

Implications of Types of Leisure Lifestyles

One of the most extensive and classic studies of lifestyles among retired persons was conducted by Osgood (1983), who examined the patterns of retirement lifestyles among residents of three age-segregated retirement communities in Florida and Arizona. Data were obtained from in-depth interviews in three retirement communities: blue-collar mobile home residents in Florida, upper-middle-class condominium dwellers in Florida, and a self-sufficient community of private homeowners in Arizona. Six major types or patterns of lifestyles were found in these communities:

1. **Organizers**—busy, dedicated, involved in organizations and clubs, younger and healthier.
2. **Joiners**—moderately active in formal activities organized by others.
3. **Socializers**—gregarious, friendly, but not formally active.
4. **Humanitarians**—helping others less fortunate, older and in worse health.
5. **Recreationalists**—very involved in selected activities, affiliated with others with similar interests; recreation is central to them.

6. **Retirees**—lack clear social roles, older and in worse health, may have been active earlier, but now are withdrawn from others.

Osgood found the majority of residents to be joiners, socializers, humanitarians, or recreationalists.

Although results of this study might vary as a function of geographic region and socioeconomic status, they build an important data base for future leisure programming, of which there is great need (Leitner & Leitner, 2004; Mcguire, Boyd, & Tedrick, 2004). Information regarding the lifestyles and interests of residents of retirement communities is also important because as more people live to advanced old age and move to such locales, planners and developers will need information about what types of services and activities should be available to residents. Diversity in persons' skills and interests and flexibility in what activities are available as well as in the nature of the programs housing such activities will be key to meeting middle-aged and older persons' needs for leisure services.

Comparatively speaking, little research has been conducted regarding leisure activities in adulthood, perhaps because of the shift in views about leisure as an activity versus leisure as a state of mind, i.e., serious leisure (see above). Most of what is available is cross-sectional and focuses on level of leisure activities versus their meaningfulness. One major reason for this lack of research is that leisure tends to be in opposition to the traditional work ethic in our society.

Check Your Learning 8-3

Identify the following terms or concepts:

> Leisure competence
> Intrinsic vs. extrinsic influences
> Serious leisure
> Continuity of leisure
> Protestant work ethic
> Active vs. passive leisure
> Limiting factors
> Prohibiting factors

- List and give an example of the five categories of leisure activities.

- What factors affect participation in leisure activities?

- Why do Americans need to learn to live with leisure?

- Describe leisure activities during young adulthood.

- Describe leisure activities during middle age.

- Describe leisure activities during old age.

- What is serious leisure?

- What is the relationship between work and leisure?

- Why is leisure competence important?

Learning Activity: Ask two people in each category: young adults, middle-aged adults, and older adults, what types of leisure activities in which they participate.

Summary

While **retirement** usually implies **disengagement** from the work role, individuals seem to go through distinct phases of adjustment to retirement—**honeymoon**, **disenchantment**, and **stabilization**. The decision to retire and the impact of retirement are influenced by a number of factors, the most important of which are health status and retirement preparation. Relative to the past, patterns of labor force participation and retirement are changing.

The major factors influencing the decision to retire voluntarily are both **personal** and **institutional** in nature. Institutional factors such as the organization's mandatory retirement policy are out of the control of the individual. The major personal factors related to the decision to retire are: health status, occupational level, retirement preparation, economic climate, personal financial situation, age, gender, work satisfaction, and personal attitudes. There are **individual differences** in reasons for retirement, and such differences mediate the effects of retirement on the individual and society.

Leisure was defined as any activity in which individuals engage during free time, though defining leisure clearly is difficult. Developing **leisure competence** is a lifelong process. There are numerous ways to classify leisure activities, and the selection of and participation in them are affected by many factors, such as personal interest, health, and economic resources.

Participation in leisure activities during adulthood seems to be important to well-being. Research indicates there are certain types of leisure activities that are characteristically engaged in by people of different ages. Moreover, with increasing age, there is a general decrease in the overall frequency of participation in activities, with a shift away from **active** to more **passive** activities. These patterns of leisure activity, as well as **leisure lifestyles**, are influenced by numerous factors such as health condition, financial resources, and transportation.

Chapter 9
The Social-Environmental Context of Adulthood and Aging

Adulthood and the Environment

The roles that we play, our interactions with others in the context of these roles, as well as the cultural or societal expectations of us as parents, teachers, spouses, or workers collectively define the **social-environmental context** of adulthood. Our focus in this chapter is to explore the larger social context in which we age. This is the multifaceted environment which we must continually be aware of and adapt to so that we can be happy, healthy, and productive, and maintain satisfying relationships to others. It should not be surprising to learn that even gross cultural or historical changes can influence our behavior, given our discussion of the impact of cultural changes on personality (see Chapter 6) and intelligence (see Chapter 3) in adulthood.

Roles in Adulthood:
Coping with Changes in the Environment

Much of our adult lives is spent dealing with the demands on us as a consequence of the many **roles** that we play - as a husband or wife, as a parent, as an employee, or as a caregiver or friend to someone else. In light of the fact some adults often play many roles that may conflict with one another, these conflicts require us to change our behavior and make demands on our time. Thus, the complexity of our lives, as well as the rapidity of the changes we must face in our roles as spouses, parents, workers, or caregivers are a source of stress for many adults. Thus, it is usually in the context of the roles that we play as adults that we attempt to cope with the en-

vironment, as well as with **changes** (see Box A) in our lives linked to the roles that we play.

Not only must we deal with the many obligations that our roles require, but we also must interact with others who are also responding to us in the context of the roles that they too must play, perhaps as parents, teachers, fellow employees, supervisors, or service providers. Though we may not always be aware of it, we must also react to changes or events which impact the institutions that such persons represent, e.g., the school system, the work environment. Thus, cultural expectations regarding how we are supposed to behave as parents, as husbands or wives, as workers, or as adult children caring for aging parents also influence our behavior in light of the many roles that we often must play.

What complicates matters is that the social-cultural context in which our roles and those of others are embedded also changes (Schaie & Elder, 2005). These changes affect how people organize their lives, and in some cases, they exert a profound influence on how persons define themselves. For example, the Great Depression, World War Two, the Korean War, and the Women's Movement each affected specific cohorts of men and women in shaping their identities, family lives, values, and careers (Stewart & Healy, 1989; Stewart & Ostrove, 1998; Elder, 1999; Laub & Sampson, 2005). It remains to be seen whether events such as 9/11 or the recession of 2008-2009 have a comparable long-term impact on the lives of adults. There is little argument, however, in stating that these events indeed affected millions of adults in a variety of ways, even if such effects are short-lived.

Box A

Are Our Roles Changing?

Are our roles as adults changing? Riley (1994) argues that our currently **age-differentiated** society will eventually give way to an **age-integrated** one. An age-differentiated society makes distinctions between the roles played by younger versus older persons, whereas in an age-integrated society, no such distinctions are made. Age will therefore lose its power to limit persons' opportunities to participate in roles specific to education, work, and retirement. This change is imminent because there is a **structural lag** between changes in persons' lives and the societal institutions that define our roles as adults and children. For example, changes in the birthrate and in life expectancy have altered the number of frail older persons who need support, and have caused a change in the institution of retirement. Older students are more prevalent on many college campuses. Older retirees are often rehired by the same company for which they once worked to serve as men-

tors to younger employees who can benefit from their experience and wisdom. It is not uncommon for persons to begin entirely new careers as "entrepreneurs" after they have retired from more traditional jobs, or for persons to redefine their lives as caregivers for their grandchildren, or to become involved in their communities as volunteers. It is also not uncommon to find teenagers to be working part-time along with middle-aged and older employees, or to find older children teaching younger children in the primary and secondary schools (Riley & Riley, 1994). Such changes will require a fundamental shift in our values and expectations about roles that are appropriate for younger and older persons, as well as for men and women. Moreover, institutions such as higher education and the workplace will need to be flexible in order to accommodate these changes without being destroyed in the process.

Understanding and Describing
the Environment

Adult Development in Context

Many times thus far we have referred to the developing individual in the **context** of biological, psychosocial, and cultural-environmental changes or influences. What exactly do we mean by this? Likewise, as obvious as it seems, defining exactly what we mean by "the environment" can be difficult as well (see Box B).

To the extent that there is something systematic and age-related about our behavior, the **age continuum** serves as our **individual time line** (Neugarten, 1973), which begins at birth and ends with death (see Chapter 1). This age continuum serves as a focus or basis for the interaction of what might be termed various sectors, arenas, or dimen-

sions of influence. The **intrapersonal** dimension deals with our feelings, goals, abilities, or attitudes, in short, how we internally represent—at present, in the past, and with respect to the future—our experiences. Learning, memory, intelligence, personality, and sensation/perception are all quite relevant to the intrapersonal dimension of development. The **interpersonal** dimension reflects our relationships with others in a number of contexts or situations—as workers, parents, children, or spouses. The **biological** dimension most directly relates to issues important to most adults such as health and illness, death, longevity, and sexuality, while the **cultural** dimension not only encompasses issues of socialization, attitudes toward aging, work, and retirement, but also relates to questions of mental and physical health care.

Because we do not age "in parts," each of the

Box B

Defining the Environment in Adulthood

What is the environment? Ecological or environmental psychologists (Wacker, 2002; White, 1999) define the term very broadly because people and their environments necessarily interact and sometimes influence one another. Consider the environment to be **multifaceted** – complex and interactive. One aspect of the environment and our relationship to it must be understood in light of our relationship to other aspects of the environment as well as their relationship to one another. Being able to carefully define those aspects of the environment is key to understanding the impact of and interactions with the environment on adults of all ages.

Physical Environment - Those aspects of the environment that relate to whether you live in a city or a small town, a rural or an urban area; whether you can walk or must drive to school or work; whether you live on the first or second floor of your apartment complex; whether you must park your car outside your house or in your garage; where the nearest bank, gas station, hospital, shopping mall, coffee shop, or grocery store might be in terms of their nearness to your house or apartment. Do you live by yourself or do you share a house or an apartment? Do you live in a cool, temperate, or hot climate? Does it rain a great deal where you live? Is it typically windy? The physical aspects of the environment can be objectively defined in terms of indicators such as temperature, distance, or annual rainfall.

Subjective Environment - Those aspects of the environment that you evaluate as being meaningful or not, important or unimportant, or pleasant or unpleasant to you. Thus, we all have our favorite places to eat or shop, our favorite parts of town or even cities in which to live. Thus, when asked to describe your living environment, you might choose to emphasize those aspects of it which you value and ignore those which are unimportant to you.

Functional Environment - Those aspects of the environment with which you routinely interact or actually use, to include stores you shop at, areas of town you visit, or services which you use. These most likely reflect the subjective environment that you have defined for yourself, but they need not be akin to the physical environment as it exists objectively. You may not travel to certain areas of town because you fear for your safety, or you may not shop at certain stores because the sales clerks are rude or because the prices are too high. On the other hand, you (hopefully) only go to the hospital or to your doctor's office when you, or someone you care about, is ill. Thus, though they are not routinely used, these aspects of the functional environment can, under certain circumstances, be quite important in influencing our health and well-being as adults.

Interpersonal Environment – Those aspects of the environment which are necessarily defined by your relationships with others. Thus persons you list as important to you or as people upon whom you depend for help, support, or who provide you with a specific service or form of help (e.g. your doctor, accountant, home health care nurse) define the interpersonal environment.

above dimensions or sectors of development over-laps with and affects the others. For example, our health (biological dimension) both is affected by and affects (1) our awareness (intrapersonal dimension) of the importance of eating a balanced diet or exercising, which are influenced by what we read or hear about in the news (cultural dimension); (2) our prevailing attitudes (intrapersonal dimension) toward and access to health care (cultural dimension); as well as (3) our relationships with others who provide this care or who are affected by our own ill health (interpersonal dimension).

Our discussion also suggests that each of these dimensions is itself changing, along a **historical time** continuum (Schaie & Elder, 2005). Each point in history serves as a reference point, and thereby defines the larger context for our development. Besides changes in individuals, we must also consider changes in our culture that vary with the ebb and flow of historical changes that help to define the context of development. These cultural changes affect us at each phase of the life cycle. We label this historical continuum **contextual time**. We might draw several samples of a person's behavior at various chronological age points in time, each must be considered a small slice of the individual's life in the context of the influence of intrapersonal, interpersonal, biological, and cultural factors.

As you read about the various sectors of adult development and aging in this text, try not only to think in terms of their relationship to one another and their influence on your own development, but also try to envision how **changes** in these sectors over perhaps the last decade have affected development in adulthood. For example, how have advances in medical care and social services impacted changes in life expectancy (Chapter 2)? How have changes in men's and women's roles affected marriage and parenting (Chapters 4 and 5)? How have changes in the work world affected career choice among younger and middle aged persons (Chapter 7)? How have changes in life expectancy affected the ability of adult children to care for their parents and grandparents (Chapters 5 and 10)? How has divorce affected the role of grandparent (Chapter 5)?

Understanding adult development in this way will help you realize that your own development and aging are best understood in **relative** terms, that is, relative to how each of the sectors or dimensions in your own life is interacting across the lifecycle and relative to changes in each sector across contextual time.

Check Your Learning 9-1

Define the following terms and concepts:

> Social environmental context
> Intrapersonal dimension of development
> Interpersonal dimension of development
> Biological dimension of development
> Cultural dimension of development
> Individual versus contextual time
> Age continuium
> Historical time
> Age differentiated vs. age integrated
> Environment
> Multifaceted

- How do the roles we play in adulthood affect our interactions with others in the environment?

- How does a contextual view of adulthood help us to understand adult development?

- What are the sectors or dimensions of adult development? How do they relate to one another?

- What is the transactional model of Lawton and Nahemow?

Bronfenbrenner's Ecological Approach
Another way of understanding the social-environmental aspects of development is to study the environment in terms of its impact on the adult. The Bronfenbrenner and Morris (2006) **ecological approach** to development identifies five levels of environmental influence, ranging from very intimate and narrow to very broad (see Table 9-1). This ap-

Table 9-1

Bronfenbrenner's Ecological Approach

Relationship to Individual	Level	Examples
Most Immediate	Microsystem	Home, school, work
	Mesosystem	Connections between home and school
	Exosystem	Educational systems, transit systems
	Macrosystem	Cultural beliefs, political ideology
Least Immediate	Chronosystem	Changes in person/environment (family structure, war)

proach sees the person within the context of these multiple environments. Bronfenbrenner and Morris discuss several layers of the environment that are relevant to adulthood and aging: the **microsystem, mesosystem, exosystem, macrosystem,** and the **chronosystem.**

A **microsystem** is the everyday environment of home, school, work, or neighborhood, including relationships with spouse, children, friends, classmates, teachers, employers, or coworkers. For most of us, it is that aspect of the environment of which we are most aware. Recall in Chapters 4 and 5 that we discussed our **convoy of support**, which was largely defined in terms of the microsystem—those most immediate to us who could support us in times of stress or change. Thus, questions relating to parenthood or the work role are relevant here. How does a new baby affect the parents' lives? How is one expected to deal with coworkers?

The **mesosystem** is the interface among various microsystems—connections between home and school, between work and home, or between work and the neighborhood. In this case, questions that relate to the relationship between work and family are often asked. How does one balance time at home with an increase in the hours one is expected to be at work because of a product deadline? How does divorce affect a person's performance at work? How does unhappiness on the job affect the relationship

between husband and wife? How does the quality of the elementary school one's child attends, or for that matter, the influence of other children at this school, influence decisions parents make about raising a child?

The **exosystem** reflects connections between a microsystem and outside systems or institutions. In this case, the effects on the adult are explained in terms of the indirect impact of those institutions on the person. For example, how does a community's transit system affect job opportunities or the accessibility of social services? Does television programming that illustrates violence cause people to venture out less in the evenings for fear of crime? How does neighborhood crime affect an older adult's mobility?

The **macrosystem** consists of general cultural expectations, such as predominant beliefs and ideologies, or prevalent economic and political policy. How is an individual affected by living in a capitalist or socialist society? What are cultural standards for being a good husband or wife? A good parent? How do economic priories espoused by the party in power affect the allocation of funds for social services to minorities or older persons?

Last, the **chronosystem** speaks to the dimension of **change** or **consistency** in aspects of the person and the environment. This can include changes in family structure, place of residence, or employment, as well as larger cultural changes such as wars and economic cycles. Changes in cultural expectations regarding the parent or the work role, as well as demographic shifts that may affect family structure or caregiving roles also help to define the chronosystem.

As change is a necessary part of development in adulthood, it is often the chronosystem with which we must deal that often makes an impact on us. Cultural shifts in our ideas about child-rearing (Chapter 4), work and retirement (Chapters 7 and 8), the impact of technology on our mental skills (Chapter 3), how persons who are depressed or have a form of dementia are best treated (Chapters 10 and 11), and our ideas about many aspects of death and dying (Chapter 12) clearly have the potential to alter the decisions we make about parenting our children, selecting an occupation, retiring, caring for a dying family member, or coping with the death of a husband, wife, parent, or child. What was comfortable and acceptable in each of these respects 10 years ago has changed, and these changes force us to live our lives differently.

Person-Environment Fit

The notions of person-environment fit and a related concept, **developmental niche**, were presented and discussed in Chapter 1. Rather than reintroduce them here, we expand on the notion of how we interact with our environments in ways that are both productive and destructive to use personally, physically, and interpersonally.

Briefly, throughout adulthood, most aspects of our behavior or performance can be understood in terms of our interactions with the many aspects of the environment that define our everyday lives. In light of the adult's **degree of competence** (skills, abilities, personality characteristics) and the **demands** or **"press" of the environment** (its complexity, novelty, difficulty, or potential to change rapidly or in unknown ways), we might observe some behavioral manifestation of person-environment fit, as well as the individual's unobservable emotional state that accompanies this behavior (Lawton & Nahemow, 1973). Of course, adults vary

in terms of how competent they are. Some are brighter or healthier or have more interpersonal or material resources than do others. Likewise, some persons have more demanding jobs, are raising more children, or experience greater conflicts about the importance they place on being a good parent or being successful in their career. Our **internal representation** of the external world mediates this person-environment interaction. By internal representation, we mean the person's perceptions or views about his or her environment.

Applying Person-Environment Fit to Everyday Life

You might understand the concept of person-environment fit more easily by considering the example of your being employed at a demanding job, such as word processing in a busy office. If you are not adept at word processing or cannot meet deadlines, we might say that your individual competence at work is impaired. This would define a poor fit between your skills and the demands of your job, leading to being demoted or fired, or perhaps at home, becoming angry with your spouse or children. If your boss is very demanding or you have a tight schedule, the press of these demands will likely influence your work performance, the level of stress you are experiencing, and perhaps even your relationships with coworkers, regardless of how skilled you are. Even the most skilled word processor has limits! It is even possible that if you are exceptionally skilled, because the demands of your job are *not* great enough, you may not pay attention to the task at hand because you are easily distracted or even bored because things are moving too slowly for you. Thus, your work performance could suffer.

Coping with Person-Environment Fit

What might you do to adapt to such work situations? You might (a) work overtime or at lunch to upgrade your skills or lessen your workload during the day; (b) enroll in a class or training program to enhance your computer/word processing skills; (c) use a technique like relaxation to enable you to deal better with the stressfulness of your work demands with your anger or depression resulting from your boss's criticism of your work; (d) reassess your skills and ask to be assigned less work; or perhaps (e) seek a less demanding position elsewhere.

As you recall from Chapter 1, when you have made the necessary adjustments so that your skills and abilities match the demands of the environment, you have reached your personal **adaptation level** or **comfort zone of functioning**. When you exceed this comfort zone, negative affect (e.g., anger, depression, negative evaluations of self) increases and performance decreases are often the result. For example, if you normally word process 6 pages per hour, 7 or 8 might be a challenge. However, being asked to do 10 pages per hour would cause you to make more mistakes. You might become irritable or tire more easily. While slowing down to 7 pages per hour make actually increase your speed and efficiency, it may not be sufficient to satisfy your boss, keep up with your coworkers, or meet an important deadline. Of course, your personal adaptation level might be different from that of your parents, coworkers, friends, or roommates.

Developmental Niche

The concepts of person-environment fit and adaptation level are very similar to what we discussed in Chapter 1 as a **developmental niche** (Wachs, 1996). To reiterate, a person's developmental niche is defined in terms of the culture or environment in which the individual best functions. In theory at least, persons select those environments in which they can function most comfortably: those that are most **congruent** with their skills and abilities productively; enable them to express their convictions and values; and enable them to mature in the context of the roles they are playing, e.g., parent, spouse, worker.

Influences on the Developmental Niche in Adulthood: The Healthy and Not-So-Healthy

In theory, persons select a developmental niche that is positive for them. We all make the best decisions in light of our life situations. Perhaps we have been simply blessed with good judgment, are highly

Figure 9-1. A developmental niche which is positive is one where the environment matches the individual's needs and skills.

educated, and have been lucky enough to have been in good health for most of our lives. Perhaps we grew up with loving parents who were interested in our growth and development, or had stimulating and caring teachers from whom we have learned about making life decisions and from whom we were able to seek advise and counsel.

For some adults however, those developmental niches that might enhance one's growth may not be available. Additionally, persons select those that **inhibit** rather than make more likely their growth and development (Wachs, 1996). Many factors may act to **restrict** one's choices in selecting a niche that is positive in nature. For example, having to cope with chronic illness in oneself or in a loved one, the lack of a desirable marital partner, being widowed, discovering that a desired job or career is closed off to you, a lack of parenting skills, being poorly educated, being isolated from others, succumbing to peer pressure, or experiencing depression can all undermine your ability to select a niche for yourself that facilitates your health, well-being, or job performance. This ill-advised choice of a niche may further restrict your choice of friends, a marital partner, or a career. It may cause you to try to adapt to a niche whose demands are personally unacceptable or unacceptable to your family or subculture. This may cause you to become even *less* able to meet the new demands of coping with new situations at work, at school, or in your personal life.

Regarding our developmental niche, we should not fail to appreciate how we **appraise** or **evaluate** those experiences and situations about which we must make decisions (see Chapter 6). Thus, how we **assess** what happens to us in adulthood, as well as our efforts to exercise either primary or secondary control over the many events that we experience as adults, will influence person-environment fit and developmental niche. As our niche changes in response to decisions we make on the basis of this appraisal, it may be necessary to **reappraise** the "new" niche so that we can assess whether further adjustments in our behavior are necessary to reestablish a niche that is positive for us.

Others' expectations regarding the decisions and choices we make can also contribute in positive or negative ways to the quality of our own person-environment fit and our developmental niche. For example, cultural and family members' expectations about whether we should spank our children, how much independence to allow them, whether we should become involved in the church, whether we should be politically active, whether we should pursue a given career, marry, or have children often have a major influence on our lives, as well as help determine the **consequences** of making a good or a poor decision. Thus, finding one's personal level of adaptation or selecting a positive developmental niche is not done in a vacuum. The expectations of the culture or subculture of friends and family are important factors in understanding the social-environmental aspects of adult development and aging.

Being aware of these influences on you should make it obvious that there is much truth in saying that "no man is an island" in terms of our development as adults. That is, adult development is best understood in **relative** terms—**relative to the social-environmental context in which our development in adulthood takes place**. Thus, there is no one "best" way in which to age. We all age in unique ways, some of which are adaptive, and others of which are not (see Chapters 1 and 10).

We are all constantly making decisions and choices to "select" an environment that is in tune with our skills, needs, and personalities. We try to find a developmental niche that is positive for us. Yet, these choices may be closed off to us for many reasons, and the environments that we then select for ourselves may have negative consequences for us in terms of our health, our personal adjustment and happiness, our roles as parents, spouses, or workers, as well as for our performance in the workplace or at school. The choices we make can either strengthen or worsen the fit with our environment, and thus our new "niche" can be either positive or negative in nature.

Check Your Learning 9-2

Define the following terms and concepts:

> Ecological approach to adulthood
> Mesosystem
> Exosystem
> Macrosystem
> Chronosystem
> Person-environment fit
> Adaptation level
> Developmental niche
> Congruence
> Microsystem

- What is Bronfenbrenner's ecological approach?

- What is person-environment fit? Why is it important in understanding how adults cope with the environment?

- What are some factors that either enhance or inhibit the choice of a developmental niche?

- How do poor choices and decisions affect our developmental niche?

Person-Environment Fit and Developmental Niche in Adulthood

The concepts of person-environment fit and developmental niche are relevant in many ways to our lives in adulthood. For example, Holland's theory of occupational selection (see Chapter 7) stresses the congruence between one's career and one's personality. In designing jobs or tasks, one might want to maximize the "fit" between one's skills and the requirements of the task. This approach to job design is termed **human factors** because it recognizes the importance of matching a person's capabilities to, for example, how the knobs, buttons, and displays in an automobile instrument panel are placed so that they can most easily be seen and used without interfering with one's driving (see Chapters 2 and 7). Moreover, in adjusting to a new job, the accurate assessment of the match between the individual's skills, needs, and personality to (a) relationships with coworkers (whether they are cooperative or competitive); (b) the requirements of the job (whether one has or can acquire the requisite job skills); (c) relationships with authority figures (whether one feels supported by or can influence those in positions of authority); (d) the physical demands or hazards of a given career; and (e) one's needs for leisure time, plans for retirement, or desire to be promoted are all critical (Newman & Newman, 2009). Deciding whether (or when) to retire (see Chapter 8) often involves an assessment of the match between one's values about work, retirement, and leisure and the rewards of either working or retiring.

Person-environment fit is also important in love and marriage. In selecting a potential mate and in understanding interpersonal attraction, the extent to which one is **similar to**, or **complements** another underlies ideas about who might fall in love with whom, or who might make the best husband or wife (see Chapter 4). In selecting friends, whether one gives as much as one receives (equity) often determines whether a friendship endures. Whether caregiving is perceived as stressful or not often hinges on whether its demands are in proportion to the rewards of caring for a family member (see Chapters 4 and 5). In later life, the extent to which a variety of social and medical services are available and adequate to meet the needs of the older person and his or her family often influence the older adult's health, well-being, and ultimate survival. Even dying (see Chapter 12) can be understood in terms of the match between the dying person's needs and the ability and desire of family members to meet such needs.

In adulthood, the concept of the match between the person and the social environment can be quite useful in understanding how individuals of varying ages deal with a variety of **age-graded developmental tasks** (see Chapter 1).

Making Choices about Alternative Paths of Adult Development

Before we discuss developmental tasks in adulthood, it is important to note that there are many individuals who simply do not think of their lives as a series of age-related stages or adjustments to developmental tasks. We might call such persons "free spirits" or "nonconformists." They value the freedom to "do their own thing." Yet, this may come at the cost of being totally responsible for the consequences of their decisions, rejection by others who are uncomfortable with their lifestyle, and difficulties on the job or in everyday life because of others' lack of understanding or rejection of their value systems and decisions. These, of course, are outcomes and consequences that may indeed be valued by some persons and not others.

At this point in your life, do you take a risk to forge a path different from what is normal for your age or gender? This speaks to the importance of **individual differences in adult development** (see Chapter 1). For example, for every person that marries and has children, there is someone who chooses not to marry and still to have children, or not to marry at all. There are those who are comfortable with a clear career path working for others, and there are persons who choose to be self-employed or not work at all. Some persons retire "on time" and others retire earlier or later than the norm (e.g., at age 65), and still others never retire. These choices have the potential to enhance our satisfaction with life or worsen the fit between ourselves and our everyday work or interpersonal environments. Which type of person do you think you will be?

Developmental Tasks in Adulthood: Young Adulthood

Establishing a Lifestyle

In young adulthood, many of the decisions and choices we make to select a positive niche or good fit to our environment are carried out in light of the establishment of a **lifestyle** (Newman & Newman, 2009). One's lifestyle is a manner of constructing one's life that is translated into decision, actions, or choices one makes in light of role conflicts, role demands, personality characteristics, health, personal and professional goals, and relationships with others (Lombardi et al., 1996). Our lifestyle determines how we use our time and our resources to solve problems. Thus, lifestyle affects the extent to which our personal convoy (see Chapters 4 and 5) carries out its function of providing us with emotional or material support in times of need, crisis, or transition. Our lifestyle also influences how we carry out our roles in the context of the immediate or extended family, at work, or in the larger context of our interactions with others at school, at church, or as members of the nearly endless variety of clubs and organizations that demand our time.

As we age, a number of normative or non-normative events (see Chapter 1) can exert a very powerful influence on our lifestyle, such as accidents, illnesses, job loss or job change, divorce, the birth of our children, grandparenting, retirement, widowhood, or cognitive or physical incapacitation due to a stroke or Alzheimer's disease. Thus, nearly all of the many dimensions of adulthood and aging that we discuss in the text **both influence and are influenced by** changes in our lifestyle. The impor-

tant dimensions of lifestyle include the tempo of activities, the balance between work and leisure, the focus of our time and energy in specific life arenas, and the establishment of social relationships of varying degrees of intimacy (Newman & Newman, 2009).

Meeting One's Needs for Intimacy

In young adulthood, persons are often confronting with the task of selecting someone through whom they can meet their intimacy needs—the need to care for and be cared for by someone else without restrictions (Newman & Newman, 2009). Many aspects of the environment as defined by Bronfenbrenner and Morris (see above) might make this task easier or more difficult. For example, living in a rural area, being socially isolated, wishing to marry someone of a different ethnicity or race, having a demanding work schedule, or delaying marriage until a career has been established may interfere with the selection of someone with whom to share personal intimacy. Likewise, expectations driven by one's **social clock** (that one is expected to accomplish certain things at certain times in one's life) vary by social class (Newman & Newman, 2009). This can either impede or enhance one's marriageability—whether one is expected to marry early or late, or whether one is expected to put off marriage until either a career choice or an education is finalized. Such expectations vary by gender, with men having more clearcut criteria than women. Men are often expected to have achieved some career stability before they marry (Craig-Bray, Adams & Dobson, 1988). On the other hand, men who are more highly educated marry somewhat earlier than do their female counterparts, who are more able to support themselves and can therefore delay marriage somewhat (Teachman, Polonko & Scanzoni, 1987).

Having a Child

Even deciding on whether and/or when to have a child may be determined in part by one's perception of the environment, as when couples delay parenthood until one or both have completed their education or have steady incomes. The decision to have children can therefore be influenced by cultural changes in the context in which such decisions are made, e.g., are jobs available to both husband and wife? Will both receive maternity leave when the child is born? Among both married and single adults, access to oral contraceptives and other methods of birth control such as condoms, diaphragms, or spermicides now permits them to actively plan for the possible birth of a child, or delay it altogether, just as legal abortion can allow a couple to terminate a pregnancy, though it may come at the cost of criticism from family and friends (Wang & Buffalo, 2004). There is no guarantee, moreover, that the decision to terminate a pregnancy will be viewed similarly within the couple (Holmberg & Wahlberg, 2000). Issues of grief will need to be discussed and resolved within the couple (see Chapter 12). On the other hand, for couples who are childless, techniques such as in vitro fertilization or artificial insemination can make having and raising a child a reality (Siegelman & Rider, 2006). The power to make such decisions is obviously a consequence of both changes in attitudes toward such issues as well as medical advances. For couples marrying 50 years ago, such decisions, with their attendant joys, disappointments, risks, and responsibilities, were not possible.

Establishing a Career

Particularly so for young adults, **work** (see Chapter 7), exerts a powerful influence on our lifestyle, principally because of its demands on our time and because socioeconomic status is for the most part tied to how much we earn from our employment (Newman & Newman, 2009). Our work also influences how much time we are able (or willing) to spend with our spouse and children, how much leisure time we have, and/or whether we even develop any leisure activities (see Chapters 7 and 8). Our work often influences who our friends are likely to be, as well as the depth and breadth of our friendships with others (see Chapters 4 and 5). If we are divorced or single, our work may exert a particularly powerful influence on how we spend our time, in lieu of time that we might spend with a spouse or children. Indeed, because work often serves to structure our lives in young and middle adulthood, the **absence** of work, either via the loss of a job (or in retirement), both frees up and restricts the nature of relationships with others for many adults. Thus, economic ups and downs that affect the marketplace, the availability of a particular career, as well as legal restrictions on discrimination that is racial, gender, or age-specific in nature all represent cultural forces that are exosystemic or macrosystemic in nature that influence the impact of work in adulthood. Indeed, whether one can be forced to retire at a given age, or whether one is granted leave from work responsibilities due to caregiving responsibilities or death are also impacted by cultural expectations regarding aging, grief, and bereavement (see Chapters 10 and 12).

Developmental Tasks in Adulthood: Middle Adulthood

In midlife, managing a career (see Chapter 7), raising one's children, or evaluating the quality of one's marriage or of one's life in general, the degree to which one's expectations and goals were met is important in deciding on whether one is "on time" or "off time." This sense of "timeliness" thus influences our views of our careers as successful, whether we have succeeded as a parent, whether our marriage is satisfying, and whether we feel satisfied with our lives (Newman & Newman, 2009).

Raising a Family

As younger and middle-aged parents, we are to varying degrees all influenced by prevailing wisdom regarding how we should raise our children. For example, the roles of authoritarian, laissez-faire, or authoritative parent (Baumrind, 1971) have at varying times each been viewed as an optimal parenting style. Moreover, changes in men's and women's roles that are driven by demographic shifts (e.g., that women outlive men) or by forces such as the Women's Movement influence whether we might socialize our children along gender-specific lines. Changes in men's and women's roles also influence whether a man might raise his children as a "house-husband," or in the event of divorce, whether he would be viewed as a fit parent and consequently be awarded custody of his children. Indeed, dual career families, which impact on the allocation and sharing of child rearing responsibilities, are a direct consequence of changes in men's and women's roles. Moreover, the prevalence of single parent families, same-sex families, and stepfamilies is influenced by cultural changes in the attitudes toward divorce and toward persons with different sexual orientations (Kimmel, Rose, & David, 2006).

Caring for One's Parents in Midlife

Many middle-aged persons must care for an aging parent due to ill health or widowhood (see Chapters 4, 5, 10, and 11). That nursing homes even exist is a function of the increasingly older age that persons now attain, requiring that they be cared for by someone other than the family (Combrink-Graham, 1985). This is in contrast to earlier times when families cared for their own elderly because of a lack of formal care alternatives. Compared to Caucasian families who hold an "accepting" attitude toward outside help, a "rejecting" attitude toward outside assistance is characteristic of a variety of minority groups such as African Americans or Hispanics (Gelfand, 2003), who prefer to care for frail family members themselves, and who often seek outside help as a last resort. It is because of sociodemographic shifts, e.g., slowing of the birth rate, the increase in teenage pregnancies, that women outlive men, the later age at which marriage occurs, the experience of caregiving has changed, resulting in fewer younger persons to care for an increasing proportion of frail older persons, where the burdens of such responsibilities often fall on women (see Chapters 4 and 5).

Generativity in Midlife

The concepts of person-environment fit and developmental niche are relevant to the adult's selecting an environment that is both nurturant and supportive, as well as being able to foster one's own personal and professional goals in the context of caring for others—one's children and parents (Newman & Newman, 2009). Being able to do this allows one to feel **generative**—a feeling of productivity and creativity (Erikson, 1963). The most direct expression of generativity is in having children and raising them, as well as in caring for one's parents (Newman & Newman, 2009). In providing such care, our own sense of **ego strength** or **self-efficacy** (Bandura, 1989) is strengthened because caregiving allows you to feel that your own life as well as the lives of others are under your control or personal direction. Your own values and goals can be expressed in raising your children and caring for your parents. Feeling personal satisfaction in a "job well done" both defines this sense of self-efficacy and is influenced by it. Through caring for others that you love, you are demonstrating that you can express what is important to you as well as fulfilling your obligation as both a loving child (to your parents) and as a caring parent (to your children). When persons' prime focus is to improve the quality of life in those that they care for, this is termed **generative caregiving** (Phillips & Reed, 2009).

In deciding who they will marry, what career they will pursue, where they will live, and whether to have children, persons must understand themselves as well as be able to set goals for themselves in their lives and in their work that are personally meaningful. Thus, having a viable identity, but yet giving oneself "time" to find out who one actually is and wants to be (Newman & Newman, 2009) is quite important in being able to lovingly and unselfishly care for others, be they one's child, a grandchild, or a parent or grandparent.

In successfully caring for others, we must also be able to anticipate their needs, while permitting them to make choices that reflect their own needs, wishes, skills, and values, rather than those that we would choose for them. To accomplish this task, it is important that we accurately and honestly evaluate our own needs and motives for providing such care. For example, we might be consumed by our own unmet goals in influencing what our children choose to major in while at college, or in deciding

---

Box C

Volunteerism in Adulthood

Many middle-aged and older adults become involved in nonpaid volunteer work (e.g., **Retired Senior Volunteer Program, Meals on Wheels, Foster Grandparent Program, Peace Corps, Senior Companionship, Senior Corps of Retired Executives**). Doing so gives such persons a sense of purpose, helps them structure their day, serves as a hedge against the stress of work, and clearly gives them satisfaction in they are helping others. From an organizational point of view, volunteers are a source of experienced and reliable workers who cost the employer little and consequently, provide quality work at little financial risk to the organization. In a large study of volunteerism and aging, Morrow-Howell (2010) found that rates of volunteering do not decline until people are well into their 70s, with older persons committing more time to volunteer work than younger persons. However, the greatest rate of volunteer involve-

ment is found among persons who are middle-aged, where those whose work and family roles are more involved tend to engage in more volunteer work (Hooyman & Kiyak, 2011). Volunteering to help others contributes to self-esteem and is an expression of social support provided to others (Thomas, 2009). Encouraging and maintaining volunteerism among middle-aged and older persons, especially after a traumatic event such as the death of a spouse, is vitally important to older persons and those that they help through their volunteer activities (Butrica, Johnson, & Zedlewski, 2009; Donnelly & Hinterlong, 2009). Whether volunteerism is a valued attribute by society contributes to whether persons see such activity as desirable, admirable, or beneficial to themselves and to others (Hank & Erlinghagen, 2009; Hooyman & Kiyak, 2011; Rozario, 2006-2007).

---

whether to attend college at all. Likewise, we might care for a parent because it enables us to retain a sense of power over them, borne of resentment over their treatment of us when we were children. This is termed **role reversal**. Alternatively, we might care for them out of love and a genuine concern for their well-being. This is termed **filial maturity** (Blenkner, 1965).

Other Interactions with the Social Environment in Adulthood

Other activities which reflect middle-aged (and younger) adults' involvement in the social environment are **volunteer activities** to help disabled, poor, or elderly persons (see Box C), including involvement in self-help groups that deal with parenting, grief and bereavement, addictive/compulsive behaviors, family abuse, divorce or childbirth; lifelong

learning; and grandparenting (see Newman & Newman, 2009; Smith, 2003). Most are somewhat informal in nature, are self-led by peers, and for the most part, free to those who are interested in participating. Though their efficacy is often difficult to establish, they do meet the needs for support, help, and personal growth that many young and middle aged persons have.

While making choices regarding where to live are often imposed on older adults, for younger and middle-aged adults, choices regarding where to live are often tied to either leaving home for the first time to attend college or work, or to job changes, particularly so for those who are still establishing their careers, (see Chapter 7). Moreover, while most persons purchase their first home in their late 20s or early 30s, increasing numbers of younger adults, some of whom are married and/or have their own children, return home to live close to or with their parents (Connidis, 2010). While job changes are responsible for such relocation for some individuals (see Chapter 7), the loss of a job, divorce, or widowhood is responsible for the return of adults to their parents' homes for others.

Changing One's Environment in Adulthood

The concepts of person-environment fit and developmental niche also suggest that we, as young, middle-aged, and older adults, are able to change our environments when necessary. For example, this might occur at work (one changes jobs when work becomes unsatisfying or too stressful), in retiring or taking on a bridging job to ease the transition from full-time employment to retirement (see Chapters 7 and 8), in deciding to buy a new car or a new house, in seeking professional help to relieve marital conflict or personal distress, in deciding to sell one's home and move into an assisted living facility, or perhaps in deciding that divorce is preferable to an unhappy marriage. Being able to successfully make these decisions requires an accurate assessment of our own and others' needs, as well as that of the work environment, the neighborhood, and the larger community in which we carry out our roles. Our environments therefore both limit and are changed by the many decisions we make in adulthood.

The decision to change one's environment is also reflected in the many ways in which adults are involved in the community. This might be expressed in many ways: becoming involved in a crime-watch program to make the neighborhood safe, doing volunteer work at a local hospital or church, coaching Little League baseball, becoming a youth leader at church or Boy Scouts/Girl Scouts, joining a service organization such as Kiwanis Club, doing volunteer work at a school, or becoming politically active, e.g., running for city council or a seat on the local school board.

We can also change our everyday environment by becoming involved in a support group to help others who are facing a divorce, having a child, or grieving the loss of a parent. Each of these activities and roles acknowledges that **our social world**

is important enough to us to become actively involved in and to influence. It consequently enables us to create an environment in which our own needs and goals are met, as well as fostering positive relationships with family members, friends, neighbors, coworkers, and fellow citizens.

Check Your Learning 9-3

Define the following terms and concepts:

> Lifestyle
> Intimacy
> Social clock
> Generativity
> Self-efficacy
> Role reversal
> Filial maturity
> Generative caregiving

- What are some examples of both poor and good "matches" between the person and the environment in adulthood?

- How do person-environment fit and developmental niche influence our development in young adulthood?

- How do person-environment fit and developmental niche influence our development in midlife?

- Why is it important that adults can change their environments when necessary?

Developmental Tasks in Adulthood: Late Adulthood

In later life, our lifestyle is often dictated by whether we are caring for a husband or wife, whether we are widowed or not, our health, whether we live on a fixed income that is adequate to meet our needs, and how we experience the role of retiree. For many older persons, a major disrupting influence on the lifestyle to which they have become accustomed is having to relocate to the home of a son or daughter, transitioning into an assisted living environment, or being admitted to a nursing home, each of which may be brought about by a serious illness or the death of a spouse, bringing up questions about whether one can continue to live independently or not. Indeed, interactions with the social-environmental context in adulthood are often brought into sharp focus for a son or daughter who is a caregiver, as well as for many older women who must care for an older, frail spouse. This underscores the importance of making decisions to change the older adults' lifestyle **collaboratively**. Both generations participate actively in making such decisions, based upon an accurate assessment of the older person's preferences, cognitive/decision-making abilities, and everyday living skills (see Chapter 10).

The Use of Medical and Social Services and Older Persons

For many older persons, except for close friends or family, regular contact with persons who provide a variety of social and medical services defines their interactions with the social environment. As more persons live into their 70s, 80s, and beyond, the demands for all types of social-medical services is expected to increase (Wacker & Roberto, 2008) a direct function of the aging of the Baby Boomer generation (see Chapter 1). Likewise, the relative percentage of black, American Indian, Asian American, and Hispanic elderly are expected to increase dramatically in the next several decades, as are the numbers of elderly persons who live alone (Wacker & Roberto, 2008). This presents challenges to those who develop social policy to design such services with the needs of ethnically diverse older persons in mind. This holds true for the design of mental health services (see Chapter 11) and an awareness of end-of-life decision making (see Chapter 12). Older persons who live alone will also likely require more supportive services designed to maintain them in the community. Both **activities of daily living** (ADLs, e.g., dressing, grooming, eating, bathing) and **instrumental activities of daily living** (e.g., IADLs, shopping, meal preparation,

money management, transportation use) are likely to be the focus of such services.

Housing in Later Life

For many older persons, deficits in ADLs and IADLs are caused by declines in functioning due to illness, isolation, widowhood, an inability to pay for services critical to independent living, or an inability to make needed repairs and upkeep on the home. These make necessary the relocation from home to some alternative housing arrangement. This may be either a **congregate housing facility**, where persons can live in an apartment and still have access to needed social or medical services, or an **assisted living facility**, where persons live as independently as possible, but have ongoing access to some personal care, health-related, or emergency assistance services. Here residents have the benefit of being supervised, should they need help, on a 24-hour basis. Another option is to live in a **continuing life care community**, where for a fee, persons are guaranteed continuing care as their health demands escalate, permitting them to live out the remainder of their lives in an environment that is designed to meet their needs. A **residential care home** offers assistance to those elderly persons who need it so that they might continue to live independently (Wacker & Roberto, 2008). Still other older persons, particularly if they are living on extremely limited incomes, end up living in **single room occupancy (SRO) hotels**, which are often located in inner cities, with barely adequate facilities. Still others who are not well off financially choose to share a house with someone younger, or they may live in federally mandated public housing, wherein older renters pay no more than 30% of their adjusted monthly income (Wacker & Roberto, 2008). Some older adults who are homeless may frequent meal programs or community shelters, and drift in and out of hospitals as their health improves or worsens. Some suffer from chronic physical or mental disabilities (see Table 9-2).

On either end of the housing continuum is **planned independent housing**, which meets the housing needs of independent living older adults

Table 9-2

Housing Choices in Later Life

Facility	Degree of Independence
Public Housing/Retirement Communities	Much
Continuing Life Care Community	Much, but varies as the individual's needs vary
Congregate Housing	Much, but varies as the individual's needs vary
Residential Care Homes, Assisted Living	Moderate
Home-Based with ADL/IADL assistance	Moderate
Single Room Occupancy Hotels (SROs)	Moderate
Planned Independent Housing	Moderate
Nursing Homes (Skilled/Intermediate Levels of Care)	Least

Source: Wacker and Roberto (2008).

but provides no supportive services. In some cases, older adults can continue to live semi-independently, with periodic assistance from persons who provide home health care and can assist the elder with both ADLs and IADLs (see above).

What many families fall back on to enable a family member to live as independently as possible is **home health care**, which varies in terms of the degree to which such services promote independence. Skilled nursing care, nonmedical home care, and hospice care are the main types of home health care (Wacker & Roberto, 2008). Such care may or may not primarily focus on ADLs or IADLs. Complementing home health care are **respite services**, designed to alleviate the stress and burden to family members who are caregivers, especially those who are 24-hour/day care providers. Respite services may be provided in the home or may take the form of adult day care, especially for persons suffering from dementia (Wacker & Roberto, 2008). **Tranportation services** may also aid in helping older adults maintain their independence, so they

do not become homebound or have to move in with a son or daughter. For example, public transit or specialized transportation can serve adults and older persons who are visually impaired, have difficulty in walking or ascending/descending stairs, are dependent upon a walker, cane, or wheelchair to get around, or are low income (Wacker & Roberto, 2008).

Nursing homes also help to define the housing continuum in later life. Nursing homes vary in terms of the **level of care** that is provided: There are those which deliver **skilled** nursing care to persons who are the most impaired, those whose level of care is **intermediate**, and those termed **residential care facilities** (Haber, 1987), where the level of nursing care provided is minimal. As might be expected, skilled care is the most expensive, and residents often reside in the nursing home for 6-10 years or longer until their death. In all cases, social support services are also provided, such as activity programs, mental health care, rehabilitation care, or units designed to care for persons with

Alzheimer's disease (see Chapter 10). For some persons whose health difficulties are less severe, a stay in a nursing home may be limited. After they have been rehabilitated they can return to the community.

In some cases, nursing homes provide respite care for stressed caregivers, post-operative acute care for those recently hospitalized, specialized care for those suffering from Alzheimer's disease (see Chapter 10), or end-of-life care to dying persons (see Chapter 12). Key to matching the level of care to the older person's needs as well as obtaining timely and accurate information about care options are **information and referral services**, often coordinated by a case manager or a geriatric care manager. Such persons get needed information for families, provide timely referrals to providers of quality services, advocate for the family, solve problems in either getting care or receiving quality care, aid in decision making, and follow up with families to ensure that things are going smoothly and as expected (see Paggi, 2010; Wacker & Roberto, 2008). Especially when family must make decisions about a parent's care long distance, information and referral services are critical in identifying a local resource person who can explore care options and coordinate care.

The costs of nursing home care, which can easily exceed $50,000 annually, are principally paid by **Medicaid**, a federal insurance program that provides matching funds to the states to pay for the medical care of low-income elderly persons. The costs of nursing home care are also paid by **Medicare**, which is part of the Social Security system. Medicare provides some support, but not total coverage to pay for the medical costs of any individual over the age of 65. Such persons pay a monthly premium. Medicare coverage is also restricted in the terms of the length of medical care provided in a hospital or nursing home. Those with such coverage can extend their benefits by paying a supplemental monthly premium (Gottlieb, 1992).

Persons can also defray the cost of nursing home care ahead of time by purchasing **long-term care insurance**, which typically pays a fixed amount for long-term care on a daily basis, and whose premiums vary with the age at which one purchases such insurance. Monthly premiums are lower the younger one is when purchasing long-term care insurance. Long-term care insurance becomes increasingly difficult to get as one's health declines and can be quite expensive in some cases.

Residing in a nursing home can be quite debilitating for some older persons, especially if they are depressed (Rubinstein & Lawton, 1997), alone, and **lack control** over the everyday aspects of their existence (Rodin, 1986). Issues of wandering and pacing among cognitively impaired nursing home residents have led to modifications in the environment, creating highly structured or protected walking areas. These limit aimless wandering, yet permit persons who are restless to walk safely, contributing to peace of mind that a parent or grandparent is safe (Day, Carrepon, & Stump, 2001). Thus, the match between persons' needs and desire for control, the extent to which they are cognitively impaired, their ability to assume greater degrees over control and decision making in everyday life, and the physical, interpersonal, and service-oriented aspects of the nursing home are important to older persons and their families (Curtiss, Hayslip, & Dolan, 2007).

Key to providing quality long-term (nursing home) care are: ensuring adequate levels of trained nursing staff, providing opportunities for continued staff training and advancement, maximizing staff retention over time, monitoring the stress levels of staff, protecting residents from abuse and ensuring their right to quality and humane care, and having a defined program that involves family in care decisions (Wacker & Roberto, 2008).

Community Support Systems in Later Life

Transactions between the older persons and the social environment can take place in the context of other **community-based long-term care services**. These services are quite varied, such as visiting nurses programs, home health aid services, programs in which prepared meals are delivered to elderly persons in their homes on a daily basis, and transportation services (see above). With such support, older persons can **age in place,** and therefore remain independent for as long as possible. For some families, respite programs for caregivers of persons with Alzheimer's disease may either substitute for or supplement help which the older person's convoy of support, i.e., family, friends, is unable or unwilling to provide (see Chapters 4 and 5) .

Older Adults' Involvement in the Community

Other more varied services and opportunities for older persons which require that they interact in the social environment involve attendance and involvement in **senior center** activities such as dancing, reading, consumer awareness, caring for one's own health, filing one's taxes, maintaining good nutrition, accessing local transportation, or legal aid (Krout et al, 1990). Many persons see senior centers in a negative light, thinking they are just for "old people," while others are attracted to them because of a desire to remain active and engaged, or because of the programs that are offered (see Box D).

Other programs focus on building **intergenerational relationships**, wherein grandparents are matched with adolescents so that the latter can profit from the advice and love of persons who have already raised children of their own. Many older persons derive a great deal of satisfaction from doing **volunteer work** (see Box C). The Retired Senior Volunteer Program (RSVP) is the largest federally funded program of its kind in the nation (Kelly, 1991), where older persons with specific skills and interests are matched with existing community needs in such arenas as providing tax assistance, home care, Medicare counseling, home repair assistance, telephone reassurance, being a foster grandparent, or being a senior companion to someone who is frail or homebound and living alone. Volunteerism among older persons therefore represents a good example of the application of the concepts of person-environment fit and developmental niche to enhance well-being in later life.

Other means by which older persons interact with the social environment are through becoming involved in post-retirement work or leisure opportunities (see Chapter 8), and by enrolling in formal or informal educational programs and courses (see Chapter 3), such as a local lifelong learning program, Elderhostel, or returning to school to acquire new knowledge or earn a college degree. Older persons can, via their interactions with mental health professionals (see Chapters 10 and 11), in light of the congruence of the older person's capabilities, self-assessments, and the expectations of others, be influential in deciding on a given therapeutic approach and whether such an approach might be effective or not (see Chapter 11).

Enhancing Older Persons' Use of Services and Programs

Of course, the challenge for many physicians, psychologists, program directors, nurses, and social workers is to make older persons aware of their services so that they might be used. Moreover, involving older persons in the variety of community-based roles and activities requires that their motivations for doing so be understood. How can this be accomplished? One approach that has proven helpful is the **Health Belief Model** , which stresses that persons must first **perceive themselves to be vulnerable** to a problem for which the program or service can address, and therefore exert personal control over the problem by accessing services. Using such services protects persons from the negative consequences of, for example, a decline in one's health or isolation from others (Rosenstock et al., 1988). The use of services or programs is enhanced by **cues to action**, which are external stimuli that make the person aware of the need to deal with the problem.

Additional approaches (see Wacker & Roberto, 2008) that might help to explain the use of programs and services by older persons include **reactance theory** (Brehm, 1966). Reactance theory predicts that programs which are perceived as enhancing freedom and autonomy are more likely to be utilized. **Attribution theory** (Fisher et al.,

Box D

Senior Centers

It took over 65 years for senior centers to evolve so that they could offer multiple services geared towards older adults. The first senior center was constructed in New York City in 1943 to help alleviate loneliness among older adults (Leanse, Tiven, & Robb, 1977). In 1965 the Older Americans Act (OAA) helped create and support senior centers as a main resource for older adults in the community (Wacker & Roberto, 2008). The 1973 amendment to the OAA made services for older adults a focal point and allowed for a range of delivery of services. The amendment also introduced the term **multipurpose senior centers** (Wacker & Roberto, 2008), which offer health-related (including mental health), social, nutritional, and educational services, in addition to recreational activities for older adults.

Senior centers have become a major community institution that are geared toward maintaining good mental health and preventing the deterioration of mental, social, and emotional functioning of older adults (NISC, 1978). They can offer social support, reduce loneliness and depression, and enhance life satisfaction. Available literature suggests that senior centers have complied with the terms of the AAA mandates on senior centers. A study conducted by Aday (2003) surveyed 734 senior centers attendees in Florida, Maine, Iowa, New Hampshire, Texas, and Tennessee; of those surveyed, over 75% reported that the senior center helped them to remain independent.

The Older Americans Act has defined certain criteria to enable one to attend a multipurpose senior center. One of those criteria is that the individual be 60 years old or older (some cities have lowered this to age 50) to be a participant. Recent research has found that senior center use increases with age, up to 85, which suggests that the younger older adults that attend senior centers are "aging in place" (Wacker & Roberto, 2008). **Do you agree with age as a criterion for being able to utilize senior center services?** Calsyn and Winter (1999) found that race was not a predictor of senior center participation but reported that overall, 8% of participants were black, 5% were Hispanic, and 2% were Asian and Native American. Older minority adults are underrepresented at most senior centers with the exception of those centers that primarily serve them within the community, which are more often than not located in minority neighborhoods.

Senior centers have traditionally offered recreational and leisure activities such as bingo, dominoes, card games, board games, a nutritional lunch, and arts/crafts. Due to the demand in services from more active older adults, senior centers have begun to offer exercise classes (e.g., T'ai Chi, yoga), trips to outside venues (e.g., festivals, ballgames), oil painting classes, cookoffs, line dancing, foreign language classes, computer classes, senior dances, balloon volleyball, and musical entertainment. Other services include information and referral, outreach, transportation services, health education, health screenings (City of Dallas: Senior Services, 2009), home delivered meals, friendly visits, telephone buddies, consumer information, crime prevention, financial/ tax assistance, housing information, legal assistance, assistance with Social Security and Medicare, adult day care services, job training and placement, protective services, and peer counseling (City of Culver, 2009).

Though there are senior centers available to older adults, there are nevertheless barriers that prevent the older adult from using them, including the lack of bilingual staff, the lack of other persons from the participant's culture attending a program, a lack of awareness of available senior center programs, a lack of understanding regarding what available senior center programs offer, a lack of experience in using public transportation and taxi service, and a lack of intergenerational activities (Fairfax County, 2006). A significant and particularly troublesome barrier to the use of senior centers is one's attitude toward aging—feeling "too young" to be attending a senior center (Di & Berman, 2000). A lack of childcare assistance may also discourage older adult caregivers raising grandchildren (see Chapter 5). According to Wacker and Roberto (2008), senior centers will be challenged to respond to the needs and demands of a new generation of older adults. Senior centers of the future must reflect the diversity of potential attendees and the diversity of other social services that are available.

Source: Rhynes (2009). *The use of senior centers by grandparents raising grandchildren.* Dissertation, University of North Texas

---

1983) suggests that persons attempt to interpret both their own and others' behavior so they can make sense of what happens to them. For example, if the desire to help is seen as genuine, and the problem is one that most persons experience, then help is likely to be requested. **Equity or social exchange theory** (Walster et al., 1973) predicts that when persons feel that they cannot reciprocate (a condition of inequity), they are less likely to ask for assistance. Thus persons will use services to a greater extent when they feel they are also giving back to an equal degree. They do not feel indebted, and can reciprocate the help that they are receiving. The **social behavior model** (Anderson, 1995) suggests that some persons are more predisposed toward using services than others, that they must have the family, personal, and community resources to enable them to access services, and that they must need such services. Last, the **threats to self-esteem model** (Fisher et al., 1983) predicts that when receiving help as personally threatening (e.g., making them feel inferior or inadequate), persons will be less likely to seek assistance.

Thinking about these different approaches to enhancing older persons' use of services and programs should make us aware that programs and services to older persons must be designed with the older persons' needs and values in mind. Services which make people feel dependent, guilty, indebted, or inferior are less likely to be used at all, or at least not used in a timely manner.

Person-Environment Fit and Quality of Life in Late Adulthood

The match between the needs of the older person and the ability of the environment (programs and services that are both available and perceived as both helpful and valuable) will determine the quality and quantity of life for the older adult. For example, perceiving where one lives as "home" suggests that one can remain autonomous, that one's identity as an individual is preserved, and that one can make preparations for death.

In terms of the variety of community-based services and programs for older adults discussed above, such activities must not only meet the older adults' objective needs for service, but they must also be perceived as both helpful and valuable to one's health and well being. When the fit between the older adult and the environment is a good one, the developmental task of promoting intellectual vigor, which makes possible the processes of **life review** and **introspection**, leading to a sense of **integrity** - - a feeling of completeness about one's life, can be achieved (Newman & Newman, 2009). A good match between the older person's needs and the environment also permits the redirection of one's energy into new roles and life tasks which may be brought about by declines in one's health, grandparenthood, retirement, or widowhood. Thus, later life, as might *also* be characteristic of young and middle adulthood, can be full of choices and opportunities for personal growth that respect the individuality of the process of development in adulthood. Such choices enhance rather than inhibit creativity, satisfying personal relationships, happiness and life satisfaction.

Check Your Learning 9-4

Define the following terms and concepts:

Baby Boomers
Activities of daily living
Instrumental activities of daily living
Life care community
Residential care home
SRO
Health Belief Model
Attribution
Social exchange
Assisted living
Long-term care insurance
Information and referral services
Adult day care
Planned independent housing
Nursing homes/long-term care
Level of care
Home health care
Medicare/Medicaid
Personal control
Reactance
Integrity
Congregate housing
Collaborative decision making
Respite care
Social behavior model

• What demographic changes are likely to affect the demand for medical and social services of future cohorts of elderly persons?

• What demographic changes are likely to affect caregiving for frail or impaired elderly?

• Why is the older person's choice of housing important to person-environment fit?

• What are information and referral services and why are they important?

• How does being involved in the community affect person-environment fit in later life?

• How might older persons' use of social services be enhanced?

• How can person-environment fit affect the quality of life?

Summary

This chapter discussed the social-environmental context of adult development and aging. Interacting with others in the environment is often done in the context of roles that both we and others must play. The complexity of our lives can in part be understood in light of the demands that such roles make on us, changes and conflict between such roles, and our interactions with other persons as well as the institutions which define their roles as well.

Several approaches to understanding the environment in adulthood were discussed, all of which help to define the relationship of the adult to the larger context in which development in adulthood can be understood. The **adult-in-context** model discusses several sectors or dimensions of adult development which interact with one another, and whose interactions changes over both the lifetime of the individual and historical time, which marks changes in the culture. Other approaches to understanding the environment in adulthood that are valuable are Bronfenbrenner's **ecological model**, as well as the concepts of **person-environment fit** and **developmental niche**. In each case, adults are constantly in the process of appraising the environment, making decisions that translate into behavioral, interpersonal, and emotional outcomes, and reappraising the consequences of these decisions into order to arrive at their respect adaptation level or positive developmental niche. The concepts of person-environment fit and developmental niche are important to understanding how young adults and middle-aged persons deal with a variety of developmental tasks, such as seeking intimacy, establishing a career, establishing a lifestyle, raising a family, caring for older parents, or gaining a sense of **generativity.**

In later life, person-environment fit and developmental niche are relevant to understanding the use of social and medical services, the choice of housing, and the involvement in the community so that one can redirect one's energy into new roles. Ultimately, the fit between the adult and the environment is crucial in determining the quality of life for adults of all ages.

Chapter 10
Mental Health and Psychopathology

Mental Health in Adulthood

One in four adults (26.2%) suffers from some form of diagnosable mental illness in any one year, and these estimates do not vary appreciably by age in adulthood (National Institute of Mental Health, 2010). Moreover, these figures have not changed a great deal in the last decade; 2003 estimates suggested that between 14 and 25% of older persons suffered from mental illness (NIMH National Advisory Mental Health Council Workgroup on Aging Research, 2003), with similar rates of mental illness for children and older adults.

As the proportion of middle-aged and older persons increases (see Chapter 1), the likelihood of these persons experiencing some form of mental illness also increases. Mental illness is expensive. The costs of treating mental illness comprise 7% of all health care costs, and if Alzheimer's disease and substance abuse are included, this figure rises to 10% (National Institute of Mental Health, 2010). Consequently, as the incidence (new cases) and prevalence (overall cases, new and old) of mental illness increase, a greater proportion of health care dollars will be used to treat the emotional problems that many persons experience from time to time.

As with health care, there is evidence of mental health disparities in later life across gender and socioeconomic status (Miech, Eaton, & Brennan, 2005). Thus, among all adults, and perhaps among specific subgroups of older adults, emotional difficulties will likely continue to be a serious concern that may require the help, especially given the aging of Baby Boomers. This trend was recognized at the 2005 White House Conference on Aging, which voted to make the diagnosis, assessment, and treatment of mental illness and depression among older persons a priority, as was the strengthening of the Medicare program for senior adults, and greater attention to the geriatric education and training of health care professionals and paraprofessionals (Stambor, 2006). Indeed, recently (August, 2010), geropsychology was officially recognized as a clinical subspecialty by the American Psychological Association.

This chapter focuses upon the **continuum** of **mental health—mental illness**, with a particular emphasis upon late adulthood. Information about mental health in adulthood can be valuable in alerting mental health personnel to the disorders older or younger persons are especially prone to experience. It can also be helpful in affecting the design and implementation of mental health services, especially for persons who are physically ill or isolated from others.

What Is Abnormal? What Is Healthy?

We probably know more about what mental health is **not** than about those qualities **positively** defining mental health in adulthood. The terms **normal** and **abnormal** are difficult to define precisely, in that the criteria for each change with time and with society's expectations (Nevid, Rathus, & Green, 2008). Once a behavior is **labeled** abnormal or deviant, it immediately becomes the concern of a qualified professional (i.e., a psychologist, psychotherapist, or a psychiatrist), and implies that the behavior is disruptive, unlawful, or harmful to oneself or others. Yet, it is clear that we should put as much emphasis on strengths (health, vitality, positive adjustment) as we do on mental illness (deficits, problems and difficulties) (see Box A).

What then is abnormal? Many instances of abnormal behavior in later life are **co-morbid** (co-exist) with physical disorders (see Box B), as well as with other psychological difficulties. For example, anxiety and depression frequently occur together. To complicate matters, it is important to realize that while behaviors that are harmful to individuals are often considered abnormal, such behaviors are often quite adaptive for many aged persons. For example, feeling depressed at the death of one's spouse, being frightened because of a serious illness, feeling anxious about being relocated to a nursing home, or being resistant to expectations by nursing home staff to behave "appropriately" (e.g., by taking your medicine, or generally being a good "patient") may be quite natural given the circumstances. On the other hand, if our behaviors interfere with our relationships with others or our work and *cause* our health to deteriorate, one would likely suspect a problem. For example, not eating or sleeping, not taking or abusing medications, hitting someone else for no reason, or secluding oneself, might all be reasons for concern. We might be especially worried if these behaviors occurred together, rather than in isolation, or if they persisted over time.

Most of us experience stressful experiences in adulthood (*USA Today,* May 18, 2010), and often report feeling "stressed-out" regarding difficulties in dealing with our job situations, the economy in general, work, or health (*Stress in America,* 2008 as cited in the *American Psychologist*, December, 2008, p. 29). However, it is only when one experiences marked intellectual or memory declines, changes in sleeping patterns, sexual disinterest, or a preoccupation with death should a mental health problem be suspected (see Chapter 12).

Careful attention to each individual's current life circumstances, family support system, and life history can help identify behaviors that may signal emotional distress and enable one to decide whether a given person's behaviors or feelings are a legiti-

mate response to stress, loss, or change. Indeed, adults of all ages also vary in their response to life changes. For example, two persons who each experience the same life event (e.g., divorce) will vary in their response to it; some persons will respond by becoming depressed or by being preoccupied with the event, while others will not. Such events also **transform** persons' self-images, create **life changes**, or cause persons to be **preoccupied** with the event long after it has occurred (Lieberman & Peskin, 1992). Thus, the impact of events such as a job change or a divorce can be either positive or negative.

Our ideas about what is abnormal in adulthood will likely change as (1) future cohorts of elderly persons become more highly educated and thus more psychologically sophisticated (see Chapter 11), (2) mental health services occur in the natural helping network of the aged persons (druggists, beauticians, mailmen, custodians, or peers), (3) mental health-oriented programs emphasize wellness, life review, bereavement, caregiver support, or even self-help, and (4) the public is educated about adult development and aging. This is important because our ideas about (a) whether we have a problem and (b) the nature and severity of that problem are each key to our seeking help and assistance in a timely way from a qualified mental health professional (Knight, 2004).

DSM-IV

At the present, the diagnosis of mental illness in adulthood is made using the **Diagnostic and Statistical Manual of Mental Disorders** (1994, 5th ed.) **(DSM-IV)** of the American Psychiatric Association. It helps to define mental disorders and enables clinicians, researchers, and practitioners to communicate about abnormality using the same language. DSM-IV not only provides professionals with a working set of definitions that aid diagnosis and treatment, but it also, in some cases, provides information about etiology and specifies the criteria for making a diagnosis.

DSM-IV uses a multi-axial (multidimensional) system so that each individual can be comprehen-

Box A

Successful Aging

Successful aging is perhaps the goals for most persons, young and old. Do you have a plan to age successfully? To **age well**? In a series of landmark writings, Rowe and Kahn (1997, 1998) define successful aging in terms of three key components: (1) having a **low probability of disease and disease-related disability**, (2) having **high cognitive and physical functional skills**, and (3) **being actively engaged with life.** To reflect the emphasis on the positive aspects of growing older, publications entitled *Aging Well* (www.agingwell mag.com) as well as a related e-newsletter (AW_Newsletter@gvpub.com) are available to both professionals and laypersons of all ages. A *Positive Aging Newsletter* (Kenneth and Mary Gergen, info@healthandage.com) also exists for those who want to learn more about successful aging.

While these domains of successful aging overlap and collectively define aging well for many persons, having a set of meaningful **spiritual beliefs** (Atchley, 2009) or **religious involvement** is also important to many older adults and enables them to persist through hard times. Other key attributes that might define successful aging are **personal resilience** or **hardiness** (Crowley et al., 2003) and **motivational reserve** (having a sense of purpose, not allowing oneself to be defined by others, being proactive).

Among successful agers, we see a spirit of **optimism and adventure about life** and a **propensity to take risks and set out on a new course in life**, despite formidable odds and adverse experiences such as poor health, loneliness, or forced retirement. Lawrence-Lightfoot (2009, p. x) gives us several examples of people who despite their age have set a new course for themselves in later life: "In Vermont, a 72-year-old realtor whose business had 'shrunk to nothing' said she'd signed up for a stint in the Peace Corps in Senegal; she feels that for the first time that 'she is making a difference on our planet.' A 72-year-old obstetrician in Texas felt "burnt out" from the tedium of his practice . . . so he returned to his childhood love of Broadway theatre, plunged back into training, and is now performing the classic songs on cruise liners."

Yet, people can age successfully even if they must live with illness, loss, or isolation from others. They seem to have found a way to deal with life's surprises, joys, and disappointments. They derive happiness and satisfaction from everyday pursuits, be they tending to their plants, reading, caring for a loved pet, crocheting, cooking, being with children and grandchildren, traveling, or doing volunteer work. Perhaps they spend time simply sitting in the park, enjoying the birds and the squirrels, or walking in the morning or in the evening. They have much peace and are quite happy. They most likely have raised families, been happily married, and have accepted the ups and downs of work and retirement. They are content to accept what life offers them, and control that which they can control, and not worry about the rest.

Using Rowe and Kahn's (1997, 1998) criteria, a national study by McLaughlin et al. (2009) estimated that approximately 12% of older adults were aging successfully in any one year.

Do you think this estimate is accurate? Why or why not?

How do you define successful aging?

Box B

Examples of Relationships between Mental and Physical Health in Older Adults

The Impact of Psychogenic Stress that Leads to Physical Health Consequences

Example: Anxiety—gastrointestinal symptoms
    The accurate diagnosis of gastrointestinal (GI) symptoms can be very difficult in the elderly, with research showing that as many as 5 of 9 older persons with GI trouble may experience psychogenic problems that lead to their physical discomfort.

The Effect of Physical Disorder that Leads to Psychiatric Disturbance

Example: Hearing loss—onset of delusions
    More than 25% of the elderly have a hearing impairment; a sensory-deprivation phenomenon may lead to psychotic symptoms in certain vulnerable individuals; an increased frequency of hearing loss has also been identified in older adults with late-onset schizophrenia.

The Interplay of Coexisting Physical and Mental Disorders

Example: Congestive heart failure + depression—further cardiac decline
    Cardiac disorder and depression are two of the most common health problems of the elderly. A covert depression could bring about indirect suicidal behavior acted out by failure on the part of the patient to follow a proper schedule of medication; the resulting clinical picture could then be one of further deterioration in overall cardiac capacity.

The Impact of Psychosocial Factors on the Clinical Course of Physical Health Problems

Example: Diabetic with infected foot, living in isolation—increased risk of losing foot
    Isolation can mean an absence of adequate social supports to help with proper medical management and follow-up. More than two in five older women and nearly one in six older men live alone.

Source: Cohen (1992).

---

sively evaluated for purposes of either planning a treatment program or predicting therapeutic outcome. Axes I and II encompass all of the mental disorders. Axis II deals with personality disorders and mental retardation, and Axis I includes all other mental disorders. Axis III includes physical disorders and conditions. Each axis forms a dimension that refers to a unique bit of information about the individual. Each individual is assessed along each axis, and the first three axes represent the official diagnostic assessment. Axes IV and V supplement the first three and are useful in arriving at a more complete understanding of the individual for treatment purposes. Axis IV deals with psychosocial and environmental problems and Axis V focuses upon a global assessment of the individual's functioning. Multiple diagnoses within axes are possible. Usually, the clinician can reach a *principal* diagnosis (usually on Axis I), referring to the condition for which the individual was recommended to be assessed or admitted to care, and specific diagnostic criteria are available for each disorder.

We recommend the use of DSM-IV with **caution**. While practitioners need to refer to DSM for hospital diagnoses or insurance forms, they should evaluate the definitions and classifications carefully since these may not always clearly reflect reality; older persons are no exception in this respect. DSM-IV's developers stress the fact that errors are possible with any categorical system, and the use of DSM-IV requires extensive training. Of course, clinical experience, psychological tests, and interviews with family can also tell us about the older person we are treating. DSM-5 is currently under development, and is purported to be more research-based and more patient-friendly; it is projected to be released in 2013 (American Psychiatric Association, 2010).

In this chapter, we concentrate on those aspects of abnormal behavior unique to older persons. We must not forget, however, that many of the factors contributing to these problems are *not* age related. This sensitivity is perhaps the most important issue in best deciding how to treat the older person experiencing emotional problems (Knight, 2004).

Check Your Learning 10-1

Define the following terms and concepts:

> Abnormal vs. normal
> DSM-IV
> Co-morbidity
> Successful aging

- Why should mental health and mental illness be viewed along a continuum?

- What characteristics define a behavior as abnormal?

- What is DSM-IV? How is it used in diagnosis?

- Why are ideas about normal and abnormal behavior in adulthood and later life important?

Alzheimer's Disease

Alzheimer's disease (AD) has become a major public health problem, with nearly 5 million persons being diagnosed with this very debilitating disorder; by 2050, 11 to 16 million persons are predicted to have AD (Alzheimer's Association, 2010). Worldwide, 26.6 million people are estimated to have Alzheimer's dementia, with 460,000 new cases occurring every year (one new case every 70 seconds in the United States) (Alzheimer's Association, 2010; Ferri et al., 2005). By 2050, 100 million people worldwide are predicted to have AD (Hareyan, 2007), and one new case every 33 seconds is predicted by 2050 (Alzheimer's Association, 2010). By 2010, Medicare costs for the care of Alzheimer's patients were predicted to reach nearly $50 billion, an increase of over 50% relative to 2000, and the average lifetime cost for someone with Alzheimer's disease is nearly $175,000 (Alzheimer's Association, 2005). The cost of health care triples for persons with Alzheimer's disease (Alzheimer's Association, 2010).

The diagnosis of Alzheimer's disease, a form of **dementia,** can be very disruptive and indeed devastating for older persons and their families, who often suffer from feelings of anger, frustration, hopelessness, and burden. For example, they struggle with the decision that the older person can no longer drive (Carr, Shead, & Storandt, 2005). This is especially so in cases of early-onset dementia, where families and especially children fear that they too will soon develop the disease at an early age, i.e., one's 40s and 50s (Reiswig, 2010). Indeed, many families struggle with the decision to inform the patient that he or she has AD, thinking that it best that persons not know or that should they know, they would become depressed, or even worse, attempt suicide. In this context, Dr. Jack Kevorkian's first patient, whose life he helped end via assisted suicide (see Chapter 12) was a 43-year old woman who learned that she had been diagnosed with Alzheimer's dementia.

For many Alzheimer's patients and their families, support groups (often sponsored by the

---

Box C

Can a Person with Alzheimer's Disease Still Learn?

Cameron Camp and his colleagues have demonstrated that after as many as two brief training sessions, memory-impaired elderly persons could remember the name of a staff person using the **spaced retrieval technique** (Camp, 2006; Camp & Foss, 1997; Camp, Foss, Stevens & O'Hanlon, 1996). This technique initially involves presenting the client with the name to be learned and the client's repeating the name. Sixty seconds later, the client's inability to remember the name was verified. Subsequently, this process was repeated with the staff member seated across from the older client. A correct answer caused the interval to the next test trial to increase; an incorrect answer caused it to decrease. Between trials, client and examinee engaged in social conversation as a distractor. Intervals between trials increased from 5 seconds to 120 seconds. One week later, the process was repeated, with trial intervals increasing from 120 seconds to 240 seconds. Between trials, music notes prompted the client's recall. One week later, the client was able to spontaneously recall the name of the staff member; this was maintained 6 months later. The advantages of this technique are that clients can experience immediate success at remembering and that it is less cognitively demanding than other more elaborate memory enhancement techniques such as the method of loci (see Chapter 3). The entire technique is social. Talking and playing music or games occur between trials. Thus, it is less threatening and more enjoyable to the memory-impaired elder, who may already be sensitized to memory deficits and failures.

Camp (2006) argues that spaced retrieval has many advantages that make it a viable therapeutic option for persons with mild to moderate dementia: it is (1) it is beneficial and of low risk to the client, (2) it is compatible with the goals and values of many institutions caring for older persons, (3) it is simplistic and therefore easily and rapidly disseminated, (4) it has trialability because it can be tested on a small scale before widespread adoption, and (5) it has observability. Others can observe its effects and how it should be conducted before attempting to use spaced retrieval themselves.

Alzheimer's Association), education about the disease—its symptoms and course—and respite care for family caregivers are all very important (see Chapter 11). They help caregivers cope with the demands of caregiving, inform them of what is likely to occur in the future regarding the progression of the disease, relieve feelings of isolation and frustration in being able to get help and support from one another, and give people hope (see Box E).

The term **dementia** refers to a cluster of disorders which produce both cognitive and emotional changes in the older adult and, more often than not, lead to eventual mental deterioration over which the patient has little control. The causes of dementia receiving the most attention at present are **multi-infarct dementia** and **Alzheimer's disease**. The dominant feature of true, organically based dementia is **brain cell** (neuronal) **loss** or **impairment** (see Chapter 2). While these brain cell losses are *correlated* with a number of behavioral changes, definitive answers on *why* brain cells degenerate have yet to be discovered. Once the exact cause of dementia is identified, treatments, which may range from drug treatment, exercise, mental stimulation, or some form of counseling, can be developed (see Box D). At present, treatment focuses upon the reduction of symptoms (in the earliest stages of the disease) and more generally, improving the quality of life for the persons with AD.

Research has isolated a specific protein, labeled

Box D

Preventing Alzheimer's Disease and Cognitive Decline in Later Life

To many older persons and their adult children, preventing the loss of their skills as they age and, indeed, preventing Alzheimer's disease (AD) are among their greatest concerns. How can each be prevented or minimized? According to the *Agency for Healthcare Research and Quality* (2009), based upon a review of all of the available evidence (over 250 scientific studies), the following conclusions were reached:

1. Not smoking, engaging in cognitively stimulating and complex activities, engaging in non-physical/noncognitive leisure activities, and remaining physically active are all associated with higher levels of cognitive functioning in later life.

2. Remaining physically active, being cognitively engaged, and making efforts to enhance one's cognitive skills are each associated with a lowered risk for Alzheimer's disease.

3. Diabetes, genetic predisposition (APOE e4 gene), smoking, and depression are all associated with an increased risk of AD *and* cognitive decline.

4. A Mediterranean diet (one with limited meats and sweets; moderate amounts of poultry, eggs, and cheese; lots of fish, seafood, fruits, and vegetables), cognitive engagement, and remaining physically active are all associated with an decreased risk of AD *and* cognitive decline.

beta-amyloid, that kills brain cells, which is particular to Alzheimer's disease (Selkoe, 1991; Welsh-Bohmer & Warren, 2006). In such cases, these proteins are located in certain areas of the brain and not others. Recent research suggests that as *beta-amyloid* proteins break down with age, they form "clumps" which accumulate in the brain. In response to these clumps of protein, the brain forms senile plaques, which may actually therefore serve a protective function in absorbing the clumps of protein (Alzheimer's: A new theory. *AARP Bulletin*, September 2010, pp. 10-11). We have also learned that for the form of Alzheimer's disease which occurs early (before age 60), there is a genetic mutation which seems to run in families For some persons, Alzheimer's disease can occur as early as age 30 (Alzheimer's Association, 2005; Selkoe, 1991). This form of Alzheimer's disease is relatively infrequent (occurring in 2% of cases), however. In addition to age (greater increases after age 85), family history is the most important risk factor for Alzheimer's disease (Welsh-Bohmer & Warren, 2006). AD was

the sixth leading cause of death in the United States in 2006 (Alzheimer's Association, 2010).

Statistically speaking, gender (favoring women) and age predict the incidence of AD (Alzheimer's Association, 2010). On the other hand, being highly educated seems to lower one's risk of developing AD-related pathological changes in brain cells (Brayne & Keage, 2010), as does being cognitively engaged in everyday life (see Box D). Indeed, Boyle (2010) found that persons with a **sense of purpose in life** (being able to derive meaning from one's experiences, behaving in a goal-directed and purposeful manner) were less likely to develop AD.

Alzheimer's disease, named for its discoverer, Alois Alzheimer, in 1907, affects from between 4 and 6% of those of 65 and older (Welsh-Bohmer & Warren, 2006); 20% of those aged 85 or older exhibit signs of dementia, and persons age 85 and older comprise 50% of all cases of AD. AD accounts for nearly 50% of all cases of dementia in later life, followed by multi-infarct dementia (12-20%). It is not uncommon for persons, if they are diagnosed

Box E

Caregiving: A Thankless Job?

Caregiving costs U.S. businesses $13 billion a year in dealing with the effects of caregiving on their employees (MetLife, 2010). For many employees, their caregiving responsibilities per se or the impact of caregiving on their physical and mental health—termed **caregiver burden**—cause them to miss work, perform more poorly at work, or quit their jobs. Indeed, anyone who has cared for a loved one, especially on a 24-hour, 7 days-a-week basis will tell you that **caregiving** is at once exhausting, depressing, frustrating, and satisfying—whether it is caring for an ill or dying husband, wife, parent, or child, or in raising a grandchild in the event of an adult child's inability to parent, incarceration, divorce, or death (see Chapters 4, 5, and 12). In this respect, *The 36-Hour Day* accurately captures the positive and the negative sides of caregiving, especially for persons caring for a loved one with dementia (Mace & Rabins, 2006). It is fairly common to find caregivers to feel helpless, isolated, alone, angry, and resentful, and to experience not only psychological stress, but also impaired physical health. In one study (Monin et al., 2010), spouses' blood pressure actually increased in merely witnessing the suffering of a partner carrying a heavy log for several minutes and displaying in a facial expression the stress of doing so.

Many caregivers express concerns about the changing nature of their relationship with the person they are caring for. They lack accurate information about the illness from which a loved one is suffering, lack support from friends and family in carrying out their caregiving responsibilities, lack respite care in helping them deal with the demands and stress of caregiving, and express concerns about their own financial futures and physical/mental health. In advance of active caregiving, persons would do well to anticipate its demands and establish a network of support (Hayslip, Han, & Anderson,

2008). **Caregiving tasks** can include shopping, household cleaning and maintenance, helping an ill relative take medications, managing the care recipient's legal and financial affairs, keeping the person safe, getting needed medical care, dealing with the emotional, cognitive, or behavioral difficulties of the person being cared for, and managing ADLs and IADLs.

Reflecting the emotional toll that caregiving takes, a 60 year-old woman wrote to her sister:

> "I'm sitting here in the living room, and mom is talking in her sleep. I hate this. I feel at times it's like a death watch. She's just so worn out and her heart is tired. . . . I was thinking today what I would say to you if she dies. I can't stand the thought of it. How do you want me to tell you?"

What is key to the survival of the caregiver is **self-care**:

1. Accurately assessing the impact of caregiving on yourself.
2. Asking for help when needed and getting needed emotional and instrumental support from others.
3. Taking purposeful and proactive steps toward caring for your physical and mental health.
4. Developing coping skills to deal with stress.
5. Avoiding isolation from friends and family.
6. Getting respite care.
7. Being willing to realistically assess whether the task of caregiving is beyond your personal and financial resources.
8. Being aware of the need to change your approach to coping with the stresses of caregiving.
9. Being willing to decide whether the many adjustments to your identity as well as

your personal life, lifestyle, work and career aspirations, or even your marriage are necessary, and worth all that you are sacrificing.

10. Looking as caregiving as an act of love.
11. Emphasizing your strengths as a caregiver.

later in life, to live 10 or more years with the disease, though they live half as long as similarly aged persons without AD (National Institute of Mental Health, 2006).

We now know that Alzheimer's disease is a specific disorder, **not** simply normal aging or senility. As there are other types of dementia, a careful diagnosis should be sought, particularly in the early stages of the disease; AD is considered a **diagnosis of exclusion**—a diagnosis of Alzheimer's disease can be positively verified only by a histological exam (an after death analysis of brain tissue), though imaging techniques (e.g. PET scans, MRIs) can aid in diagnosis. Early-onset dementia of the Alzheimer's type is generally more rapid and progressive than is late-onset Alzheimer's disease (Heston & White, 1991), and is often genetic in nature (the gene APOE-e4). The presence of higher than normal concentrations of **senile plaques** (clusters of dead or dying neurons) and **neurofibrillary tangles** (bundles of twisted neural fibers) in the cerebral cortex is adequate to identify Alzheimer's disease (see Chapter 2). In addition, persons with Alzheimer's disease commonly show decreased levels of cortical neurotransmitters (acetylcholine, norepinephrine) (Bondareff, 1986). There is also a suspected link between increased levels of aluminum and the formation of tangles (Gatz et al., 1996), but the evidence for this association is not consistent.

Alzheimer's Disease: The Clinical Picture

Often, persons who are injured and taken to the emergency room or are in jail or in intensive care (particularly if they have been drinking or are on medication) may act confused and have difficulty answering questions. This contributes to *falsely diagnosed* dementia of the Alzheimer's type. Personality changes such as depression and withdrawal (Devanand et al., 1996; Storandt & VandenBos, 1994), anxiety, agitation, loss of interest in work, inability to concentrate, or denial of problem may act as first signals regarding the onset of Alzheimer's disease. In this respect, in *Alzheimer's from the Inside Out*, Taylor (2007) has poignantly written about the experience of having Alzheimer's disease, and talks about his fears of losing his skills to perform everyday tasks, fears of deterioration, the struggle to communicate with others, and the loss of *himself* as the disease progresses. Helplessness, frustration, anger, sadness, and indeed, thankfulness at having a loving wife to support him all characterize his response to his disease. Sadly, individuals do die from AD or AD-related complications, and it is commonplace for family to report "losing" the persons many times as the disease worsens, prior to the individual's actual death (see Box E). They thus grieve anticipatorily (see Chapter 12) in advance of a loved one's death (Holley & Mast, 2010).

Balsis, Carpenter, and Storandt (2005) found that among persons who went on to be diagnosed with AD, increased rigidity, apathy, egocentricity, and less emotional control were most common, relative to persons who had no clinical indication of the disease. Bachman and Associates (2005) found that several years before diagnosis, persons who were subsequently identified as having AD demonstrated clear declines in cognitive functioning, episodic memory (see Chapter 3), perceptual speed, and executive functioning (planful problem solving, decision making), with smaller deficits in verbal ability, attention, and visuospatial skills. Importantly, these changes are greater and more severe than those linked to normal aging. Collectively, they

---

Box F

Mild Cognitive Impairment

Mild cognitive impairment (MCI) refers to a complex of cognitive and to an extent, personality changes that are intermediate between normal aging and Alzheimer's disease (AD), where each overlaps with the other to an extent. Cognitively speaking, one's memory skills or ability to think in abstract terms, as well as the ability to make decisions critical to everyday living are central to the diagnosis of MCI. While persons suffering from MCI or what is termed "preclinical dementia" exhibit memory complaints and memory impairments, such difficulties do not normally interfere with everyday functioning. They can continue to live independently. However, from a "latent" phase (normal aging), such difficulties, which can be verified via cognitive testing, progress gradually until they reach a threshold where they are clearly observable in their impact of persons' ability to remember things that they once had little difficulty with. These deficits are typically verified via corroboration by family member and extensive cognitive testing. At this point, a diagnosis of AD might be made. Central nervous system degeneration, injury, or cardiovascular problems (e.g., high blood pressure) seem to be causally related to MCI, and individuals who are genetically predisposed toward AD are more likely to develop MCI.

MCI is **clinically heterogenous**. Some persons exhibit memory symptoms, some experience general cognitive difficulties, others exhibit difficulties in thinking quickly about objects in space (perceptual speed), and still others experience difficulties in making decisions and planful thinking (executive functioning). Still others experience gradual declines in all of these areas, and may respond to such declines with anxiety or depression when it becomes clear that they cannot cope with or compensate for such declines.

These declines generally predict some form of dementia (e.g., AD, vascular dementia, frontotemporal dementia), and appear 3-5 years in advance of a formal clinical diagnosis of dementia. Consequently, individuals and families should be alert to cognitive changes persons experience that are progressive in nature, even if persons seem to be functioning adequately in everyday life. MCI is considered to be early-stage AD, in that (a) similar neurological changes underly both, and (b) the cognitive difficulties persons with MCI experience are progressive. Fortunately, research suggests that any number of cognitive interventions (e.g., memory training) may be potentially helpful in treating the symptoms of MCI (Jean et al., 2010).

Sources: Bachman et al. (2005), Morris et al. (2001), Smith & Rush (2006).

---

describe a syndrome defined as **mild cognitive impairment (MCI)** (Peterson et al., 2001; Smith & Rush, 2006). Often, though not always, MCI has been preceded by normal cognitive functioning, and evolves into diagnosable (possible, probable, then definite) Alzheimer's type dementia (Smith & Rush, 2006) (see Box F).

Episodic (situational) memory loss for new in-

formation is the major symptom of preclinical AD/MCI, and may be the cause of many behavior and personality changes that coincide with the early development of the disease. Indeed, among persons with a history of AD in their families (e.g., a parent with the disease), anxiety, symptom seeking (e.g., subjective memory assessments), and the perception that one's symptoms resemble those of an afflicted parent were common (Hodgson & Cutler, 2003).

Ironically, many patients are generally somewhat puzzled, if not somewhat unconcerned about their memory loss and about errors in judgment as the disease worsens. They may have become quite skilled at covering up the difficulties they are having, deny that such changes are occurring, or find ways of compensating for the memory, decision making, or attentional problems they are experiencing, e.g., by taking notes, becoming more organized, relying on a spouse. From an occasional absent-mindedness, Alzheimer's disease worsens to a point where the individual loses memory for all remembered and learned routines, facts, and information (e.g., one's name or the name of a spouse). Daily life eventually becomes chaotic and confusing when one cannot remember how to put on a jacket, change the TV channel, or brush one's teeth. Disregard for one's manners and morals, unforeseen mood swings from laughter to tears, or a sudden turnabout from love to hate are not uncommon. As noted above, the individual may not recognize those whom he or she has loved deeply for years. Controls over physical functions are also impaired. Walking becomes an unsteady shuffle. Posture sags and appetite decreases. Hallucinations of sight and sound occur. Bowel and bladder control is lost. Disorientation in space and time is pervasive. The individual may wander aimlessly and eventually become unable to communicate. The Alzheimer's patient becomes increasingly difficult for others to relate to, understand, and care for. Finally, the patient may fall into a coma, which results from secondary infections such as pneumonia. At this point, Alzheimer's disease is virtually indistinguishable from other forms of dementia (Welsh-Bohmer & Warren, 2006). Ultimately, persons die from the combined effects of the disease itself on critical organ systems functions, or from the effects of having been bedridden for quite some time.

The symptoms of Alzheimer's disease, though they vary somewhat from patient to patient, are often most obvious in its early stages, when persons are still intact enough to realize that they are not as functional as they once were. At this point, depression is common (Storandt & VandenBos, 1994); persons try to compensate for their failings, or may persist in denying that they are even ill. They may write notes to themselves to help them remember things, or they might make excuses to others when they lose their way, e.g., saying they had to work late to conceal the fact that they got lost on the way home from work. Family members may reinforce this denial, preferring to see the patient's memory difficulties as just a part of the aging process (Pollitt et al., 1989). As time passes, however, the above symptoms do worsen, and the person loses the essence of who he or she is—common words and expressions, important and meaningful associations, treasured memories. Upon death, in addition to evidence of organic deterioration, i.e., senile plaques and neurofibrillary tangles, the brain may appear small, with **convolutions** being smaller and **fissures** being wider than normal (see Chapter 2). While we know that beta-amyloid proteins contribute to plaques and tangles, how such proteins are formed is still a mystery (Selkoe, 1991; Welsh-Bohmer & Warren, 2006). In many cases, the **primary** (cognitive) features of Alzheimer's disease are often impossible to separate from those that are **secondary** (emotional) to structural losses in brain cells (Storandt & VandenBos, 1994). Indeed, a true **functional** disorder—one that creates difficulties in everyday functioning for the aged individual *despite* intact brain function e.g., anxiety and depression (see below)—may coexist with dementia.

A diagnosis of Alzheimer's disease is best viewed descriptively. That is, it is based on symptoms and tells us little about **etiology** (the underlying cause). It does not suggest any specific treatment. Usually, a diagnosis of Alzheimer's disease is made only after other causes for the individual's difficulties in concentration, memory, or abstract reasoning have been ruled out (Gilhooly et al., 1986). Clinically, the symptoms of all forms of dementia are similar and overlap with those of the normal aging process (see Chapter 3) (Gilhooly et al., 1986). However, as noted above, dementia is **not** an inevitable consequence of the aging process.

Age (statistically speaking), gender, having had a head injury, and genetic predisposition (genetic mutations on chromosomes 1, 14, or 21) are often used a predictors of the risk of developing Alzheimer's disease (Smith & Rush, 2006).

Generally speaking, the diagnosis of Alzheimer's disease should be comprehensive, excluding other illnesses such as vascular dementia, Parkinson's disease, Huntington's chorea, AIDS dementia, dementia due to head injury, alcoholism-related dementia, reversible conditions such as normal pressure hydrocephalus, hypothyroidism, delirium, vitamin B12 deficiencies, depression, cardiovascular illness, strokes, and the effects of medications (e.g., antidepressants, sedatives, blood pressure medication, anticonvulsants, and antihistamines) (Houston & Bondi, 2006). This assessment should also be repeated over time to ascertain declines in functioning. An extensive battery of neuropsychological tests and a functional (ADL/IADL) assessment, in addition to CT scans, MRIs, or PET scans are necessary to conclusively identify likely AD (Welsh-Bohmer & Warren, 2006).

Recently, driven by the public's desire to learn of a diagnosis of AD as early as possible, especially given the apparent success of drugs such as Aricept and Memantine in treating memory loss among Alzheimer's disease patients (see Potyk, 2005 and Chapter 11), many persons have used a self-administered home diagnostic test, stressing the identification of olfactory (smell) dysfunction. Such test's marketing and its general use by the public should be viewed with extreme caution. Screening tests are not necessarily diagnostic, test results may be misunderstood or misused, and persons testing positive may lack options for treatment. Indeed, the use of such tests is described as "inappropriate and unethical" by Kier and Molinari (2003). At the minimum, they create many problems for physicians, insurers, and employers who are confronted with numerous legal complications, in part because this test's use is not regulated by the Federal Drug Administration (Kapp, 2003). Thus, the use of this test or any other *single* test to detect AD is controversial.

Unfortunately, complicating matters for AD sufferers is the fact that recent FDA clinical trials suggest that drugs such as Aricept may be limited in their success in treating the symptoms of AD (Kernisan, 2010, www.caring.com). Though they are beyond the scope of our discussion here, an in-depth presentation of experimental pharmacological approaches to treating AD can be found in *Treating Dementia: Is There a Pill for It?* (Ballinger et al., 2009).

Closely related to Alzheimer's disease is **frontotemporal dementia (FTD)**, which is sometimes referred to as **Pick's disease**. FTD is much rarer than is Alzheimer's. Strub and Black (1981) suggest that those with Pick's disease suffer from a unique form of neuronal loss, are socially inappropriate, slovenly, and unconcerned, despite cognitive intactness. Personality changes and expressive language difficulties are its manifestations, rather than difficulties with memory and judgment, as is true for AD (Alzheimer's Association, 2010). FTD typically emerges in one's 50s and 60s, and evolves over 5-10 years ending in the patient's being in a vegetative state and ultimate death. In contrast, Alzheimer's patients are neat and quite social, have substantial intellectual loss, and the disease appears later in life. The two dementias are difficult to tell apart, except among the most astute and experienced clinicians (Welsh-Bohmer & Warren, 2006).

Other Forms of Dementia

Multi-infarct (vascular) dementia, which is commonly believed to be next most common in later life (Alzheimer's Association, 2010), consists of gradual, yet somewhat progressive intellectual impairment. It is typically brought on by a series of strokes, stemming from partial or complete blockage of cerebral blood vessels, though several specific varieties of vascular dementia actually exist (Cato & Crosson, 2006). Such strokes can be quite severe, leaving the patient paralyzed, with severely impaired speech, impaired language, and a loss of the ability to recognize objects. In some cases, strokes are fatal. In many cases, abrupt changes in movement or memory function occur, followed by periods of mild recovery. Senile plaques and neurofibrillary tangles are typically absent. Multi-infarct dementia comprises 12 to 20% of all dementias (Alzheimer's Association, 2010; Welsh-Bohmer & Warren, 2006), second only to Alzheimer's disease. Its onset is somewhat earlier, yet more irregular than that of Alzheimer's disease, and definite cerebrovascular lesions (**infarcts**)—the loss of brain tissue that results in a softening of the brain from impaired blood flow—are present. In multi-infarct dementia, personality and insight into one's behavior are relatively unimpaired until late in the disorder, and emotional lability is common (Heston & White, 1991). While memory loss is thought to be "spotty," high blood pressure often is present. With hypertensive medication and/or surgery, vascular disorders leading to multi-infarct dementia can be prevented. Moreover, changes in diet and exercise, treatment of diabetes mellitus, and discouraging the use of alcohol and tobacco can be quite helpful (Bondareff, 1986). The diagnosis of vascular dementia (and of AD as well) can be helped via an complete history from the patient or family, and vascular dementia-related damage using CT scans of the brain and PET scans to identify brain infarcts and their location.

Among the other dementias that have been defined symptomatically is **Huntington's chorea**, which is comparatively rare and thought to be genetic in origin. It is accompanied by peculiar, writhing movements which are easily identified by a physician. **Parkinsons's disease** is a degenerative neuromuscular disease involving the progressive loss of motor control. It may also produce dementia in its latter stages. **Normal pressure hydrocephalus** is a treatable accumulation of cerebrospinal fluid producing dementia-like symptoms. In some cases, **AIDS** can produce dementia, and there also exists a rare viral form of dementia termed **Creutzfeldt-Jacob disease**. Its onset is, in contrast to Alzheimer's, usually well-defined; death occurs relatively quickly (within 2 months) (see Zarit & Zarit, 2007). **Lewy body dementia (LBD)** is characterized by abnormal protein deposits in the brain (named after Friederich Lewy who discovered them in the early 1900s). Symptoms of LBD overlap with other forms of dementia (e.g., Parkinson's disease), and are highly variable over time (hours or days). At one moment the person may be attentive and alert and in the next, may be confused. Persons with LBD often suffer from sleep disorders, fall often, sometimes lose consciousness, and are quite sensitive to neuroleptic (anti-psychotic) medications. While persons may live 5-7 years with the disease, its diagnosis and treatment are poorly defined.

As we mentioned above, the diagnosis of Alzheimer's disease and its distinction from other forms of dementia require a **thorough** physical, neurological, and cognitive evaluation by an interdisciplinary team of professionals (Green, 2000). A thorough family history, psychological testing to assess cognitive and personality functioning, a complete physical and neurological exam, as well as an assessment of the drug regimen the individual may be under are all essential. When other causes of Alzheimer's can be ruled out, a probable diagnosis can be confirmed by reassessing the individual over a period of 3-6 months to observe progressive changes in intellectual functioning.

Check Your Learning 10-2

Define the following terms and concepts:

> Senility
> Dementia
> Multi-infarct dementia
> Neurofillibrary tangles
> Mild cognitive impairment
> Sense of purpose in life
> Alzheimer's disease
> Beta-amyloid protein
> Senile plaques
> Fronto-temporal dementia
> Caregiver burden
> Multi-infarct dementia

- What is dementia? Of what value is it in diagnosis?

- What are the typical symptoms of Alzheimer's disease? What is its typical course?

- Why is Alzheimer's disease termed a diagnosis of exclusion?

- What are the typical symptoms of multi-infarct dementia?

- What are the precursors of diagnosable Alzheimer's disease?

- What are other forms of dementia other than Alzheimer's disease?

Disorders that Mimic Dementia

In addition to separating the dementias from one another, one must be sensitive to those conditions that symptomatically *mimic* irreversible organicity but *are treatable and reversible* (Gatz et al., 1996; Heston & White, 1991). In many respects, as we noted above, this distinction has tremendous importance for elderly persons and their families. Writing them off as "senile" may overlook a variety of conditions that, if left untreated, can deteriorate to the point where they do become irreversible. Reversible dementia-like conditions may be caused by prescription drug toxicity, the side effects of drugs (e.g., sedatives, anti-agitation drugs), drug interactions **(polypharmacy)** (LaRue, Dessonville, & Jarvik, 1985; Zarit & Zarit, 2007), infections, neurosyphilis, cerebral tumors, metastatic cancerous tumors (those that have spread to the brain from the lungs), and alcohol or drug abuse (Cato & Crosson, 2006; Heston & White, 1991; Welsh-Bohmer & Warren, 2006). In truth, nearly **50** conditions can cause symptoms of dementia (Alzheimer's Association, 2010; Zarit & Zarit, 2007).

Delirium

Another condition that may mimic dementia is **delirium**, which appears to be dementia-like but is in fact treatable. Delirium, if treated, is generally short-lived (less than a week), but if left untreated, can result in permanent cerebral damage and death (Knight, 2004; Raskind & Peskind, 1992). It too may result from drug toxicity, simple exhaustion, a

blow to the head, heart disease, malnutrition, anemia, diabetes, fluid-electrolyte disturbances, hepatitis, fever, or acute alcoholic intoxication (Knight, 2004; Zarit & Zarit, 2007). Symptoms of delirium such as agitation, paranoia, depression, disorientation, incontinence, lethargy, and sleeplessness have been documented as consequences of drug toxicity or drug interactions in aged persons, particularly with barbiturate use (Heston & White, 1991). Such problems can be easily misinterpreted as reflecting organicity or a functional disorder.

Alcoholism

Alcoholism can play a central role in influencing cognitive functioning, also leading to the misdiagnosis of dementia in aged persons (Cato & Crosson, 2006; Knight, 2004; Welsh-Bohmer & Warren, 2006; Zimberg, 1987). In alcoholism, cognitive losses are much less severe, as is disorientation, but emotional lability is often present. Delirium tremens (DTs) and hallucinations are common during withdrawal. If left untreated, an **alcoholic dementia** characterized by memory loss and falsification to fill in gaps (Korsakoff's syndrome) that is indistinguishable from other dementias usually appears after chronic alcohol abuse (Raskind & Peskind, 1992). Thus, while mild to moderate alcohol consumption seems to have positive health benefits for older women only (Balsa et al., 2008), this does not suggest that drinking more will lead to greater such benefits!

Common Functional Disorders

In discussing **functional disorders** in the aged, we will confine our discussion to depression and suicide, paranoia, schizophrenia, anxiety, and personality disorders. Sleep disturbances and hypochondriasis are more properly thought of as *outgrowths* of the above functional problems.

Depression

Depression is the most common functional disorder in aged persons, with estimates for depressive **diagnoses** as high as 15% (Blazer, 2002; Fiske, 2006). On the other hand, depressive **symptoms** are quite common in later life (70%), and depressive symptoms generally increase with increasing age in later life (Davey, Halverson, Zonderman, & Costa, 2004), and coexist with symptoms of anxiety. It is very important that transient depressive reactions (sadness) be separated from prolonged dysfunctional depressions in bereaved aged persons, often referred to as **complicated** or **pathological bereavement**, meaning that the response of depression is *out of proportion* to the loss; it is unrealistic, self-destructive, and harmful to oneself or others (see Chapter 12). For those (1) who are in poor health, (2) who have the fewest and most limited range of coping skills, (3) who are isolated from others, or (4) who are in situations they feel are beyond their control (like being institutionalized or forcibly retired), pathological depression in later life as a response to loss is more likely (Knight, 2004). Unfortunately, less than half of older persons who are depressed or anxious see a need for help with their feelings, though as depressive symptoms worsen or if persons have a history of depression or anxiety, their perceived need for help and care increases (Garrido, Kane, Kaas, & Kane, 2009).

The likelihood of depression increases as symptoms become more persistent over time (e.g., 2-3 weeks), especially if depressed mood and a loss of pleasure in everyday activities define such symptoms, according to DSM-IV (1994). Depression involves losses that are "narcissistic" in character (valued aspects of oneself). For example, the loss of one's health, a significant person, one's status at work or in the community, one's cognitive abilities (refer to our above discussion of mild cognitive impairment and dementia), or a part of one's body through illness or surgery are all terribly central to most of us. What is critical is not the loss per se but the *perception that this loss cannot be replaced*. In this respect, Cicirelli (2009) found that the death of a sibling and the closeness of the relationship to that sibling predicted depression in later life.

Unfortunately, older adults often feel that depression accompanies the aging process – that experiencing depression is inevitable if one lives long enough (Law, Laidlaw, & Peck, 2010). For this reason, older persons are often reluctant to admit feeling depressed, and may mask their depression through a variety of ego defense mechanisms, such as denial, counterphobic defenses (overcompensation), somatic complaints, and hypochondriasis (Blazer, 2002). In diagnosing depression, it is important to separate depression-related somatic (bodily) disturbances from genuine physical illnesses. Depression may also precede or result from a serious illness or pain (Parmalee et al., 1991), or it may be a by-product of drug effects in aged persons (Zarit & Zarit, 2007).

Older persons who are depressed manifest two major symptoms (Blazer, 2002; Fiske, 2006; Scogin, 1994): **depressive mood** (sadness, guilt, hopelessness, helplessness) and **reduced behavior** (giving up, apathy). Those who are depressed often feel excessively guilty, are aggressive, or feel anxious. Negativism and other cognitive disturbances (limited attention, disorganized thought, short-term memory loss) and a variety of physical complaints (indigestion, sleeplessness) and suicidal ideas are also often present. Indeed, older persons who are depressed have more cognitive difficulties (Beaudreau & O'Hara, 2009). Indeed, depression can coexist with dementia-related cognitive impairments though they are separate disorders (Teri & Reifer, 1987).

Newmann et al. (1991) discovered that older persons expressed their depression in terms of **depletion,** or **subthreshhold depression** (Adams, 2001; Hybels, Blazer, & Pieper, 2001). They felt worthless, had lost interest in daily activities, had lost their appetites, felt hopeless, and frequently thought about death and dying, but they do not meet the clinical (DSM-IV) criteria for diagnosable major depressive disorder. When manic behavior accompanies depression, the latter is termed **bipolar;** if no mania is present, depression is termed **unipolar** (Nevid, Rathuus, & Green, 2008).

Depression in younger and older persons does share many common features. For example, in a study of over 4,500 adults aged 50 and over, Lewinsohn et al. (1991) found that depression is more strongly associated with everyday stress, less support from and interaction with others, less interpersonal skills and fewer pleasurable activities.

Moreover, depressed persons typically think more irrationally, have more negative expectations of themselves and about the future, and tend to externalize success (Lewinsohn et al., 1991). While what was unique to older persons who were depressed was *poor health,* in general, however, complaints about memory, sleep difficulties, and low self-esteem all correlated with depression and were independent of age (Lewinsohn et al., 1991). .

Though one might think that depressed persons might recognize that learning new techniques for coping with their problems can be helpful, depression seems to feed upon itself. Foster and Gallagher (1986) found that depressed elders made less use of **information seeking** (finding out more, seeking advice from others) and of **problem solving** (taking specific action) than did younger depressives. Elderly depressed persons, relative to non-depressed ones, were also more likely to use **emotional discharge** (verbal outbursts, drug use, eating, smoking) as coping techniques. Moreover, depressed aged persons rated these efforts as less helpful. Maiden (1987) found elderly depressed women to experience **personal helplessness** ("I will fail at this task") while non-depressed older women expressed a more generalized (and less devastating) type of **universal helplessness** ("Everyone would fail at this task"). Interestingly, given the isolation that dementia caregivers experience, it is not surprising that they would experience feelings of depression in dealing with the loss of a family member due to Alzheimer's disease, where dealing with caregiving demands on a daily basis, having little income, and not being able to get adequate (long-term) care for an impaired family member are all associated with depression in such persons (Robinson et al., 2009) (see Box E).

As we mentioned above, in order for accurate diagnosis and treatment, physical causes for depression must be ruled out. This is often difficult because in many cases, physical and mental illness go hand in hand (see Box G). In these cases, the treatment of depression may consist of providing support in time of loss and drug therapy (lithium, tricyclics), though illness may alter the body's response to drugs (Salzman & Nevis-Olsen, 1992).

In addition, individual psychotherapy, cognitive "restructuring" of the environment, exercise, or lessening isolation can be most helpful in treating depression (Gallagher & Thompson, 1996; Hindrichsen & Clougherty, 2006; Qualls & Knight, 2006; Zeiss & Steffen, 1996) (see Chapter 11).

Depression, where affective symptoms predominate, must also be separated from dementia, where cognitive symptoms are most characteristic. Such misdiagnosed depression has been termed **pseudodementia** (Salzman & Shader, 1979). Depression may or may not exist with accompanying cognitive impairment, and depression can coexist with dementia. While persons who are depressed often complain of memory problems, subsequent testing does not bear out their supposed memory deficits (Snarski & Scogin, 2006). If depression is "masked" via physical complaints (fatigue, loss of appetite, constipation, sleeplessness), these "symptoms" help persons **deny** the fact that they are depressed yet permit them to legitimately ask for help. Ironically, because these symptoms serve a useful function in "protecting" the person, they are often not given up and thus resist treatment.

The National Institute of Mental Health (2003) suggests older adults ask themselves the following questions as an indication that they might be depressed: Do I feel (1) nervous or empty, (2) guilty or worthless, (3) very tired and slowed down, (4) not enjoy things the way I used to, (5) restless and irritable, (6) like no one loves me, (7) like life is not worth living? In addition, persons should ask themselves if they are sleeping or eating more or less than usual, or if they are having persistent headaches, stomach aches, or physical pain. These are often signs of depression in later life, and they **can** be treated! Depression is **not** a part of normal aging!

Depression in later life can stem from a variety of causes. It may be related to changes in neurotransmitter substances with age, hormonal changes, structural/vascular changes in the brain, or persons can be genetically predisposed toward depression (Blazer, 2002; Fiske, 2006). It can, as noted above, be a reaction to loss or exist as a response to loneliness. Fiori, Antonucci, and Cortina (2006) found

---

Box G

Symptoms of Depression in Later Life

Emotional: Dejected mood or sadness, loss of interest, sense of failure, irritability, worry, helplessness and hopelessness.

Cognitive: Pessimism, rumination about problems, poor memory, complaints about memory, difficulty in concentrating, delusions, hallucinations, suicidal thoughts, self-blame.

Physical/Somatic: loss of appetite, fatigue, sleep disturbances, weight loss.

Appearance: stooped posture, sad face, withdrawal, suspiciousness, hostility, confusion, unkempt appearance, weight loss, difficulties in elimination.

Psychomotor: slowed speech, slowed movements, shuffling slow gait.

Psychomotor agitation: continued motor activity, wringing of hands, picking of skin, pacing, restless sleep, grasping others.

Sources: Blazer (2002), Fiske (2006), Barusch & Wilby (2010).

---

that among older persons, the absence of family in the context of friends was less important in explaining depression than was the absence of friends in the context of family, and that the **quality** of social support was important in explaining the ability of one's social network of support (family and friends, see Chapters 4 and 5).

Depression can also be a secondary consequence of drug or alcohol abuse, physical illness (e.g., dementia, cardiovascular illness), exposure to negative life events, or everyday social stress. Though it may be difficult to assess, depression can also be existential in nature, reflecting the perception that life is meaningless (Blazer, 2002; Fiske, 2006). In this context, we discuss suicide.

Check Your Learning 10-3

Define the following terms and concepts:

Delirium
Alcoholic dementia
Depletion
Cognitive, affective, somatic aspects of depression

Pseudodementia
Depression
Complicated bereavement
Bipolar vs. unipolar depression
Personal vs. universal helplessness

- What is common to depression in younger and older adults? What is different?

- What factors lead to depression in older persons?

- With what disorders is depression often confused?

Suicide

The suicide rate among young adults has increased over the last decade, with firearms, poisoning, and hanging/suffocation being the principal means of ending one's life (Lubell et al., 2008). Depression and a lack of support from others are triggers for suicidal thoughts in college-age students (Calderia et al., 2010), who are showing up at campus counseling centers with serious psychological difficulties (Munsey, 2010).

The rates of successful suicides are greater in older persons than in any other age group, particularly so for elderly white males (Zarit & Zarit, 2007). Though older persons composed but 13% of the population, they accounted for 18% of all suicides in 2000 (National Institute of Mental Health, 2003). This is despite the fact that suicide rates increased for all age groups over the last decade (see Blazer, 2002). While cross-sectional data suggest that suicide rates for aged persons are higher, longitudinal data suggest otherwise (Koenig & Blazer, 1992). Blazer (1986) found a cohort effect in acceptance of suicide, where younger generations were **more** positive than were older ones; moreover, even older cohorts reported being more accepting than when they were young. Such generational shifts pose special challenges for those in the field of suicide prevention, wherein suicide may be a more acceptable alternative to dying in pain, losing one's dignity at the end of life, or living life alone, perhaps in a nursing home.

Depression is the single most common element in suicide, regardless of age and most persons attempt suicide following a depressive episode (see Fiske, 2006; Laidlaw, 2006). Suicide rates for teenagers are increasing and while their relative frequency is low, suicide among young children has also gained increasing attention (Nevid, Rathus & Greene, 2008). Women who are middle-aged also seem be vulnerable (Humphrey & Palmer, 1990-91) as do persons from the Baby Boomer generation, due to economic pressures and competition for jobs (Koenig & Blazer, 1992).

What are some of the reasons older adults commit suicide? Those who attempt suicide are more likely to have suffered the loss of a close relative in the past than otherwise, as through death or divorce (Perkins & Tice, 1994). For some elders, ageism, poor health, isolation, or marital conflict accompanying the withdrawal from the work force, not retirement **per se**, may contribute to lessened self-esteem and depression in the aged (Zarit & Zarit, 2007). Koenig and Blazer (1992) emphasize that poor health, especially if it is accompanied by pro-

tracted severe pain, often predicts suicide after retirement. Much depends on the *value* attached to the retirement by the older person (see Chapters 8 and 9). Not surprisingly, alcoholism and suicide seem to be highly related (Osgood, 1990).

In terms of the likelihood of someone committing suicide, race (white), gender (male), older age (75+), income (less), and either a recent physical illness or significant loss put people at greater risk for suicide among those older persons who are depressed (Blazer, 2002; Fiske, 2006). When these factors are combined, one's risk of suicide increases dramatically.

While the overall suicide rate is 10 cases per 100,000 persons, in older adults, it is 15 per 100,000 persons, and more common among men and those who are widowed or divorced (Zarit & Zarit, 2007). Unfortunately, older adults are more often likely to successfully commit suicide, relative to younger persons, who are more likely to attempt suicide, but who are less successful in doing so (Zarit & Zarit, 2007). Older adults also see suicide as more acceptable, more normal, more lethal, and less influenced by a strong religious conviction (Segal, Mincic, Coolidge, & O'Riley, 2004).

Among older persons, suicide sometimes accompanies the news of a serious illness. Providing support and alternatives to suicide and making people aware of how their distress is impairing their ability to realistically assess and solve their problems are very important (Laidlaw, 2006; Pierpont & McGinty, 2005). Moreover, being assertive and directive when necessary, and simply being with those who are at risk are the most important elements in averting a suicide attempt. In this respect, older adults are less likely to endorse depression-related suicidal thoughts than are younger adults (Balsis & Cully, 2008).

One should **not** misinterpret suicidal younger persons or females as just "wanting attention" or assume that older persons or males do not want to be prevented from killing themselves. The fact is that if persons truly wish to kill themselves, they can do so without ever communicating that intent to anyone. Many persons who do leave notes or contact suicide prevention centers *do* want help. Consequently, *all* references to an individual's killing himself should be taken seriously. The costs of not doing so are too great.

For many persons, young and old, taking their own lives may be a final expression of the wish to control the little that they have that is valued. Elderly suicides have been described by Kastenbaum (2009) as **egoistic.** They reflect the decision that the **quality** of one's life is **more important** than its **quantity**. Tthis perception is therefore based in the older person's crossing the **line of unbearability** (Kastenbaum, 2009). This "line" varies from person to person, depending upon what "quality of life" means to each individual; for some it may be living in constant pain; for others it may be not being able to care for oneself or make decisions about one's life.

Egoistic suicides involve few commitments to interpersonal or cultural values often resulting in or stemming from social isolation. Hence, for some elderly persons, the suicide act is highly individualistic and very serious in its intent, e.g., involving the use of firearms (Kaplan et al., 1994; Pierpont & McGinty, 2005). This makes it particularly difficult to mobilize effective support upon which the older person can rely in crisis when dealing with stress and/or loss.

In a landmark study of older male suicides, Miller (1979) found that aged men who committed suicide visited their physicians a month prior to their deaths. Perhaps these physicians were not skilled in "picking up on" the cues these men were providing them. Ironically, Miller (1979) found 60% of his sample to have given a clue as to their impending suicide; over a third of their family had admitted to acknowledging such clues! Yet 23% did not recognize such clues; many did nothing even when they were given advance notice! Miller (1979) states regarding suicide prevention, "Although they (the research team) emphasized outreach services are imperative to reach depressed people who may have become withdrawn and isolated, they felt the ulti-

mate answer would be for **old age itself to offer the elderly something worthwhile for which to live**" (p. 19). Education about suicide per se should be directed toward elderly persons, their families, physicians, and the general public (Osgood, 1990). Suicide *is* preventable.

Suicide in Institutions

Death within institutions (nursing homes, mental hospitals, geriatric wards) is commonplace for many elderly persons (see Chapter 12). Institutions such as these are seen (accurately or not) by many aged persons as depersonalizing, dehumanizing, lonely places—places to go where one dies. Miller (1979) states that the *mere prospect* of being institutionalized was enough to precipitate a suicide for some elderly men. When overt, quick means of taking one's life are not available, many elderly persons resort to other methods: starving, refusing to follow the physician's orders, voluntary isolation, behaving dangerously, excessive drinking/drug abuse, or smoking. These behaviors may be regarded by staff and other residents as "problems" in themselves.

Nelson and Faberow (1980) have termed such methods of suicide **indirect self-destructive behavior (ISDB)**. Clearly, institutionalization (as do other life changes) clearly has the potential for eliciting suicide-like behavior in those older persons who do not see relocation in a positive light, or who are already depressed or hopeless. In this respect, attention to older suicides in either primary care hospitals or nursing homes is key, highlighting the need for not only prevention, but also the need to train staff to recognize older persons in long-term care environments who may be thinking about ending their lives (Cukrowicz et al., 2009; Mezuk et al., 2008; Reiss & Tishler, 2008a, 2008b; Tadros & Salib, 2007). Suicide in nursing homes is a serious and under-recognized problem whose incidence is indeed increasing. Likewise, suicides among veterans receiving care from the Veteran's Administration (VA) are increasing. This is now recognized as a serious problem requiring greater efforts in prevention and proactive monitoring of veterans' thoughts and feelings as well as increasing the availability of therapy to help such persons.

Anxiety

We have all felt anxious from time to time. However, persons who are chronically anxious often appear tense, hyperactive, and are apprehensive and vigilant about what terrible thing might happen next. While we know comparatively little about chronic **anxiety** in later adulthood, Burke et al. (1990) found that scores on a self-report measure of anxiety generally decreased across age up to age 69 and accelerated thereafter; women were more anxious than men. Teachman (2006) found levels of anxiety to decline in young adulthood, followed by a slow, but steady decline into later life. Wetherell, Gatz, and Peterson (2001) found that anxiety predicted depression among older persons, and that anxiety, rather than depression, correlated with a lack of well-being. Anxiety and depression are frequently co-morbid in later life (Zarit & Zarit, 2007).

A key component of anxiety is the perception that one cannot control it. Moreover, as is true for depression, if anxiety symptoms typically last over a 2-3 week period, or if they persist off and on for 6 months, as per DSM-IV (1994), a formal diagnosis is likely. For many persons, physical illness (e.g., cardiovascular, respiratory illness, hormonal changes, menopause, dementia, delirium, epilepsy, drug intoxication, withdrawal from alcohol or sedatives) is often accompanied by anxiety (Zarit & Zarit, 2007). Poor health (cardiovascular, neurological, cancer-related, respiratory), relocation stress, isolation, or fears about loss of control may precipitate anxiety reactions (Zarit & Zarit, 2007).

Anxiety reactions may be especially dysfunctional among the very old (75+), who are predominantly women (Sheikh, 1992). Transient anxiety is episodic—a reaction to a stressful life event or a loss. Estimates for transient anxiety reactions may be high as 20% in some studies (Zarit & Zarit, 2007), though the frequency of anxiety disorders is less so in later life (3-5%) than for anxiety symptoms. Anxiety symptoms (e.g., restlessness, fatigue,

difficulty concentrating, irritability, muscular tension, sleep disturbances) that interfere with one's relationships and work performance, or undermine one's health and well-being should be taken seriously. Closely related to anxiety are **adjustment disorders**, whose symptoms are similar to those of anxiety and depression, but are in response to a stressful life event (Zarit & Zarit, 2007).

Paranoid Reactions

Paranoid symptoms (delusional or hallucinatory persecutory ideas) *may* accompany dementia, coexist with severe depression, or simply be a response to isolation or to sensory or cognitive losses (accusations of being talked about, food being poisoned, mail being stolen). Paranoid reactions must be viewed in light of older persons' attempts to "make sense" of their everyday environment via the projection of hostile or persecutory intent onto others, rather than wildly bizarre delusions. Such accusations are somewhat logical. In these cases, providing cues for forgetfulness (a system to keep track of when the "forgotten" letter was written), treating the sensory deficit (more seasoning on food, a hearing aid), explaining major changes (relocation) before they occur, and communicating clearly with those who are sensorily impaired often improve matters greatly. Paranoia in such cases certainly should *not* be interpreted as a reason for institutionalizing an older individual.

Another manifestation of paranoia is paranoid psychosis, where the quality of a person's delusions is quite bizarre, e.g., threats of being poisoned, being spied upon by the CIA, being monitored by electronic equipment (see Knight, 2004). Older paranoics typically have not had much contact with others and are consequently difficult to treat when they present for the first time in late life. Indeed, older paranoiacs are difficult to treat (e.g., with psychotropic drugs) because of their intense distrust of others. In many causes, older persons with such ideas live their lives as social isolates and may simply seem "odd" to others. They are not schizophrenic, where delusions are more systematic, organized, and bizarre (e.g., one is being plotted against by the police, poisonous gasses are being pumped into one's room). Paranoid reactions some-times accompany dementia (Knight, 2004; Zarit & Zarit, 2007). They may also be acute, short-term responses to being hospitalized or transferred to a nursing home. Paranoid symptoms may coexist with mania or depression. Paranoid reactions in older persons appear to be exaggerations of existing per-sonality characteristics, where for example, the normally withdrawn person develops delusions of passivity of influence by others.

Schizophrenia

Schizophrenia is comparatively rare in late adulthood and has not received a great deal of at-tention (Knight, 2004; Zarit & Zarit, 2007), though it had been predicted that the number of older adults with schizophrenia will increase in the next decade (Palmer, Heaton, & Jeste, 1999). It may be that persons do not live long enough to be counted as having been diagnosed as schizophrenic. Most older "schizophrenics" were most likely diagnosed much earlier in life and simply grow old in an institution, though it sometimes happens that schizophrenia appears for the first time in later life (Cohen, 2003; Knight, 2004). It is unclear whether older schiz-ophrenics' symptoms worsen or not, relative to when they were younger (Jeste et al., 2003). Older chronic paranoid schizophrenics, while more upset by their symptoms, sometimes seem to make better social adjustments than when they were younger (Zarit & Zarit, 2007). If they have grown old in an institu-tion, they often have a characteristic "burned out" appearance. They walk around in a stupor or sim-ply lie on the floor. They may utter incoherent, ani-mal-like sounds or be mute; they may smack their lips, grimace, or slobber like infants. They show little cognitive activity, stemming from years of medications to control outbursts of anger brought on by delusions or the dull sameness of institutional life. They often have a fixed stare with dark circles under their eyes accompanied by a plodding-like gait (Nevid, Rathus, & Green, 2008).

We know comparatively little about what causes the schizophrenia that develops in late life (termed **paraphrenia** in Britain), largely because many schizophrenics do not survive into old age. Most

older persons who develop schizophrenia for the first time in later life are women, and are of the paranoid type; they are often isolated and have fewer emotional and interpersonal resources in coping with their illness (Jackson, Meeks, & Vititoe, 2002; Zarit & Zarit, 2007). Differential diagnosis (versus dementia or delirium) is key to an accurate picture of late life schizophrenia. Extensive schizophrenia-like paranoid delusions do, however, sometimes accompany dementia, e.g., "ideas of reference" (oth-ers are looking at/talking about him or her), severe hypochondriacal delusions (cancer, syphilis), or manic behavior (having extraordinary amounts of energy that must be released). Knight (2004) notes that the current cohort of older schizophrenics would more likely have received community-based men-tal health care, as opposed to institutional care, and consequently, may have a harder time adjusting to everyday life, often ending up in substance abus-ing, high-crime, poor neighborhoods.

Drug Use and Abuse among Older Persons

Who has not resorted to taking some sort of pain medication for a headache? How common is alco-hol consumption at parties, weddings, or simply a get-together among friends? Yet, unique concerns come up when one asks "How might younger, middle-aged, and older adults come to use or abuse drugs?" Several ideas have been proposed: (1) one may be genetically predisposed to substance use, so the "high" that persons feel when they use a drug (even caffeine) becomes biologically ingrained; (2) the use of the drug is maintained because of its ef-fects on arousal, self-worth, depression and anxi-ety; (3) the drug's use is classically conditioned (paired with a variety of powerful stimuli); (4) we learn through observation that a drug's effects are pleasurable; (5) drug use is a function of early es-tablished oral personality traits; or (6) drug use is an outgrowth of the availability of drugs, making drug use attractive via the media or peer pressure (Nevid, Rathus & Greene, 2008). While overall il-licit drug use has declined relative to the late 70s/ early 80s, the use of LSD, marijuana, and cigarette smoking has increased since the early 1990s among

Box H

Personality Disorders in Later Life

Segal, Coolidge, and Rokowsky (2006) have written about **personality disorders in later life.** Personality disorders have a **pervasive** quality to them, wherein they are stable over time, reflect qualities and behaviors that are **rigid and inflexible**, and are **at odds with cultural expectations regarding typical behavior.** They are **clearly maladaptive** and often are not diagnosed or treated until later life.

Individuals with personality disorders report that regardless of whether their behavior is adaptive or not, it "feels right—it feels like me" (Segal et al., 2006, p. 290). They have **little insight** into why they feel and act as they do and what their impact is on others. Such persons externalize their difficulties—it's other people, not me. They have difficulty seeing themselves changing. Their feelings, thoughts, and behaviors are narrow and inflexible.

Despite concerns about DSM-IV criteria for personality disorders as they apply to older adults (Segal et al., 2006), examples of personality disorders they discuss that one finds among older persons are:

- **Cluster A**: **paranoid** (pervasive distrust and suspicion of others); **schizoid** (a pattern of social isolation and detachment); **schizotypal** (acute discomfort with close relationships, eccentric behavior).
- **Cluster B**: **antisocial** (pattern of disrespect for others' feelings and rights);

borderline (unstable relationships, impulsive); **histrionic** (excessive emotionality and attention-seeking, superficiality), **narcissistic** (grandiose, needs for admiration, lack of empathy).
- **Cluster C**: **avoidant** (social inhibition, sensitive to negative evaluation); **dependent** (excessive dependence on others, needs to be taken care of); **obsessive-compulsive** (preoccupied with orderliness and perfection).
- **Cluster D**: **depressive** (pervasive depressive thoughts), and **passive-aggressive** (negative attitudes and passive resistance to others).

Morse and Lynch (2004) found Clusters A and C to be the most common in later life.

If persons have survived life into old age, those with personality disorders typically have a more difficult time coping with changes in their physical appearance, illness, sensory loss, widowhood, and increased dependency, due to their ways of coping and relating to others that have never been adaptive, and into which they have little insight. In some cases (e.g., borderlines), their symptoms seem to abate with aging. They are often unhappy, having alienated themselves from loved ones, lonely, and understandably difficult to care for and treat. They pose a challenge for nursing home staff, health care personnel, family, and professional therapists.

college students (Nevid, Rathus & Greene, 2008). While alcohol consumption has declined somewhat, drinking, and especially binge drinking, remains a problem on many college campuses.

It is not unheard of to find middle-aged persons who are addicted to either illicit or prescription drugs to control pain, depression, or anxiety.

Also, because of the many chronic health problems many older persons experience, they often must take several medications (Storandt, 1994). Unfortunately, older persons account for almost half of all deaths from either adverse drug reactions or misuse of prescription medications. Compared to younger age groups, elderly persons not only take many more drugs, but also consume a wider variety of drugs. This is partially a result of the numerous chronic physical conditions that increase with age for which drugs are prescribed (e.g., hypertension, congestive heart failure, ischemic heart disease). Moreover, elderly persons are also more likely to have obtained multiple prescriptions for these chronic conditions (Glantz & Backenheimer, 1988; Zarit & Zarit, 2007).

Aged individuals are also the largest consumers of **over-the-counter (OTC) drugs**. While older persons rarely abuse illegal drugs, there has been some concern about the abuse of OTC medications, such as sedatives and laxatives, and the possible consequences of this abuse for the older person's health, such as excessive weight loss and chronic intestinal inflammation. Tragically, many elderly persons may be inadvertently endangering their health and even their lives. Sadly, too, in many cases, medication-related problems are reasons for institutionalization. Blazer (2002) notes that alcohol is the most commonly used drug by older persons, though its use is less frequent relative to younger or middle-aged persons, in part because of cohort differences (older cohorts are less likely to have drunk alcohol regularly), and the fact that younger alcoholics do not survive into old age. Older persons may drink less alcohol because they can are less able to metabolize alcohol (see below).

As people age, there are a number of physiological changes that impact how the body responds to drugs. These changes are expressed in terms of their impact on the initial **absorption** of the drug from the gastrointestinal tract, the **distribution** of the drug in the circulatory system, the **metabolism** of the drug into a different form that can be used by the body, and finally, the **elimination** of the drug from the body (Cherry & Morton, 1989). Decreases in lean body mass and water content and increases in adipose tissue all influence how a drug is initially absorbed, distributed, and later metabolized (Cherry & Morton, 1989). The length of time it takes for half the drug to be eliminated from the individual's system is referred to as the drug's **half-life**. For aged persons, in most cases the half-life of most drugs is greater. For persons with chronic or acute illness, the likelihood of **polypharmacy** (the use of many drugs simultaneously) is greater, and the illness itself undermines the body's ability to absorb, metabolize, and excrete drugs, further contributing to drug toxicity and/or polypharmacy. Consequently, dosages should be individualized. Older cohorts express more temperance and are less permissive or condoning in their attitudes toward the use of alcohol (Benshoff & Roberto, 1987).

Alcohol abuse can be a serious problem among aged persons, though its frequency seems to decline somewhat in later life (Breslow, Faden, & Smothers, 2003; Moos, Schutte, Brennan, & Moos, 2004; Zarit & Zarit, 2007). It seems to be more common than is drug abuse among older adults and can be a problem for some older persons, who may or may not be lifelong drinkers or fit the stereotype of the "down-and-out" alcoholic (Zarit & Zarit, 2007). For this reason, it is important to understand *why* some people continue to drink heavily into old age or why others begin to drink later in life. In many cases, depression, as well as an inability to cope with losses associated with retirement, spousal bereavement, illness, marital discord, or loneliness contribute to both of these patterns, and as alcohol is a depressant, depression may follow from alcohol use as well (Blazer, 2002; Zarit & Zarit, 2007). Indeed, the psychosocial stresses some persons experience in later life outweigh the negative effects of the use of alcohol itself (Cantor & Koretzky, 1989). Moreover, symptoms such as slurred speech, an atoxic gait, sleep disturbances, or confusion can be misinterpreted as symptoms of dementia, or even due to normal aging. In extreme cases, Korsakoff's syndrome and alcohol-induced dementia can be created by years of hard drinking, as can cirrhosis of the liver, cardiovascular, pancreatic, and kidney disorders. An accurate diagnosis is important, especially given that it is likely the older person will deny drinking, and because alcohol abuse often creates social and interpersonal problems for the older person. Questions regarding the extent of change in recent behavior and personality, as well as those regarding isolation or conflict with others, deficits in self-care and in routine everyday transactions (e.g. appointments, income management), troubles with the law, and episodes of memory loss or confusion are important ones to ask of family or friends.

For those aged alcoholics who do seek treatment, the outlook is good, i.e., detoxification, followed by inpatient/outpatient care of both a medical and psychosocial nature (Benshoff & Roberto, 1987), especially for the unimpaired older client (Cantor & Koretzky, 1989). Restoring fluid and electrolyte balance is key, as is attending the nutritional deficits and a lack of self-care (e.g., not bathing or shaving, poor dental hygiene). After the older alcoholic has been stabilized, the task remains to remain drug or alcohol free, especially since even prescription medications often interact with alcohol in later life (Zarit & Zarit, 2007). One plan is to utilize a contract between the older person and the family stipulating a daily intake of antabuse, and that no alcohol will be consumed lest the person experiences severe physical symptoms (e.g., difficulty breathing, vomiting, chest pains). Educating the person and family about the long-term negative effects of alcohol on memory can be helpful, as well as attendance at support groups (Alcoholics Anonymous) (Blazer, 2002).

Drug Adherence in Older Persons

Once a proper drug regimen has been established, monitoring drug adherence by aged persons is critical. Older persons often willfully fail to comply with a physician's prescriptions in a variety of ways: (a) taking drugs **not** prescribed, (b) **failing** to take drugs that **are** prescribed, (c) **not knowing** the proper schedule of drugs to be taken in a specified dose, and (d) **knowing** but **failing** to take proper dosages at correct intervals (Brown & Park, 2003; Park & Kidder, 1996). Of course, when older patients are unable to clearly read medicine labels, fail to remember where bottles of pills/capsules are stored, or have more than one drug (with varying dosages) involved, noncompliance is a serious problem. Doctor-patient communication is vital in this respect, where drug education, the use of both written and oral teaching aids, ensuring comprehension,

and education and support in the use of written memory aids to ensure compliance are all important (Brown & Park, 2003; Park & Jones, 1997). For some elderly, self-taught aids, facilitated by computer-software designed to "remind" the individual to take the medication, may even be possible.

Check Your Learning 10-4

Define the following terms and concepts:

> Suicide
> ISDB
> Paraphrenia
> Half-life
> Egoistic suicides
> Adjustment disorders
> Anxiety
> Paranoia
> Personality disorders
> Drug use and misuse
> Polypharmacy
> Alcohol abuse

- Why would an older person commit suicide?

- What steps could be taken to lessen suicide among older adults?

- What factors lead to anxiety among older persons?

- What theories attempt to explain drug use in adulthood?

- What are the unique aspects of drug use among older persons?

- How can adherence to drugs among older persons be improved?

- Is there more than one type of older person who drinks? How can this difference be understood?

Assessment

An in-depth discussion of the assessment of older persons can be found in Kaszniak (1996), Kane and Kane (2000), and Zarit and Zarit (2007), especially as it relates to aiding in **differential diagnosis** (e.g., in making the distinction between depression and dementia) and the evaluation of affective functioning, competence, decision-making skills, driving, and the capacity to functioning independently. The assessment of aged persons however, generally varies in terms of the *level* of skill that is being assessed. For example, we might be interested in strength or range of motion, ADLS/IADLs, learning/memory, or social skills (Kemp & Mitchell, 1992; Pearson, 2000). As a general rule, before conducting an assessment, one should be clear in defining for what **purpose** an interview, questionnaire, psychological test, or clinical examination is being done. This should be clearly explained to the older individual and the family. For example, assessments might be used to measure the effects of a given intervention, or to aid a counselor in reaching a decision about an individual's adjustment to changed life roles (for instance, the viability of retirement). Assessment might also be used to establish job-related competence/retraining or to determine levels of competence or self-care regarding relocation (Kaszniak, 1996).

In general, scales with demonstrated **reliability** and **validity** should be utilized (Anastasi & Urbina, 1997). This is no less true for older persons. Briefly, a scale is **reliable** (stable) if it yields similar scores (scores that correlate highly with one another) at two occasions for a given individual. A **valid** scale measures what it intends to measure when judged against some external criterion of that quality. In general, measures that are valid are almost always reliable, but the opposite need not be the case. Scales that have age-corrected norms and are supplemented by reliability and validity are especially valuable. Above all, assessments should be **comprehensive**, and should ideally be conducted at least **twice** by **different** examiners, and results should be interpreted in light of the individual's

health, level of education, and family history (Kane, 2000). Extensive **functional behavioral assessment** procedures that involve structured interviews have been developed for this purpose—for example, the Older Americans Resources and Services (OARS) questionnaire (Fillenbaum, 1990). These interviews (1) identify the problem and (2) understand its history and relationship to the older person's current situation (Kemp & Mitchell, 1992; Pearson, 2000).

Whenever possible, instructions should be personalized. Care should be taken to first establish trust and rapport in order to allay the person's fears and anxiety about the assessment itself or the consequences of the assessment. Particular care should be taken to use materials and techniques that are concrete, clear, and easily seen and heard. Assessments should be done in a relaxed, nonthreatening, familiar atmosphere, and should not be so long as to needlessly fatigue or irritate the individual. Mounds of information do not compensate for common sense, good clinical judgment, sensitivity, experience, and interpersonal skills.

Errors in Diagnosis

When a diagnosis of, for example, depression or dementia is falsely made, it is termed a **false positive** error. When such conditions are assumed not to exist when they are in fact present, a **false negative** error has been made. This is especially critical if the disorder is one that will cause the individual to deteriorate further and harm him or her irreversibly if left untreated. Depending on what effects falsely diagnosing a problem that is not present may have, each error in judgment can result in serious consequences for older persons and their families. For example, diagnosing someone as depressed rather than as demented makes it more likely that the individual will receive treatment for the latter. In contrast, falsely diagnosing someone as having dementia (Alzheimer's disease, multi-infarct dementia) may overlook a disorder that, if left untreated, produces irreversible damage or worse still, leads to death (e.g., depression). Due to age bias, clinicians may be more likely to make a diagnosis

---

Box I

Strength-Based Approaches to Later Life Adjustment

Strength-based approaches to understanding older persons, assessing them, and treating them share several core characteristics as they relate to the provision of health care, developing consumer awareness, adjustment to retirement, long-term care, and counseling and therapy. These characteristics are:

1. Assuming that older clients indeed have skills, resources, and capacities to help them solve problems and adjust.
2. The relationship between the older client and the professional helper is collaborative rather than hierarchical (e.g., the therapist knows best, is the expert). Rather than being problem-based, therapy is solution-based.

3. The emphasis of helping efforts is to build upon the client's strengths and life experiences in a time-efficient manner.
4. Therapists are not bound by their assumptions about age or diagnostic categories. Each older client is treated as an individual.

Source: J. Ronch and J. A. Goldfield (2003), *Mental wellness and aging: Strength-based approaches.* Baltimore, MD: Health Professions Press.

---

of dementia versus depression, *given the same symptoms*, if the "patient" is old versus being young (Knight, 2004).

Optimally Mentally Healthy Aged Persons

What is optimally mentally healthy has a universal quality to it. Clearly, although we have discussed for the most part, psychopathology and abnormal behavior in this chapter, it is equally important to emphasize what has been termed a **strength-based approach** to older persons (Ronch & Goldfield, 2003) (see Box I). This stresses the adaptive qualities that persons possess in terms of the use of wisdom, judgment, and experience, being resilient in the face of stress, feeling empowered, and caring for and treating older persons.

Hellebrandt (1980) has written about those characteristics associated with what are called the **advantaged aged**. This term refers to the well-educated, reasonably healthy, financially secure, independent-living elderly person. She talks of these individuals not **feeling** old, accepting their physical/health-related limitations, and being preoccu-

pied with meaningful activities of their *own* choosing. Moreover, they held very **individualistic** feelings about work and retirement and about religion (or a personally meaningful set of values). Last, they exhibited a notable lack of fears about death, and rarely reminisced about the past. This illustrates **flexibility** in adapting to life's pleasures and problems, which is important in being mentally healthy **at any** age.

Why are some elders more adaptive than others? Valliant and Valliant (1990) tested over 200 healthy college students in the early 1940s and reinterviewed them four times over the next 40 years. Persons who enjoyed positive mental health in their 50s had come from intact homes and had trusting relationships with their parents that permitted some autonomy and initiative. Persons with the poorest mental health later in life were most likely to have used mood-altering drugs before the age of 50. Jones and Meredith (2000) found that adolescents who were psychologically healthier were more likely to maintain and even gain in this respect when they were middle-aged and older. We see that developing a flexible, yet adaptive attitude toward life in young adulthood contributes to mental health in later life. This has been termed **planful competence** (Clausen & Jones, 1998). Forstmeier and Maercker (2008) found that persons who had a history of being more highly motivated in that they were **self-directed** enjoyed better cognitive and emotional health as older adults. Moreover, thinking about life experiences in more positive terms, termed the **positivity effect**, and being more able to regulate one's emotions (especially intense and negative feelings) seems to contribute to better adjustment in later life (Schiebe & Carstensen, 2010). Being emotionally bonded to a "significant other" (sibling, spouse, friend) also seems to contribute to emotional stability in old age. Persons who are ill or isolated often lack this special person, who serves as a "buffer" or **confidant** (see Chapters 4 and 5).

Fostering **positive** mental health in old age might be achieved by stressing its developmental antecedents. What appears to be a consequence of old age upon close scrutiny often emerges as an individualized lifelong pattern of coping, which may be very adaptive, or it may be very ineffective. Increased self-confidence and self-reliance, healthy attitudes about one's strengths and weaknesses, learning and maintaining effective coping skills, and an active approach toward the environment are prerequisites for mental health in **both** young and elderly persons (Valliant & Valliant, 1990). Unrealistic expectations of self, narrowness of experience, emotional fragility, resistance to criticism, and a restrictive environment encourage **unhealthy** styles of coping in **both** the young and the old.

In closing, we want to reaffirm the necessary balance between (a) the emotional and cognitive difficulties that some adult do indeed experience and (b) the positive, adaptive qualities and resources that we all possess. Rowe and Kahn (1998) suggest that positive mental health and **successful aging** (see Box A) are a combination of many factors: personal vitality, resilience, adaptive flexibility, autonomy and control that are realistic and possible, integrity, and a good person-environment "fit."

It has been said that if you want to be happy in later life, (1) have something to do, (2) have someone to love and who loves you, (3) have something

to hope for, and (4) have something (or someone) to believe in. Persons who have successfully aged take care of themselves both physically and mentally. They have satisfying relationships with others. They get regular physical and mental exercise. Importantly, they seem to find a way to get the most out of whatever life brings them--good or bad. Perhaps they were much like this as younger persons. Maybe it's not too late to start?

Check Your Learning 10-5

Define the following terms and concepts:

  Assessment
  Planful competence
  False positive error
  Positive mental health
  Successful aging
  Positivity effect
  Reliability
  Validity
  Optimally mentally healthy persons
  False negative error
  Strength-based approach
  Functional behavioral assessment

- What factors should be kept in mind when assessing older persons?

- Who are mentally healthy older adults?

- What is the difference between reliability and validity?

- What are the advantages of a strength-based approach to mental health in later life?

Summary

Information about **mental health** and mental illness across the adult lifespan must be viewed with caution for a number of reasons. Mental health and mental illness are best thought of as ends of a **continuum**. This is particularly important in that mental health has rarely been defined, especially with the aged, and has been traditionally seen as the absence of mental illness. A variety of approaches have been proposed to understand this continuum with the aged; each has strengths and weaknesses that must be kept in mind in defining mental illness and in planning mental-health interventions with the aged.

Of major importance is separating **reversible** and **irreversible** forms of **dementia** as well as separating **dementia** and **depression** in the aged. The confusion of these categories termed **pseudo-dementia** often leads to improper treatment of or no treatment at all for aged persons and their families. While forms of dementia such as **Alzheimer's disease, multi-infarct dementia**, and **depression** have received the most attention, other disorders such as **anxiety**, **paranoia**, and **schizophrenia** are less well understood. Depression is, in some respects, unique in older persons, yet in other ways it is expressed universally. As depression is a key element in **suicide**, its assessment should be done carefully, especially since suicides in late life are often self-contained, and difficult to prevent. The **assessment** of mental health and mental illness should be **purposeful** and as **comprehensive** as possible, in order to enable one to make as **reasonable** an interpretation as possible in light of the older person's goals, needs, resources, and capabilities. While mental illness does occur, particular attention should be paid to **optimally mentally healthy** persons who are older. They have much to teach us about **successful aging**.

Chapter 11
Intervention and Therapy

Mental Health Services: Equally Helpful for All Adults?

It is the rare person who does not need help or advice from someone else from time to time. Most of us rely on others in times of need or severe stress, and it is the mental health professional to whom we often turn when we experience emotional problems that are beyond our own resources to handle effectively.

Between 15% and 25% of the 28 million older Americans suffer from mental health problems (see Chapter 10), and if middle-aged persons are included in these figures, the need for help increases still further (Knight, Kaskie, Shurgot, & Dave, 2006). Mental health care demands were expected to increase as the Baby Boom generation ages (Koenig, George & Schneider, 1994). In light of the increasing numbers of middle-aged and older persons in the U.S. population (see Chapter 1), this prediction is likely to be borne out.

Despite the need for mental health care among adults, not all persons get the help that their illness requires. According to a report released by the National Institute of Mental Health (Kessler et al., 2005), only one-third of Americans who suffer from some form of mental illness receive professional treatment (more often than not in the form of drugs prescribed by a physician). Moreover, a report "Therapy in America- 2004" (http://tinyurl.com/18r) indicated that while 27% of adults (59 million people) received some form of mental health treatment, a third of those needing help do not get it, due to a lack of confidence, cost, and a lack of health insurance. Most persons lacked information about selecting a therapist, relying upon their physicians' recommendation. While women were more likely to seek and get help, men feared being stigmatized should getting help go on their "record."

As a discussion of all possible forms of treatment with adults of all ages is beyond our scope here, in this chapter we will discuss the variety of treatment approaches with middle-aged and older adults, given the age bias in treatment and referral (American Psychological Association, 2004; Karel et al., 2010). In many respects however, therapy and intervention with aged people is in principle much like that with young adults (Knight, 2004), and fortunately, a great deal of research has demonstrated that older adults are *equally* amenable to change (Baltes, 1997; Knight, 2004; Knight et al. 2006). Ideally, this should provide additional impetus for professionals to actively treat elderly clients by focusing on their potential for change in the context of the relationship with a counselor or therapist. Indeed, some evidence suggests that more recently born cohorts of older persons hold more positive views toward mental health and mental health services than their predecessors (Currin, Hayslip, Schneider, & Kooken, 1998), though such attitudes have stabilized over the past decade (Currin, Hayslip, & Temple, 2011).

Barriers to Mental Health Services

Many have expressed great concern about the underutilization of mental health services by elderly adults (Knight et al., 2006). Unfortunately, despite a more positive outlook about adulthood and aging (see Chapter 1), negative expectations about older people continue to influence mental health services. For example, persons who are disabled or mentally retarded may be denied continued eligibility to community-based services because they are too old, and persons may be refused admission to a nursing home if the reason for their disability is a mental disorder (Lebowitz & Niederehe, 1992). Additionally, rehabilitation services often have a strong job component to them; their goal is to provide the disabled individual with everyday living skills as well as job skills. Older persons who may be suffering from *both* a chronic physical illness and a mental disorder and who may not want or need job skill training often have no rehabilitation services that are designed with them in mind. Moreover, meal services, housing, senior centers, or day care services (see Chapter 9) are not designed for people with more serious mental disorders. For these reasons, older adults often "fall through the cracks" of available community services. These dilemmas present challenges to mental health services planners so that all adults are served equally. Garrido, Kane, Kaas, and Kane (2009) found that among community-residing older adults, degree of depression and anxiety symptoms influenced a perceived need for mental health care and that only 11% of older persons indicated a need for help.

External barriers to mental health care refer to the objective, observable aspects of the mental health system itself. While many older adults seek "basic services," such as housing, meals, or income assistance, what are offered are often "life enhancing" services, such as socialization, growth experiences, and activity programs. Clearly, this suggests that mental health service providers need to more carefully design and implement their programs so that they will be perceived as acceptable by would-be older clients. Thus, many types of services could be provided at **multiple levels** (Brim & Phillips, 1988) depending upon the individual's need in a variety of settings. For example, we could treat individuals, families, or even change cultures or societies to enhance the individual's adjustment. Services could be provided by professionals, para-

professionals, and peers (Yang & Jackson, 1998). **Coordination of services** of the community-based, institutionalized, and individual types is essential (Lebowitz & Niederehe, 1992). We have all probably experienced trying to get answers from service providers and felt like "we got the runaround." In this respect, relying upon aging services providers may lessen the problem of access to services by would-be middle-aged and older clients (Kaskie, Linkins, & Estes, 2002). **Transportation** to where services are offered may also be a problem for older persons who cannot drive or afford transportation, for whom mass transit may not be available, or who live alone or in a rural area. Providing services that are **affordable** is also a major barrier to their use by older adults, raising Medicare ceilings on reimbursement for mental health services provided by *all* professionals *qualified* to deliver such services has helped matters greatly since psychologists' services have been for some time reimbursable under Medicare (Norris, Molinari, & Rosowsky, 1998). Yet recent cuts in Medicare benefits (21%) passed by Congress in mid-2010 will undoubtedly undermine older adults' access to all types of health care services because mental health professionals and physicians will be less likely to take older persons on as clients if their bills are to be paid by Medicare. (see Table 11-1). Paying for and supporting mental health services for those who are uninsured remains a challenge (National Mental Health Information Center, 2010). Such services might be in the form of community-based mental health care, pastoral counseling, self-help groups, or public assistance.

We all bear some of the burden of paying for services for adults of all ages, in terms of taxes and health insurance premiums. Mental health disorders cost the U.S. economy about $194 billion annually in terms of direct medical care costs, as well as losses of work productivity (Shern et al., 2008). These cost estimates to provide such care are likely to rise, influenced by the demand for mental health services and the ability of managed care to keep pace with the cost of providing such services (see Frank & McGuire, 2000). The **design of existing**

Table 11-1

Medicare Coverage of Mental Health Services

Medicare Part A: Inpatient Care: Mental Health Care Provided in a Hospital: psychiatric, skilled nursing facility

Applies to services designed to identify, diagnose, and treat mental health problems.
Lifetime limit of 190 days of specialty inpatient care for serious, recurring mental illness, after which care must be provided in a general hospital.

Expenses subject to deductibles and copayments.

Medicare Part B: Outpatient Care

Covers mental health services provided by a qualified medical doctor, clinical psychologist, clinical social worker, clinical nurse specialist, nurse practitioner, or physician's assistant.

Applies to mental health services that are typically provided outside a hospital and those provided in the hospital's outpatient department that do not require an overnight stay.

Examples of such services: individual or group therapy, family counseling, testing and evaluation, activity or occupational therapy that is part of one's mental health treatment, prescription medication that cannot be self-administered, laboratory tests, partial hospitalization (more intense treatment outside the doctor's or therapist's office that substitutes for inpatient treatment).

Expenses subject to copayments and deductibles.

What Medicare will not cover: Meals and transportation to and from mental health services, support groups meeting outside the doctor or therapist's office, testing or training for job skills, self-administered prescription medication.

Source: *Medicare and Your Mental Health Benefits* (2000). Health Care Financing Aministration, U.S. Dept. of Health and Human Services, Baltimore, MD

---

services is another external barrier. Existing services may be overburdened, personnel may be poorly trained (see Table 11-2), or services may not be geared to deal with elderly patients. For example, making home visits, and offering services in contexts particular to older persons, e.g., a senior center, a church, or public housing, would improve access to services.

Internal barriers primarily reflect **client or therapist attitudes and biases**, and contribute to a lack of interest in the treatment of elderly adults, often resulting in no care at all or at best, poor quality of care (Knight, 2004; Pepin, Segal, & Coolidge, 2009). For example, a belief in the pervasiveness of Alzheimer's disease leaves many professionals helpless, thinking that memory difficulties are a normal sign of aging that do not require professional intervention, or that only drugs and not psychotherapy can be effective in treating depression. All of this ultimately discourages many professionals from helping middle-aged and older persons. Unfortunately, *some* middle-aged and older adults may also hold such beliefs. In this respect, Webb, Jacobs-Lawson, and Waddell (2009) found that older adults themselves saw older persons (women) with schizo-phrenia as dangerous, and thought that older persons with anxiety/depression had themselves to blame for their illness. These expectations are the basis for the stigma attached to being mentally ill and discourage older persons from seeking help. Even having a hearing loss is stigmatizing to older persons (Wallhagen, 2009).

Complicating matters, Wetherall et al. (2009) found older adults to be less accurate than younger adults in identifying the symptoms of anxiety and depression, interfering with the timely search for help for such older adults. Hayslip et al. (2011) found older adults in rural areas to hold more negative mental health attitudes than their urban counterparts, interfering with seeking help in underserved rural areas.

We should be cautious about interpreting older persons as resistant to seeking help, and it would be inaccurate to assume that older adults are *necessarily* more reluctant to seek help than are younger adults (Robb, Haley, Becker, Polivka, & Chwa, 2003). While older persons may be equally willing to seek help, their *access to services* may interfere with efforts to get professional assistance ((Knight et al., 2006). In this respect, cultural values and biases need to be considered in assessing needs for mental health care among older persons (Crowther et al., 2006; Woods & Laidlaw, 2010). Older adults do see some forms of therapy, i.e., cognitive therapy or cognitive therapy and medication, to be acceptable in treating depression (Hanson & Scogin, 2008).

Another factor behind the lack of mental health care to elderly patients is **countertransference**. This means that the therapist projects personal negative feelings about aging, death or loss onto the elderly client, interfering with diagnosis and treatment. Both caring for one's elderly parents and for one's children intensifies the therapist's countertransference, leading to (a) unrealistic demands for a cure, (b) a parental "know it all" attitude, or (c) hostility, pity, or sympathy toward elderly people as individuals who cannot care for themselves (American Psychological Association, 2004). Complicating mat-ters is the older person's **transference** to the counselor, e.g., seeing him or her as a parent or a child figure, as one who is to be "taught," as an authority figure, or as a long lost sexual object. For these reasons, once therapy has ended, breaking off the relationship with the therapist may be difficult (Knight, 2004).

Adapting Therapy to Middle-Aged and Older Persons' Needs

Recognizing and handling these feelings require that goals for therapy must be set and adhered to in light of the client's needs, abilities, and resources, but with a large measure of empathy for both the physical and the interpersonal losses the older person may have experienced (Knight, 2004). Respecting persons *as individuals,* encouraging independent decision making, and having a knowledge of community resources are also important. Ultimately, the individual's dignity and self-respect must be preserved throughout the course of therapy. These factors are especially important given the suspicion and distrust with which some older clients may approach therapy. Many elderly people prefer to help themselves rather than turn to others, based in a work ethic that emphasizes independence at all costs (Knight, 2004). In some cases, changing the environment in which the older person lives, rather than changing the older person per se, can be just as helpful and less disruptive, as can providing information and education. In some cases then, there is wisdom in adhering to the notion that " If it ain't broke, don't try to fix it."

It may also be that middle-aged and older persons do not think in psychological terms, preferring to see matters in terms of a physical illness or as a consequence of normal aging. This may be why families do not seek professional help for a family member who may be suffering from some form of dementia (Pollitt et al., 1989). In seeking help for mental health difficulties, one **first** must label a problem as psychological, **second** the problem's severity must be evaluated, **third**, the decision that professional is help is appropriate must be made, **fourth**, one must decide to seek that help, assum-

Table 11-2

Guidelines for Psychological Practice with Older Adults

In 2003, the American Psychological Association developed guidelines defining the standards of competence for those psychologists engaged in clinical work with older adults, in an effort to improve the quality of mental health services offered to such persons. These guidelines encompassed the following issues:

1. Attitudes toward providing professional help: staying within one's own scope of competence; making referrals when necessary; recognizing the impact of ageistic attitudes on one's assessment and treatment of an older client; getting necessary consultation about such issues.

2. Developing knowledge about: the biological, health-related, and psychosocial aspects of aging; theory and research in aging; diversity issues (race, gender, ethnicity, sexual orientation, disability status, urban/rural residence).

3. Developing knowledge about: cognitive changes with aging; problems in everyday living; accommodating assessment instruments for use with older clients; developing skills in cognitive screening and functional assessment.

4. Developing knowledge about: current theory, research and practice regarding methods of intervention with older adults and their efficacy; adapting interventions for use with older persons; providing services in setting particular to older adults' everyday lives; using health promotion and preventative interventions; proving consultant services to older adults, their families, and other health care professionals; being aware of the legal and ethical issues in providing services to older adults.

5. Continuing to educate professionals regarding developments in theory, research, and practice with older adults via continuing education, training, supervision, and consultation.

Source: Guidelines for Psychological Practice with Older Adults, *American Psychologist, 2004, 59,* 236-260; Karel et al. (2009), Attitude, knowledge, and skill competencies for practice in professional geropsychology: Implications for training and building a geropsychology workforce. *Training and Education in Professional Psychology, 4,* 75-84.

ing it is available, and **fifth,** a specific mental health professional must be selected (Hayslip et al., 2011; Knight, 2004). Table 11-3 summarizes the barriers to mental health services we have discussed.

In an influential paper on therapy and aging, Gottesman, Quarterman and Cohn (1973) note that with older persons, one's choice of treatment should **always** involve (a) the **capacities** (physical, emotional, cognitive) of the elderly individual, (b) **societal demands** regarding "appropriate" behavior for the aged, (c) **expectations of significant others,**

and (d) what the elderly person expects of **himself/herself.** Not only are these issues for elderly people, but they are also important concerns for adults of all ages.

More recently, Knight (2004) has advocated a **Contextual, Cohort-Based, Maturity, Specific Challenge Model** to understand mental illness and its treatment among older adults. This model argues that older adults are **more mature** (e.g., they are more cognitively and emotionally complex; they have more life experience) than younger adults, but

Table 11-3

Barriers to the Use of Mental Health Services by Older Adults

Internal	External
Therapist ageistic biases	Lack of coordination and timely referrals
Countertransference	Lack of transportation
Stereotyping of older persons	Costly/poorly reimbursed
Older persons are not psychologically minded	Large patient loads
Self-help mentality of older persons	Poorly designed services
Therapist transference	Poorly trained staff
Stigma of getting help	Emphasis upon age-related problems
Lack of knowledge	
Fear of being judged as mentally ill	

Sources: Pepin, Segal & Coolidge (2009), Hayslip et al. (2010).

are also likely to be dealing with **more difficult challenges** (disability, chronic illness, grief, caregiving demands). That they are members of a **different cohort** (see Chapter 1) requires that therapy be designed with their values, life experiences and historically based attitudes toward mental health care in mind (see Currin, Hayslip, Schneider, & Kooken, 1998). Moreover, such help can be offered in a **variety of contexts** (age-segregated communities, senior centers, medical settings, nursing homes, senior service and recreation centers).

Thinking about how to conduct therapy with older persons as well as those middle-aged persons soon to be old (one can join the American Association of Retired Persons at age 50!) requires sensitivity to a number of issues (see Knight, 2004), and results in the necessity to *adapt* therapy in several ways in working with middle-aged and older persons. Indeed, the "client" may be both the middle-aged child *and* the adult parent, as in the case of difficulties in caregiving. Thus, relationship issues should be the focus of therapy, rather than seeing the problem as lying within the older person, i.e., that he or she is difficult to care for.

Among the important adaptations that may be necessary with older clients are: slowing the pace of therapy; recognizing older persons' difficulties in processing information and their particular memory failures (see Chapter 3); acknowledging that they may have developed coping skills that are effective; and realizing that they may have greater expertise and knowledge about relationships (see Chapter 6). Likewise, older adults may be more emotionally complex, have greater crystallized skills, and be more amenable to monitoring and regulating extreme emotions that might interfere with the course of therapy (Knight, 2004). Moreover, as middle-aged and older persons are members of a different birth cohort, they may be less highly educated (generally and with regard to their knowledge of therapy), use different words to express themselves, and have values about issues relevant to getting professional help (that men and women are/are not different, that women should get married and have children versus pursuing a career, that divorce is disgraceful, that one's emotions at a loved one's death should be private, that one should be able to fend for himself/herself when things get tough) that may differ from persons born at a different historical time (see Knight, 2004). The older person's cultural values should be respected as well in assessing and treating mental illness (Woods & Laidlaw, 2010).

The therapist should also understand the social context that defines the lives of many middle-aged and older persons. For example, an older client may be retired, living on a fixed income, and dependent upon Medicare or Medicaid. That person may be a victim of ageist attitudes regarding Alzheimer's disease or older persons' sexuality, or have a real history of being discriminated against because of age, illness, or disability. That person's everyday life is likely to be defined by interactions with service providers and other middle-aged and older adults (Knight, 2004). Therapists who can work effectively with middle-aged and older persons should also be knowledgeable about the array of social and medical services available to older persons, be capable of making informed, timely and effective referrals, and be prepared to act as an advocate and caseworker for the older client if necessary to ensure that this person gets the needed help.

Comparatively recently, the needs of older persons residing in long-term care (LTC) institutions, i.e., nursing homes, have begun to be addressed on a larger scale than in the past (see Zarit & Zarit, 2007). Delineating the psychotherapeutic skills practitioners need to help persons receiving LTC, understanding healthcare policy in light of such persons needs, and stimulating research on psychotherapy in LTC environments have been discussed by many with the goal of improving the quality of care such persons receive (Burns, 2008; Powers, 2008a, 2008b).

Check Your Learning 11-1

Define the following terms and concepts:

External barriers
Internal barriers
Transference
Countertransference

- What barriers to mental health care for older persons must be overcome?

- Why is the distinction between transference and countertransference important in working with older clients?

- Why are cohort effects in demands for mental health services important?

- By what process do adults come to use the services of a mental health professional?

- What adaptations to therapy are necessary with older clients?

- What is the Contextual, Cohort-Based, Maturity, Specific Challenge Model of mental illness and its treatment? Why is it helpful?

- In what ways does Medicare support mental health treatment with older adults?

- What skills should professionals have who treat older adults and their families?

Evidence-Based Research on Therapy in Later Life

Before we present specific forms of therapy that may be used with adults and older persons, it is important to realize that our views about therapy in adulthood, and especially in later life, are now being driven by evidence-based research. It examines many studies, (a **meta-analysis**) versus a single study or two, to determine whether persons who receive help are better off than those who do not or whether one form of therapy is more effective than another. This work, stressing the results of empirical research rather than clinically based work, suggests that such techniques as relaxation training, CBT, supportive (psychoeducational programs, social support), cognitive therapy, and behavioral interventions to improve caregiver problem solving are each potentially helpful in treating such problems as insomnia, caregiver distress, anxiety, behavioral disturbances in persons with dementia, and depression (Gatz, 2007; Gallagher-Thompson & Coon, 2007; Logsdon & Teri, 2007; McCurry et al., 2007; Scogin & Yon, 2006; Sorell et al, 2007). Not only should **evidence-based findings** help to guide one's choice of therapy, but it is also important to realize that private health insurance companies and Medicare utilize such findings in determining for what kinds of help they will pay a health/ mental health care provider.

Approaches to Therapy and Counseling with Adults

Freud contended that middle-aged and older adults were not good candidates for therapy.

> On the one hand, near or above the fifties the elasticity of the mental processes, on which the treatment depends, is as a rule lacking— older people are no longer educable—and, on the other hand, the mass of material to be dealth with would prolong the duration of the treatment indefinitely. (Freud, 1924, pp. 258-259)

Yet, because age fails to predict who can be helped, for all adults, the therapist should be primarily concerned with improving the **quality** of life, not necessarily just its quantity. More specific goals in therapy with adults and older persons are: (1) insight into one's behavior, (2) symptom relief, (3) enhancing coping skills in light of one's life situation, (4) improving the ability to make independent decisions, (5) facilitating activity and independence, (6) becoming more self-accepting, and (7) improving interpersonal relationships. These are goals for adults of **all** ages! Each goal will be more or less important depending on the individual's physical health, strengths, and resources, as well as the therapist's own biases.

Relying on a single approach virtually guarantees an unsatisfying helping experience for *both* the counselor and the client. Wherever possible however, try to put the treatment of adults who vary in age into an adult developmental perspective. That is, therapy with adults of all ages shares many common features. As many therapies are closely derived from a more basic theory of personality, we recommend re-reading Chapter 6 on Personality Development. Doing so will enable you to achieve a fuller understanding of the relationship between personality theory and psychotherapy/counseling in adult-

hood. Moreover, try to think in terms of the therapeutic *options* open to the aged person in distress. The array of counseling and intervention approaches used with aged persons is presented in Table 11-4.

Individual Psychotherapy—Psychoanalysis

Psychoanalysis (Freud, 1924) is based on the assumption that through insight (aided by the guidance of a therapist) one may come to grips with troublesome emotions that have been repressed via unconscious defense mechanisms. While such defenses ordinarily operate very efficiently, a breakdown in one's defenses leads to anxiety. Anxiety is a sign that the control exercised by the ego (being reality-oriented) over both the id (composed of instincts, wishes, drives) and the superego (referring to one's morals, ideals) is weakening. Through free association, such conflicts between the ego, id, and superego, normally unconscious, are made conscious, and their meaning interpreted to the client by the therapist (see Hall & Lindzey, 1985).

Unfortunately, Freud saw few older clients (even clients in their 40s and 50s), and was quite skeptical about his technique's success with elderly persons. He assumed that the effort required to change persons whose defenses had been overused for years was not worth the limited time left to them. However, changes in technique have allowed the therapist to be more supportive and make use of the aged person's defense mechanisms. The older person's needs to be dependent on the therapist, i.e., transference, would instead be encouraged (Knight, 2004; Semel, 1996).

Instead of classical psychoanalysis, which requires insight into one's own dynamics and is often quite lengthy, some now advocate brief psychoanalytic therapy with the aged, where more realistic goals of reducing anxiety and restoring the person to a more functional state can be achieved (Silberschatz & Curtis, 1991), termed **time-limited** psychodynamic therapy (Nordus & Nielsen, 1999). Rather than spend years in therapy, clients spend 3-4 months and focus on improving interpersonal relationships and skills that affect them on a daily basis, rather than achieving "insight" into long-held,

Table 11-4

Counseling Strategies with Older Persons

Approach	Examples	Domains of Use	Advantages	Disadvantages
Psychoanalytic	Time-limited therapy Classical psychoanalysis	Emotional and behavioral difficulties	Helpful in some cases, especially if goals are short-term in nature	Difficult to document objectively; can be very long; only certain aged can benefit
Cognitive	Alter thinking strategies and problem solving/ coping skills	Adjustment to life change, stress reduction, cognitive change	Easily used by most older persons	Real-life environment may not support new thinking skills; not all aged can benefit
Behavioral	Define undesirable and desirable behavior in behavioral terms; reinforce desired behavior; withdraw reinforcers from undesired behavior	All types of general behavioral problems	Easily learned; outcomes timelyif used correctly	Does not address itself to the social context that influences behaviors, ethical concerns
Family	Alter patterns of communication and behavior within the family	All types of family dysfunction	Can be used with a variety of family-related problems (marital, caregiving)	Difficult to document
Group	Small group dynamics are used to help persons profit from feedback from others facing similar difficulties	Help persons deal with emotional, behavioral, and interpersonal difficulties in the context of a group setting	Builds on the older person's dependency needs; creates sense of safety; can be issue-oriented	Benefits difficult to document; only certain aged can benefit

repressed feelings and experiences. Pathogenic (abnormal, destructive) beliefs about oneself rooted in one's childhood can instead be dealt with through therapy by clearly defining goals for the client. As middle-aged and older clients may believe that they are too old to change or simply unworthy of help, they may "test" the therapist by being hostile, late for appointments, arguing with the therapist, or being passive. All of these maneuvers are designed to find out if the painfully destructive beliefs about oneself formed in childhood need to be maintained, or whether they can be challenged. They should *not* be interpreted as evidence for the adult's rigidity or resistance to therapy—"a lost cause."

An interesting theme that emerges in time-limited therapy with adults is **survivor guilt** (Silberschatz & Curtis, 1991). As adults grow older and witness the physical decline and death of friends and family, they become increasingly prone to experience guilt over having outlived these loved ones. Survivor guilt may even explain why some adults allow themselves to be abused at the hands of their grandchildren or children (see Chapters 4 and 5). Because they feel guilty about past failures as parents, or because they outlived a spouse, they may feel that they "deserve" to be abused. Ironically, it is because they have limited time left to live that enables many adults to be able to work through trauma. The older client has less time to waste, and is more willing to use this time wisely in therapy (Silberschatz & Curtis, 1991). Reports of classic psychoanalysis are rare with older clients (see Semel, 1996), and they are often poorly designed and documented. However, recent well-designed studies indicate that psychoanalytic therapy can be quite helpful, leading to less anxiety, less depression, greater self-esteem, and more functional behavior (see Cohler, 1998; Semel, 1996). Good candidates for psychanalysis should have some insight into their own unconscious motives, be committed to changing, be able to tolerate very strong emotions, and have had some success in relating to others (Myers, 1991). Certainly, psychoanalysis should not be dismissed, but perhaps reserved for highly verbal, insightful older clients, and realistically, classical psychoanalysis is rarely practiced with older persons.

Life Review Therapy

An extension of psychoanalytic thought is to be found in life review therapy (see Knight, 2004). Life review therapy is more extensive than a simple recall of the past, although reminiscence is important in this approach (Haight & Haight, 2007). Obtaining an extensive autobiography from the elderly person is important, allowing the elder the opportunity to put his life in order. The use of music, art, photographs, or even an actual trip to a memorable place in one's past can help clients focus on themselves. Key elements in life review therapy are: (1) it is **structured** to guide persons through memories of their lives, (2) **duration** - six to eight 1-hour sessions seem to be adequate for most older persons, (3) **individuality**- the life review reflects a unique relationship between the therapeutic listener and a life reviewer, and (4) **evaluation-** the life reviewer evaluates why life was lived in the way it was, and this is key to acceptance (Haight & Haight, 2007). Constructing one's genealogy or family tree can also bring the positive and negative aspects of the past to the present. Resolving internal conflicts, improving relationships with one's family, making decisions about success and failure, resolving guilt, clarifying one's own

values, and simply "getting out" one's feelings about painful past experiences are all benefits of the life review (Knight, 2004), which often accompanies grief over a loved one's death. Life review therapy may be successfully conducted individually or in a group setting. However, the life review can be a frustrating, painful experience for many aged, who require emotional support from a counselor in order to deal with the by-products of this process, and the contents of life review can be negative (Knight, 2004). Many older persons have led hard, frustrating lives that forced them to make choices that they regretted (e.g., not finishing high school). Many lack someone to confide in, with whom such confidences may be shared.

Group Therapy

The distinguishing feature of group therapy with aged persons is that dependency needs can be used to their best advantage (Spayd & Smyer, 1996). As many older persons are isolated, group therapy may be especially suited to them. It may also be quite helpful for adult caregivers, who often must shoulder the burden of caring for an ill or dying family member (Waters, 1995). In many cases, simply being with others makes one feel safe. Problems, fears, and hidden emotions can be shared with others. These may range from relationship difficulties, to illness, retirement, or simply feeling alone or less worthy. Face-to-face contact, touching another person, and sharing experiences are quite important to many middle-aged and older adults, in contrast to younger adults, for whom making and breaking relationships is more common and for whom touching is less comforting. Group therapy for younger people seems to be a bit more impersonal or less intimate.

Group therapy can take many forms, ranging from issue-oriented (life event) discussion groups to groups designed to stimulate interaction among group members (Zarit & Zarit, 2007). Groups can also be designed to promote independence and a positive sense of self. Common themes often include social losses, independence, illness, sensory loss, death, caregiving, or loneliness (Spayd & Smyer, 1996). Groups are typically short-term (when used within the institution) and informal in nature. They may be self-help, educational in nature, or more formally therapeutic. Both self-help and educational groups may not carry the stigma of being "in therapy." Group therapy is often used in a variety of settings in combination with art therapy, dance therapy, or music therapy for elderly persons, and is especially appropriate for older persons living in long-term care environments (Spayd & Smyer, 1996).

Recent empirical analyses of the impact of group therapy on caregiver well-being and burden suggest that while group interventions are not very effective in this regard, they may be very helpful in alleviating care receiver symptoms via changing the interaction of caregiver and care receiver (Sorensen et al., 2002).

In working with older adults in a group (or individual) setting, one needs to realize that physical or sensory losses may dictate slower paced and shorter counseling sessions (Knight, 2004). Moreover, using properly designed written materials (large, clear, bold print, nonglare paper) and having adequate lighting are very important. Sessions must be held at locations that are easily accessible for those who have difficulty walking. Conducting sessions in areas that lack background noises that would interfere with hearing is also essential. Groups may also need to be smaller to lessen the elder's confusion and fatigue, and plans need to be made with each group member as to what he/she will do when the group ends. Group work may not be advisable for older adults who are severely disturbed, aggressive, extremely introverted, or disoriented (Spayd & Smyer, 1996).

Family Therapy

Family therapy can also help older persons whose difficulties are communicative in nature (Qualls, 1999; Yorgason, Miller, & White, 2009). Family therapy can aid in adjustment to roles such as retirement or grandparenthood. It can help resolve problems accompanying caring for an ill spouse, institutionalizing of one's parent(s) or spouse, or conflicts arising when an older parent is being cared for at home by a middle-aged child.

Each family member can be involved in setting up clear expectations for behavior, improving communication, lessening distrust and guilt, or dealing with hostility and anxiety. Family therapy can help couples reestablish intimacy, learn to enjoy life without being preoccupied with illness, enable them to nurture and let go of children, and help them grieve over losses of loved ones. Family therapy is also appropriate in dealing with parent-child conflicts elicited by the parent's remarriage after the divorce or death of a spouse, struggles for power within the home, restrictions on the aged person brought about by ill health, or by the divorce of an adult child. In these cases, the major benefits of family therapy are allowing each person to express his or her own feelings, explore options, and increase sensitivity to others' points of view. A **family systems** approach now characterizes views about the family (Qualls, 1999) where problems are understood in terms of **patterns of family interaction**. In dealing with families, both parents and children need to be understood as developing individuals. However, interactions among dyads in the family, e.g., parent-child, sibling-sibling, husband-wife, each of which is also changing, are also important in understanding how families cope with life transitions or crisis. It is for this reason that family therapy must encompass *all* members of both the nuclear and extended family. For example, the family therapist might relabel a problem in terms of the *relationship* rather than the characteristics of specific individuals (Qualls, 1999).

Family Therapy and Psychological Interventions with Caregivers

Zarit and Zarit (2007), Sorenson, King, and Pinquart (2007) and Knight, Kaskie, Shurgot, and Dave (2006) have all discussed the potential of family therapy to solve a number of problems and choices families with older members often face, such as deciding about whether to institutionalize an elderly parent, or selecting alternatives to institutionalization, such as day care or home care. Family therapy can help children cope with the terminal illness of an older family member, or help them care for a parent who has been diagnosed with

Alzheimer's disease (see Chapter 10). For example, Knight (2004) suggests that giving information, active problem solving, support and one-on-one counseling can help families make decisions about caring for a family member with dementia. When feelings of isolation and burden can be dealt with, the stress of coping with the death of a loved one or in caring for a family member who has Alzheimer's disease can be relieved. Moreover, feelings of guilt that often accompany grief over the decision to institutionalize an older parent can be lessened, leaving the family intact (Aneshensel, Pearlin, Mullan, Zarit & Whitlatch, 1995). If properly handled, such issues can actually *strengthen* the family's feelings of closeness, love, and interdependence (see Table 11-5). Moreover, the institutionalized elder need not give up control over his/her life, yet can accept help from others without feeling dependent upon them. Thus, families can avoid feeling overwhelmed by guilt, anger, or a sense of hopelessness or helplessness. In in-depth discussion of the assessment of family caregivers as well as interventions with them, paralleling the above, can be found in Qualls & Zarit (2009).

Among the interventions that can be helpful to family caregivers are those emphasizing relaxation, the purposeful scheduling of pleasant and enjoyable activities and events, changing the manner in which the caregiver appraises the caregiving situation, developing new caregiving skills, and getting involved in a support group (which may or may not be equally helpful for all caregivers) (see Knight, 2004). In some cases, when the caregiver's distress is severe, and he or she is manifesting signs of depression or anxiety that interfere with not only caregiving, but the caregiver's own physical and mental well-being, one-on-one psychotherapy may be helpful (Knight, 2004). A particular problem arises when the caregiver and care recipient do not agree on the nature of the difficulties experienced in provided care, to the detriment of the care provider (Lyons, Zarit, Sayer, & Whitlatch, 2002).

Formal research with caregiver interventions has yielded somewhat disappointing results. For example, a series of caregiver interventions encompassed by the **REACH** study (Resources for Enhancing Alzheimer's Caregivers' Health) study (Gitlin et al., 2003; Schulz et al., 2003) found mild positive benefits of psychological interventions on caregiver burden and caregiver depression across multiple sites in the United States. It compared several different types of interventions (psychoeducational and skill-based training, individual information and support, group and family systems therapy, home-based environmental interventions, automated telecare communication system) with one another and against a control group (those not receiving any intervention), focusing upon Alzheimer's caregivers. Some caregivers (women, those who were less highly educated) benefited more than others, and results for some sites were more positive than for others. A recent meta-analysis (an analysis of the pattern of findings of different research projects) of caregiver intervention studies also found mild, though consistent effects for psychoeducational and psychotherapeutic interventions with caregivers, with positive benefits being smallest for Alzheimer's caregivers (Sorensen, Pinquart, Habil, & Duberstein, 2002; Sorenson, King, & Pinquart, 2007).

In evaluating the impact of interventions with caregivers, it is important to assess not only measured effects (e.g., changes in test scores), but also **clinically meaningful outcomes**, such as recognizing the need to institutionalize a family member when one can no longer carry on, being able to competently provide care for a longer period of time, improvements in one's mood (anger, depression), lowered blood pressure, greater caregiver self-efficacy/self-confidence, or improvements in everyday functioning among those receiving care (Schulz et al., 2002).

Check Your Learning 11-2

Define the following terms and concepts:

Time-limited therapy
Survivor guilt
Life review

Table 11-5

Common Caregiver Concerns Amenable to Family Therapy

Improving Coping Skills

Time management: Includes problems of the caregiver not having enough time for personal activities. Problems inferring an inability to manage time or to be organized also belong here.
Dealing with stress: Includes problems regarding coping with stress and anxiety, especially from caregiving.
Other coping mechanisms: Includes problems that emphasize the caregiver's realization of the need to develop/use various coping mechanisms such as forbearance, assertiveness, sharing feelings and concerns over caregiving with others, enhancing personal control, and modeling peers.

Family Issues

Regarding husband: Includes problems regarding such concerns as lack of time to spend with husband, motivating him to become more involved in caregiving and the impact of caregiving on marriage.
Regarding siblings: Includes problems having to do with both getting siblings to assume more responsibility in caregiving and the caregiver's feelings of anger and resentment toward siblings.
Regarding caregiver's children: Includes problems focused on the impact or issues that caregiving has raised for the caregiver's children.

Responding to the Older Person's Care Needs

Emotional and behavioral problems: Includes problems involving issues that are primarily psychological or behavioral in nature, such as dealing with the older person's affect, cognitive problems, motivation, involvement in daily living tasks, and relationships with people other than the caregiver.
Physical safety: Includes problems focused on the older person's physical well-being and overall safety such as handling medical emergencies, concern over the older person's physical limitations, and cognitive difficulties that might prove hazardous in everyday life.
Legal and financial concerns: Includes problems involving the older person's legal and financial affairs.

Quality of Relationship with Older Adult

Includes problems regarding the caregiver's feelings toward older care recipient, the wish to avoid conflict, the older person's inability to respond to the caregiver's needs, being the central figure in the older adult's life, and having quality communication with the older person.

Eliciting Formal and Informal Support

Includes problems involving the caregiver's recognition of the need for or attempt to get assistance with caregiving duties from sources including relatives other than spouse, respite services, and community services.

Guilt and Feelings of Inadequacy

Guilt: Includes problems regarding any expression of guilt whatsoever by the caregiver.
Feelings of inadequacy: Includes problems over the caregiver's feelings relating to low self-esteem, lack of confidence, and lack of self-acceptance.
Long-term planning: Includes problems focused on planning for an older person's future, including such issues as considering or applying for nursing home care, and discussions with the elder or other family members about future caregiving arrangements, wills, powers of attorney, and funeral planning.

Sources: Smith et al. (1991), LoboPrabbu, Molinari, & Lomax (2007), Fingerman et al. (2009).

Family system
Evidence-based research
Reminiscence
Group therapy
Family therapy
REACH study

• What factors influence the effectiveness of therapy with adults and older persons?

• What is survivor guilt? Why is it important?

• For what types of difficulties is group therapy or family therapy appropriate?

• How can caregivers be helped via family therapy and other forms of intervention?

• What is evidence-based research? Why is it important regarding therapy with adults and older persons?

Behavioral Interventions

Behavior therapy is most often used in an institutional, inpatient setting, where control over reinforcers (rewards) and those behaviors one wants to change is more likely. According to this approach, application of a behavioral strategy requires three primary tasks be carried out: (1) a definition and assessment prior to intervention of the desired **target behavior**; (2) the identification of a **reinforcer**, defined as a stimulus whose impact makes the desired behavior **more frequent** or of **longer duration**, noting that this reinforcer may be self-administered or administered by the therapist; and

(3) the establishment of specific **behavior-reinforcer contingencies**.

Positive reinforcing stimuli, leading to pleasurable events, **negative reinforcing** stimuli, which provide relief from aversive events, or **punishing** stimuli, which decrease the frequency of a behavior by providing unpleasant consequences, may all be used for the purpose of defining such contingencies, though punishing stimuli should be used as a last resort. A variation on this approach is the **token economy**, where patients can earn tokens for desired behaviors, which can be later exchanged for appropriate rewards (Fisher, Harsen, & Hayden, 2000; Zarit & Zarit, 2007). Another technique that can be used by the behavior modifier involves positively reinforcing a behavior which **competes** with the unwanted target behavior (e.g., rewarding self-care behaviors that compete with aggressive behaviors). **Contracting** is a form of behavior modification that deserves mention. In contracting, the client and therapist arrive at a mutually agreed upon, clearly specified goal. Being able to jointly define this goal may in itself promote a sense of control and independence for some elderly persons. Of all the forms of intervention with older persons we discuss, behavior therapy is perhaps easiest to document and there is ample, well-designed research to support its efficacy in dealing with a variety of behavior problems, (Fisher, Harsen, & Hayden, 2000; Zeiss & Steffen, 1996). For example, overly dependent interactions with other elderly persons as well as with nursing home staff, incontinence, assertive behavior, withdrawal, inappropriate sexual behavior, wandering, anxiety, and self-care can all be treated behaviorally (Smyer et al., 1990). Many of these behaviors are a consequence of being institutionalized and have been termed **excess disabilities** (Kahn & Miller, 1978).

Behavioral technology with younger and older people has a number of advantages. It can be readily measured and its effects easily assessed, goals can be objectively defined, and it can be carried out and understood by staff if they are trained in its use (Zeiss & Steffen, 1996). Relative to drug therapy and aversive behavioral interventions (e.g., time out procedures), positive behavioral interventions, such as reinforcing the individual if an inappropriate behavior has not occurred, are more acceptable to older persons (Burgio & Sinnott, 1990). Behavior therapy can also be tailored to the individual patient, and behavioral procedures are relatively brief and economical. However, it requires a great deal of expertise to use effectively, and its use can create some ethical questions, particularly when it is used with impaired, institutionalized, or isolated older adults. Intervention for intervention's sake is not always in the older person's best interests. It may be more feasible to change the environment per se, or to leave things as they are. These concerns are very important if one is unsure of the consequences of a given treatment.

Cognitive Behavior Therapy

Closely related to behavioral approaches is cognitive behavior therapy (e.g., Meichenbaum, 1989). In general cognitive behavior therapists believe that the way a person **thinks** largely determines the way he or she feels. In other words, thought causes emotional response. **Cognitive behavior therapy (CBT)** is an attempt to help the client change his or her maladaptive thinking habits to relieve emotional disturbances such as depression, anger, and anxiety. Ellis (1962) views this process in an **A-B-C** fashion. A is designated as the event that the client thinks is causing the anxiety, depression, etc. The emotional disturbance lies at point C. A client might believe that, for example, her depression (C) is being caused by her getting old (A). Ellis insists that age (A) is not causing the depression (C). Instead,

the depression (C) is attributed, not to aging (A), but to the woman's **belief** (B) about her own aging; this belief about aging is the culprit. In this case, the woman might erroneously believe that being old means that she is a person unworthy of respect or love. Elderly persons, perhaps lacking realistic feedback about themselves from others, often make "thinking errors" that are not realistic (Hayslip & Caraway, 1989). For example, irrational assumptions about one's age or about the loss of skills may lead to feelings of self-depreciation in many aged persons. These feelings can lead to anger, guilt, and depression.

Cognitive techniques instruct the elder to substitute more rational thoughts for these irrational ones and have been discussed in detail by Laidlaw (2006). Laidlaw stresses the advantages of CBT: (1) CBT focuses on "**the here and now,**" (2) CBT develops **practical problem solving skills,** (3) CBT sessions are **structured,** (4) CBT emphasizes **self-monitoring**—individuals are taught to recognize maladaptive thinking and develop techniques to change, (5) CBT uses a **psycho-educational approach** emphasizing the connections between thoughts, mood, and behavior in understanding one's problems and ways of changing, and (6) CBT is **goal-oriented** and challenges negative beliefs about aging.

Laidlaw, Thompson, Dick-Siskin, and Gallagher-Thompson (2003), taking an evidence-based approach (see page 253), have reviewed the extensive literature on CBT with older persons. They have found ample evidence to support its use in treating older persons who are depressed (especially if combined with drug therapy for those who depression is biologically based; see Chapter 10), those who are anxious or suffering from panic attacks, and those who are having difficulty sleeping (see also Knight et al., 2006). Cognitive behavioral approaches to therapy have been successfully used to treat a variety of cognitive and emotional problems in the aged, i.e., memory loss, response slowness (Laidlaw et al., 2003). Moreover, CBT is effective in treating anxiety and depression in older adults (Crowther, Scogin, & Norton, 2010; Moss

& Scogin, 2008; Stanley et al., 2009) as well as depression/caregiver burden (Martire et al., 2010).

While the similarities outweigh the differences in cognitive therapy with younger versus older adults, there are a few aspects of cognitive behavioral therapy that are unique to older adults (Laidlaw, 2006; Laidlaw et al., 2003). For example, the therapist must be more flexible, special attention should be given to cohort differences in education and interests, an assessment of one's physical history must be made, and a conference with the client's physician and family should be arranged. In addition, the therapist may have to be more active with older clients, keeping them focused on the issue at hand, and should expect the pace of therapy to be slower, due to fatigue or resistance in giving up long-held assumptions about oneself or others.

As the name suggests, CBT uses *both* cognitive and behavioral approaches to treat the client. CBT seems to work best with people who experience depression that is **exogenous**—a reaction to recent stress—versus depression that is **endogenous**—depression that is lifelong; even persons with mild dementia can benefit (Laidlaw, 2006; Laidlaw et al., 2003)

Interpersonal Psychotherapy

A recent approach to working with older persons is termed **interpersonal psychotherapy** (Hindrichsen, 2006; Hindrichsen & Clougherty, 2007), and it focuses on relationships with others, both at present and in the past (as when a loved one has died). It is short term, and goal-oriented, where the therapist desires to provide the person with a sense of mastery over his or her role, lessen isolation from others, foster a sense of group belonging, and enable the person to find new meaning in life. All of these goals are especially important when the older person's convoy of support (see Chapters 4 and 5) has deteriorated due to death or relocation. **Interpersonal therapy** (see Box A) assumes that all problems can be understood in terms of interpersonal relationships, and thus in contrast to analytic therapy, makes no assumption about an underlying cause for depression or anxiety (Hindrichsen, 2006). In therapy, techniques such as reassurance,

clarifying one's emotional state, improving communication skills, and the clarification/testing of the patient's perceptions of relationships with others are all used. The focus is on the "here and now." Interpersonal therapy is very effective in treating depression as well as preventing its reoccurrence (Miller et al., 2001, 2003), in helping elderly persons adapt to life transitions such as caregiving or retirement, lessening difficulties in grieving (see Chapter 12), treating anxiety (Wetherell, Gatz, & Craske, 2003), and resolving interpersonal conflicts (Knight et al., 2006).

Specialized Treatments for the Older Adult

Reality Orientation

Reality orientation (RO) stresses the lessening of confusion/disorientation (primarily within the institution), and may be highly structured, stressing orientation to time, place, and person. The impact of RO is equivocal, though recent research is more positive in this respect, at least in demonstrating the short-term effectiveness of reality orientation (Spector, Davies, Woods, & Orrell, 2001). While RO may temporarily improve orientation to time and place, more permanent, "deeper" changes in mood and cognitive status do not necessarily follow. The use of RO should be flexible and probably limited to those aged who are not profoundly deteriorated (Zarit & Zarit, 2007). The less disoriented patient may become hostile if needlessly exposed to RO, requiring more staff time and effort to deal with this anger (Storandt, 1983).

Environmental Change

A number of what may be termed **environmental changes** may also be appropriate and helpful in some situations (Day, Carreon, & Stump, 2000; Knight, 2004; Waters, 1995). Many of these changes can be especially helpful for persons suffering from dementia (Day et al., 2000; Knight et al., 2006). Simply clarifying or highlighting (making more discriminable) aspects of the environment may reduce anxiety, disorientation, and confusion in elderly people suffering from Alzheimer's disease. Moreover, there are many positive benefits to older

Box A

Interpersonal Therapy and Problem-Solving Therapy

In **Interpersonal therapy** (IPT), changing the nature of one's interactions with others and acquiring better communication skills in the context of treating depression are key elements. IPT is (1) time-limited, (2) focuses upon one or two problem areas that the client has identified as problems, (3) is directed to current rather than remote relationships, (4) focuses on interpersonal rather than intrapersonal issues, and importantly, (5) changes the ways in which persons deal with problematic interpersonal issues.

IPT begins by identifying the client's depression symptoms. It allows the patient to adopt "the sick role," evaluates the need for medication in treatment, and most important, helps the client understand the relationship between the depression and the interproblems that are being experienced by the person. IPT is next explained and treatment goals are outlined. Problem areas (grief, role disputes, role transitions) and the client's interpersonal deficits, including isolation from others, are discussed. Developing a support system, learning new interpersonal skills, and forming new relationships in light of one's acquired understandings are stressed in IPT. Finally, the therapist terminates the therapeutic relationship, being sure to acknowledge the loss the client is experiencing and stressing that the person is now competent and able to function independently of the therapist.

The evidence for the effectiveness of IPT on depression is substantial. It "fits" older adults well and is acceptable to them. Whether it is effective for older adults who are severely depressed remains to be seen.

Closely related to IPT in its practical and short-term nature is **Problem-solving therapy** (PST), whose primary focus is mobilizing the client's resources, to deal with both everyday difficulties and major life transitions. The goal is to develop effective problem-solving skills that either do not exist or are not being used because of poor self-efficacy. In PST, problems are identified and decision-making strategies developed to meet the client's goals. Persons are aided in implementing the solutions they have developed in concert with the therapist, relying upon past successes to facilitate the acquisition of new skills.

Sources: Arean & Huh (2006), Hindrichsen & Cloughtery (2007).

people such as improved physical health, morale, and enhanced self-esteem, when they are given control over certain aspects of their everyday environment (Schulz & Hanusa, 1978; Winningham & Pike, 2007). For example, being able to set one's own visiting hours, being able to have plants in one's room, and being able to choose from a variety of foods for dinner can all be quite beneficial to persons who are institutionalized or lack control over their everyday lives (Hayslip & Caraway, 1989). While these approaches would certainly not seem to be "therapy" in a traditional sense, they do possess a great deal of promise in this regard as "envi-ronmental" approaches to treatment, especially for persons with dementia, who are not likely candidates for other forms of therapy and intervention (see Table 11-6)

Pet Therapy

Pet therapy is not unique, because it can be used with many individuals, such as abused children, the physically handicapped, or the mentally retarded. However, the therapeutic use of **pets** in the treatment of older persons who are institutionalized or isolated suggests that there are some **short-term** benefits to be gained. For example, persons have

---

Box B

Validation Therapy: Help for Disoriented Older People

Validation therapy was developed by Naomi Feil, a social worker, to help restore some measure of functioning to severely impaired older people. In contrast to reality orientation, whose goal is to keep the disoriented older person attuned to reality—today's date, where one is living, time of day—validation therapy accepts the disoriented older person as he or she is at present (Feil, 2002). Validation also helps us understand the reason behind a disoriented older person's feelings, whether anger, sadness, fear, or happiness.

Feil feels that in the disoriented old, early learned emotional memories replace intellectual thinking, preventing them from functioning in the world as it is now. To validate is to acknowledge the feelings of the old person, who has returned to the past to survive (Feil, 2002). In a sense, the validation therapist helps the old person replace intellect with feelings to restore a sense of self-worth. This enables him or her to reduce the stress of living in a world that may no longer be meaningful, to justify continuing to live and, of course, to feel happier. Validation therapy also enables the helper to become comfortable with the disoriented old.

Instead of labeling as demented those who may appear to be mindlessly preoccupied with past memories or any emotionally significant past experience, validation therapy tries to understand such behavior as a coping mechanism the elder uses to survive—to deal with losses in the face of a limited, or at least emotionally barren, existence. According to Feil, the failure to resolve the past leads to vegetation. However, through validation therapy, the disoriented person can experience resolution.

---

more positive feelings about themselves, increase interaction with others, feel less depressed, and improve their cognitive functioning as a function of animal-assisted therapy (Barker & Wolen, 2008; Morrison, 2007; Richsen, 2010). Not only are dogs, cats, birds (even turtles!) loveable and affectionate, but their care also demands a certain amount of responsibility. This allows one to shift the focus from personal anxieties or dissatisfactions with life to the welfare of an animal who wants and needs love and care. In using pet therapy, the older person may gain a sense of control over his/her own feelings as well as over the immediate situation (Connelly & MacDonald, 1993). Pets can also be used to elicit life history information from the individual that may be of importance, for example, childhood experiences with pets (Brickel, 1984). Such information can therefore be obtained in a nonthreatening way. Feelings about one's past, e.g., life events where a pet was present, or about present feelings of depression can be discussed in a situation where the animal provides a sense of security and both psychological/tactile comfort. Often, caring for a pet may lessen isolation from others; it is very difficult to pout or be grumpy with a loveable dog or cat! Despite its common sense potential to improve depression, the effects of pet therapy are difficult to document. Recent work however, suggests that animal-assisted therapy may have documented benefits for older persons (Barker & Wolen, 2008; Morrison, 2007; Richsen, 2010).

Check Your Learning 11-3

Define the following terms and concepts:

Behavior therapy
Positive reinforcing stimuli
Cognitive therapy
Reality orientation
Pet therapy
Problem-solving therapy

Table 11-6

Suggestions to Enhance the Therapeutic Potential of Dementia Care Environments

- Create a noninstitutional environment (homelike furnishings, personalizing one's room) that promotes positive well-being, especially in dining areas.
- Avoid sensory overload and overstimulation. It increases confusion and agitation, and undermines self-esteem and interactions with others
- Reduce glare, provide more contrast, minimize confusion concerning the perception of depth (use ramps instead of stairs), and provide more overall levels of (bright) light without creating glare.
- Make rooms smaller.
- Separate cognitively unimpaired residents from those with dementia.
- Use covers over panic bars and doorknobs to prevent unwanted exiting the premises.
- Provide access to the outdoors to maintain a homelike environment, accommodate activity, and increase persons' exposure to light and sun.
- Make toilets more visible to reduce incontinence.
- Make bathing less stressful: Provide persons with a choice of a tub bath or shower, give them extra space and provide grab bars to avoid falls and increase a sense of security and privacy. Avoid unfamiliar procedures such as bathtub lifts, specialized tubs, and provide persons with mats, handrails, and adequate light with which to bathe comfortably and safely

Source: Day, Carreon, & Stump (2000). The therapeutic design of environments for people with dementia: A review of the empirical research. *The Gerontologist, 40,* 397-416.

Negative reinforcing stimuli
Contracting
A-B-C paradigm
Environmental change
Interpersonal therapy

- What special considerations underlie behavioral and cognitive therapy with older persons?

- Why could changing one's environment be as effective as changing the person?

- What specialized treatments for older people are available? Are they effective?

- What environmental changes might be helpful for persons with dementia?

Psychopharmacological (Drug) Treatments

While an extensive discussion of drug therapy with adults is beyond our scope, drug treatment with adults has been a clear option in the treatment of such disorders as schizophrenia, anxiety, or depression, and while drug treatment may be risky, it is nevertheless an option for some aged persons (Schneider, 1995). Importantly, the cognitive difficulties experienced by some older persons may interfere with the ability to understand medication information (Brown & Park, 2003), as well as the ability to adhere to a medication prescription regimen (Israel, Morrow, Brewer, & Figueredo, 2006).

Several major categories of drugs have been used with the aged. **Antipsychotic** drugs are commonly used to treat agitation, violent behavior, irrational behavior, and perceptual disturbances (hallucinations) accompanying paranoid state/late life schizophrenia. Side effects often include tremors or agitation. **Major tranquilizers** used to treat psychosis, and with older persons, reduced dosage levels and/or "drug holidays" are recommended. **Antidepressant drugs** often interact with a variety of foods (e.g., cheese, caffeine); **tricyclics** can create many problems, such as arrhythmia, strokes, myocardial infarctions, and tachycardia, for those aged persons with cardiovascular disorders. **Antimanics** (lithium) often produce side effects of nausea, central nervous system toxicity, and confusion. **Antianxiety drugs** (barbiturates) often produce "paradoxical" symptoms (excitement), and other minor tranquilizers can be addictive. A variety of **cognitive-acting** drugs (e.g., hydrergine) are used to reverse cognitive impairment.

Older persons are particularly sensitive to drug effects. Substantial individual differences exist in the response to psychopharmacological agents among older people (Gray & Hayslip, 1990). Haley (1996) emphasizes the importance of the clinician's knowledge about medications that may create problems for older clients, particularly those that produce symptoms such as sedation and delirium. Depression and impaired cognitive functioning are also side effects which can be dangerous to the extent that they may be misdiagnosed. Because older persons are likely to be taking many medications (both prescribed and over the counter drugs) for both medical and psychological illness, the potential for harmful drug interactions is greater.

Consultation with a geriatric physician is especially important (Haley, 1996). An outstanding example of the successful use of drug therapy with older persons is the use of antidepressant medication in concert with cognitive behavior therapy to treat endogenous depression (Blazer, 2002). There is evidence that using drugs such as Aricept and Memantine to treat memory loss associated with Alzheimer's disease may be helpful (Hayslip & Madden, 2005), though their long-term effects have been recently challenged. A recent study (Reynolds & Associates, 2006) even suggests that antidepressant medication may be more effective than therapy in preventing relapses from major depression in older persons.

As Blazer (2002) notes, when treating older adults pharmacologically, taking a thorough drug history, specifically targeting symptoms to be treated, administering starting doses at least a third to half as strong as the suggested adult dose, and being very clear with the patient, family, and friends regarding the drug regimen are all quite desirable. This would suggest that such persons are educated about what drugs to take, in what doses to take them, and when to take them. They are aware of drug and/or food interactions, what side effects to expect, and the importance of getting rid of expired prescriptions. Drug therapy should also be coordinated with one's pharmacist to avoid problems, and frail older persons may need help in opening child-safe pill bottles.

Societal Intervention as Therapy

In addition to changing the individual, we might also want to alter the environment or context in which that person functions. This underscores the concept of **levels of intervention** (Danish, 1981) — intervention at many levels (individual, family, society). Interventions at the **physical/social environment** level can be quite effective, in place of or in combination with treatment at the individual or family level (see Table 11-4). Attention needs to be given to both the **microenvironment** (home, institution, i.e., activities programs, rehabilitation), and the **macroenvironment** (neighborhood, community, subculture) as targets for intervention (see Chapter 9). For example, intergenerational relationships (see Chapters 4 and 5) affect older persons' sense of independence, and demographic shifts influence both worker-retiree ratios and the experience of retirement (see Chapters 7 and 8). These are likely targets for societal change. Moreover, divorce rates that increase may create in older parents a sense of failure in raising their children; such persons may end up raising their grandchildren (Hayslip & Kaminski, 2005; Hayslip & Page, 2011) (see Chapters 4 and 5). Additionally, the changing work involvement of women affects how they define their roles, as well as decisions the couple may make regarding child care and parenting (see Chapter 4).

Clearly, these broader social influences will affect future cohorts of older people. Not only will their role commitments and relationships to those who are younger change, but also what they expect of themselves, as well as what others expect of them will be altered as our culture changes. Counselors and therapists need to be aware of these influences, much as they need to be skilled in various therapeutic techniques in order to facilitate the "fit" between older people and their environment.

Intervention at a broader societal level may indeed be helpful and necessary (Knight, 2004). Altering attitudes toward middle-aged and older adults and therefore enabling them to increase their reliance on the community, family, and friends are examples of such intervention. Indeed, altering attitudes toward aging and older persons, especially among young children, may have enormous benefit for future generations of older adults to enable them to **age successfully** (see Chapter 10): helping them prevent disease and disability (see Chapter 2), maintaining their physical health and cognitive functioning (see Chapters 2 and 3), and being meaningfully engaged in life pursuits and relationships with others that are satisfying (see Chapters 6 and 9).

Moreover, the development of services (home-based care, outreach, hospice care, foster grandparent programs, widow-to-widow programs) geared to older persons may prove to be as effective as intervention at the individual level (see Chapter 9). The counselor will often utilize the above resources as well as many of the above various treatments in combination to achieve a more effective solution for the patient and family.

As we become aware of the role many factors play in the development difficulties for which professional help is warranted, our concern has increasingly shifted toward **prevention** as a form of intervention (Knight, 2004; Knight, Kaskie, Shurgot, & Dave, 2006). Prevention that is **timely**, properly **targeted**, and **strategic** (flexible, individualized) is most likely to be effective. Those who are now old, families of impaired adults, and the general public are common targets of prevention. The **level** at which prevention is targeted is important as well. For example, we might choose to focus on the individual, the family, one's reference (peer) group, or society.

Prevention may also be most useful for persons who value **self-help.** One major advantage of self-help is that it need not occur in a therapist's office. It can take place in **nontraditional** settings (therapeutically speaking), e.g., senior centers or community centers. The timing of prevention may dictate its effectiveness, referring to whether education, advocacy, seeking support, or consultation is initiated earlier or later in development of a problem. For example, knowing that proper diet and exercise are important to one's health in adulthood may be to varying degrees helpful, depending upon when one begins to exercise regularly and restrict one's fat intake. For those who can do so early, before they become obese or suffer a cardiovascular illness (stroke, heart attack), making these changes can be quite effective. In order for preventative interventions to work, they of course must be acceptable to the individual. For example, if one is convinced that weight loss or developing communication skills will enhance the quality (and quantity) of one's life, then chances are greater that preventative behavior changes will be maintained over the long haul. We might begin an exercise program, enroll in a human relations course, or seek professional help.

In light of issues about development and aging we raised in Chapter 1, counselors who deal with adults of **all** ages should come to terms with what they expect from younger versus older clients. What kinds of assumptions do they made about adults of varying ages? Are clients dealt with on an age-related basis or are other factors taken into account in assessment and therapy? Clearly, counselors' views about human development based upon comparisons between the young and the old, as well as their own recollections of youth, all play an important role in how effective they will be with clients of all ages. Moreover, beliefs about aging and personality change (see Chapter 6) are likely to have an important bearing on whether a person chooses to work with adults of all ages, or with older clients at all. They also influence which approaches are selected for use with a particular client. We recommend striking a balance between acquiring specialized knowledge about the assessment and therapy of adults of a given age range versus developing a more flexible, *individualized* approach, Here the basic competences in assessment, therapeutic approaches, and community psychology are all developed. Indeed, such a philosophy has characterized our discussion of adulthood throughout this text.

Above all, the dignity and individuality of the person must be maintained to ensure that regardless of the quantity of the years the individual has accrued, the *quality* of his/her life can be improved. Through the helping efforts of others, we can learn new skills, gain insight into ourselves, improve our relationships with others, and express our innermost private feelings. Most of us can benefit in these ways from help of many kinds. As growth and change are realities for all adults, professional helpers can assist us in facilitating our own personal growth and development throughout the adult years.

Check Your Learning 11-4

Define the following terms and concepts:

> Drug therapy
> Polypharmacy
> Societal intervention
> Prevention as intervention

- Why could societal intervention be effective in changing the individual?

- What are the advantages and disadvantages of drug therapy with elderly persons?

- Why can prevention be an effective form of intervention?

- Generally speaking, what considerations are most relevant in designing and carrying out interventions with older adults?

Summary

Several therapeutic options currently exist for elderly persons after they decide to see a therapist. These options include **psychodynamic, behavioral, cognitive, group, family,** and **pharmacological treatment**. More specialized approaches include **life review, interpersonal therapy, environmental change, reality orientation,** and **pet therapy**. Not only should one examine the feasibility of different approaches with different types of older clients, but their efficacy should be established. More recently, many have advocated **self-help** or psychotherapy in **nontraditional** settings as alternatives to more formal types of interventions with the aged. Regardless of the nature of the help provided, it should be directed at **multiple levels** (individual, family, community, subcultural) and be geared to the needs, interests, capabilities, and goals of the individual. Such help, to be most effective, should be **preventative** in nature.

Chapter 12
Death and Dying

"We all have to go sometime!" "Gettin' old beats the alternative!" "I'm dying to go." These statements reflect the curiosity **and** repulsion we feel at the thought of death. Likewise, we may slow down to get a good look at an accident, or be curious about what happens to the body at the moment of death or thereafter. By confronting death and dying on a *personal* level, we can face our feelings about our own or another's death. Moreover, we can better understand the role that death plays in our daily lives.

Acknowledging death's ongoing presence in our lives is healthy. It helps us treasure who and what we have. It helps us keep things in perspective. It keeps us from taking life for granted. Perhaps most importantly, it helps us appreciate all that life has to offer: our family, treasured friends, enjoying the beauty of a spring morning or a tranquil sunset, hearing a bird chirping, or a dog barking, or the sound of someone's voice. Being aware of how precious others are to us is brought into focus by death. Elizabeth Kubler-Ross, a pioneer in the movement to bring death out in the open, said it best in talking about **unfinished business**—regrets about what we should or should have done or said that cannot be taken back when others we care about die, or when we die.

> When a patient has no unfinished business there is a sense of peace and harmony, a sense of having done what needed to be done. It is like a housewife who has put her children to bed at night. The dishes are washed and the dining room table is cleaned, and she has a sense of having done everything she wanted to do and had planned to do during the day. She can take her shower and go to bed. She has a sense of pride, a feeling of accomplishment, and it is okay now for her to go to sleep. That, in the simplest words I know is the finishing of unfinished business (Kubler-Ross & Warshaw, 1978, p. 55).

Having no unfinished business would be a great goal for all of us, because we are never guaranteed tomorrow. It could be taken from us, or from others whose relationships we cherish, in a split second. Acknowledging that life is precious in this way is both the most difficult and the most rewarding insight that we can acquire by studying death and dying.

For many of us, our own death seems distant. Indeed, it is comparatively rare for young adults to die, unless their deaths are violent. Yet, as young adults, we must face the loss of important persons in our lives—friends who die tragically in car accidents, from drug overdoses, via suicide, or from a terminal illness, and our parents and grandparents. These deaths remind us that we too will not live forever. For those who are middle-aged, the physical realities of aging (see Chapter 2) as well as the increased likelihood of losing our parents or age peers due to cancer or heart disease bring death closer. For older persons, death is almost a fact of life. In seeing loved ones die, many of whom are persons with whom we have shared our lives, the reality of our own death perhaps is most evident (see DeVries, Bluck, & Birren, 1993).

Our response to and awareness of death can be understood at many levels: (1) the **personal** level, as we reflect on the loss of our own lives, changes in our bodies as we age, or what it might be like to have a serious illness such as cancer or AIDS, (2) the **interpersonal** level, as when our relationships to others (friends, family members, coworkers, fellow students) are changed through death, and (3) at the **societal or cultural** level, as when important public figures (entertainers, politicians) die, or when people die under adverse circumstances, for example, on September 11, 2001, during the Iraq war, or because of hurricanes Katrina or Ike. Indeed, there is clear evidence that persons' attitudes toward death, dying, and bereavement have undergone a cultural shift, perhaps in response to the increased power of medical science to cure disease, the enhanced visibility of death in media coverage (see King & Hayslip, 2002), or the advent of hospice care (Hayslip & Peveto, 2005).

Each of these levels of understanding is closely intertwined, and just as our personal awareness of death waxes and wanes over time, so too does that of our culture. When either personal or cultural events exceed our threshold, we talk about them and think about them intensely. As time passes and these events become less salient at both a personal and a cultural level of awareness, we become less concerned or preoccupied with them, and eventually, it may seem as if they have never happened at all. Of course, our awareness may again increase when we are reminded of those events or new events occur. Consider your response to deaths due to the flu epidemic, 9/11, mass killings, or natural disasters. Likewise, reflect on losses in your life that you have experienced.

It has been said that "looking at death is like looking into the sun"—we can only do either for a short time lest we get hurt or injured. For this reason, the insights we gain about death through being exposed to it in various ways are likely to be temporary. Lessons about life are likely to be learned and relearned later. Consider our discussion about death and dying in adulthood to be the beginning of a personal journey for you.

Definitions of Death

What is death? This seems an obvious enough question. Yet, death means different things to different people, and approaches to defining death do not always agree. By one standard, an individual is dead, yet by another, that person is alive! The most widely held definition of death in the United States is broadly known as the **legal-medical** definition of death, used by many courts of law today, and embodied by the Uniform Definition of Death Act (1994). It encompasses two types of death, of which **clinical death** is one variety. The criteria for clinical death are having one's heart and breathing cease spontaneously. There are no reflexes. In clinical death, however, resuscitation **is** possible. The second type of death is called **brain death**, where one's brain cells die, reflected in a flat EEG for a certain period of time (24 hours), the absence of reflexes, and no spontaneous heart or respiratory activity, excluding body temperature (below 90°F) and the presence of drugs that suppress central nervous system activity (Corr, Nabe, & Corr, 2009). It refers to the brain's inability to integrate key bodily systems (heart, lungs) necessary for life, based upon the central nervous system's loss of functioning. When the central nervous system fails, circulation and breathing come to a halt shortly thereafter. Key to brain death is the **irreversibility** of damage to the central nervous system, which supports circulatory and respiratory functions, and the lack of an individual's ability to sustain such functioning in the absence of some form of medical intervention, e.g., life support (Corr, Nabe, & Corr, 2009). Of course, it may be that while the more primitive part of the brain, the brain stem, can remain intact, which can support breathing and circulation, the person's ability to think, reason, interact with others, and make decisions is lost because of damage to the neocortex. Under such circumstances, is the person alive or dead? Much then, depends upon our criteria for biological death, and the weight we place on our ability to think and make decisions.

Using other criteria, death can occur in the **absence** of changes in the brain or vital organ sys-

---

Box A

Self-Reflection

Ask yourself the following questions and write down your answers. Look them over in a while. How did you feel when answering these questions? How did you feel later when reading your answers?

Where am I in my life span? At what point do I consider myself? Have I lived 25% of my life? 50%? 75%?

At what age do I expect to die? How do I expect to die?

Do I have a will or power of attorney?

Have I made plans for my funeral? What would I want said about me at my funeral?

What should I be doing that I am not doing now?

What should I stop doing that I am doing now?

Do I have any unfinished business with

people I love?

What can I do to finish this unfinished business?

How lately have I said to someone I love:

I love you.
I care about you.
You mean the world to me.
I am sorry.
I forgive you.
I am listening to you.

What do I want to do with the remainder of my life?

If I were to die tomorrow, what would I do today?

If I were to die tomorrow, what would people remember about me?

---

tems. For example, **social death** occurs when the person is abandoned or isolated from others (Pattison, 1977). Many critically ill adults, those who are institutionalized (persons in prison, in a nursing home, or in mental hospitals), or persons who are severely impaired, die a social death even though they are quite "alive" by other criteria (see above). What often follows social death is **psychic death**; feelings of profound depression, loneliness, and feeling a lack of control over one's life are common in persons who are psychically dead (Pattison, 1977). Sadly, social death **does** cause some to give up on life, and they die a psychic death. We might even say that persons who have died a psychic death have died spiritually, i.e., their soul, or will to live, has left them, even though they are very much biologically alive.

The multiple classifications of death lead to some perplexing legal and moral issues as evidenced by a number of cases presented in the newspapers and on television, most notably that of Karen Ann Quinlan who, through a mix of drugs and alcohol, was brain dead, yet was being supported via a respirator, or more recently, the death of Terri Schaivo, who was comatose, whose heart had stopped and led to the oxygen deprivation of her brain; she subsequently had been connected to a feeding tube (Corr, Nabe & Corr, 2009). Even after Ms. Quinlan was disconnected, she continued to breathe on her own for some time (10 years) before she "died." In the case of Mrs. Schaivo, after much legal maneuvering on both sides over several years, her feeding tube was ultimately removed, and she died approximately a month later. In neither case had each woman signed an **advanced directive,** a legal document making one's wishes known regarding the type of end-of-life care one wishes, e.g., whether a person would like his or her life extended via the use of medical technology. Advanced directives encompass both **living wills** and **durable powers of at-**

torney for health care, documents that make possible others' knowledge about one's wishes at the end of life when that individual cannot make his or her wishes known because of incapacitation, e.g., being in a coma or in a persistent vegetative state.

The principal difficulty created by the many definitions of death are that the criteria for death do not provide any objective or agreed-upon basis for a scientific or legal decision about who is alive and who is not. Consequently, moral values, legal precedent, cultural biases, or religious beliefs come into play, all of which do not necessarily agree on what is best for the dying person and his or her family. For example, by one standard (brain death) an individual is dead; by another (clinical death), the person is alive. Who is to decide? The physician? The family? The legal system? These multiple definitions of death thus raise "gray" issues as to **who** should make the decision about when a life has ceased to exist. It is at this point that the **value** of a person's life comes into play. While the lives of the young, the powerful, or the productive are valued, those of the old, the powerless, and the non-productive seem less worthy (DeSpelder & Strickland, 2009).

That these issues are on our minds is evidenced by several cultural events. For example, Oregon voters in 1994 passed an amendment to the state constitution permitting physician-assisted suicide (Quill, 1996) for persons who are hopelessly terminally ill. Most everyone is aware of (and has an opinion about!) Dr. Jack Kevorkian's having attended the deaths of many seriously ill persons in Michigan. Moreover, the best selling book for many months in 1991 was *Final Exit*, by Derek Humphrey, which explained rational suicide. Likewise, Nuland's (1994) *How We Die* was a bestseller. *All of Us* by Anderson (1996) and *Final Exam: A Surgeon's Reflections on Mortality* by Chen (2007) explored our culture's unique orientation toward death, popularly referred to as a "death-denying" culture. *Learning to Fall: The Blessings of an Imperfect Life* by Simmons (2000), *Robbery and Redemption: Cancer as Identity Theft* by Fiedler (2009), and *The Last Lecture* by Rausch (2008) have all helped sensitize us to the difficulties *and* blessings persons experience in confronting serious illness and death. Likewise, *Wisdom of Our Fathers* by Russert (2006), *Fathers Aren't Supposed to Die* by Shine (2000), and *On Grieving the Death of a Mother* by Smith (1994) helped persons deal with the death of a parent in a way that was culturally unprecedented, as did *Don't Ask for the Dead Man's Golf Clubs* by Kelly (2000) regarding how to communicate with grieving persons.

Check Your Learning 12-1

Define the following terms and concepts:

> Death
> Clinical death
> Social death
> Psychic death
> Brain death
> Unfinished business
> Levels of understanding regarding death and
>   dying
> Living wills
> Durable powers of attorney for health care

- What approaches have been taken in defining death?

- What are the implications of the varying criteria for death?

- Why is an awareness of death important in everyday life?

- At what levels can death and dying be understood?

Meanings of Death

What death means to us personally dictates how we live our lives as well as how we react to death. Death is often seen as the ultimate **loss** in our lives. Death may involve losses of several kinds: (1) the loss of ability to have experiences, (2) the loss of our ability to predict subsequent events (after death), (3) the loss of our bodies, (4) the loss of our ability to care for persons who are dependent on us, (5) the loss of a loving relationship with our family, (6) the loss of the opportunity to complete treasured plans and projects, and (7) the loss of being in a relatively painless state (Kastenbaum, 2009). For still others, death may mean **punishment** for one's sins presumably linked to one's feelings about the afterlife. Death may also be seen as a **transition**, a stopping point between one form of existence and another.

What is meaningful about life is highly subjective and varies by age. For example, Reker, Peacock, and Wong (1987), found that in general, older persons reported more purpose in life than did the young and were more death accepting. Yet, the oldest-old (75+ years) and the young (16-29 years) experienced the most meaninglessness in life, most lacked goals, and felt the most free-floating anxiety. Wong (2000) notes the contradiction in using successful aging (see Chapter 10) as a barometer for what is meaningful in life, especially with regard to what is personal and spiritual in nature, not just what makes people happy or involves productive activity.

Hayslip and Peveto (2005) found that older persons had made more preparations for death, were less death anxious, thought about death more frequently, and were more accepting of death, all relative to younger persons. Generally speaking, this would suggest that death was more meaningful to them. They were, however, no more likely to believe in the afterlife.

Death may also mean that we use our **time** judiciously, as well as helping us to order our lives (Kastenbaum, 2009). Without such orderliness, nothing would be any more important than anything else! Indeed, it is often only when we nearly lose someone that we truly appreciate how special he or she is to us. When we "run out of time," some things become more important to us than they were before. This awareness of time is a central idea in what we discuss in Chapter 6 pertaining to **socioemotional selectivity**—that an awareness of time causes us to shift our priorities from relationships that provide us with information to those that provide us with emotional support. For some persons, simply living life on a day-to-day basis is more important than being preoccupied with future goals and plans. Ultimately, the meaning of death is unique to each individual, in part dependent upon whether one is young or old.

Responses to Death and Dying

What life and death **mean** to us is likely to influence how we **respond** to death. When you think of death, how do you feel? Anxious? Peaceful? Depressed? While **fear** and **anxiety** are not the only ways in which we respond to our death, they have received considerable research attention within the last 20 years (Neimeyer, Moser, & Wittkowski, 2003). While some might express anxiety over the variety of losses thought to accompany **death**, others may fear the loss of **control** over and **dignity** in their everyday lives that may come about as a function of **dying**. People who are dying are often isolated from others in an institutional setting such as a nursing home or hospital, where dying in such situations can be very depersonalizing.

Research suggests that **death** concerns must be separated from those relating to the **dying process**. Furthermore, fears about one's **own** death may differ from those surrounding **significant others**. Moreover, we may or may not be **consciously aware** of our fears about death or dying. Not feeling particularly death anxious may simply reflect a person's success at **denial**, in which case such fears may surface at a covert, unconscious level (Kastenbaum, 2009). For example, Galt and Hayslip (1998) found that while older persons **and** younger persons did not differ in consciously expressed death fear, older persons experienced more covert (unconscious) death fear than did the young, but reported less overt (conscious) fear. Hayslip, Luhr, and Beyerlein (1991) found that while men with AIDS and healthy men expressed similar degrees of conscious death fear, terminally ill men experienced more covert death fears. Hayslip, Guarnaccia, Radika, and Servaty (2002) found that conscious and unconscious death fear were negative related, suggesting that the successful denial of one's conscious fears is related to greater such fears at the unconscious level of awareness. It may be that in the face of imminent death, individuals need to consciously deny their fears about dying in order to continue functioning on a daily basis (Hayslip, Servaty, Christman & Mumy, 1996-1997). The death anxious individual may have many physical complaints, have difficulty sleeping, change his/her eating habits, have difficulty in completing a task, or show an overconcern with the welfare of others. In such cases, individuals do not **report** being anxious or concerned about death or dying, but inexplicably experience a number of these difficulties (Bassett, 2007; Firestone, 1993; Wass & Neimeyer, 1995). Individuals aware of imminent death may give away valued personal possessions, be unable to complete everyday tasks, or be excessively concerned over the welfare of others (Kastenbaum, 2009). Among older persons, poor physical health, psychological difficulties (e.g., depression), being institutionalized, a lack of social support from others, and being less religious are all associated with greater fears about death (Cicirelli, 2002). On the other hand, having a greater purpose in life and being intrinsically religious (referring to one's beliefs rather than to one's behaviors) is associated with less death anxiety (Hui & Fung, 2009).

It is important to realize that defenses against fear of death can be adaptive, if they are not over-used (Hayslip, 2003). Moreover, denial can take on various forms, such as selectively ignoring those things which make us anxious, compartmentalizing our feelings, or hiding our feelings from others (Kastenbaum, 2009).

Reflecting the understanding of death at a cultural level, McCoy, Pyszcynski, Solomon, and Greenberg (2000) have proposed a **terror management theory**, which asserts that humans overcome their fear of death and ultimate annihilation by adopting a *cultural worldview* that says that what happens to us is "controllable, fair and just" (p. 39). The chaos in our lives that is created by the ever-present threat of death from diseases such as cancer or AIDS, or from the threat of nuclear destruction or a pandemic (e.g., the bird flu) is minimized by adapting a worldview that emphasizes order and control over our lives, and living on through our accomplishments. Such a worldview is a form of denial, which is adaptive, according to terror management theory. Consistent with terror management theory, Cicirelli (2006) found that the discrepancy between desired and expected time left to live elicited more fear of physical loss through death among mid-old (75-84) than among young-old (60-74) persons. Wink and Scott (2005) found that when older persons' religious practices and their beliefs in an afterlife were consistent with one another, they feared death and dying to a lesser extent.

Contrary to what we might expect, elderly persons do not **report** fearing death **per se** (Cicirelli, 2002; Galt & Hayslip, 1998). They do, however, fear to a great degree the **dying process**—pain, dying alone, or the loss of control over everyday events or bodily functions. Where these fears are clearly justified, ending one's own life or preferring to die may be seen as preferable to suffering a painful, lonely death for some individuals, or feeling unloved and rejected by family (see Corr, Nabe, & Corr, 2009). For some persons, who are able to make life and death decisions and demonstrate their competence in the face of insurmountable odds, "letting go" of life is easier. For others, concerns about pain and suffering simply mask deeper feelings of loneliness and rejection—such persons have suffered a social death. What they want and need is to be cared **about**.

Our feelings about death may determine the quality of life we have left to live. One response to death or dying may be termed **overcoming** (Kastenbaum, 2009). Overcomers see death as the enemy, as external, or as a personal failure. Others may show a **participatory** response to death. Participators see death as internal, as an opportunity to be reunited with a loved one, and as a natural consequence of having lived. It appears that as one approaches death, one becomes more participatory (Kastenbaum & Aisenberg, 1976). Yet, it may be very difficult to adopt a participatory response to death. Death is often violent in nature, and we literally may not see death, as it often occurs in institutions such as hospitals or nursing homes. Medical science can now cure diseases and extend lives that would have ended 20 years ago. Indeed, we have

---

Box B

Overcoming and Participating as Responses to Death

Overcomers	Participators
Are often younger.	Are often older.
Are often male.	Are often female.
Tend to come from highly industrialized, technology-driven, paternal cultures.	Tend to come from cultures that are agrarian, maternal.
The environment is a resource to be used.	The environment is valued for itself.
See death in terms of technology.	See death in terms of relationships.
Emphasize competitiveness, self-reliance.	Emphasize cooperation with others.
See life and death as opposites	Life and death are complementary.
Death is the end of life.	Death means the future of a new life.
Death is failure.	Death is a reward.

Sources: Kastenbaum & Aisenberg (1976); Kastenbaum (1978, 2009).

---

come to "expect" that medicine can cure anything, and so the inability of medical science to triumph over death is seen as a failure. All of these factors push us in the direction of attempting to "overcome" death. Recent work discussed by Kastenbaum (2009) suggests that personifications of death have changed somewhat, with older age being less connected to such views, and a greater increase in female personifications among women. For men, death is still predominantly male, but men are now more likely to describe death as "cold and remote." This might suggest that men are becoming more overcoming in their response to death, and that among women, a participatory response is increasingly more common.

Check Your Learning 12-2

Define the following terms and concepts:

Death as loss
Purpose in life
Death anxiety
Conscious death fear
Unconscious death fear

Overcoming
Participating
Terror management theory

- What factors influence fear of death in adulthood?
- What are the meanings that death may have?
- What are the differences in death fear across age in adulthood?
- How does terror management theory explain death anxiety?

Death and Dying in Young Adulthood

For young adults, death comes for the most part unexpectedly. Rather than dying because of disease, when young adults die it is often by accident or through violence (Corr, Nabe & Corr, 2009). While it is the rare younger person who dies of cancer or heart disease, fatal illnesses such as AIDS are increasing among young adults (Corr, Nabe, & Corr, 2009). In most cases, however, death is due to homicides, auto or motorcycle accidents, or in some cases, because of war (Kochanek et al., 2004).

Regardless of the cause of death, the process of dying disrupts relationships with parents, children, and spouses, interferes with one's future goals and plans, and often undermines one's sense of attractiveness and sexuality. Understandably, a terminal illness or a sudden death leaves family and friends feeling frustrated, angry, and lonely. Because death in young adulthood is nonnormative (see Chapter 1), individuals feel angry and cheated that the personal or career goals they have set for themselves are never going to be reached. If individuals have children, they must experience the sadness of not seeing their children grow up, marry, and raise their own children. This is often experienced as **sorrow**.

Terminal Illness

If young adults are suffering from AIDS or cancer, they face many difficulties. At present AIDS is without a cure, though education about the disease, better methods of prevention, and recent advances in drug treatment have improved the quality and quantity of life for persons with AIDS. AIDS victims and their families are often isolated, and feel both shame and guilt over having contracted a disease, which many persons still often inaccurately associate with homosexuality. AIDS sufferers are often discriminated against at work, have difficulty in getting insurance coverage, and even have problems in getting adequate medical care. As a result, they often deny their diagnosis or hide their symptoms from others. Additionally, AIDS victims who keep to themselves inadvertently deny others the opportunity to offer support. At present, isolation is the AIDS victim's major enemy (Corr, Nabe & Corr, 2009).

Persons who have cancer also face discrimination (even if they are in remission, getting health insurance may be impossible) and must cope with the loneliness that accompanies their illness. As Kastenbaum (2009) has observed, dying persons must deal with their own and others' reactions to (1) changes in their appearance, (2) the fear that "what they have" is contagious, (3) their presumed loss of ability to make choices and decisions, (4) the ultimate permanent loss of this person through death, (5) fears about what lies ahead after death, (6) a lack of time in accomplishing what needs to be accomplished, and (7) losing the experience of oneself. These are difficult and indeed anxiety-evoking issues with which persons who are dying as well as their families are confronted.

The desperation of dying persons' situation is reflected in a terminally ill mother's desire to maximize the quality of time she had left with her children and her husband.

> She tried to fill their minds with beautiful memories, of princess parties and waterslide rides, pancakes at IHOP on Sunday mornings. She longed to wrap her children in a protective spell. She knew what was coming would leave a part of them forever empty . . . As her husband walked into the bedroom, she spoke to him softly "I think I'm dying." "I think so too." he said. He crawled into bed beside her, and they were quiet. (Scant Time to Mother, *Dallas Morning News*, Thompson, August 1, 2010).

What is key is realizing that it is a *person* who is dying. He or she is losing *everything*, and not only are beliefs about life and death challenged (I am immortal, I have control), but relationships with others are inevitably altered. "I am alone in my dying, no one can do that for me" (Edmondson, *personal communication*, 2010). These feelings and ideas are indeed difficult for those of us who are healthy to comprehend until we actually face our own deaths.

Both AIDS sufferers and their families grieve over the many losses that death brings. Yet, ironically, they are not permitted to grieve as others do because they are blamed for this illness. We term this special sense of loss as **disenfranchised grief**, because individuals who die of AIDS are often held responsible for their illness (Doka, 2008). Consequently, both those with AIDS and their survivors are stigmatized, making adjustment both before and after death more difficult. Disenfranchised grief

Adults Speak

Terminal Illness

Being faced with a terminal illness forces us to reevaluate our lives. A 27-year old woman dying of cancer with perhaps two weeks to live talks about the impact of her illness on her values and relationships:

I now see things in a much different light. Even though I will probably die young, I don't just sit around and wait for it. Actually, no one is given any more time than I am. We wake each morning to a new day, and that is all. No one is promised ahead of time that they will be here for spring vacation, for the wedding in August, or even for the dentist appointment next Thursday. We are all equal in that we have one day to fill with anything we please. The quality of life lived each day is more important than how long we live. . . . I am not the only one in the boat but no one else can do my living or dying for me. (Rosenbaum, 1980, p.19)

often accompanies deaths due to Alzheimer's disease, suicide, or deaths in prison or in the commission of a crime, alcohol or drug-related deaths, as well as death of older persons (Jones & Beck, 2006-2007; Walter & McCoyd, 2009).

While young adults with cancer are also isolated and are often discriminated against at work (even if they are in remission), they nevertheless face unique problems. They may have to cope with seemingly endless visits to physicians, painful diagnostic procedures, disfiguring surgery, or either chemotherapy or radiation therapy. Moreover, there is no guarantee that these treatments will be effective, or if the cancer is in remission, that it will not return. Despite their illness, young adults' needs for intimacy, autonomy, and dignity must be met (Oltjenbruns, 2001; Walter & McCoyd, 2009). A semblance of a family and social life must be maintained, which can be difficult for those who are weak or who have lost weight or whose appearance has changed due to surgery, chemotherapy, or radiation therapy.

In the case of any terminal illness, be it cancer, AIDS, or Alzheimer's disease, the person's **dying trajectory** (Field, 2009; Glaser & Strauss, 1968)—how rapidly and how regularly does the disease progress—and the **awareness context**—how

knowledge about the disease (its progression, prognosis, potential for treatment or remission) is shared among family, the dying person, and health care professionals (physicians, nurses)—are key to one's quality of life (Glaser & Strauss, 1968).

When the dying trajectory is rapid and unpredictable, as with communicable diseases, versus when it is more prolonged and predictable, as with degenerative diseases, how information and feelings are shared—whether an open awareness context for communication exists—is important to decision making and continuing to live fully in the face of death. Unfortunately, many family members or professionals feel the need to "manage" communication, perhaps to "protect" the dying person from the bad news of a terminal diagnosis or prognosis, in a way that is not straightforward and honest, leaving dying persons and their families feeling angry and disenfranchised (Hayslip, Hansson, Starkweather, & Dolan, 2009). Especially noteworthy are the difficulties physicians and nurses have in truth telling, and providing information to patients and families enabling them to make end of life decisions (Levetown, Hayslip, & Peel, 1999). This difficulty in communication is termed **communication apprehension** regarding dying persons. In this respect, project SUPPORT (SUPPORT

Principal Investigators, 1995) was not successful in altering physicians' end of life communication skills, stance toward cure-oriented treatments at the end of life, and the overuse of pain medication. Indeed, the quality of pre-death communication between the eventually bereaved persons and the individual who is dying predicts emotional distress after the latter's death (Metzger & Gray, 2008). Moreover, purposeful efforts by medical personnel to provide palliative (symptom or pain reducing) care for dying persons improves their quality of life (Casarett et al., 2008). This care involves providing spiritual or emotional support, treating the dying person with respect and dignity, and including symptom management, as in improving access to home care or supportive care for the family after a loved one dies (Casarett et al., 2008).

Being able to be painfree, maintaining hope in the face of death, clarifying or even creating a spiritual self, and seizing the opportunity to make life-changing choices are some of the positive outcomes that can accompany dying (Fleming & Hagan, 2010). Since these goals are not always met in supporting patients near death as well as their families, we obviously still have a long way to go in improving end of life care for dying persons and their families.

Loss of a Child

Young adults who lose children through death, particularly if those children die at a relatively young age, grieve for long periods of time (Lohan & Murphy, 2005-2006a, 2005-2006b; Rubin and Malkinson, 2001; Walter & McCoyd, 2009). Parents of young children who have died are often forced to be physically and emotionally separated from their dead child, especially if the child has died in childbirth or shortly thereafter. Funerals may be avoided because it is assumed that they would be too upsetting, further interfering with the couple's healthy expression of feelings. Parent may assume that **they** are responsible and that they should have done something to prevent their child's death. They often feel alone, angry, and resentful toward others, and may be disappointed in one another. Ulti-

mately, this child's death challenges feelings of **parental omnipotence**—that feeling that because they are parents, they *should* be able to "fix" everything in their child's life. Their greatest fear as a young parent is that their child may die suddenly and they will be powerless to prevent it. The death of a very young child can have serious consequences for the family as a whole—leading to divorce, physical/mental illness, or school difficulties (Murphy, 2008; Oltjenbruns, 2001).

Parents' responses to the death of a child can be understood at two levels: (1) the disruption the death causes them personally—how their everyday functioning, feelings, relationships to other family members, work performance, health are affected; and (2) their relationship to the deceased child—how parents maintain and ultimately change their image of and feelings about the child they have lost—their memories, images, and redefinition of their relationship to their child over time (Rubin & Malkinson, 2001).

The death of a child affects the family as a whole. Relationships between husbands and wives are altered, especially if they are grieving the loss in different ways. Men and women often differ in their response to loss (Hansson, Hayslip, & Stroebe, 2007). They may feel a profound sense of guilt (Corr, Nabe & Corr, 2009) at having not been able to prevent their child's death, or even feel that they caused it to happen. Grandparents grieve as well and are faced with supporting their adult children and dealing with their own feelings of loss (Reed, 2000). Likewise, siblings must cope with the loss of a brother or sister. They may need the attention of parents and yet feel guilty in asking for such support. For families where an atmosphere of **open communication** between husband and wife and between parents and children exists, grief work is easier to accomplish. Understanding why their child died, and that it was not their fault helps to make sense of the death. Some families seek professional help to assist them in working through their grief. For others, community support is very important. One such self-help group is **The Compassionate Friends**, where parents who have lost children can come together to share their feelings as well as to

---

Box C

The Compassionate Friends: Support for Bereaved Parents

Despite the fact that a child's death is quite traumatic, many families have nowhere to turn when a child dies. The pain of losing a child to an accident, a suicide, a homicide, an illness, or in childbirth is far-reaching, intense, and lonely.

Parents often simply need to be in the presence of others who understand and acknowledge the pain of their loss, who have felt the emotions they are feeling. Others need to talk openly about their loss, and it is important for them to share their feelings with others. These emotions may range from extreme sadness to guilt, anger, self-doubt, and hopelessness. Some parents who have suffered and learned to live with and grow from the loss of their child can offer support. Thy can serve as sounding boards, confidants, or even "psychological punching bags." They offer hope and compassion to those parents who have suffered a loss so devastating that it is too terrible to discuss with anyone. While many find their faith to be a source of strength, no religious creed or affiliation is involved. Ideally, parents can get beyond the hurt and remember their children with love,

yet with a touch of sadness. A parent expressed her feelings in a poem she entitled "Remembrance."

REMEMBRANCE

I see your smile in the brightness of the
  summer sun.
A gentle breeze is the touch of your hand on
  mine.
A wave breaks softly on the shore, and I hear
  you whisper,
"Remember me".

A winged bird begins its flight into the distant
  sky.
The sound of children's laughter fills the air.
The evening stars become your eyes, and I
  reply—
"You are ever near".

Priscilla D. Kenney
TCF, Kennebunk, ME

---

help one another cope with the death of a loved son or daughter. Indeed, parents who have fewer difficulties in coping with the death of a child remember the child's good qualities (termed a continuing bond, Corr, Nabe, & Corr, 2009) and even idealize the child as a role model in the face of the suffering the child experienced prior to death (Ronen et al., 2009-2010).

A young woman who decides to have an abortion also faces a unique sense of loss. Even if she freely chose abortion, she may nevertheless experience more anger, guilt, or depression, and she may also face rejection from, or be judged by, family or friends who feel that abortion is morally wrong. For these reasons, it may take some time for the individual to come to terms with her abortion, and

to fully resolve her grief over the loss of a child (Kesselman, 1990). Other losses in young adulthood are often extremely difficult to cope with because of the sudden and often unforeseen nature of a parent's or friend's death (Walter & McCoyd, 2009). Providing emotional support to and acknowledging the depth of their grief are quite important. In case of a death due to suicide, young adults may not get the help that they need and want in helping them cope with their feelings, complicating the adjustment to a friend's suicide (Dyregrov, 2009). Equally important is normalizing young parents' feelings of anger, envy, jealousy, and guilt regarding the loss of their child and their feelings towards others whose children are still living (Barr & Cacciatore, 2007-2008). If the death of a partner/

Losing a Spouse in Young Adulthood

The grief that young adults feel at losing a spouse lingers for a long time. Three years after losing his wife of 2 years to a car accident at the age of 25, this young widower wrote:

> The experience of grief and healing is not magical, and it doesn't leave you immune to the pain of loss. Many people have said to me, "You have really become a strong person by surviving Becky's death." Maybe it's true that I am more capable of handling life's crises than I was before widowhood. Maybe my grief has inspired me not to give up when I try to meet other challenges in life. The pain of grief, however, is one that seared me, and one that can quickly rise within me. One day when I was at a lake with my cousin, we became a part of a search party to find a 5-year-old girl. On the third cross, my cousin located the child and pulled her from the lake. She was dead from drowning. I stood by the shore and stared at this child while the medics worked on her. Like Becky, she looked so alive and yet was dead. In the background her mother screamed, "Oh my God, no my baby, please don't take my baby." I watched and felt helpless. Later, when I cried in the shower that evening my tears were for the child and for her mother. There were also tears for myself. I cried for losing the someone I loved so early in my adult years, so suddenly and so completely. (Lichtenberg, 1990, p. 89)

He writes, "I learned you cannot grieve alone; grief is frightening due to its immense range and the intensity of feelings it provokes; and even when healing occurs, there remains a heightened sensitivity to loss" (p. 83).

Source: Lichtenberg (1990). Remembering Becky. *Omega, 21*, 83-89.

---

spouse is sudden, persons must reinvent themselves and learn to go on in life without this person. They must function independently, while at the same time deal with the sadness, loneliness, and the lack of a future with this special person (Rodger et al., 2006-2007).

Death in Middle Adulthood

For adults who are in their 40s and 50s, the possibility of their own death becomes real. For many, the time they have left to live now exceeds the time elapsed since their birth, promoting at the least, a heightened sense of time, and at worst, a full blown crisis. At this point, they may be caring for an aging parent or have already suffered the loss of a parent. Cancer, heart disease, stroke, heart attacks, and rarer diseases such as amyotrophic lateral sclerosis (ALS) and multiple sclerosis are the major killers of middle-aged adults (see Chapter 2). For men, lung, colorectal, and prostate cancer become major concerns, while for women, lung, breast and colorectal cancer are the most common (American Cancer Society, 2009).

For individuals facing a terminal illness, however, reevaluating life and its meaning are likely consequences (see Table 12-1). The quality of one's relationships as well as one's achievements and goals is assessed with a finality that was never present before. Goals can never be achieved and relationships can never be fulfilled. For these reasons, it may be important to the dying person to continue to carry out the roles of father, mother, spouse, mentor, friend, or worker. Plans for the future must

Table 12-1

Issues and Tasks Related to Coping with Cancer

I. **ISSUE: Discovery of cancer.**
ADAPTIVE TASK: To seek appropriate treatment.

II. **ISSUE: Primary treatment.**
ADAPTIVE TASK: To recognize and cope with the situation and one's emotional reactions and to integrate the experience of illness with the rest of one's life.

III. **ISSUE: Damage to one's body from the cancer and/or treatment.**
ADAPTIVE TASK: To mourn the loss, replace or compensate for lost parts or functions, and maximize other potentials in order to maintain a sense of self-esteem and intactness.

IV. **ISSUE: Returning to normal activities and maintaining continuity in life roles.**
ADAPTIVE TASK: To understand and communicate one's changed attitudes, needs, and limitations in a way that permits functioning within one's social and physical environment with a minimum of constriction of one's life.

V. **ISSUE: Possibility of recurrence and progression of the disease.**
ADAPTIVE TASK: To learn to cope with this uncertainty and to continue appropriate medical follow-up.

VI. **ISSUE: Persistent or recurrent disease.**
ADAPTIVE TASK: To exercise freedom of choice when possible and accept one's dependence on others when necessary, while continuing appropriate treatment.

VII. **ISSUE: Terminal illness.**
ADAPTIVE TASKS: To prepare for the final separation from family and friends, to put one's affairs in order, to use medical and personal resources to minimize pain, and to retain as much self-sufficiency and personal dignity as possible.

Source: Cook, A. S., & Oltjenbruns, K. A. (1998). Dying and Grieving: Lifespan and family perspectives (p. 338). New York: Holt, Reinhardt, and Winston.

be made. "Unfinished business" (Kubler-Ross, 1969) must be settled. One's affairs must be put in order; the security of a business must be ensured; a child's college education must be paid for. For these reasons, discussing one's obligations and responsibilities is critical, so they are not unmet after death. As do young adults, middle-aged persons face a series of adjustments in the face of cancer, e.g., seeking appropriate treatment, coping with its side effects, dealing with remissions and relapses, accepting the end of life (Oltjenbruns, 2001; Walter & McCoyd, 2009) (see Table 12-1). If the individ-

ual's cancer is incurable, then the rights and obligations of the person as a dying individual come into play (see Box D), and ultimately, issues surrounding end-of-life decision making become relevant (see Box E).

In the context of Bronfenbrenner's (1979) notion of *structural lag*, i.e., the delay between an event's occurrence and that event's impact on individuals, it is important to recognize that a number of cultural shifts have driven attitudinal changes toward end-of-life care. For example, the rise in deaths due to AIDS, the passage of the Patient Self-

Box D

The Dying Person's Bill of Rights

I have the right to be treated as a living human being until I die.

I have the right to maintain a sense of hopefulness, however changing its focus may be.

I have the right to be cared for by those who can maintain a sense of hopefulness, however changing this might be.

I have the right to express my feelings and emotions about my approaching death in my own way.

I have the right to participate in decisions concerning my care.

I have the right to expect continuing medical and nursing attention even though "cure" goals must be changed to "comfort" goals.

I have the right not to die alone.

I have the right to be free from pain.

I have the right to have my questions answered honestly.

I have the right not to be deceived.

I have the right to have help from and for my family in accepting my death.

I have the right to die in peace and dignity.

I have the right to retain my individuality and not be judged for my decisions, which may be contrary to beliefs of others.

I have the right to discuss and enlarge my religious or spiritual experiences, whatever these may mean to others.

I have the right to expect that the sanctity of the human body will be respected after death.

I have the right to be cared for by caring, sensitive, knowledgeable people who will attempt to understand my needs and will be able to gain some satisfaction in helping me face my death.

Source: A Barbus, <u>American Journal of Nursing</u>, 1975, <u>1</u>, 99.

Determination Act in 1991, the implementation of advanced directives legislation by many states, and the growth of consumer groups and private foundations (e.g., Project Death in America of the Open Society Institute, Hospice Foundation of America, Nathan Cummings Foundation, Robert Wood Johnson Foundation) have led to recognition of patients' rights and improvements in end-of-life situations. All have come together to bring end-of-life issues to the forefront of the public's consciousness. Perhaps more obviously, several high profile cultural events have caused questions regarding the moral and legal parameters defining end-of-life decisions to be raised. Such events include the controversy surrounding Dr. Jack Kevorkian, who was ultimately convicted of murder in 1999 for his role in ending the life of Thomas Youk (Dr. Kevorkian was released from prison in late 2009); the passage of the Oregon Death with Dignity Act in 1994; and the deaths of Karen Ann Quinlan (1975), Nancy Cruzan (1983), and Terry Schiavo (2005). They present physicians, health care personnel, lawyers, ethicists, and perhaps most poignantly dying persons and their families with choices that are un-

Box E

Decision Making at the End of Life

Psychologists, lawyers, ethicists, physicians, and family members of dying persons have become increasing vocal about family members' ability and opportunity to make choices as their lives come to an end. In light of these concerns, it would not be surprising to observe that our culture has changed over time in ways that not only influence persons' attitudes toward end of life issues, but create many personal dilemmas for such persons in making decisions about the quality of their own or others' lives. For example, the decision to abandon further treatment and the availability of hospice care have likely altered the context in which families make decisions about the quality of care provided to terminally ill family members (Hayslip & Hansson, 2006).

Such issues revolve around: truth telling in the event of a terminal diagnosis or prognosis, the acceptability of life-extending medical treatments that may prolong suffering at the expense of longer life, the withdrawal of life-sustaining treatment, and the acceptability of physician-assisted suicide. Indeed, persons differ with regard to their views on such issues, and such variability is linked to age, race/ethnicity, gen-

der, religious or spiritual beliefs (Doka, 2009), and individual competence as in the case of someone with advanced dementia (Hayslip et al., 2009). Thus, every dying person's ability to make end-of-life choices is unique. Families should of course be involved and thus, the impact of such decisions is influenced by the family's burden of care, financial situation, values regarding life and death, and patterns of communication (Wells-DiGregario, 2009). Such choices are often ambiguous (Kleespies et al., 2009).

Blevins and Werth (2006) argue that to improve matters, education of the public, family members, and health care professionals is necessary. The provision of interdisciplinary end-of-life care, the proactive formation of public policy, and the informed use of end-of-life research are also necessary. The goal is that the interests of the physician do not conflict with those of the dying person and the family, so that dying patients can die dignified and meaningful deaths, based upon the opportunity to make informed choices about the end of their lives.

precedented in terms of their impact on the quality of life for such persons, their families, and those persons for whom such decisions are both possible and inevitable.

The other major ways in which death affects middle-aged individuals is through the loss of one or both parents, and less commonly in dealing with the death of a former spouse (Oltjenbruns, 2001; Walter & McCoyd, 2009). As individuals age, the aging and eventual death of their parents are more likely. When a parent dies, the likelihood of one's own death becomes greater. It is for this reason that the death of a parent may cause them to redefine

their own roles as parents, and become attuned to their responsibilities in the family as the now oldest child (Corr, Nabe, & Corr, 2009). Much depends upon the nature of the death (sudden or not) as well as how families deal with the news (by either avoiding the topic, distorting the intent of the message, or accepting the news) that death is both imminent and desired by the older parent (Corr, Nabe, & Corr, 2009; Moss et al., 2005).

The fact that a parent is still alive serves as a "psychological buffer" against death (Moss & Moss, 1983). As long as a parent is alive, one can still feel protected, cared for, approved, and even scolded.

Stripped of this "protection," one must acknowledge that he/she is now the senior member of the family, and that death is a certainty. While children certainly mourn and grieve over the loss of their fathers, mothers may represent the last evidence of one's family or origin, as women typically outlive men. The death of a parent may also have special significance for men versus women. For an adult male, the death of his father may represent the loss of a trusted friend, a role model, and a valued grandparent, especially if he has male children of his own, as his identity is in part tied to that of his father. An important part of raising his own son may be in telling stories about his own father, and in encouraging his son to feel closer to his deceased grandfather. For an adult female, her mother's death may heighten her own feelings as a mother, particularly if she and her mother have remained close over the years and have shared child-raising experiences. A parent's death symbolizes many things—one's own mortality, independence from authority, attachment, and love. For many middle-aged persons, a parent's death coincides with either personal, marital, or work crises, and in some cases, the loss of a parent seemed to intensify a couple's marital difficulties (Rosenblatt & Barner, 2006).

Death and Aging

Late adulthood is often a period in our lives that we unfortunately often come to think of in terms of loss, i.e., good health, relationships with others, and status in the community as independent and productive persons (Kastenbaum, 2009). Perhaps the most important losses thought to accompany getting older are those of one's spouse, a sibling (Moss, Moss, & Hansson, 2001), and, ultimately, the loss of one's own life.

Older people are likely to have had more death experiences (parents, siblings, friends) than younger people. This has several consequences: (1) the future seems more definite rather than being infinite—when we are very young, being 60 or 70 seems a long way off!; (2) older people may see themselves as less worthy because their future is

more limited; (3) desirable roles are closed off to them; and (4) not knowing what to do with one's "bonus time" on earth, one may think that he/she has already "used up" what years were available. Lastly, as more friends and relatives die, older persons become more attuned to sadness and loneliness, and to signals from their bodies that say that death is near.

Kastenbaum (1978) suggested that the **principle of compensation** may preserve a sense of continuity and fairness about life and death for some persons. This principle suggests that just as we may have been left a penny (or perhaps with inflation, a dollar) to compensate for a lost tooth as children, older or terminally ill persons are compensated for the losses of health and ultimately life itself by the promise of eternity. Near death, persons are assumed to acquire a kind of spiritual wisdom that lets them view death more positively. The principle of compensation reinforces the practice of **regressive intervention** that there is nothing more that could have been done for the old person. Interestingly, older persons who are dying rarely say that the afterlife is a compensation for death (see Hayslip & Peveto, 2005; Kastenbaum, 1978). For these reasons, we may feel prepared to deal with the death of someone who is older, whereas we are caught off guard when someone young dies. Indeed, the value of older persons' lives suddenly becomes an issue when one must argue that such persons, if they are dying, have "the right" to adequate medical care, must be able to maintain their identities as individuals, be convinced that their lives still have value, and be able to participate in decisions about their lives (Corr, Nabe, & Corr, 2009). If the dying person were younger, would these same questions be raised? Would we need to protest when it has been proposed that in the event of a bird flu pandemic, that younger persons, who presumably have more (re)productive years ahead of them, be vaccinated first (*Dallas Morning News*, May 12, 2006)? While this may seem logical, would you argue this with regard to your grandparents?

Indeed, many ideas about aging tend to reinforce the association between older persons and death, leading to the conclusion that death/dying is "more natural" or "more appropriate" for older persons versus the young. For example, **integrity** (a sense of completeness) or **disengagement** (withdrawal from others) have each been attributed to later life (see Chapter 6). Instead of seeing disengagement or life review as characteristic of all elderly persons, we might instead view such processes as being characteristic of some persons more than others irrespective of age, consistent with personality traits or specific life experiences. In contrast to this negative outlook regarding older persons and death, Cicirelli (1997) found that despite a low quality of life, older persons preferred to maintain life at all costs if they were to have a terminal illness. Only a minority wished to end life through suicide, euthanasia, or physician-assisted suicide. Interestingly, older persons' attitudes toward end-of-life issues often differ from those of younger persons, wherein an acceptance of death and their spiritual beliefs seem to make older persons more amenable to making end-of-life choices e.g., completing an advanced directive (Hayslip et al., 2009).

Older persons may experience some difficulty in discussing such issues with children and grandchildren, due to the latter's resistance in doing so (Moore & Sherman, 1999). Whether support from others during the dying process is conflict-filled or not influences older persons' desire to hasten death (Schroepfer, 2008). How much and in what areas of life older persons can exercise both primary (over themselves and their bodies) and secondary (how they react to dying) control in the last chapter of their lives is key to their quality of life (Schroepfer, Noh, & Kavanaugh, 2009). Indeed, one's "mindframe" toward dying likely influences older persons' stance regarding end-of-life choices. In this respect, Schroepfer (2006) found six mindframes among terminally ill older persons: (1) neither ready nor accepting, (2) not ready but accepting, (3) ready and accepting, (4) ready, accepting, and wishing death would come, (5) considering a hastened death, but having no specific plan, and (6) considering a hastened death and having a specific plan.

Check Your Learning 12-3

Define the following terms and concepts:

> Principle of compensation
> Regressive intervention
> Integrity
> Disengagement
> Disenfranchised grief
> Awareness contexts
> Dying trajectory

- What difficulties do adults facing a terminal illness experience?

- What is unique about the loss of a child?

- What is unique about the loss of a parent?

- What is unique about grief in younger, middle-aged, or elderly persons?

Bereavement—Surviving Loss

Regardless of age, the loss of a child, parent, sibling, spouse, or grandparent is likely to be one of the most disruptive life events that we experience. Referring to someone as **bereaved** simply indicates that the person has survived another person's death, while **grief** is the term we use to refer to the manner in which one deals with or responds to this loss; **mourning** simply indicates a socially condoned way of expressing one's grief (i.e., at a funeral) or acknowledging that a life has ended (Kastenbaum & Costa, 1977).

Older people clearly must deal more frequently with the loss of a spouse. By the age of 65, 50% of women have lost their husbands; by the age of 75, two-thirds are widowed (Corr, Nabe, & Corr, 2009). Anyone, however, who may have to deal with several closely spaced deaths might not have the opportunity to do the **grief work** necessary to "work through" each loss, termed **bereavement overload**. Such persons may appear depressed, apathetic, or suffer from physical problems (Kastenbaum, 1978).

Adults Speak

A Widow's Grief

"Widow" is a harsh and hurtful word. It comes from the Sanskrit and it means "empty." I have been empty too long. I do not want to be pigeon-holed as a widow. I am a woman whose husband has died, yes. But not a second-class citizen, not a lonely goose. I am a mother and a working woman and a friend and a sexual woman and a vital woman. I am a person. I resent what the term "widow" has come to mean. I am alive. I am part of the world. Today I carry the scars of my bitter grief. In a way I look upon them as battle stripes, marks of my fight to attain an identity of my own. But today I am someone else. I am stronger, more independent. I have more understanding, more sympathy. A different perspective.

Source: Caine, L. (1974). *Widow*. New York: William Morrow.

Since such deaths are often sudden, persons who are left behind suffer from **acute grief**, commonly believed to be more difficult to cope with (Oltjenbruns, 2001). Not only are older persons likely to experience bereavement overload, but those who lose family via accidents or violence as well as professionals who must deal with the dying (police, firemen, EMTs) suffer from the burden of losing many persons all at once.

Grief is often composed of many different types of responses (affective, behavioral, physical), and seemingly contradictory emotions (Stroebe, Hansson, Stroebe & Schut, 2001; Weiss, 2008). For example, one can simultaneously experience an intense desire to hold on to the image/memory of the dead spouse, guilt, anger, or relief (Oltjenbruns, 2001; Weiss, 2008). Accepting such emotions seems to positively predict bereavement outcome (Corr, Nabe, & Corr, 2009). Likewise, grief forces us to think about the world and our relationships differently (Wortman & Silver, 2001). The importance of remaining in touch with someone as a crucial element in the surviving spouse's ultimate survival has been emphasized (Morgan, 1989). This is important because those who are bereaved are often avoided and treated as if they are sick; and loneliness not surprisingly is bereaved persons' major difficulty.

It seems that persons who are not themselves bereaved have a difficult time understanding how bereaved persons think or feel. For example, Williams-Conway et al. (1991) found that professionals attributed more distress and difficulty in adjusting to their husbands' deaths than did widows themselves, while widows yearned more strongly for their husbands and felt more isolated than professionals judged them to feel. However, when persons were asked to imagine bereavement, and their responses were compared to those who had lost a loved one to a variety of causes, perceptions were surprisingly similar, except that people could not predict the experience of suicidal bereavement regarding the amount and helpfulness of contact with others. For most bereaved individuals, feelings of **isolation** and **separateness** from others are major obstacles to asking for and receiving help.

Abnormal (maladaptive) grief frequently involves a long-term change in the individual's typical behaviors, i.e., chronic depression, extended denial of the death, self-abusive/self-destructive behavior, and isolation from others (Lindemann, 1944). Normal adaptive grief may or may not last for an extended time period (e.g., 2-3 years), depending upon a number of factors (personality, health, relationship with the deceased person, support from others). Even the loss of a beloved pet can evoke intense feelings which take time to resolve. While for many persons, grief does follow a predictable course, adjustment to the loss of a loved one is nevertheless a complex process, composed of many emotions that necessitate changes in one's relationships with friends, family, and coworkers, others, views about oneself, as well as impacting one's health, one's roles as a citizen in the community and as a coworker (Schuchter & Zisook, 1993).

As grief is inherently complex and composed of physical sensations, feelings, thoughts, many persons report behaving in ways and feeling emotions which may seem strange and indeed contradictory (Corr, Nabe, & Corr, 2009). They may see or hear the deceased person (Sanger, 2009), want to join them in death, engage in obsessive-compulsive behaviors (cleaning the house over and over), or adopt some of the symptoms of the disease that killed a loved one. (For example, a widow may develop a cough after the death of her husband who had smoked all of his life and died from emphysema, lung cancer, or a heart attack). While there is much debate about what defines pathological grief and how it should be understood and measured (Parkes, 2005-2006), most grief is healthy. Most persons eventually cope with their losses and reestablish a balance that incorporates the experience of having lost a loved one through death.

It is important to recognize that responses to loss among adults and older persons are quite diverse. The quality of one's relationship to the deceased persons, one's religious or spiritual beliefs, the cause of death, pre-death health status, and social support from others all contribute to differences between persons in coping with loss (Hansson, Hayslip, & Stroebe, 2007). Over time (e.g., in the year or two after death), persons adjust differently as well. Some are resilient, some experience a "spike" in symptoms of grief (e.g., sadness and depression) followed by improvements later on, others experience depression after the death which persists over time, and others who were depressed before the death respond least adaptively (Bonanno, Wortman, & Neese, 2004). Above all, it is important not to be judgmental, not to give advice that is not asked for, and to be unconditionally supportive of the grieving person's behaviors or feelings, unless you sense that this person is a danger to himself or others. In other words, be the friend that you would want others to be for you, should your loved one die (see Box F).

Grief in Adulthood

Widowhood

Relative to widows, we know comparatively little about how men cope with the loss of a spouse, though recent work suggests that men are quite resilient in the face of the deaths of their wives (Carr, 2006; Moore & Stratton, 2002). They are able to cope with the death—its emotional and practical aspects—and emerge with greater feelings of control and self-confidence. Since women outlive men, widowerhood is less common. For this reason, support from other men who have lost their wives is likely to be scarce (Lund, 2000). There is some evidence that men's and women's adjustment to loss are indeed different, with women being intuitive (they express their emotions) and men being instrumental (they focus on practical matters, work, and problem solving) (Martin & Doka, 2000). Yet, a classic 2-year longitudinal study by Lund, Caserta and Dimond (1986) suggested that widows **and** widowers tended to face common problems in bereavement, suggesting that the loss of one's spouse is a universal adjustment for both men and women.

In general, several factors seem to put bereaved persons at risk for both psychological and health-related difficulties: sudden or especially violent deaths, feelings of ambivalence toward and dependence upon the person who has died, poor health prior to bereavement, other coexisting crises in a person's life, the loss of a parent or child, and a lack of social support from others after the death (Moss, Moss, & Hansson, 2001). Lund, Dimond, Caserta, Johnson, Poulton, and Connelly (1986-87), for example, found that elderly persons who were poor copers expressed lower self-esteem prior to bereavement, had more confusion, a greater desire to die,

Box F

Helping Others Cope with Grief and Loss

1. More important than anything is to **listen, listen, and listen! Be there in body and in spirit.** You do not have to have all the answers, either.

2. Be an **active listener**. Really attend to what the other person needs and wants to share. Make it clear by your facial expression, tone or voice, and body language that you care and that you are indeed listening. Ask "How are you?" "Is there anything I can do?"- Several requests may be necessary for those who think they can "go it on their own."

3. **Try to remember how you felt when you lost someone special**—your emotions, behaviors, and thoughts. What did someone say or do that made you feel more comfortable? Less alone? More accepting of your loss and the changes in your life that your loss brought about? This will make it easier to relate to them, even if their loss is different than yours. **Remember, everyone grieves in a unique way.**

4. **Make a mental note of how healthy people appear to be**. Do they appear to be taking care of themselves? Have their self-care behaviors changed since their loss?

5. **Do not offer advice unless it is asked for**. Even if it is, be very cautious in giving advice. What worked for you may not work for someone else.

6. **Be accepting and uncritical** of what people are saying or doing, unless it is clear that they are acting in a way that is harmful to them or to others. If so, try to find a professional helper to intervene. Go with them to the appointment if necessary.

7. **Take the opportunity to go out of your way to support them**. Call or drop by. Most persons report that feeling lonely, feeling different from others, and being judged by them are the major difficulties as grieving people that they face.

8. **Try to strike a balance** between asking them what they need and what you can do, and their need for help and support from you. Try not to be a pest, but do not say "call me when you need me." Make it clear that you are always available, but on their terms, not yours.

9. **Normalize their feelings**. This assures them that what they are feeling and thinking about is probably not as weird, unusual, or bad as they think. Talk about what interests them, be it cooking or baseball. Have a meal together. Ask them what they would enjoy doing and offer to do that together.

10. **Stress that the process of coping with a loss is difficult, and that it is an ongoing process. There are no time limits on grief. There is no one best way to grieve.**

11. Stress that with patience, self-care, and the opportunity to be with and talk with others, **persons will eventually come full circle.** They will be whole again, but yet different than the way they were before.

12. Stress that there will be **good days and bad days**, pleasant feelings and not-so-pleasant feelings.

13. **Keep your feelings separate from theirs**. If you have the need to talk, find someone who can listen. Being with them may arouse feelings and thoughts in you that may need a bit of support from someone else.

14. **Your opinions on what they "should be doing or feeling" are irrelevant**.

15. **Empathize** with them. **Reflect** their thoughts and feelings in what you say or do. **Be a friend.**

cried more, and were less able to keep busy shortly after the death. Van der Houwen, Stroebe and Stroebe (2010) found that a lack of social support predicted more intense grief and depression in survivors, while being more anxiously attached (see Chapters 4, 5 and 6) and having lost a partner predicted more emotional loneliness. Ben-Zur and Michael (2009) found that widowed persons negatively evaluated themselves relative to others, and that this negative evaluation was related to less well-being. If such persons have suffered a stigmatizing loss (e.g., a death due to suicide), they are at greater risk for depression, difficulties in grieving, having suicidal thoughts, and are less likely to be open to mental health assistance (Feigelman, Gorman, & Jordan, 2009; Johnson et al., 2009). Additionally, if they have endured many years of caring for someone with Alzheimer's disease, which in addition to the death of a child (Corr, Nabe, & Corr, 2009), would be considered a "high grief" death, they may be a greater risk for bereavement difficulties (Sanders et al., 2008). Especially among older men, those who are depressed after a death are three times more likely than married men to commit suicide (Li, 1995). For these reasons, we should be especially concerned about someone who has experienced a number of the above high risk events that coincide with bereavement, where maladaptive bereavement adjustment can interfere with one's development (Shapiro, 2008). Such persons may be at risk for poorer physical and psychological health.

Grief clearly has the potential to negatively impact persons in many ways: personally, physically, and relationship-wise (Weiss, 2008). For many, losing someone evokes a kind of unreality: that the rules of life have been broken somehow.

A young woman who had lost two friends in the last year said.

"I know what matters. I know that bad things happen to good people. And yes, good things happen to bad people. I just don't know what to do about it. . . . But why does a good person who only loved, who wanted nothing but the best, who celebrated life, why does she end up with tubes everywhere? Why does she have to decide that it is time for the tubes to come out, time to face death? Is she scared? Is she angry? Is there any peace in such a moment?"

In thinking about grief's impact on us, we should perhaps be concerned for those who are most vulnerable to its negative impact. Especially for males whose wives die, in terms of health, well-being, and mortality, grief can have especially negative effects. The odds of dying increase after the death of a spouse (see Elwert & Christakis, 2008). Yet, many *positive* outcomes can accompany grieving. Values about life and relationships can be redefined, and one can become more attuned to one's feelings and can develop new coping skills (Corr, Nabe, & Corr, 2009). One can "re-make" or reconstruct life as one understands it so that it is more meaningful, and grow personally from the experience of grief (Neimeyer, 2005-2006). Recognizing that one's *relationship* with someone who has died (e.g., a spouse, a child, a parent) does *not* end with death is a valuable insight that bereavement can provide. Many persons emerge stronger than they were before, having *survived* the experience of having grieved (Corr, Nabe, & Corr, 2009). Indeed, being more resilient and being a spiritual person are resources that enable persons to survive the demands of coping with the loss of a loved one (Rossi, Bisconti, & Bergeman, 2007; Sandler, Wolchik, & Ayers, 2008; Wortmann & Park, 2008). It may *also* be that bereavement creates resilience in people and enables them to become more spiritual.

Whether older persons "grieve" in different ways in the process of adjusting to loss versus the young, is a matter of some disagreement. Some discuss stages of grief: (1) initial shock/disbelief, (2) a working through of one's feelings and a review of one's relationship with the deceased, and (3) a restructuring phase, where "life moves on" which may last for varying periods of time (Cook & Oltgenbruns, 1998; Parkes, 1996; Worden, 2002). Maciejewski et al. (2007) found evidence for a stagelike progression of grief over a 2-year period:

(1) disbelief, (2) yearning, (3) anger, (4) depression, and (5) acceptance. Holland and Neimeyer (2010) found mixed support for a stage approach to grief among persons who had experienced both natural and violent deaths, where stages seemed to apply to grief over shorter periods of time (less than 2 years); nearly all persons eventually came to accept the death. For longer periods of time (2 years or more), Holland and Neimeyer (2010) found that anniversary reactions were more common.

A newer approach to grief, termed the **Dual Process Model** (Stroebe & Schut, 1999), emphasizes the oscillation between **loss-oriented** and **restoration-oriented** processes over time, where persons go back and forth between coping with the loss they have experienced (feeling overwhelmed by grief, breaking bonds with the deceased person) and building a new life for themselves (adjusting to life changes, developing new interests and relationships). This dual process model is more realistic if one thinks of grief as like the tide—it comes in and goes away.

In many respects, we continue to grieve, even in small ways, long after someone we love has died. Thus, "getting over" one's grief and returning to "normal" are clearly inaccurate ways of thinking about adjusting to loss. Indeed, it is a process wherein we are **returned to wholeness** via our experience in coping with the pain of loss. Yet, it is very important to realize that in some ways, grief is forever.

It is commonly believed that younger persons have a more difficult time adjusting to the loss of a spouse than do older individuals, though given the variability among older persons in their responses to loss, this conclusion may be premature. For a young person, a spouse's death may force the young person into child care or work responsibilities for which he or she is unprepared. As widowhood in young adulthood is relatively uncommon, other men and women may not be available as models for how to survive alone. Indeed, while some have found younger persons who are widowed to make poorer adjustments than do older persons, others do not. For example, Thompson et al. (1989) discovered

that while older bereaved spouses were initially more distressed than nonbereaved spouses, 2 years later there were few differences between the groups. In a unique study of older women's grief, Sable (1991) found that within 3 years, older women's grief does subside. Yet, while some older women do eventually move on with their lives, others do not seem to be able to do so. In Sable's (1991) study of bereaved women, 78% thought they would never get over their loss; they simply learned to live with it. Moreover, older women adjusted to loss more negatively than did younger women. This is contrary to the myth that says because older women are more prepared for their husbands' eventual deaths they will adjust more quickly and more completely. While the quality of the marital relationship is important in yearning for a deceased spouse, it does, however, appear that **yearning** for the dead spouse is a universal experience among those whose marriages have broken by death (Stroebe, Abakoumkin, & Stroebe, 2010).

It is important to understand that coping with loss in middle and later life is often preceded by an extensive period of caregiving, where for some older persons, the death of a spouse (or a parent) represents the end of a chronic stressor rather than an event which signals the beginning of a series of adjustments (Wolff & Wortman, 2006). For some middle-aged and older persons, however, the effects of caregiving are long-lasting in terms of their impact on physical and mental health (Schulz et al., 2001). Much depends upon the coping and emotional regulation skills of the griever, his/her health and social support, and the demands of caregiving itself. Other variables are whether the care recipient was cognitively impaired or in pain, other work or family demands on the caregiver, and whether the caregiver derives satisfaction from providing care (Hansson, Hayslip, & Stroebe, 2007). For many caregivers, dependent upon the quality of their relationship to the person for whom they provided care, whether they had support from family and friends, and the degree to which a loved one had suffered and was in pain, the death of that person could be a relief.

In families where an older spouse dies, both the surviving spouse **and** the adult children have suffered a loss. For example, Bass et al. (1990) found that spouses were more negatively affected by the death than were children, yet they tended to become more socially active after the death than their children, perhaps in an effort to rebuild support from others that was lacking prior to the spouse's death. While children tried to emotionally prepare themselves for a parent's death, this seemed to make adjustment more difficult. Findings such as these should alert us to our own biases about **anticipatory grief** (that being prepared emotionally for the death makes things easier). They should also help us recognize the tremendous psychological burden spouses carry in caring for a dying husband or wife.

The Loss of an Adult Child

Approximately 10% of adults over the age of 60 experience the death of a grown child (Moss, Lesher, & Moss, 1986-1987; Moss, Moss, & Hansson, 2001). Not only is the death of an adult child untimely, but a lifelong parent-child bond is severed forever. Because this loss is comparatively rare, others who have experienced the loss of a grown child are comparatively rare and therefore unavailable to provide needed emotional support (Moss et al., 1986-1987). If a son or a daughter had grandchildren, grandparents may have to raise these children themselves, and yet be faced with caring for themselves (Hayslip & Kaminski, 2005; Hayslip & Glover, 2008-2009; Hayslip, Shore, Henderson & Lambert, 1998). When an adult child dies, the entire family's relationships are affected. Surviving siblings must deal with their own loss as well, influencing their relationships with one another as well as with older parents. Support groups such as The Compassionate Friends (see Box C) can be very helpful in providing an atmosphere of acceptance and emotional support for parents whose children have died. Guilt, anger, and depression may cloud family relationships, impede communication, and disrupt family-helping patterns and family rituals. For the surviving parent, hope for the future may

be eroded. When a child dies, our own mortality (and immortality) is shaken; we can no longer share in the joy of their lives. Indeed, grandparents grieve as well over the death of a grandchild (Reed, 2000). When the death of a grown child is experienced by elderly parents and grandparents, grief reactions are often very intense and prolonged (Rubin & Mallkinson, 2001; Walter & McCoyd, 2009). Older persons who lose adult children through death experience a special sense of failure that is difficult to deal with. Very few adults expect to bury their own children.

Grief Work

Grief is termed **work** because acknowledging and working through our feelings, as well as reorganizing our lives takes great effort. While we often **grieve anticipatorily** (before a person actually dies), some of our grief can also be experienced at a funeral or memorial service honoring the life of the person who has died. Funerals and other forms of ritual serve to structure our emotions at a time when we might otherwise be overwhelmed (Corr, Nabe & Corr, 2009). We may busy ourselves making funeral arrangements or entertaining relatives with little or no time to really be alone and reflect on how we are feeling.

Major functions of funerals are (1) to provide a socially acceptable, healthy means to prepare the body for burial (its **secular** function) and (2) to provide a symbolic rite of passage from the state of living to the state of being dead (its **sacred** function) (Schulz, 1978). Moreover, funerals can provide **psychological** support to the bereaved family and others who have suffered the loss. It is clear, however, that some persons do have more difficulty in coping with funerals (Hayslip et al., 2007). Yet, being less death anxious, having better mental health, and having more previous experience with funerals predict more positive attitudes toward the funeral (Hayslip et al., 2005-2006).

Funerals as a ritual marking death have changed in many ways (see Box G), perhaps indicating that they fulfill their function of supporting bereaved persons more adequately than in the past (Irion,

Box G

The Changing Funeral

Irion (1990-1991) has made a classic intensive study of funerals as cultural rituals that symbolize our feelings about losing a loved one. He contends that, because we are more aware of the psychological aspects of grief, funerals as rituals to facilitate grief work have changed in many ways. For example:

1. **Pastoral funeral orders to instruct clergy have become more sensitive to the needs of mourners**. These needs may be psychological or spiritual, and they clearly go beyond where to stand or what gestures to make. Being aware of the mourner's need to express grief, get support from others, and accept the reality of death is important.

2. **Funeral orders recognize that the funeral is a community function, not a private exercise**. Funerals bring people together. Death signals the loss of a part of the community. Active participation by the community is encouraged. Recognizing ethnicity, race, family, and regional customs is essential to the extent that community values as well as individual ones are reflected at the funeral.

3. **Funeral services show awareness of the importance of facing the reality of death**. The reality of the death of a loved one and its pain are brought home by viewing the body. The funeral involves a separation from the body of the deceased person. It communicates a sense of finality.

4. **The funeral is set within the context of the mourning process**. Funerals acknowledge that grief is an extended process that takes time. The survivors must not be forgotten after the funeral and will require extended pastoral support.

5. **Funerals are responsive to the dynamics of pluralism**. Funerals recognize the needs of people of different faiths and ethnic backgrounds. One "standard" funeral cannot serve everyone.

6. **Funerals recognize that there are ministries other than those of the clergy**. Laypeople and funeral directors are acknowledged as playing an important, emotionally supportive role in ministering to bereaved family members.

Source: Irion, P. E. (1990-1991). Changing patterns of ritual response to death. **Omega**, 22, 159-172.

These changes in the rituals of funerals can make them more responsive to the needs of mourners, helping them to better cope with grief and loss. Indeed, memorial services, organ donations, nontraditional funerals, and unique rituals (e.g., scattering the ashes from an airplane) are all evidence that the funeral as a ritual has become more **individualized**; this tends to be the preference of younger persons versus older persons, who prefer more traditional funeral services (Hayslip, Servaty, & Guarnaccia, 1999).

1990-1991). Indeed, nontraditional funerals are likely to become the norm for future cohorts (see Hayslip, Servaty, & Guarnaccia, 1999).

Coping with a Terminal Illness

If we assume that persons who are terminally ill, are "ready to die," we may tragically deny them the opportunity to deal with what Kubler-Ross (1969) terms **unfinished business**. Quite often, discussions about death and dying are seen as depressing or sad and consequently to be avoided with others who are dying, regardless of age. Acknowledging any and all needs is the key to helping those adults who are struggling with their mortality or who are dying (Kubler-Ross, 1969). Since the publication in 1969 of *On Death and Dying*, where Kubler-Ross's "stages," through which persons progress in reacting to their impending deaths are outlined, her stages have been overinterpreted (Kastenbaum, 1998). These stages consist of (a) **denial** (no, not me), (b) **anger** (directed at doctors, nurses, or those who will go on living), (c) **bargaining** (with others (God) in order to prolong life), (d) **depression** (a reaction to one's worsening symptoms or deterioration knowing that death will follow), and (e) **acceptance** (a sense of readiness about death, but without a loss of hope that life could be prolonged if a cure were found).

Dismissing a person's behavior as "just anger" may ignore very important external reasons (family conflicts, poor quality of care) for that anger. A patient's purported "denial" may also reflect a "mutual pretense" regarding not discussing death that the patient and the medical/staff family have agreed upon during the course of care, robbing the dying person of the opportunity to draw others closer as well as finish unfinished business. It also denies those who are in a position to help the dying person the opportunity to learn about life from someone else. Kubler-Ross teaches us to deal with dying persons "where they happen to be at the moment" (emotionally speaking). The same can certainly be applied to those who are experiencing anticipatory grief prior to a loved one's death. If we fail to recognize that every person's feelings about his/her own

(or another's) impending death are unique, we deny that person the right to make (or not make) decisions about life as well as death. These may be decisions that one may desperately want and need to make in order that one (or his/her loved one) may die "an appropriate death" (DeSpelder & Strickland, 2009; Hayslip & Hansson, 2006). In relating to those who are bereaved and grieving, we should recognize that grief is very personal. For example, it might be useful to explore whether the grieving person believed that the death was preventable or not, and to evaluate the strength of his/her relationship to the deceased (Guarnaccia, Hayslip & Pinkenburg-Landry, 1999).

What emotions people express near death seem to vary with a number of factors. One's race and degree of impairment seem to influence expectations of death (Williams et al., 2006). In a unique study of dying persons, Wu (1990-1991) found that family support and age determined how dying persons felt about life and death. Younger terminally ill patients expressed more bargaining and complaints (anger), while older patients expressed more depression and acceptance. Those with immediate family support felt more fearful and were less depressed than persons without family support. Moreover, younger persons who lacked support were more angry than those with meaningful family ties, while levels of support were not important for older persons (Wu, 1990-1991).

Whether persons are aware of their terminal diagnosis and impending death also seems to influence their emotions. In general, persons who are close to death are not more likely to mention the afterlife as a source of strength (Kastenbaum, 1998), and they seem to mention religion less often (Baugher et al., 1989-1990). Overall, there is little evidence for increased withdrawal from others as nearness to death increases, as might be predicted from Kubler-Ross's theory, assuming such persons are either depressed or accepting. Indeed, the quality of care they receive and the nature of their relationships with family and friends are the most important factors in determining the quality of life for dying persons.

Box H

Culture and Death

In caring for dying persons and in working with grieving individuals, the unique role that culture plays in enabling one to understand them is key to providing effective and compassionate care. Fleming (2010) notes that professionals should never assume that the values and wishes of their patients necessarily mirror their own. End-of-life discussions, feelings about and attitudes toward death are often influenced by one's cultural background. For example, while U.S. culture tends to favor the rights of individuals to make end-of-life choices, Asian, European, and Middle Eastern cultures are less consumed by the necessity of informing dying persons of their diagnosis or prognosis, as well as less predisposed toward the individual making end-of-life choices independent of cultural traditions and family wishes. Thus, one may working with a patient who will not even discuss euthanasia, admit to being fearful or being in pain, disagree about what kind of end-of-life care is desirable or acceptable, believe in the afterlife, feel that grief is private or that persons should recover from their loss and move on with their lives.

Though there are differences within cultures, it is helpful to contrast **individualistic** cultures from **collectivistic** cultures, where the former emphasize self-reliance and independence, and the latter emphasize familial bond, responsibility, and family traditions and obligations (Hayslip & Han, 2009). Whether one's identity is centrally defined by culture or whether the culture is actively experienced on an everyday basis is key to understanding cultural influences on death, dying, and bereavement.

Understandably then, definitions of quality of life and death itself, death rituals and customs surrounding dying and grieving, patterns of grieving, and openness to discussing issues surrounding death and end-of-life care will likely vary across persons based on the degree to which they are acculturated into the dominant culture and the extent to which a culture shares common values and ideas about dying and grieving. Importantly, culture is distinct from race or ethnicity.

Each culture has a **cultural script** (Rosenblatt, 2008) by which it influences persons in that culture. Culture is broadly defined as a social entity with shared values and mores about behaviors. The influence of a given cultural script is felt in our actions, preferences, values, customs, and rituals (Hayslip & Han, 2009). The cultural script may or may not mirror the beliefs of the person from that culture. As cultures necessarily change over time, their influence on persons' ideas, values, and behaviors pertinent to death and dying will also change. Similar to the cultural script is a culture's **death system** (Kastenbaum, 2009), which frames beliefs, behaviors, values, and rituals regarding death, dying, and grieving.

Key to being able to work with culturally diverse persons is **cultural competence**: being knowledgeable about cultural scripts, being informed about cultural differences, and being able to ask culturally sensitive questions that reflect the person's belief system and values regarding death and dying, end-of-life choices, and grieving.

Psychotherapy with Dying Persons

For the most part, discussions of death among those in the counseling professions are rare. Levy (1990), however, discusses therapy with terminally ill persons in the context of "humanizing death" (p. 189). As long as the patient is alive, the goal of all forms of therapy is simply to enhance the quality of life for both patient and family and to help them cope with the disease. Therapists must have confronted their own issues regarding death and loss, and must actively listen and be present in the moment with the dying person to be effective (Blumenfield & Tiamson-Kassab, 2010).

A major problem for dying patients is that psychological dysfunction that can be treated is often overlooked. Depression and anxiety, when they occur, are treatable in terminally ill persons (Coppola & Trotman, 2002). Depression is an understandable reaction to the perception that one's illness is terminal, though only 25% of dying people develop serious depression (Kiume, 2008). Feelings of abandonment by friends, coworkers, one's physician and even one's family can contribute to depression in persons who have lost all hope in the promise of a long life or even an abbreviated life.

Learning to cope with fears of losing control and being dependent and adapting to the physical losses that accompany dying are issues that can be addressed in therapy. The therapist can also help the patient and family make important decisions, e.g., planning a funeral, considering life-sustaining treatments as well as choosing to cease such treatment, making a decision to enter hospice care, and in some cases, entertaining physician-assisted suicide (Coppola & Trotman, 2002).

As persons who are depressed often entertain suicide, the therapist must inquire as to what the dying person is actually thinking about. If suicidal thoughts are uncovered, then treatment of the underlying depression can proceed. For persons who are severely depressed, antidepressives may be prescribed (see Chapter 10 and 11). When individual therapy is warranted, spouses and family members need also to be involved, as dying affects the whole family. Communication patterns can be observed and if necessary changed, and couples can explore other ways of sharing innermost feelings when their physical expression is muted by the disease process (Levy, 1990). Group therapy is also an option for some dying persons who can receive valuable support from other group members. Importantly, relationships with others can be strengthened, and fears about being alone can be confronted and worked through.

Psychotherapy with dying persons is necessarily short-term in nature, and is not focused on changing the individual per se. It is focused on making an **appropriate death** (the one that the person wants) possible (see Glaser & Strauss, 1965). It can allow persons who are dying to feel "safe" in making difficult choices and enable them to withdraw from others when necessary. They can "let go," and they can be helped to make meaning of their lives (Cohen, 2004). Techniques such as life review (see Chapter 11) can be helpful, and persons can express their feelings of anger and injustice at having their lives cut short, deal with the guilt they may feel in "abandoning" their families, and experience some normalcy amid the crisis that dying presents (Culkin, 2002).

The therapist's role does not end when the patient dies. Surviving family need support in ventilating feelings, and in dealing with guilt, anger, or grief after death, as well as in going on with their lives. Talking about the details of death, actively discussing the lost family member, and confronting one's needs for intimacy (for the spouse) are issues that the therapist can explore with the family after death (Levy, 1990). For persons who are near death, the therapist's primary role is to remain emotionally supportive, to encourage the patient to remain active in decision making, and to help the patient combat the side effects of the disease itself and of drugs by using techniques such as relaxation or self-hypnosis (Levy, 1990). The therapist can indeed become quite close to the dying person—as close as family.

Communicating with Others about Death and Dying

Because of the "pornographic" nature of death in our culture, we may avoid discussing those very things that some people have a real need to confront, under the assumption that these issues are either already settled, private, or simply too terrible to talk about (DeSpelder & Strickland, 2009; Kastenbaum, 2009). It is important to realize that for some adults, death may actually be positive. Ultimately, going with, "what is in your gut" may be best. A look, a hug, or a squeeze may be more comforting than anything you can say.

Box I

"What Is Hospice?"

What is it about hospice that is so special? A 29-year-old woman dying of cancer with perhaps two weeks to live talked about what made hospice special:

> "Here I am treated as a person. I have a sense of my dignity. Well, I don't mean that, it sounds so proud, but here I am simply myself, and no one minds. I am glad to live each day now, one at a time. I like to nap in the afternoons, but I am so busy here, it is actually hard for me to fit that in. So many people—friends I didn't know cared for me, people I used to work with—have written to me, come to visit me and so forth, now that I am here and it is all right to say what is happening."
> (Stoddard, 1980, pp. 4-5)

The needs of each person are better served by exploring what death **means** to him or her. Is death positive or negative? A door to something larger? Or a wall—the end of everything we know? This approach is particularly important in that chronological age is a poor predictor of death concerns (Kastenbaum, 2009). What in life does this individual value? How important are such things as family, health, religion, or work? What does the individual expect the future to bring? How important are friends? Kastenbaum and Aisenberg (1976) have noted that older persons **personalize** death more often than do the young. This personalization, for example, may take the form of wanting to be reunited with a departed loved one. In this light, family, professionals, and others interested in helping adults of all ages should develop helping skills that facilitate the expression of each individual's feelings about such issues (Corr, Nabe & Corr, 2009). For many persons (young and old), simply being taken seriously and listened to is a long-forgotten experience.

Hospice Care

Within the past three decades, **hospice care** for the terminally ill has emerged as a viable alternative to hospital deaths, which are often depersonalizing, lonely, painful experiences for both the dying persons and their families (Hayslip, 1997; Hayslip & Hansson, 2006). Hospice care, originally popularized in England by Cecily Saunders at St. Christopher's Hospice in London, spread to the United States in the early 1970s, in the form of New Haven Hospice located in New Haven, Connecticut. Since then, literally thousands of hospices have sprung up around the country (National Hospice and Palliative Care Organization, www.nhcpo.org).

Hospices can take on many forms: home-care based, hospital-based, a freestanding unit, or wholly volunteer. Many care for elderly patients, most of whom have cancer. It is not, however, uncommon for hospices to care for dying children (pediatric hospices do exist) or younger and middle-aged adults who may be dying of ALS, end-stage renal disease, cancer, AIDS, Alzheimer's disease, or a traumatic life-ending injury. While the term "hospice" originally referred to a "way station" to care for travelers on their journey, in modern times, it has come to represent an attitude toward making persons' lives as full as possible until they die. Persons who are still living can avoid the "social death" we discussed earlier.

Characteristics of hospice care include (1) pain/symptom control, (2) lessening isolation, (3) physician-directed services, (4) treatment on a 24-hour per day basis of both the patient and family, (5) the involvement of an interdisciplinary team (i.e., one's personal physician, hospice medical director, nurses, home health aides, volunteers, social worker, physical therapists, clergy, counselors, speech/occupational therapists, (6) bereavement follow-up of the family after death, (7) the use of volunteers, and (8) the opportunity for staff support (of one another) to lessen burnout and facilitate their own grief when a patient dies. Hospice provides the following services to dying persons and their families: pain management; counseling; providing needed medications, equipment, and medical supplies; caregiving instruction to the family; assisting the family throughout the dying process with matters pertaining to the legal (e.g., wills, advanced directives) or financial (e.g. filing private insurance or Medicare claims) aspects of dying; and supporting the family after the death. In some cases, patients may spend short intervals of time in the hospital or nursing home as their medical needs change or the family is in need of respite from the stresses of caregiving. Thus, the focus of hospice is not only on the physical care of the patient, but also on the psychological, spiritual, and emotional care of the patient and family.

Access to hospice is variable across geographic regions and is now more commonly offered in larger hospitals and more accessible when hospice care is reimbursable under the Medicare Hospice Benefit (Goldsmith et al., 2008). However, one's private insurance may also help pay for the costs of providing such care to dying persons (Blevins & Worth, 2006; Corr, Nabe, & Corr, 2009, National Hospice and Palliative Care Organization, 2010).

While most hospice personnel agree on the philosophical basis of hospice, there is less consensus on issues such as the extent of a patient's control over his/her life, the origins of hospice, and the suitability of hospice for all patients. Perhaps this lack of agreement underscores the importance of treating every dying patient as an individual. Patients in hospice have the same "rights" to quality care (see above) as do those receiving care in a hospital. Most important for persons who are dying, hospice permits them to make decisions and exercise control over their lives in a warm, caring, and comparatively pain-free atmosphere. Thus, hospice, in many cases, simply supports each patient and family in making all types of decisions related to family matters, funeral planning, wills, grieving, where death will occur, and most importantly, with whom, under what conditions, and how death will happen (Kastenbaum, 2009).

For many persons who value personal control or wish to be close to their loved ones, hospice care is a viable alternative. For others, who need the security of a hospital or who have always depended on others to make decisions for them, hospice would likely be inappropriate. In spite of its emphasis on the dignity and self-worth of the dying person, it is not a panacea for the problems many dying persons face on a daily basis. Further, as Hine (1979-1980) has discussed, responsibilities associated with hospice home care are those which all families do not wish to or cannot bear.

Educating persons about hospice care and palliative (pain reducing) care is important, as many are not aware of what hospice and palliative care are and where they might be available (Winter, Parker, & Schneider, 2007). While hospice cares for dying persons and their families, its real value, perhaps, is to teach us to cherish and nurture our relationships with others while we can.

Euthanasia

Euthanasia literally translated means "good death" (DeSpelder & Strickland, 2009). Given the comparatively recent advances in medical technology that allow for the extension of human life, and concerns about fatal illnesses such as AIDS, Alzheimer's disease, and certain forms of cancer, the dying person, family, and physicians may agonize over whose wishes are to be respected if the dying person is near death, in pain, or is on life-supportive machinery. If one is suffering from Alzheimer's disease, has had a massive stroke, is in a coma, or is a newborn, that person cannot speak up— who decides? the physician? the family? the state? God? At what point do we cease to try to extend someone's life? What if the person were to recover from a "fatal" illness or were to come out of an apparently irreversible coma? What if a cure were found? As opposed to euthanasia or physician-assisted suicide, what about hospice care as an alternative solution? Is being removed from a respirator or having artificial hydration and nutrition (e.g., a feeding tube) a blessing or is it murder?

The issues regarding the ethics of euthanasia are complex. Indeed, while euthanasia suggests the dying persons does not actively participate in the decision to end life, this is not the case for physician-assisted suicide (Corr, Nabe, & Corr, 2009). The complexity of these issues has been highlighted by Dr. Jack Kevorkian's quest to legitimize physician-assisted suicide in Michigan, the Supreme Court's 1997 ruling that there is no constitutional right to assisted suicide, the passage of (and legal challenges to) Proposition 16 in Oregon legalizing physician-assisted suicide in 1994, and the publicity surrounding the death of Terri Schaivo in 2005. Some may object to **active euthanasia**, defined as cutting someone's life short to relieve needless suffering or to preserve individual dignity. Instead, **passive euthanasia**, defined as failing to use life-saving measures that might otherwise prolong someone's life, may be more acceptable to others. Yet, all forms of euthanasia might be equally repulsive to other persons based on their philosophical or religious beliefs. Terminal care is costly; a family's finances and insurance coverage can be sapped over an extended period of time.

A consideration in euthanasia or physician-assisted suicide is that caring for a dying family member who is suffering and will never recover can be excruciating. Interestingly, Cicirelli (2002) found only a minority of aged persons to favor ending their lives via physician-assisted suicide or euthanasia. Williams et al. (2007) found a clear majority of adults to not only favor passive euthanasia, but to agree with **physician-assisted suicide**; most did not wish for life-sustaining treatments for themselves, but felt otherwise when it came to their partners. The opposite pattern was true for euthanasia (Williams et al., 2007). Interestingly in this respect, husbands and wives may not agree (Zettle-Watson et al., 2008).

The individual can state his/her right to die by writing a **living will,** or what is now termed an **advanced directive**. The living will is a directive that impels the physician to cease using artificial means of prolonging life when there is no realistic hope for recovery, allowing the individual to die naturally. The physician, not legally bound to execute the document, can under these circumstances exercise his/her best professional judgment. In some cases, the living will may be reexecuted. Alternatively, one may not be competent to sign a living will when seriously ill. A person writes a living will for many reasons—due to financial pressure or out of the wish to make death and grieving easier or more predictable for oneself or one's family. Fear of prosecution or legal action may cause the physician to not support the patient's wishes or to discourage a living will altogether. Wanting to speed up the dying process and end suffering, the physician could take matters into his/her own hands. What is dignified or merciful to one person may not be acceptable to another. While living wills are not legally binding in all states, frank, open discussion with one's physician and family can heighten the chances of one's wishes being carried out (see Corr, Nabe & Corr, 2009).

What has replaced the living will is the Patient Self-Determination Act (1991), which is a federal law specifying the means by which dying persons can competently participate in treatment decisions (Kastenbaum, 2009). While it is not without its problems, it goes a long way toward empowering persons who are dying. Likewise, given the controversy surrounding Dr. Jack Kevorkian's efforts to promote physician-assisted suicide, Compassion in Dying, a nonprofit organization in Washington has proposed a set of guidelines and safeguards to protect both the patient and the physician in aiding the patient and his/her family to make decisions about how life will end.

In 1997, the Florida Commission on Aging with Dignity created a document, which is widely available entitled *Five Wishes*, which combines many of the key elements of living wills and advanced directives. It allows one to specify (1) the person I want to make health care decisions for me when I can no longer make them myself, (2) the kind of medical treatment I want/don't want if I am incapacitated, (3) how comfortable I want to be, (4) how I want people to treat me, and (5) what I want my loved ones to know (Aging with Dignity, 2001). This document may set the standard for allowing persons to specify important end-of-life choices that make dying more meaningful to them and their families.

As Corr, Nabe and Corr (2009) suggest, the arguments for and against euthanasia are many. Several problems complicate each point of view: death isn't usually instantaneous, medical ethics is not well-defined, conflicts of interest are inevitable, and ultimately decisions about the quality, value, or worth of human life are involved. What if euthanasia got out of hand and was used to eliminate "inferior" people? This is termed the **slippery slope** argument (Corr, Nabe & Corr, 2009). Who decides when to end a life? Is ending a life defensible legally? Morally? These issues will continue to be debated in the years to come.

Check Your Learning 12-4

Define the following terms and concepts:

> Grief
> Depression
> Acceptance
> Active euthanasia
> Passive euthanasia
> Hospice care
> Physician-assisted suicide
> *Five Wishes*
> Cultural scripts
> Cultural competence
> Appropriate death
> Grief work
> Anticipatory grief
> Maladaptive grief
> Bereavement
> Mourning
> Dual Process Model
> Anger
> Denial
> Bargaining
> Slippery slope

- Is grief best described in stages or as a process? Why?

- Are bereaved people at risk? In what ways?

- What is unique about the loss of an adult child?

- Of what value is psychotherapy with dying persons?

- Of what value is the work of Kubler-Ross?

- What are some important factors to keep in mind in talking about death and dying with adults of varying ages?

- Do men and women grieve differently?

- How important is culture in understanding death?

A Final Word

The essential aloneness of those who are grieving or dying, fear, a lack of knowledge, and the inability to communicate prevent helpers, families, and friends from "getting in touch" with adults who face life without a husband or wife, or who are coping with a terminal illness, be they older persons or younger adults. A respect for the individuality of every life is perhaps the most important quality to recognize and develop in dealing with each person. Being sensitive to these wishes is perhaps the essential skill that we can nurture in helping adults deal with their own deaths, and in counseling those who are coping with the loss of a significant other.

The issues discussed here are those that persons of all ages face: desiring control over our lives, wanting to be loved and cared for, being treated with respect and dignity as individuals, and perhaps most importantly, appreciating the intertwining of life and death. As Wass and Corr (1981) have noted, "We cannot grasp or evaluate the proportions and the significance of life if we do not bring death into the picture. Just as death must be construed through life, so also life must eventually be seen in the context of death. Certainly death is not the only perspective from which to understand life, but . . . it is indispensable as a constitutive element of human existence" (p. 7).

Life and death *are* necessarily intertwined. We can indeed learn a great deal about living by confronting our fears about dying, and discussing what is important to us in life and death with our friends and family. While this may seem be a foreboding task, "climbing this emotional hill" is something from which we can grow personally.

Summary

This chapter dealt with a variety of issues pertaining to **death** and **dying** in adulthood. Death can mean many things, and defining death is a complex process that depends upon the criteria that are used to delineate life and death. The understanding of what one means when **fear of death** is stated is also multifaceted, and fear of death is multidimensional and can exist at both conscious and unconscious levels of awareness. Fears about **death** need to be separated from those about the **dying process** or the **afterlife**. In addition to fear, **overcoming** and **participating** are common responses to death among adults.

Death for the most part is foreign to the lives of most young adults. Yet, sudden deaths that are accidental and/or violent are not uncommon, and terminal illness and the loss of a child do affect some young persons. For middle-aged persons, the possibility of their own mortality and the loss of parents are the major aspects of death that persons confront during midlife. Older persons think about death more often than do younger persons, and personalize it more frequently as well. Their responses to death are highly variable, but do seem to be related to a number of factors, most notable health status and institutionalization. For older persons, the losses of a spouse, a sibling, and an adult child are the most common ways in which death affects them.

Grief and **bereavement** are distinct from one another. Grief is a complex and ongoing process which requires a series of adjustments to a different lifestyle and relationships with others, as well as to the emotional burdens of coping with the loss of a relationship. While older versus younger widows and widowers may cope with different short-term and long-term issues, **loneliness** remains the chief problem for those who are bereaved, regardless of age.

In working with the dying person, as **Kubler-Ross's** stage theory implies, it is most important to recognize each person's feelings as unique, and to deal with each individual in a nonjudgmental manner. In this respect, **hospice** has provided many terminally ill persons and their families with alternatives to dying in an institution. Its chief characteristics are pain/symptom control, 24-hour care, treatment of the patient and family as a unit, and bereavement follow-up.

Euthanasia and physician-assisted suicide are highly controversial areas regarding the quality versus the quantity of life. Distinctions between **active** and **passive** euthanasia can be made, and there are age, sex and racial differences regarding its acceptance. While **living wills** and **advanced directives** have helped structure decisions regarding euthanasia, there remain numerous issues that complicate their utility in many situations.

Most important in talking with adults about death is the recognition that each person is a **unique individual**. Open, honest communication that reflects an appreciation for the needs and values of both dying person and the family seems to work best.

Glossary

Absolute threshold The minimum level of stimulus energy/intensity required for the individual to detect stimulation.

Accommodation The process whereby the eye adjusts itself to attain maximal image resolution (clarity).

Accommodation versus assimilation Piagetian styles of interacting with the environment. Accommodation involves changing one's behavior to fit the environment, while assimilation involves changing the environment to suit one's behavior.

Active euthanasia Doing something to cut life short for those who are in pain or suffering.

Active leisure activity Refers to activities such as exercising, jogging, playing sports, or going to restaurants. The primary focus of these leisure activities is active "doing" and/or participation.

Activities of daily living (ADL) Basic skills such as bathing, dressing, or eating that enable persons to function independently on a daily basis.

Activity theory Theory that suggests that the older individual who manages to resist withdrawal from the social world and remains active will maintain life satisfaction.

Adaptation The change in sensitivity of the eye as a function of change in illumination. There are two types: dark adaptation—improvement in sensitivity to light in a dark environment; and light adaptation—increased sensitivity to light in a light environment.

Adaptation level The process whereby individual receptor processes (hearing, vision) tend to function at a comfortable level relative to the external stimulation, so that a stimulus of a given magnitude is perceived as neither strong nor weak.

Advanced directive A document that allows one to state his or her wishes regarding end-of-life care should that person no longer be able to make such decisions and communicate them to others.

Age associated memory impairment (AAMI) Normal and reliable age-related declines in short-term memory performance.

Age Discrimination in Employment Act (ADEA) Federal law enacted in 1967 to prohibit age discrimination in employment. Amended in 1974 and 1978 to provide more comprehensive coverage.

Age function A statement of the relationship between a given variable and chronological age.

Ageism Discrimination or bias against persons due to their age.

Age-normative influences Factors that are general to development, are highly related to chronological age, and are presumed to affect everyone of a given chronological age range similarly.

Aging The biological, psychological, and sociological aspects of growth and development across the life span.

Aging process A complex emphasizing change and affected by many biological, psychological, sociological, and environmental factors.

Alzheimer's disease A form of dementia characterized by a higher than normal incidence of senile plaques and neurofibrillary tangles in brain tissue.

Anticipatory grief Preparation or rehearsal for death prior to its actual occurrence.

Anxiety An emotional disorder characterized by excessive worry and apprehension.

Arteriosclerosis Progressive hardening of blood vessel walls with age.

Atherosclerosis Progressive narrowing of blood vessel walls with age.

Attachment An emotional bond that develops between children and their parents. Often viewed as the foundation upon which other interpe-=rsonal relationships are built.

Attribution The process of interpreting or making inferences about one's own or another's behavior.

Audition The hearing sense.

Baby Boom generation Persons born during the period from approximately 1946 to 1964 during which there was a high birthrate in the United States.

Behavior therapy Form of therapy where rewarding and punishing stimuli in the environment are manipulated to bring about desired behavior(s).

Bereavement overload The inability to work through the deaths of loved ones that occur close to one another in time.

Beta-amyloid protein Abnormal protein that interferes with the brain cell's function, thought to be responsible for Alzheimer's disease.

Biological age Biological age has two aspects. It can be considered to be the relative age or condition of the individual's organ and body systems. Also, it refers to individuals' present position relative to their potential life span, which varies from species to species.

Biological death The cessation of function or irreversible damage to certain critical organs or organ systems.

Bipolar versus unipolar depression Depression characterized by mood swings (bipolar) versus predominately sad affect (feeling low) (unipolar).

Bona fide occupational qualification (BFOQ) An ability, trait, or factor that is considered to be related to job performance.

Brain death Death via the cessation of higher order brain activity.

Brain plasticity The capacity of the brain to regenerate or compensate for losses in brain cells.

Bridge employment Jobs which serve to make the transition from full-time employment to retirement less difficult.

Career A planned, coherent, organized sequence of positions that have meaning for the individual.

Career indecision The inability to choose a particular occupation, or difficulty in deciding whether to change occupations or remain in the same occupation.

Caregiver burden The subjective feeling of stress and frustration in caring for an elderly family member.

Cautiousness Being conservative in decision making and with respect to many aspects of behavior.

Cerebral death The cessation of brain activity for a given period of time (e.g., 24 hours), often termed brain death.

Clinical death The cessation of spontaneous heart and respiratory activity.

Cognitive behavior therapy Form of therapy emphasizing internal cognitions or ideas about oneself or the environment as key concepts in bringing about behavior change.

Cognitive personality theory Approach to personality emphasizing one's perceptions or cognitions about experiences or events.

Cognitive versus noncognitive influences Referring to the distinction between factors (noncognitive) that influence performance on tests of learning or memory (e.g., fatigue) and those processes (cognitive) that the tests are designed to reflect (e.g., learning, memory.)

Cohort A group of individuals sharing a common set of experiences (e.g., individuals born at a given point in history who, by virtue of their birth data, experience certain sets of events at roughly the same time in their development).

Cohort sequential design A replication of a longitudinal study with different cohorts.

Collaborative choices Life choices made by two persons that reflect joint decision making and each person's needs and values.

Collagen A fibrous protein present in connective tissue (ligaments, muscles, joints, bones).

Competence The skills and abilities of the individual that enable him/her to adequately cope with the the environment.

Complementarity Theory of mate selection that suggests that opposites attract.

Complicated bereavement Adjustment to loss that is characterized by a susbstantial degree of self-destructive behavior and depression.

Compromise and circumscription Making career choices that do not suit one based upon gender stereotypes.

Congruence The extent to which the demands of the environment match the skills of the individual.

Convoy Personal network of friends and family members who accompany us throughout the life cycle.

Countertransference The difficulties experienced by a younger therapist who is treating an older client (e.g., feelings about one's parents may be projected upon the older client).

Crossover effect The fact that for more recent cohorts black females' life expectancy will exceed that of white males.

Cross-sectional design A design which compares two or more age groups at one time of measurement.

Cross-sequential design The replication/generalization of a time lag design to other times of measurement and cohorts.

Crystallized ability Acculturated skills that build upon one another and remain stable across most of adulthood.

Cultural competence Being sensitive to persons of other cultures and being able to ask culturally relevant and culturally sensitive questions.

Cultural ethics Prevailing attitudes of a society at a particular point in time that determine how individuals view their relationship with society and others at all points in the life span.

Cultural script A culture's set of expectations and influences on death and dying.

Custodial grandparents Grandparents who have assumed parental responsibility for a grandchild.

Death anxiety Fear of death, dying, or the afterlife, which may or may not be consciously expressed.

Death system A particular culture's set of expectations on death, dying, and grieving.

Death versus dying The moment of death versus the process of days' or weeks' duration leading up to death.

Death with dignity Death that is "appropriate" (of the individual's choosing) and that preserves the person's sense of respect and honor.

Decision/premotor time In a perceptual-motor reaction time task, the time lapsed from the onset of the stimulus to the initiation of the response to that stimulus.

Deep friendships Friendships based on intimate feelings between individuals.

Delirium A temporary state of confusion that is often misdiagnosed as dementia.

Dementia A cluster of behaviors or characteristics (e.g., disorientation) common to many diagnostic entities ranging from depression to Alzheimer's disease.

Developmental niche The fit between the individual and his/her physical and social environment.

Developmental tasks Behaviors, activities, skills, or milestones that individuals are expected to accomplish by their culture during specific stages of the life cycle. For instance, in our culture these include activities for the adult such as obtaining a driver's license and voting.

Deviation IQ A method of computing an intelligence quotient based upon deviations from the mean.

Dialectical operations Theory of Riegel that suggests internal factors (genetically preprogrammed instinctual behaviors, traits, characteristics, physiological state) and external factors (aspects of the physical environment, cultural components) continuously influence and are influenced by each other.

Difference threshold The degree to which a stimulus (e.g., sound, light) must be louder or brighter to be perceived as such.

Disengagement theory Theory that suggests that with increasing age individuals withdraw (disengage) from society and society withdraws (disengages) from the individual. There are two types of disengagement, psychological and social. The theory has been reformulated to account for individual differences.

Dual process model of grief The experience of grief that emphasizes the shift from loss-oriented functioning to restoration-oriented functioning.

Ecological validity Refers to the ability of tasks or tests to reflect everyday requirements (e.g., the real-life ecology of learning).

Elder abuse Psychological, physical, or financial neglect or active harm of older persons by others.

Empty nest Refers to the time when all the children have left the home. Its impact may be positive or negative.

Emotional support Support that is affective in nature.

Encoding The interpretation or giving of meaning to information so that it may be stored and retrieved.

Engaged lifestyle A lifestyle that is mentally and emotionally stimulating, thought by many to be a key element in the aging of our cognitive skills.

Environment The multileveled aspects of the context in which persons are embedded, including the physical/objective, subjective, interpersonal, and functional environment.

Environmental press The demandedness of the environment with respect to one's skills and abilities.

Everyday intelligence Intelligence applied to everyday cognitive functioning that is adaptive.

Everyday memory Memory for facts, events, names, faces, etc., that are important to that person's everyday physical and psychological functioning.

Evidence-based research The impact of therapy that is based upon empirical findings to reach conclusions.

Evolutionary sensence Explains aging in terms of genetic influences which are passed down from generation to generation.

Exchange theory Theory that has been adapted to help explain negative attitudes toward aging. Suggests individuals attempt to maximize rewards and reduce costs in interpersonal relationships.

Exercised versus unexercised abilities Denny's notion that abilities maintain themselves with age if they are used; those that are not used (unexercised) decline.

Explicit versus implicit memory Explicit memory requires purposeful effort to recall information while implicit memory involves the casual if not unintentional acquisition of seemingly irrelevant information in the process of learning a task.

Extended family Close relatives such as aunts, uncles, cousins, and grandparents.

False negatives Error of diagnosis where a disorder is diagnosed as absent when it is, in fact, present.

False positives Error of diagnosis where a disorder is falsely diagnosed as present when it is not.

Family systems theory An approach to understanding and treating families that emphasizes the entire family as a system of interrelating individuals.

Family-to-work spillover A form of role conflict where one's family responsibilities interfere with work performance.

Field dependence/independence A construct developed to explain individual differences in perception. Persons who are field dependent make judgments that are heavily influenced by the surrounding, immediate environment, while field independent persons' judgments are not influenced by the immediate environment.

Filial maturity When adult children no longer view their parents only as parents but as real people who need their help.

Filial responsibility Refers to the perceived obligation (frequently determined by law, custom, or personal preference) with regard to the various types of services and social support that children should provide for their older parents.

Filter theory of mate selection Theory of mate selection that suggests that in selecting a mate people do so via the use of a hierarchical set of "filters." The person who passes through each of these filters is the person we marry.

Fluid ability Cognitive skills that are independent of acculturated influences and that decline with increased age.

Flynn effect The tendency for IQ scores to improve over the last several decades.

Frontotemporal dementia A form of dementia characterized by personality change and language difficulties, distinct from Alzheimer's disease. Also called Pick's disease.

Functional ability An individual's ability to care for himself/herself or the ability to cope in a given situation.

Functional age Judging persons on their ability to function or perform a job adequately as opposed to their chronological age.

Functional analysis An analysis of an individual's behavior in relation to the function it serves in managing the environment.

Functional disorders Behavioral changes that are problematic, whose causes can be attributed to psychogenic versus organic factors. Functional disorders can coexist with organicity.

Gender roles Those behavior patterns (culture specific) that are considered appropriate and often specific to each gender, which are formed (acquired) early in life and are maintained until death.

Gender splitting As found by Levinson for women, a sense of the expectation that there are roles appropriate for men and women.

General adaptation syndrome Selye's notion of the body's three-phase reaction to stress or illness (alarm, resistance, exhaustion).

Generational stake The tendency of older generations to report more closeness to those who are younger versus the latter's reporting less closeness to the former.

Generative caregiving Caregiving that is unselfish and that has the care receiver's well-being as a first priority.

Generativity Erikson's notion that suggests persons who are middle-aged find ways of being creative or productive as a way of ensuring that they will live on after their death.

Genetic biological theories of aging Theories of aging that emphasize the formation of genetic structures as explanations for the aging process.

Glare sensitivity Sensitivity to bright light that results in unpleasantness or discomfort and/or that interferes with optimum vision.

Grandparental styles Modes of interacting with one's adult children and grandchildren (e.g., formal versus involved styles) and the meaning attached to the grandparent role.

Grief versus bereavement Grief refers to the expression of feelings about a loss, while bereavement simply indicates that one has experienced a loss.

Group therapy A form of therapy where individuals in a group setting share experiences under the guidance of a group leader.

Half-life The length of time it takes for half the drug which has been taken to be fully metabolized and eliminated from the person's system.

Health belief model A theory about behavior change which emphasizes that persons must first feel vulnerable to a problem and with the support of others and cues to change their behavior, will actually do so.

History-normative influences Factors or events that occur at a specific point in time (day, year, month) and theoretically impact upon everyone in that society or culture.

Horizontal career move A move from one career to another.

Hospice A philosophy of caring for the terminally ill and their families emphasizing individualized care over cure and bereavement counseling.

Identity style One's style of interacting with others that influences self-concept and self-esteem.

Illusion of absolute safety Gould's concept stressing the false myth of safety learned during childhood, that one eventually gives up in adulthood.

Implicit versus explicit theories of intelligence Implicit theories of intelligence refer to ideas about what intelligence is, while explicit theories refer to the abilities we use when we behave intelligently.

Indirect self-destructive behavior (ISDB) Taking one's life covertly or indirectly within an institution by becoming combative, not taking medication, not eating, etc.

Individual differences Refers to differences between persons on any trait, behavior, ability, or performance skill at any given point in time.

Informal role types According to Rosow, informal role types assume no institutional status but have definite roles attached to them. These include family scapegoat, heroes, criminals, etc.

Information processing approach to aging A framework which suggests that once a person has received stimulation from the environment, this stimulation (information) must pass through several distinct information processing stages before a response occurs.

Institutional role types According to Rosow, an institutional role type assumes a given status for a person who has defined roles. These include such factors as social class, gender, race, and age.

Instrumental activities of daily living (IADL) More advanced everyday skills such as driving, shopping, or housecleaning that enable persons to live independently.

Instrumental leisure activity Leisure activity that is in the service of attaining a goal or producing a result.

Instrumental support Support that applies to helping persons manage their affairs and cope with everyday tasks

Integrity A sense of completeness about one's life characterized by an acceptance of death (Erikson).

Intellectual plasticity The view that suggests older adults' intellectual skills are quite plastic or malleable with training or intervention.

Intelligence General index of an individual's ability to behave intelligently in situations or in tests designed to elicit such behaviors.

Interdependence Referring to the interrelatedness of events in our lives. Each influences and is influenced by the other.

Interest-related friendships Friendships that are based on some similarity of lifestyle or interest. These may include plants, pets, hobbies, or sports.

Interindividual differences Refers to differences between persons on any trait, behavior, ability, or performance skill at any given point in time. *See* Individual differences.

Interiority Neugarten's term for the tendency to become preoccupied with one's inner experiences (intrapsychic level) with increased age.

Interpersonal/problem solving therapy Therapy that focuses upon the interpersonal difficulties of the client and which stresses the changing and development of the client's problem-solving skills

Intimacy Erikson's notion that applies to young adults, who are thought to be seeking a meaningful relationship with another person as an extension of the love they received from their parents.

Intraindividual changes Refers to changes within an individual over time on any trait, behavior, ability, or performance skill.

Intraindividual differences Refers to differences between traits, behaviors, abilities, or performance levels within a person at any one point in time.

Intrapsychic Refers to internal personality dynamics.

Intrinsic leisure activity Activities that are inherently satisfying to the individual.

Intrinsic (primary) versus extrinsic (secondary) influences on life expectancy Intrinsic factors (e.g., genetic inheritance, race) contribute directly to life expectancy, while extrinsic factors (smoking, exercise) have an indirect influence on life expectancy.

Kinship network The extended family—aunts, uncles, and cousins. *See* Extended family.

Knowledge acquisition components Aspects of intelligence that help us gain new knowledge.

Learned helplessness The perception that the correlation between one's behavior and desired outcomes is minimal.

Learning Learning is the acquisition of information and facts via experience.

Leisure Typically refers to a person's activities during free time. Can include work or may simply be a state of mind.

Leisure competence The development of satisfying leisure activities. Implies understanding the meaning of leisure for you personally.

Leisure lifestyles Patterns of activity among retirees. Researchers classify these individuals into categories on the basis of their primary leisure activities.

Lewy body dementia Dementia that is defined by abnormal protein deposits in the brain.

Life expectancy How long on the average one is expected to live; it is species specific.

Life review The internal process by which the individual comes to terms with crises, problems, conflicts, etc., in an effort to make sense out of personal life experiences via reminiscence.

Life-span developmental model A view that sees development as the result of an interdependence between internal and external factors throughout the course of the life span.

Life structure Levinson's concept emphasizing the overall plan of one's life, composed of many interrelated aspects (e.g., work vs. family).

Line of unbearability One's personal equation governing suicide as an end to life where life's quality is emphasized over its quantity.

Lipofuscin Aging pigment that accumulates in certain organ systems with age.

Living will A provision by which the individual directs the physician or family not to needlessly sustain that individual's life if such acts would prolong suffering. Sometimes referred to as an advanced directive.

Longevity The theoretical upper limit of the lifespan; it is species specific.

Longitudinal design A design which follows a specific cohort of people as they age over time

Maturational ground plan The biologically determined sequence one progresses through, according to Erikson's psychosocial stages.

Mechanics versus pragmatics of intelligence Distinction by Baltes emphasizing basic fundamental intellectual skills (mechanics) versus the use of intellectual skills that are more applied or adaptive, e.g., wisdom (pragmatics).

Memory The storage and retrieval of facts over time.

Menopause The cessation of menstruation and the ability to bear children. Usually occurs in one's late 40s or early 50s.

Mentor One who guides or advises another in terms of either occupational or personal goals, behaviors, etc.

Meta-analysis Understanding a phenomenon based upon an analysis of the picture created by available research versus relying upon a single study.

Metacomponents Aspects of intelligence that help us make decisions and adapt to the environment.

Metamemory One's memory for what is in one's memory, to include self-assessment or self-estimates of one's memory capacity or efficiency.

Midlife crisis A personal sense of upheaval experienced by some men and women in their 40s, 50s, and 60s.

Mild cognitive impairment A condition characterized by personality change and gradual loss of cognitive functioning that often precedes Alzheimer's disease.

Milieu therapy A form of therapy often used within institutions where all aspects of the interpersonalenvironment are changed to facilitate the individual's adaptation or adjustment (e.g., interactions with staff).

Mnemonic devices Referring to a variety of techniques by which learning and memory performance may be improved.

Motor-cognitive rigidity Refers to the degree to which an individual can shift without difficulty from one activity to another.

Motor time In a perceptual-motor reaction time task, the time lapse from the initiation of the response to the stimulus to the completion of that response.

Multidimensional change Refers to numerous changes in different types of ability, skill, and behavior simultaneously within an individual over time.

Multidirectional change Numerous behaviors and traits that exhibit different types of change (e.g., increases and decreases in functioning) along the course of development.

Multi-infarct dementia Dementia produced by small strokes producing clusters of dead neurons or infarcts that create disturbances in the flow of blood to the brain.

Neurofibrillary tangles Intertwined nerve fibers that interfere with brain cell function.

Neurotransmitter substances Various chemicals (e.g., acetylcholine) that make possible communication across synapses between brain cells.

Noise Background interference that interferes with the ability to detect a stimulus.

Nongenetic biological theories of aging Theories of aging that emphasize changes in cells and tissues with age after they have been formed.

Nonnormative influences Factors that are not related to age or history and that affect specific individuals during the life cycle. These factors cannot be attributed to the normal process of development or to the impact of environmental, cultural, societal events.

Normal versus pathological aging Normal aging occurs in the absence of disease, while pathological aging is caused by disease. This distinction is similar to that between primary and secondary aging.

Nuclear family The traditional nuclear family in American society is one in which there is a husband, wife, and children.

Obsolescence A pattern of career change where the older worker has fallen behind in the mastery of new skills and knowledge on the job.

Occupational development Refers to the selection and choice of an occupation during the life course. Often called career development.

Occupational developmental tasks The particular goals, activities, or skills associated with a specific occupation.

Occupational role The behaviors, status, and traits associated with a specific occupation. Occupations vary in terms of the expectancies of society and others with regard to behaviors and activities.

Old age dependency ratio The ratio of older persons who are receiving retirement or health care benefits relative to the number of younger person whose earnings support such funds.

Optimists Persons who look forward to desirable events and who look on the bright side of even negative events

Osteoporosis The process of our bones hardening or becoming brittle with age, linked to a reduction of bony material. This results in greater fragility and is related to a deficit in calcium.

Overcoming A style of dealing with death that emphasizes death as failure.

Paired associates task Task where the learner is to associate and recall certain stimuli (S) that have been paired with specific responses (R).

Paradoxical directives Suggestions by the therapist to the client not to engage in a behavior designed to reveal its self-defeating nature and establish control over that behavior.

Paranoia Feelings of persecution or suspiciousness.

Paraphrenia Term given to schizophrenia appearing for the first time in later life.

Parkinson's disease A form of dementia characterized by cognitive dysfunction accompanied by psychomotor disturbances, e.g., involuntary trembling or tremors.

Participating A style of dealing with death that emphasizes the interrelatedness of life and death as natural partners.

Passive euthanasia Failing to do something that would otherwise extend the life of a terminally ill person.

Passive leisure activity Refers to activities such as reading or watching television in the home.

Pattern recognition Involves recognizing a specific stimulus pattern from a group of stimulus patterns or displays.

Perception The interpretation of sensory stimulation.

Perceptual inference Theory that suggests that older adults do not utilize incomplete information as effectively as young adults.

Perceptual information processing model Model of perception that suggests the abilities of perceptual style, selective attention, and perceptual motor reaction time are related to behavior or performance.

Performance components Various mental operations such as making comparisons, which help us to solve problems.

Peripheral explanations for RT slowing View the loss of response speed with age as due to decrements in the sense organs and/or peripheral nervous system.

Peripheral field The outer areas of the visual field. The visual field is the extent of physical space visible to an eye in a given position—that whole area you see.

Periphery That aspect of personality that is situational and behavioral, according to Maddi.

Personality disorders Characteristic patterns of relating to others and coping with change which are at odds with cultural expectations of adaptive behavior.

Personality-perceptual rigidity Refers to an individual's ability to adjust readily to new surroundings and changes in cognitive and environmental patterns.

Personality "types" Neugarten's clusters of personalities whose styles differ and who vary regarding life satisfaction.

Personalization of death Giving death a personal meaning (e.g., death means being reunited with loved ones).

Personal/subjective age The age that one privately feels.

Personal versus universal helplessness Personalized, idiosyncratic feelings about helplessness versus generalized ideas about helplessness that apply to all people.

Person-environment interaction Theory that suggests that all aspects of behavior and performance can be conceived of as a result of the interaction or transaction between the individual and the environment.

Pet therapy Form of therapy using real or plush animals as aids in reestablishing caring relationships with others.

Physiological theories of aging Theories of biological aging that emphasize breakdown of certain organs or organ systems.

Pick's disease A form of dementia that is genetic in origin. Now referred to as frontotemporal dementia.

Plasticity The quality of being able to change or be flexible, especially with regard to brain function, learning, memory, or intelligence

Pluralism Refers to the fact that development takes on many forms.

Positivity effect Referring to the tendency to recall life experiences in positive terms or to recall positive experiences more easily.

Postformal thinking An adaptive form of intelligence that characterizes much of adulthood, often termed problem finding rather than problem solving.

Poverty level index A dollar figure set by the government to officially designate individuals as living below the poverty line, for purposes of eligibility for federal assistance.

Presbycusis The most common hearing disorder of older adults. It is characterized by a progressive bilateral loss of hearing for tones of high frequency due to degenerative physiological changes in the auditory system as a function of age.

Presbyopia The progressive decline with age in the eye's ability to focus on near objects. Results mainly from a loss of elasticity in the lens.

Primary appraisal An initial evaluation of an event as stressful or not.

Primary memory Memory for material whose limit is 5 to 7 bits of information.

Primary mental abilities Theory of intelligence hypothesizing seven major abilities—the focus of Schaie's work on the aging of intelligence.

Prime age Designation varies substantially as a function of specific occupation. The U.S. Bureau of Labor Statistics considers the ages between 25 and 54 to be prime age for a worker.

Principle of compensation The perception that terminally ill persons are compensated for the loss of life by the promise of eternity.

Process approach to personality Theory of personality which stresses traits, life scripts, and self-regulation.

Progeria A disease process that rapidly accelerates the physical signs and symptoms of aging.

Programmed senescence Explaining aging in terms of a biological clock which controls the aging process.

Prospective memory Memory for facts or actions to be performed in the future.

Protestant work ethic Traditional work value that views work as sacred and something to be engaged in and enjoyed.

Pseudodementia The misdiagnosis of depression as dementia in older persons.

Psychic death Extreme withdrawal from others, often characterized by giving up.

Psychoanalytic model Views development as instinctual and biologically based, progressing through a series of discontinuous psychosexual stages that are quantitatively different.

Psychodynamic therapy Freud's psychoanalytic therapy emphasizing free association, insights provided by the therapist, and the uncovering of unconscious material embedded in one's childhood experiences.

Psychological age Refers to the adaptive capacities of the individual, such as coping ability or intelligence.

Psychometric tradition Perspective emphasizing the construction of empirically derived tests with established reliability and validity to assess intelligence or personality.

Psychopharmacological therapy Drug therapy. Often contraindicated with elderly persons due to unwanted side effects of many medications. Can be used with other forms of therapy.

Psychosocial crises Erikson's sequence of individual-social choices that face all persons at various points in their lives (e.g., intimacy vs. isolation).

PXO theory A theory of interpersonal attraction that says that persons are influenced by person (P), environment (X), and the other person in the relationship (O).

Rating of living theory Theory that explains aging in terms of diminished energy and resources available to repair one's body

Reality orientation (RO) Form of therapy stressing reorientation of self to time and place on a daily basis.

Recognition versus recall Methods of studying memory processes (retrieval, encoding), presenting tasks where cues for the information exist (recognition) versus those where such cues must be generated (recall).

Registration The process of taking in information or stimulation so that it may be processed.

Regression to the mean The tendency for individuals with high or low scores to regress or change in the direction of the average for the group.

Regressive intervention Doing little or nothing for someone who is terminally ill because that person is beyond all help.

Relabeling A technique frequently used in cognitive or family therapies where the "problem" is redefined so as to enable the client to see things from a new perspective.

Reminiscence The process of looking back on one's life, central to the life review.

Remotivation therapy A form of therapy assuming that the healthy portion of the person's personality can be activated via restructuring the real environment with the help of the therapist and others.

Resilience The quality of being able to rebound or bounce back from adversity or negative experiences. Sometimes referred to as hardiness.

Response bias Term used in laboratory investigation of cautiousness. Refers to the particular response characteristics of individuals—their criteria for making a response.

Retirement Voluntary or mandated withdrawal from the work force.

Retrieval The "getting out" of information from memory storage.

Reversible (acute) versus irreversible (chronic) dementia Referring to the distinction between dementias whose cause can be identified and whose symptoms can be reversed (e.g., malnutrition) versus those whose causes are organic and presumed irreversible (e.g., brain cell loss).

Role change A role shift that involves the complete shifting from one type of role to another. An example would be a change from student to teacher.

Roles Roles are the behaviors, traits, and characteristics expected by others for individuals who occupy a specific social position in society.

Role transition A role shift that involves the evolution of one form of a specific role to another form of that same role. An example would be a shift from mother to grandmother.

Rote versus mediated learning Rote learning is learning via simple repetition, whereas mediated learning relies on a scheme or mnemonic (e.g., i before e except after c). Some tasks and some persons tend to favor one type of learning over the other.

Sandwich generation The generation of middle-aged persons who are both raising adolescent children and caring for aging parents.

Schizophrenia General term suggesting symptoms that imply a break with reality (e.g., delusions or hallucinations).

Secondary appraisal Deciding upon one's available options in coping with change.

Secondary memory Memory for material whose span exceeds the capacity of primary memory (5 to 7 digits). Often referred to as short-term memory. Requires active rehearsal.

Secular versus sacred function of funerals Secular aspects of funerals refer to their function in disposing of the body, while their sacred function refers to the memorialization of life and transition to death.

Selective attention The control of information processing so that a particular source of information is processed more fully than any other simultaneous sources of information.

Selective dropout The tendency for certain types of persons to drop out of a longitudinal study.

Selective exposure The formulation of a belief or attitude on the basis of limited information—not having observed all possible instances.

Selective sampling The tendency for certain types of persons to volunteer for research.

Selective survival The tendency for certain persons to be more likely to survive than others.

Semantic versus episodic memory Refers to the distinction between the recall of general information (e.g., what a plane is) and the recall of specific details (e.g., dates, places; for instance, the date and destination of your last plane trip).

Senile plaques Clusters of dead or dying neurons that interfere with brain function and that are especially present in the brains of persons with Alzheimer's disease.

Sensation The reception of physical stimulation and the translation of this stimulation into neural impulses.

Sensory memory Memory that is preattentive— it requires no conscious effort or attention. Material is processed solely in terms of its physical (visual, aural) features.

Sensory receptors Structures that receive and register stimulation from the environment. Each primary sense has specific receptors.

Serial learning task Task where the learner is required to learn and recall items in a given order (e.g., as presented).

Serious leisure Leisure that is carried out with passion and commitment.

Skilled care A term denoting the level of care offered in nursing homes; skilled care demands more staff time and effort to care for impaired or physically dependent elderly persons than does unskilled or intermediate care.

SOC (Selection, Optimization, Compensation). A process of adapting to the aging process emphasizing the selection of meaningful activities and skills, their optimization through practice, and one's ability to compensate for decline via the use of such skills and activities.

Social age Refers to the social habits and roles of the individual relative to the expectations of society.

Social clock Expectations about the timing of various events, behaviors, and activities along the lifecycle with regard to their being "on" or "off" time.

Social death Death via the cessation of interpersonal relationships, i.e., being treated as if one were dead.

Socialization The process that molds each of us into a member of a particular society or subculture through our acquisition of the roles appropriate to our age, gender, social class, or ethnic group.

Social learning theory Personality theory that emphasizes the role of models who serve as guides for the construction of internal standards of behavior.

Socioadaptational Refers to adaptation at the level of roles and relationships with others.

Socioemotional selectivity The process by which individuals make choices about relationships with others based on their awareness of the limited time left for them to live.

Solidarity model A model of intergenerational relationships emphasizing the role of older parents in maintaining connections within the expanded family system.

Somesthesis Our sensitivities to touch, vibration, temperature, kinesthesis, and pain are collectively referred to as somesthesis since they arise from normal and intensive stimulation of the skin and viscera.

Sorrow A form of anticipatory grief. Acknowledging that one's future is limited due to imminent death.

Speed versus accuracy trade-off Accuracy is stressed at the expense of speed in performing a psychomotor task; often characteristic of older persons.

Stage theory of dying Kubler-Ross's notion that dying patients go through discrete stages (denial, anger, bargaining, depression, acceptance) in coping with impending death.

Stage theory of mate selection The process by which individuals are attracted to one another, fall in love, and marry. This process is defined in terms of discrete stages corresponding to the deepening and stability of the relationship, and in part by stimulus variables and social role expectations.

Stereotype Beliefs, attitudes, or expectations about individuals from a specific group that are presumed solely on the basis of the individual's membership in that group.

Stereotype threat The impact that being exposed to negative stereotypes of aging has on one's health or performance.

Storage Memory process whereby information is organized in some fashion. Storehouse of information that has been encoded and that will be retrieved.

Strengths-based model An approach to mental health emphasizing the positive attributes, resources, and strengths of individuals.

Styles of grandparenting Different approaches taken by middle-aged and elderly persons toward defining the role of grandparent (e.g., reservoir of family wisdom, parent surrogate).

Survivor guilt Feelings of guilt over having survived a loved one's death.

Synchrony Referring to the coordination of events in our lives so that they complement one another.

Task pacing The slowing down of presentation rates so that learning and memory can be improved.

Tenuous role types According to Rosow, tenuous role types reflect persons in definite social positions (status) who do not have well-defined functions or roles. These include the aged and the unemployed.

Terminal change (drop) The decline in functioning that precedes death by 3 to 5 years.

Tertiary appraisal Reevaluating one's actions as successful or not in coping with change.

Tertiary memory Memory for overlearned, meaningful material that is relatively permanent and whose capacity is unlimited. Often termed long-term memory.

Time lag design A design that assesses cultural change.

Time sequential design A design that replicates a cross-sectional study at another time of measurement.

Trait An internal quality or characteristic reflected in behavior that is consistent across situations.

Transactional model Point of view stressing the individual's interaction or transaction with the environment, as a means of understanding how persons adapt to or cope with change.

Transference The attribution to the therapist of positive or negative qualities by the client.

Transformations Gould's notion that through experience we are transformed into adults, having shed several myths about the world, ourselves, and our parents collective referred to as the myth of absolute safety.

Types of widows Research by Lopata indicates that there are a number of types of widows; each type has a specific set of characteristics. These types include liberated women, merry widows, working women, widow's widows, traditional widows, and grieving women.

Unfinished business Feelings of not having said or done what was important after a loved one dies, leading to feelings of guilt or regret.

Unretiring A pattern of some persons who have been retired wherein they return to the work force on a full-time basis.

Validation therapy A form of therapy with extremely impaired elders where the authenticity of the person's feelings and experiences is acknowledged rather than challenged.

Value-based occupational choice Making career choices based upon one's personally meaningful set of values.

Vertical career move A move to a higher level of responsibility within a specific career.

Vigilance The ability to maintain attention to a task for a sustained period.

Visual acuity The eye's ability to resolve detail. It is most often equated with accuracy of distance vision compared to the hypothetical normal person.

Vocational maturity Super's index of the congruence between one's vocational behaviors and societal expectations. Varies by stage of the occupational life cycle.

Yearning Referring to the sense of missing another who has died.

Wisdom factor The use of one's experience or life perspective to aid in adaptation to the aging process.

Work-to-family spillover Referring to the impact of work responsibilities on one's family role. performance

Bibliography

Abeles, N. (1997) *What practitioners should know about working with older adults*. Washington, DC: American Psychological Association.

The ache age. (1989, December 29). *USA Weekend*, pp. 4–5.

Acierno, R., Hernandez, M. A., Amstadter, A. B., Resnick, H., Steve, K., Muzzy, W., & Kilpatrick, D. G. (2010). Prevalence and correlates of emotional, physical, sexual, and financial abuse and potential neglect in the United States: The National Elder Mistreatment Study. *American Journal of Public Health, 100*, 292–297.

Acitelli, L. K., Douvan, E., & Veroff, J. (1997). The changing influence of interpersonal perceptions on marital well-being among black and white couples. *Journal of Social and Personal Relationships, 14*, 291–304.

Ackerman, P. (1996). A theory of adult intellectual development: Process, personality, interests, and knowledge. *Intelligence, 22*, 227–257.

Ackerman, P. (2000). Domain-specific knowledge as the "dark matter" of adult intelligence: Gf Gc, personality and interest correlates. *Journal of Gerontology: Psychological Sciences, 55B*, P69–P84.

Ackerman, P. L., & Beier, M. E. (2003). Intelligence, personality, and interests in the career choice process. *Journal of Career Assessment, 11*, 205–218.

Adams, G. A., & Beehr, T. A. (2003). *Retirement: Reasons, processes, and results*. New York: Springer.

Adams, G., & Rau, B. (2004). Job seeking among retirees seeking bridge employment. *Personnel Psychology, 57*, 714–744.

Adams, K. B. (2001). Depressive symptoms, depletion, or developmental change? Withdrawal, apathy, and lack of vigor in the Geriatric Depression Scale. *Gerontologist, 41*, 768–777.

Aday, R. (2003). *Identifying import linkages between successful aging and senior center participation*. www.aoa.gov/prof/agingnet/Seniorcenters/NICS.pdf

Aday, R. H., & Kano, Z. M. (1997). Attitudes toward caring for aging parents: A comparison of Laotian and U.S. students. *Educational Gerontology, 23*(2), 151–167.

Adelman, M. (1990). Stigma, gay life-styles, and adjustment to aging: A study of later-life gay men and lesbians. *Journal of Homosexuality, 20*, 7–32.

Administration on Aging. (1991). Exercise isn't just for fun. *Aging, 362*, 37–40.

Agency for Healthcare Research and Quality. (2010). *Preventing Alzheimer's disease and cognitive decline*. Rockville, MD: Department of Health and Human Services.

Aging with Dignity. (2001). *Next steps: Discussing and coping with serious illness*. Tallahassee, FL: Author.

Ainsworth, M. D. S. (1989). Attachments beyond infancy. *American Psychologist, 44*, 709–716.

Alder, A. G., Adam, J., & Arenberg, D. (1990). Individual differences assessment of the relationship between change and initial level of adult cognitive functioning. *Psychology and Aging, 5*, 560–568.

Aldwin, C., Spiro, A., & Park, C. (2006). Health, behavior, and optimal aging. In J. Birren & K. Schaie (Eds.), *Handbook of the psychology of aging* (pp. 85–104). San Diego, CA: Academic Press.

Allaire, J. C., & Marsiske, M. (1999). Everyday cognition: Age and intellectual ability correlates. *Psychology & Aging, 14*, 627–644.

Allen, E. A., & Steffensmeier, D. J. (1989). Youth, employment, and property crime: Differential aspects of job availability and job quality on juvenile and young adult arrest rates. *American Sociological Review, 54*, 107–123.

Allen, S., & Hayslip, B. (2000). A model for predicting bereavement outcome. In D. Lund (Ed.), *Men grieving* (pp. 148–161). Amityville, NY: Baywood.

Alzheimer's Disease Association. (1995). *Is it Alzheimer's?* Chicago, IL: Author.

Alzheimer's Disease Association. (2009). *Alzheimer's disease: Basic facts and statistics*. www.alz.org/resources/ topicindex/basicfacts.asp#statistics

Amato, P. R. (2010). Research on divorce: Continuing trends and new developments. *Journal of Marriage and Family, 72*, 650-666.

American Association of Retired Persons. (1990). *Workers over 50: Old myths, new realities*. Washington, DC: Author.

American Association of Retired Persons. (2004). *Breaking the silver ceiling: A new generation of older Americans redefining the new rules of the workplace*. Congressional testimony (1/20/04). www.aarp.org/research/ press-center/testimony/ a2004–09-22.aging

American Cancer Society. (1998). *What you need to know about cancer*. Washington, DC: Author.

American Cancer Society. (2009). *Cancer: Facts and figures*. Atlanta, GA: Author.

American Medical Association. (1992). *Diagnostic and treatment guidelines on elder abuse and neglect*. Washington, DC: Author.

American Psychiatric Association. (1994). *Diagnostic and statistical manual of mental disorders* (4th rev. ed.). Washington, DC: Author.

American Psychiatric Association (2010). DSM-5. *The future of psychiatric diagnosis*. http.//www dsm5. org/ Pages/Default. aspx

American Psychological Association. (2004). Guidelines for psychological practice with older adults. *American Psychologist, 59*, 236–260.

Amick, B., McDonaough, Chang, H., Rogers, W., Pieper, C., & Duncan, G. (2002). Relationship between all-cause mortality and cumulative working life course psychosocial and physical exposures in the United States labor market from 1968 to 1992. *Psychosomatic Medicine, 64*, 370–381.

Anastasi, A., & Urbina, S. (1997). *Psychological testing*. New York: Prentice Hall.

Anderson, G., Cisneros, J., Saidpour, A., & Atchley, P. (2000). Age-related differences in collision detection during deceleration. *Psychology and Aging, 15*, 241– 252.

Anderson, R. (1995). Revisiting the behavioral model and access to medical care: Does it matter? *Journal of Health and Social Behavior, 36*, 1-10.

Aneshensel, C., Pearlin, L., Mullan, J, Zarit, S., & Whitlatch, C. (1995). *Profiles in caregiving: The unexpected career*. San Diego, CA: Academic Press.

Angerer, J. M. (2003). Job burnout. *Journal of Employment Counseling, 40*, 98-107.

Anschultz, L., Camp, C. J., Markley, R. P., & Kramer, J. J. (1987). A three-year follow-up on the effects of mnemonic training in elderly adults. *Experimental Aging Research, 13*, 141–143.

Antonucci, T. C. (1985). Personal characteristics, social support, and social behavior. In R. Binstock & E. Shanas (Eds.), *Handbook of aging and the social sciences* (pp. 94–128). New York: Van Nostrand Reinhold.

APA Monitor. (1991, July). *Women's expectations are menopause villains* (p. 14). Washington, DC: American Psychological Association.

Archer, J., & Rhodes, V. (1995). A longitudinal study of job loss in relation to the grief process. *Journal of Community and Applied Social Psychology, 5*, 183–188.

Area, P., & Huh, T. (2006). Problem solving therapy with older adults. In S. Qualls & B. Knight (Eds.), *Psychotherapy for depression in older adults* (pp. 133-151). New York: Wiley.

Armstrong-Stassen, M. & Templer, A. (2005). Adapting training for older employees: The Canadian response to an aging workforce. *Journal of Management Development, 24*, 57–67.

Arnett, J. J. (1994). Are college students adults? Their conceptions of the transition to adulthood. *Journal of Adult Development, 1*, 213–224.

Arnett, J. J. (2000). Emerging adulthood: A theory of development from the late teens through the twenties. *American Psychologist, 55*, 469–480.

Arnett, J. J. (2006). Emerging adulthood. Understanding a new way of coming of age. In J. J. Arnett & J. L. Tanner (Eds.), *Emerging adults in America: Coming of age in the 21st century* (pp. 3–20). Washington, DC: American Psychological Association.

Astin, H. S. (1984). The meaning of work in women's lives: A sociopsychological model of career choice and work behavior. *Counseling Psychologist, 12*, 117–126.

Atchley, R. C. (1999). *Social forces and aging* (9th ed.). Belmont, CA: Wadsworth.

Atchley, R. (2009). *Spirituality and aging*. Baltimore: John Hopkins Press.

Atchley, R. C., & Barusch, A. (2003). *Social forces and aging*. Belmont, CA: Wadsworth.

Austad, S. N. (2009). Making sense of biological theories of aging. In V. L. Bengston, D. Gans, N. M. Putney, & M. Silverstein (Eds.), *Handbook of theories of aging* (2nd ed., pp. 147–161). New York: Springer.

Avery, R., & Foley, R. (1988). *Fairness in selecting employees*. New York: Addison-Wesley.

Avolio, B., & Panek, P. (1981, November). *Assessing changes in levels of capacity and preferences across the working life span*. Paper presented at the Annual Meeting of the Gerontological Society. Toronto.

Ayers, C., Sorrell, J., Thorp, S., & Wetherall, J. (2007). Evidenced-based psychological treatments for late life anxiety. *Psychology and Aging, 22*, 8–17.

Backman, L., Jones, S., Berger, A., Laukka, E., & Small, B. (2005). Cognitive impairment in preclinical Alzheimer's disease: A meta-analysis. *Neuropsychology, 19*, 520–531.

Bailey, L. L. III., & Hansson, R. O. (1995). Psychological obstacles to job or career change in late life. *Journal of Gerontology: Psychological Sciences, 50B*, P280–P288.

Ballenger, J., Whitlehouse, P., Lyketsos, C., Rabins, P., & Karlawish, J. (2009). *Treating dementia: Do we have a pill for it?* Baltimore: Johns Hopkins.

Balsa, A., Homer, J., Fleming, M., & French, M. (2008). Alcohol consumption and health among elders. *The Gerontologist, 48*, 622–636.

Balsis, S., Carpenter, B., & Storandt, M. (2005). Personality change precedes clinical diagnosis of dementia of the Alzheimer's type. *Journal of Gerontology: Psychological Sciences, 60B*, P98–P103.

Balsis, S., & Cully, J. (2008). Comparing depression diagnostic symptoms across younger and older adults. *Aging & Mental Health, 12*, 800–806.

Baltes, P. B. (1968). Cross-sectional and longitudinal sequences in the study of age and generation effects. *Human Development, 11*, 145–171.

Baltes, P. B. (1993). The aging mind: Potential and limits. *Gerontologist, 33*, 580–594.

Baltes, P. B. (1997). On the incomplete architecture on human ontogeny: Selection, optimization, and compensation of developmental theory. *American Psychologist, 52*, 366–379.

Baltes, P. B., & Baltes, M. M. (1990). *Successful aging: Perspectives from the social sciences*. New York: Cambridge University Press

Baltes, P. B., & Lindenberger, U. (1997). Emergence of a powerful connection between sensory and cognitive functions across the lifespan: A new window on the study of cognitive aging? *Psychology and Aging, 12*, 12–21.

Baltes, P. B., Reese, H., & Nesselroade, J. R. (1988). *Life-span developmental psychology: Introduction to research methods*. Hillsdale, NJ: Erlbaum.

Baltes, P. B., Smith, J., Standinger, U., & Sowarka, D. (1990). Wisdom: One facet of successful aging? In M. Perlmutter (Ed.), *Late life potential* (pp. 63–82). Washington, DC: Gerontological Society.

Baltes, P. B., & Willis, S. L. (1982). Plasticity and enhancement of intellectual functioning in old age: Penn State's Adult Development and Enrichment Program (ADEPT). In F. I. M. Craik & S. E. Trehub (Eds.), *Aging and cognitive processes* (pp. 353–389). New York: Plenum.

Bambrick, P., & Bonder, B. (2005). Older adults' perceptions of work. *Work, 24*, 77–84.

Bandura, A. (1986). *Social foundations of thought and action: A social cognitive theory*. Englewood Cliffs, NJ: Prentice Hall.

Bandura, A. (1989). Regulation of cognitive processes through self-efficacy. *Developmental Psychology, 25*, 729–735.

Barbus, A. (1975). The dying person's bill of rights. *American Journal of Nursing, 1*, 99.

Barer, B. M. (1994). Men and women aging differently. *International Journal of Aging and Human Development, 38*, 29–40.

Barker, B., & Wolen, A. (2008). The benefits of human-companion animal interaction: A review. *Journal of Veterinary Medical Education, 35*, 487–495.

Barnes-Farrell, J. L. (2003). Beyond health and wealth: Attitudinal and other influences on retirement decision making. In G. A. Adams & T. A. Beehr (Eds.), *Retirement: Reasons, process, and results* (pp. 159–187). New York: Springer.

Barnes-Farrell, J. L., & Piotrowski, M. (1989). Workers' perceptions of discrepancies between chronological age and personal age: You're only as young as you feel. *Psychology and Aging, 4*, 376–377.

Barr, P., & Cacciatore, J. (2007-2008). Problematic emotions and maternal grief. *Omega, 56*, 331–348.

Barr, R. A., & Giambra, L. M. (1990). Age-related decrement in selective auditory attention. *Psychology and Aging, 4*, 597–599.

Barusch, A., & Wilby, F. (2010). Coping with symptoms of depression: A descriptive survey of community-dwelling elders. *Clinical Gerontologist, 33*, 210–222.

Bass, D. M., Noelker, L. S., Townsend, A. L., & Deimling, G. T. (1990). Losing an aged relative: Perceptual differences between spouses and adult children. *Omega, 21*, 21–40.

Bass, S. A. (2005). New models for post-retirement. In P. T. Beatty & R. M. Visser (Eds.), *Thriving on an aging workforce: Strategies for organizational and systemic change* (pp. 161–170). Malabar, FL: Krieger.

Bassett, J. (2007). Psychological defenses against death anxiety: Integrating terror management theory and Firestone's separation theory. *Death Studies, 31*, 727–750.

Baugher, R. J., Burger, C., Smith, R., & Wallston, K. (1989–1990). A comparison of terminally ill persons at various time periods to death. *Omega, 20*, 103–116.

Baumrind, D. (1971). Current patterns of parental authority. *Developmental Psychology Monographs, 4*, 1–103.

Baylor, A. M., & Spiduso, W. W. (1988). Systematic aerobic exercise and components of reaction time in older women. *Journal of Gerontology: Psychological Sciences, 43*, P121–P126.

Beatty, P. T., & Visser, R. M. (Eds.). (2005). *Thriving on an aging workforce: Strategies for organizational and systemic changes*. Malabar, FL: Krieger.

Beaudreau, S., & O'Hara, R. (2009). The association of anxiety and depressive symptoms with cognitive performance in community dwelling older adults. *Psychology and Aging, 24*, 507–512.

Beder, H. (1989). Purposes and philosophies of adult education. In S. B. Merriam & P. M. Cunningham (Eds.), *Handbook of adult and continuing education* (pp. 37–50). San Francisco: Jossey-Bass.

Beehr, T. A. (1986). The process of retirement: A review and recommendations for future investigation. *Personnel Psychology, 39*, 31–55.

Bengtson, V., Rosenthal, C., & Burton, L. (1990). Families and aging: Diversity and heterogeneity. In R. Binstock & L. George (Eds.), *Handbook of aging and the social sciences* (pp. 263–287). New York: Academic Press.

Bengtson, V., & Schrader, S. S. (1982). Parent-child relations. In D. Mangen & W. Peterson (Eds.), *Handbook of research instruments in social gerontology* (Vol. 2, pp. 115–185). Minneapolis: University of Minnesota Press.

Bennett, K. C., & Thompson, N. L. (1991). Accelerated aging and male homosexuality: Australian evidence in a continuing debate. *Journal of Homosexuality, 20*, 65–76.

Benshoff, J. J., & Roberto, K. A. (1987). Alcoholism in the elderly: Clinical issues. *Clinical Gerontologist, 7*, 3–14.

Ben-Zur, H., & Michael, K. (2009). Social comparisons and well-being following divorce and widowhood. *Death Studies, 33*, 220–238.

Berardo, F. M., Appel, J., & Berardo, D. H. (1993). Age dissimilar marriages: Review and assessment. *Journal of Aging Studies, 7*(1), 93–106.

Berg, C. A., & Sternberg, R. J. (1985). A triarchic theory of intellectual development during adulthood. *Developmental Review, 5*, 353–389.

Berger, E. (2009). Managing age discrimination: An examination of the techniques used when seeking employment. *The Gerontologist, 49*, 317–332.

Berger, R. M. (1982). The unseen minority: Older gays and lesbians. *Social Work, 27*(3), 236–242.

Berger, R. M., & Kelly, J. J. (1996). Gay men and lesbians grow older. In R. P. Cabaj & T. S. Stein (Eds.), *Textbook of homosexuality and mental health* (pp. 305–316). Washington, DC: American Psychiatric Press.

Bergman, C. S., Plomin, R., McClearn, G., Friberg, L., & Pederson, N. L. (1988). Genotype-environment interaction in personality development: Identical twins raised apart. *Psychology and Aging, 3*, 399–406.

Berkowitz, M. (1988). Functioning ability and job performance as workers age. In M. E. Borus, H. S. Parnes, S. H. Sandell, & B. Siedman (Eds.), *The older worker*. Madison, WI: Industrial Relations Research Association.

Berman, W. H., & Turk, D. C. (1981). Adaptation to divorce: Problems and coping strategies. *Journal of Marriage and the Family, 47*, 179–189.

Berrios-Allison, A. (2005). Family influences on college students' occupational identity. *Journal of Career Assessment, 13*, 233–247.

Biblarz, T. J., & Savci, E. (2010). Lesbian, gay, bisexual, and transgender families. *Journal of Marriage and Family, 72*, 480–497.

Biblarz, T. J., & Stacey, J. (2010). How does the gender of parents matter? *Journal of Marriage and Family, 72*, 3–22.

Bidwell, J., Griffin, B., & Hesketh, B. (2006). Timing of retirement: Including a delay discounting perspective in retirement models. *Journal of Vocational Behavior, 68*, 368–387.

Birren, J. E. (1964). *The psychology of aging.* Englewood Cliffs, NJ: Prentice Hall.

Birren, J. E., & Fisher, L. M. (1995). Aging and speed of behaviors: Possible consequences for psychological functioning. *Annual Review of Psychology, 46*, 329–353.

Birren, J. E., & Renner, V. J. (1980). Concepts and issues of mental health and aging. In J. E. Birren & R. B. Sloane (Eds.), *Handbook of mental health and aging* (pp. 3–33). Englewood Cliffs, NJ: Prentice Hall.

Bischman, D. A., & Witte, K. L. (1990, August). *Food identification, taste complaints, and depression in the elderly.* Paper presented at the Convention of the American Psychological Association, Boston.

Blackburn, J. A., & Papalia, D. (1992). The study of adult cognition from a Piagetian perspective. In R. Sternberg & C. Berg (Eds), *Intellectual development* (pp. 141–160). New York: Cambridge University Press.

Blair, S. L. (2010). The influence of risk-taking behaviors on the transition into marriage: An examination of the long-term consequences of adolescent behavior. *Marriage & Family Review, 46*, 126–146.

Blanchard-Fields, F. (1986). Reasoning in adolescents and adults on social dilemmas varying in emotional saliency. *Psychology and Aging, 1*, 325–333.

Blau, G. (2008). Exploring the antecedents of individual grieving stages during an anticipated worksite closure. *Journal of Occupational and Organizational Psychology, 81*, 529–550.

Blazer, D. (1986). Depression. *Generations, 10*, 21–23.

Blazer, D. (2002). *Depression in late life.* New York: Springer.

Bleidorn, W., Kandler, C., Riemannm R., Angleitner, A., & Spinath, F. M. (2009). Patterns and sources of adult personality development: Growth curve analyses of the NEO PI-R scales in a longitudinal twin study. *Journal of Personality and Social Psychology, 97*, 142–155.

Blenkner, M. (1965). Social work and family relationships in later life with some thoughts on filial maturity. In E. Shanas & G. Streib (Eds.), *Social structure and the family: Generational relations* (pp. 46–59). Englewood Cliffs, NJ: Prentice Hall.

Blevins, D., & Worth, J. (2006). Recommendations to improve psychosocial care near the end of life. In J. Werth & D. Blevins (Eds.), *Psychosocial issues near the end of life* (pp. 219–230). Washington, DC: American Psychological Association.

Block, J. (1971). *Lives through time.* Berkeley, CA: Bancroft Books.

Blumenfeld, W. J., & Raymond, D. (1993). *Looking at gay and lesbian life.* Boston: Beacon.

Blumenfield, M. (2010). Review of Handbook of Psychiatry in Palliative Medicine (2nd ed.). *American Journal of Psychiatry, 167*, 355–356.

Boerner, K. (2004). Adaption to disability among middle aged and older adults: The role of assimilative and accommodative coping. *Journal of Gerontology: Psychological Sciences, 59B*, P35–P42.

Bohannon, J. R. (1990-1991). Grief responses of spouses following the death of a child: A longitudinal study. *Omega, 22*, 109–122.

Bonanno, G. A., Wortman, C., & Neese, R. M. (2004). Prospective patterns of resilience and maladjustment during widowhood. *Psychology and Aging, 19*, 260–271.

Bond, J. B., & Harvey, C. D. (1988). *Intergenerational perceptions of family interactions.* Paper presented at the Annual Meeting of the Canadian Association of Gerontology. Halifax, NS.

Bondareff, W. (1985). The neural basis of aging. In J. E. Birren & K. W. Schaie (Eds.), *Handbook of the psychology of aging* (pp. 157–176). New York: Van Nostrand Reinhold.

Boomer beauty is in the eyes of the beholder. (1996, September). *Your Health*, 20.

Bossé, R., Aldwin, C. M., Levenson, M. R., Spiro, A., & Mroczek, D. K. (1993). Change in social support after retirement: Longitudinal findings from the normative aging study. *Journal of Gerontology, 48*(4), P210–P217.

Bossé, R., & Ekerdt, D. J. (1981). Change in self-perception of leisure activities with retirement. *Gerontologist, 21*, 650-654.

Botwinick, J. (1984). *Aging and behavior* (3rd ed.). New York: Springer.

Bowlby, J. (1969). *Attachment and loss: Attachment* (Vol. 1). New York: Basic Books.

Boyle, P., Buchman, A., Barnes, L., & Bennett, D. (2010). Effect of a purpose in life on risk of incident Alzheimer's disease and mild cognitive impairment in community-dwelling older persons. *Archives of General Psychiatry, 67*, 301–310.

Bradbury, T. N., Fincham, F. D., & Beach, S. R. (2000). Research on the nature and determinants of marital satisfaction: A decade in review. *Journal of Marriage and Family, 62*, 964–980.

Bradford, J., Ryan, C., & Rothblum, E. D. (1994). National lesbian health survey: Implications for mental health care. *Journal of Consulting and Clinical Psychology, 62*, 228–242.

Bradsher, J. E., Longino, C. F., Jackson, D. J., & Zimmerman, R. S. (1992). Health and geographic mobility among the recently widowed. *Journal of Gerontology: Social Sciences, 47*, S261–S268.

Bramlett, M. D., & Mosher, W. D. (2002, July). *Vital and health statistics: Cohabitation, marriage, divorce, and remarriage in the United States* (Series 22, Number 23). Washington, DC: National Center for Health Statistics.

Brandstadter, J. Krampen, G., & Greve, W. (1987). Personal control over development: Effects on the perception and emotional evaluation of personal development in adulthood. *International Journal of Behavioral Development, 10*, 99–120.

Brayne, C., & Keage, H. (2010). Why more education lowers dementia risk: 11% decrease in risk per year of education. *Brain*.

Brehm, J. (1966). *A theory of psychological reactance.* New York: Academic Press.

Breitenbecher, K. H. (1999). The association between the perception of danger cues and sexual revictimization. *Journal of Interpersonal Violence, 12*, 81–91.

Breitenbecher, K. H, & Gidycz, C. A. (1999). An empirical evaluation of a program designed to reduce the risk of multiple sexual victimization. *Journal of Interpersonal Violence, 12*, 14–28.

Breitenbecher, K. H., & Scarce, M. (1999). A longitudinal evaluation of the effectiveness of a sexual assault education program. *Journal of Interpersonal Violence, 11*, 40–51.

Brennan, R. T., Barnett, R. C., & Gareis, K. C. (2001). When she earns more than he does: A longitudinal study of dual-earner couples. *Journal of Marriage and Family, 63*, 168–182.

Breslow, R., Faden, V., & Smothers, B. (2003). Alcohol consumption by elderly Americans. *Journal of Studies on Alcohol, 64*, 884–892.

Brickel, C. M. (1979). The clinical use of pets with the aged. *Clinical Gerontologist, 2*, 72–74.

Bright, J. (2005). The role of chance events in career decision making. *Journal of Vocational Behavior, 66*, 561–576.

Brim, O. G., & Phillips, D. A. (1988). The life-span intervention cube. In E. M. Hetherington, R. M. Lerner, & P. B. Baltes (Eds.), *Child development in life-span perspective* (pp. 270–300). Hillsdale, NJ: Erlbaum.

Brody, E. M., Litvin, S. J., Hoffman, C., & Kleban, M. H. (1995). On having a "significant other" during the parent care years. *Journal of Applied Gerontology, 14*, 131–149.

Bronfenbrenner, U. (1979). *The ecology of human development: Experiments by nature and design.* Cambridge: Harvard University Press.

Bronfenbrenner, U., & Morris, P. A. (1998). The ecology of developmental processes. In Damon & R. Lerner (Eds.), *Handbook of child psychology: Volume 1: Theoretical models of human development* (5th ed., pp. 994–1023). Hoboken, NJ: John Wiley & Sons.

Brown, D. (2002). The role of work values and cultural values in occupational choice, satisfaction, and success: A theoretical statement. In D. Brown & Associates (Eds.), *Career choice and development* (pp. 465–509). San Francisco: Josey Bass.

Brown, S. C., & Park, D. C. (2003). Theoretical models of cognitive aging and implications for translational research in medicine. *Gerontologist, 43*, 57–67.

Bruck, C. S., & Allen, T. D. (2003). The relationship between five personality traits, negative affectivity, type A behavior, and work-family conflict. *Journal of Vocational Behavior, 63*, 457–472.

Burgio, L. D., & Sinnott, J. (1990). Behavioral treatments and pharmacotherapy: Acceptability ratings by elderly individuals in residential settings. *Gerontologist, 30*, 811–816.

Burke, K. C., Burke, J. D., Regier, D. A., & Rae, D. S. (1990). Age at onset of selected mental disorders in five community populations. *Archives of General Psychiatry, 47*, 511–518.

Bushfield, S., Fitzpatrick, T., & Vinck, B. (2008). Perceptions of impingement and marital satisfaction among wives of retired husbands. *Journal of Women and Aging, 20*, 199–207.

Butler, R. N., Walker, W. R., Skowronski, J. J., & Shannon, L. (1995). Age and responses to the Love Attitudes Scale: Consistency in structure, differences in scores. *International Journal of Aging and Human Development, 40*, 281–296.

Butrica, B., Johnson, R., & Zedlewski, S. (2009). Volunteer dynamics of older Americans. *Journal of Gerontology: Social Sciences, 64B*, 644–653.

Cagney, K. A., Browning, C. R., & Wen, M. (2005). Racial disparities in self-rated health at older ages: What difference does the neighborhood make? *Journal of Gerontology: Social Sciences, 60B*, S181-S190.

Caine, L. (1974). *Widow.* New York: William Morrow.

Calasanti, T. M. (1996). Gender and life satisfaction in retirement: An assessment of the male model. *Journal of Gerontology: Social Sciences, 51B*, S18–S29.

Calderia, K., & Vincernt, K. (2010,). Depression, lack of social support trigger suicidal thoughts in college students. *Journal of Affective Disorders.*

Calsyn, R., & Winter, J. (1999). Predicting solder adults' awareness of services. *Journal of Social Service Research, 25*, 1–14.

Camp. C. (2006). Spaced retrieval: A model for dissemination of a cognitive intervention for persons with dementia. In K. K. Attix & K. Welsh-Bohmer (Eds.), *Geriatric neuropsychology: Assessment and intervention* (pp. 275–292). New York: Guilford Press.

Camp, C., & Foss, J. (1997). Developing ecologically valid instruments for persons with dementia. In D. Payne & F. Conrad (Eds.), *Intersections in basic and applied memory research* (pp. 311–326). Mahwah, NJ: Erlbaum.

Camp, C. J., Foss, J. W., Stevens, A. B., & O'Hanlon, A. M. (1996). Improving prospective memory task performance in Alzheimer's disease. In M. A. Brandimonte, G. O. Einstein, & M. A. McDaniel (Eds.), *Prospective memory: Theory and applications* (pp. 351–367). Washington, DC: American Psychological Association.

Camp, C. J., Foss, J. W., Stevens, A. B., Reichard, C. C., McKitrick, L. A., & O'Hanlon, A. M. (1993). Memory training in normal and demented elderly populations: The E-I-E-I-O model. *Experimental Aging Research, 19*, 277–290.

Campione, W. A. (1988). Predicting participation in retirement-preparation programs. *Journal of Gerontology, 43*, 591–595.

Campos, B., Graesch, A. P., Repetti, R., Bradbury, T., & Ochs, E. (2009). Opportunity for interaction? A naturalistic observation study of dual-earner families after work and school. *Journal of Family Psychology, 23*, 798–807.

Canestrari, R. E. (1968). Age changes in acquisition. In G. A. Talland (Ed.), *Human aging and behavior* (pp. 169–187). New York: Academic Press.

Cantor, W. A., & Koretzky, M. B. (1989). Treatment of geriatric alcoholics. *Clinical Gerontologist, 9*, 67–70.

Carden, A., & Boehnlein, T. (1997). Intervention with male batterers: Continuous risk assessment. *Ohio Psychologist, 44*, 9–16.

Carlson-Jones, D., & Vaughn, K. (1990). Close friendships among senior adults. *Psychology and Aging, 5*, 451–457.

Carr, D. (2006). Methodological issues in studying late life bereavement. In D. Carr, R. Neese, & C. Wortman (Eds.), *Spousal bereavement in later life* (pp. 19–48). New York: Springer.

Carr, D., Shead, V., & Storandt, M. (2005). Driving cessation in older adults with dementia of the Alzheimer's type. *Gerontologist, 45*, 824–827.

Carson, R. C., & Butcher, J. N. (1991). *Abnormal psychology and modern life* (9th ed.). New York: HarperCollins.

Carstensen, L. L. (1992). Social and emotional patterns in adulthood: Support for socioemotional selectivity theory. *Psychology and Aging, 7*(3), 331–338.

Carstensen, L. L. (1995). Evidence for a life span theory of socioemotional selectivity. *New Directions in Psychological Science, 4*, 151–156.

Carstensen, L. L., & Cone, J. (1983). Social desirability and the measurement of well-being in elderly persons. *Journal of Gerontology, 38*, 713–715.

Carstensen, L. L., Isaacowitz, D. M., & Charles, S. T. (1999). Taking time seriously: A theory of socioemotional selectivity. *American Psychologist, 54*(3), 165–181.

Casarett, D., Pickard, A., Bailey, F., Ritchie, C., Furman, C., Rosenfeld, K., Shreve, S., Chen, Z., & Shea, J. (2008). Do palliative consultations improve patient outcomes? *Journal of the American Geriatrics Society, 56*, 593–599.

Caspi, A., & Bem, D. J. (1990). Personality continuity and change across the life course. In L. A. Pervin (Ed.), *Handbook of personality: Theory and research* (pp. 549–575). New York: Guilford Press.

Caspi, A., & Elder, G. (1986). Life satisfaction in old age: Linking social psychology and history. *Psychology and Aging, 1,* 18–26.

Caspi, A., Roberts, B. W., & Shiner, R. L. (2005). Personality development: Stability and change. *Annual Review of Psychology, 56,* 453–484.

Catalano, S. (2007). *Intimate partner violence in the United States.* Washington, DC: Bureau of Justice Statistics.

Catalano, R., Aldrete, E., Vega, W., Kolody, B., & Aguilar-Gaxiola, S. (2000). Job loss and major depression among Mexican Americans. *Social Science Quarterly, 81,* 477–487.

Cato, M., & Crosson, B. (2006). Stable and slowly progressive dementias. In K. K. Attix & K. Welsh-Bohmer (Eds.), *Geriatric neuropsychology: Assessment and intervention* (pp. 89–102). New York: Guilford Press.

Centers for Disease Control and Injury Prevention. (2009). *Falls among older adults: An overview.* Retrieved from www.cdc.govHomelandRecreational Safety/Falls/adultfalls.html.

Cerella, J., Poon, L. W., & Williams, D. M. (1990). Age and the complexity hypothesis. In L. W. Poon (Ed.), *Aging in the 1980s: Psychological issues* (pp. 332–340). Washington, DC: American Psychological Association.

Chalk, L., Meara, N., Day, J., & Davis, K. (2005). Occupational possible selves: Fears and aspirations of college women. *Journal of Career Assessment, 13,* 188–203.

Chase-Landsdale, P. L., & Hetherington, P. M. (1990). The impact of divorce on life-span development: Short and long-term effects. In P. Baltes, D. Featherman, & R. Lerner (Eds.), *Life-span development and behavior* (Vol. 10, pp. 107–151). Hillsdale, NJ: Erlbaum.

Cheng, G., & Cahn, D. (2008). Who suffers more from job insecurity? A meta-analytic review. *Applied Psychology, 57,* 272-303.

Cherlin, A. C., & Furstenberg, F. (1986). *The new American grandparent.* New York: Basic Books.

Cherlin, A. J. (1996). *Public and private families: An introduction.* New York: McGraw-Hill.

Cherry, K. E., & Morton, M. R. (1989). Drug sensitivity in older adults: The role of physiologic and pharmacokinetic factors. *International Journal of Aging and Human Development, 28,* 159–174.

Cherry, K. E., & Smith, A.D. (1998). Normal memory aging. In M. Hersen & V. Van Hasselt (Eds). *Handbook of clinical gerontology.* New York: Plenum.

Childs, H., Hayslip, B., Radika, L., & Reinberg, J. (2000). Young and middle-aged adults' perceptions of elder abuse. *Gerontologist, 40,* 75–85.

Chiriboga, D. A., Catron, L. S., & Associates. (1991). *Divorce: Crisis, challenge, or relief?* New York: New York University Press.

Cicirelli, V. G. (1985). The role of siblings as family caregivers. In W. J. Sauer & R. T. Coward (Eds.), *Social support networks and the care of the elderly* (pp. 93–107). New York: Springer.

Cicirelli, V. G. (1989). Feelings of attachment to siblings and well-being in later life. *Psychology and Aging, 4,* 211–216.

Cicirelli, V. G. (1997). Relationship of psychosocial and background variables to older adults' end of life decisions. *Psychology and Aging, 12,* 72–83.

Cicirelli, V. G. (2002). Fear of death in older adults: Predictions from Terror Management theory. *The Journal of Gerontology: Psychological Sciences, 57B,* P358–366.

Cicirelli, V. G. (2006). Fear of death in mid-old age. *Journal of Gerontology: Psychological Sciences, 61B,* P75–P82.

Cicirelli, V. (2009). Sibling death and death fear in relationship to depressive symptomatology in older adults. *Journal of Gerontology: Psychological Sciences, 64B,* 24–32.

Cicirelli, V. G. (2010). Attachment relationships in old age. *Journal of Social and Personal Relationships, 27,* 191–199.

Claes, J. A., & Moore, W. (2000). Issues confronting lesbian and gay elders: The challenge for health and human services providers. *Journal of Health and Human Services Administration* (Fall), 181–202.

Clark, R., & Spengler, J. (1980). *The economics of individual and population aging.* Cambridge: Cambridge University Press.

Clark, R. L., & Ogawa, N. (1996). Human resource policies and older workers in Japan. *Gerontologist, 36,* 627–636.

Clark, R. L., & Quinn, J. F. (2002). Patterns of work and retirement for a new century. *Generations, Summer,* 17–24.

Cleveland, J. N., & Hollmann, G. (1990). The effects of age-type of tasks and incumbent age composition on job perceptions. *Journal of Vocational Behavior, 36,* 181–194.

Clingempeel, W. G., & Segal, S. (1986). Stepparent-stepchild relationships and the psychological adjustment of children in stepmother and stepfather families. *Child Development, 57,* 474–484.

Cockburn, J., & Smith, P. T. (1991). The relative influence of intelligence and age on everyday memory. *Journal of Gerontology: Psychological Sciences, 46,* P31–36.

Cohen, G. (1992). The future of mental health and aging. In J. E. Birren, R. B. Sloane, &. G. D. Cohen (Eds.), *Handbook of mental health and aging* (pp. 893–914). New York: Academic Press.

Cohen, G. (2003). *Schizophrenia in later life: Treatment, research, and policy.* Washington, DC: American Psychiatric Association.

Cohen, G. (2005). *The Mature Mind: The power of the aging brain.* Cambridge, MA: Perseus Books.

Cohen, S, & Block, S. (2004). Issues in psychotherapy with terminally ill patients. *Palliative Support Care, 2,* 181–189.

Cohler, B. (1998). Psychoanalysis and the life course: Development and intervention. In I. Nordhus, G. VandenBox, S. Berg, & P. Fromholt (Eds.), *Clinical geropsychology* (pp. 61–78). Washington, DC: American Psychological Association.

Coleman, P. K., & Karraker, K. H. (2003). Maternal self-efficacy beliefs, competence in parenting, and, toddlers' behavior and developmental status. *Infant Mental Health Journal, 24,* 126–148.

Colman, R. J., Anderson, R. M., Johnson, S. C., Kastman, E. K., Kosmatka, K. J., Beasley, T. M., Allison, . . . Weindruch, R. (2009). Caloric restriction delays disease onset and mortality in rhesus monkeys. *Science, 325,* 201–204.

Combrink-Graham, L. (1985). A developmental model for family systems. *Family Process, 24,* 139–150.

Connelly, B., & MacDonald, B. (1993, November). *A review of pet therapy programs for the elderly and examples from Jeff's companion animal shelter.* Paper presented at the Annual Scientific Meeting of the Gerontological Society of America, New Orleans, LA.

Connodis, I. (2010). *Family ties and aging.* Thousand Oaks, CA: Pine Forge Press.

Connidis, I. A., & Davies, L. (1990). Confidants and companions in later life: The place of family and friends. *Journal of Gerontology: Social Sciences, 45,* S141– 149.

Cook, F. L. (1992). Ageism: Rhetoric and reality. *Gerontologist, 32,* 292–295.

Coppola, K., & Trotman, F. (2002). Dying and death: Decisions at the end of life. In F. Trotman & C. Brody (Eds.). *Psychotherapy and counseling with older women: Cross cultural, family, and end of life issues* (pp. 221–238). New York: Springer.

Corby, N., & Solnick, R. (1980). Psychosocial and physiological influences on sexuality in the older adults. In J. E. Birren & R. B. Sloane (Eds.), *Handbook of mental health and aging* (pp. 893–921). Englewood Cliffs, NJ: Prentice Hall.

Cornelius, S. W. (1990). Aging and everyday cognitive abilities. In T. Hess (Ed.), *Aging and cognition: Knowledge, organization, and utilization* (pp. 411–444). Amsterdam: North Holland.

Cornelius, S. W., & Caspi, A. (1987). Everyday problem solving in adulthood and old age. *Psychology and Aging, 2,* 144–153.

Cornwell, B., Schumm, L., & Laumann, E. (2008). The social connectedness of older adults: A national profile. *American Sociological Review, 73,* 185–203.

Corr, C. (1998–1999). Enhancing the concept of disenfranchised grief. *Omega, 38,* 11–20.

Corr, C., Nabe, C., & Corr, D. (1999). *Death and dying: Life and living.* Pacific Grove, CA: Wadsworth.

Corr, C. A., Nabe, C. M., & Corr, D. M. (2009). *Death and dying: Life and living* (9th ed.). Belmont, CA: Thomson.

Costa, J. J. (1984). *Abuse of the elderly.* Lexington, MA: Heath.

Costa, P. T., Jr., (1991). The use of the five-factor model: An introduction. *Journal of Personality Assessment, 57,* 393–398.

Costa, P. T., Jr., & McCrae, R. R. (1989). Personality continuity and the changes of adult life. In M. Storandt & G. VandenBos (Eds.), *The adult years: Continuity and change* (pp. 45–77). Washington, DC: American Psychological Association.

Costa, P. T., & McCrae, R. R. (1992a). Four ways five factors are basic. *Personality and Individual Differences, 13*(6), 653–665.

Costa, P. T., & McCrae, R. R. (1992b). *Professional Manual for the NEO PI-R and the NEO-FFI*. Odessa, FL. Psychological Assessment Resources, Inc.

Costa, P. T., McCrae, R., & Arenberg, D. (1983). Recent longitudinal research on personality and aging. In K. W. Schaie (Ed.), *Longitudinal studies of adult psychological development* (pp. 222–265). New York: Guilford Press.

Covey, H. C. (1989). Old age portrayed by the ages-of-life models from the middle ages to the 15th century. *Gerontologist, 29*, 692–698.

Cox, T., Jr. (1994). *Cultural diversity in organizations: Theory, research, and practice*. San Francisco: Berrett- Koehler Publishers, Inc.

Craig-Bray, L., Adams, G., & Dobson, W. (1988). Identity formation and social relations during late adolescence. *Journal of Youth and Adolescence, 17*, 173–188.

Crook, T. H., & Addely, B. (1998). *The Memory Cure*. New York: Pocket Books.

Crook, T. H., Bartus, R. T., Ferris, S. H., Whitehouse, P., Cohen, G. D., & Gershon, S. (1986). Age-associated memory impairment: Proposed diagnostic criteria and measures of clinical change [report of an NIMH work group]. *Developmental Neuropsychology, 2*, 261–276.

Crook, T. H., Zappala, G., et al. (1993). Republic of San Marino Normal Population sampling. *Developmental Neuropsychology, 9*, 103–113.

Cross, R. J. (1993). What doctors and others need to know: Six facts on human sexuality and aging. *SIECUS Report, 21*, 7–9.

Crouch, K. A. (1998). Late life job displacement. *Gerontologist, 38*, 7–17.

Crouter, A. C., & Manke, B. (1997). Development of a typology of dual-earner families: A window into differences between and within families in relationships, roles, and activities. *Journal of Family Psychology, 11*, 62–75.

Crowley, B. J., Hayslip, B., & Hobdy, J. (2003). Psychological hardiness and adjustment to life events in adulthood. *Journal of Adult Development, 10*, 237–249.

Crowther, M., Scogin, F., & Norton, M. (2010). Treating the aged in rural communities: The application of cognitive behavioral therapy for depression. *Journal of Clinical Psychology, 66*, 502–512.

Crowther, M., Shurgot, G., Perkins, M., & Rodriguez, R. (2006). The social and cultural context of psychotherapy with older adults. In S. Qualls & B. Knight (Eds.), *Psychotherapy for depression in older adults* (pp. 179-200). New York: Wiley.

Cuddy, A. J. C., Norton, M. I., & Fiske, S. T. (2005). This old stereotype: The pervasiveness and persistence of the elderly stereotype. *Journal of Social Issues, 61*, 267–285.

Cukrowicz, K., Duberstein, P., Vannoy, S., Lynch, T. McQuoid, D., & Steffens, D. (2009). Course of suicide ideation and predictors of change in depressed older adults. *Journal of Affective Disorders, 113*, 30–36.

Culkin, J. (2002). *Psychotherapy with the dying person*. www.qcc.cuny.edu/socialsciences/ppecorino/DeathandDying

Cumming, E. (1963). Further thoughts on the theory of disengagement. *International Social Science Journal, 15*, 377–393.

Cumming, E. (1975). Engagement with an old theory. *International Journal of Aging and Human Development, 6*, 187–191.

Cunningham, W. R., & Tomer, A. (1991). Intellectual abilities and age: Concepts, theories, and analysis. In E. Lovelace (Ed.), *Aging and cognition: Mental `processes, self-awareness, and interventions*. Amsterdam: North Holland.

Currin, J., & Hayslip, B. (2001, November). *Historical shifts in attitudes toward mental health among older adults*. Paper presented at the Annual Scientific Meeting of the Gerontological Society of America. Chicago.

Currin, J., Hayslip, B., Schneider, L., & Kooken, R. (1998). Cohort differences in attitudes toward mental health services among older adults. *Psychotherapy, 35*, 506–518.

Currin, J., Hayslip, B., & Temple, J. (2011, In Press). The relationship between age, gender, historical change, and adults' attitudes toward mental health services. *International Journal of Aging and Human Development*.

Curtiss, K., & Hayslip, B. (2000, November). *Conceptualizations of young, middle aged, and older adults: A test of the in group-out group hypotheses*. Paper presented at the Annual Scientific Meeting of the Gerontological Society of America. Washington, DC.

Curtiss, K., Hayslip, B., & Dolan, D. (2007). Motivational style, length of residence, and voluntariness of relocation in relation to nursing home adjustment. *The Journal of Human Behavior in the Social Environment, 15,* 13–34.

Cusack, O., & Smith, E. (1984). *Pets and the elderly: The therapeutic bond.* New York: Haworth Press.

Cutler, S., & Hendricks, J. (2001). Emerging social trends. In R. Binstock & C. George (Eds.), *Handbook of aging and social sciences* (pp. 462–502). San Antonio, TX: Academic Press.

Czaja, S. (2001). Technological change and the older worker. In J. E. Birren & K. W. Schaie (Eds.), *Handbook of the psychology of aging* (5th ed.). San Diego, CA: Academic Press.

Danaei, G., Rimm, E. B., Oza, S., Kulkarni, S. C., Murray, C. J. L. & Ezzati, M. (2010). The promise of prevention: The effects of four preventable risk factors on national life expectancy and life expectancy disparities by race and county in the United States. *Public Library of Science: Medicine, 7,* e1000248.

Danish, S. (1981). Life-span development and intervention: A necessary link. *Counseling Psychologist, 9,* 40–43.

Danish, S., Smyer, M., & Nowak, C. (1980). Developmental intervention: Enhancing life-event processes. In P. B. Baltes & O. G. Brim (Eds.), *Life-span development and behavior* (pp. 340–366). New York: Academic Press.

Davey, A., Halverson, C., Zonderman, A., & Costa, P. (2004). Change in depressive symptoms in the Baltimore Longitudinal Study of Aging. *Journal of Gerontology: Psychological Sciences, 59B,* P270–P277.

Davis, A. C. (1991). Epidemiological profile of hearing impairments: The scale and nature of the problem with special reference to the elderly. *Acta Oto-Laryngologia Supplement, 476,* 23–31.

Davis, J. (2009). *Examining career transitions during mid-adulthood through the lens of bioecological and microdevelopmental research.* Dissertation, University of North Texas.

Davy, J. A., Kinicki, A. J., & Scheck, C. L. (1991). Developing and testing a model of survivor responses to layoffs. *Journal of Vocational Behavior, 38,* 302–317.

Day, K., Carreon, D., & Stump, C. (2000). The therapeutic design of environments for people with dementia: A review of the empirical research. *Gerontologist, 40,* 397–416.

DeAngelis, T. (2010). Mapping menopause. *Monitor on Psychology, March,* pp. 44-45.

DeFrain, J. (1990-1991). The psychological effects of a stillborn on surviving family members. *Omega, 22,* 81–108.

DeFrank, R. S., & Ivancevich, J. M. (1986). Job loss: An individual-level review and model. *Journal of Vocational Behavior, 28,* 1–20.

de Graaf, C., Polet, P., & van Staveren, W. A. (1994). Sensory perception and pleasantness of food flavors in elderly subjects. *Journal of Gerontology: Psychological Sciences, 49,* P93–P99.

Deihl, M. (1998). Everyday competence in later life: Current status and future directions. *Gerontologist, 38,* 422–433.

Deihl, M., Willis, S. L., & Schaie, K. W. (1995). Everyday problem solving in older adults: Observational assessment and cognitive correlates. *Psychology and Aging, 10*(3), 478–491.

Delmore-Ko, P., Pancer, S. M., Hunsberger, B., & Pratt, M. (2000).Becoming a parent: The relation between prenatal expectations and postnatal experiences. *Journal of Family Psychology, 14* (4), 625-640.

DeMaris, A., & MacDonald, W. (1993). Premarital cohabitation and marital instability: A test of the unconventionality hypothesis. *Journal of Marriage and the Family, 55,* 399–407.

Demming, J., & Pressy, S. (1957). Tests indigenous to the adult and older years. *Journal of Counseling Psychology, 4,* 144–148.

Dendinger, V. M., Adams, G. A., & Jacobson, J. D. (2005). Reasons for working and their relationship to retirement attitudes, job satisfaction and occupational self-efficacy of bridge employees. *International Journal of Aging & Human Development, 61*(1), 21–35.

DeSpelder, L. A., & Strickland, A. L. (1996). *The last dance: Encountering death and dying.* Palo Alto, CA: Mayfield.

DeSpelder, L. A., & Strickland, A. L. (2009). *The last dance: Encountering death and dying* (8th ed.). New York: McGraw-Hill.

Devany, S., & Kim, H. (2008). Older self-employed workers and planning for the future. *Journal of Consumer Affairs, 42,* 123–130.

Devenand, D., Sano, M., Tang, M., Taylor, S., Gurland, B., Wilder, D., Stern, Y., & Mayeaux, R. (1996). Depressed mood and the incidence of Alzheimer's disease in the elderly living in the community. *Archives of General Psychiatry, 53*, 175–182.

DeVries, B., Bluck, S., & Birren, J. E. (1993). Understanding death and dying from a life span perspective. *Gerontologist, 33*, 366–372.

De Young, R. (1999). Environmental psychology. In D. Alexander & R. Fairbridge (Eds.). *Encyclopedia of environmental science* (pp. 1–4). Hingham, MA: Kluwer.

Di, J., & Berman, J. (2000). Older New Yorkers' use of senior services: Effect of family support networks. *The Gerontologist, 40*, 390.

DiGiovanna, A. (1994). *Human aging: Biological perspectives*. New York: McGraw-Hill.

Dittman, C. (2005). Generational differences at work. *Monitor on Psychology, 36*, 54–55.

Dixon, R. (1989). Questionnaire research on metamemory and aging: Issues of structure and function. In L. Poon, D. Rabin, & B. Wilson (Eds.), *Every-day cognition in adulthood and late life* (pp. 394–415). New York: Cambridge University Press.

Dogma overturned. (1998, November). *Scientific American*, pp. 19–20.

Doka, K. J. (1989). Loss upon loss: The impact of death after divorce. *Death Studies, 10*, 441–449.

Doka, K. (2008). Disenfranchised grief in historical and cultural perspective. In M. Stroebe, R. Hansson, H. Schut, & W. Streobe (Eds.), *Handbook of bereavement research and practice* (pp. 223–240). Washington, DC: American Psychological Association.

Doka, K. (2009). Religious and spiritual perspectives on life-threatening illness, dying, and death. In J. Worth & D. Blevins (Eds.), *Decision making near the end of life: Recent developments and future directions* (pp. 281–300).New York: Routledge.

Donkin, R. (2010*). The future of work*. New York: Palgrave Macmillan.

Donnelly, E., & Hinterlong, J. (2010). Changes in social participation and volunteer activity among recently widowed older adults. *The Gerontologist, 50*, 158-169.

Doppelt, J. E., & Wallace, W. L. (1955). Standardization of the Wechsler Adult Intelligence Scale for older persons. *Journal of Abnormal and Social Psychology, 51*, 312–330.

Dorfman, L. T. (1989). Retirement preparation and retirement satisfaction in the rural elderly. *Journal of Applied Gerontology, 8*, 432–450.

Dorrell, B. (1991). Being there: A support network of lesbian women. *Journal of Homosexuality, 20*, 89–98.

Dunn, S. (2005). Effective strategies for training older workers. In P. T. Beatty & R. M. Visser (Eds.), *Thriving on an aging workforce: Strategies for organizational and systematic change* (pp. 70–79). Malabar, FL: Krieger.

Duxbury, L., Higgins, C., & Lee, C. (1994). Work-family conflict: A comparison by gender, family type, and perceived control. *Journal of Family Issues, 15*, 449–466.

Dykstra, P. A. (2006). Off the beaten path: Childlessness and social integration in late life. *Research on Aging, 28*, 749–767.

Dyregrov, K. (2009). How do the young suicide survivors wish to be met by psychologists? A user study. *Omega, 59*, 221–238.

Eagly, A. H., & Wood, W. (1999). The origins of sex differences in human behavior: Evolved dispositions versus social roles. *American Psychologist, 54*, 408–423.

Eby, L., Maher, C., & Butts, M. (2009). The intersection of work and family life: The role of affect. *Annual Review of Psychology, 61*, 599–622.

Edelstein, B., & Segal, D. (2011). Assessment of emotional and personality disorders in older adults. In K.W. Schaie & S. Willis (Eds.), *Handbook of the psychology of aging* (7th ed.) (pp. 325–338). Amsterdam: Elsevier.

Edwards, M. (2004). As good as it gets. *AARP: The Magazine*, Nov.-Dec., 35–51, 74–75.

Ekerdt, D. J. (1989). Retirement preparation. In M. P. Lawton (Ed.), *Annual review of gerontology and geriatrics* (Vol. 9, pp. 321–356). New York: Springer.

Ekerdt, D. J. (1998). Workplace norms for the timing of retirement. In K. Schaie & C. Schooler (Eds.), *Impact of work on older adults* (pp. 101–123). New York: Springer.

Ekerdt, D. (2010). Frontiers of research on work and retirement. *Journal of Gerontology: Social Sciences, 65B*, 69–80.

Ekerdt, D. J., & Bosse, R. (1985). An empirical test for phases of retirement: Findings from the Normative Aging Study. *Journal of Gerontology, 40*, 95–101.

Ekerdt, D. J., & Vinick, B. H. (1991). Marital complaints in husband-working and husband-retired couples. *Research on Aging, 13*, 364–382.

Ekerdt, D. J., Vinick, B. H., & Bosse, R. (1989). Orderly ending: Do men know when they retire? *Journal of Gerontology: Social Sciences, 44*, S28–35.

Elder, G. H. (1979). Historical change in life patterns and personality. In P. B. Baltes & O. G. Brim (Eds.), *Life-span development and behavior* (pp. 117–159). New York: Academic Press.

Elder, G. H. (1986). Military times and turning points in men's lives. *Developmental Psychology, 22*, 233–245.

Elder, G. H. (1999). *Children of the great depression: Social change in life experience.* Boulder, CO: Westview Press.

Ellis, A. (1962). *Reason and emotion in psychotherapy.* New York: Lyle Stuart.

Elwert, F., & Christakis, N. (2008). The effect of widowhood on mortality by the causes of death of both spouses. *American Journal of Public Health, 98*, 2092–2099.

Erber, J., & Long, B. (2006). Perceptions of forgetful and slow employees: Does age matter? *Journal of Gerontology: Psychological Sciences, 61B*, P333–P339.

Erikson, E. H. (1963). *Childhood and society* (2nd ed.). New York: Norton.

Evercare (2010). *100 @ 100 Survey.* Available on-line at: Evercare100at100.com.

Everett, C., & Everett, S. (1994). *Healthy divorce.* San Francisco: Jossey-Bass.

Faberow, N. L., Gallagher-Thompson, D., Gilewski, M., & Thompson, L. (1992). Changes in grief and mental health of bereaved spouses of older suicides. *Journal of Gerontology: Psychological Sciences, 47*, P357–P366.

Farmer, H. S. (2002). *Diversity and women's career development.* Belmont, CA: Sage.

Farraro, K. F. (1992). Cohort changes in images of older adults, 1974–1981. *Gerontologist, 32*, 296–404.

Farraro, K. F. (2001). Aging and role transitions. In R. H. Binstock & L. K. George (Eds.), *Handbook of the social sciences and aging* (5th ed.), pp. 313–332. San Diego, CA: Academic Press.

Fassinger, R. E. (1990). Causal models of career choice in two samples of college women. *Journal of Vocational Behavior, 36*, 225–248.

Fassinger, R., & Schossberg, N. (1992). Understanding the adult years: Perspectives and implications. In S. Brown & R. Lent (Eds.), *Handbook of counseling psychology* (pp. 217–249). New York: Wiley.

Feigelman, W., Gorman, B., & Jordan, J. (2009). Stigmatization and suicide bereavement. *Death Studies, 33*, 591–608.

Feigelman, W., Jordan, J, & Gorman, B. (2009). Personal growth after a suicide loss: Cross sectional findings suggest growth after loss may be associated with better mental health among survivors. *Omega, 59*, 181–202.

Feil, N. (1989). *Validation: The Feil method.* Cleveland, OH: Author.

Feil, N. (2002). *The validation breakthrough* (2nd ed.). Baltimore: Health Professions Press.

Feilfel, H., & Stack, S. (1987). Old is old is old? *Psychology and Aging, 2*, 409–412.

Feinstein, L., Bynner, J., & Duckworth, K. (2006). Young people's leisure contexts and their relation to adult outcomes. *Journal of Youth Studies, 9*, 305–327.

Ferri, C., & Prince, M. (2005). *Worldwide incidence of dementia set to double every 20 years.* Retrieved from http://www.alzscot.org/pages/media/ worldwideincidence.htm

Ferrini, A., & Ferrini, R. (1993). *Health in the later years.* Dubuque, IA: Brown-Benchmark.

Field, D. (1991). Continuity and change in personality in old age: Evidence from five longitudinal studies. *Journal of Gerontology: Psychological Sciences, 46*, P271–274.

Field, D., & Milsap, R. E. (1991). Personality in advanced old age: Continuity or change? *Journal of Gerontology: Psychological Sciences, 46*, P299–308.

Field, M. (2009). How people die in the United States. In J. Worth & D. Blevins (Eds.), *Decision making near the end of life: Recent developments and future directions* (pp. 63-76). New York: Routledge.

Fillenbaum, G. G. (1990). *Multidimensional functional assessment of older adults.* Hillsdale, NJ: Erlbaum.

Filsinger, E., & Sauer, W. (1978). An empirical typology of adjustment to aging. *Journal of Gerontology, 33*, 437–445.

Fincham, F. D. & Beach, S. R. H. (2010). Marriage in the new millennium: A decade in review. *Journal of Marriage and Family, 72*, 630–649.

Findsen, B. (2005). *Learning later.* Malabar, FL: Krieger.

Finkelstein, L. M. (2005). Intergenerational issues inside the organization. In P. T. Beatty & R. M. Visser (Eds*.), Thriving on an aging workforce: Strategies for organizational and systemic change* (pp. 104–111). Malabar, FL: Krieger.

Finley, N. J., Roberts, M. D., & Banahan, B. F. (1988). Motivators and inhibitors of attitudes of filial obligation toward aging parents. *Gerontologist, 28*, 73–78.

Fiori, K., Antonucci, T., & Cortina, K. (2006). Social network typologies and mental health among older adults. *Journal of Gerontology: Psychological Sciences, 61B*, P25–P32.

Firestone, R. W. (1993). Individual defenses against death anxiety. *Death Studies, 17*, 497–515.

Fisher, J., Harsen, C., & Hayden, J. (2000). Behavioral interventions for patients with dementia. In V. Molanari (Ed.), *Professional psychology in long-term care: A comprehensive guide* (pp. 179–200). New York: Hatherleigh Press.

Fisher, J., Nadler, A., & Whitcher-Adams, S. (1983). Four conceptualizations of reactions to aid. In J. Fisher , A. Nadler, & B. De Paulo (Eds.), *Nebraska Symposium on Motivation* (pp. 151–174). Lincoln: University of Nebraska Press.

Fiske, A. (2006). The nature of depression in later life. In S. Qualls & B. Knight (Eds.), *Psychotherapy for depression in older adults* (pp. 29–44). New York, NY: Wiley.

Fleming, D. (2010). Cultural sensitivity in end-of-life decisions. In D. Fleming & J. Hagan III (Eds). *Care of the dying patient* (pp. 84–100). Columbia, MO: Univ. of Missouri Press.

Fleming, D., & Hagan III, J. (2010). *Care of the dying patient*. Columbia, MO: Univ. of Missouri Press.

Flynn, J. R. (1999). Searching for justice: The discovery of IQ gains over time. *American Psychologist, 54*, 5–20.

Fontana, L. & Klein, S. (2007). Aging, adiposity, and calorie restriction. *Journal of the American Medical Association, 297*, 986–994.

Foster, J., & Gallagher, D. (1986). An exploratory study comparing depressed and nondepressed elders' coping strategies. *Journal of Gerontology, 41*, 91–93.

Fouad, N. (2007). Work and vocational psychology: Theory, research, and applications. *Annual Review of Psychology, 58*, 543–564.

Fozard, J. E., Vercruyssen, M., Reynolds, S. L., Hancock, P. A., & Quilter, R. E. (1994). Age differences and age changes in reaction time: The Baltimore longitudinal study of aging. *Journal of Gerontology: Psychological Sciences, 49*, 179–189.

Fozard, J. L. (1990). Vision and hearing in aging. In J. Birren & K. Schaie (Eds.), *Handbook of the psychology of aging* (pp. 150–171). New York: Academic Press.

Fozard, J. L., & Gallagher, D. (1986). An exploratory study comparing depressed and nondepressed elders' coping strategies. *Journal of Gerontology, 41*, 91–93.

Fozard, J. L., & Gordon-Salant, S. (2001). Changes in vision and hearing with aging. In J. Birren & K. W. Schaie (Eds.), *Handbook of the psychology of aging* (5th ed.) (pp. 241–266). San Diego, CA: Academic Press.

Frank, R., & McGuire, T. (2000). *The mental health economy and mental health economics*. http:/www.mentalhealth.samhsa.gov/publications/ allpubs/ sma01–3537/chapter8.asp

Franklin-Panek, C. (1978). Effects of personal growth groups on the self concept and decision making ability of normal adults. *Psychology, 15*, 25–29.

Fredrickson, B. L., & Carstensen, L. (1990). Choosing social partners: How old age and anticipated endings make people more selective. *Psychology and Aging, 5*, 335–347.

Freeman, F. M., & Williams, C. L. (1987, September-October). Minorities face stubborn inequalities. *Perspective on Aging (National Council on Aging), 32*, 15–17.

Freud, S. (1924). *On psychotherapy. Collected papers of Sigmund Freud* (Vol. 1, pp. 249–263). London: Hogarth Press.

Friend, R. A. (1991). Older lesbian and gay people: A theory of successful aging. *Journal of Homosexuality, 20* (3/ 4), 99–118.

Friese C., Becker G., Nachtigall R.D. (2008). Older motherhood and the changing life course in the era of assisted reproductive technologies. *Journal of Aging Studies, 22*, 65–73.

Fronstein P., & Salisbury, D. L. (2005). Rising health care costs and the aging workforce. In P. T. Beatty & R. M. Visser (Eds.), *Thriving on an aging workforce: Strategies for organizational and systemic change* (pp. 132–142). Malabar, FL: Krieger.

Fullerton, H. N. (2005). The workforce of tomorrow. In P. T. Beatty & R. M. Visser (Eds.), *Thriving on an aging workforce: Strategies for organizational and systemic change* (pp. 14–25). Malabar, FL: Krieger.

Fung, H., & Carstensen, L. (2003). Sending memorable messages to the old: Age differences in preferences and memory for advertisements. *Journal of Personality and Social Psychology, 85,* 163–178.

Fyock, C. D. (2005). Effective strategies for recruiting and retraining older workers. In P. T. Beatty & R. M. Visser (Eds.), *Thriving on an aging workforce: Strategies for organizational and systemic change* (pp. 51– 62). Malabar, FL: Krieger.

Gallagher, D., & Thompson, L. (1996). Applying cognitive behavioral treatments to the common psychological problems of later life. In S. Zarit & B. Knight (Eds.), *A guide to psychotherapy and aging* (pp. 61–82). Washington, DC: American Psychological Association.

Gallagher, S. K., & Gerstel, N. (1993). Kinkeeping and friend keeping among older women: The effect of marriage. *Gerontologist, 33,* 675–681.

Gallagher-Thompson, D. (2007). Evidence-based treatments for distress in family caregivers of older adults. *Psychology and Aging, 22,* 37–51.

Gallo, W. T., Bradley, E. H., Siegel, M., & Kasl, S. V. (2000). Health effects of involuntary job loss among older workers: Findings from the health and retirement survey. *Journal of Gerontology: Social Sciences, 55B,* S131–S140.

Galt, C., & Hayslip, B. (1998). Age differences in levels of overt and covert death anxiety. *Omega, 37,* 185–200.

Gardner, H. (1983). *Frames of mind: The theory of multiple intelligences.* New York: Basic Books.

Garrido, M., Kane, R., Kaas, M., & Kane, R. (2009). Perceived need for mental health care among community-dwelling older adults. *Journal of Gerontology: Psychological Sciences, 64B,* 704–712.

Gelfand, D. (2003). *Aging and ethnicity* (2nd ed.). New York: Springer.

Gentry, M., & Schulman, A. D. (1988). Remarriage as a coping response for widowhood. *Psychology and Aging, 3,* 191–196.

George, L. K. (1990). Social structure, social processes, and social-psychological states. In R. Binstock & L. K. George (Eds.), *Handbook of aging and the social sciences* (pp. 186–204). New York: Academic Press.

George, L. K., Fillenbaum, G. G., & Palmore, E. (1984). Sex differences in the antecedents and consequences of retirement. *Journal of Gerontology, 39,* 364–371.

George, L. K., & Weiler, S. J. (1981). Sexuality in middle and late life: The effects of age, cohort, and gender. *Archives of General Psychiatry, 38,* 919–923.

Gibson, H. (2006). Leisure and later life: Past, present, and future. *Leisure Studies, 25,* 397–401.

Gidycz, C. A., Coble, C. N., Latham, L., & Layman, M. J.(1993). A sexual assault experience in adulthood and prior victimization experiences: A prospective analysis. *Psychology of Women Quarterly, 17,* 471–475.

Gidycz, C. A., Hanson, K., & Layman, M. (1995). A prospective analysis of the sexual relationships among sexual assault experiences: An extension of previous findings. *Psychology of Women Quarterly, 19,* 5–29.

Gilbert, N. (2005). Family life: Sold on work. *Society, 42,* 12–17.

Gilbert, N. (2005). What do women really want? *Public Interest, 158,* 21–38.

Gilford, R. (1984). Contrasts in marital satisfaction throughout old age: An exchange-theory analysis. *Journal of Gerontology, 39,* 325–333.

Gilhooly, M., Zarit, S., & Birren, J. E. (1986). *The dementias: Policy and management.* Englewood Cliffs, NJ: Prentice Hall.

Gilmer, T., Ojeda, V., Fuentes, D., Criado, V., & Garcia, P. (2009). Access to public mental health services among older adults with severe mental illness. *International Journal of Geriatric Psychiatry, 24,* 313–318.

Ginzberg, E. (1971). *Career guidance.* New York: McGraw-Hill.

Gitlin, L. N., & Associates (2003). Effect of multicomponent interventions on caregiver burden and depression: The REACH multisite initiative at 6-month follow-up. *Psychology and Aging, 18,* 361–374.

Glamser, F. D. (1981). The impact of preretirement programs on the retirement experience. *Journal of Gerontology, 36,* 244–250.

Glamser, F. D., & Hayslip, B. J. (1985). The impact of retirement on participation in leisure activities. *Therapeutic Recreation Journal, 19*, 28–38.

Glantz, M. D., & Backenheimer, M. S. (1988). Substance abuse among elderly women. *Clinical Gerontologist, 8*, 3–26.

Glaser, B., & Strauss, A. (1968). *Time for dying*. Chicago: Aldine.

Glazer, S., & Nielson, N. L. (2000). Work and nonwork predictors of employees' retirement ages. *Journal of Vocational Behavior, 57*(2), 206–225.

Gold, D., & Arbuckle, T. (1990). Personality, cognition, and aging. In E. Lovelace (Ed.), *Aging and cognition* (pp. 351–378). Amsterdam: North Holland.

Goldenberg, I., & Goldenberg, H. (1991). *Family therapy: An overview*. Pacific Grove, CA: Brooks/Cole.

Goldsmith, B., Deitrich, J., Du, Q., & Morrison, R. (2008). Variability in access to hospital palliative care in the United States. *Journal of Palliative Medicine, 11*, 1094–1102.

Goleman, D. (1995). *Emotional intelligence*. New York: Bantam.

Goodstein, R. K. (1982). Individual psychotherapy and the elderly. *Psychotherapy: Theory, Research and Practice, 19*, 412–418.

Gorchoff, S. M., John, O. P., & Helson, R. (2008). Contextualizing change in marital satisfaction during middle age. *Psychological Science, 19*, 1194–1120.

Gottesman, L. E., Quarterman, C., & Cohn, G. (1973). Psychosocial treatment of the aged. In C. Eisdorfer & M. P. Lawton (Eds.), *The psychology of adult development and aging* (pp. 378–427). Washington, DC: American Psychological Association.

Gottfredson, L. (2002). Gottfredson's theory of circumscription, compromise, and self-creation. In D. Brown & Associates (Eds.), *Career choice and development* (pp. 85-148). San Francisco: Josey Bass.

Gottlieb, G. (1992). Economic issues and geriatric mental health. In J. Birren. R. Sloane, & G. Cohen (Eds.), *Handbook on mental health and aging* (pp. 873–890). San Diego, CA: Academic Press.

Gould, R. (1980). Transformations in mid-life. *New York University Education Quarterly, 10*, 2–9.

Gowan, M. A., Riordan, C. M., & Gatewood, R. D. (1999). Test of a model of coping with involuntary job loss following a company closing. *Journal of Applied Psychology, 84*, 75–86.

Grandparents raising kids: Rising number, rising stress. (2010, September 1). *Dallas Morning News*.

Green, J. (2000). *Neuropsychological evaluation of the older adult*. San Diego, CA: Academic Press.

Green, R. J., Bettinger, M., & Zacks, E. (1996). Are lesbian couples fused and gay male couples disengaged? Questioning gender straightjackets. In J. Laird & R. J. Green (Eds.), *Lesbians and gays in couples and families* (pp. 185–230). San Francisco: Jossey-Bass.

Gregoire, J., & van der Linden, M. (1997). Effect of age on forward and backward digit spans. *Aging, Neuropsychology, and Cognition, 4*, 140–149.

Greller, M., & Richtenmeyer, S. (2006). Changes in social support for professional development and retirement preparation as a function of age. *Human Relations, 59*, 1213-1234.

Griffin, J., & McKenna, K. (1998). Influences on leisure and life satisfaction of elderly people. *Physical & Occupational Therapy in Geriatrics, 15* (4), 1998.

Gruenewald, T., Karlamangla, A., Greendale, G., Singer, B., & Seean, T. (2009). Increased mortality risk in older adults with persistently low or declining feelings of usefulness to others. *Journal of Aging and Health, 21*, 398–425.

Guarnaccia, C., Hayslip, B., & Pinkenberg-Landry, L. (1999). Influence of perceived preventability of death and emotional closeness to the deceased on grief: A test of Bugen's model. *Omega, 39*, 261–276.

Guidelines for psychological practice with older adults. (2004). *American Psychologist, 59*, 236–260.

Guttman, D. (1975). Parenthood: A key to the comparative study of the life cycle. In N. Datan & L. Ginsburg (Eds.), *Life-span developmental psychology: Normative life crises* (pp. 167–184). New York: Academic Press.

Haan, N. (1972). Personality development from adolescence to adulthood in the Oakland growth and guidance studies. *Seminars in Psychiatry, 4*, 399–414.

Haan, N., Millsap, R., & Hartka, E. (1986). As time goes by: Change and stability in personality over 50 years. *Psychology and Aging, 1*, 220–232.

Haber, P. (1987). Nursing homes. In G. Maddox (Ed.), *Encyclopedia of Aging*. New York: Springer.

Hagestad, G. O. (1985). Continuity and connectedness. In V. L. Bengtson & J. F. Robertson (Eds.), *Grandparenthood* (pp. 31–48). Beverly Hills, CA: Sage.

Hagestad, G. O., & Neugarten, B. L. (1985). Age and the life course. In R. Binstock & E. Shanas (Eds.), *Handbook of aging and the social sciences* (pp. 35–61). New York: Van Nostrand Reinhold.

Haight, B., & Haight, B. (2007). *The handbook of structured life review*. Baltimore: Health Professions Press.

Haley, W. E. (1996). The medical context of psychotherapy with the elderly. In S. Zarit & B. Knight (Eds.), *A guide to psychotherapy and aging* (pp. 221–240). Washington, DC: American Psychological Association.

Hall, C., & Lindzey, G. (1985). *Theories of personality*. New York: Wiley.

Hall, D. T., & Mirvis, P. H. (1995). The new career contract: Developing the whole person at midlife and beyond. *Journal of Vocational Behavior, 47*, 269–289.

Hamby, S. (2009). The gender debate about intimate partner violence: Solutions and dead ends. *Psychological Trauma: Theory, Research, Practice, and Policy, 1*, 24–34.

Hamill, S.B., & Goldberg, W. A. (1997). Between adolescents and aging grandparents: Midlife concerns of adults in the "sandwich generation." *Journal of Adult Development, 4*, 135–147.

Hanson, A., & Scogin, F. (2008). Older adults' acceptance of psychological, pharmacological, and combination treatments for geriatric depression. *Journal of Gerontology: Psychological Sciences, 63B*, P245–P248.

Hanson, K. A., & Gidycz, C. A. (1993). Evaluation of a sexual assault prevention program. *Journal of Consulting and Clinical Psychology, 6*, 1046–1052.

Hansson, R. O., Dekoekkoek, P. D., Neese, W. M., & Patterson, D. W. (1997). Successful aging at work: Annual review 1992–1996: The older worker and transitions to retirement. *Journal of Vocational Behavior, 51*, 202–233.

Hansson, R. O., Hayslip, B., & Stroebe, M. (in press). Grief and bereavement. In J. Blackburn & K. Dulmus (Eds.), *Handbook of gerontology: Evidence-based approaches to practice and policy*. New York: Wiley.

Hardy, M. (2006). Older workers. In R. Binstock & L. George (Eds.), *Handbook of aging and the social sciences* (pp. 202–219). San Diego, CA: Academic Press.

Hareven, T. (2001). Historical perspectives on aging and family relations. In R. Binstock & C. George (Eds.), *Handbook of aging and social sciences* (pp. 141–159). San Antonio, TX: Academic Press.

Hartmann, H., English, A., & Hayes, J. (2010). *Women's and men's employment and unemployment in the Great Recession*. Institute for Women's Policy Research Publication, accessed: http://www.iwpr.org/pdf/C373womeninrecession.pdf

Harju, E. L. (2002). Cold and warmth perception mapped for age, gender, and body area. *Somatosensory & Motor Research, 19*, 61–75.

Harmon, L. W. (1989). Longitudinal changes in womens' career aspirations: Developmental or historical? *Journal of Vocational Behavior, 35*, 46–63.

Harper, M., & Shoffner, M. (2004). Counseling for career development after retirement: An application of the theory of work adjustment. *Career Development Quarterly, 52*, 272–284.

Harrington, M. P. (1992). Advantages and disadvantages of multigenerational family households: Views of three generations. *Journal of Applied Gerontology, 11*, 457–474.

Harris, R. L., Elliott, A. M., & Holmes, D. S. (1986). The timing of psychosocial transitions and changes in women's lives: An examination of women aged 45 to 60. *Journal of Personality and Social Psychology, 51*, 409–416.

Hartup, W. W. (1989). Social relationships and their developmental significance. *American Psychologist, 44*, 283–292.

Hary, J. (1983). Gay male and lesbian relationships. In E. D. Macklin and R. Rubin (Eds.), *Contemporary family forms and alternative lifestyles: Handbook on research and theory*. Newbury Park, CA: Sage.

Havighurst, R. J. (1972). *Developmental tasks and education* (3rd ed.). New York: McKay.

Havighurst, R. J. (1982). The world of work. In J. Wolman (Ed.), *Handbook of developmental psychology* (pp. 771–787). Englewood Cliffs, NJ: Prentice Hall.

Havighurst, R. J., Neugarten, B. L., & Tobin, S. (1961). The measurement of life satisfaction. *Journal of Gerontology, 16*, 134–143.

Hawkins, A. J., Christiansen, S. L., Sargent, K. P., & Hill, E. J. (1993). Rethinking fathers' involvement in child care. *Journal of Family Issues, 14*, 531–549.

Hayden, K., & Sano, M. (2006). Pharmocological and other treatment strategies for Alzheimer's disease. In K. K. Attix & K. Welsh-Bohmer (Eds.), *Geriatric neuropsychology: Assessment and intervention* (pp. 414–455). New York: Guilford Press.

Hayflick, L. (1988). Biological aging theories, In G. Maddox Ed.), *Encyclopedia of aging* (pp. 64–68). Englewood Cliffs, NJ: Prentice Hall.

Hayflick, L. (1994). *How and why we age.* New York: Ballantine.

Hayflick, L. (2000). The future of aging. *Nature, 408*, 267–269.

Hayslip, B. (1988). Personality-ability relationships in aged adults. *Journal of Gerontology: Psychological Sciences, 43*, P74–84.

Hayslip, B. (1989). Alternative mechanisms for improvements in fluid-ability performance in aged persons. *Psychology and Aging, 4*, 122–124.

Hayslip, B. (1997). Hospice care. In J. E. Birren (Eds.), *Encyclopedia of gerontology* (pp. 318–334), San Diego, CA: Academic Press.

Hayslip, B. (2003). Death denial: Hiding and camouflaging death. In C. D. Bryant (Ed*.), Handbook of death and dying: V1-The presence of death* (pp. 34–42). Newbury Park, CA: Sage.

Hayslip, B. (2011). Job loss transition for families. In M. J. Craft-Rosenberg (Ed.), *Handbook of family health.* Thousand Oaks, CA: Sage.

Hayslip, B., Booher, S. Riddle, R., & Guarnaccia, C. (2005-2006). Proximal and distal antecedents of funeral attitudes: A multidimensional analysis. *Omega: Journal of Death and Dying, 52,* 121–142.

Hayslip, B., Booher, S. K., Scoles, M. T., & Guarnaccia, C. (2006-2007). Assessing adults' difficulty in coping with funerals. *Omega: Journal of Death and Dying, 55,* 97–119.

Hayslip, B., & Caraway, M. (1989). Cognitive therapy with aged persons: Implications of research design for its implementation and evaluation. *Journal of Cognitive Psychotherapy, 3*, 255–271.

Hayslip, B., & Glover, R. (2008-2009). Custodial grandparenting: Perceptions of loss by traditional grandparent peers. *Omega: Journal of Death and Dying, 58,* 165–177.

Hayslip, B., & Goldberg-Glen, R. (2000). *Grandparents raising grandchildren: Theoretical, empirical, and clinical perspectives.* New York: Springer.

Hayslip, B., Guarnaccia, C., Radika, L., & Servaty, H. (2002). Death anxiety: An empirical test of a blended self-report and projective measurement model. *Omega, 44*, 277–294.

Hayslip, B., & Han, G. (2009). Cultural attitudes towards death, dying, and bereavement: An overview. In K. J. Doka (Ed.), *Living with grief: Cultural diversity* (pp. 5-20). Washington, DC: Hospice Foundation of America.

Hayslip, B., Han, G., & Anderson, C. L. (2008). Predictors of Alzheimer's disease caregiver depression and burden: What non-caregiving adults can learn from active caregivers. *Educational Gerontology, 34,* 945–970.

Hayslip, B., & Hansson, R. O. (2006). Hospice. In J. E. Birren (Ed.), *Encyclopedia of gerontology* (pp. 1–10). Oxford: Elsiever.

Hayslip, B., Hansson, R., Starkweather, J., & Dolan, D. (2009). Culture, individual diversity, and end-of-life decisions. In J. Werth & D. Blevins (Eds.), *Decision-making near the end of life: Recent developments and future directions* (pp. 301-324). Oxford, UK: Routledge.

Hayslip, B., & Kaminski, P. (2005). Grandparents raising grandchildren: A review of the literature and implications for practice. *Gerontologist, 45*, 262–269.

Hayslip, B., Kennelly, K., & Maloy, R. (1990). Fatigue, depression, and cognitive performance among aged persons. *Experimental Aging Research, 16*, 111–115.

Hayslip, B., & Leon, J. (1992). *Hospice care.* Beverly Hills, CA. Sage.

Hayslip, B., Luhr, D., & Beyerlein, M. (1991). Levels of death anxiety in terminally ill men: A pilot study. *Omega, 24*, 13–20.

Hayslip, B., & Maiden, R. (2005). Cognitive loss. In C. Dulmus & C. Rapp-Paglicci (Eds.), *Handbook of preventative interventions for adults* (pp. 27–55). New York: Wiley.

Hayslip, B., Maiden, R. J., Thomison, N., & Temple, J. R. (2010). Mental health attitudes among rural and urban older adults. *Clinical Gerontologist, 33,* 1–17.

Hayslip, B., & Page, K. S. (in press). Grandparent-grandchild/great-grandchild relationships. In R. Blieszner & V. H. Bedford (Eds.), *Handbook of aging and the family*. New York, NY: Praeger.

Hayslip, B., & Panek, P. (1993). *Adult development and aging*. New York: HarperCollins.

Hayslip, B., Panek, P., & Stoner, S. (1991). Cohort differences in Hand Test performance: A time-lagged analysis. *Journal of Personality Assessment, 54,* 704–710.

Hayslip, B. & Patrick, J. (2003*). Working with custodial grandparents*. New York: Springer.

Hayslip, B. & Peveto, C. (2005). *Cultural changes in attitudes toward death, dying, and bereavement*. New York: Springer.

Hayslip, B., Servaty, H., Christman, T., & Mumy, E. (1996–1997). Levels of death anxiety in terminally ill persons: A cross validation and extension. *Omega, 34,* 204–218.

Hayslip, B., Servaty, H., & Guarnaccia, C. (1999). Age cohort differences in perceptions of funerals. In B. deVries (Ed.), *End of life issues: Interdisciplinary and multidimensional perspectives* (pp. 23–36). New York: Springer.

Hayslip, B. J., Jr., Shore, R. J., Henderson, C. E., & Lambert, P. L. (1998). Custodial grandparenting and the impact of grandchildren with problems on role satisfaction and role meaning. *Journal of Gerontology: Social Sciences, 53B,* S164–S173.

Hayslip, B. J., Jr., & Sterns, H. (1979). Age differences in relationships between crystallized and fluid intelligences and problem-solving. *Journal of Gerontology, 34,* 404–414.

Hedge, J., Borman, W., & Lammlein, S. (2005). *The aging workforce: Realities, myths, and implications for organizations*. Washington, DC: American Psychological Association.

Heilbronn, L. K., de Jonge, L., Frisard, M. I., DeLany, J. P., Larson-Meyer, D. E., Rood, J., Nguyen, T., Ravussin, E. (2006). Effect of 6-month calorie restriction on biomarkers of longevity, metabolic adaptation, and oxidative stress in overweight individuals: A randomized controlled trial. *Journal of the American Medical Association, 295,* 1539-1548.

Hellebrandt, F. (1980). Aging among the advantaged: A new look at the stereotype of the elderly. *Gerontologist, 20,* 404–417.

Helson, R., & Moane, G. (1987). Personality change in women from college to mid-life. *Journal of Personality and Social Psychology, 53,* 176–186.

Hendrick, C., & Hendrick, S. S. (1986). A theory and method of love. *Journal of Personality and Social Psychology, 50,* 392–402.

Henry, N. J. M., Berg, C. A., Smith, T. W., & Florsheim, P. (2007). Positive and negative characteristics of marital interaction and their association with marital satisfaction in middle-aged and older couples. *Psychology and Aging, 22,* 428–441.

Hershey, D. A., Walsh, D. A., Read, S. J., & Chulef, A. S. (1990). The effects of expertise on financial problem solving: Evidence for goal-directed problem solving scripts. *Organizational Behavior and Human Decision Processes, 46,* 77–101.

Hess, T. (2006). Attitudes toward aging and their effects on behavior. In J. Birren & K. Schaie (Eds.), *Handbook of the psychology of aging* (pp. 379–407). San Diego, CA: Academic Press.

Heston, L. L., & White, J. A. (1991). *The vanishing mind*. New York: Freeman.

Hetherington, E. M., Cox, M., & Cox, R. (1985). Long-term effects of divorce and remarriage on the adjustment of children. *Journal of the American Academy of Child Psychiatry, 24,* 518–530.

Hickson, F. C., Davies, P. M., Hunt, A. J., & Weatherburn, P. (1992). Maintenance of open gay relationships: Some strategies for protection against HIV. *AIDS Care, 4,* 409–419.

Hindrichsen, G. (2006). Interpersonal therapy with older adults. In S. Qualls & B. Knight (Eds.), *Psychotherapy for depression in older adults* (pp. 111–132). New York: Wiley.

Hindrichsen, G. (2008). Interpersonal therapy as a treatment for depression in later life. *Professional Psychology, Research and Practice, 39,* 306–312.

Hindrichsen, G. (2010). Public policy and the provision of psychological services to older adults. *Professional Psychology, Research, and Practice, 41,* 97–103.

Hindrichsen, G., & Cloughtery, K. (2006). *Interpersonal therapy for depressed older adults*. Washington, DC: American Psychological Association.

Hine, V. (1979-1980). Dying at home: Can families cope? *Omega, 10,* 175–187.

Hobdy, J., Hayslip, B., Kaminski, P., Crowley, B., Riggs, S., & York, C. (2007). The role of attachment style in coping with job loss and the empty nest in adulthood. *International Journal of Aging and Human Development, 65,* 335–371.

Hodgson, L., & Cutler, S. (2003). Looking for signs of Alzheimer's disease. *International Journal of Aging and Human Development, 56*, 323–344.

Hodson, D. S., & Skeen, P. (1994). Sexuality and aging: The hammerlock of myths. *Journal of Applied Gerontology, 13*, 219–235.

Hoffman, L. W. (1989). Effects of maternal employment in the two-parent family. *American Psychologist, 44*, 283–292.

Hoffnung, M. (2004). Wanting it all: Career, marriage, and motherhood during college education women's 20s. *Sex Roles, 50*, 711–723.

Hogan, M. (2005). Physical and cognitive activity and exercise for older adults. *International Journal of Aging and Human Development, 60*, 95–126.

Holland, J. (1994). Separate but equal. In M. Savickas & R. Lent (Eds.), *Convergence in career development theories: Implications for science and practice* (pp. 45-51). Palo Alto, CA: CPP Books.

Holland, J., & Neimeyer, R. (2010). An examination of stage theory of grief among individuals bereaved by natural and violent causes: A meaning-oriented contribution. *Omega, 61*, 103–120.

Holley, C., & Mast, B. (2010). Predictors of anticipatory grief in dementia caregivers. *Clinical Gerontologist, 33*, 223–236.

Holmberg, L., & Wahlberg, V. (2000). The process of decision-making in abortion: A grounded theory study of young men in Sweden. *Journal of Adolescent Health, 26*, 230–234.

Holmes, B. J. & Johnson, K. R. (2009). Adult attachment and romantic partner preference: A review. *Journal of Social and Personal Relationships, 26*, 833–852.

Holmes, J. H., & Rahe, R. H. (1967). The social readjustment rating scale. *Journal of Personality and Social Psychology, 11*, 213–218.

Hooker, K., & McAdams, D. P. (2003). Personality reconsidered: A new agenda for aging research. *Journal of Gerontology: Psychological Sciences, 58B*, P296–P304.

Hooker, K., & Ventis, D. G. (1984). Work ethic, daily activities, and retirement satisfaction. *Journal of Gerontology, 39*, 478–484.

Hooyman, N., & Kiyak, H. (2011). *Social Gerontology: A multidisciplinary perspective*. Boston: Allyn & Bacon.

Horn, J. L. (1978). Human ability systems. In P. Baltes (Eds.), *Life-span development and behavior* (Vol. 1, pp. 211–256). New York: Academic Press.

Horn, J. L., & Hofer, S. (1992). Major abilities and development during the adult period. In R. Sternberg & C. Berg (Eds.), *Intellectual Development* (pp. 44–99). New York: Cambridge University Press.

Hornblower, M. (1997). Great expectations. *Time*, June 8, pp. 58–65.

Horne, H. L., Lowe, J. D., & Murry, P. D. (1990, August). *Anxiety of young adults over expected caregiver role*. Paper presented at the Annual Meeting of the American Psychological Association, Boston.

Houston, W., & Bondi, M. (2006). Potentially reversible cognitive symptoms in older adults. In K. K. Attix & K. Welsh-Bohmer (Eds.), *Geriatric neuropsychology: Assessment and intervention* (pp. 103–130). New York: Guilford Press.

Howath, T. B., & Davis, K. L. (1990). Central-nervous system disorders in aging. In E. Schneider & J. Rowe (Eds.), *Handbook of the biology of aging* (pp. 306– 329). New York: Academic Press.

Howell, W. C. (1997). Forward, perspectives, and prospectives. In A. D. Fisk and W. A. Rogers (Eds.), *Handbook of human factors and the older adult* (pp. 1–6). Academic Press: New York.

Hoyer, W. J., & Rybash, J. (1994). Characterizing adult cognitive development. *Journal of Adult Development, 1*, 7–12.

Hoyer, W. J., & Verheagen, P. (2006). Memory aging. In J. Birren & K. W. Schaie (Eds.), *Handbook of the psychology of aging* (pp. 209–232). San Diego, CA: Academic Press.

Huang, Q., & Sverke, M. (2007). Women's occupational career patterns over 27 years: Relations to family of origin, life careers, and wellness. *Journal of Vocational Behavior, 70*, 369–397.

Hudson, F. M. (1999). *The adult years: Mastering the art of self-renewal*. New York: Jossey-Bass.

Hudson, F. M. (2002). *The adult years* (2nd ed.). San Francisco: Jossey-Bass.

Huffman, K. (2007). *Psychology in action* (8th ed.). New York: Wiley.

Hui, V. & Fung, H. (2009). Mortality anxiety as a function of intrinsic religiosity and perceived purpose in life. *Death Studies, 33*, 30–50.

Hultsch, D. F., & Dixon, R. A. (1990). Learning and memory in aging. In J. E. Birren & K. W. Schaie (Eds.), *Handbook of the psychology of aging* (pp. 258–274). New York: Academic Press.

Hultsch, D. F., MacDonald, W. S., & Dixon, R. A. (2002). Variability in reaction time performance of younger and older adults. *Journals of Gerontology: Psychological Sciences, 57B*, P101–PI15.

Hummert, M. (1990). Multiple stereotypes of elderly and young adults: A comparison of structure and evaluations. *Psychological and Aging, 5*, 182–193.

Hummert, M. (1999). A social cognitive perspective on age stereotypes. In T. Hess & F. Blanchard-Fields (Eds.), *Social cognition and aging* (pp. 175–196). San Diego, CA: Academic Press.

Humphrey, D. (1991). Final exit. New York: Dell.

Humphrey, J. A., & Palmer, S. (1990–991). The effects of race, gender, and marital status on suicides among young adults, middle-aged adults, and older adults. *Omega, 22*, 277–286.

Hwalek, M. A., Neale, A. V., Goodrich, C. S., & Quinn, K. (1991). The association of elder abuse and substance abuse in the Illinois elder abuse system. *Gerontologist, 36*, 694–700.

Hybels, C., Blazer, D., & Pieper, C. (2001). Toward a threshold for subthreshold depression: An analysis of the correlates of depression by severity of symptoms using data from an elderly community sample. *Gerontologist, 41*, 357–365.

Ingersoll-Dayton, B., Neal, M. B., & Hammer, L. B. (2001). Aging parents helping adult children: The experience of the sandwiched generation. *Family Relations: Interdisciplinary Journal of Applied Family Studies, 50*(3), 263–271.

Ingersoll-Dayton, B., & Saengtienchai, C. (1999). Respect for the elder in Asia: Stability and change. *International Journal of Aging and Human Development, 48*, 113–130.

Irion, P. E. (1990-1991). Changing patterns of ritual response to death. *Omega, 22*, 159–172.

Iso-Ahola, S. E., Jackson, E., & Dunn, E. (1994). Starting, ceasing, and replacing leisure activities over the lifespan. *Journal of Leisure Research, 26*(3), 227–249.

Iwasaki, Y., MacKay, K. J., & Risstock, J. (2004). Gender based stress among professional managers: An exploratory qualitative study. *International Journal of Stress Management, 11*, 56–79.

Jackson, E., Meeks, S., & Vitotoe, E. (2002). Life events, distress, symptoms, and functioning in late-life severe mental illness. *Journal of Mental Health and Aging, 8*, 59–87.

Jackson, J., Antonucci, T., & Gibson, R. (1990). Cultural, racial, and ethnic minority influences on aging. In J. Birren and K. W. Schaie (Eds.), *Handbook of the psychology of aging* (3rd ed.) (pp. 103–123). San Diego, CA: Academic Press.

Jackson, T. (1999). Differences in the psychosocial experiences of employed, unemployed, and student samples of young adults. *Journal of Psychology, 133*, 49–60.

Jacobs-Lawson, J., Hershey, D., & Neukam, K. (2004). Gender differences in factors that influence time spent planning for retirement. *Journal of Women & Aging, 16*, 55-69.

Jacque, E. (1965). Death and the mid-life crisis. *International Journal of Psychoanalysis, 46*, 502–514.

James, W. B., & Maher, P. A. (2004). Understanding and using learning styles. In M. W. Galbraith (Ed.), *Adult learning methods: A guide for effective instruction* (pp. 119–136). Malabar, FL: Krieger.

Jandeska, K. E., & Kraimer, M. L. (2005). Women's perceptions of organizational culture, work attitudes, and role modeling behaviors. *Journal of Managerial Issues, 17*, 461–478.

Jean, L., Bureron, M., Thivierge, S., & Simard, M. (2010). Cognitive intervention programs for individuals with mild cognitive impairment: Systematic review of the literature. *The American Journal of Geriatric Psychiatry, 18*, 281–296.

Jenkins, S. R. (1989). Longitudinal predictors of women's careers: Psychological, behavioral, and social-structure influences. *Journal of Vocational Behavior, 34*, 204–235.

Jeste, D., Twamley, E., Eyler, C., Zorrilla, L., Golshan, S., Patterson, T., & Palmer, B. (2003). Aging and outcome in schizophrenia. *Acta Psychiatricia Scandinavica, 107*, 336–343.

Job loss: How to cope (2006). http://careerplanning about.com/od/jobloss/a/job_loss.htm

Johnson, C. L. (1988). Active and latent functions of grandparenting during the divorce process. *Gerontologist, 28*, 185–191.

Johnson, C. L., & Troll, L. E. (1994). Constraints and facilitators to friendships in late life. *Gerontologist, 34*, 79–87.

Johnson, J., First, M., Block, S., Vanderwerker, L., Kivin, K., Zhang, B., & Prigerson, H. (2009). Stigmatization and receptivity to mental health services among recently bereaved adults. *Death Studies, 33*, 691–711.

Johnson, M. M. S. (1990). Age differences in decision making: A process methodology for examining strategic information processing. *Journal of Gerontology, 45,* P75–78.

Johnson, R. (2009). The recession's impact on older worker. *Public Policy and Aging Report, 19,* 26–30.

Johnson, R., & Schaner, S. (2005). *The value of unpaid activities by older Americans tops $160 billion per year.* Perspectives on Productive Aging, Brief No. 4, Washington, DC: The Urban Institute.

Johnston, W. B. (1987). *Workforce 2000: Work and workers for the 21st century.* Indianapolis, IN: Hudson Institute.

Jones, C., & Meredith, W. (2000). Developmental paths of psychological health from early adolescence to later adulthood. *Psychology and Aging, 15,* 351–360.

Jones, D., & McIntosh, B. (2010). Organizational and occupational commitment in relation to bridge employment and retirement intentions. *Journal of Vocational Behavior, 76,* 1-14.

Jopp, D., & Hetzog, C. (2010). Assessing adult leisure activities: An extension of a self-report activity questionnaire. *Psychological Assessment, 22,* 108–120.

Kahn, R., & Antonucci, T. (1980). Convoys over the life course: Attachment, roles, and social support. In P. B. Baltes & O. G. Brim, Jr. (Eds.), *Life-span development and behavior* (Vol. 3, pp. 254–286). New York: Academic Press.

Kahn, R., & Miller, N. (1978). Assessment of altered brain function in the aged. In M. Storandt, I. Siegler, & M. Elias (Eds.), *The clinical psychology of aging* (pp. 43– 69). New York: Plenum.

Kaminski, P., & Hayslip, B. (2006). Gender differences in body esteem among older adults. *Journal of Women and Aging, 18,* 19–35.

Kane, M., Lacey, D., & Green, D. 2009). Investigating social work students' perceptions of elders' vulnerability and resilience. *Social Work in Mental Health, 7,* 307–313.

Kane, R. (2000). Choosing an assessment tool. In R. L. Kane & R. A. Kane (Eds.), *Assessing older persons: Measures, meaning and practical application* (pp. 1–16). New York: Oxford.

Kane, R. L., & Kane, R. A. (2000). *Assessing older persons: Measures, meaning, and practical application.* New York: Oxford.

Kaplan, M. S., Adamek, M. E., & Johnson, S. (1994). Trends in firearm suicide among older American males: 1979–1988. *Gerontologist, 34,* 59–65.

Kapp, M. B. (2003). Should home screening tests for Alzheimer's disease be regulated? *Gerontologist, 43,* 292–294.

Karel, M., Knight, B., Duffy, M., Hindrichsen, G., & Zeiss, A. (2010). Attitude, knowledge, and skill competencies for practice in professional geropsychology: Implications for training and building a geropsychology workforce. *Training and Education in Professional Psychology, 4,* 75–84.

Karlamangla, A., Tinetti, M., Guralnik, J., Studenskil, S., Wetle, T., & Reuben, D. (2007). Comorbidity in older adults: Nosology of impairment, diseases, and conditions. *Journals of Gerontology: Biological Sciences/Medical Sciences, 62,* 296–300.

Karp, D. A. (1988). A decade of reminders: Changing age consciousness between fifty and sixty years old. *Gerontologist, 28,* 727–738.

Kaskie, B., Linkins, K., & Estes, C. (2002). The role of the aging network in identifying and providing care to older adults with mental illnesses. *Journal of Mental Health and Aging, 8,* 241–253.

Kastenbaum, R. (1978). Death, dying, and bereavement in old age: New developments and their possible implications for psychosocial care. *Aged Care and Services Review, 1,* 1–10.

Kastenbaum, R. (1992). *The psychology of death.* New York: Springer.

Kastenbaum, R. (1998). *Death, society, and human existence.* Boston: Allyn & Bacon.

Kastenbaum, R. (2006). *Death, society, and human experience* (9th ed.). Boston: Allyn and Bacon.

Kastenbaum, R. (2009). *Death, society, and human experience* (10th ed.). Boston: Allyn and Bacon.

Kastenbaum, R. (2009). Should we manage terror—If we could? *Omega, 59,* 271–304.

Kastenbaum, R., & Aisenberg, R. (1976). *The psychology of death.* New York: Springer.

Kaszniak, A. W. (1996). Techniques and instruments for assessment of the elderly. In S. Zarit & B. Knight (Eds.), *A guide to psychotherapy and aging* (pp. 163–219). Washington, DC: American Psychological Association.

Kausler, D. (1991). *Experimental psychology and human aging* (2nd ed.). New York: Springer-Verlag.

Kausler, D. (1994). *Learning and memory in normal aging.* San Diego, CA: Academic Press.

Kawachi, I., Daniels, N., & Robinson, D. E. (2005). Health disparities by race and class: Why both matter. *Health Affairs, 24*, 343–352.

Keene, J. R. (2005). Balancing work and caregiving. In P. T. Beatty & R. M. Visser (Eds.), *Thriving on an aging workforce: Strategies for organizational and systemic change* (pp. 112–120). Malabar, FL: Krieger.

Keith, P. M., Hill, K., Goudy, W. J., & Powers, E. A. (1984). Confidants and well-being: A note on male friendships in old age. *Gerontologist, 24*, 318–320.

Kelly, J. R. (1983). *Leisure identities and interactions.* London: Allen & Unwin.

Kelly, J. R. (1988). Leisure in later life: Roles and identities. In N. J. Osgood (Ed.), *Life after work: Retirement, leisure, and the elderly.* New York: Praeger.

Kelly, J. R. (1996a). Activities. In J. E. Birren (Ed.), *Encyclopedia of Gerontology: Age, aging, and the aged* (Vol. 1, pp. 37–49). San Diego, CA: Academic Press.

Kelly, J. R. (1996b). *Leisure.* Englewood Cliffs, NJ: Prentice Hall.

Kelly, J. R., Steinkamp, M. W., & Kelly, J. R. (1986). Later-life leisure: How they play in Peoria. *Gerontologist, 26*, 531–537.

Kelly, T. (1991). *Volunteerism legislation. In Resourceful aging: V.2-Volunteerism.* Washington, DC: American Association of Retired Persons.

Kemp, B. J., & Mitchell, J. (1992). Functional assessment in geriatric mental health. In J. E. Birren, R. B. Sloane, & G. D. Cohen (Eds.), *Handbook of mental health and aging* (pp. 672–698). New York: Academic Press.

Kennedy, G. F. (1990). College students' expectations of grandparent and grandchild role behaviors. *Gerontologist, 30*, 43–48.

Kennelly, K. J., Hayslip, B., & Richardson, S. K. (1985). Depression and helplessness-induced cognitive deficits in the aged. *Experimental Aging Research, 8*, 165–173.

Kenshalo, D. R. (1977). Age changes in touch, vibration, temperature, kinesthesis, and pain sensitivity. In J. E. Birren & K. W. Schaie (Eds.), *Handbook of the psychology of aging* (pp. 562–579). New York: Van Nostrand Reinhold.

Kesselman, I. (1990). Grief and loss: Issues for abortion. *Omega, 3*, 241–248.

Kessler, R. C., Demler, O., Frank, R., Olfson, M., Pincus, H., Walters, E., Wang, P., Wells, K., & Zaslavsky, A. (2005). Prevalence and treatment of mental disorders from 1990 to 2003. *New England Journal of Medicine, 352*, 2515–2523.

Kier, F. J., & Molanari, V. (2003). "Do it yourself" dementia testing: Issues regarding and Alzheimer's home screening test. *Gerontologist, 43*, 295–301.

Kim, J., Kwon, J., & Anderson, E. (2005). Factors related to retirement confidence: Retirement preparation and workplace financial education. *Financial Counseling and Planning, 16*, 77–89.

Kim, J. E., & Moen, P. (2002). Retirement transitions, gender, and psychological well-being: A life-course, ecological model. *Psychological Sciences and Social Sciences, 57B*(3), P212–P222.

Kimmel, D. C. (2004). Issues to consider in studies of midlife and older sexual minorities. In G. Herdt & B. de Vries (Eds.), *Gay and lesbian aging: Research and future directions* (pp. 265–283). New York: Springer.

Kimmel, D., Rose, T., & David, S. (2006). *Lesbian, gay, bisexual, and transgender aging: Research and clinical perspectives.* Columbia, NY: Columbia University Press.

King, J., & Hayslip, B. (2002). The media's influence on college students' views of death. *Omega, 44*, 37–56.

Kinicki, A. J., & Latack, J. C. (1990). Explication of the construct of coping with involuntary job loss. *Journal of Vocational Behavior, 36*, 339–360.

Kinney, J. M., & Cart, C. S. (2006). Not quite a panacea: Technology to facilitate family caregiving for elders with dementia. *Generations, Summer*, 64–66.

Kinney, J., Ishler, K., Cavanaugh, J., & Pargament, K. (2003). The use of religious coping by caregivers of spouses with dementia. *Journal of Religious Gerontology, 14*, 171–188.

Kinsella, K., & Wan He (2009). *An aging world 2008.* U.S. Census Bureau, International Population Reports, P95/09-1, U.S. Government Printing Office, Washington, DC.

Kirchmeyer, C. (2002). Gender differences in managerial careers: Yesterday, today, and tomorrow. *Journal of Business Ethics, 37*, 5–24.

Kirkclady, B. D., Shephard, R. J., & Furnham, A. F. (2002). The influence of type A behavior and locus of control upon job satisfaction and occupational health. *Personality and Individual Differences, 33*, 1361–1371.

Kitson, G. C., & Morgan, L. A. (1990). Consequences of divorce. *Journal of Marriage and the Family, 52*, 913–924.

Kivett, V. R. (1991). Centrality of the grandfather role among older rural black and white men. *Journal of Gerontology: Social Sciences, 46*, S250–S258.

Kjonniksen, L., Anderssen, N., & Wold, B. (2009). Organized youth sport as a predictor of physical activity in adulthood. *Scandinavian Journal of Medicine & Science in Sports, 19*, 646–654.

Kleemeier, R. W. (1962). *Intellectual change in the senium*. Proceedings of the Social Statistics Section of the American Statistical Association, 1, 290–295.

Kleespies, P., Miller, P., & Preston, T. (2009). End of life choices. In J. Worth & D. Blevins (Eds.), *Decision making near the end of life : Recent developments and future directions* (pp. 119–142). New York: Routledge.

Kline, D. W., & Scheiber, F. (1985). Vision and aging. In J. E. Birren & K. W. Schaie (Eds.), *Handbook of the psychology of aging* (2nd ed., pp. 296–331). New York: Van Nostrand Reinhold.

Kline, D. W., & Scialfa, C. T. (1997). Sensory and perceptual functioning: Basic research and human factors implications. In A. D. Fisk and W. A. Rogers (Eds.), *Handbook of human factors and the older adult* (pp. 27–54). Academic Press, New York.

Klume, S. (2008). *Psychotherapy for the dying*. http://psychcentral.com/blog/archives/2008/04/18/psychotherapy-for-the-dying.

Knight, B. G. (1996). Overview of psychotherapy with the elderly: A contextual cohort based maturity specific challenge model. In S. Zarit & B. Knight (Eds.), *A guide to psychotherapy and aging* (pp. 17–34). Washington, DC: American Psychological Association.

Knight, B. (2004). *Psychotherapy with older adults*. Thousand Oaks, CA: Sage.

Knight, B., Kaskie, B., Shurgot, G., & Dave, J. (2006). Improving the mental health care of older adults. In J. E. Birren & K. W. Schaie (Eds.), *Handbook of the psychology of aging* (pp. 407–424). San Diego, CA: Academic Press.

Knight, B. G., & Qualls, S. H. (1995). The older client in developmental context: Life course and family systems perspectives. *Clinical Psychologist, 48*, 11–17.

Kochanek, K. D., Murphy, S. L., Anderson, R., & Scott, S. (2004). *Deaths: Final data for 2002. National Vital Statistics Reports, 53*(5). Hyattsville, MD: National Center for Health Statistics.

Koenig, H. G., & Blazer, D. G. (1992). Mood disorders and suicide. In J. E. Birren, R. B. Sloane, & G. D. Cohen (Eds.), *Handbook of mental health and aging* (pp. 380–409). New York: Academic Press.

Koenig, M. H., George, L., & Schneider, R. (1994). Mental health care for older adults in the year 2020: A dangerous and avoided topic. *Gerontologist, 34*, 674–679.

Kogan, N. (1990). Personality and aging. In J. E. Birren & K. W. Schaie (Eds.), *Handbook of the psychology of aging* (pp. 330–346). New York: Academic Press.

Kornhaber, A. (1996). *Contemporary grandparenting*. Thousand Oaks, CA: Sage.

Koropeckyj-Cox, T. (1998). Loneliness and depression in middle and old age: Are the childless more vulnerable? *Journals of Gerontology: Social Sciences, 53B*, S303–312.

Kosnik, W., Winslow, L., Kline, D., Pasinki, K., & Sekular, R. (1988). Visual changes in daily life throughout adulthood. *Journal of Gerontology: Psychological Sciences, 43*, P63–70.

Kotch, J. B., & Cohen, S. R. (1985-1986). SIDS counselors' reports of own and parents' reactions to reviewing the autopsy report. *Omega, 16*, 129–139.

Kotter-Gruhn, D., Scheibe, S., Blanchard-Fields, F., & Baltes, P. B. (2009). Developmental emergence and functionality of sehnsucht (life longings): The sample case of involuntary childlessness in middle-aged women. *Psychology and Aging, 24*, 634-644.

Kozma, A., & Stones, M. (1986). Social desirability in measures of subjective well-being: A systematic evaluation. *Journal of Gerontology, 42*, 56–57.

Krause, N. (1994). Stressors in salient social roles and well-being in later life. *Journal of Gerontology: Psychological Sciences, 49*, P137–P148.

Krause, N. (2001). Social support. In R. H. Binstock & L. K. George (Eds.), *Handbook of aging and the social sciences* (5th ed.) (pp. 272–294). San Diego, CA: Academic Press.

Kreider, R. M. & Elliott, D. B. (2009). *America's Families and Living Arrangements: 2007*. Current Population Reports, P20-561. U.S. Census Bureau, Washington, DC.

Krout, J., Cutler, S., & Coward, R.T. (1990). Correlates of senior center participation: A national analysis. *Gerontologist, 30*, 72–79.

Krumboltz, J., & Henderson, S. (2002). A learning theory for career counselors. In S. Niles (Ed.), *Adult career development: Concepts, issues, and practices* (pp. 39–56). Tulsa, OK: National Career Development Association.

Kubanoff, B. (1980). Work and nonwork: A review of models. *Psychological Bulletin, 88*, 60–77. Kubler-Ross, E. (1969). *On death and dying*. New York: Macmillan.

Kubler-Ross, E., & Warshaw, M. (1978). *To live until we say goodbye*. New York: Prentice Hall.

Kuhn, M. E., & Bader, J. E. (1991). Old and young are alike in many ways. *Gerontologist, 31*, 273–274.

Kunz, J., & Kunz, P. R. (1995). Social support during the process of divorce: It does make a difference. *Journal of Divorce and Remarriage, 24*, 111–119.

Kurdek, L. A. (1995). Lesbian and gay couples. In A. R. D'Augelli and C. J. Paterson (Eds.), *Lesbian, gay, and bisexual identities over the lifespan: Psychological perspectives* (pp. 243–261). New York: Oxford University Press.

Labouvie-Vief, G. (1985). Intelligence and cognition. In J. E. Birren & K. W. Schaie (Eds.), *Handbook of the psychology of aging* (2nd ed.) (pp. 500–530). New York: Van Nostrand Reinhold.

Lachman, M. E. (2001). *Introduction*. In M. E. Handbook of midlife development (pp. xvii–xxvi). New York: Wiley.

Lachman, M. E., & Leff, L. (1989). Perceived control and intellectual functioning: A five-year longitudinal study. *Developmental Psychology, 25*, 722–728.

Lachman, M. E., Lewkowicz, C., Marcus, A., & Peng, Y. (1994). Images of midlife development among young, middle-aged, and older adults. *Journal of Adult Development, 1*, 201–212.

Lahner, J., & Hayslip, B. (2005, August). *Employee age and reactions to downsizing*. Paper presented at the Annual Convention of the American Psychological Association. Washington, DC (Refereed).

Laidlaw, K. (2006). Cognitive behavior therapy with older adults. In S. Qualls & B. Knight (Eds.), *Psychotherapy for depression in older adults* (pp. 83–110). New York, NY: Wiley.

Laidlaw, K., Thompson, L., Dick-Siskin, L., & Thompson, D. G. (2003). *Cognitive behavior therapy with older people*. New York: Wiley.

Lakatta, E. G. (1990). Heart and circulation. In E. Schneider & J. Rowe (Eds.), *Handbook of the biology of aging* (pp. 181–218). New York: Academic Press.

Landauer, T. K. (1989). Some bad and some good reasons for studying memory and cognition in the wild. In L.W. Poon, D. C. Rubin, & B. A. Wilson (Eds.), *Everyday cognition in adulthood and late life* (pp. 116–125). Cambridge: Cambridge University Press.

Lang, F. R., & Carstensen, L. (1994). Close emotional relationships in later life: Further support for proactive aging in the social domain. *Psychology and Aging, 9*, 315–324.

Langdridge, D., Connolly, K., & Sheeran, P. (2000). Reasons for wanting a child: A network analytic study. *Journal of Reproductive and Infant Psychology, 18*(4), 321–338.

Larson, E., Wang, L., Bowen, J., McCormick, W., Teri, L., Crane, P., & Kukull, W. (2006). Exercise is associated with reduced risk for incident dementia among persons 65 years of age and older. *Annals of Internal Medicine, 144*, 73–81.

Larson, R., Mannell, R., & Zuzanek, J. (1986). Daily wellbeing of older adults with friends and family. *Psychology and Aging, 1*, 117–126.

Larsson, M., Finkel, D., & Pederssen, N. L. (2000). Odor identification: Influences of age, gender, cognition, and personality. *Journals of Gerontology: Psychological Sciences, 53B*, P304–P31O.

LaRue, A., Dessonville, C., & Jarvik, L. F. (1985). Aging and mental disorders. In J. E. Birren & K. W. Schaie (Eds.), *Handbook of the psychology of aging* (pp. 664–702). New York: Van Nostrand Reinhold.

Laub, J., & Sampson, R. (2005). Coming of age in wartime: How World War II and the Korean War changed lives. In K. Schaie & G. Elder (Eds.), *Historical influences on lives and aging* (pp. 207–228). New York: Springer.

Laurenceau, J-P., Barrett, L. M., & Rovine, M. J. (2005). The interpersonal process model of intimacy in marriage: A daily diary and multilevel modeling approach. *Journal of Family Psychology, 19*, 314–323.

Law, J., Laidlaw, K., & Peck, D. (2010). Is depression viewed as an inevitable consequence of aging? The "understandability phenomenon" in older people. *Clinical Gerontologist, 33*, 194–209.

Lawrence-Lightfoot, S. (2009). *The Third Chapter: Passion, Risk, and Adventure in the 25 Years after 50*. New York: Crichton Books.

Lawton, M. P. (1975). The Philadelphia Geriatric Morale Scale: A revision. *Journal of Gerontology, 30*, 85–89.

Lawton, M. P. (1983). Environment and other determinants of well-being in older persons. *Gerontologist, 23*, 349–357.

Lawton, M. P., & Nahemow, L. (1973). Ecology and the aging process. In C. Eisdorfer & M. P. Lawton (Eds.), *The psychology of adult development and aging* (pp. 619–674). Washington, DC: American Psychological Association.

Lazarus, L.W., & Folkman, S. (1984). *Stress, appraisal, and coping*. New York: Springer.

Lazarus, R. S., & Delongis, A. (1983). Psychological stress and coping in aging. *American Psychologist, 38*, 245–254.

Leana, C. R., Feldman, D., & Tan, G. Y. (1998). Predictors of coping behaviors following a layoff. *Journal of Organizational Behavior, 19*, 85–97.

Leanse, J., & Wagner, L. (1977). *Senior Centers: A Report of Senior Group Programs in America*. Washington, DC: National Council on the Aging.

Lebowitz, B., & Niederche, G. (1992). Concepts and issues in mental health and aging. In J. Birren, R. Sloane, & G. Cohen (Eds.), *Handbook of mental health and aging* (pp. 3–27). San Diego, CA: Academic Press.

Lee, G. R., Netzer, J. K., & Coward, R. T. (1995). Depression among older parents: The role of intergenerational exchange. *Journal of Marriage & the Family, 57*(3), 823–833.

Lee, I. M., & Paffenbarger, R. S, Jr. (2000). Associations of light, moderate, and vigorous intensity physical activity with longevity. The Harvard Alumni Health Study. *American Journal of Epidemiology, 151*, 293–299.

Lee, J. A. (1991). Through the looking glass: Life after Isherwood—A conversation with Don Bachardy. *Journal of Homosexuality, 20*, 33–64.

Lee, K. (2005). Coping with career indecision: Differences between four career choice types. *Journal of Career Development, 31*, 279–289.

Leerkes, E. M., & Burney, R. V. (2007). The development of parenting efficacy among new mothers and fathers. *Infancy, 12*(1), 45-67.

Leitner, M. J., & Lietner, S. F. (2004a). *Leisure in later life* (3rd ed., pp. 421–433). New York: Haworth Press.

Leitner, M. J., & Leitner, S. F. (2004b). Sexuality in later life. In M. J. Leitner & S. F. Leitner (Eds.), *Leisure in later life* (3rd ed.). New York: Haworth Press.

Lemon, B., Bengtson, V., & Peterson, J. (1972). An explanation of the activity theory of aging: Activity tapes and life satisfaction among in-movers to a retirement community. *Journal of Gerontology, 27*, 511–523.

Lent, R., Brown, S., & Hackett, G. (2002). Social cognitive career theory. In D. Brown & Associates (Eds.), *Career choice and development* (pp. 255–311). San Francisco: Jossey Bass.

Lerner, R. M. (1996). *Concepts and theories of human development*. Reading, MA: Addison-Wesley.

Lerner, R. M. (2002). *Concepts and theories of human development* (3rd ed.). Mahwah, NJ: Erlbaum.

Levetown, M., Hayslip, B., & Peel, J. (1999). The development of the physicians' end of life attitudes scale. *Omega, 40*, 323–332.

Levinson, D. J. (1978). *The seasons of a man's life*. New York: Knopf.

Levinson, D. J. (1986). A conception of adult development. *American Psychologist, 41*, 3–13.

Levinson, D., & Levinson, J. (1996). *The seasons of a woman's life*. New York: Ballantine.

Levy, B. (1996). Improving memory in old age by implicit self-stereotyping. *Journal of Personality and Social Psychology, 71*, 1092–1107.

Levy, B., Hausdorff, J., Hencke, R., & Wei, J. (2000). Reducing cardiovascular stress with positive self-stereotypes of aging. *Journal of Gerontology: Psychological Sciences, 55B*, 205–213.

Levy, B., Slade, M., & Gill, T. (2006). Hearing decline predicted by elders' stereotypes. *Journal of Gerontology: Psychological Sciences, 61B*, P82–P89.

Levy, B., Slade, M., & Kasl, S. (2002). Longitudinal benefit of positive self-perceptions of aging on functional health. *Journal of Gerontology: Psychological Science, 57B*, 409–417.

Levy, B., Slade, M., Kunkel, S., & Kasl, S. (2002). Increased longevity from positive self-stereotypes of aging. *Journal of Personality and Social Psychology, 83*, 261–270.

Levy, B., Slade, M., May, J., & Caracciolo, E. (2006). Physical recovery after acute myocardial infarction: Positive age self-stereotypes as a resource. *International Journal of Aging and Human Development, 62*, 285–302.

Levy, S. M. (1990). Humanizing death. In G. Herek, S. Levy, S. Maddi, Taylor S., & Wertleib D. (Eds.), *Psychological aspects of serious illness* (pp. 189–213). Washington, DC: American Psychological Association.

Lewinsohn, P. M., Rohde, P., Seeley, J. R., & Fischer, S. A. (1991). Age and depression: Unique and shared effects. *Psychology and Aging, 6*, 247–260.

Li, G. (1995). The interaction effect of sex on the risk of suicide in the elderly. A historical cohort study. *Social Science and Medicine, 40*, 825–828.

Lichtenberg, P. (1990). Remembering Becky. *Omega, 21*, 83-89.

Lieberman, M. A. (1975). Adaptive processes in later life. In N. Datan & L. Ginsburg (Eds.), *Life-span developmental psychology: Normative life events* (pp. 135– 159). New York: Academic Press.

Lieberman, M. A., & Peskin, H. (1992). Adult life crises. In J. E. Birren, R. B. Sloane, & G. D. Cohen (Eds.), *Handbook of mental health and aging* (pp. 120–146). New York: Academic Press.

Liebowitz, B., & Niederehe, G. (1992). Concepts and issues in mental health and aging. In J. E. Birren, R. B. Sloane, and G. D. Cohen (Eds.), *Handbook of mental health and aging* (pp. 3–25). New York: Academic Press.

Lincoln, K. D., Taylor, R. J., Bullard, K. M., Chatters, L. M., Woodward, A. T., Himle, J. A., & Jackson, J. S. (2010). Emotional support, negative interaction and DSM IV lifetime disorders among older African Americans: findings from the national survey of American life (NSAL). *International Journal of Geriatric Psychiatry, 25*, 612–621.

Lindau, S., Schumm, L., & Laumann, E. (2007). A study of sexuality and health among older adults in the United States. *New England Journal of Medicine, 357*, 762–774.

Lindemann, E. (1944). The symptomatology and management of acute grief. *American Journal of Psychiatry, 101*, 141–148.

Lindley, L. (2005). Perceived barriers to career development in the context of social cognitive career theory. *Journal of Career Assessment, 13*, 271–287.

Lindsey, E. W., Mize, J., & Pettit, G. S. (1997). Mutuality in parent-child play: Consequences for children's peer competence. *Journal of Social and Personal Relationships, 14*, 523–538.

Livingston, G., & Cohn, D. (2010). *More women without children*. Pew Research Center Publications: Social Trends, June 25, 2010. Accessed: http:// pewresearch.org/assets/pdf/758-childless.pdf.

LoboPrabhu, S., Molinari, V., & Lomax, J. (2006). *Supporting the caregiver in dementia: A guide for health professionals*. Baltimore, MD: Johns Hopkins.

Lockenhoff, C., Terracciano, A., & Costa, P. (2009). Five factor personality traits and the retirement transition: Longitudinal and cross sectional associations. *Psychology and Aging, 24*, 722–728.

Lodgson, R., McCurry, S., & Teri, L. (2007). Evidenced-based psychological treatments for disruptive behaviors in individuals with dementia. *Psychology and Aging, 22*, 28–36.

Logan, R. (1986). A reconceptualization of Erikson's theory: The repetition of existential and instrumental themes. *Human Development, 29*, 125–136.

Lohan, J., & Murphy, S. (2005-2006a). Mental distress and family functioning in bereaved parents: Case examples and intervention challenges. *Omega, 52*, 307–322.

Lohan, J., & Murphy, S. (2005-2006b). Mental distress and family functioning among married parents bereaved by a child's sudden death. *Omega, 52*, 295–307.

Lombardi, D., Melchior, E., Murphy, J., & Brinkerhoff, A. (1996). The ubiquity of lifestyle. *Individual Psychology, 52*, 31–41.

Long, G. M., & Crambert, R. F. (1990). The nature and basis of age-related changes in dynamic visual activity. *Psychology and Aging, 5*, 138–143.

Long, H. B. (1990). Educational gerontology: Trends and developments in 2000–2010. *Educational Gerontology, 16*, 317–326.

Lopata, H. Z. (1975). Widowhood: Societal factors in life-span disruptions and alternatives. In N. Datan & L. Ginsburg (Eds.), *Life-span developmental psychology: Normative life crises* (pp. 217–234). New York: Academic Press.

Lorsbach, T. C., & Simpson, G. B. (1988). Dual-task performance as a function of adult age and task complexity. *Psychology and Aging, 3*, 210–212.

Lowis, M., Edwards, A., & Burton, M. (2009). Coping with retirement: Well-being, health, and religion. *Journal of Psychology, 143*, 427–448.

Luescher, K., & Pillemer, K. (1998). Intergenerational ambivalence: A new approach to the study of parent child relations in later life. *Journal of Marriage & the Family, 60*(2), 413–425.

Lund, D. (2000). Men coping with grief. Amityville, NY: Baywood.

Lund, D., Caserta, M. S., & Dimond, M. F. (1986). Gender differences through two years of bereavement among the elderly. *Gerontologist, 26,* 314–320.

Lund, D., Dimond, M., Caserta, M., Johnson, R., Poulton, J., & Connelly, J. (1986–1987). Identifying elderly with coping patterns two years after bereavement. *Omega, 16*, 213–224.

Lyons, K., Zarit, S., Sayer, A., & Whitlatch, C. (2002). Caregiving as a dyadid process: Perspective of caregiver and receiver. *Journal of Gerontology: Psychological Sciences, 57B*, P195–P204.

Maas, H., & Kuypers, J. (1975). *From thirty to seventy*. San Francisco: Jossey-Bass.

MacDonald, W. L., & DeMaris, A. (1995). Remarriage and the frequency of marital conflict. *Journal of Marriage and the Family, 57*, 387–398.

MacDonald, W. L., & DeMaris, A. (1996). Parenting stepchildren and biological children: The effects of stepparent's gender and new biological children. *Journal of Family Issues, 17*, 5–25.

Mace, N., & Rabins, P. (2006). *The 36-hour day*. Baltimore: Johns Hopkins Press.

Macklin, E. (1987). Nontraditional family forms. In M. Sussman & S. Sternmetz (Eds.), *Handbook of marriage and the family* (pp. 320–354). New York: Plenum.

MacLennan, B. W. (1992). Stressor reduction: An organizational alternative to individual stress management. In J. C. Quick, L. R. Murphy, and J. J. Hurrell, Jr. (Eds.), *Stress and well-being at work: Assessments and interventions for occupational mental health* (pp. 79–95). Washington, DC: APA.

Maddi, S. (1990). *Personality theories: A comparative analysis*. Homewood, IL: Dorsey Press.

Maddox, G. L. (1965). Fact and artifact: Evidence bearing on disengagement theory from the Duke Longitudinal Study. *Human Development, 8*, 117–130.

Maiden, R. J. (1987). Learned helplessness and depression: A test of the reformulation model. *Journal of Gerontology, 42*, 60–64.

Mani, A. (2004). Choosing the right pond: Social approval and occupational choice. *Journal of Labor Economics, 22*, 835–861.

Many Americans retire years before they want to: When it comes to retirement, 59 is the new 65. *USA Today*, July 10, 2006, pp.1–2.

Markides, K. S. (1983). Minority aging. In M. Wiley, B. Hess, & K. Bond (Eds.), *Aging in society* (pp. 115–137). Hillsdale, NJ: Erlbaum.

Markos, L. (2005). Building an age-friendly workplace. In P. T. Beatty & R. M. Visser (Eds.), *Thriving on an aging workforce: Strategies for organizational and systemic change* (pp. 112–120). Malabar, FL: Krieger.

Marshall, V. W., & Levy, J. A. (1990). Aging and dying. In R. Binstock & L. George (Eds.), *Handbook of aging and the social sciences* (pp. 245–267). New York: Academic Press.

Marsiske, M., & Margrett, J. (2006). Everyday problem solving and decision-making. In J. Birren & K. W. Schaie (Eds.), *Handbook of the psychology of aging* (pp. 315–342). San Diego, CA: Academic Press.

Marsiske, M., & Willis, S. L. (1995). Dimensionality of everyday problem solving in older adults. *Psychology & Aging, 10*, 269–283.

Martin, C., & Doka, K. (2000). *Men don't cry: Women do: Transcending gender stereotypes of grief*. Philadelphia: Burner-Mazel.

Martire, L., Schulz, R., Reynolds, C., Karp, J., Gildingers, A., & Whyte, E. (2010). Treatment of late-life depression alleviates caregiver burden. *Journal of the American Geriatrics Society, 58*, 23–29.

Masters, W. H., Johnson, V. E., & Kolodny, R. C. (1992). *Human sexuality*. New York: HarperCollins.

Matthews, S. H., Werkner, J. E., & Delaney, P. J. (1990). Relative contributions of help by employed and nonemployed sisters to their elderly parents. *Journal of Gerontology: Social Sciences, 49*, S36–44.

Matthias, R. E., Lubben, J. E., Atchison, K. A., & Schweitzer, S. O. (1997). Sexual activity and satisfaction among very old adults: Results from a community-dwelling medicare population survey. *Gerontologist, 37*, 6–14.

McBride, H. (2003). Young scientist: Women mentoring women. *Nature, 426*, 588.

McCary, J., & McCary, S. (1982). *McCary's human sexuality*. Belmont, CA: Wadsworth.

McConatha, J. T., Schnell, F., Volkwein, K., Riley, L., & Leach, E. (2003). Attitudes toward aging: A comparative analysis of young adults from the United States and Germany. *International Journal of Aging and Human Development, 57*, 203–215.

McCortney, A., & Engels, D. (2003). Revisiting the work ethic in America. *Career Development Quarterly, 52*, 132–140.

McCoy, S. K., Psyszcynski, T., Solomon, S., & Greenberg, J. (2000). Transcending the self: A terror management perspective on successful aging. In A. Tomer (Ed.), *Death attitudes and the older adult* (pp. 37–63). Philadelphia: Brunner-Routledge.

McCrae, R. R. (1982). Age differences in the use of coping mechanisms. *Journal of Gerontology, 37*, 454–460.

McCrae, R. R. (1989). Age differences and changes in the use of coping mechanisms. *Journal of Gerontology: Psychological Sciences, 44*, P161–169.

McCrae, R. R., & Costa, P. T. (1990). *Personality in adulthood*. New York: Guilford Press.

McCullock, B. J. (1990). The relationship of intergenerational reciprocity of and to the morale of older parents: Equity and exchange-theory comparisons. *Journal of Gerontology: Social Sciences, 44*, S150–155.

McGuire, F. A., Boyd, A. K., & Tedrick, R. E. (2004). *Leisure and aging: Ulyssean living in later life* (3rd ed.). Champain, IL: Sagamore.

McGuire, F. A., Dottavio, D., & O'Leary, J. T. (1986). Constraints to participation in outdoor recreation across the life-span: A nationwide study of limitors and prohibitors. *Gerontologist, 26*, 538–544.

McIlroy, J. H. (1984). Mid-life in the 1980s: Philosophy, economy, and psychology. *Personnel and Guidance Journal, 62*, 623–628.

McLaughlin, A. (1989). *Older worker task force: Key policy issues for the future*. Washington, DC: U.S. Department of Labor.

McLaughlin, S., Connell, C., Heeringa, S., Li, L., & Roberts, J. (2009). Successful aging in the United States: Prevalance estimates from a national sample of older adults. *Journal of Gerontology: Social Sciences, 65B*, 216–226.

Meara, E. R., Richards, S., Cutler, D. M. (2008). The gap gets bigger: Changes in mortality and life expectancy, by education, 1981-2000. *Health Affairs, 27*, 350–360.

Medicare and your mental health benefits (2000). Health Care Financing Administration, U.S. Department of Health and Human Services, Baltimore.

Megan, J., & Kleiber, D. (2008). Reduction in leisure activity and well-being during the transition to widowhood. *Journal of Women and Aging, 20*, 83–98.

Mehta, C. M., & Strough, J. (2009). Sex segregation in friendships and normative contexts across the life span. *Developmental Review, 29*, 201–220.

Meichenbaum, D. (1989). *Cognitive behavior modification: An integrative approach*. New York: Plenum.

Mellor, M. J., & Rehr, H. (2005). *Baby boomers: Can my eighties be like my fifties?* New York: Springer.

Menac, V. (2003). The relation between everyday activities and successful aging: A 6-year longitudinal study. *Journal of Gerontology: Social Sciences, 58B*, S74–S82.

Merz, B. (October, 1992). Why we get old. *Harvard Health Letter*, 9–12.

MetLife (2010). *Caregiving employees' health problems can cost U.S. companies a potential $13.4 billion yearly*. www.maturemarketinstitute.com.

Metzger, P., & Gray, M. (2008). End-of-life communication and adjustment: Pre-loss communication as a predictor of bereavement-related outcomes. *Death Studies, 32*, 301–325.

Meyer, B. J., Russo, C., & Talbot, A. (1995). Discourse comprehension and problem solving: Decisions about the treatment of breast cancer by women across the life span. *Psychology & Aging, 10*, 84–103.

Mezuk, B., Prescott, M., Tardiff, K., Vlahov, D., & Galea, S. (2008). Suicide in older adults in long term care: 1990 to 2005. *JAGS, 56*, 2107–2111.

Miech, R., Eaton, W., & Brennan, K. (2005). Mental health disparities across education and sex: Prospective analysis examining how they persist over the life course. *Journal of Gerontology: Health inequities across the life course, 60B*, 93–95.

Miller, M. (1979). *Suicide after sixty: The final alternative*. New York: Springer.

Miller, M., Cornes, C., Frank, E., Ehrenpreis, L., Silberman, R., Schlernitzauer, M., et al. (2001). Interpersonal psychotherapy for late-life depression: Past, present, and future. *Journal of Psychotherapy Research & Practice, 10*, 231–238.

Miller, M., Frank, E., Cornes, C., Houch, P., & Reynolds, C. (2003). The value of maintenance interpersonal therapy (IPT) in older adults with different IPT foci. *American Journal of Geriatric Psychiatry, 11*, 97–102.

Miller, R. A. (1990). Aging and the immune response. In E. Schneider & J. Rowe (Eds.), *Handbook of the biology of aging* (pp. 157–180). New York: Academic Press.

Moen, P., & Wethington, E. (1999). Midlife development in a life course context. In S. L. Willis & J. D. Reid (Eds.), *Life in the middle* (pp. 3–23). San Diego, CA: Academic Press.

Moject, J., Christ-Hazelhof, E., & Heidema, J. (2001). Taste perception with age: Generic or specific losses in threshold sensitivity to the five basic tastes. *Chemical Senses, 26*, 845–860.

Monge, R. H., & Hultsch, D. (1971). Paired-associate learning as a function of adult age and the length of the anticipation and inspection intervals. *Journal of Gerontology, 26*, 157–162.

Monin, J., Schulz, R., Feeny, B., & Cook, T. (2010). Attachment insecurity and perceived partner suffering as predictors of personal distress. *Journal of Experimental Social Psychology*.

Montalvo, B. (1991). The patient chose to die. Why? *Gerontologist, 31*, 700–703.

Montepare, J., & Lachman, M. (1989). You're only as young as you feel: Self-perceptions of age, fears of aging, and life satisfaction from adolescence to old age. *Psychology and Aging, 4*, 73–78.

Moore, A., & Stratton, B. (2002). *Resilient widowers: Older men speak for themselves*. New York: Springer.

Moore, C., & Sherman, S. (1999). Factors that influence elders' decisions to formulate advanced directives. *Journal of Gerontological Social Work, 31*, 21–39.

Moos, R., Schutte, K., Brennan, P., & Moos, B. (2004). Ten year patterns of alcohol consumption and drinking problems among older women and men. *Addiction, 99*, 829–838.

Morgan, D. L. (1989). Adjusting to widowhood: Do social networks really make it easier? *Gerontologist, 29*, 101–107.

Morris, J., Storandt, M., Miller, J., McKeel, D., Proce, J., Rubin, E., & Berg, L. (2001). Mild cognitive impairment represents early-stage Alzheimer's disease. *Archives of Neurology, 58*, 397–405.

Morrison, M. (2010). *Health benefits of animal-assisted intervention*. http://chp.sagepub.com/content/12/1/51.abstract.

Morrow-Howell, N. (2010). Volunteering in later life: Research frontiers. *Journal of Gerontology: Social Sciences, 65B*, 461–469.

Morse, J. Q., & Lynch, T. R. (2004). A preliminary investigation of self-reported personality disorders in late life: Prevalence, predictors of depressive severity and clinical correlates. *Journal of Aging and Mental Health, 8*, 307–315.

Mosher, W. D., & Pratt, S. (1990). Contraceptive practice in the United States, 1982–1988. *Family Planning Perspectives, 22*, 198–205.

Moss, K., & Scogin, F. (2008). Behavioral and cognitive treatments for geriatric depression: An evidence-based perspective. In D. Gallagher-Thompson, A. Steffen, & L. Thompson (Eds). *Handbook of cognitive and behavioral therapies with older adults* (pp. 250-265). New York: Springer.

Moss, M. S., Lesher, E. L., & Moss, S. Z. (1986-1987). Impact of the death of an adult child on elderly parents: Some observations. *Omega, 17*, 209–218.

Moss, M. S., & Moss, S. Z. (1983). The impact of parental death on middle-aged children. *Omega, 14*, 65–75.

Moss, M., Moss, S., & Hansson, R. (2001). Bereavement and old age. In M. Stroebe, R. O. Hansson, W. Troebe, & H. Schut (Eds.), *Handbook of bereavement research: Consequences, coping, and care* (pp. 241–260). Washington, DC: American Psychological Association.

Moss, S., Moss, M., Black, H., & Rubinstein, R. (2005). How family members respond to residents' wish to die. *Omega, 51*, 301–322.

Mroczek, D., Spiro, A., & Griffen, P. (2006). Personality and aging. In J. Birren & K. W. Schaie (Eds.), *Handbook of the psychology of aging* (pp. 363–378). San Diego, CA: Academic Press.

Mui, A. C. (1993). Self-reported depressive symptoms among black and Hispanic frail elders: A sociocultural perspective. *Journal of Applied Gerontology, 12*, 170–187.

Munsey, C. (2010). More students—with more serious psychological issues—are showing up at campus counseling centers. *APA Monitor on Psychology, April,* p. 10.

Muratore, A., & Earl, J. (2010). Predicting retirement preparation through the design of a new measure. *Australian Psychologist, 45,* 98–11.

Murphy, L. R., Hurrell, Jr., J. J., & Quick, J. C. (1992). Work and well-being: Where do we go from here? In J. C. Quick, L. R. Murphy, and J. J. Hurrell, Jr. (Eds.), *Stress and well-being at work: Assessments and interventions for occupational mental health.* Washington, DC: APA.

Murphy, S. (2008). The loss of a child: Sudden death and extended illness perspectives. In M. Stroebe, R. Hansson, H. Schut, & W. Streobe (Eds.), *Handbook of bereavement research and practice* (pp. 375–396). Washington, DC: American Psychological Association.

Murstein, B. I. (1982). Marital choice. In J. Wolman (Ed.), *Handbook of developmental psychology* (pp. 652–666). Englewood Cliffs, NJ: Prentice Hall.

Myers, W. A. (1991). *New techniques in the psychotherapy of older patients.* Washington, DC: American Psychiatric Press.

National Bureau of Labor Statistics. (2009a). *Labor force statistics from the Current Population Survey.*http://data.bls.gove/PDQ/outside.jsp? survey=1n.

National Bureau of Labor Statistics. (2009b). *Unemployed persons by age, sex, race, Hispanic or Latino ethnicity, marital status, and duration of employment.* ftp:/ftp.bls.gov/pub/suppl/empsit.cpsseea36.txt

National Cancer Institute. (1996). *What you need to know about cancer.* Washington, DC: DHEW.

National Center for Educational Statistics. (2005). *Total fall enrollment in degree granting institutions by attendance status, age, and sex, 1970–2014.* Washington, DC: U.S. Department of Education.

National Council on the Aging. (2000, March). *Myths and realities: 2000 survey results.* Washington, DC: National Council on the Aging.

National Institute of Health. (2006). *Aging under the microscope.* National Institute on Aging Office of Communications and Public Liaison, Bethesda, MD. Available: www.nia.nih.gov

National Institute of Mental Health. (2003a). *Mental health for a lifetime: Research for the mental health needs of older Americans.* Report of the National Advisory Mental Health Council's Workgroup on aging research. Washington, DC.

National Institute of Mental Health. (2003b). *Older adults: Depression and suicide facts.* Washington, DC. Retrieved from www.nimh.nib.gov/publict/elderlydepsuicide.cfm

National Institute of Mental Health. (2006). *The members count: Mental disorders in America.* Retrieved from www.nimh.nih.gov/publicat/ numbers.cfm

National Institute of Mental Health. (2009). *The impact of mental illness on society.* http://nimh.nih.gov/health/topics/statistics/index.shtml

National Mental Health Information Center (2010). *How to pay for mental health services.* http://mental health.samhsa.gov.

Neimeyer, R. A. (1998). Death anxiety: State of the art. *Omega, 36,* 97–120.

Neimeyer, R. (2005-2006). Complicated grief and the quest for meaning. *Omega, 52,* 37-52.

Neimeyer, R. A., Moser, R. P., & Wittkowski, J. (2003). Assessing attitudes toward dying and death: Psychometric considerations. *Omega, 47,* 45–76.

Neisser, U., Boodoo, G., et al. (1996). Intelligence: Knowns and unknowns. *American Psychologist, 51,* 77–101.

Nelson, E. A., & Dannefer, D. (1992). Aged heterogeneity: Fact or fiction? The fate of diversity in gerontological research. *Gerontologist, 32,* 17–23.

Nelson, F., & Faberow, N. (1980). Indirect self-destructive behavior in the nursing-home patient. *Journal of Gerontology, 35,* 949–957.

Netz, Y., Wu, M. J., Becker, B. J., & Tennenbaum, G. (2005). Physical activity and psychological well-being in advanced age: A meta-analysis of intervention studies. *Psychology & Aging, 20,* 272–284.

Neugarten, B. L. (1968). The awareness of middle age. In B. L. Neugarten (Ed.), *Middle-age and aging: A reader in social psychology* (pp. 93–98). Chicago: University of Chicago Press.

Neugarten, B. L. (1973). Personality change in late life: A developmental perspective. In C. Eisdorfer & M. P. Lawton (Eds.), *The psychology of adult development and aging.* Washington, DC: American Psychological Association.

Neugarten, B. L. (1976). Adaptation and the life cycle. *Counseling Psychologist, 6,* 16–20.

Neugarten, B. L. (1977). Personality and aging. In J. E. Birren & K. W. Schaie (Eds.), *Handbook of the psychology of aging* (pp. 626–649). New York: Van Nostrand Reinhold.

Neugarten, B. L., & Datan, N. (1973). Sociological perspectives on the life cycle. In P. B. Baltes & K. W. Schaie (Eds.), *Life-span developmental psychology: Personality and socialization* (pp. 53–69). New York: Academic Press.

Neugarten, B. L., & Hagestad, G. (1976). Aging and the life course. In R. H. Binstock & E. Shanas (Eds.), *Handbook of aging and the social sciences* (pp. 35–57). New York: Van Nostrand Reinhold.

Neugarten, B. L., & Neugarten, D. A. (1987). The changing meaning of age. *Psychology Today, 21*, 29–33.

Neugarten, B. L., & Weinsten, K. K. (1964). The changing American grandparent. *Journal of Marriage and the Family, 26*, 199–204.

Neumann, J., Engle, R., & Jense, J. (1991). Changes in depression symptoms experiences among older women. *Psychology and Aging, 6*, 212–222.

Nevid, J., Rathus, S., & Green, B. (2008). *Abnormal psychology in a changing world*. Upper Saddle River, NJ: Prentice Hall.

Newman, B., & Newman, P. (2009). *Development through life: A psychosocial approach* (8th ed.). Belmont, CA: Thomson.

Newson, R. S., & Kemps, E. B. (2005). General lifestyle activities as a predictor of current cognition and cognitive change in older adults. *Journal of Gerontology: Psychological Sciences, 60B*, P113–P120.

Ng, T., & Fedlman, D. (2008). The relationship of age to ten dimensions of job performance. *Journal of Applied Psychology, 93*, 392–423.

Niles, S., & Harris-Bowlsbey, J. (2005). *Career development interventions in the 21st century*. Upper Saddle River, NJ: Pearson.

Nordus, I., & Nielsen, G. (1999). Brief dynamic psychotherapy with older adults. *Journal of Clinical Psychology, 55*, 935–947.

Norris, M., Molinair, V., & Rosowsky, E. (1998). Providing mental health care to older adults: Unraveling the maze of Medicare and managed care. *Psychotherapy, 35*, 490–497.

Norton, A. J., & Glick, P. C. (1986). One-parent families: A social and economic profile. *Family Relations, 35*, 9–17.

Novak, M., & Guest, C. (1992). A comparison of the impact of institutionalization on spouse and non-spouse caregivers. *Journal of Applied Gerontology, 11*, 379–394.

Novatney, J. P. (1990, November). *Grandparents' ties to step- and biological grandchildren*. Paper presented at the Annual Scientific Meeting of the Gerontological Society. Boston.

Nuland, S. B. (1994). *How we die*. New York: Vintage.

Oberg, P., & Tornstam, L. (2003). Attitudes toward embodied old age among Swedes. *International Journal of Aging and Human Development, 56*, 133–244.

Occupational stress, strain, and coping across the lifespan. *Journal of Vocational Behavior, 27*, 98–108.

Ochs, A. L., Newberry, J., Lenhardt, M. L., & Harkins, S. W. (1985). Neural and vestibular aging associated with falls. In J. E. Birren & K. W. Schaie (Eds.), *Handbook of the psychology of aging* (pp. 378–399). New York: Van Nostrand Reinhold.

Oliver, M. B., & Hyde, J. S. (1993). Gender differences in sexuality: A meta analysis. *Psychological Bulletin, 114*, 29–51.

Olshansky, S. J., Goldman, D. P., Zheng, Y., & Rowe, J. W. (2009). Aging in America in the Twenty-first Century: Demographic Forecasts from the MacArthur Foundation Research Network on an Aging Society. *Milbank Quarterly, 87*, 842–862.

Oltjenbruns, K. A. (2001). Developmental context of childhood: Grief and regrief phenomena. In M. Stroebe, R. O. Hansson, W. Troebe, & H. Schut (Eds.), *Handbook of bereavement research: Consequences, coping, and care* (pp. 169–198). Washington, DC: American Psychological Association.

Osgood, N. J. (1990). *Prevention of suicide in the elderly* [unpublished manuscript]. Virginia Commonwealth University: Richmond, VA.

Osipow, S. H. (1987). Counseling psychology: Theory, research, and practice in career counseling. *Annual Review of Psychology, 38*, 257–278.

Osipow, S., & Doty, L. (1985). Job stress across career stage. *Journal of Vocational Behavior, 16*, 26–32.

Osipow, S. H., Doty, R. E., & Spokane, A. R. (1985).

Osipow, S. H., & Fitzgerald, L. F. (1996). *Theories of career development*. Boston: Allyn and Bacon.

Padula, M. A. (2001). Reentry women: A literature review with recommendations for counseling and research. *Journal of Counseling & Development, 73*, 10–16.

Paggi, K. (2010). *Caregiver eletter: Because we choose.* http://www.kaypaggi.com/

Palmer, B., Heaton, S., & Jeste, D. (1999). Older patients with schizophrenia: Challenges in the coming decades. *Psychiatric Services, 50*, 1178–1183.

Panek, P. E. (1997). The older worker. In A. Fisk & W. Rodgers (Eds.), *The handbook of human factors and the older adult* (pp. 363–394). San Diego, CA: Academic Press.

Panek, P. E., & Reardon, J. (1987). Age and gender effects on accident types for rural drivers. *Journal of Applied Gerontology, 6*, 332–346.

Panek, P. E., & Rush, M. C. (1981). Simultaneous examination of age-related differences in the ability to maintain and reorient auditory selective attention. *Experimental Aging Research, 7*, 405–416.

Panek, P. E., Staats, S., & Hiles, A. (2006). College students perceptions of job demands, recommended retirement ages, and optimal age of performance in selected occupations. *International Journal of Aging and Human Development, 62*, 87–116.

Paraman, R., & Giambra, L. (1991). Skill development in vigilance: Effects of event rate and age. *Psychology and Aging, 6*, 155–169.

Park, D., & Jones, T. (1997). Medication adherence and aging. In A. D. Fiske & W. A. Rogers (Eds.), *Handbook of human factors and the older adult* (pp. 257–288). San Diego, CA: Academic Press.

Park, D., & Kidder, D. (1996). Prospective memory and medication adherence. In M. Brandimonte, G. Einstein, & M. McDaniel (Eds.), *Prospective memory: Theory and applications* (pp. 369–390). Mahwah, NJ: Erlbaum.

Parkes, C. (2005-2006). Guest Editor's conclusions: Symposium on complicated grief. *Omega, 52*, 107–114.

Parkes, C. M., & Weiss, R. S. (1983). *Recovery from bereavement.* New York: Basic Books.

Parkes, M. (1996). *Bereavement: Studies of grief in adult life.* London: Routledge.

Parmalee, P. A., Kleban, M. H., Lawton, M. P., & Katz, I. R. (1991). Depression and cognitive change among institutionalized aged. *Psychology and Aging, 6*, 504–511.

Parmalee, P. A., & Lawton, M. P. (1990). The design of special environments for the aged. In J. E. Birren & K. W. Schaie (Eds.), *Handbook of the psychology of aging* (pp. 55–68). San Diego, CA: Academic Press.

Patel, D. (2005). The workplace tomorrow. In P. T. Beatty & R. M. Visser (Eds.), *Thriving on an aging workforce: Strategies for organizational and systemic change* (pp. 14–24). Malabar, FL: Krieger.

Patrick, J. H., Cottrell, L. E., & Barnes, K. A. (2001). Gender, emotional support, and well-being. *Sex Roles, 45*, 15–29.

Patrick, J. H., & Hayden, J. M. (1999). Neuroticism, coping strategies, and negative well-being among caregivers. *Psychology and Aging, 14*, 273–283.

Patrick, J. H., & Murphy, M. D. (2004). *Dynamic information search strategies: Age & decision quality interactions.* Paper presented at the 10th annual Cognitive Aging Conference, Atlanta, GA. April, 2004.

Patrick, J. H. & Strough, J. (2004). Everyday problem solving: Experience, strategies and behavioral intentions. *Journal of Adult Development, 11*, 9–18.

Patrick, J. H. & Tomczewski, D. K. (2008). Custodial grandfathers: The new forgotten caregiver? *Journal of Intergenerational Relationships, 5*, 113–116.

Patterson, C. (2005, January). *Generational diversity: Implications for consultation and teamwork.* Paper presented at the meeting of the Council of Directors of School Psychology Programs on generational differences, Deerfield Beach, FL.

Pattison, E. M. (1977). *The experience of dying.* Englewood Cliffs, NJ: Prentice Hall.

Peacock, E. W., & Talley, W. M. (1985). Developing leisure competence: A goal for late adulthood. *Educational Gerontology, 11*, 261–276.

Pearce, S. D. (1991). Toward understanding the participation of older adults in continuing education. *Educational Gerontology, 17*, 451–464.

Pearlin, L., Mullan, J. T., Semple, S., & Skaff, M. (1990). Caregiving and the stress process: An overview of concepts and their measures. *Gerontologist, 30*, 583–594.

Pearlin, L., Pioli, M. F., & McLaughlin, A. E. (2001). Caregiving by adult children: Involvement, role disruption, and health (pp. 238–254). In R. H. Binstock & L. K. George (Eds.), *Handbook of aging and the social sciences* (5th ed.). San Diego, CA: Academic Press.

Pearlin, L., & Skaff, M. (1995). *Stressors and adaptation in later life. In M. Gatz (Ed.), Emerging issues in mental health and aging* (pp. 97–123). Washington, DC: American Psychological Association.

Pearson, J., Hunter, A., Ensminger, M., & Kellam, S. (1990). Black grandmothers in intergenerational households: Diversity in family structure and parenting involvement in the Woodlawn community. *Child Development, 61,* 434–442.

Pearson, V. I. (2000). Assessment of function in older adults. In R. L. Kane & R. A. Kane (Eds.), *Assessing older persons: Measures, meaning and practical application* (pp. 17–48). New York: Oxford.

Pederson, J. (1998). Sexuality and aging. In I. Nordhus, G. VandenBos, S. Berg, & P. Fromholt (Eds.). *Clinical geropsychology* (pp. 141–145). Washington, DC: American Psychological Association.

Pepin, R., Segal, D., & Coolidge, F. (2009). Intrinsic and extrinsic barriers to mental health care among community-dwelling younger and older adults. *Aging & Mental Health, 13,* 769–777.

Peplau, L. A. (2003). Human sexuality: How do men and women differ? *Current Directions in Psychological Science, 12,* 37–40.

Peplau, L. A. & Fingerhut, A. W. (2007). The close relationships of lesbians and gay men. *Annual Review of Psychology, 58,* 405–424.

Peppers, L. (1987). Grief and elective abortion: Breaking the emotional bond. *Omega, 18,* 1–12.

Perkins, K., & Tice, C. (1994). Suicide and older adults: The strengths perspective in practice. *Journal of Applied Gerontology, 13,* 438–454.

Perlmutter, M., & Hall, E. (1992). *Adulthood development and aging.* New York: Wiley.

Perlmutter, M., & Nyquish, L. (1990). Relationships between self-reported physical and mental health and intelligence performance across adulthood. *Journal of Gerontology: Psychological Sciences, 45,* P145–155.

Perls, T. T. (2006). The different paths to 100. *American Journal of Clinical Nutrition, 83,* 484–487.

Perls, T. T., Bochen, K., Freeman, M., Alpert, L., & Silver, M. H. (1999). Validity of reported age and centenarian prevalence in New England. *Age and Aging, 28,* 193–197.

Peterson, R. C., Doodey, R., Kurz, A., Mohs, R., Morris, J., Rabin, P., et al. (2001). Current concepts in mild cognitive impairment. *Archives of Neurology, 58,* 1985–1992.

Phillips, L., & Reed, P. (2010). End-of-life caregivers' perspectives on their role: Generative caregiving. *The Gerontologist, 50,* 204–214.

Piaget, J., & Inhelder, B. (1969). *The psychology of the child.* New York: Basic Books.

Pierpont, J. H., & McGinty, K. (2005). Suicide. In C. N. Dulmus & L. Rapp–Paglicci (Eds.), *Preventative interventions for adults* (pp. 56–75). New York, NY: Wiley.

Pillemer, K., & Suitor, J. J. (1998). Violence and violent feelings: What causes them among family caregivers? In R. K. Bergen (Ed.), *Issues in intimate violence.* Thousand Oaks, CA: Sage.

Pinquart, M., & Schindler, I. (2007). Changes of life satisfaction in the transition to retirement: A latent class approach. *Psychology and Aging, 22,* 442–455.

Plotnick, R. D. (2009). Childlessness and the economic well-being of older Americans. *Journals of Gerontology: Social Sciences, 64B,* S767–776.

Pollitt, P. A., O'Connor, D. W., & Anderson, I. (1989). Mild dementia: Perceptions and problems. *Aging and Society, 9,* 261–275.

Pomin, K., Pederson, N., McClearn, G., Nesselroade, J., & Bergman, C. (1988). EAS temperaments during the last half of the life-span: Twins reared apart and twins reared together. *Psychology and Aging, 3,* 43–50.

Poon, L. (1985). Differences in human memory with aging. In J. E. Birren & K. W. Schaie (Eds.), *Handbook of the psychology of aging* (pp. 427–462). New York: Van Nostrand Reinhold.

Pope, M., & Schulz, R. (1991). Sexual attitudes and behavior in mid-life and aging homosexual males. *Journal of Homosexuality, 20,* 169–178.

Potyk, D. (2005). Treatments for Alzheimer's disease. *Southern Medical Journal, 98,* 628–635.

Powell, D. (1994*). Profiles in cognitive aging.* Cambridge, MA: Harvard University Press.

Powers, D. (2008a). Psychotherapy in long term care: I. Practical considerations and the link to policy and advocacy. *Professional Psychology, Research and Practice, 39,* 251–256.

Powers, D. (2008b). Psychotherapy in long term care: II. Evidence-based psychological treatments and other outcome research. *Professional Psychology, Research, and Practice, 39,* 257–263.

Price, R., Choi, J., & Vinokur, A. (2006). Links in the chain of adversity following job loss. How financial strain and loss of personal control lead to depression, impaired functioning, and poor health. *Journal of Occupational Health Psychology, 7,* 302–312.

Qassis, S., & Hayden, D. C. (1990). Effects of environment on psychological well-being of elderly persons. *Psychological Reports, 66,* 147–150.

Qualls, S. (1999). Family therapy with older adult clients. *Journal of Clinical Psychology, 55,* 997–990.

Quam, J. K., & Whitford, G. S. (1992). Adaptation and age-related expectations of older gay and lesbian adults. *Gerontologist, 32,* 367–374.

Quandt, S. A., McDonald, J., & Arcury, T. A. (2000). Nutritional self-management of elderly widows in rural communities. *Gerontologist, 40*(1), 86–96.

Quill, T. (1996). *A midwife through the dying process.* Baltimore: Johns Hopkins University Press.

Rabins, P. V. (1992). Schizophrenia and psychotic states. In J. E. Birren, R. B. Sloane, & G. D. Cohen (Eds.), *Handbook of mental health and aging* (pp. 464–477). New York: Academic Press.

Ragland, D. R., Satariano, W. A., & Macleod, K. E. (2004). Reasons given by older people for limitation or avoidance of driving. *Gerontologist, 44,* 237–244.

Rando, T. A. (1984). *Grief, dying, and death: Clinical interventions for caregivers.* Champaign, IL: Research Press.

Raskind, M. A., & Peskind, E. R. (1992). Alzheimer's disease and other dementing disorders. In J. E. Birren, R. B. Sloane, & G. D. Cohen (Eds.), *Handbook of mental health and aging* (pp. 478–516). New York: Academic Press.

Raymo, J. M., Liang, J., Sugisawa, H., Kobayashi, E., & Sugihara, Y. (2004). Work at older ages in Japan: Variation by gender and employment status. *Journal of Gerontology: Social Sciences, 59, B,* SI54–S163.

Reed, M. (2000). *Grandparents cry twice: Help for bereaved parents.* Amityville, NY: Baywood Publishers:

Reedy, M. N., Birren, J. E., & Schaie, K. W. (1982). Age and sex differences in satisfying love relation ships across the life-span. *Human Development, 24,* 52–66.

Reese, C., Cherry, K., & Norris, L. (1998). *Practical memory concerns of older adults.* Unpublished manuscript. Louisiana State University.

Reid, J. D. (1995). Development in late life: Older lesbian and gay lives. In A. R. D'Augelli & C. J. Patterson (Eds.), *Lesbian, gay, and bisexual identities over the lifespan: Psychological perspectives* (pp. 215–240). New York: Oxford University Press.

Reinke, B. J., Holmes, D. S., & Harris, R. L. (1985). The timing of psychosocial changes in women's lives: The years 25 to 45. *Journal of Personality and Social Psychology, 48,* 1353–1364.

Reiss, S., & Tishler, C. (2008). Suicidality in nursing home residents: Part I. Prevalence, risk factors, methods, assessment, and management. *Professional Psychology: Research and Practice, 39,* 264–270.

Reiss, S., & Tishler, C. (2008). Suicidality in nursing home residents: Part II. Special issues. *Professional Psychology: Research and Practice, 39,* 271–275.

Reiswig, G. (2010). *The thousand mile stare: One family's journey through the struggle and science of Alzheimer's.* Boston: Nicholeas Brealey Publishing.

Reitzes, D. C., & Mutran, E. J. (2004). Grandparenthood: Factors influencing frequency of grandparent-grandchild contact and grandparent role satisfaction. *Journal of Gerontology: Social Sciences, 59B,* S9–S16.

Reker, G. T. (1997). Personal meaning, optimism, and choice: Existential predictors of depression in community and institutional elderly. *Gerontologist, 37,* 709–716.

Reker, G. T., Peacock, E. J., & Wong, T. P. (1987). Meaning and purpose in life: A life-span investigation. *Journal of Gerontology, 42,* 44–49.

Rennison, C. M. & Welchans, S. (2002). *Intimate partner violence.* Washington, DC: Bureau of Justice Statistics.

Reynolds, C., & Associates (2006). Maintenance treatment of major depression in old age. *New England Journal of Medicine, 354,* 1130–1138.

Reynolds, D., & Kalish, R. (1976). Death rates, ethnicity, and the ethnic press. *Ethnicity, 3,* 305–316.

Rhyne, D. (1981). Bases of marital satisfaction among men and women. *Journal of Marriage and the Family, 43,* 941–954.

Ribas, R. de C., & Bornstein, M. H. (2005). Parenting knowledge: Similarities and differences in Brazilian mothers and fathers. *Inter-American Journal of Psychology, 39*, 5–12.

Rice, F. P. (1993). *Intimate relationships, marriages, and families.* Mountain View, CA: Mayfield.

Richardson, V. (1993). *Retirement counseling.* New York: Springer.

Richeson, N. (2010). *Effects of animal-assisted therapy on agitated behaviors and social interactions of older adults with dementia.* http://aja.sagepub.com/content/18/6/353.abstract.

Riediger, M., Li, S., & Lindenberger, V. (2006). Selection, optimization, and developmental mechanisms of adaptive resource allocations: Review and preview. In J. Birren & K. W. Schaie (Eds.), *Handbook of the psychology of aging* (pp. 289–314). San Diego, CA: Academic Press.

Riegel, K. F. (1975). Adult life crises: A dialectical interpretation of development. In N. Datan & L. Ginsburg (Eds.), *Life-span development psychology: Normative life crises* (pp. 99–128). New York: Academic Press.

Riegel, K. F. (1976). The dialectics of human development. *American Psychologist, 31*, 689–700.

Rife, J., & Kilty, K. (1989-1990). Job-search discouragement and the older worker: Implications for social work practice. *Journal of Applied Social Sciences, 14*, 71–94.

Riggio, H. R., & Desrochers, S. J. (2006). Maternal employment: Relations with young adults' work and family expectations and self-efficacy. *American Behavioral Scientist, 49*(10), 1328–1353.

Riley, M. W., & Riley, J. W. (1994). Aging and society: Past, present, and future. *Gerontologist, 34*, 436–444.

Rix, S. E. (1990). *Older workers.* Santa Barbara, CA: ABC-CLIO.

Robb, C., Haley, W., Becker, M., Polivka, L., & Chwa, H. (2003). Attitudes toward mental health care in younger and older adults: Similarities and differences. *Journal of Aging and Mental Health, 7*, 142–152.

Robbins, A. (2005). *Conquering your quarterlife crisis.* New York: Penguin Books.

Roberto, K. A., & Scott, J. P. (1986). Friendships of older men and women: Exchange patterns and satisfaction. *Psychology and Aging, 1*, 103–109.

Roberto, K. A., & Stroes, J. (1992). Children and grandparents: Role influences and relationships. *International Journal of Aging and Human Development, 34*, 227–239.

Roberts, B. W., Caspi, A., & Moffitt, T. E. (2003). Work experiences and personality development in young adulthood. *Journal of Personality and Social Psychology, 84*, 582–593.

Roberts, P., & Newton, P. M. (1987). Levinsonian studies of women's adult development. *Psychology and Aging, 2*, 154–163.

Robertson, A. (2000). I saw the handwriting on the wall: Shades of meaning in reasons for early retirement. *Journal of Aging Studies, 14*(1), 63–79.

Robertson-Tchabo, E., Hausman, C., & Arenberg, D. (1976). A classical mnemonic for older learners: A trip that works! *Educational Gerontology, 1*, 215–216.

Robinson, J., Sareen, J., Cox, B., & Bolton, J. (2009). Correlates of self-medication for anxiety disorders: Results from the National Epidemiologic Survey on Alcohol and Related Conditions. *Journal of Nervous and Mental Disease, 197*, 873–878.

Robinson, O., Demetre, J., & Corney, R. (2010). Personality and retirement: Exploring the links between the Big Five personality traits, reasons for retirement and the experience of being retired. *Personality and Individual Differences, 48*, 797–797.

Rodger, M., Sherwood, P., O'Connor, M., & Leslie, G. (2006-2007). Living beyond the unanticipated death of a partner: A phenomenological study. *Omega, 54*, 107–134.

Rodin, J. (1986). Aging and health: Effects of the sense of control. *Science, 233*, 1271–1276.

Rogers, W. A. (1997). Individual differences, aging, and human factors: An overview. In A. D. Fisk & W. A. Rogers (Eds.), *Handbook of human factors and the older adult* (pp. 151–170). New York: Academic Press.

Ronch, J. L., & Goldfield, J. A. (2003). *Mental wellness in aging: Strength-based approaches.* Baltimore: Health Professions Press.

Ronen, R., Packman, W., Field, N., Davies, B., Kramer, R., & Long, J. (2009-2010). The relationship between grief adjustment and continuing bonds for parents who have lost a child. *Omega, 60*, 1–32.

Rook, K. S. (1987). Reciprocity of social exchange and social satisfaction among older women. *Journal of Personality and Social Psychology, 52*, 145–154.

Rook, K. S. (2009). Gaps in social support resources in later life: An adaptational challenge in need of further research. *Journal of Social and Personal Relationships, 26*, 103–112.

Roseman, I. (1980). Bodily changes with aging. In E. W. Busse & D. G. Blazer (Eds.), *Handbook of geriatric psychiatry* (pp. 125–146). New York: Van Nostrand.

Rosen, B., & Jerdee, T. H. (1988). Managing older workers' careers. In G. R. Ferris & K. M. Rowland (Eds.), *Research in personnel and human resources management* (Vol. 6, pp. 37–74). Greenwich, CT: JAI Press.

Rosenbaum, E. H. (1980). The doctor and the cancer patient. In M. Hamilton & H. Reid (Eds.), *A hospital handbook: A new way to care for the dying.* Grand Rapids, MI: Eerdmans.

Rosenberg, S., Rosenberg, H., & Farrell, M. (1999). The midlife crisis revisited. In S. Willis & J. Reid (Eds.), *Life in the middle: Psychological and social development in middle age* (pp. 47–77). San Diego, CA: Academic Press.

Rosenblatt, P. (2008). Grief across cultures: A review and research agenda. In M. Stroebe, R. Hansson, H. Schut, & W. Streobe (Eds.), *Handbook of bereavement research and practice* (pp. 207–22). Washington, DC: American Psychological Association.

Rosenblatt, P., & Barner, J. (2006). The dance of closeness-distance in couple relationships after the death of a parent. *Omega, 53*, 277–294.

Rosenbloom, C. A., & Whittington, F. J. (1993). The effects of bereavement on eating behaviors and nutrient intakes in elderly widowed persons. *Journal of Gerontology: Social Sciences, 48*, S223–S229.

Rosenstock, J., Strecher, V., & Becker, M. (1988). Social learning theory and the Health Belief model. *Health Education Quarterly, 15*, 175–183.

Rosenthal, C., & Marshall, V. (1983). *The head of the family: Authority and responsibility in the lineage.* Paper presented at the Annual Scientific Meeting of the Gerontological Society of America. Chicago.

Rosenthal, C. J., Martin-Matthews, A., & Matthews, S. H. (1996). Caught in the middle? Occupancy in multiple roles and help to parents in a national probability sample of Canadian adults. *Journal of Gerontology: Social Sciences, 51B*, S274–S283.

Rosow, I. (1985). Status and role change through the life cycle. In R. Binstock & E. Shanas (Eds.), *Handbook of aging and the social sciences* (p. 693). New York: Academic Press.

Ross, N., Bisconti, T., & Bergeman, C. (2007). The role of dispositional resilience in regaining life satisfaction after the loss of a spouse. *Death Studies, 31*, 863–883.

Rossi, A. F., & Rossi, P. H. (1990). *Of human bonding: Parent-child relationships across the life course.* New York: Aldine.

Roth, S., & Cohen, J. L. (1986). Approach-avoidance and coping with stress. *American Psychologist, 41*, 813–819.

Rowe, G. (1990, November). *Retirement transition of state employees: A ten-year follow-up.* Paper presented at the Annual Meeting of the Gerontological Society. Boston.

Rowe, J., & Kahn, R. (1987). Human aging: Usual and successful. *Science, 237*, 143–149.

Rowe, J., & Kahn, R. (1995). *Successful aging.* New York: Dell.

Rowe, J., & Kahn, R. (1997). Successful aging. *Gerontologist, 37*, 433–440.

Rowe, J. W., & Kahn, R. L. (1998). *Successful aging: The MacArthur Foundation Study.* New York: Pantheon.

Rozario, P. A. (Winter, 2006-2007). Volunteering among current cohorts of older adults and Baby Boomers. *Civic Engagement in Later Life,* 31–35.

Rubenstein, R., & Lawton, M. P. (1997). *Depression in long term and residential care: Advances in research and treatment.* New York: Springer.

Rubin, S. S., & Malkinson, R. (2001). Parental response to child loss across the life cycle: Clinical and research perspectives. In M. Stroebe, R. Hansson, W. Stroebe, & H. Schut (Eds.), *Handbook of berevement research* (pp. 219–240). Washington, DC: American Psychological Association .

Rudberg, M. A., Furner, S. E., Dunn, J. E., & Cassel, C. K. (1993). The relationship of and hearing impairments to disability: An analysis using the longitudinal study of aging. *Journal of Gerontology: Medical Sciences, 48,* M261–M265.

Russell, M. J., Cummings, B. J., Profitt, B. F., Wysocki, C. J., Gilbert, A. N., & Cotman, C. W. (1993). Life span changes in the verbal categorization of odors. *Journal of Gerontology: Psychological Sciences, 48*, P49–P53.

Russell, M. M.. & Visser, R. M. (2005). Partnering career development and human resources. In P. T. Beatty & R. M. Visser (Eds.), *Thriving on an aging workforce: Strategies for organizational and systemic change* (pp. 92–101). Malabar, FL: Krieger.

Ruth, J., & Coleman, P. (1996). Personality and aging: Coping and management of the self in later life. In J. Birren & K. Schaie (Eds.), *Handbook of the psychology of aging* (308–322). San Diego, CA: Academic Press.

Ryan, E., Giles, H., Bartolucci, G., & Henwood, K. (1986). Psycholinguistic and social psychological components of communication by and with the elderly. *Language and Communication, 6,* 1–24.

Rybash, J. M., Hoyer, W. J., & Roodin, P. A. (1986). *Adult cognition and aging.* Elmsford, NY: Pergamon Press.

Ryff, C. D. (1984). Personality development from adulthood and aging. In P. B. Baltes & O. G. Brim (Eds.), *Life-span development and behavior* (pp. 244–279). New York: Academic Press.

Ryff, C. D. (1989). In the eye of the beholder: Views of psychological well-being among middle-aged and older adults. *Psychology and Aging, 4,* 195–210.

Sable, P. (1991). Attachment, loss of spouse, and grief in elderly adults. *Omega, 23,* 129–142.

Sachs, R., Chrisler, J. C., & Devlin, A. S. (1992). Biographic and personal characteristics of women in management. *Journal of Vocational Behavior, 41,* 89–100.

Salthouse, T. A. (1992). The information processing perspective on cognitive aging. In R. Sternberg & C. Berg (Eds.), *Intellectual development* (pp. 261–277). New York: Cambridge University Press.

Salthouse, T. A. (1993). Attentional blocks are not responsible for age-related slowing. *Journal of Gerontology: Psychological Sciences, 48,* P263–P270.

Salthouse, T. A. (1998). Cognitive and information processing perspectives on aging. In I. Nordhus, G. VandenBos, S. Berg, & P. Fromholt (Eds.), *Clinical gerontology* (pp. 49–60). Washington, DC: American Psychological Association.

Salthouse, T. A. (2006). Mental exercise and mental aging: Evaluating the validity of the "use it or lose it" hypothesis. *Perspectives on Psychological Science, 1,* 24–45.

Salzman, C., & Nevis-Olsen, J. (1992). Psychopharmacologic treatment. In J. E. Birren, R. B. Sloane, & G. D. Cohen (Eds.), *Handbook of mental health and aging* (pp. 722–763). New York: Academic Press.

Salzman, C., & Shader, R. (1979). Clinical evaluation of depression in the elderly. In A. Raskin & L. Jarvik (Eds.), *Psychiatric symptoms and cognitive loss in the elderly: Evaluation and assessment techniques* (pp. 39–74). Washington, DC: Hemisphere.

Sammartino, F. J. (1987). The effect of health on retirement. *Social Security Bulletin, 50,* 31–47.

Sanders, S. C. (1993). Risk factors in bereavement outcome. In M. Stroebe, W. Stroebe, & B. Hansson (Eds.), *Handbook of bereavement: Theory, research, and intervention* (pp. 255–270). New York: Cambridge University Press.

Sanders, S., Ott, C., Kelber, S., & Noonan, P. (2008). The experience of high levels of grief in caregivers of persons with Alzheimer's disease and related dementia. *Death Studies, 32,* 495–523.

Sandler, I, Wolchik, S., & Ayers, T. (2008). Resilience rather than recovery: A contextual framework on adaptation following bereavement. *Death Studies, 32,* 59–73.

Sands, L. P., & Meredith, W. (1989). Effects of sensory and motor functioning on adult intellectual performance. *Journal of Gerontology: Psychological Sciences, 44,* P56–58.

Sanger, M. (2009). When clients sense the presence of loved ones who have died. *Omega, 59,* 69–89.

Sauremann, H. (2005). Vocational choice: A decision making perspective. *Journal of Vocational Behavior, 66,* 273–303.

Savickas, M., and Associates (2009). Life designing: A paradigm for career construction in the 21st century. *Journal of Vocational Behavior, 75,* 239–250.

Schaie, K. W. (1965). A general model for the study of developmental problems. *Psychological Bulletin, 64,* 92–107.

Schaie, K. W. (1970). A reinterpretation of age-related changes in cognitive structure and functioning. In L. Goulet & P. Baltes (Eds.), *Life-span developmental psychology: Research and theory* (pp. 486–508). New York: Academic Press.

Schaie, K. W. (1979). The primary mental abilities in adulthood: An exploration in the development of psychometric intelligence. In P. Baltes & O. Brim (Eds.), *Life-span development and behavior* (Vol. 2, pp. 68–115). New York: Academic Press.

Schaie, K. W. (1996). Intellectual development in adulthood. In J. Birren & K. Schaie (Eds.), *Handbook of the psychology of aging* (pp. 266–286). San Diego, CA: Academic Press.

Schaie, K. W. (2005). *Developmental influences on adult intelligence*. New York: Oxford.

Schaie, K. W., & Edler, G. H. (2005). *Historical influences on lives & aging*. New York: Springer.

Schaie, K. W., & Labouvie-Vief, G. (1974). Generational versus ontogenetic components of change in adult cognitive behavior: A 14-year cross-sequential study. *Developmental Psychology, 10,* 305–320.

Schaie, K. W., & Willis, S. L. (1986). Can decline in adult intellectual functioning be reversed? *Developmental Psychology, 22,* 223–232.

Schaie, K. W., & Willis, S. L. (1996). Psychometric intelligence and aging. In F. Blanchard-Fields & T. Hess (Eds.), *Perspectives on cognitive change in adulthood and aging* (pp. 293–324). New York: McGraw-Hill.

Schaie, K.W., Willis, S. L., & O'Hanlon, A. (1994). Perceived intellectual change over seven years. *Journal of Gerontology: Psychological Sciences, 49,* P108–P118.

Scheibel, A. (1992). Structural changes in the aging brain. In J. Birren, R. Sloane, & G. Cohen (Eds.), *Handbook of mental health and aging* (pp. 147–174). New York: Academic Press.

Scheibel, F. (2006). Vision and aging. In J. Birren & K. W. Schaie (Eds.), *Handbook of the psychology of aging* (pp. 129–162). San Diego, CA: Academic Press.

Scheier, M. F. & Carver, C. S. (1985). Optimism, coping, and health: Assessment and implications of generalized outcome expectancies. *Health Psychology, 4,* 219–247.

Schiff, W., Oldak, R., & Shah, V. (1992). Aging persons' estimates of vehicular motion. *Psychology and Aging, 7,* 518–525.

Schiffman, S. (1997). Taste and smell losses in normal aging and disease. *Journal of the American Medical Association, 278,* 1357–1362.

Schlenberg, J., Wasworth, K., O'Malley, P., Bachman, J., & Johnston, L. (1996). Adolescent risk factors for binge drinking during the transition to young adulthood. *Developmental Psychology, 32,* 659–674.

Schlossberg, N. (1989). *Overwhelmed: Coping with life's ups and downs* (pp. 28–29). Lexington, MA: Lexington Books.

Schmidt, A. M., & Padilla, A. (1983). Grandparent-grandchild interaction in a Mexican American group. *Hispanic Journal of Behavioral Sciences, 5,* 181–198.

Schmitt, M., Kliegel, M., & Shapiro, A. (2007). Marital interaction in middle and old age: A predictor of marital satisfaction? *International Journal of Aging and Human Development, 65,* 283–300.

Schneider, L. S. (1995). Efficacy of clinical treatment for mental disorders among older persons. In M. Gatz (Ed.), *Emerging issues in mental health and aging* (pp. 19–71). Washington, DC: American Psychological Association.

Schooler, C. (1987). Effects of complex environments during the life-span: A review and theory. In C. Schooler & K. W. Schaie (Eds.), *Cognitive functioning and social structure over the life course* (pp. 24–29). Norwood, NJ: Ablex.

Schroepher, T. A. (2006). Mind frames toward dying and factors motivating their adoption by ill elders. *Journal of Gerontology: Social Sciences, 61B,* S129–S139.

Schroepfer, T. (2008). Social relationships and their role in the consideration to hasten death. *The Gerontologist, 48,* 612–621.

Schroepfer, T., Noh, H., & Kavanaugh, M. (2009). The myriad of strategies for seeking control in the dying process. *The Gerontologist, 49,* 755–766.

Schrof, J. M. (1994). A lens on maturity. *U.S. News & World Report, 116,* 66–69.

Schulter, S., & Zisook, S. (1993). The course of normal grief. In M. Stroebe, W. Stroebe, & B. Hansson (Eds.), *Handbook of bereavement: Theory, research, and intervention* (pp. 23–42). New York: Cambridge University Press.

Schultz, K. (2003). Bridge employment: Work after retirement. In G. A. Adams & T. A. Beehr (Eds.), *Retirement: Reasons, process, and results* (pp. 214–241). New York: Springer.

Schultz, R. (1978). *The psychology of death, dying and bereavement*. Reading, MA: Addison-Wesley.

Schultz, R., & Associates. (2002). Resources for enhancing Alzheimer's caregiver health (REACH). Overview, site-specific outcomes, and future directions. *Gerontologist, 43,* 514–520.

Schulz, R., Beach, S. R., Lind, B., Martire, L., Zdaniuk, B., Hirsch, C., Jackson, S., & Burton, L. (2001). Involvement in caregiving and adjustment to the death of a spouse. *Journal of the American Medical Association, 285,* 3123–3129.

Schulz, R., & Hanusa, B. H. (1978). Long-term effects of control and predictability enhancing interventions: Findings and ethical issues. *Journal of Personality and Social Psychology, 35*, 1194–1201.

Schultz, R., & Heckhausen, J. (1996). A life span model of successful aging. *American Psychologist, 51*, 702–714.

Schulz, R., Martire, L., Jennings, J., Lingler, J., & Greenberg, M. (2010). Spouses' cardiovascular reactivity to their partners' suffering. *Journal of Gerontology, 65B*, 195-201.

Schwartz, B., & Reisberg, D. (1991). *Learning and memory*. New York: Norton.

Schwerha, D. J., & McMullin, D. L. (2002). Prioritizing ergonomic research in aging for the 21st century American workforce. *Experimental Aging Research, 28*, 99–110.

Scogin, F. (1994). Assessment of depression in older adults. In M. Storandt & G. VandenBos (Eds.), *Neuropsychological assessment of dementia and depression in older adults: A clinician's guide* (pp. 61–80). Washington, DC: American Psychological Association.

Scott, D., & Willits, F. K. (1998). Adolescent and adult leisure patterns: A reassessment. *Journal of Leisure Research, 30,* 319–330.

The search for the fountain of youth. (1990, March 5). *Newsweek*, pp. 44–47.

Segal, D. L., Coolidge, F. L., & Rosowsky, E. (2006). *Personality disorders and older adults: Diagnoses, assessment, and treatment*. New York: Wiley.

Segal, D., Mincic, M., Coolidge, F., & O'Riley, A. (2004). Attitudes toward suicide and suicidal risk among younger and older persons. *Death Studies, 28*, 671–678.

Seligman, M. E. P. (1991). *Learned optimism*. New York: Knopf.

Selkoe, D. J. (1991, November). Amyloid protein and Alzheimer's disease. *Scientific American*, 68–78.

Seltzer, M., Greenberg, J., & Krauss, M. (1995). A comparison of coping strategies of aging mothers of adults with mental illness or mental retardation. *Psychology and Aging, 10,* 64–75.

Selye, H. (1976). *The stress of life* (rev. ed.). New York: McGraw-Hill.

Seman, T. E, & Adler, N. (Spring, 1998). Older Americans: Who will they be? *Phi Kappa Phi Journal*, 22–25.

Shapiro, E. (2008). Whose recovery, of what? Relationships and environments promoting grief and growth. *Death Studies, 32*, 40–58.

Shea, G. F., & Haasen, A. (2005). *The older worker advantage: Making the most of our aging workforce*. Westport, CT: Praeger.

Shea, L. (1988). Grandparent-adolescent relationships as mediated by lineage and gender. *Dissertation Abstracts International, 49*, 351A.

Shehan, C. L., Berardo, F. M., & Vera, H. (1991). Women in age-discrepant marriages. *Journal of Family Issues, 12*(3), 291–305.

Shehan, C. L., & Dwyer, J. W. (1989). Parent-child exchanges in the middle years: Attachment and autonomy in the transition to adulthood. In J. A. Mancini (Ed.), Aging *parents and adult children*. Lexington, MA: Lexington Books

Sheikh, J. I. (1992). Anxiety and its disorders in old age. In J. E. Birren, R. B. Sloane, & G. D. Cohen (Eds.), *Handbook of mental health and aging* (pp. 410–432). New York: Academic Press.

Sherman, A. M., de Vries, B., & Lansford, J. E. (2000). Friendship in childhood and adulthood: Lessons across the life span. *Aging and Human Development, 51,* 31–51.

Shern, D., & Moran, H. (2008). Medicaid managed care and the distribution of societal costs for persons with severe mental illness. *American Journal of Psychiatry, 165*, 254–260.

Shiferaw, B., Millelmark, M. B., Wofford, J. L., Anderson, R. T., Walls, P., & Rohrer, B. (1994). Defining elder abuse. *Gerontologist, 34*, 123–125.

Shock, N. (1977). Biological theories of aging. In J. Birren & K. Schaie (Eds.), *Handbook of the psychology of aging* (pp. 103–115). New York: Van Nostrand Reinhold.

Siegelman, B., & Rider, T. (2006). *Life span human development*. Belmont, CA: Thomson.

Siegler, I. (1989). Developmental health psychology. In P. Costa, M. Gatz, B. Neugarten, T. Salthouse, & I. Siegler (Eds.), *The adult years: Continuity and change*. Washington, DC: American Psychological Association.

Silberschatz, G., & Curtis, J. T. (1991). Time-limited psychodynamic therapy with older adults. In W. Myers (Ed.), *New techniques in the psychotherapy of older clients* (pp. 95–110). Washington, DC: American Psychiatric Press.

Silverstein, M. (2006). Intergenerational family transfers in social context. In R. Benstock & L. George (Eds.), *Handbook of aging and the social sciences* (pp. 166– 181). San Diego, CA: Academic Press.

Simonton, D. K. (1990). Creativity and wisdom in aging. In J. E. Birren & K. W. Schaie (Eds.), *Handbook of the psychology of aging* (pp. 320–329). New York: Academic Press.

Simonton, D. K. (1998). Career paths and creative lives: A theoretical perspective on late life potential. In C. Adams-Price (Ed.), *Creativity and successful aging* (pp. 3–20). New York: Springer.

Sinnott, J. (1989). General systems theory: A rationale for the study of everyday memory. In L. W. Poon, D. C. Rubin, & B. A. Wilson (Eds.), *Everyday cognition in adulthood and late life* (pp. 59–72). Cambridge: Cambridge University Press.,

Sinnott, J. (1996). The developmental approach: Postformal thought as adaptive skill. In F. Blanchard-Fields & T. Hess (Eds.), *Perspectives on cognitive change in adulthood and aging* (pp. 358–386). New York: McGraw-Hill.

Sinnott, J. D. (1998). *The development of logic in adulthood: Postformal thought and its applications*. New York: Plenum.

Slavek, S. (1995). Presenting social interest to different lifestyles. *Individual Psychology, 51,* 166–177.

Small, B. J., Hertzog, C., Hultsch, D. F., & Dixon, R. A. (2003). Stability and change in adult personality over 6 years: Findings from the Victoria Longitudinal Study. *Journal of Gerontology: Psychological Sciences, 58B,* P166–P176.

Smith, A. D. (1996). Memory. In J. Birren & K. W. Schaie (Eds.), *Handbook of the psychology of aging* (pp. 236–250). San Diego, CA: Academic Press.

Smith, D., & Moen, P. (2004) Retirement satisfaction for retirees and their spouses: Do gender and the retirement decision-making process matter? *Journal of Family Issues, 25,* 262–269.

Smith, G. (2003). How caregiving grandparents view support groups: An exploratory study. In B. Hayslip & J. H. Patrick (Eds.), *Working with custodial grandparents* (pp. 69–92). New York: Springer.

Smith, G., & Rush, B. (2006). Normal aging and mild cognitive impairment. In K. K. Attix & K. Welsh-Bohmer (Eds.), *Geriatric neuropsychology: Assessment and intervention* (pp. 27–56). New York: Guilford Press.

Smith, G. A., & Brewer, N. (1995). Slowness and age: Speed-accuracy mechanisms. *Psychology and Aging, 10,* 238 247.

Smith, G. C., Smith, M. F., & Toseland, R. W. (1991). Problems identified by family caregivers in counseling. *Gerontologist, 31,* 15–23.

Smola, K. W., & Sutton, C. D. (2002). Generational differences: Revisiting generational work values for the new millennium. *Journal of Organizational Behavior, 23,* 363–382.

Smulyanm, L. (2004). Redefining self and success: Becoming teachers and doctors. *Gender and Education, 16,* 225–245.

Snarski, M, & Scogin, F. (2006). Assessing depression in older adults. In S. Qualls & B. Knight (Eds.), *Psychotherapy for depression in older adults* (pp. 45–78). New York: Wiley.

Sneed, J., & Whitbourne, S. (2003). Identity processing and self consciousness in middle and later adulthood. *Journal of Gerontology: Psychological Sciences, 58B,* P313–P320.

Snowden, D. (2001). Aging with grace. New York: Bantam.

Sorensen, S., Pinquart, M., Habil, D., & Duberstein, P. (2002). How effective are interventions with caregivers? An updated meta-analysis. *The Gerontologist, 42,* 356–372.

Sorkin, D. H., & Rook, K. S. (2006). Dealing with negative social exchanges in later life: Coping responses, goals, and effectiveness. *Psychology and Aging, 21,* 715–725.

Spayd, C., & Smyer, M. (1996). Psychological interventions in nursing homes. In S. Zarit & B. Knight (Eds.), *A guide to psychotherapy and aging* (pp. 241–268). Washington, DC: American Psychological Association.

Speas, K., & Obenshain, B. (February, 1995). *AARP: Images of aging in America* (Final Report). Chapel Hill, NC: FGI Integrated Marketing.

Spector, A., Davies, S., Woods, B., & Orrell, M. (2001). Reality orientation for dementia: A systematic review of the evidence of effectiveness from randomized controlled trials. *Gerontologist, 40,* 206–212.

Spencer, S.M., Schulz, R., Rooks, R.N., Albert, S.M., Thorpe, Jr., R.J., Brenes, G.A., Harris, T.B., Newman, A.B. (2009). Racial differences in self-rated health at similar levels of physical functioning: An examination of health pessimism in the Health, Aging and Body Composition Study. *Journal of Gerontology: Social Sciences, 64B,* 87–94.

Spitze, G., Logan, J. R., Joseph, G., & Lee, E. (1994). Middle generation roles and the well-being of men and women. *Journal of Gerontology: Social Sciences, 49,* S107–S116.

Spitzer, M. E. (1988). Taste acuity in institutionalized and noninstitutionalized elderly men. *Journal of Gerontology: Psychological Sciences, 43,* P71–P74.

Staats, S. (1996). Youthful and older biases as special cases of a self-age optimization bias. *International Journal of Aging and Human Development, 43,* 267–276.

Staats, S., Colbert, B., & Partlo, C. (1995). Uplifts, hassles, and quality of life in older workers. In M. J. Sirgy & A. C. Samli (Eds.), *New dimensions in marketing/ quality-of-life research* (pp. 117–135). Westport, CT: Quorum.

Stagner, R. (1985). Aging in industry. In J. E. Birren & K. W. Schaie (Eds.), *Handbook of the psychology of aging* (2nd ed.) (pp. 789–817). New York: Van Nostrand Reinhold.

Stambor, Z. (February, 2006). Bracing for the baby boom. *Monitor in Psychology* (pp. 30–31).

Stanley, M. Rhoades, H., Kunik, M., & DeBakey, M. (2009). Cognitive behavior therapy for older patients with generalized anxiety disorder. A reply. *JAMA, 302,* 487.

Stanley, M., Wilson, N., Novy, D., Rhoades, H., Wagener, P., Greisinger, A., Cully, J., & Kunik, M. (2009). Cognitive behavior therapy for generalized anxiety disorder among older adults in primary care: A randomized clinical trial. *JAMA, 301,* 1460–1467.

Stebbins, R. (2004). *Between work and leisure.* New Brunswick, NJ: Transaction Publishers.

Stein, J. A., Newcomb, M. D., & Bentler, P. M. (1990). The relative influence of vocational behavior and family involvement on self-esteem: Longitudinal analyses of young adult women and men. *Journal of Vocational Behavior, 36,* 320–328.

Steinmetz, S., Clavan, S., & Stein, K. F. (1990). The relative influence of vocational behavior and family involvement on self esteem: Longitudinal analysis of young adult women and men. *Journal of Vocational Behavior, 36,* 320–328.

Stern, D., Song, Y., & O'Brien, B. (2004). Company training in the United States 1970–2000. What have been the trends over time? *International Journal of Training and Development, 8,* 191–209.

Sternberg, R. J. (1985). Cognitive approaches to intelligence. In B. B. Wolman (Ed.), *Handbook of human intelligence: Theories, measurements, and applications* (pp. 59–118). New York: Wiley Interscience.

Sternberg, R. J. (1988). The triarchic mind. New York: Viking.

Sternberg, R. J. (1991). Theory-based testing of intellectual abilities: Rationale for the triarchic abilities test. In H. Rowe (Ed.), *Intelligence: Reconceptualization and measurement* (pp. 183–202). Hillsdale, NJ: Erlbaum.

Sternberg, R. J. (2007). Triangulating love (Ch. 30, pp. 331-374). In T. J. Oord (Ed.), *The Altruism Reader: Selections from writings on love, religion, and the sciences.* West Conshohocken, PA: Templeton Foundation Press.

Sternberg, R. J., Conway, B., Keton, J., & Bernstein, M. (1981). People's conceptions of intelligence. *Journal of Personality and Social Psychology, 41,* 37–55.

Sterns, H. L., Barrett, G. V., & Alexander, R. A. (1985). Accidents and the aging individual. In J. E. Birren & K. W. Schaie (Eds.), *Handbook of the psychology of aging* (2nd ed., pp. 703–721). New York: Van Nostrand Reinhold.

Sterns, H. L., & Gray, J. H. (1999). Work, leisure, and retirement. In J. Cavanaugh & S. Whitbourne (Eds.), *Gerontology* (pp. 355–390). New York: Oxford.

Sterns, H. L., & Huyck, M. H. (2001). The role of work in midlife. In M. Lachman (Ed.), *Handbook of midlife development* (pp. 447–486). New York: Wiley.

Sterns, H. L., & Kaplan, J. (2003). Self management of career and retirement. In G. A. Adams & T. A. Beehr (Eds.), *Retirement: Reasons, process, and results* (pp. 188–13). New York: Springer.

Sterns, H. L., & Sterns, A. A. (2005). Past and future directions for career development theory. In P. T. Beatty & R. M. Visser (Eds.), *Thriving on an aging workforce: Strategies for organizational and systemic change* (pp. 81–91). Malabar, FL: Krieger.

Stevens, J. C., Cruz, L. A., Marks, L. E., & Lakatos, S. (1998). A multimodal assessment of sensory thresholds in aging. *Journals of Gerontology: Psychological Sciences, 53B,* P263–P272.

Stevens-Long, J. (1984). *Adult life: Developmental processes* (2nd ed.). Palo Alto, CA: Mayfield.

Stewart, A. J., & Healy, J. M. (1989). Linking individual development and social changes. *American Psychologist, 44*, 30–42.

Stewart, A. J., & Ostrove, J. M. (1998). Women's personality in middle age: Gender, history, and midcourse corrections. *American Psychologist, 53*, 1185–1194.

Stewart, A. J., Ostrove, J. M., & Helson, R. (2001). Middle aging in women: Patterns of personality change from the 30s to the 50s. *Journal of Adult Development, 8*, 23–37.

Stewart, A. J., & Vandewater, E. A. (1999). "If I had it to do over again . . .": Midlife review, midcourse corrections, and women's well-being in midlife. *Journal of Personality and Social Psychology, 76*, 270–283.

Sticker, M. (March, April, 1997). Age discrimination in employment. *Modern Maturity*, 77–79.

Storandt, M. (1983). *Counseling and therapy with older adults*. Boston: Little, Brown.

Storandt, M. (1994). General principles of assessment of older adults. In M. Storandt and G. VandenBos (Eds.), *Neuropsychological assessment of dementia and depression in older adults: A clinician's guide*. (pp. 7–32). Washington, DC: American Psychological Association.

Storandt, M., & VandenBos, G. (1994). *Neuropsychological assessment of dementia and depression in older adults: A clinician's guide*. Washington, DC: American Psychological Association.

Strain, L. A., Grabusic, C. C., & Searle, M. S. (2002). Continuing and ceasing leisure activities in later life: A longitudinal study. *Gerontologist, 42*(2), 217–223.

Strauss, E., McDonald, S. W. S., Hunter, M., Moll, A. & Hultsch, D. F. (2002). Intraindividual variability in cognitive performance in three groups of older adults: Cross-domain links to physical status and self-perceived affect and beliefs. *Journal of the International Neuropsychological Society, 8*, 893–906.

Stroebe, M. S., Hansson, R. O., Stroebe, W., & Schut, H. (2001). Future directions in bereavement research. In M. Stroebe, R. O. Hansson, W. Sroebe, & H. Schut (Eds.), *Handbook of bereavement research: Consequences, coping, and care* (pp. 741–766). Washington, DC: American Psychological Association.

Stroebe, M. S., & Schut, H. (1999). The dual process model of coping with bereavement: Rationale and description. *Death Studies, 23*, 197–224.

Stroebe, M. S., Stroebe, W., Hansson, R., & Schut, H. (2001). *Handbook of bereavement research*. Washington, DC: American Psychological Association.

Stroebe, W., Abakoumkin, G., & Stroebe, M. (2010) Beyond depression: yearning for the loss of a loved one. *Omega, 61*, 85–102.

Strough, J., Patrick, J. H., Swenson, L. M., Cheng, S., and Barnes, K. A. (2003). Collaborative everyday problem solving: Interpersonal relationships and problem dimensions. *International Journal of Aging and Human Development, 56*, 43–66.

Strub, R. L., & Black, F. W. (1981). *The mental status exam in neurology*. Philadelphia: Davis.

Sullivan, K., & Mahalik, J. (2000). Increasing career self efficacy for women: Evaluating a group intervention. *Journal of Counseling and Development, 78*, 54–62.

Sum, S., Mathews, R. M., Pourghasem, M., & Hughes, I. (2009). Internet use as a predictor of sense of community in older people. *CyberPsychology and Behavior, 12*, 235–239.

Sung, K. (1990). A new look at filial piety: Ideals and practices of family-centered parent care in Korea. *Gerontologist, 30*, 610–617.

Super, C., & Harkness, S. (1986). The developmental niche. *International Journal of Behavioral Development, 9*, 545–569.

Super, D. E. (1990). A life-span, life space approach to career development. In D. Brown, L. Brooks, & Associates (Eds.), *Career choice and development* (2nd ed.) pp. 197–261). San Francisco: Jossey-Bass.

Super, D. E., Osborne, W., Walsh, D., Brown, S., & Niles, S. (1992). Developmental career assessment and counseling: The C-DAC model. *Journal of Counseling and Development, 7*, 74–80.

Super, D. E., Savakis, M. L., & Super, C. M. (1996). The life-space, life span approach to careers. In D. Brown & L. Brook (Eds.), *Career choice and development* (pp. 114–128). San Francisco: Jossey-Bass.

Super, D. E., Thompson, A., & Lindeman, R. (1988). *Adult Career Concerns Inventory: Manual for research and exploratory use in counseling*. Palo Alto, CA: Consulting Psychologists Press.

SUPPORT Principal Investigators. (1995). A controlled trial to improve care for seriously ill hospitalized patients: The SUPPORT study. *Journal of the American Medical Association, 274*, 1591–1598.

Sussman, M. B. (1985). The family of old people. In R. Binstock & E. Shanas (Eds.), *Handbook of aging and the social sciences* (pp. 415–449). New York: Van Nostrand Reinhold.

Swan, G. E., Dame, A., & Carmelli, D. (1991). Involuntary retirement, Type A behavior, and current functioning in elderly men: 27-year follow-up of the Western Collaborative Group study. *Psychology and Aging, 6*, 384–391.

Swanson, H. L. (1999). What develops in working memory? A life span perspective. *Developmental Psychology, 35*, 986–1000.

Sweeney, M. M. (2010). Remarriage and stepfamilies: Strategic sites for family scholarship in the 21st century. *Journal of Marriage and Family, 72*, 667–684.

Szinovacz, M. (2003). Contexts and pathways: Retirement as an institution, process, and experience. In G. A. Adams & T. A. Beehr (Eds.), *Retirement: Reasons, process, and results* (pp. 6–52). New York: Springer.

Szinovacz, M., & Davey, A. (2004). Retirement transitions and spouse disability: Effects on depressive symptoms. *Journal of Gerontology: Social Sciences, 59B*, S333–S342.

Szinovacz, M., & Davey, A. (2005). Predictors of perceptions of involuntary retirement. *Gerontologist, 45*, 36–47.

Szinovacz, M., & Davey, A. (2005). Retirement and marital decision making: Effects on retirement satisfaction. *Journal of Marriage and Family, 67*(2), 387–398.

Tadros, G., & Salib, E. (2007). Elderly suicide in primary care. *International Journal of Geriatric Psychiatry, 22*, 750–756.

Tang, M., Fouad, N. A., & Smith, P. L. (1999). Asian Americans' career choices: A path model to examine factors influencing their career choices. *Journal of Vocational Behavior, 54*, 142–157.

Tangri, S., & Jenkins, S. (1992). The women's life-paths study: The Michigan graduates of 1967. In D. Shuster & K. Hulbert (Eds.), *Women's lives through time: Educated American women of the 20th century* (pp. 20–35). San Francisco: Jossey-Bass.

Tanner, J. L. (2006). Recentering during emerging adulthood: A critical turning point in life span human development. In J. J. Arnett & J. L. Tanner (Eds.), *Emerging adults in America: Coming of age in the 21st century* (pp. 21–56). Washington, DC: American Psychological Association.

Tausig, M., & Fenwick, R. (1999). Recession and well-being. *Journal of Health and Social Behavior, 40*, 1–16.

Taylor, A. (2005). It's for the rest of your life: The pragmatics of youth, decision making. *Youth and Society, 36*, 471–503.

Taylor, K. M., & Popma, J. (1990). An examination of the relationships among career decision-making, self-efficacy, career-salience, locus of control, and vocational indecision. *Journal of Vocational Behavior, 37*, 17–31.

Taylor, M. A., & Doverspike, D. (2003). Retirement planning and preparation. In G. A. Adams & T. A. Beehr (Eds.), *Retirement: Reasons, processes, and results* (pp. 53–82). New York: Springer.

Taylor, M. A., Schultz, K. S., & Doverspike, D. (2005). Academic perspectives on recruiting and retaining older workers. In P. T. Beatty & R. M. Visser (Eds.), *Thriving on an aging workforce: Strategies for organizational and systemic change* (pp. 43–50). Malabar, FL: Krieger.

Taylor, R. (2007). *Alzheimer's from the inside out*. Baltimore: Health Professions Press.

Teachman, J., Plonko, K., & Scanzoni, J. (1987). Demography of the family. In M. Sussman & S. Steinmatz (Eds.), *Handbook of marriage and the family* (pp. 3–57). New York: Plenum.

Thoits, P. A. (1992). Identity structures and psychological well-being: Gender and marital status comparisons. *Social Psychology Quarterly, 55*, 236–256.

Thomas, H. (1980). Personality and adjustment to aging. In J. Birren & R. B. Sloane (Eds.), *Handbook of mental health and aging* (pp. 285–309). Englewood Cliffs, NJ: Prentice Hall.

Thomas, J. L. (1986). Gender differences in satisfaction with grandparenting. *Psychology and Aging, 1*, 215–219.

Thomas, J. L. (1989). Gender and perceptions of grandparenthood. *International Journal of Aging and Human Development, 29*, 269–282.

Thomas, J. L. (1990). The grandparent role: A double bind. *International Journal of Aging and Human Development, 31*, 169–177.

Thomas, J. L. (1993). Concerns regarding adult children's assistance: A comparison of young-old and old-old parents. *Journal of Gerontology: Social Sciences. 48*, S315–S322.

Thomas, J. L., & King, C. M. (1990, August). *Adult grandchildren's views of grandparents: Racial and gender effects.* Paper presented at the annual meeting of the American Psychological Association, Boston.

Thompson, L. W., Breckenridge, J. N., & Gallagher, D. (1984). Effects of bereavement on self-perceptions of physical health in elderly widows and widowers. *Journal of Gerontology, 39*(3), 309–314.

Thompson, L. W., Davies, R., & Gallagher, D. (1986). Cognitive therapy with older adults. *Clinical Gerontologist, 5*, 245–279.

Thompson, L. W., Gallagher-Thompson, D., Futterman, A., Gilewski, M. J., & Peterson, J. (1991). The effects of late-life spousal bereavement over a 30-month interval. *Psychology and Aging, 6*, 434–441.

Thompson, L. W., Gantz, F., Florsheim, M., DelMaestro, S., Rodman, J., Gallagher-Thompson, D., & Bryan, S. (1991). Cognitive-behavioral therapy for affective disorders in the elderly. In W. Myers (Ed.), *New techniques in the psychotherapy of older clients* (pp. 3–20). Washington, DC: American Psychiatric Press.

Thompson, L. W., & Walker, A. J. (1989). Gender in families: Men and women in marriage, work, and parenthood. *Journal of Marriage and the Family, 51*, 845–871.

Thorton, W., & Dumke, H. (2005). Age differences in everyday problem solving and decision making effectiveness: A meta-analysis. *Psychology and Aging, 20*, 85–99.

Tokar, D. M., & Jome, L. M. (1998). Masculinity, vocational interests, and career choice traditionality: Evidence for a fully mediated model. *Journal of Counseling Psychology, 45*, 424–435.

Tomlin, A. M., & Passman, R. H. (1991). Grandmothers' advice about disciplining grandchildren: Is it accepted by mothers, and does its rejection influence grandmothers' subsequent guidance. *Psychology and Aging, 6*, 182–189.

Topa, G., Moriano, J., Depolo, M., Alcover, C., & Morales, J. (2009). Antecedents and consequents of retirement planning and decision-making: A meta-analysis and model. *Journal of Vocational Behavior, 75*, 38–55.

Toseland, R., & Smith, G. (1990). Effectiveness of individual counseling by professional and peer helpers for family caregivers of the elderly. *Psychology and Aging, 5*, 256–263.

Troll, L. (1980). Grandparenting. In L. Poon (Ed.), *Aging in the 1980s: Psychological issues* (pp. 475–481). Washington, DC: American Psychological Association.

Trotter, S. (1986). Three heads are better than one. *Psychology Today, 20*, 56–62.

Turner, M. J., Scott, J. P., & Bailey, W. C. (1990, November). *Factors impacting attitude toward retirement and retirement-planning behavior among midlife university employees.* Paper presented at the Annual Scientific Meeting of the Gerontological Society, Boston.

Twenge, J. M. (2000). The age of anxiety? Birth cohort change in anxiety and neuroticism, 1952–1993. *Journal of Personality and Social Psychology, 79*, 1007–1021.

Twenge, J. M. (2001). Birth cohort changes in extraversion: A cross temporal meta-analysis, 1966–1993. *Personality and Individual Differences, 30*, 735–748.

Udry, J. R. (1974). *The social context of marriage.* New York: Lippincott.

Uhlenberg, P. (1996). The burden of aging: A theoretical framework for understanding the shifting balance of caregiving and care receiving as cohorts age. *Gerontologist, 36*(6), 761–767.

Uhlenberg, P., & Hammill, B. G. (1998). Frequency of grandparent contact with grandchildren sets: Six factors that make a difference. *Gerontologist, 38*, 276–285.

U.S. Bureau of the Census. (1997). *Current population reports.* Washington, DC: U.S. Government Printing Office.

U.S. Bureau of the Census. (2000). *Current population reports.* Washington, DC: U.S. Government Printing Office.

U.S. Bureau of the Census (2005). *Families and living arrangements.* www.census.gov/Press-release/www/ release/archives/families—households.

U.S. Bureau of the Census (2008). *National Population Projections.* Available at http://www.census.gov/population/www/projections/2008projections.html

U.S. Bureau of the Census (2008). *S0103. Population 65 Years and Over in the United States.* Accessed: http://factfinder.census.gov

U.S. Department of Health and Human Services, Administration for Children and Families, Administration on Children, Youth and Families, Children's Bureau. (2010). *Child Maltreatment 2008*. Available from http://www.acf.hhs.gov/programs/cb/stats_research/index.htm#can.

U.S. Department of Labor. (2002). *Lost work time injuries and illnesses: Characteristics and resulting time away from work, 2000*. Bureau of Labor Statistics: Washington, DC.

U.S. Bureau of Labor Statistics. (2001, March 30). *Mass layoffs in February 2001*. United States Department of Labor. Retrieved from http://www.bls.gov/schedule/archives/mmls_nr.htm

Valacek, D., & Sterns, H. (1981, November). *Task analysis and training: Applications from the lab to the field*. Paper presented at the annual scientific meeting of the Gerontological Society of America. Toronto, Canada.

Valcour, M., & Ladge, J. (2008). Family and career path characteristics as predictors of women's objective and subjective career success: Integrating traditional and protean career explanations. *Journal of Vocational Behavior, 73*, 300–309.

Valliant, G. (2002). *Aging well: Surprising guideposts to a happier life*. Boston: Little Brown.

Valliant, G. E., DiRago, A. C., & Mukaml, K. (2006). Natural history of male psychological health, XV: Retirement satisfaction. *American Journal of Psychiatry, 163*, 682–688.

Valliant, G. E., & Valliant, C. O. (1990). Natural history of male psychosocial health, XII: A 45-year study of predictors of successful aging at age 65. *American Journal of Psychiatry, 147*, 31–37.

Van der Houwen, K., Stroebe, M., Stroebe, W., Schut, H., van den Bout, J., & Wijngarrds-De Meij, L. (2010). Risk factors for bereavement outcome: A multivariate approach. *Death Studies, 34*, 195–220.

Vannoy, D. (1995). A paradigm of roles in the divorce process: Implications for divorce adjustment, future commitments, and personal growth. *Journal of Divorce and Remarriage, 24*, 71–87.

Van Solinge, H., & Henkens, K. (2005). Couples' adjustment to retirement: A multi-actor panel study. *Journal of Gerontology: Psychological and Social Sciences, 60B*, S11–S20.

Van Viane, A., & Fischer, A. (2002). Illuminating the glass ceiling: The role of organizational culture preferences. *Journal of Occupational and Organizational Psychology, 75*, 315–337.

Vercruyssen, M. (1997). Movement control and speed of behavior. In A. D. Fist and W. A. Rodgers (Eds.), *Handbook of human factors and the older adult* (pp. 55–86). New York: Academic Press.

Verhaeghen, P. (2000). The interplay of growth and decline: Theoretical and empirical aspects of plasticity of intellectual and memory performance in normal old age. In R. Hill, L. Bachman, & A. Neely (Eds.), *Cognitive rehabilitation in old age* (pp. 3–22). New York: Oxford University Press.

Verrillo, R. T., & Verrillo, V. (1985). Sensory and perceptual performance. In N. Charness (Ed.), *Aging and human performance* (pp. 1–46). New York: Wiley.

Vincent, G. K., & Verkoff, V. A. (2010). *The next four decades: The older population in the United States: 2010 to 2050*. U.S. CENSUS BUREAU, P25-1138.

Visser, R. M., & Beatty, P. T. (2005a). Achieving organizational and systemic change. In P. T. Beatty & R. M. Visser (Eds.), *Thriving on an aging workforce: Strategies for organizational and systemic change* (pp. 183–192). Malabar, FL: Krieger.

Visser, R. M., & Beatty, P. T. (2005b). Introduction. In P. T. Beatty & R. M. Visser (Eds.), *Thriving on an aging workforce: Strategies for organizational and systemic change* (pp. 3–12). Malabar, FL: Krieger.

Vuchinich, S., Hetherington, E. M., Vuchinich, R. A., & Clingempeel, W. G. (1991). Parent-child interaction and gender differences in early adolescents' adaptation to stepfamilies. *Developmental Psychology, 27*, 618–626.

Wachs, T. (1996). Known and potential processes underlying developmental trajectories in childhood and adolescence. *Developmental Psychology, 32*, 796–801.

Wacker, R., & Roberto, K.. (2008). *Community resources for older adults*. Thousand Oaks, CA: Pine Forge Press.

Wagner, N., Hassanein, K., & Head, M. (2010). Computer use by older adults: A multidisciplinary review. *Computers in Human Behavior, 26*, 870–882.

Wahl, H. W., & Krause, A. (2005). Historical perspectives of middle age within the life span. In S. L. Willis & M. Martin (Eds.), *Middle adulthood: A life span perspective* (pp. 3–34). Thousand Oaks, CA: Sage.

Waldron, V. R., Gitelson, R., & Kelley, D. L. (2005). Gender differences in social adaptation to a retirement community: Longitudinal changes and role of mediated communication. *Journal of Applied Gerontology, 24*, 283–298.

Wallerstein, A. (1989). *Second chances*. New York: Ticknor & Fields.

Walster, E., Berscheid, E., & Walster, G. (1973). New directions in equity research. *American Journal of Health Promotion, 3*, 47–52.

Walter, C., & McCoyd, J. (2009). *Grief and loss across the lifespan: A biopsychological perspective*. New York: Springer.

Ware, L., & Carper, M. (1982). Living with Alzheimer's disease patients: Family stresses and coping mechanisms. *Psychotherapy: Theory, Research. and Practice, 19*, 472–481.

Wass, H., & Corr, C. (1981). *Helping children cope with death: Guidelines and resources*. Washington, DC: Hemisphere.

Wass, H., & Neimeyer, R. (1995). *Dying: Facing the facts*. New York: Taylor & Francis.

Waters, E. B. (1995). Let's not wait till it's broke: Interventions to maintain and enhance mental health in later life. In M. Gatz (Ed.), *Emerging issues in mental health and aging* (pp. 183–210). Washington, DC: American Psychological Association.

Webb, A., Jacobs-Lawson, J., & Waddell, E. (2009). Older adults' perceptions of mentally ill older adults. *Aging & Mental Health, 13*, 838–846.

Wechsler, D. (1981). *WAIS-R administration and scoring manual*. New York: Psychological Corp.

Weeks, G. R., & Wright, L. (1985). Dialectics of the family life cycle. *American Journal of Family Therapy, 27*, 85–91.

Weisman, A. (1990–1991). Bereavement and companion animals. *Omega, 22*, 241–248.

Weiss, R. S. (1974). The provisions of social relationships. In Z. Rubin (Ed.), *Doing unto others* (pp. 17–26). Englewood Cliffs, NJ: Prentice Hall.

Weiss, R. (2008). The nature and causes of grief. In M. Stroebe, R. Hansson, H. Schut, & W. Stroebe (Eds.), *Handbook of bereavement research and practice* (pp. 29–44). Washington, DC: American Psychological Association.

Weiss, R., & Mirin, S. (1987). *Cocaine*. Washington, DC: American Psychiatric Association.

Welford, A. T. (1977). Motor performance. In J. E. Birren & K. W. Schaie (Eds.), *Handbook of the psychology of aging* (pp. 450–496). New York: Van Nostrand Reinhold.

Wells-DiGregario, S. (2009). Family end-of-life decision making. In J. Worth & D. Blevins (Eds.), *Decision making near the end of life* (pp. 247–280). New York: Routledge.

Welsh-Bohmer, K., & Warren, L. (2006). Neurodegenerative dementias. In K. K. Attix & K. Welsh-Bohmer (Eds.), *Geriatric neuropsychology: Assessment and intervention* (pp. 56–88). New York: Guilford Press.

Wetherell, J., Gatz, M., & Craske, M. (2003). Treatment of generalized anxiety disorder in older adults. *Journal of Consulting and Clinical Psychology, 71*, 31–40.

Wetherell, J., Gatz, M., & Pedersen, N. (2001). A longitudinal analysis of anxiety and depression symptoms. *Psychology and Aging, 16*, 187–195.

Whitbeck, L. B., Simons, R. L., & Conger, R. D. (1991). The effects of early family relationships on contemporary relationships and assistance patterns between adult children and their parents. *Journal of Gerontology: Social Sciences, 46*, S330–337.

Whitbourne, S. K. (1985). *The aging body: Physiological changes and psychological consequences*. New York: Springer-Verlag.

Whitbourne, S. K. (1986). *The me I know: A study of adult identity*. New York: Springer-Verlag.

Whitbourne, S. K. (1987). Personality development in adulthood and old age: Relationships among identity style, health, and well-being. In K. W. Schaie & C. Eisdorfer (Eds.), *Annual Review of Gerontology and Geriatrics* (pp. 189–216). New York: Springer.

Whitbourne, S. K. (1998).Physical changes in the aging individual: Clinical implications. In I. Nordhus, G. VandenBos, S. Berg, & P. Fromholt (Eds.), *Clinical geropsychology* (pp. 79–108). Washington, DC: American Psychological Association.

Whitbourne, S. K. (1999). Physical changes. In J. C. Cavanaugh & S. K. Whitbourne (Eds.), *Gerontology: An interdisciplinary perspective* (pp. 91–122). New York: Oxford.

White, L. K. (1990). Determinants of divorce: A review of research in the eighties. *Journal of Marriage and the Family, 52*, 904–912.

Who should get bird flu vaccine first? (2006, May 12). *Dallas Morning News.*

Wicker, A. (2002). Ecological psychology: Historical contexts, current conception, prospective directions. In R. Bechtel & A. Churchman (Eds.), *Handbook of environmental psychology* (p. 124). Hoboken, NJ.: John Wiley.

Wilcoxon, S. A. (1987). Grandparents and grandchildren: An often-neglected relationship between significant others. *Journal of Counseling and Development, 65,* 289–290.

Williams, B., Lindquist, K., Moodt-Ayers, S., Walter, L., & Covinsky, K. (2006). Functional impairment, race, and family expectations of death. *Journal of the American Geriatrics Society, 54,* 1682–1687.

Williams, J. G., & Solano, C. H. (1983). The social reality of feeling lonely: Friendship and reciprocation. *Personality and Social Psychology Bulletin, 9,* 237–242.

Williams-Conway, S., Hayslip, B., & Tandy, R. (1991). Similarity of perceptions of bereavement experiences between widows and professionals. *Omega, 23,* 37–52.

Willis, S. (1996). Everyday competence in elderly persons: Conceptual issues and empirical findings. *Gerontologist, 36,* 595–601.

Wilson, D., & Palha, P. (2007). A systematic review of published research articles on health promotion at retirement. *Journal of Nursing Scholarship, 39,* 330–337.

Wilson, M. N. (1989). Child development in the context of the black extended family. *American Psychologist, 44,* 380–385.

Wink, P., & Scott, J. (2005). Does religiousness buffer against fear of death and dying in late adulthood? Findings from a longitudinal study. *Journal of Gerontology: Psychological Sciences, 60B,* P207–P214.

Winningham, R., & Pike, N. (2007). A cognitive intervention to enhance institutionalized older adults' social support networks and decrease loneliness. *Aging and Mental Health, 11,* 716–721.

Winston, N., & Barnes, J. (2007). Anticipation of retirement among Baby Boomers. *Journal of Women and Aging, 19,* 137–144.

Winter, L., & Parker, B. (2007). Current health and preferences for life-prolonging treatments: An application of prospect theory to end-of-life decision making. *Social Science and Medicine, 65,* 1695–1707.

Wolf, R. S., & Pillmer, K. (1994). What's new in elder abuse programming? Four bright ideas. *Gerontologist, 34,* 126–129.

Wolff, K., & Wortman, C. (2006). Psychological consequences of spousal loss among older adults: Understanding the diversity of responses. In D. Carr, R. Neese, & C. Wortman (Eds.), *Spousal bereavement in late life* (pp. 81–116). New York: Springer.

Wong, J., & Hardy, M. (2009). Women's retirement expectations: How stable are they? *Journal of Gerontology: Psychological and Social Sciences, 64B,* 77–86.

Wong, P. T. (2000). Meaning in life and meaning in death in successful aging. In A. Tomer (Ed.), *Death attitudes and the older adults* (pp. 23–36). Philadelphia: Taylor and Francis.

Woods, B, & Laidlaw, K. (2010). Editorial. Cultural issues—introduction to special section. *Aging & Mental Health, 14,* 245–246.

Worden, J. W. (2002). *Grief counseling and grief therapy: A handbook for the mental health practitioner.* New York: Springer.

Work in America Institute. (1980). *The future of older workers in America: New options for an extended working life.* Scarsdale, NY: Author.

Wortman, C., & Silver, R. (2001). The myths of coping with loss revisited. In M. Stroebe, R. O. Hansson, W. Stroebe, & H. Schut (Eds.), *Handbook of bereavement research: Consequences, coping, and care* (pp. 405–430). Washington, DC: American Psychological Association.

Wortmann, J., & Park, C. (2008). Religion and spirituality adjustment following bereavement: An integrative review. *Death Studies, 32,* 703–736.

Wrightsman, L. S. (1988). *Personality development in adulthood.* Newbury Park, CA: Sage.

Wu, K. (1990–1991). Family support, age, and emotional states of terminally ill cancer patients. *Omega, 22,* 139–152.

Yang, J., & Jackson, C. (1998). Overcoming obstacles in providing mental health treatment to older adults: Getting in the door. *Psychotherapy, 35,* 498–505.

Yaremko, S. K., & Lawson, K. L. (2007). Gender, internalization of expressive traits, and expectations of parenting. *Sex Roles, 57,* 675–687.

Yeung, D., & Fung, H. (2009). Aging and work: How do SOC strategies contribute to job performance across adulthood? *Psychology and Aging, 24,* 927–940.

Yorgason, J., Miller, R., & White, M. (2009). Aging and family therapy: Exploring the training and knowledge of family therapists. *American Journal of Family Therapy, 37*, 28–47.

Youngjohn, J., Larrabee, G. J., & Crook, T. H. (1991). First last names and the grocery list selective reminding test: Two computerized measures of everyday verbal learning. *Archives of Neuropsychology, 6*, 287–300.

Zacher, H., & Frese, M. (2009). Remaining time and opportunities at work: Relationships between age, work characteristics, and occupational future time perspective. *Psychology and Aging, 24*, 487–493.

Zarit, S., & Knight, B. (1996). Introduction: Psychotherapy and aging. Multiple strategies, positive outcomes. In S. Zarit & B. Knight (Eds.), *A guide to psychotherapy and aging* (pp. 1–16). Washington, DC: American Psychological Association.

Zarit, S., & Zarit, J. (2007). *Mental disorders in older adults: Fundamentals of assessment and treatment.* New York: Guilford Press.

Zelinski, E., Crimmins, E., Reynolds, S., & Seeman, T. (1998). Do medical conditions affect cognition in older adults? *Health Psychology, 17*, 504–512.

Zimberg, S. (1987). Alcohol abuse among the elderly. In L. Carstensen & B. Edelstein (Eds.), *Handbook of clinical gerontology* (pp. 57–65). New York: Praeger.

Zohoori, N. (2001). Nutrition and healthy functioning in the developing world. *Journal of Nutrition, 131*, 2429–2432.

Index